The Thinking Past

The Thinking Past

Questions and Problems in World History to 1750

Adrian Cole and Stephen Ortega

New York Oxford
OXFORD UNIVERSITY PRESS

Oxford University Press is a department of the University of Oxford.
It furthers the University's objective of excellence in research,
scholarship, and education by publishing worldwide.

Oxford   New York
Auckland   Cape Town   Dar es Salaam   Hong Kong   Karachi
Kuala Lumpur   Madrid   Melbourne   Mexico City   Nairobi
New Delhi   Shanghai   Taipei   Toronto

With offices in
Argentina   Austria   Brazil   Chile   Czech Republic   France   Greece
Guatemala   Hungary   Italy   Japan   Poland   Portugal   Singapore
South Korea   Switzerland   Thailand   Turkey   Ukraine   Vietnam

For titles covered by Section 112 of the US Higher Education
Opportunity Act, please visit www.oup.com/us/he for the
latest information about pricing and alternate formats.

Published by Oxford University Press
198 Madison Avenue, New York, NY 10016
http://www.oup.com

Oxford is a registered trade mark of Oxford University Press.

Library of Congress Cataloging-in-Publication Data
Cole, Adrian, 1967–
    The thinking past : questions and problems in world history to 1750 / Adrian Cole and Stephen Ortega.
      pages cm
    Includes bibliographical references and index.
    ISBN 978-0-19-979462-1 (paperback : acid-free paper)
    1. World history—Textbooks. 2. World history—Problems, exercises, etc. 3. History,
Ancient—Textbooks. 4. History, Ancient—Problems, exercises, etc. I. Ortega, Stephen. II.Title.
    D21.C6816 2015
    909—dc23

                                                                2014007044

Printing number: 9 8 7 6 5 4 3 2 1

Printed in the United States of America
on acid-free paper

This book is for Hilary Janet Cole.
We all miss you. As you knew we would.

And for my beloved wife, Katy McCann.
No, this is not Pride and Prejudice. *But it's all I got. For now.*
                                                    —*Adrian Cole*

For their unwavering support though the years, I dedicate this
book to my wife Nancy and my daughter Ana.
                                                    —*Stephen Ortega*

Brief Contents

Detailed Contents

Earliest Orgins to 10,000 BCE

*What evolutionary advantages did early humans possess that
allowed them to dominate other species? This chapter examines
discoveries in evolutionary psychology, anthropology, and
archaeology that shed light on what separated humans from the rest
of the animal world. We discuss the fossil record, the place of
prehistoric technology, and the role of social factors such as
language as drivers of human evolutionary success. We also
question the notion of dominance and success.*

10,000 BCE to 5000 BCE

*Sedentism and the subsequent evolution of complex societies greatly
expanded the scope of human dominance. In this chapter we explore
why humans settled in villages, including material and cultural*

Chapter 5   ## Was Greece the First Democracy?   163
1000 BCE to 300 CE

*Was Greece really the "birthplace of democracy"? A significant
amount has been written about the existence of shared governance
in Greece and about Greek exceptionalism, and the West has
traditionally held up Greek democracy as the first flowering of a
treasured cultural tradition. Is this fair? This chapter discusses what
constituted Greek "democracy" and examines what forms of
government existed elsewhere during the same time period, in an
attempt to frame Greece's achievements in a global context.*

Chapter 6   ## What Is an Empire?   199
550 BCE to 400 CE

*The Axial Age saw a massive expansion of the human community
into large empires. What constituted an empire? In what ways did
the Roman, Greek, Persian, and Chinese Empires represent a
variation from former states? Were empires a Eurasian tradition?
This chapter explores how the aforementioned empires constituted
new territorial entities, what mechanism they used to function, how
they developed, and why they collapsed. In exploring these
questions we also look at how the expansion of these states led to
new sets of power relations among all those caught in the empire's
influence.*

Chapter 13   # What Changed in Global Interactions Between 1450 and 1750?   475

Historian Victor Lieberman has noted that there was a pattern at play between 1450 and 1830 in which "localized societies in widely separated regions coalesced into larger units—politically, culturally, and commercially." This sounds relatively harmless when put like that, but the process of expanding states created turmoil, forging the world we live in today in a crucible of war, disease, competition, and innovation. Rival powers competed globally, ethnicities blended, and religions clashed, merged, splintered, and disappeared. Money and goods were exchanged on an unprecedented scale, and the profits paid armies, explorers, and missionaries, while merchants, princes, and pirates looked for new ways to get rich, generate taxes, and maintain power.

List of Maps

MAPS:

Preface

Three years ago while teaching the first half of world history, Stephen was visited by a student who inquired about a long textbook chapter on early empires, "What do I need to know"? At first, the question perplexed him, and his initial reply was "Everything that is important." But upon further reflection, Stephen realized that his answer had been evasive. He had not given the student a satisfactory explanation as to what to focus on and what to study.

The world history classroom presents many challenges in terms of the range of events, people, places, and political developments that potentially constitute a meaningful curriculum. On many occasions, both the instructor and the students find themselves dazed by the huge amount of information that requires coverage. One solution has been to cram in as much material as possible so that the student has remedial knowledge of as many places and time periods as possible. Replicating the "Plato to NATO" approach of Western civilization courses, the macro view seems to satisfy the need for extensive exposure to a wide array of peoples and cultures.

But to what end is this approach directed? Does skimming along the surface of human and nonhuman history meet the needs of contemporary world history students? Does it provide the necessary skill set for further intellectual pursuits? Changes in the twenty-first-century classroom and recent shifts in academic pedagogy suggest that information for information's sake is in the process of being phased out for a problem-/case-based approach to learning. Students now are being asked to learn material outside of the class so that they can engage in active classroom discussion and participate in different group activities.

Part of the challenge for the world historian is figuring out how this type of "flipped-classroom" pedagogy can be applied in a setting where the "sage on the stage" approach is replaced by more interactive forms of learning. Asked to regularly participate, students are being required not to memorize but to think about and to evaluate the reliability of different sources of information.

This book is based on the premise that asking questions and evaluating sources represents a new and insightful way of presenting material on world history. While content on states such as the Songhay, the Ming, and the Aztecs and on nomadic people remains an important part of the work, we believe that the classroom experience of debating different issues such as the origins of war and the nature of empire serves as a solid foundation for actually thinking about world history.

Each chapter in *The Thinking Past* is based on a question that has been generated in an actual class discussion. Thus, student inquiries about the importance of technology, the significance of cross-cultural contact, and the exceptionalism of the Renaissance serve as the basis of the book's subject matter and address issues that have relevance both for specific periods and for today. While the questions are broad, they seek to give students a comparative understanding of issues related to diverse areas such as Africa, Asia, and Europe.

The comparisons and the different arguments should be seen as a starting-off point for further discussion about the different issues and questions that the book raises. They should not be seen as the final word but instead as means to engage students in how history is written, argued, and debated.

The close reading of primary and secondary texts in each chapter provides the instructor with the opportunity to look further into how different arguments have been constructed and how primary sources can be used as supporting evidence. While the *Secret History of the Mongols* provides important information on the life of Chinggis Khan, the work also raises questions as to its reliability in writing the history of Mongol relations with sedentary people.

Our answer to challenges inherent in taking on a problem approach to studying world history is to bring on the debate. Recent studies on success in the classroom provide ample evidence that the successful student is the engaged student, who not only is involved in classroom discussions but can also evaluate the viability of different sources of information. While traditionally textbooks have been thought of as background for class lectures and discussions, our text looks to bring weekly reading assignments into the classroom so that students feel prepared to ask questions and engage in discussion.

In deciding from chapter to chapter not to be as comprehensive in our coverage of different places, we believe that the examples we cite and the perspectives we give will provide instructors with the opportunity to introduce ideas of their own that either support or challenge existing arguments. Ideas about democracy and the Renaissance are not provided to give preference to Europe but instead to consider how ideas and periods that students are familiar with can be applied within a world historical framework. Questions are raised about the nature of different empires such as the Roman and the Han, about the transfer of technology, and about the motivations of conquerors from the crusaders to the Mongols to give the student a reference point that she or he can apply to issues that apply globally.

The goal here is accessibility. A less formal language is used, to make the book more appealing to a student readership. Contemporary examples are used, to provide insight and to ask if presentist approaches work in the study of history. While trying to cater to student needs, we also feel that the work does not lack academic rigor. The arguments and the sources that are used include the most contemporary approaches to the study of world history. The book is both user-friendly and academically challenging in a similar manner to great classroom debates. This approach makes sense because the idea for the book comes directly from the classroom experience.

Introduction

They went ashore and looked about them. The weather was fine. There was dew on the grass, and the first thing they did was to get some of it on their hands and put it to their lips, and to them it seemed the sweetest thing they had ever tasted.
VINLAND SAGAS

This simple passage tells of an event in history, the magnitude of which is hard to convey in writing. The Viking subjects of the passage had just landed on the North American coast, the first humans ever to cross the Atlantic. Although their settlements did not last, as later European ones did, the process of the two hemispheres coming together after millennia of separation and mutual ignorance had begun. In light of this, how incredible do those simple sentences now sound?

Although often buried by weighty compendia of facts, history is really about moments like this: a sense of wonder, a hankering to know "what was it like," in the past—to be a soldier in the Han army on campaign against the fearsome barbarians beyond the wall or an Aztec peasant catching her first glimpse of the Spaniards in what would be Mexico or an early hominid scavenging on the baking plains of the Serengeti.

Without a sense of wonder about the past, the hard work of history—the detailed analysis of data or the decoding of ancient documents—would be drudgery, pure and simple. History is only illuminated as a live, relevant discipline when people poke their heads through the pages of a book and remind us that beyond the theories and dates, the point of this work is to understand something about human beings in the past. For this reason we have attempted, in this volume, to bring some of these people back to life, while situating them in their historical contexts and looking at the larger forces which weighed on their lives.

But in many ways writing a "world history" is impossible. Too much has occurred to too many individuals, nations, empires to truly do justice to the past of the entire planet. Too many questions clamor to be answered in the discipline of history as it is that to contain them all neatly between the covers of a readable volume seems like a Herculean task (or a fool's errand). Not only is there too much ground to reasonably cover in a book, but for every assertion there is a counterassertion. There is an old adage about how when you have three economists in a room they will produce five competing theories on any problem. Well, the same is true for historians; all the data that need to be considered in the realm of world history admit to multiple interpretations, expanding the amount of work for the historian.

But other, more basic problems face the history writer. For example, where does one start? Should we commence with what some people consider the onset of history (writing)? Or should we roll the start date back to the evolution of our species (as we chose to do), which conflates world history with human history? Or should we instead go back to the big bang—necessitating forays into various scientific fields and risking befuddling ourselves and even our readers?

Once we've established a start date, which of the millions of possible questions and stories should we privilege in these inadequately few pages? Should we measure various populations and give each group equal time according to its numbers? (In a very rough sense, this may be what most world histories do—less is obviously written about lightly populated places.) Figuring out what to discuss is the most vexing challenge. What, in other words, should be included and what should be excluded? Such editorial decisions unavoidably privilege some places, events, and people at the expense of others for the simple reason that you cannot include it all. However, since many people and places have been excluded in the past for murkier reasons—prejudice or feelings of superiority—the problem of content continues to be highly charged. Any world history writer can be virtually guaranteed that a reviewer whose specialty is, for example, India will find insufficient data on . . . India. Likewise China, Europe, and Africa (and every other place or polity we have neglected to mention).

So perhaps the first point to make is that our world history, like any other, is necessarily just that—*our* world history. It deals with issues chosen by us as important, interesting, or controversial. It does not in any way purport to be comprehensive, complete, all-encompassing, or ultimately authoritative. Content itself is not a fixed object—historical matter, unlike physical matter, is elusive, mercurial, and ever-changing; every generation has its own ideas as to what content *is,* what historical "facts" *are,* and what is proper material for consideration.

If this is true, then it follows that a world history book should not doggedly march through a recitation of things that happened (the "one darn thing after another" school of history) but should instead present the reader with ideas and arguments, for what is history, after all, other than multiple ideas and arguments about the past and its peoples? And what is the business of history but the process of generating ideas and arguments—based on the available sources (some better than others)? The past, being past, is impossible to know completely. It has taken its place in multiple memories and, as such, is vulnerable to the vagaries thereof and to the more purposeful perversions of the present—such as propaganda and revisionism. Attempts to know the past, therefore, will always be incomplete; and the best we can do is to examine the evidence, discuss the merits of different ideas, and recognize history as a type of rhetoric.

This is precisely what we have attempted to do here. What you will not find in these pages, therefore, is a descriptive account of everything that has happened to humans on earth; we have not written a full record of the human past. Instead, we have generated multiple questions about the past, which allow us to explore major themes in world history, using the "content" as examples. The resultant book allows students of world history to gain an idea of the breadth of debates and arguments that abound in the discipline and acquire a sense of how history is one of the rhetorical subjects, as are all the humanities. It has, perhaps, never been truer that historical positions are largely subjective. Scholars today have questioned everything. Take, for example, the raging debate about why the West is "ahead" or has more power or is richer or any iteration of these ideas. Not only do multiple, contradictory theories exist—such as long-term "lock-in" theories suggesting a certain inevitability to Western superiority and short-term accident theories— but different scholars question the notion of the West and East as artificial constructs, pulling out the rug from under the entire debate. Other major debates continue; for example, were there multiple hominids living simultaneously on earth, or are different fossil specimens really radically different individuals of the same species? Paleoanthropology is particularly rife with major arguments because it is a relatively young discipline, and we've only begun to dig up the earth's secrets.

The result for the history student? We hope that in reading these chapters students will begin to appreciate that there are few invulnerable ideas and, further, that most of what we consider "content," the bread and butter of history, is comprised of ideas, constructed in language, with insufficient data. The facts of history are, therefore, only as solid as the evidence upon which they rest and the coherence and persuasiveness of the arguments that those facts help to create.

If, therefore, we can help to generate discussion in class, then our job has been done. Hopefully, you will find, as teachers and students alike, enough in these pages to get a sense of the complexity of history, spark debate, and generate a desire for further research and reading. Hopefully, the book will force students to think critically about the past and such thinking will empower students far more than any rote memorization of randomly chosen facts.

Although somewhat thematic (with chapters on war, politics, religion, etc.), the book is nonetheless largely chronological. We begin with the story of evolution, described while discussing the idea of human dominance, then progress through sedentism, farming, and the urban revolution, which looks at the earliest river valley civilizations. Chapter 4 looks in depth at warfare, going back where necessary to look at its earliest history, and then discussing it in the ancient world. Chapters 5, 6, and 7 tackle early precursors of "democracy," empire, and universal religions, respectively, and as such linger in the ancient world but keep moving forward, through the Olmecs, the Romans, Han, Persians, Mauryan Indians, and ancient Greeks among others. Chapter 8 takes a similarly broad time frame, looking at the history of trade, starting with the earliest evidence thereof and continuing through the ancient Silk Road, trans-Saharan, Mayan, and pre-Islamic trade and Islamic Arabia. Chapter 9 explores technology's place in ancient history, culminating with Song China but including roughly contemporaneous societies and their technologies globally. Chapter 10 examines environmental factors in history between about 1100 and 1400, exploring, among others, the Norse of Greenland, the Maya, the American Southwest, and the plague of the fourteenth century. Chapter 11 discusses medieval conquerors, largely the Mongols but also the Delhi Sultanate, the crusaders, Mamlukes, and the Iberian Reconquista. Chapters 12 and 13 extend the chronology into the early modern period, with discussions of the notion of "renaissance" and expansion globally.

We should mention here that we have attempted to overcome traditional excessive focus on Europe to the exclusion of other parts of the world. Our chapters on the Renaissance and democracy (12 and 5, respectively) attempt to break free from the exclusively European hold on these two concepts and look at how we can apply them more inclusively, taking a broad view of global renaissances and looking at early expression of participatory politics around the ancient world.

The chapters of this book all follow a similar pattern. The opening, or hook, sets the scene, taking an event or idea from the chapter, and expands on it. With the introduction you will find a map, which locates the places discussed in the chapter. Subsequent sections tackle major subquestions, within a chapter's more general question. Throughout the text we have included the voices not only of the primary sources—the historical actors themselves—but also of historians—the secondary sources—giving the reader a window into ongoing debates and research.

The Thinking Past

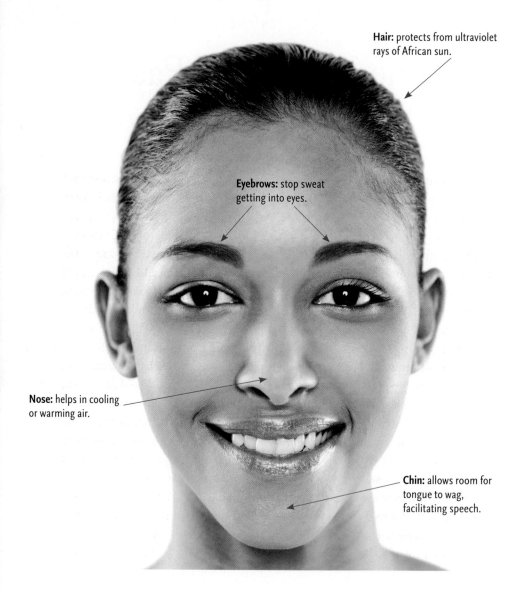

Hair: protects from ultraviolet rays of African sun.

Eyebrows: stop sweat getting into eyes.

Nose: helps in cooling or warming air.

Chin: allows room for tongue to wag, facilitating speech.

What does the face mean?

Chapter 1

Why Are Humans Dominant?

Earliest Origins to 10,000 BCE

Through the Looking Glass

Next time you happen to look in a mirror, stop and ponder this: staring back at you is an animal. All jokes aside, this is a *real* animal, related in biology and history to creatures of the barnyard, the jungle, the African plains, and even the deepest oceans. Sometimes it is easy to forget the animal part of our existence, especially if you look around at what humans have done. Looking in the mirror seems to emphasize this point (what other animal does this?). You might be accustomed to looking into the mirror in order to get a fix on your appearance, but mirror-gazing, as anthropologists Chris Stringer and Robin McKie put it, "reveals many telling clues about our evolution as intelligent and ultimately world-conquering primate foragers, and about our long march to 'civilization.'"[1] Stringer offers a whirlwind tour of our faces: Starting at the top, with our hair—a holdover from our more hirsute ancestors—we kept it on our heads to shield our brains from the ultraviolet rays of the African sun (hair in armpits and groins covers glandular areas and helps circulate pheromones, the smells by which many animals communicate). Our eyebrows, more subtle than an ape's brow ridges, keep the sweat out of our eyes. As for our noses, they help minimize or maximize heat loss as we exhale, those evolved for tropical climates tending to be broader, while cooler climates favor narrower designs. The chin provides room for our tongues to waggle around; this is perhaps the one thing that distinguishes us above all else from our cousins in the animal kingdom, as language was a key component of the human career and a major part of the answer to this chapter's question,

---

[1] Chris Stringer and Robin McKie, *African Exodus: The Origins of Modern Humanity* (New York: Henry Holt, 1996), 224.

3

why dominant? What our mirror-gazing shows us, then, is that underneath the deceptive, modern clutter of our hairstyles and eye shadow, we are, as Harvard anthropologist David Pilbeam has said, just a "rather odd African ape."[2]

THINKING ABOUT DOMINANCE

In What Sense, Dominant?
- "By 'dominant,' Darwin was referring to dominance within the animal kingdom, and this is a simple fact—explaining why humans keep other animals in zoos and not vice versa."

How Did the Human Body Evolve?
- Over thousands of years individuals increasingly inherited bipedalism, while those who did not went to the leopards. That is the meaning of "survival of the fittest."

What Differentiated the Intellectual Life of *Homo sapiens* from That of Their Forbears?
- There might have been ancient advantages to possessing the "gift of the gab," or being good at prehistoric pickup lines, competence in language itself being an indication of intelligence and, therefore, an advantage when choosing a mate.

What Role Did Sociability Play in Evolution?
- Language is the glue that holds human society together, allows learning between the generations, and the sharing of knowledge between groups. It also created cohesion within groups and allowed them to increase their population and eventually colonize the earth.

Conclusion
Yet all of our innovations come with a cost: overpopulation and pollution. Perhaps these are also a consequence of our vision of ourselves as somehow outside of nature.

---

[2]   Stringer and McKie, *African Exodus,* 225.

Introduction

In what follows we will take a whirlwind tour of human evolution, by way of answering the chapter's title question. We will explore how, from about 7 million years ago to the early prehistory of the human species about 200,000 years ago, humans developed a set of what paleoanthropologists (those who study early human remains) refer to as "adaptations," which over the millennia allowed them to become increasingly dominant in their environments. *Adaptations* are characteristics, of body and behavior, which animals develop—through the lengthy and unending process of evolution—that enable them to better succeed in their given environments. In the case of humans, these adaptations included the ability to walk on two legs (bipedalism); the ability to use stone tools, starting sometime before 2.5 million years ago; the ability to control fire, sometime around 1.5 million years ago; and the habit of group sociability, made possible largely by the acquisition of language. This in turn allowed for larger group sizes, which in itself was a benefit for survival and was the context within which a complex human culture was able to develop.

While all these adaptations unfolded—experts disagree on exactly how and when each one appeared—the human animal became increasingly able to exploit its ecological niche. Initially, this was limited to the dry grasslands of the eastern African savanna, which humans shared with other mammals. But a massive volcanic eruption nearly extinguished the species some 70,000 years ago. In the aftermath, the remaining human population retrenched to southern Africa and thereafter developed, with extraordinary rapidity, a new set of skills that turned them from big-cat prey of the savanna to the world's deadliest primate.

Human success is to be measured against that of other animals. And we outnumber all other mammals on the planet and behave so differently that we no longer even consider ourselves part of the animal kingdom. Part of the reason for this is that our adaptations have allowed us to break out of local ecosystems and colonize all of the earth—an unprecedented step for an animal and made possible by our possession of complex culture, such as making clothes for northern latitudes and domesticating species when foraging fell short. Such adaptability has led *Homo sapiens* to be the most dominant mammal on the planet.

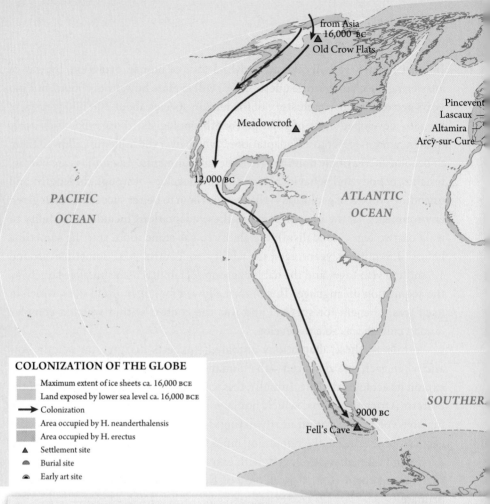

COLONIZATION OF THE GLOBE

- Maximum extent of ice sheets ca. 16,000 BCE
- Land exposed by lower sea level ca. 16,000 BCE
- → Colonization
- Area occupied by H. neanderthalensis
- Area occupied by H. erectus
- ▲ Settlement site
- ⬭ Burial site
- ⬱ Early art site

from Asia
16,000 BC
Old Crow Flats

Meadowcroft ▲

12,000 BC

Pincevent
Lascaux
Altamira
Arcy-sur-Cure

PACIFIC OCEAN

ATLANTIC OCEAN

SOUTHER.

9000 BC
Fell's Cave ▲

Human beings evolved in Africa then left it to colonize the globe. Their possession of complex symbolic thought a▮ environments, allowing them to populate the earth. The "African Origin" of humankind is now widely accepted, on t▮

MAP 1.1   COLONIZATION OF THE GLOBE

TIMELINE*

☀ **7,000,000 million years ago**
Last known ancestor of chimps and humans.
Climate cooling. Thinning of forest cover.

☀ **1.8 million years ago**
Homo Ergaster; first migrations
of hominids out of Africa

☀ **6,000,000 to 4, 5000,000 million years ago**
Evolution of bipedal apes (Australopiths)

☀ **2.5 million years ago**
Homo Habilis

*All dates approximate

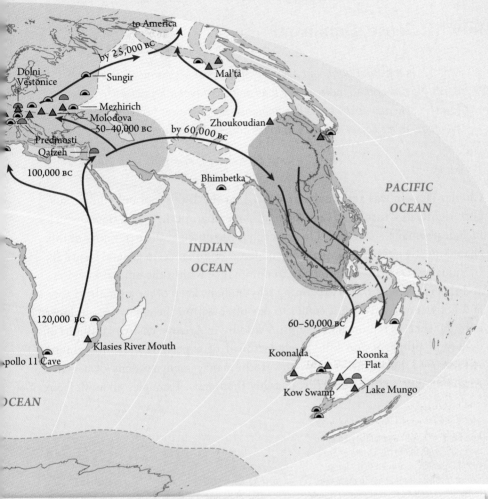

to America

by 25,000 BC

Dolni
Vestonice — Sungir
Mal'ta

— Mezhirich
Molodova
50–40,000 BC
Zhoukoudian

by 60,000 BC

Predmosti
Qafzeh

100,000 BC

Bhimbetka

PACIFIC
OCEAN

INDIAN

OCEAN

120,000 BC

Klasies River Mouth

60–50,000 BC

Apollo 11 Cave

Koonalda
Roonka
Flat

OCEAN

Kow Swamp
Lake Mungo

...nguage, and the adaptability which follows from these characteristics, have enabled humans to thrive in different
...asis of fossil and DNA evidence.

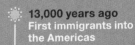

100,000–50,000 years ago
First Homo Sapiens migrate
out of Africa

13,000 years ago
First immigrants into
the Americas

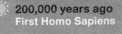

200,000 years ago
First Homo Sapiens

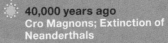

40,000 years ago
Cro Magnons; Extinction of
Neanderthals

In What Sense, Dominant?

Man . . . is the most dominant animal that has ever appeared on this earth. He has spread more widely than any other highly organized form. . . . He manifestly owes this immense superiority to his intellectual faculties, to his social habits, and to his corporeal structure.

CHARLES DARWIN, *THE DESCENT OF MAN*

Charles Darwin was amazingly far-sighted for the 1860s: not only did he suspect, rightly as it turns out, that *hominids*—members of the genus *Homo*, which includes humans—originated in Africa, but the quote at the beginning of this chapter neatly answers the question about our dominance, in general terms. By "dominant," Darwin was referring to dominance within the animal kingdom, and this is a simple fact—explaining why humans keep other animals in zoos and not vice versa. When it comes to our place within the environment, however, our success is more ambiguous: A wildfire in Arizona destroys millions of dollars of property and kills a whole squad of expert, veteran firefighters. A category-5 hurricane swamps the storm-management systems of a major American city, killing hundreds, possibly thousands. Examples abound, from

Ape-man   Darwin was lambasted upon the publication of *On the Origin of Species* (1859), in which he argued that *Homo sapiens* evolved from apes. To most eyes today, however, what is really funny is how Victorian society thought it amusing that humans were even part of the animal kingdom.

China, India, Australia, wherever weather and other natural phenomena happen. Included as part of the environment we can list microbes, invisible "germs," which have brought devastation to human populations on multiple occasions and doubtless will again. Throughout this volume we will see cases of humanity's helplessness against nature, revealing how it is questionable to think in terms of human dominance over it. Nonetheless, humans have managed to reach an accommodation with their various environments, adapting as necessary to changes in temperature and climate, manipulating the environment, and even inventing vaccines against diseases. Weathering disasters and enjoying triumphs, humans have found that their relationship with the environment has been among the most important factors in their various histories.

> ☀ Weathering disasters and enjoying triumphs, humans have found that their relationship with the environment has been among the most important factor in their various histories.

Darwin highlighted three key elements of our domination of the animal kingdom: our physical (or "corporeal") structure, our intellectual faculties, and our social habits. Scholars today cite the same elements in discussing how humans became what they are. Between Darwin's time and ours the details have been largely filled in and his theories often proven, or refined, by later discoveries. These three elements combined to create an unstoppable human momentum, making us what the paleoanthropologist Richard Klein has called a "geologic force," changing the planet forever.

We have even developed elaborate ideologies and religions, which posit our difference from other animals, sometimes inventing gods that gave us "dominion" over the earth, sometimes going one step further and fashioning ourselves as gods. But what is the basis of this feeling, if not borne out by biology? The geographical spread of humans is one way in which we differ from other animals. Most large mammals thrive in specific habitats: apes in the jungles, horses on the steppe, hyenas on the savanna, etc. But humans have managed to survive and flourish everywhere, adapting themselves to the environment as needed. Population is another major difference. The very adaptability that enabled us to colonize the planet allowed us to gain dominance over creatures fiercer and stronger than ourselves. Better protected and better fed, our population grew to unprecedented levels. Most large mammals number in the thousands or hundreds of thousands. Lions, another top-of-the-food-chain predator, restricted to Africa, number in the tens of thousands. African elephants number some half a million. We number in the billions.

Difference can also be seen in the extent to which we change our environment and control other creatures within it. While we are not alone in altering our habitats to suit our needs, we exceed all limits. Many animals eat other animals, for example; but the human animal has wiped out entire species, such as in the "megafauna" extinctions closely associated with the work of

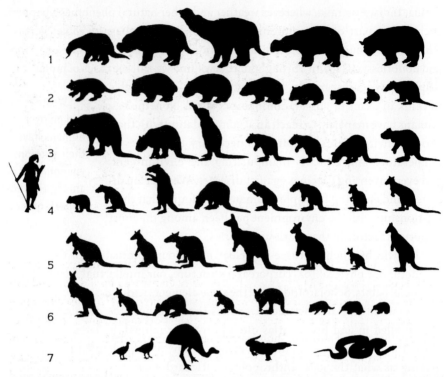

The Hunter and the Hunted   While disease or climate change may have played a role, humans remain high on the list of suspects as the large prehistoric species, or "megafauna," disappeared soon after their arrival in Australia and the Americas. This drawing shows the progressive extinction of different species of animals caused by humans.

Homo sapiens. "The evidence is fairly straightforward," says biologist Niles Eldredge. "Wherever we went, many other species seem to have become extinct shortly after our arrival."[3] Whether it is Madagascar or the Caribbean islands, Australia or North America, prime hunting targets disappeared.[4] Some scholars see our evolution as big-game hunters as the moment at which we achieved such fateful separation from nature; at that point in time we altered the balance between ourselves and our environment, embarking on a course to possible ecocide. In addition to exterminating species, we have domesticated species, allowing for a stable food supply and changing the relationship between ourselves and nature even further.

Power within or even over the environment can be measured by a creature's ability to get work done or by energy output. Until fairly recently humans were

[3]   Niles Eldredge, *Dominion: Can Nature and Culture Co-Exist?* (New York: Henry Holt, 1995), 83.
[4]   The human role in megafauna extinctions is still debated, the other prime suspects being disease and climate change.

Dominant?   Coming down from the trees entailed some big risks. Early hominids were more hunted than hunter.

relatively limited in this, relying on human (often slave) labor and animal power (horses, oxen, camels, elephants, etc.). Then they discovered fossil fuels, and this triggered an unprecedented change in what was possible. But this discovery precipitated unforeseen consequences. "It is nothing short of alarming," says paleoanthropologist Ian Tattersall, "how human intervention is affecting a huge array of processes that will clearly be reflected in the record available to future geologists, should there be any."[5] Just as the success of some of the earliest humans prompted them to leave their homes and seek new ones, having overpopulated and depleted their resource base, could our own success be the key to our undoing? The natural world has shown us, repeatedly, that our dominance over it is illusory.

How Did the Human Body Evolve?

In throwing a stone or spear, and in many other actions, a man must stand firmly on his feet; and this again demands the perfect co-adaptation of numerous muscles. To chip a flint into the rudest tool, or to form a barbed spear or hook from a bone, demands the use of a perfect hand.

CHARLES DARWIN, *THE DESCENT OF MAN*

In order to achieve such a world-changing status, we needed a vehicle (the human body). While we share many characteristics with chimps (and 95% of our DNA), we are also separated by major differences of appearance and behavior. At some

---

5   Ian Tattersall, *Masters of the Planet: The Search for Our Human Origins* (New York: Palgrave Macmillan, 2010), 231.

point in the distant past (researchers believe between 6 and 8 million years ago) African apes split into two groups, one spawning a host of hominid creatures, from one of which modern humans evolved (we still don't know which one) and one that evolved into modern chimps.

To understand this process, we need to go back to the eastern Africa of around 7 million years ago and consider an imaginary scenario: An ape comes down from a tree in the Rift Valley, the giant gorge that runs down the eastern side of that continent. For millions of years its kind have been able to gather food without leaving the trees because the canopy was so thick—a real jungle. They could stay aloft, easily traveling between trees in search of fruit, without having to come down, a risky proposition bearing in mind the predators below.

But the climate is cooling, and the arctic ice caps are expanding, sucking so much moisture out of the world that the Mediterranean Sea has dried up. This aridity has affected Africa as well: what had been thick jungle—a good place for apes—is becoming woodland; and the rains, which had been year-round, are becoming seasonal, meaning that fruit is less abundant.

"The [climate] change spelled doom for many forest-adapted species, including a variety of apes," says Richard Klein of Stanford University.[6] It was now necessary to hop down and race around to another tree to look for fruit because the space between trees was increasing. The problem of walking and chewing gum comes to mind here: being a creature that needs all four limbs to walk, it can either carry fruit or walk. Not both. The ape pushes itself up until it is standing on two legs. Not only can it use its arms to carry, but it can see much farther over the long grass and can run for the trees if it spots a leopard.

WHAT IS THE SIGNIFICANCE OF BIPEDALISM?

Bipedalism, or walking on two legs, is one of the key adaptations that comprise the human corporeal structure (the first of Darwin's three main points) and one of the key elements paleoanthropologists use to classify hominids, the early ones often being called "bipedal apes." We should stress at this point that the ability to see over long grass while gathering fruit, what many scholars have seen as the reason that bipedalism took hold, is now in dispute as new hominid fossils suggesting bipedal traits have been discovered from periods in which tree cover was still abundant. Other researchers have shown that bipedalism is a more efficient mode of locomotion (an ape uses the same amount of energy to move 6 miles as a human does to clock 11). Others still have suggested that an upright stance maintains body temperature, thus allowing

---

[6]   Richard G. Klein, *The Dawn of Human Culture,* with Blake Edgar (New York: John Wiley & Sons), (2002), 55.

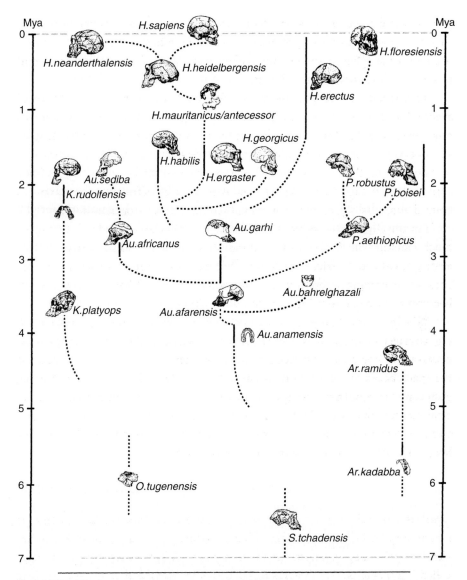

Hominid Evolution   Fossil remains are insufficient for a full picture of hominid evolution. So far paleontology is a case of fill-in-the-blanks. This is one tentative sketch of some of the possible relationships.

hominids to stay cool on the baking plains of the Serengeti. But for several million years trees and grasslands coexisted, the Serengeti still being a geography of the future.

Why apes became bipedal remains, as Ian Tattersall puts it, "One of the most fundamental mysteries in all of paleoanthropology."[7] He points out that with all

---
[7]   Tattersall, *Masters of the Planet*, 231.

the downsides that came with leaving the trees—such as leopard attacks—hominids must have already been comfortable standing up *in the trees*. This makes sense for many of the earlier species of bipedal apes from 7 to 4 million years ago, largely because of their size. Some ranging to 100 or 120 pounds, flitting about in the upper canopy was not an option for them. But clinging onto lower branches, sleeping in trees, and avoiding predators were vital requirements for the job; and for this they would have needed to hold their trunks upright while operating in the branches. But how and exactly when this happened we still do not know.

The anatomy of bipedalism represented a major change from what preceded it: the entire spinal column and the head have to be balanced over the pelvis, requiring muscular redistribution and neural rewiring. And while walking upright provided multiple benefits, such as freeing our hands to do other things, it also had multiple downsides, such as wear and tear on hips and knees and complications for childbirth. The latter cannot be understated—they still make childbirth a surprisingly dangerous proposition for both mother and baby today (every 90 seconds somewhere in the world a woman dies from childbirth) and they go some way to determining modern gender roles. "For the first hominids it was certainly a huge gamble," says Tattersall, "albeit one that eventually paid off in spades."[8]

We have discussed why, but how did this change occur? Darwin's theory of evolution operated by what he called "descent with modification." In the case of bipedal apes, for example, an individual might have a small physical variation—a quirk—which made walking on two legs easier (a narrower pelvis, a big toe that lined up with the others). While there was no need to walk on two legs, this quirk remained just that—an eccentricity. But if environmental changes meant that this quirk allowed the individual to survive to pass on its DNA, then it was likely to become mainstream in a population. Tattersall's idea that apes were already standing on two legs in the trees before they committed to the ground might well make sense if they were too heavy to caper about on branches on all fours. Then later, it seems, their ability to totter on two legs made ground life much easier. "Life on the ground," says Klein, "presented new challenges and opportunities that favored those individuals whose anatomy and behavior gave them a reproductive edge, however slight, over their peers. In retrospect, it appears that the most important anatomical advantage was an enhanced ability to walk and run bipedally."[9]

Over thousands of years individuals increasingly inherited this trait, while those without it went to the leopards. That is the meaning of "survival of the fittest."

---

8   Tattersall, *Masters of the Planet*, 15.
9   Klein, *Dawn of Human Culture*, 55.

WILL THE EARLIEST HOMINID PLEASE STAND UP?[10]

Often referred to as the "Holy Grail" of paleoanthropology is the earliest common ancestor of the chimp and the human being—that is to say, the evolutionary moment when apes split into two branches of the same family. This scholarly and scientific discipline is a minefield; based on fossil discoveries, researchers spend years piecing bones together to finally make pronouncements about their specimens. Whenever a new discovery is made it overturns the apple cart and prompts researchers to question all their assumptions. In general terms, however, we can begin our search for early hominids between around 6 and 4.5 million years ago, at a time in which eastern Africa's forest mass was breaking up. From the outer limits of this time period, until about 200,000 years ago, multiple human-like creatures (what archaeologist Ian Morris has called "ape-men," for ease of reference) appear in the fossil record. It is a strange thought, no doubt, but until about 40,000 years ago several different species of hominids existed simultaneously. Imagine if this were the case today; if we think chimps are uncanny in their resemblance to us, how much more so might different hominids have been?

> Imagine if this were the case today; we think chimps are uncanny in their resemblance to us, how much more so might different hominids have been?

You can visit some of the contenders for "earliest hominid" in the "Primary Sources" section at the end of this chapter. For more details on their various characteristics. Until recently, the earliest hominid specimen was Lucy, a partial skeleton found in Ethiopia in 1974 and named *Australopithecus* (literally, "southern ape") *afarensis* (from the Afar district of that country). The difference between australopithecines and apes was largely one of *morphology* (shape). Morphology tells us more than what creatures looked like; it allows us to make inferences about a species' behavior. Teeth, for example, are very telling. Chimps and gorillas like to eat fruit and other soft vegetative matter. Their large canine teeth are mostly for shows of aggression (in males). Molars are relatively small in comparison to later hominids because soft fruit does not require much chewing. Later australopithecines began to show increasingly large molars, which are good for chewing tough roots, leafy material, and other less digestible foods—like seeds and nuts, the food most readily available in a dryer environment in which trees were less dominant (woodlands and grasslands, not jungles). The fossil clues therefore point to the existence of a creature that was eating a varied diet, distinctly different from that of other apes, made up of the foods common in its new, woodland environment.

Lucy, only some 3 feet high, was upright-walking, although she still showed signs of being a regular tree-user—notably, the shape of her fingers and arms, built for climbing. A thousand miles south from where Lucy was found, at Laetoli in

---

[10]   This clever pun of a subtitle was borrowed from Tattersall, *Masters of the Planet*, 3.

Three Million Years Ago   Two hominids walked across an ash field during the course of a volcanic eruption near Laetoli, Tanzania. Being australopithecines, they might have felt vulnerable to other wild animals on this open plain; but they were probably heading for an area that was wooded. They left a trail of footprints, recorded in the ash as it hardened. What was most important about the Laetoli find was that it was clear that their gait was bipedal: they walked upright.

Tanzania, researchers made another unprecedented find; footprints from 3.6 million years ago. Two individuals had walked—upright—across a layer of wet volcanic ash that had later hardened, preserving the event. The exact species remains in question, but it is certain that someone was walking upright at this point in time.

In reality, however, it may be misleading to think of Lucy as either part ape or part human; she represented something altogether different: "her species . . . had hit upon a unique solution to the challenges of living and moving in the new environments presented to them by climate change."[11]

Since the 1970s, however, the date of the earliest hominid has been pushed back. Researchers have discovered multiple new specimens, none of them conclusively representing the "common ancestor." If anything, these finds have opened the door to new ways of conceiving early hominids and the evolution of humans. Instead of seeing human evolution as a straight line of descent, one species neatly evolving into another, in an easily traceable route, researchers now see a tangled web of species, some of them dead ends, disappearing from the record altogether, others evolving into different species. There were, in other words, multiple species in the millions of years

---

[11]   Ibid., 31

before humans appeared, all exploiting different environments in different ways. One of these, *Ardipithecus ramidus* ("Ardi"), discovered in the early 1990s but not put together and fully analyzed for another decade, briefly looked like a hit but then came under intense scrutiny. Subsequent analysis has created disagreement among researchers, in particular over the specific physical attributes of the fossil. Nonetheless, Ardi has helped to establish the view that there was a diversity among hominids in this period, all the more remarkable in light of the fact that we are now the only one.

WHAT SOCIAL CHANGES ACCOMPANIED PHYSICAL CHANGES IN HOMINIDS?

The evolution of corporeal structure had wide-ranging effects on hominid life. "Something that many people don't care to think about," says linguist Dereck Bickerton, "is that our early ancestors were prey more often than predators."[12] For Lucy and the australopithecines, there was no shortage of predators, including giant versions of what are today small vermin: "it's more than likely that some of our ancestors suffered the ignominious fate of being eaten by weasels. Some of them, it's pretty certain, were eaten by birds."[13]

This is evidence of precisely how dangerous it was to come down from the trees and, perhaps, why so much time elapsed before it seems that hominids gave up on them entirely. Australopithecine fossils show no dramatic change for several million years. Lucy's species alone lasted some 900,000 years; that's about four times as long as humans have been around, so far. But between 3 and 2 million years ago something new and significant showed up and would begin to tip the balance in the battle against the weasels.

Evidence of tool use suggests an evolutionary development, both cultural and biological, because there must, many scholars think, have been a change in the brain in order to allow this new behavior. As always, we look for some cause for this change. Why millions of years of stasis and then, quite suddenly, this? An intensification of the cooling trend may have increased the savanna to the detriment of the woods. This forced early hominids to venture farther into the arid grasslands, in search for food. Although these australopithecines and other early hominids were largely vegetarian, they began at some point to supplement their diets with meat, most of it scavenged from big-cat kills, morsels of raw flesh.

What does tool use have to do with eating meat? Well, put yourself back in eastern Africa, around 2.5 million years ago. Although it's drier than it was 5 million years ago, it's not a fully fledged savanna yet. Away in the distance you

---

[12] Dereck Bickerton, *Adam's Tongue: How Humans Made Language, and How Language Made Humans* (New York, Hill and Wang, 2009), 113.
[13] Ibid., 114

Homo Habilis Widely
thought to have been the
toolmaker, but the possibility
remains that australopithecines,
such as Lucy, may have made
them too.

hear a repetitive, methodical thumping sound. In the shade of a clump of trees
you spot a creature that looks weirdly familiar—human and yet not. This is the
first member of the genus *Homo*, a successor to Lucy. This one is still hairy but a
little taller, competent on two legs, and a little more human in the face than Lucy
but with brow ridges and a sloping face, with no real "nose" to speak of.

More significantly, however, it is holding a sharp piece of stone with which it is
hacking away at the carcass of a gazelle killed and left by a lion. The archeologist Louis
B. Leakey called this creature *Homo habilis*, or "handyman"; and true to its name, it is
using a tool. That piece of rock is not just something plucked from the ground (as you
would have done). It is fashioned from a larger piece of rock for that express purpose.
Stone-tool remains have been dated slightly older than the oldest *habilis* fossils, so it is
also possible that a late australopithecine did this, though we do not know whether
they used just any old stone lying around or fashioned one specifically. Klein suggests
that the jury is still out but only for want of more evidence.

If coming down from the trees represented the first major event in the story of
human domination of the animal kingdom and (to a lesser extent) the planet, the
second was tool use. Archeologists have discovered thousands of examples of these

primitive hand tools in Ethiopia at a site at the Awash River, as well as in the Olduvai George in Tanzania and in parts of Kenya. These stones were flaked by a process of bashing them together at an oblique angle to produce a sharp cutting edge. The core stone from which flakes were broken was probably useful as a chopper, and the flakes provided more specialized, smaller blades for more delicate operations. These tools could be used for slicing through tough tendons and removing muscle from bone, something that *habilis*—and you too—was very ill-equipped to do by hand. The rock could also be used to smash bone wherein lay high-protein marrow. Now *habilis* could do what lions and hyenas do with their teeth.

Tool use and *carnivory*, or the eating of meat, evolved together, one skill feeding the other. The more meat gleaned from a carcass, the more protein to feed the brain, a very energy-hungry organ. "Its use of stone tools conferred a reproductive advantage over other individuals who could not do likewise, and those who could soon increased in number."[14] This creature's brain is significantly bigger than that of earlier australopithecines, getting as large as 650 CC (versus the 3–400 CC of many australopithecines). Ounce for ounce the brain consumes *twelve times* as much energy as muscle. Fully *one-fifth* of the body's caloric intake goes into the brain— that's 20% of our energy for an organ that represents only 2% of our body weight. This is not so surprising, perhaps, when you consider how all those tools extend the range of our abilities and how much carrying around that big brain seems to pay off.

We have little information about *habilis* lives, except for the fact that they were exploiting more protein from their surroundings. This in itself suggests greater subtlety of observation and mental capacity than their predecessors and earlier, full-time leaf-eaters. Klein also agrees that while apparently beyond the grasp of modern chimpanzees to effectively bash stones together to get a cutting edge, it still represents a very primitive skill. As Tattersall puts it, "There's no question that with the invention of stone tools we are witnessing a major hominid life-style change. . . . Nonetheless . . . I doubt very much whether if through some miracle we could meet them in the flesh, we would intuitively wish to describe much about them as functionally human."[15] The debates continue however. One surrounds the possibility that *habilis* practiced some sort of rituals around burial. *Habilis* bones have been found to have been "defleshed" before burial, a common practice among early humans, usually not associated with cannibalism. Even cannibalism, however, was rarely just cannibalism, as anthropologist Paul Taçon puts it: "Instead, it more often was heavily ritualistic with formalized cultural elements."[16]

---

[14] Klein, *Dawn of Human Culture*, 64.

[15] Ian Tattersall, *Becoming Human: Evolution and Human Uniqueness* (New York: Harcourt Brace, 1998), 134.

[16] Paul S. Taçon, "Identifying Ancient Religious Thought and Iconography: Problems of definition, preservation, and interpretation," in *Becoming Human: Innovation in Prehistoric Material and Spiritual Culture*, ed. Colin Renfrew and Iain Morley (Cambridge: Cambridge University Press, 2009), 65.

WHERE IS THE HUMAN/APE BOUNDARY?

After borrowing the chopper from *habilis* and satisfying your appetite for a gory meal of raw meat, you fast-forward to see if things are more to your liking, say, 1.8 million years ago. You might notice that the cooling phase has further intensified. Now *this* is a true savanna.

In the distance you see someone walking (or are they running?) toward you. He seems to be a man and tall. But how can this be? Have we reached "real" humans yet? Well, we have and we haven't. At 1.8 million years ago a species comes on the scene known as *Homo ergaster*, "working man." He is fully upright, standing up to 6 feet tall. Many paleoanthropologists consider this the first "true" human. His brain, however, is some three-quarters of that of a modern human. But *ergaster* is done with trees, period, and fully committed to this savanna. And in this species we have something that is recognizably human. As the Harvard historian Daniel Lord Smail so memorably put it, "if they chose to have sex in public you would feel shocked or embarrassed rather than giggly."[17] This may sound puerile at first, but it is in fact a profound distinction. The same, he opines, would not be true of australopithecines, who would not look out of place in a cage at the zoo.

Homo Ergaster ("Working Man")   Like us but not quite. What is the dividing line between humans and other hominids? Are we just "a rather odd African ape?"

[17]   Daniel Lord Smail, *On Deep History and the Brain* (Berkeley: University of California, 2008), 191.

The fossil record with *ergaster* allows us to draw other conclusions about them. There was little size difference between male and female remains, suggesting a more cooperative social organization featuring less male-on-male aggression, as in other primate societies, and more male–female cooperation. It's likely that a nursing mother needed the extra calories provided by a dedicated mate since she was at home with baby, unlike a baboon mother that could go and forage while her newborn clung to her belly with prehensile, gripping fingers.

These aspects of *ergaster* life are hugely significant, for they begin to prefigure much of later human social life, in particular the relationship between the sexes. Before you start envisioning sensitive new-age males, there was likely, in addition to cooperation, increased separation of gender roles because of the infant's dependency on the mother. Such gender roles have been a foundational aspect of most human cultures until very recently, when cultural developments have allowed some societies to challenge them radically.

NEW SPECIES, NEW TOOLS?

Ergaster's invention of the bifaced hand axe meant more meat. This tool, signifying what archeologists call the "Acheulian period" of technology, represents the next great revolution in becoming human; after the innovation of using tools comes their refinement. This instrument, neatly chipped on both sides and remarkably standardized, differs markedly from the early stone flakes, which were made by a less thoughtful, bashing process, producing a variety of different shapes. Acheulian technology spread with this species as it made its way out of Africa in the first wave of human migrations, and it turns up all over Eurasia, over hundreds of thousands of years, with astounding conformity.

And it is this migration out of Africa that makes *ergaster* a true milestone in human evolution, beginning the colonization of all the earth's environments, as we mentioned earlier. This appears to have happened almost as soon as *ergaster* evolved, 1.8 million years ago. Fossils from Java, in particular, suggest their presence. Remains have shown up in China and parts of eastern Asia of a species that subsequently became extinct, known as *Homo erectus*, or "upright man," probably a descendant of *ergaster*. In Europe, *ergaster* evolved over a couple of different species into the Neanderthals, who also lived in southwest Asia and parts of the Middle East. And it was most probably from African *ergaster* that modern humans evolved in Africa some 200,000 years ago. By the time they, too, migrated out of the continent there were several other species of hominids in the world, but ultimately only one would survive. Migration, beyond the specific seasonal migrations seen with many animals, is to become a hallmark of human history and will take them to every corner of the earth.

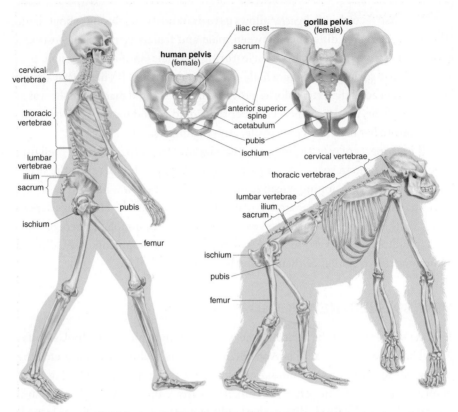

Bipedalism   Was bipedalism more efficient? Did it enable a view over the savanna grasses, or help to keep hominids cool? Whatever the reason, it involved a re-structuring of the entire skeleton with far-reaching consequences. Once upright, we left the trees, made tools, became big game hunters, developed language, symbolic thought, culture, and populated the planet.

Some scientists argue that what is really revolutionary about *ergaster* is that it appears to have started to cook its food. This is important because cooking allows nutrients to be released, therefore providing more benefit, especially to the brain. In general, animal size is limited by the amount eaten. Gorillas, for example, need to spend all day eating because of their slow digestive process and the chewiness of leaves and roots. When humans began applying heat to tough fibers and meat, more nutrition was instantly available to them, freeing up energy for brain growth.[18] There is, however, controversy about whether the use of fire can be conclusively proved at this point.

WHERE DID *HOMO SAPIENS* EVOLVE?

In 1998 a team of fossil hunters at the Awash River in Ethiopia discovered fossilized human skulls near a village called Herto. The Herto skulls were the same size as

---

[18]   See, for example, Richard Wrangham, *Catching Fire: How Cooking Made Us Human* (New York: Basic Books, 2009).

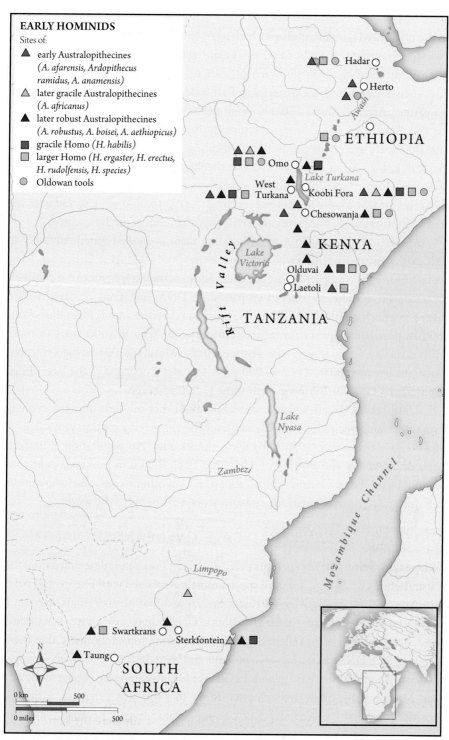

EARLY HOMINIDS

Sites of:

▲ early Australopithecines
(*A. afarensis, Ardopithecus ramidus, A. anamensis*)

△ later gracile Australopithecines
(*A. africanus*)

▲ later robust Australopithecines
(*A. robustus, A. boisei, A. aethiopicus*)

■ gracile Homo (*H. habilis*)

□ larger Homo (*H. ergaster, H. erectus, H. rudolfensis, H. species*)

○ Oldowan tools

Hadar

Herto

Awash

ETHIOPIA

Omo

Lake Turkana

West Turkana

Koobi Fora

Chesowanja

KENYA

Lake Victoria

Olduvai

Laetoli

TANZANIA

Rift Valley

Lake Nyasa

Zambezi

Mozambique Channel

Limpopo

Swartkrans

Sterkfontein

Taung

SOUTH AFRICA

N

0 km 500
0 miles 500

MAP 1.2 EARLY HOMINIDS   Most notable are archeological sites along the Rift Valley, the giant gorge running along Africa's eastern side, including areas in Ethiopia, Kenya, and Tanzania. These have given up evidence of humanity's earliest origins. Other important sites include those in South Africa.

23

those of modern humans, perhaps a bit bigger, around 1450 CC. What was really interesting was that the skulls, dated by measuring the radioactive elements in volcanic ash surrounding the fossils, were somewhere in the region of 165,000 years old. Geneticists claim that the ancestors of all modern humans can be traced back to eastern Africa, around 200,000 years ago. The Herto fossils were the closest to this date to be found, and subsequently fossils were found dated to around 195,000 years ago, more completely vindicating geneticists' claims. These are the earliest known signs of what many archeologists call "anatomically modern" humans. Their morphology, in other words, was indistinguishable from ours; and it is likely that if you were to pass one on the street, you would not respond with the kind of horror-movie stare you gave to that *ergaster* you met on the savanna.

Analysis of modern DNA has found that there is greatest genetic diversity in Africa, suggesting that this is where our species has lived the longest. Geneticists have, in fact, been able to pinpoint a part of eastern Africa as the likely home of our common ancestor. From there, as generations passed on DNA, mutations occurred within genes on a fairly regular basis, giving rise to greater diversity among individuals. This human population spread throughout Africa, in the first 100,000 years or more of its existence, finally leaving Africa between 100,000 and 50,000 years ago, reaching Australia between 60,000 and 40,000 years ago, and crossing over the land bridge from Siberia into North America only some 13,000 years ago.

Until recent decades, some scholars argued that modern humans evolved from different species in Afro-Eurasia, over the course of a million years. This is now largely disproved, as Richard Klein points out: "No population in eastern Asia or anywhere else outside of Africa has been shown to possess a gene that cannot be traced to a recent African ancestor."[19] In other words, all *Homo sapiens* are descended from original African ancestors, who peopled the world.

DID *HOMO SAPIENS* ERADICATE THE NEANDERTHALS?

Whereas for many years it was assumed that modern Europeans descended from the Neanderthals, an ancient hominid species mostly associated with Europe and western Asia, anthropologist Chris Stringer has argued that Neanderthals were on a separate evolutionary line—a dead-end line in fact. Only very recently was it discovered, upon analysis of Neanderthal DNA gleaned from bone fragments, that there was very little DNA shared between humans and Neanderthals. Although some geneticists claim that there is (genetic) evidence for interbreeding between humans and Neanderthals, many archeologists doubt that this was extensive. Stringer's position was that the Neanderthals became extinct largely because they were

---

[19]   Klein, *Dawn of Human Culture*, 246.

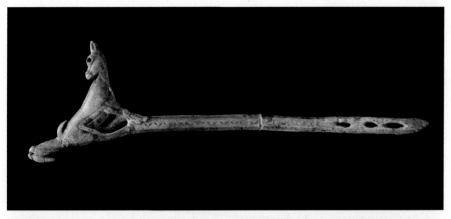

Dominating Weapon   Cro-Magnon, the first *Homo sapiens* in Europe, are widely believed to have either exterminated or outcompeted the Neanderthals. This spear-thrower made of reindeer antler was part of their armory.

outcompeted by modern humans (in Europe these were known as "Cro-Magnon," from the remains at Cro-Magnon in France). They may, in addition, have been actively exterminated by humans, although this is still a hypothesis.

When the Cro-Magnon humans appeared in Europe some 40,000 years ago they found Neanderthals already well established. Neanderthals were well adapted to the cold as Europe was in the late stages of the last Ice Age. Their bodies (short and squat) enabled them to tolerate the temperatures as their stature was such that it minimized heat loss. They hunted large mammals, which were then plentiful, and ate mostly meat. In comparison to humans, their brains were as large, possibly even larger. Yet Neanderthals showed far fewer signs of the kind of complex behavior—symbolic and ritualistic—that most experts associate with humans, and this might have been the cause of their ultimate undoing.

Geneticists claim, from analysis of modern human populations, that the humans who arrived in Europe some 40,000 years ago had come via central Asia, after their original migration from Africa, where they learned their extremely effective hunting skills. Instead of the thrusting spears favored by Neanderthals, they used throwing spears and other implements that allowed them to take down large prey without endangering themselves. The Neanderthals' preferred hunting techniques, while successful for millennia, came at a cost: many bone fossils recovered from Europe and western Asia show high levels of damage, which is likely the result of close encounters with the large animals they hunted.

Cro-Magnons, like other early humans, were nomadic peoples, who did not appear to settle for long periods. Neanderthals, on the other hand, made more permanent camps; when they had thinned out the animals in their immediate vicinity, they would have to make longer hunting trips. Their fossilized remains frequently record signs of resultant starvation and malnutrition. As the Ice Age came to an end, around 30,000 years ago, the big game retreated to the north, following the tundra, as woodland came back to what is now Europe. The Cro-Magnon were able to adapt to these changing conditions, following smaller prey, exploiting plants as well as animals, and learning how to live off fish from rivers and lakes. It is very likely that many of these hunting and gathering behaviors were never adopted by Neanderthals, and ultimately their inability to adapt sounded their death knell.

Humans also outstripped Neanderthals in the complexity of their social life; as Chris Stringer and Peter Andrews point out, they exhibited a level of complexity close to that of modern hunter–gatherers: "They hunted, fished, traded, produced art and apparently even recorded time."[20] Language was a vital part of this. Although Neanderthals probably had some language ability, there is no evidence that they had the complexity of verbal communication that we have. This may have been why their group size was smaller than that of humans, language being a prerequisite of larger social groups, and why they did not innovate technologically and culturally to be able to survive the end of the Ice Age. The Neanderthals' history was not one of failure however. Like most other hominids, and archaic humans, their species existed far longer than we have to this point, and for most of that time they were perfectly adapted for their environments. The differences between the Cro-Magnons and the Neanderthals get to the point of what these "modern" humans really represented, which brings us to an assessment of Darwin's second major reason for human dominance, our "intellectual faculties."

What Differentiated the Intellectual Life of *Homo Sapiens* From That of Their Forbears?

Modern scholars focus on the brain as an extraordinary organ that explains much of human dominance and separation from the rest of the animal kingdom. The biologist E. O. Wilson, for example, considered the evolution of the human brain to be one of the major events in the history of the entire planet because its consequences were so far-reaching. How and why did we become so brainy?

---

[20]   Chris Stringer and Peter Andrews, *The Complete World of Human Evolution*, 2nd ed. (London: Thames and Hudson, 2011), 167.

WHAT'S SO GREAT ABOUT INTELLIGENCE?

Clearly, big brains were favored by natural selection. But why? It may seem like a no-brainer (excuse the pun), but as we have seen, all of our ancestors, from australopithecines like Lucy through *Homo ergaster*, seem to have possessed as much intelligence as they needed to survive for millennia. What accounted for such a dramatic and relentless increase from the late bipedal apes through *Homo sapiens*? According to Ian Tattersall, there are only two major motivating factors for intelligence. One is the search for food or, more broadly, the challenges of the natural habitat. The other is the social milieu or, in other words, the complexities of living in a large group (which itself is advantageous).

Processing Power   Primates, like this baboon, tend to live in large groups. The larger your group, the more processing power it takes to keep up with all the gossip. Social relations occupy much of our thoughts, as any social media user will admit.

Among most primates, the search for food is not much of a problem. As Tattersall puts it, "Some species simply snuffle, swoop, or swim around hoping to blunder into the next edible item that comes along."[21] But for others there is more to it. Some primates have to develop a mental map of the forest to know where seasonal fruit is growing and how to find it. Orangutans have this capacity, moving efficiently between trees that are only temporarily in fruit. In general, foraging animals are well equipped—even with limited processing power—to carry out their gathering. Hunting represents a greater mental challenge, although this is an everyday routine for dedicated carnivores of all sizes. Chimps are a good example of nonhuman primate omnivores. They conduct regular "organized" hunts of monkeys such as colobus, in addition to often catching and eating birds and other small mammals that happen across their path. Chimps cooperate in small groups to ensure a success that would likely be impossible without such unity of purpose. We can conclude, then, that intelligence can benefit animals in their search for food in a broad sense.

---

[21]   Tattersall, *Becoming Human*, 35.

☀ Human society is nothing if not complex, and it is not always a study in harmonious coexistence, as anyone who has a family will tell you; the big issues are the soap opera issues, which usually boil down to sex, status, and money.

Primates spend considerable time thinking about relations with others inside their own group (in the human context, "group" could be defined variously, as household, neighborhood, school, etc.). This requires skills such as manipulation, persuasion, diplomacy, secrecy, even duplicity. A telling example among baboons is a female partially hiding herself from the view of the dominant male, thus allowing a subordinate male to groom her. Human society is nothing if not complex, and it is not always a study in harmonious coexistence, as anyone who has a family will tell you; the big issues are the soap opera issues, which usually boil down to sex, status, and money. Replace money with food, and you have chimp soap opera.

Security is another obvious motivation for intelligence, and this has a social aspect. The sorts of squabbles human families have can be a matter of life and death in primate groups. Among baboons, for example, a low-ranking male may be pushed to the physical periphery of the group. This is a dangerous place to be, especially come nightfall. The high-ranking males make sure that *you* are on the outside so that *they* don't get eaten. There are echoes of this in human society, where we talk about living on the "wrong side of the tracks" or in gated communities. Rich or "high-ranking" individuals can afford a level of security that impoverished or low-status ones cannot.

So far we have some good reasons for natural selection to treat intelligence as an advantage and push for it; as Klein says, "if this advantage aids in the ability to obtain or process food, to acquire a mate, and to raise offspring to reproductive age, it is likely to spread within a population."[22] And that's just what it did.

Historian David Christian thinks that the speed of this brain increase might have been the result of a number of feedback loops. The first, linking tool use and brain size, suggests that protein gleaned by the use of tools led to an increase in brain size, which in turn led to more effective tools, which led to further brain growth: "Changes in one area (either genetic or behavioral) may have caused changes in other areas, which created new selective pressures that reinforced the original change."[23] Another feedback loop involved sociability and the brain. Socially skilled individuals may well have been able to mate more frequently and produced more offspring with similarly advanced social skills. Fond of feedback loops, Christian cites a third, which involves the evolution of more sophisticated language. Language, discussed further below, conferred advantages on individuals,

---

[22]   Klein, *Dawn of Human Culture*, 25.
[23]   Christian, *Maps of Time*, 166.

possibly from the point of view of sexual selection; in other words, there might have been ancient advantages to possessing the "gift of the gab" or being good at prehistoric pickup lines, competence in language itself being an indication of intelligence and, therefore, an advantage when choosing a mate.

The Neanderthals, and several other intermediate species preceding *Homo sapiens*, had brains as large as ours. Although several notable scholars argue that the Neanderthals had more complex and advanced societies than we once thought, most historians consider *Homo sapiens* to be the sole possessors of complex culture; and this leads to Darwin's final category of reasons for human dominance, our social habits.

What Role Did Sociability Play in Evolution?

As man is a social animal, it is almost certain that he would inherit a tendency to be faithful to his comrades, and obedient to the leader of his tribe; for these qualities are common to the most social animals. He would consequently possess some capacity for self-command. He would from an inherited tendency be willing to defend, in concert with others, his fellow-men; and would be ready to aid them in any way, which did not too greatly interfere with his own welfare or his own strong desires.

CHARLES DARWIN, *THE DESCENT OF MAN*

For many paleoanthropologists "modern" human behavior includes certain key components: the invention of new technologies; the ability to enter new environments (often using these new technologies); signs of symbolic thinking, such as artwork and, for some scholars most importantly, language; increased social organization, which would have resulted in larger group sizes; lastly, evidence of materials which do not naturally occur locally, suggesting trade. All of these behaviors were made possible by the social nature of *Homo sapiens*.

Many scholars believe that until about 50,000 years ago there were no signs of such modern behavior. *Homo sapiens*, although attaining its present anatomy about 200,000 years ago, did not behave very differently from its hominid predecessors such as *ergaster*—living in small groups, spending days bashing stones together and scavenging meat from top predators. Klein, a prominent proponent of this argument, suggests that a neurological change, which probably brought language with it, appeared 50,000 years ago; if the braincase had not increased in size during the life span of *Homo sapiens*, then something inside the brain must

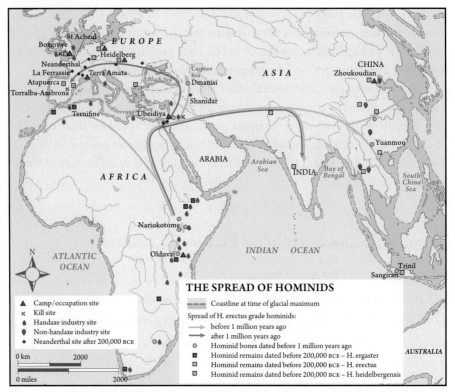

MAP 1.3   AFRICA, THE ORIGIN OF HOMINIDS WORLDWIDE   Hominids migrated out of Africa in waves, populating different niches and giving rise to separate species until all died out except Homo Sapiens. This map shows the spread of hominids out of Africa before 200,000 BCE. Compare this map with Map 1.4, which shows the colonization of the entire globe by Homo Sapiens.

have changed. With this sudden change came a host of new behaviors, mostly related to abstract thought, religion, and social life, which are seen as the breeding ground for culture—perhaps the icing on the cake as far as human dominance is concerned.

But several archeologists have challenged this theory, seeing evidence of this kind of behavior much earlier. And the argument comes down to evidence. Of particular interest are the discoveries of certain rock shelters on the South African coast, dating to around 70,000 years ago. In the Blombos Cave, archeologist Christopher Henshilwood of the University of Bergen found remains of anatomically modern humans, along with evidence of shellfish and game from the surrounding countryside. Significantly, he also unearthed the earliest evidence of bone tools, including foot-long spear points, daggers, and fishhooks. These discoveries suggested an entire industry, not just individual tools. Bones belonging

Doodles or Art?   Symbolism and art are key characteristics of modern humans. This piece of red ochre has been etched with markings. Although we will likely never know their intent, we can be fairly sure they did have some meaning. From 75,000 years ago, this is among the earliest of such items.

to multiple species of large animals were also discovered here, including giant cape buffalo, wildebeest, zebra, and bush pig, all either large or fierce and requiring considerable skill and cooperation to hunt. Putting together the tools with the bones suggests that humans at this point had become deadly big-game hunters, a new development since to that date it was largely supposed that hominids mostly scavenged their meat, hunting fewer, smaller animals as they were limited by their skills and their weapons.

Henshilwood and his team also found what are arguably the first examples of human artwork—two 70,000-year-old pieces of red ochre, engraved with geometric motifs. According to Henshilwood, these patterns showed "symbolic intent" and were likely not just doodles. While we can never know what might have been the meaning behind this art, it marks a watershed in human history; after this date we begin to see similar evidence in other parts of Africa, in particular Ethiopia, from where the first migrations of *Homo sapiens* are believed to have left, crossing over the Red Sea into southwest Asia.

Going on the theory that evolutionary change needs a prompt, climate scientists see something that would certainly account for dramatic changes at this time. Seventy thousand years ago the planet was approaching the height of an Ice Age. Then, Mount Toba, a volcano in northern Sumatra, erupted. This was no ordinary eruption; it was the largest surface eruption the earth had suffered for some 400 million years. The amount of debris it disgorged was equal to some 3,000 times that spewed out by Mount St. Helens in 1980. It left behind a crater

36 miles wide and 60 miles long. If we ever doubt the extent to which humans are at the mercy of the elements, we should stop and take a look at this event. Global temperatures plummeted overnight, by 15 to 20 degrees Fahrenheit, more in higher latitudes, as the ash cloud filled the skies with over a billion tons of stratospheric dust. A volcanic winter ensued, lasting 5 or 6 years, as ash particles blocked the sunlight. Plants withered, and species went extinct. This was almost an extinction event for humans as well. With a population probably under 10,000, the human community seems to have retrenched to the southern tip of Africa; in the struggle to stay alive innovations spread quickly, as did genes, in a reduced gene pool, giving rise to the variety of new tools, techniques, and habits mentioned already.

The American archeologists Sally McBrearty and Alison Brooks also question the human revolution theory.[24] Citing evidence from around Africa well before 50,000 years ago, they suggest that advanced toolmaking, trade, and evidence of symbolic thought were present but that they expanded only fitfully, supplying innovative solutions on an "as-needed" basis. Some behaviors, including the use of grindstones to sharpen points, the processing of color pigments, and the making of finely wrought blades, can be seen as far back as the very beginning of our species; and McBrearty and Brooks even suggest the existence of an intermediate species, very close to *Homo sapiens*, which was associated with these technologies. The humans at the South African caves, archeologists now think, were probably "preadapted" to develop a certain material culture that had been in existence in Africa possibly for millennia; they just needed the incentive to put it into effect on a full-time basis, and this is what Mount Toba provided.

HOW DID HUMANS POPULATE THE GLOBE?

We have questioned the extent to which humans dominate the planet, but their uniqueness lies in their ability to *survive* in multiple habitats, unlike most animals on the planet. Adaptability is the key here as humans have managed to change their habits to fit their geography. Humans expanded out of Africa by constant adaptation to their environment. Such migration would likely never have happened without the pressure of population growth. You can think of this process as a slow, incremental drift: A group outgrows the area it requires to feed its members, exerting pressures on relationships within and between groups and

---

[24]   Sally McBrearty and Allison S. Brooks. "The Revolution That Wasn't: A New Interpretation of the Origin of Modern Human Behavior," *Journal of Human Evolution* 39 (2000): 453–563.

on the environment upon which everybody relies. A splinter group breaks off—a few families, let's say—and moves downriver 10 or 20 miles. It was most likely this kind of process that led humans to cover the entire globe, as historian Daniel Lord Smail puts it, "like a rising tide, that swept out of Africa, then more slowly inundated the nooks and crannies of the world."[25] Some authors talk of this migration as a "journey," which gives the impression that these hunter–gatherers set out on a long-distance trek to colonize Europe or Russia. More likely, however, their movements were local, major distance only being covered over generations, as the process of relocation was repeated over and over. Recent genetic research has enabled historians to see their route in the genetic markers of aboriginal Australians, for example, which show up in the DNA of residents of India's east coast.

This suggests that humans passed that way on their way to Indonesia, leaving genetic traces behind, and eventually made it by "boat" to Australia, at the earliest some 60,000 years ago. The same groups of early humans probably branched out after leaving Africa, and some fanned northwest, toward central and western Asia, appearing there some 70,000 years ago. Descendants of these migratory peoples showed up in Siberia, and during the last great Ice Age, when the sea levels fell far below modern ones, a land bridge, Beringia, existed between Alaska and Siberia, over which the human hunters walked into the Americas. Although evidence for earlier settlement emerges from time to time, archeologist Brian Fagan puts it like this: "It is only fair to say that no archaeological site dating to earlier than 15,000 years ago in any part of the Americas has received complete scientific acceptance."[26] After about 12,000 years ago, the land bridge closed due to rising sea levels and the human population of the Americas lived in isolation for thousands of years, only linking up (traumatically) with Afro-Eurasia after 1492 (see Chapter 13).

WHAT ROLE DID LANGUAGE PLAY IN HUMAN SUCCESS?

Most of modern behavior, and Darwin's all-important social faculties, are unthinkable without human language. In fact, Darwin saw language as perhaps the central adaptation engendering all the others. "If it be maintained that certain powers, such as self-consciousness, abstraction, etc., are peculiar to man, it may well be that these are the incidental results of other highly advanced intellectual

---

[25] Smail, *On Deep History*, 193

[26] Brian M. Fagan, *Ancient North America: The Archaeology of a Continent* (London: Thames and Hudson, 2005), 85.

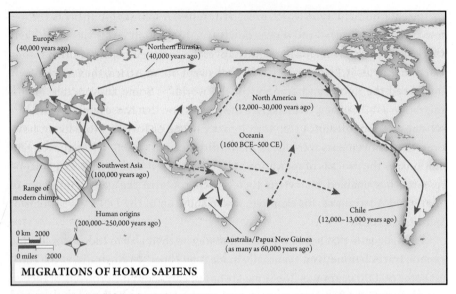

MIGRATIONS OF HOMO SAPIENS

MAP 1.4   MIGRATION OF *HOMO SAPIENS* Human migration happened over many generations as groups slowly filled their foraging ranges and moved to new ones. Crossing rivers, then oceans, they fanned out around the world.

faculties and these again are mainly the result of the continued use of a highly developed language."[27] It is the glue that holds human society together, allows learning between the generations, and the sharing of knowledge between groups. It also created cohesion within groups, allowing them to increase their population and eventually colonize the earth. "To understand when human history really began," says David Christian, "we have to understand when and how humans acquired their aptitude for symbolic language."[28] What is so complex and unique about our communication system?

The answer has to do with our use of grammar and syntax. These tools put words in the right order, creating precision and flexibility. Humans also have a capacity for abstract thinking, allowing them to consider such notions as past events, the importance of a place, the attributes of an individual or thing, or time. While apes communicate fear, joy, anger, etc., they do not discuss memories or plans for next week's fruit harvest or give complex instructions. Without grammar, syntax, and abstract thought a useful sentence, such as "a large herd of angry mammoths is coming from the southwest, three clicks away," might be reduced to a panic-inducing collection of sounds, such as "mammoths . . . herd . . . ahh!"

---

[27]   Charles Darwin, quoted in Bickerton, *Adam's Tongue,* 5.

[28]   Christian, *Maps of Time,* 151.

All animals communicate, in fact many with a dizzying array of sounds—everything, from ants to whales via gibbons, dogs, crickets, and pigeons. Some communicate vocally, others physically, and others still through smell. Says linguist Dereck Bickerton, "The means different species use for communication are so bewilderingly diverse and so different from one another that you might well think that something pretty complex is going on." But, he admits, "it isn't."[29] Research done on animal communication systems found three main areas of content: survival, mating, and what we can loosely call "social signals." These are a far cry from the elaborate messages passed between humans concerning abstract thought, memories, plans, etc. Researchers have been trying to teach chimps to talk for decades—with some success. But illustrative of their lack of facility with syntax, chimp communication was found to be of a basic nature. Herbert Terrace of Columbia University, for example, trained his chimp, Nim Chimpsky, to sign, with resultant utterances such as "Me banana you banana you me give." The chimp's mastery of grammar, however, was severely limited.

Humans are able to use a combinatorial system of both vocabulary and syntax. If we were only able to use single sounds to represent things, our vocabulary would be limited to the number of sounds we could make. But by combining sounds we are able to massively extend the range of our vocabulary (to the extent that the English language, for example, has a vocabulary of some 60,000 words, even if many of us resort to using "like" or "duh" to express ourselves). Linguist Noam Chomsky (clearly the namesake of our friend Nim Chimpsky) believes that there is such a thing as universal grammar, which is hardwired into the human brain and enables human children to understand and learn the grammar of whatever language they are born into. Looking for the origin of language, however, Bickerton has argued that language, like other adaptations, evolved through natural selection. In particular, Bickerton uses "niche construction theory," which in simple terms argues that evolution answers the problems faced in particular niches that animals construct for themselves. Language, therefore, was a response to the early human niche, which, at the time of its development, between 1 and 2 million years ago, was that of a wily scavenger on the African savanna.

Understanding how early humans lived, therefore, is the key to understanding why language might have evolved among them. Bickerton describes an imaginary scenario in which a group of humans are attempting to avail themselves of the carcass of a prehistoric elephant—a major prize for those living on the savanna. "Its hide is intact still, but other scavengers have arrived already—

---

[29] Bickerton, *Adam's Tongue*, 16.

lionlike or tigerlike creatures, some larger than those of modern times.[30]" Bickerton asks us to imagine being on the savanna and realizing that we are outgunned. You run off to collect everybody, men and women. This goes against the prevailing theories that men hunted and women foraged plants. But, as Bickerton puts it, "To go in without the women, at least all the women who aren't currently pregnant or minding babies and toddlers, would be like tying one hand behind one's back."[31] Once all the people are assembled, dozens of them, the men go in first—being wombless, they are dispensable. The women head for the meat and start carving out huge slabs, as the men, some of them being ripped apart, distract the beasts, with everything they have—Acheulian-style hand axes, rocks, sticks, flailing arms.

Such a dangerous undertaking had obvious risks and obvious rewards, and it demanded oversight. This was provided by language, which at its most basic is a form of social control. Carving up an elephant carcass before the hyenas get it required persuading people that there was a carcass "over there" that needed immediate attention, Bickerton explains. Once assembled, people needed to act together, follow the plan, and cooperate—all in real time. Bickerton makes the point that in his lectures several dozen humans sit quietly while he talks. Imagine trying that with chimpanzees. Language, with its socially controlling properties, makes this possible. Armed with this extraordinarily powerful yet invisible tool, humans were able to establish a niche as "high-end" scavengers, able to work together to outwit the fiercer and stronger creatures and survive on the open grasslands. Now the human portfolio of adaptations was sufficiently potent to take them wherever they wanted to go.

> Armed with this extraordinarily powerful, yet invisible, tool, humans were able to establish a niche as "high-end" scavengers, able to work together to outwit the fiercer and stronger creatures and survive on the open grasslands.

Conclusion: Domination and the Future

In summary, the story of human domination is long and complex, and it is certain that we have not read the final draft. Experts still wrangle about not only the details but the broad strokes as well. New discoveries in archeology force us to rethink assumptions. The adaptations that generated such population growth and migration—bipedalism, tool use, large brains, language, large group size, complex culture, and abstract thought—all contributed to our dominion. All of these adaptations, those things that made us, by anybody's estimate, truly human, were drawn upon in the development of agriculture (discussed in the next chapter); and

---

[30]   Ibid., 158.
[31]   Ibid., 161.

it was this which really cemented our hold over the planet by forever changing our relationship to nature and allowing for ever greater population growth.

The eighteenth-century writer Reverend Thomas Malthus predicted that if left unchecked the human population would increase exponentially. His conjecture was that our population would outstrip our ability to feed ourselves. As most species live within the limits of their local ecosystems, it is the environment that keeps population in check. As Niles Eldredge points out, however, "stepping outside the confines of local ecosystems, as our species began to do 10,000 years ago with the advent of agriculture, released us from these primordial constraints on our numbers."[32] Humans, who are a global species, have taken the entire planet as their ecosystem. It has so far only been our ability to innovate that has allowed us to keep feeding ourselves, with developments in agriculture such as synthetic fertilizer and intensive farming techniques.

Yet all of our innovations come with a cost: overpopulation and pollution. Perhaps these are also a consequence of our vision of ourselves as somehow outside of nature. "Ecologically speaking," says Eldredge, "culture is an enabler, a facilitator. But culture can be a disruption and a source of deep confusion. For we have come to think that we are no longer a part of nature. And that simply isn't so."[33] However distanced we may feel from nature and our biological heritage, much of our behavior arises from motivations that are lodged deeply in our evolutionary history. We are still in many ways Paleolithic people, evolved over millions of years to walk the plains of Africa, hunting, gathering, and scavenging; yet because of our culture we have developed a very different lifestyle, the foundations of which, described in Chapters 2 and 3, will remain in place for the rest of human history.

Perhaps most important is not what separates us from other animals but what unites us; the fact that we are flesh and blood and, as such, ultimately dependent on the building blocks of life—water, soil, sun. Our "dominance" is intensely relevant today as it raises many questions about the future of the human race and of the planet: Is there a limit to the planet's carrying capacity? How can we continue to maintain good standards of living while consuming so many resources and polluting at such a high rate? Many societies have faltered through overpopulation and the pressure it put on local ecosystems. But the human race, even if failing to colonize an area or sustain a society indefinitely, ultimately seems to rebound and start again or to adapt to new conditions. Will it always be so?

---

[32]   Eldredge, *Dominion*, 5
[33]   Ibid., 24.

Words to Think About

Adaptation	Bipedalism	Ecosystem
Evolution	Hominid	

Questions to Think About

- How can one speak of "human dominance?"
- What role might climate change have had in human evolution?
- How did language affect human dominance?

Primary Sources

Darwin, Charles. *The Descent of Man*. Norwalk, CT: Heritage Press, 1974.

"What Does It Mean to Be Human? Human Family Tree." National Museum of Natural History. Last modified February 16, 2014, http://humanorigins.si.edu/evidence/human-fossils/species/human-family-tree.

Secondary Sources

Bickerton, Dereck. *Adam's Tongue: How Humans Made Language, and How Language Made Humans*. New York: Hill and Wang, 2009.

Christian, David. *Maps of Time: An Introduction to Big History*. Berkeley: University of California Press, 2004.

Eldredge, Niles. *Dominion: Can Nature and Culture Co-Exist?* New York: Henry Holt, 1995.

Fagan, Brian M. *Ancient North America: The Archaeology of a Continent*. London: Thames and Hudson, 2005.

Klein, Richard G. *The Dawn of Human Culture*. With Blake Edgar. New York: John Wiley & Sons, 2002.

McBrearty, Sally, and Allison S. Brooks. "The Revolution That Wasn't: A New Interpretation of the Origin of Modern Human Behavior." *Journal of Human Evolution* 39 (2000): 453–563.

Smail, Daniel Lord. *On Deep History and the Brain*. Berkley: University of California, 2008.

Stringer, Chris, and Peter Andrews. *The Complete World of Human Evolution*, 2nd ed. London: Thames and Hudson, 2011.

Stringer, Chris, and Robin McKie. *African Exodus: The Origins of Modern Humanity*. New York: Henry Holt, 1996.

Taçon, Paul S. "Identifying Ancient Religious Thought and Iconography: Problems of Definition, Preservation, and Interpretation." In *Becoming Human: Innovation in Prehistoric Material and Spiritual Culture*, edited by Colin Renfrew and Iain Morley, 61–73. Cambridge: Cambridge University Press, 2009.

Tattersall, Ian. *Becoming Human: Evolution and Human Uniqueness*. New York: Harcourt Brace, 1998.

Tattersall, Ian. *Masters of the Planet: The Search for Our Human Origins*. New York: Palgrave Macmillan, 2010.

Wrangham, Richard. *Catching Fire: How Cooking Made Us Human*. New York: Basic Books, 2009.

For additional resources, including maps, primary sources, and visuals, web links, and quizzes, please go to **www.oup.com/us/cole**

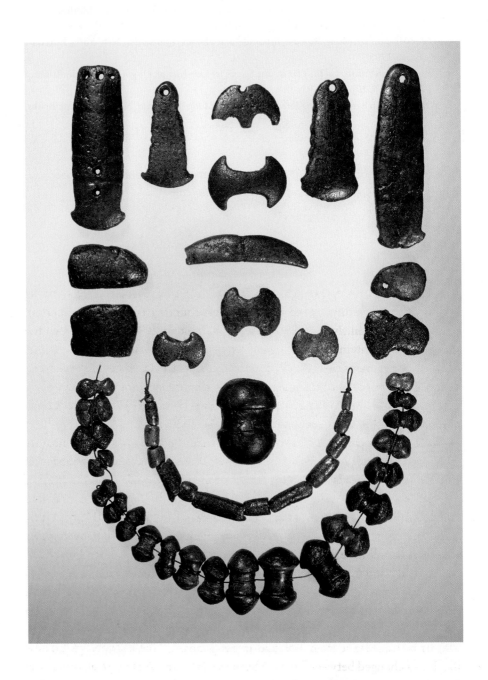

Amber Pendants from Denmark   These decorative items first appeared in Neolithic burials as people began to experiment with new materials and technologies.

Chapter 2

What Were the Consequences of Settling Down?

What Will You Put in My Grave?

Denmark, 11,000 years ago. It is safe to imagine several people standing around the freshly opened grave. They were burying a woman with a certain ritual, so it seems likely that relatives were in attendance. And we know that the grave already contained the bones of a woman buried some 12 years before. Maybe these remains were the dead woman's mother. Next to her skeleton was a decorated dagger carved from a single piece of deer bone that was left in the grave when they buried her. We can also imagine two people (men?) lowering the body of the daughter so that she lay next to her mother's skeleton.

Was sobbing part of the burial process, or did they do it in stony silence? As with much prehistory, we have to use our imagination. A young woman bends and places a string of beads next to the dead body. They are made from the teeth of wild cattle and elk. Then she adds some pendants made from the teeth of wild boar and deer. All of these materials are organic, naturally occurring, and only slightly transformed by human hands to serve as ornaments, reflecting the close relationship these people have with their surroundings and the creatures that share them.

Several hundred years go by. The grave remains undisturbed. Winter winds blow snow across it. Herds of reindeer graze on it. Then, only a few feet away, a descendant of the women is buried in his own grave. Scientists will dig him up too and will notice items of which he himself was unaware: a clay pot, a stone battle-axe, arrowheads made from flint, and amber pendants. These objects reveal how much had changed between his own burial and the burial of his relatives next to him. What was so significant about these apparently basic items? All of them had

THINKING ABOUT SEDENTISM

What Was Life Like Before Settlements? (200,000–12,000 years ago)
- Nomadic populations of the Paleolithic were strictly limited by their environment, restricting their numbers to how many they could feed.

How Did the Early Settlements Develop?
- It may be unpopular to suggest that we were forced into farming by bad weather, instead of "inventing" it in a "Eureka!" moment; but in a crude way that is what seems to have happened.

What Changes Did Sedentary Life Bring?
- Sedentism expanded the notion of private property greatly, and settled society never looked back.

Conclusion
- Whereas settling in one place may have led to agriculture and population growth and all subsequent ills, the societies that it spawned . . . created literature, science, architecture, medicine, and the culture of which we are all a part.

been quarried from the earth and *transformed* unrecognizably from their original material by technologies not in existence a few hundred years earlier. Their forms were also expressive of male status, won or maintained through violence, perhaps even "war." This man and his people represented a radical shift in human thought and behavior, having transitioned from a mobile, foraging life to a settled, agricultural one. Who were these new people, and what were the consequences of these changes?

Introduction

Hair covered his body,
hair grew thick on his head and hung
down to his waist, like a woman's hair.
he roamed all over the wilderness,
naked, far from the cities of men,

ate grass with gazelles, and when he was thirsty
he drank clear water from the waterholes
kneeling beside the antelope and deer.[1]

This excerpt from *The Epic of Gilgamesh*, often considered the "first story," was deciphered from clay tablets dug from the ruins of one of the world's first cities, Nineveh, in today's Iraq. It tells the story of the king-god of the title, a historical figure who ruled over the city of Uruk, some 5,000 years ago. Gilgamesh is strong and good-looking, but he is also arrogant and abusive of his subjects—so much so that a goddess creates Enkidu, the creature in the quote above, in appearance like an animal, eating grass with the gazelles. The idea is for Enkidu to do battle with Gilgamesh, match his strength and power, and ultimately force him to moderate his excessive behavior. Whereas Gilgamesh is a product of this new—urban—civilization, Enkidu is a primitive man, at one with nature. The Gods of Uruk cry out, "Let him be equal to Gilgamesh's stormy heart! Let them be a match for each other so that Uruk may find peace!"

For some readers *Gilgamesh* may seem like an adventure story, full of monsters, gods, demons, heroes, and villains—*Harry Potter*–esque. But historians see in *Gilgamesh* profound, contemporary themes. In particular, the work is full of ambivalence about what was possibly the greatest revolution in the history of humankind: the move from a mobile existence as hunter–gatherers to settled villages, towns, and eventually cities. We may take for granted today that our settled, agricultural way of life is as old as humanity. But seen as a proportion of the total life of our species, it was, as one scholar has written, only "yesterday" that we became sedentary.[2] In terms of long-term stability and reliability, archaeologist Peter Bellwood considers the hunting–gathering lifestyle "the most successful in Human history."[3] People today still hunt and gather, although their numbers are drastically reduced and their cultures dangerously threatened by agricultural, sedentary societies which make up the majority of the world's population. There is even a strong case to be made for the idea that the struggle between sedentary and nonsedentary people has been history's most prominent theme and that the destruction of the latter by the former represents a kind of "end of history," to the extent that mobile/nomadic lifestyles become a thing of the past completely.[4]

In this chapter we will explore the transition from a mobile life to a sedentary and eventually agricultural one. Settling in one place, or *sedentism*, had far-reaching consequences that are still relevant today. In fact, it is no exaggeration to say that all of

---

[1]   *Epic of Gilgamesh*, trans. Stephen Mitchell (New York: Free Press, 2004), 74.
[2]   Jared Diamond, *The World Until Yesterday: What Can We Learn From Traditional Societies?* (New York: Viking Adult, 2012).
[3]   Peter Bellwood, *The First Farmers: The Origins of Agricultural Societies* (Malden, Blackwell, 2005), 2.
[4]   This idea alludes to Francis Fukuyama's 1992 book *The End of History and the Last Man*, in which the author argued that the "end of history" was heralded by the conclusion of the Cold War and the collapse of communism as a credible political system.

recorded human history to date has been made possible by this one development. If the evolutionary journey described in the previous chapter set the scene for human dominance over the animal kingdom, the transition from mobile foragers to sedentary farmers described in this chapter made it irreversible. Sedentism paved the way for farming (or possibly vice versa), and with this technology we abruptly overturned everything about our existence on earth, releasing ourselves, like no other animal, from our reliance on Mother Nature. What followed included a dramatic increase in our population; the development of towns, then cities; new social, political, economic, and cultural forms and institutions; and ultimately the global civilization we have today.

Many scholars believe that relying on agriculture as a primary source of food was a consequence of sedentism, while others believe that sedentism was a consequence of agriculture. Most scholars, however, agree that the many by-products of sedentism included population growth, private property, specialization of labor and its division along gender lines, inequality of wealth, religion, disease from overcrowding and proximity to animals, and environmental degradation and pollution. Other consequences, however, included the development of writing, literature, architecture, the arts, and religion.

Sedentism and its accompanying agriculture, in other words, has a very mixed balance sheet, so we have to ask, *Has agriculture been a net loss for both humans and the planet?* In the last few decades this charge has challenged a mostly nineteenth-century argument that saw agriculture as progressive, allowing humans to reach their full cultural potential. Agriculture, it was assumed, was a natural progression from the "ignorance" of preagricultural peoples to the "advancement" of farming. These differing perspectives reflect perhaps the social context of the times and, as such, raise a core question in the practice of history: *Is it possible to consider the past without bringing along all the baggage of the present?* While people in the nineteenth century were living through a period of what was universally considered "progress"—revolutions in communication, manufacturing, medicine, and science; "good things," in other words— we are today facing more threatening crises involving human-made climate change, overpopulation, and resource depletion, all resulting from the "progress" of the last century or so. It is no surprise therefore that we should look to the origins of our civilization and wonder whether we took the right path.

What Was Life Like Before Settlements? (200,000–12,000 years ago)

To understand the consequences of settling in villages, we need to first turn our attention to the Paleolithic (beginning with human origins about 200,000 years ago and ending around 13,000 years ago). This period has often been characterized

Sedentism   New York City commemorates the twelfth anniversary of September 11, 2001. Sedentary life changes the environment in dramatic ways.

as millennia in which nothing of historical significance happened—a yawning chasm of historical emptiness. But such a view only exists because we have no written records, and as the archaeological record grows, we are beginning to fill in the blanks. Researchers have yet to dig up evidence of changes as dramatic as sedentism and agriculture however, which are the hallmarks of the Neolithic (New Stone Age) period. Having said that, the transition to sedentism was gradual, occurring over several millennia, a timescale that is difficult for most of us to fully appreciate and that spans the end of the last Ice Age.

HOW MUCH CAN WE INFER ABOUT THE PAST FROM MODERN HUNTER–GATHERERS?

Without written records many scholars draw upon studies of present-day hunter–gatherers to piece together what life must have been like for ancient human populations. Although this is a widespread practice, it is not without drawbacks; very few nomadic and/or hunter–gatherer groups remain, and those that do are rarely untouched by the modern world. Modern hunter–gatherers are restricted to a fraction of their former territories; are often in regular contact with sedentary communities, moving in and out of them for work or to trade; and are under threat of extinction. Among those that remain, the most studied are the Aborigines of Australia,

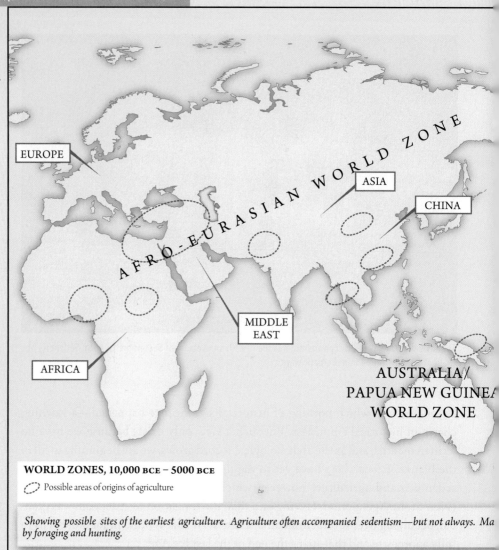

EUROPE

ASIA

CHINA

AFRO-EURASIAN WORLD ZONE

MIDDLE
EAST

AFRICA

AUSTRALIA/
PAPUA NEW GUINEA
WORLD ZONE

WORLD ZONES, 10,000 BCE – 5000 BCE

⌒ Possible areas of origins of agriculture

Showing possible sites of the earliest agriculture. Agriculture often accompanied sedentism—but not always. Ma
by foraging and hunting.

MAP 2.1   WORLD ZONES, 10,000 BCE – 5000 BCE

TIMELINE

 24,500–18,000 years ago
Height of last Ice Age

 10,500–300 BCE
Jomon Culture, Japan

ca. 12,500 BCE
Early Natufian society

ca. 10,000 BCE–6000 BCE
Neolithic Period

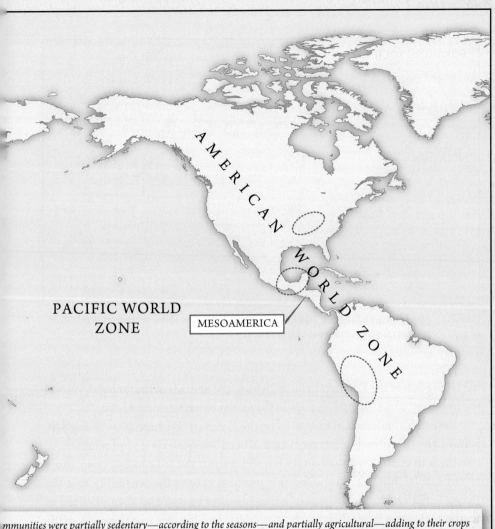

AMERICAN

WORLD

ZONE

PACIFIC WORLD
ZONE

MESOAMERICA

...mmunities were partially sedentary—according to the seasons—and partially agricultural—adding to their crops

10,000 BCE
Jericho, the "first Village"

10,800–9600 BCE
Younger Dryas

ca. 1 CE
Mound Builders of
Mississippi Valley

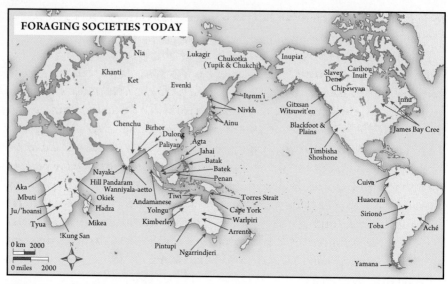

MAP 2.2   FORAGING SOCIETIES TODAY   Foraging societies have been increasingly marginalized, often to the point of extinction, in the wake of agriculture.

the !Kung San of the Kalahari in South Africa, the nomads of the far north such as the Inuit, and some "pygmy" groups in the forests of west-central Africa.

Research conducted in the 1970s on the Kalahari "Bushmen," or !Kung San, painted a picture of mobile foragers who had been living the same way for millennia, coming into contact with sedentary farmers only in the last century or so. More recent scholarship has questioned this premise, raising the possibility that the !Kung actually became sedentary hundreds of years ago and then reverted to their mobile ways later. This possibility undermines the idea that their way of life stretches back to the very earliest reaches of human existence, making them a living museum. This debate is far from concluded, but the truth will likely affect whether a reasonable understanding of ancient human foragers can be gained from what we know about the !Kung.

The historian Barbara Ehrenberg points out that several of the world's remaining hunter–gatherer groups live in similar environments to their Paleolithic forbears: The Inuit in the Arctic, familiar to Ice-Age mammoth hunters; the !Kung San in the arid South African bush, an environment similar to one in which *Homo sapiens* evolved; and the Mbuti pygmies of central Africa, who inhabit an environment similar to the hot phases, or *interglacials*, between ancient Ice Ages. "Despite these huge variations in environment," says Ehrenberg, "numerous similarities exist in the social organization of all modern foragers and we can therefore have confidence that early foragers also shared similar patterns of organization."[5]

Writer and ethnographer Elizabeth Marshall Thomas lived among the Kalahari Bushmen in the 1950s. Many of her observations, she believes, can be extended to what she calls the "Old Way," or how ancient populations of hunter–gatherers lived. She sums up the core elements of this lifeway thus: "for those who live in the Old Way, certain elements never vary. Your group size is set by the food supply, your territory must include water, the animals you hunt will always be afraid of you, and the plants will always be seasonal, so you had better remember where they grow and be there when they're fruiting."[6] While noting that many commonalities may exist between them, hunter–gatherer communities are far from identical the world over. Many differences exist: of thought, belief, and practice. Even the definition of *hunter–gatherer* is variable and elastic as different groups employed various strategies to feed themselves.

The Human Stain   Someone braved the gloom to outline this child's hand by blowing red ochre around it about 20,000 years ago. We can only guess at the significance of such art. Buried in a cave inhabited by large wild animals, who was the audience, and what was the message?

---

5   Barbara Ehrenberg, *Women in Prehistory* (Norman: University of Oklahoma Press, 1989), 51.
6   Elizabeth Marshall Thomas, *The Old Way: A Story of the First People* (New York: Farrar, Strauss and Giroux, 2006), 6.

HOW DID HUMANS LIVE AT THE END OF THE LAST ICE AGE?

In order to pick up the trail of the transition to sedentism, we need to turn our attention to the end of the last Ice Age. The archeologist Steven Mithen has attempted to give us a sense of what life was like at this time: "The world at 20,000 BC is inhospitable—a cold, dry, windy planet with frequent storms and a dust laden atmosphere.... The Sahara, Gobi, and other sandy deserts are greatly expanded in extent. Britain is no more than a peninsula of Europe, its north buried below the ice, its south a polar waste. Much of North America is smothered by a giant dome of ice."[7]

Northern peoples have been pushed together in areas that are habitable, including southwest France, Cantabrian Spain, and the river valleys of the Russian plain: "People survive wherever they can, struggling with freezing temperatures and persistent drought."[8] At Pushkari in the Ukraine, archeologists found the remains of a camp of mammoth hunters. Mithen describes five tent-like structures that form a circle on the edge of the tundra. The temperatures can dip to –30 degrees Celsius and remain there for 9 months. A few people sit around a small fire, two adults and some children, chipping flakes off stones. Next to them on the snowy ground are small piles of chips flaked off the larger pieces in their hands. Conversation is subdued—murmurs, occasional laughter, or a yelp when

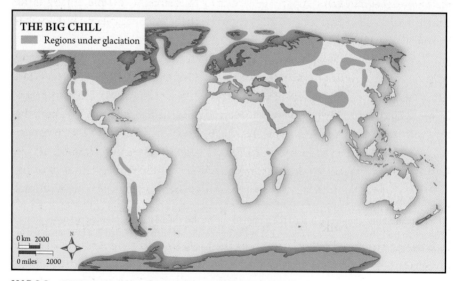

MAP 2.3   **EXTENT OF GLACIATION DURING THE ICE AGES**

---

7   Steven Mithen, *After the Ice Age: A Global Human History, 20,000 BC–5000 BC* (Cambridge, MA: Harvard University Press, 2004), 8.
8   Ibid.

someone hits her thumb. A group of men and women are busy butchering a reindeer they killed when it wandered away from the herd. The teeth will be used as pendants, the organs eaten as delicacies, the bones saved for fuel. At one edge of the camp lies a heap of giant tusks, hacked from mammoths. They use these to create impressive arched doorways for their dwellings, large domed structures. The leg bones of the creatures create the vertical supports, and jawbones are stacked on each other for walls. Hides are stretched over the structure, competently stitched together to keep out the worst of the freezing winds. From our perspective it is outlandish, but for these people its just ho-hum, daily life.

The flint-chippers will never know the balmy temperatures of the Holocene period which is coming. The earth will be in the grip of this Ice Age for another 2,000 years or more. These people live near the edge of the glacier, as far north as is possible if you are the kind of person who needs to eat. They choose to live here because this is where the mammoth herds feed, and they are dedicated mammoth hunters. They are highly skilled at what they do, and they have a diverse armory, including long tapered spears tipped with finely wrought, sharp flint points, attached, or *hafted*, with resin and plant fibers to the shaft. They have bows and arrows, similarly tipped with even finer points. They have mastered fire; make warm, fur-lined garments; and have a deep understanding of, and no doubt respect for, their prey. Like all other people on earth at this time, this group is mobile. But, like many others, they have found that they can stay put in one place for long stretches of time, as long as the herds remain. These practices would account for the relative complexity and durability of their dwellings—why invest in building if you are not going to use it?

Around the world, although there may be fewer than 1 million people (and nobody in the Americas, which most archeologists think were not peopled until about 13,000 years ago), people are exploiting different resources. Tasmania, says Mithen, is considerably warmer at this period than the frozen north, and here the locals are hunting wallabies in the grasslands. People are fishing in the river Nile and the Mediterranean. In southern France, one of the major redoubts of the Ice Age, other mammoth hunters are busy deep inside subterranean caverns, erecting scaffolding to reach the rocky ceilings; lighting their way with animal fat; possibly ingesting mind-altering herbs; creating giant murals of horses, mammoth, and *aurochs* (wild cattle); and making silhouettes of their children's hands by blowing powdered red ochre against the rock, all of this—despite, or because of, getting high—with a deadly earnest, spiritual intent. Although the archeological data from China are more scattered, the Baiyanjiao Cave, in Guizhou Province, provides evidence of hunter–gatherers reliant on annual slaughters of migrating horse and deer, like their Ice-Age cousins of Europe. While in south Asia archeological data are similarly scant, evidence demonstrates that hunter–gatherers were active in these areas at or soon after 20,000 years ago.

"Something's just not right—our air is clean, our water is pure, we all get plenty of exercise, everything we eat is organic and free-range, and yet nobody lives past thirty."

Quality of Life   Paleolithic people suffered from lack of medical care, animal attacks, and accidents. Early Neolithic lifespans were similarly short. The reason for Neolithic population growth was not related to increases in longevity but fertility. If you are not on the move constantly you can handle the logistics of child-rearing more easily. Humans can reproduce in their teens. Living to thirty allows plenty of time to have children!

WHAT IS THE SIGNIFICANCE OF GROUP SIZE?

A global population of 1 million seems pretty paltry. A mid-size American city, such as Austin, Texas, contains about that many people today; and the entire planet now hosts some 8 billion souls. Nomadic populations of the Paleolithic, however, were strictly limited by their environment, restricting numbers to how many it could feed. This did not change until the advent of sedentism and agriculture, which allowed for greater population growth. Paleolithic groups were likely to have contained around 20–50 members of an extended family, or clan. These clans, or "bands," would have interacted with other bands to share food and exchange mates. Women more frequently left the group to find mates, thus maintaining a healthy gene pool. Meetings of clans would have probably occurred during seasons of abundance, so exchanges of people and goods could take place. These meetings are still in evidence among Australian Aborigines and are known as *corroborees*.

To revisit that idea of the environment restricting population, consider this: mobile foraging requires a large range to effectively feed people, about 10 square miles per person (as opposed to 50 people per square mile, which can be supported by agriculture). Marshall Thomas found this to be the case in the Kalahari in the 1950s. To maintain this arrangement, different strategies would have been applied to birth control, including long periods of nursing, which limits fertility; abortion (both "mechanical" and herbal); and almost certainly infanticide, most notably of twins or sickly infants. Infanticide was an indication of how seriously Paleolithic groups took their dependence on nature as they could not afford to feed too many mouths. Because of these small populations, the historian Cynthia Stokes Brown argues that in all probability before 5,000 years ago no more than 500 people were ever gathered in one place.[9]

WAS PALEOLITHIC LIFE A STRUGGLE FOR SURVIVAL?

Until quite recently the received wisdom about the Paleolithic was summed up by seventeenth-century English philosopher Thomas Hobbes' declaration in his book *Leviathan* (1651) that the period offered "no culture of the earth; no navigation . . . no account of time; no arts; no letters; no society; and which is worst of all, continual fear, and danger of violent death; and the life of man, solitary, poor, nasty, brutish and short."[10] But is that fair?

We should not underestimate the challenges of the Old Way (many of us would be hard-pressed to endure it). Yet Hobbes was in effect voicing a common discomfort on the part of settled people at the idea of the nomadism of our early ancestors. More recent research suggests that hunter–gatherers would not recognize this characterization of their life. The anthropologist Marshall Sahlins, who referred to the Paleolithic as the "original Affluent Society," argued that Stone-Age societies met the needs of people better than do modern ones because they had few needs. This "Zen" path to affluence defined the Paleolithic in Sahlin's view.[11]

Studies of foragers in Australia showed that most people only worked 4–5 hours a day in tasks related to subsistence. Moreover, this work was intermittent; when the goal was met and people were fed, the work stopped and people gossiped, slept, and participated in other "leisure-time" activities. Studies from other foraging societies suggested similar findings. The "work ethic," which is such an important part of modern societies, was not well represented in this ethnographic research; instead, an emphasis was placed on social life, leisure time, and other "nonproductive" activities.

Further, in contrast to the Hobbesian view—which supposes a ceaseless struggle to generate enough calories—the diets of modern foragers are surprisingly varied and nutritious. This corresponds with what we know of ancient foragers, whose bones tells us that they were strong and healthy and that they lived off a wide variety of staples. We can conclude from that—and from modern

9   Cynthia Stokes Brown, *Big History: From the Big Bang to the Present* (New York: New Press, 2007), 58.
10   Thomas Hobbes, *Leviathan: Or the Matter, Forme and Power of a Commonwealth, Ecclesiastical and Civil* (Cambridge: Cambridge University Press, 1904), 84.
11   Marshall Sahlins, *Stone Age Economics* (New York: Aldine de Gruyter, 1972).

☀ Ironically, perhaps, today's trendy "Paleo diet" seeks to recapture some of the health benefits of prehistory and avoid a less healthy focus on carbohydrates, grains, and processed food.

foragers—that they had an encyclopedic knowledge of the plants and animals upon which they depended. They knew when certain fruits or grains would be in season and understood the migratory habits and behavior of mammals and birds. This knowledge meant that they were unlikely to suffer from starvation. Ironically, perhaps, today's trendy "Paleo diet" seeks to recapture some of the health benefits of prehistory and avoid a less healthy focus on carbohydrates, grains, and processed food.

WERE HUNTER–GATHERERS MORE EGALITARIAN?

Being mobile made it almost impossible to accumulate possessions as we understand them today. Everything you owned needed to be portable. Food was gathered and eaten in "real time," meaning that there was very little storage and surplus, making wealth inequality much more difficult. When you needed food, you went hunting. Spoils from the hunt were usually shared among participants of the band, or among kin, reciprocity being an important principle in daily life. Anthropologist Robert Wright notes, "the best place for [an Eskimo] to store his surplus is someone else's stomach."[12] This strategy would ensure reciprocal generosity in the future.

This lack of surplus represented an obstacle to the development of social hierarchies (or "haves" and "have-nots") as control over surpluses creates social inequalities. Such egalitarianism was supported by the scant need for leadership. Anthropologists consider the maximum leaderless group size to be about 150. Larger groups generally require rules to regulate interactions between people and authority of some sort to organize the kinds of collective labor that is required for life in a larger community (building projects, agricultural tasks, military activities).

Key to the notion of egalitarianism is the role of gender in early communities. Ehrenberg describes how over the last 30 years or so some feminist anthropologists have searched for evidence of matriarchal societies (defined, in her words, as "a society in which women not only have equality with men, but also control, power, dominance"[13]). Most scholars agree, she notes, that no societies today can be described as matriarchal, so the inference applies that, in all probability, ancient ones did not exist either. However, says Ehrenberg, anthropologists have looked at a range of traditional societies and found that "the status of women is

---

[12]   Robert Wright, *NonZero: The Logic of Human Destiny* (New York: Random House, 2000), 20.
[13]   Ehrenberg, *Women in Prehistory*, 63.

regularly higher in forager groups than in any other type."[14] This might be related to private property or the lack thereof. Ehrenberg adds that "one key to this equality is the lack of private property or possessions within the society, and the impossibility for a nomadic forager band of storing food. One person cannot therefore own more than another, nor can dependence or debt to another build up in a way which makes oppression and submission a likely outcome."[15]

But there are other categories of social hierarchy. Hunter–gatherer/nomadic groups often have notions of seniority based on kinship or abilities—most notably of hunting or other essential activities. Strict hierarchies exist among several types of apes that are often highly patriarchal, centering around a male and "his" females.

Modern Aboriginal Woman with Barramundi
Traditionally, fishing would have been a co-ed activity among hunter–gatherers.

This kind of "pecking order" is seen in many other mammal communities. Many scholars of prehistory have concluded that divisions of labor also meant that women for the most part performed more of the "gathering," while men hunted. Fishing would have been a co-ed activity, while weapon making was a male domain and tools such as pots, baskets, and other items related to the domestic realm were generally made by women. Ehrenberg notes that women's gathering probably produced the majority of the food as meat from hunting could not be relied upon. Marshall Thomas describes the Kalahari gender divisions: "Women provided the foods that sustained people, which they did by normal gathering, and men provided the food that people liked the best and valued most highly, the meat of the important antelope."[16] One can see from this that the specifics of these "gendered" tasks have consequences for how gender might have been viewed among such groups and how they were differently valued.

---

[14]   Ibid.
[15]   Ibid.
[16]   Marshall Thomas, *The Old Way*, 175.

Again, it should be noted that these observations may not apply equally to all mobile groups. It is also possible that our understanding of such gendered divisions at this time are obscured by our modern preconceptions and that women and men did not adhere rigidly to proscribed roles or that gender divisions were more complex and ambiguous than we think. Anthropologists Hetty Jo Brumbach and Robert Jarvenpa, for example, through their studies of the oral traditions of the Chipewyan population of northeastern Saskatchewan, concluded that the hunting/gathering division was more nuanced: "although the women we studied do not dispatch large mammals as frequently as do men, they are inextricably involved in the broader system of provisioning through pursuit, harvesting, and processing of mammals, fish, and birds."[17] Other archeologists from around the world have attempted to glean information on gender from sites where remains of settlements have yielded clues as to differences in women's and men's work, and the results often suggest the centrality of women in the entire food-acquisition process, as well as the difficulty of separating roles of prehistoric work. Another anthropologist, Rita P. Wright, has questioned the concept of "separate spheres"—in which men and women performed mutually exclusive jobs—suggesting that we should ask not *in what way* but *whether* these spheres were indeed separate.[18]

WHAT ARE THE DIFFERENCES IN WORLDVIEWS AND RELIGION BETWEEN FORGING AND SEDENTARY SOCIETIES?

Ancient foragers, like many of today's nomadic peoples, were animists, believing that nonhuman entities possessed personhood and that animals and plants had their own reason, language, consciousness, and moral sense. The environment was full of "personages," whether animal or human. There was a sense of continuity, therefore, between the human, animal, and spirit worlds. No hard-and-fast divisions existed between these realms as they do in sedentary agricultural societies, and humans were very much enmeshed in nature, arising from the ground to which they owed their existence. Although we understand them poorly, cave paintings from around the Paleolithic world were likely an expression of a human search for identity, between the spirit world and the often threatening and dangerous world of nature. Images of "wild nature" appeared well into the Neolithic era, when this negotiation was still going on.

---

[17] Hetty Jo Brumbach and Robert Jarvenpa, "Woman the Hunter: Ethnoarchaeological Lessons from Chipewyan Life-Cycle Dynamics," in *Women in Prehistory: North America and Mesoamerica,* ed. Cheryl Claassen and Rosemary A. Joyce (Philadelphia: University of Philadelphia Press, 1997), 21.

[18] Rita P. Wright, "Women's Labor and Pottery Production in Prehistory," in *Engendering Archaeology: Women and Prehistory,* ed. Joan M. Gero and Margaret W. Conkey (Oxford: Basil Blackwell, 1991), 196.

Animal Fresco from Çatal Hüyük in Turkey   "Wild nature" played a prominent part in the imagery of this Neolithic town. People lived in close proximity to a natural world that both provided and threatened.

How Did the Earliest Human Settlements Develop?

Agriculture and sedentism are by no means the same thing, but their relationship is extremely close; and most likely one led to the other, although there is scholarly debate about which one. Both farming and sedentism are linked to another major event, global climate change. It may be unpopular to suggest we were forced into farming by bad weather, instead of "inventing" it in a "Eureka!" moment; but in a crude way that's what seems to have happened. The archeologist Graeme Barker sees the climate/agriculture relationship like this: "At the global scale, a key driver of subsistence change was clearly climate change, however uncomfortably that fits with the post-modern tendency to privilege human agency and to discount all other factors shaping human decision-making as crude functionalism or environmental determinism."[19] Other archeologists, for example, Jacque Cauvin of France, see the onset of agriculture and sedentism not as a consequence of changing climate but as an expression of changing human habits—putting the human agency back into the phenomenon. He suggests that there were even cognitive developments that allowed, or encouraged, humans to live together in permanent settlements and farm. While there may be some truth in this theory, especially in the idea that group get-togethers were

---

[19]   Graeme Barker, *The Agricultural Revolution in Prehistory: Why Did Foragers Become Farmers?* (Oxford: Oxford University Press, 2006), 398.

probably festive—fun, in other words—people had been getting together for thousands of years like this, so why the change and why now?

HOW DID HUMANS RESPOND TO ANCIENT CLIMATE CHANGE?

Twenty thousand years ago, when our friends were chipping flints around the fire in the Ukraine, marks the peak of the last Ice Age, known as the Last Glacial Maximum (LGM, ca. 26,500–20,000 years ago). Much of the world's moisture was locked up in giant ice caps that spread out from both poles. The several millennia following this saw global temperatures rise and fall rapidly in a confusion of weather but generally trending toward warmer temperatures. But then, between 12,700 and 10,800 BCE, the climate underwent a rapid and intense warming accompanied by increased moisture. Were you to have lived through this period you might have assumed, cheerily, that the Ice Age was history; but then, perhaps within a decade, this warming period came to a screeching halt, and temperatures plummeted again globally, hurling the planet back into the Ice Age for over 1,000 years, causing humanity to utter a communal groan. This period, known as the Younger Dryas, lasted from 10,800 to 9600 BCE. It ended, however, as abruptly as it had begun; and another warmer, wetter period set in. At this point the Ice Age really can be classified as "history," and our present climatic period, the Holocene, had begun.

Notwithstanding that communal groan, bearing in mind geographical differences, global weather, like today, affected people differently in different places. So much so in fact that Harvard archeologist Ofer Bar-Yosef considers it inappropriate to talk of the "Ice Age" as there was no ice south of Europe, except

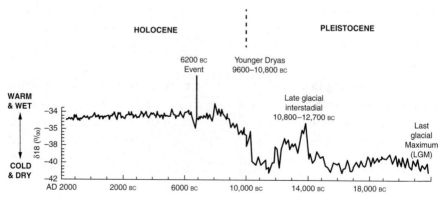

Global Temperatures Measured from Ice Cores in Greenland   Such changes in global weather had dramatic effects on human behavior, most notably affecting sustenance, and played a key role in the development of agriculture.

on top of mountains.[20] One site, on the banks of the Sea of Galilee, in modern Israel, flourished. At Ohalo, the environment provided multiple plant and animal resources, including nuts, seeds, berries, and acorns (when ground and cooked they lose their bitterness); fish and shellfish from the lake; small mammals, like fox and hare, from nearby oak forests and woodland; as well as the more significant gazelle. The inhabitants of this camp were still mobile at the LGM, although the natural abundance around them enabled them to remain in one place for some time. A fire seems to have ended the settlement, and as Mithen points out, "had they been farmers rather than hunter–gatherers, the fire would have destroyed more than brushwood huts; most likely timber-built dwellings, animal pens, fences, and stored grain; their flocks may have fled or died in the flames. Rather than abandoning the site to nature, farmers would have had to remain and rebuild."[21] But not being fully tied to the land, they were free to relocate.

With the rise in temperature and moisture following the LGM, foraging improved for most communities. A large region of the Middle East, known as the Fertile Crescent, was particularly resource-rich. This area stretches from southern Israel up to northern Syria and into southern Turkey, turning southeast in an arc into Iraq. In the middle of this area, at the Shukbah Cave in the Judean hills, archeologist Dorothy Garrod of Cambridge University made a groundbreaking discovery in the 1930s. She found a settlement with certain characteristics that would be found later in multiple sites all over a large area of Israel, Lebanon, and Syria. The Natufians, as these people came to be known, were partially or fully sedentary and lived in what are now considered the earliest known "villages." The dwellings were circular and partly dug into the ground, with timber posts supporting roofs of brush and wood. Dated to around 12,500 BCE, these sites occupied areas of hilly woodlands. Less dry than the area is today, it was full of small mammals—fox, hare, rabbit, birds such as partridges and duck, and larger game such as wild boar, aurochs, and gazelle. In the plains near the lake they also enjoyed an abundance of plant species, such as lentils, peas, and multiple nuts and berries.

Most interesting to Garrod, however, were the number of *sickles* she found (bone implements with finely chipped stone flakes embedded in them as blades). These tools had been used for cutting stems of cereals or harvesting. Were the Natufians farmers? Paleobotanists, who study ancient plant remains, determined that the Natufians relied heavily on large stands of cereals. Garrod concluded that

---

[20]   Ofer Bar Yosef, Conversation with the authors, March 2011.

[21]   Mithen, *After the Ice Age*, 21.

these cereals were farmed. On later analysis they turned out to have been wild, meaning that while these early Natufians were harvesting like farmers, they were probably not sowing the seeds and were therefore "collectors" more than farmers.

Archeologist Kent Flannery described the kind of foraging we see with the early Natufians as the "Broad Spectrum Revolution." Other historians have referred to the period as one of "intensification," meaning that people were starting to use a smaller territory more intensely, rather than ranging widely in a larger territory like traditional hunter–gatherers do. One reason for this shift is that globally, especially in Ice-Age Europe and Russia, humans had hunted many species to extinction. Between this development and the changing climate, humans had to look to other, smaller species and plants to make up the shortfall. One mammoth alone would supply a family with almost 3 weeks of meat, in addition to endless bones for fuel, weapons, and building material and hides for clothes and shelter. You need a lot of bunnies to do that.

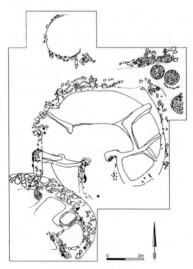

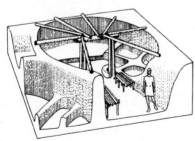

Plan and Reconstruction of a Natufian House at the Syrian Site of Mureybet III

"In the Natufian period, ample evidence suggests that sedentary life had begun in earnest," says archeologist Peter Akkermans. "A possible reason for this is the increasing abundance of wild resources made available by the amelioration of the climate, with the result that people no longer needed to range over large territories to meet their subsistence needs."[22] In other words, people settled in permanent camps, or villages, here because they could. A threshold had been reached, and humans had put down permanent roots.

Bar-Yosef spent 11 seasons excavating another Natufian site, the Hayonim Cave, in the Judean hills, beginning in 1964. In the cave he found six circular structures, about 6.5 feet in diameter with drystone walls and paved floors. Like all Natufian sites, the cave had its own "cemetery." Natufians buried their

---

[22]   Peter M. M. G. Akkermans and Glenn M. Schwartz, *The Archaeology of Syria: From Complex Hunter–Gatherers to Early Urban Societies (ca. 16,000–300 BC)* (Cambridge: Cambridge University Press, 2003), 25.

dead near their dwellings, along with treasured items such as beads, carved bones, and seashells. Here was evidence of a wholly new kind of living, signaling the end of the Old Way as the only way. In fact, says Bar-Yosef, underscoring the significance of sedentism, "I suggest that we should also refer to the formation of Early Natufian hamlets as the onset of 'history.'"[23]

WHAT IS THE HISTORICAL SIGNIFICANCE OF THE NATUFIANS?

Cornflakes have a surprisingly glorious prehistory; the Natufian relationship with cereals largely explained their—and others'—sedentism. The early Middle Easterners were surrounded by large stands of wheat, which they harvested, removing the seed heads, grinding them, and making porridge or possibly even a form of pita or flatbread. This advanced level of working with a single plant led Bar-Yosef to perhaps the most important conclusion about them: "The Natufian culture played a major role in the emergence of the early Neolithic farming communities, or what is known as the Agricultural Revolution."[24]

Sedentary lifestyles resulted in higher populations; decreasing spacing between childbirth, increased life expectancy and fertility, a more regular diet, and the need for more people to assist in seasonal harvests of wild plants all added up to more people. Yet there were further consequences: "These larger populations ultimately depleted resources and stressed carrying capacities. This development led to increased intensive use of wild grains, ultimately resulting in domestication."[25] Domestication, which we will explore later (see "What Is Agriculture?"), was the process of selecting specific species of animals and plants for farming. Explaining this point further, Mithen adds, "I suspect that the stands of wild cereals, the groves of nut trees, the patches of lupins, wild peas, and lentils were treated as a wild garden. . . . Dorothy Garrod may have been wrong to think of the Natufian people as farmers; but they were most certainly rather special gardeners."[26] Again, we see that agriculture as we know it did not appear overnight but developed in fits and starts over generations—a changing relationship between humans and their environment.

Natufian society's sedentism is interesting for another reason. One-quarter of all Natufian burials thus far discovered involved people with rich ornamentation; the rest had little or nothing. This suggests wealth inequality. Mithen thinks

---

[23]   Ofer Bar-Yosef, "Warfare in Levantine Early Neolithic: A Hypothesis To Be Considered," *Neo-Lithics* 1 (2010): 6–10.

[24]   Ofer Bar-Yosef, "The Natufian Culture in the Levant: Threshold to the Origins of Agriculture," *Evolutionary Anthropology* 6, no. 5 (1998): 159–177.

[25]   Alan H. Simmons, *The Neolithic Revolution in the Near East: Transforming the Human Landscape* (Tucson: University of Arizona Press, 2007), 15.

[26]   Mithen, *After the Ice Age*, 36.

that these resources may have been connected to their control of trade in seashells, used as symbolic decorations and as gifts in exchanges and important in cementing relationships between groups. "Wealth and power," says Mithen, "had evidently been dependent on sedentary village life."[27]

WERE THE NATUFIANS THE ONLY EARLY SETTLED PEOPLE?

Although they were probably among the earliest, and certainly the best documented, the Natufians were not alone in settling in one place because the living was easy. Around the world at the beginning of the Holocene, people were intensifying their food gathering and staying put longer, usually in coastal or river environments where marine resources could be harvested year-round and supplemented by the newly available wild resources of plants and animals. In Australia there is evidence of much more varied stone tools in the millennia after the Ice Age. As in other places, stone spear tips were so well made they were often treated as ritual objects and traded long distance. In the state of Victoria, archeologists discovered the remains of eel traps made from strips of bark and plaited rushes with a willow hoop for a mouth. These traps caught so many eels that substantial and relatively permanent settlements developed around eel-rich bodies of water.

In South Korea, around 13,000 BCE, communities were living in what appear to have been semisedentary camps along riverbanks, living off salmon, shellfish, and game such as deer and boar, as well as foraging nuts, berries, and edible plants. Evidence suggests that these people were gathering enough resources to store in pits and ceramic containers. As with other affluent foragers, notably in sub-Saharan Africa, food was so readily available that there was no need to farm, for several thousand more years. In coastal Japan, the Jomon culture was creating the first ever pottery vessels, which they decorated with cord or rope marks (the definition of *Jomon*). They too were living off a combination of marine resources and land animals. Their fishing skills, however, were advanced; and their trash heaps produced bones of sea lion, seal, mackerel, tuna, shark, and dolphin (the first sushi, perhaps?). This evidence indicates that they not only had fishing tools, like spears and nets, but offshore fishing vessels as well. Other areas in which people utilized rich marine resources included the Pacific Northwest of North America, which is still known for its (dwindling) salmon runs; the eastern coastal woodlands of the same continent; and coastal Peru. All of these cultures

---

[27]   Ibid., 50.

Jomon Village   The Jomon culture encapsulates Japan's Neolithic and lasted from ca. 10,000 to ca. 300 BCE. Different phases within this period saw different cultural styles and practices, but for much of the Jomon period people hunted, fished, and practiced horticulture, with farming and domesticated species appearing at the very end of the period.

were laying the foundations for later human societies, the consequences of which would be far-reaching.

WHAT WERE THE CONSEQUENCES OF THE YOUNGER DRYAS (10,800–9600 BCE)?

During the Younger Dryas, or "the big freeze," some communities became more mobile, especially in the southern part of the Fertile Crescent. Many permanent camps were abandoned and villages left to disintegrate. The climate change (dramatic and fast) rendered these environments drier, meaning that plants and animals dwindled or disappeared. The Natufian homeland of the Mediterranean hills and the Jordan valley, once a forager's paradise, became bleak. Many groups pulled up stakes and moved in an attempt to find the game that had retreated to warmer or wetter climates. In particular, the abundant wild stands of cereals, which had been a mainstay of the Natufian diet, shrank drastically, as Bar-Yosef says: "the two major outcomes of the cold and dry conditions were a decrease in the natural production of the C3 plants, such as the cereals, and a reduction in the geographic distribution of natural stands of wild cereals to the western wing of the Fertile Crescent."[28] When the crops left, people had to move.

---

[28]   Bar-Yosef, "The Natufian Culture in the Levant," 166.

But instead of the Younger Dryas simply creating a return to the *status quo ante* (foraging), not all went "walkabout" (as the Australians Aborigines refer to mobility). Some began to plant seeds. If early "seed" agriculture started in the Younger Dryas, it was a struggle as the plants needed help—watering weeding, tending; plants, as any gardener knows, don't always grow themselves. Places like Jericho were more suited to this agriculture—or horticulture—because it was situated on alluvial soils of lakes, exposed by the shrinking water levels. In these conditions the wild seeds of wheat and barley could be grown with some work.

In the Palestine hills, a little north of the Dead Sea, Jericho is often cited as the first agricultural village. Mithen imagines it at the end of the Younger Dryas, when the weather was improving: "Willows, poplars and fig trees surround the village, evidently fed by a local spring and growing luxuriantly in the new warm, wet world of the Holocene. . . . Many trees have been felled to provide building material and to create small fields for barley and wheat. Whether such crops are biologically domestic or wild seems unimportant, as the new world of farming has certainly arrived."[29]

In all probability, early forms of agriculture were being practiced in villages of the Fertile Crescent such as Jericho during the Younger Dryas. But at its end, the weather warmed and the rains returned, making conditions optimal for agriculture more widely. This fact, along with the likelihood that Jericho and other places in the region were probably regional hubs in networks of exchange (early forms of trade), encouraged further sedentism. In the several millennia following the end of the Younger Dryas, evidence of domesticated—and therefore agricultural—plants shows up independently in several places on earth. In the Americas, for instance, teosinte, the wild ancestor of corn, one of the most successful plants in the world today, was domesticated around this time. Says archeologist Bruce Smith: "The Younger Dryas climatic episode could perhaps have been the external stress, reducing available wild food sources, that caused hunter–gatherer societies to turn to cultivation in efforts to increase their after-harvest reserves of grain."[30] Such developments took time. But bearing in mind we've seen 190,000 years of human existence without domestication or developed agriculture, a few thousand years qualifies as a revolution. Archeologists differ on how many places developed agriculture independently. Some say as many as eight, while some, like Bar-Yosef, think it as little as three—the Fertile Crescent, Mesoamerica, and the river valleys of China. Other places, he says, probably learned about it from those three and developed their own agriculture later.[31] The cold snap, therefore, probably forced people to pay more attention to the plants and animals they depended on, especially since

[29]   Mithen, *After the Ice Age*, 56.
[30]   Bruce D. Smith, *The Emergence of Agriculture* (New York: Scientific American Library, 1998), 79.
[31]   Bar-Yosef, Personal communication with authors, March, 2011.

they had tasted the sedentary life, had increased their populations, and in some cases had found it impossible to revert to the "Old Way" of hunting–gathering.

WHAT IS AGRICULTURE?

If sedentism led to growth in population, full-blown agriculture really raised the stakes. But what, exactly, do we mean by *agriculture*? Farmers, or those who practice agriculture, routinely alter their natural environment to favor the species, both plant and animal, that people like to eat. As opposed to simply picking and harvesting what nature has grown, farmers deliberately sow (preselected) seeds in ground they prepare for the best advantage of the specific seed. Weeding and watering artificially benefit the plants and guarantee larger harvests.

☀ The cold snap, therefore, probably forced people to pay more attention to the plants and animals they depended on, especially since they had tasted the sedentary life, had increased their populations, and in some cases had found it impossible to revert to the "Old Way" of hunting–gathering.

Such intensive cultivation raises the productivity of the species. Farmers consistently pick the largest, most fruitful specimens and keep their seeds for future planting. Over generations, the species of plant would be transformed so that the large, fruitful seed head would be the norm, not the exception. Many characteristics were—unconsciously—"selected" for in this process, including natural resistance to pests and an ability to thrive on less water. As opposed to natural selection, which we discussed in Chapter 1, this process is known as *artificial selection*. This, when applied to both plants and animals, is what is known as *domestication*.

Over generations humans began to notice that herds of animals (such as wild goat and later sheep in the Fertile Crescent) could be controlled. Humans

SW Asia	wheat goats cattle barley sheep pigs				camel	
South Asia		cattle	cotton	chicken		
East Asia		rice, millet	pigs, water-buffalo			
Africa			donkey	domestic cat	millet, sorghum	yam oil palm
Meso-america	gourds	squash	beans, peppers	maize		
North America					sunflower, marsh elder, chenopod	
South America	manioc, squash	gourds, lima beans		Ilama, alpaca, cotton, potato		

8000   6000   4000   2000

Years BCE

Schematic Chronology of Domestication in Different World Regions

began to corral animals that were particularly docile and manageable. Whereas in nature females may have chosen large aggressive males as mates, farmers put smaller, less aggressive males together with females to mate. What was the result? Domestic animals became almost always smaller than their wild ancestors (this holds true for goat, dog, and cow in particular). Early herders would also have bred animals for desirable traits, such as small horns, quick growth, and large udders for producing milk. Domestication then, whether in plants or animals, was a process of genetic modification of the species by direct human control.

At the very simplest level humans have been agriculturalists for most of their life as a species. Not only is it likely that we began "farming" in one manner or another long before the agricultural "revolution" of 10,000 years ago, but we are not the only species that domesticates others. Ants, for example, "domesticate" aphids, corralling them, protecting them from predators, and periodically "milking" them by stroking them with their antennae, to generate honeydew, which the ants eat. Leaf cutter ants also "farm" a kind of fungus, by feeding it grass.

Identifying the beginnings of agriculture, therefore, is hard. Barker thinks that finding this specific date depends upon your definition of *agriculture*: "In one sense, husbandry is as old as the history of *Homo sapiens*," he says. "Burning the landscape to enhance food supplies is certainly as old as the first modern humans who reached South East Asia (at least) 45,000 years ago, and possibly as old as 100,000 years in Africa."[32] Barker goes on to quote the archeologists E. S. Higgs and M. R. Jarmon: "Domestication can be regarded as a long-term process whose limit at one end is defined by the present day, and at the other only by the earliest date that anyone has yet had the temerity to propose."[33]

Farming was not, therefore, an all-or-nothing proposition. Nor were the effects of population growth and climate change globally equal. People, in other words, found their way to farming through different paths, some, as in Latin America, domesticating plants—such as teosinte as well as squash and beans, before becoming fully sedentary. By around 6000 BCE (much later than the Natufians) foraging populations in tropical South America were "practicing increasingly interventionist strategies of plant use including forest clearance, ground preparation, plant tending, and in one instance even small-scale irrigation."[34] Agriculture—or some version of it—in other words, preceded sedentism in this case. In many areas, societies mixed cultivation of plants with herding and foraging habits for centuries, before they committed to full-time farming.

---

[32]   Barker, *The Agricultural Revolution in Prehistory*, 396.
[33]   Ibid., 397.
[34]   Ibid., 263.

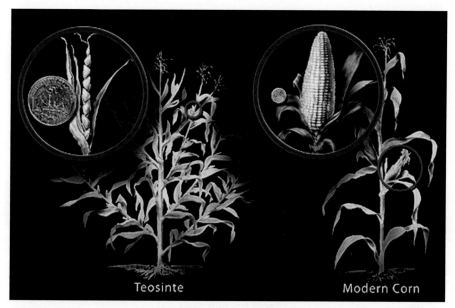

Teosinte, the Wild Ancestor of Domesticated Corn   Generations of selecting large cobs resulted in this radical change in the species. Could there be a more graphic representation the intervention strategies settled humans took to increase their food supply?

What Changes Did Sedentary Life Bring?

In the Hebrew story of Cain and Abel, Cain "worked the soil" and Abel "kept flocks." One, in other words, was a farmer and the other, a herder. The two brothers brought offerings to God, Abel a portion of meat from his flock and Cain some of the "fruits of the soil." But God preferred Abel's offering over Cain's, suggesting that the Hebrews, a nomadic, herding people, favored that way of life. Needless to say, Cain was put out. As the historian Steven Stoll tells it, "God tells Cain to get over it. Cain broods, and then bludgeons his brother to death."[35] For this crime God curses him and sends him to live in the Land of Nod, "East of Eden."[36] Again, like in *Gilgamesh*, we hear echoes of a deep ambivalence about these changing ways of life. What was it that worried people about living the settled life of the farmer?

Common sense might tell you that settling down was a good thing, but the payoff was not so clear-cut. Sedentism had its price. Negative consequences derived from the existence of a larger population, perhaps the most important

---

[35]   Steven Stoll, "Agrarian Anxieties," *Harper's Magazine* (July 2010), 6, 8–9.
[36]   Genesis, chapter 4.

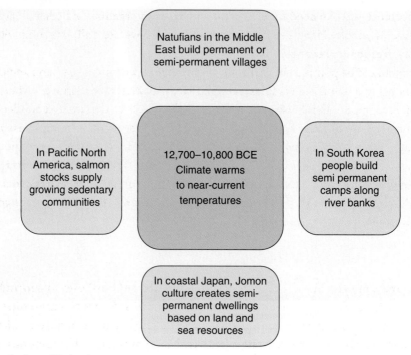

Beginnings of Sedentism

difference from mobile groups that had small populations of 20–50 people. According to research conducted by Massimo Livi-Bacci, there may have been as few as 500,000 humans on earth 30,000 years ago. By 10,000 years ago this figure had reached 6 million. By 5,000 years ago, when we see the first cities and "complex" societies, an estimated 50 million people lived on the planet.[37] At this point the population was doubling every 1,600 years, whereas in the Paleolithic it was doubling every 6,000 years.

Hunter–gatherers needed to limit their populations to a level that could be sustained by their environment, yet farmers were less restricted. More children put demands on the food supply but also provided more hands to help with the work. The growth in population density is vividly represented by the differences between early Natufian sites such as the Haynom Cave in Israel, of 12,000 to 13,000 BCE, which had a population of dozens and later Neolithic settlements such as Jericho and Mureybet in Syria, which were home to hundreds of people. With such a dramatic growth in numbers, social change happened. Of particular

---

[37]   Massimo Livi-Bacci, *A Concise History of World Population* (Oxford: Blackwell, 1992).

importance was the need for leadership and rules to organize and control large groups of people. Here, perhaps, began the debate we are still wrestling with today: freedom or security?

It should be pointed out that some archeologists see hunter–gatherer societies as being much more complex, hierarchical, and sedentary than has hitherto been recognized. Thomas Emerson, for example, points to the "mound builders" of the Mississippi River basin (from around 2,000 years ago) as being a case in point. This society, among others, created monumental architecture without either clear social hierarchies or permanent, sedentary villages.[38] Although chronologically much later, there may well have been parallels between the social worlds of the Near East and the Americas in these different eras. This is an ongoing debate within the archeology of prehistory.

HOW DID SEDENTISM AFFECT SOCIAL STRUCTURE?

Research into the burial practices of the Natufians led Bar-Yosef to conclude that social differences developed among the more sedentary communities. A correlation therefore seems to have existed with sedentism and inequality, although it becomes more acute with full-blown agricultural communities. Archeologists working at Çatal Hüyük, on Turkey's Anatolian plain, for instance, dated to some 9,000 years ago, see the social structure there, with a population of several thousand nonagricultural foragers, as largely egalitarian. Farming villages—and towns—were different, however, especially where there were signs of major building projects. The village of Jericho was famous for its tower and wall, built around 9000 BCE. When the wall was built the town probably had a population of around 1,000, far larger than any earlier village. Its wall was over 13 feet high and almost 6.5 feet across at its base. The tower was 26.25 feet high and 29.5 feet across at its base. It has been estimated that at least 100 men working for 100 days would have been necessary to create it. Was it the first public works project? "What is clear," says Mithen, "is that with the construction of the wall and the tower, people were creating architecture and communal activity on quite a new scale. A new phase of history had begun."[39] Who decided who made the bricks, who carried them to the site, who hauled them to the top of the tower, and who cleaned up? It is easy to imagine this project involving some level of coercion.

---

[38] Dale L. McElrath, Andrew C. Fortier, and Thomas Emerson, "An Introduction to the Archaic Societies of the Midcontinent," in *Archaic Societies: Diversity and Complexity Across the Midcontinent*, ed. Thomas E. Emerson, Dale L. McElrath, and Andrew C. Fortier, 3–22 (Albany, NY: SUNY Press, 2009).

[39] Mithen, *After the Ice Age*, 60.

The Tower at Jericho, ca. 9000 BCE   The first public works project? Who organized, who worked, and why did they do it?

Whether from trading seashells or controlling the harvests, property was being accumulated in many Neolithic villages across the Near East. Other Neolithic sites hint at inequalities in private wealth. Archeologists at Jerf el Ahmar in Syria found a large, multichambered storage room, which could have been communal but could equally have been private, a sign of individual wealth. Whether private or public, this structure was the scene of a violent confrontation: before being burned to the ground, someone was decapitated, after being splayed out on the ground, in what was possibly a ritual killing.

Just like searching for the origins of agriculture, looking for the origins of private property can take us back far beyond the Neolithic. Marshall Thomas mentions how the Kalahari nomads recognized the ownership of some hollow trees, which held rainwater long after the rains had stopped. These were life-giving during the dry season and, therefore, prized almost as much as wells. In another example, archeologist Colin Renfrew notes that the domestication of the dog, which occurred before the end of the last Ice Age, marks a kind of private property, bearing in mind how dogs are extremely "owner-focused." But such examples aside sedentism expanded the notion of private property greatly, and settled society never looked back.

Notwithstanding these signs of social differences in the early Neolithic period, it is not until the later Neolithic that these changes become dramatic, especially for gender roles. Several millennia after the development of farming, however, we see men playing much more of a role in "plow" agriculture. As farming began to play a larger role in food production than hunting and as farmers began to use more animals—for traction, manure, and milk, in addition to meat—women became increasingly marginalized. Ehrenberg calls this "the great male takeover bid" and dates it to somewhere around 3000 BCE, the era in which the world's first major agrarian "civilizations" appear (see Chapter 3).[40]

WAS DEFENSE A MOTIVATION FOR SETTLING DOWN?

Looking at the reconstructions of the Neolithic town of Çatal Hüyük, you get the distinct impression that it was built for security. Why else would people crowd themselves together so much, especially since for thousands of years humans had ranged widely? Their dwellings, situated on a broad, open plain with views in all directions, were all connected to each other, forming one giant structure. Houses

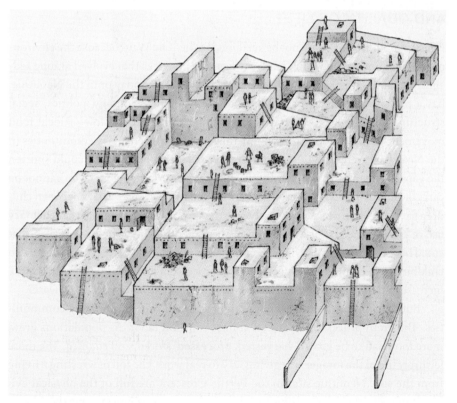

Çatal Hüyük in Turkey   The city had no streets; access to dwellings was via the rooftops. Easier to defend that way? Safety in numbers?

---

[40]   Ehrenberg, *Women in Prehistory*, 99.

were entered not through doorways but through holes in the roof, and inhabitants could navigate the village not through streets—there were none to speak of—but across the tops of their dwellings. Few explanations other than security have been put forward for this arrangement. Bar-Yosef thinks it likely that violence was endemic in this period, although he concedes that the evidence, so far, is not conclusive. What is suspicious, though, are signs of the frequent abandonment of villages and evidence of the existence of a very large number of specialized stone blades and spear points.[41]

Bearing in mind the relatively light population density of the Paleolithic, probably less violence took place than in the Neolithic. Conflict usually arises over issues such as control over resources. With a growing population and where resources needed to be guarded—such as cultivated wheat fields or storage bins—the incentive for conflict would have been greatly enhanced.

HOW DID DIET AFFECT POPULATION, HEALTH, AND QUALITY OF LIFE?

But such populations could not be sustained in the "Old Way" because the environment could not provide for it. With the farming practices that evolved among sedentary societies, their diet had to change. Diet, whether today or in the Neolithic, has a profound impact on all aspects of life, affecting economy, politics, social structure, and the health of individuals (think of the recent slow or local food movements and the political economy they represent). Sedentary communities in the Near East were able to increase their population because they could shorten the gaps between births. When you have to move camp frequently, you cannot be carrying lots of babies. Hunter–gatherers tended to have larger delays between children to ensure the first was walking before the second came along. But the sedentary use of grains—rice in Asia and corn in the Americas—provided a foodstuff that could be fed to infants, allowing for earlier weaning and for shorter spacing between childbirth. As communities became food processors and eventually farmers, the increase in population was a blessing not a curse—*many hands make light work*.

But the work was probably not as light as it had been for foraging communities. The grain processing required almost constant labor. As populations grew, more food had to be grown, harvested, processed, stored, and *guarded*. The more leisurely life of the forager was giving way to real work, the toil of wresting a living from the soil. Neolithic sites in the Fertile Crescent are full of the physical evidence of such labor: processing equipment such as stone mortars, pestles, grinding stones, and pits for storage. The size and weight of many of these indicated

---

[41]   Bar-Yosef, "Warfare in Levantine Early Neolithic."

that a community resided permanently at a site as grinding stones carved from massive rocks are not easy to pick up and throw into a bag. Their very presence gives us a clue to the origin of the common term "the daily grind."

Ancient bones also tell us about how much work these new grain processors and early farmers were doing. One of the most famous studies of the consequences to human health of the adoption of agriculture was from the Syrian Neolithic site of Abu Hureya, occupied twice, the first time as a hunter–gatherer village from 11,500 to 10,000 years ago. These people gathered a wide range of fruits, nuts, seeds, and berries, as well as einkorn and emmer wheat, oats, and barley, in addition to hunting gazelle seasonally. The second time, from about 10,800 to 7,000 years ago, with an unexplained abandonment lasting some 200 years, they returned as farmers.

Skeletal studies from bones of this period reveal back deformities from carrying heavy loads and damage to the feet, knees, and hips from lengthy, arduous work kneeling to pound grains. According to Theya Molleson, then of the Natural History Museum in London, most of the grain preparation work was done by women, with the men most probably focused on hunting and the heavier agricultural work (although it's likely that women were responsible for early developments in planting and harvesting).[42] Women were not the only ones to suffer however. The eating of so many grains had an "appalling" effect on everyone's teeth as hard kernels and small stones inevitably become mixed with the grains unless effectively sifted. Other health consequences, especially of full-blown agriculture of the later Neolithic, included starvation and famine, resulting from failures of crops (when you rely on increasingly small numbers of plants, should they fail, there is no back-up plan) as well as disease, which became a major problem when farmers began to domesticate and live close to animals. Animal-borne disease plays a vital and terrible role in subsequent human history, as we shall read in later chapters.

Abu Hureya in Syria, occupied in two distinct periods, the first time by hunter–gatherers and the second, by farmers.

---

[42]   Theya Molleson, "The Eloquent Bones of Abu Hureya," *Scientific American* (August 1994).

WHAT BELIEF SYSTEMS DID EARLY SEDENTARY HUMANS HAVE?

In the *Epic of Gilgamesh*, the hero and his sidekick Enkidu go to the Cedar Forest to kill the monster Hambaba, who guards the forest for the gods. After killing the monster and cutting him into pieces, the duo set about decimating the forest:

> They took their axes and penetrated
> Deeper into the forest, they went
> Chopping down cedars, the wood chips flew,
> Gilgamesh chopped down the mighty trees
> Enkidu hewed the trunks into timbers.[43]

But it was not timber they were after. It was the glory of having killed the monster and triumphing over nature itself. What looks to us like a human-made, environmental disaster is an ancient affirmation of human power over the often terrifying natural world. Clearly, by the time of Gilgamesh, the hunter–gatherer worldview, which saw humans as embedded within nature, was long gone. Nature, with its droughts and floods and wild animals, was the enemy; humans stood alone.

Religion, as we know it, was born in the Neolithic era. Very little is known of the spiritual life of the Paleolithic, except what we can infer from modern hunter–gatherers. And while no written records remain from the Neolithic, archeological evidence of ritualism suggests that a spiritual life and complex ideas about the afterlife were present. The remains of artwork, especially at places such as Çatal Hüyük, suggest that "wild nature" played a large part in the thoughts and beliefs of the inhabitants. Paintings of vultures taking headless corpses into the sky suggest a link between these animals and the afterlife. Other Neolithic sites in the Near East suggest a rich spiritual life, with the natural world playing a starring role. At Göbekli Tepe in Turkey, archeologists discovered what they identified as a sprawling ritual complex, littered with large stones upended in the ground, engraved with pictures of wild animals such as foxes and lions. Apparently absent of dwellings, historians think that this site must have had religious significance and was a place for meeting and worship of some sort for clans, possibly being used by hundreds of people at a time.

As humans renegotiated their relationship with the natural world, they also came to see the spiritual world differently. The starkest difference, perhaps, was the development of deities that ultimately controlled the fate of humans. By

---

[43]   *Epic of Gilgamesh*, 128.

Göbekli Tepe in Turkey   This sprawling ritual center, possibly hosting hundreds at a time, underlines the idea that prehistoric humans had a rich spiritual life.

5,000 years ago, in complex societies such as those found in Mesopotamia (see Chapter 3), gods represented the major aspects of human life: the sky god, the earth mother, as well as local deities that ruled over specific cities. These beings demanded worship and either rewarded or punished people according to their whims and the quality of that worship. The development of such religions reflected the ambivalent position of agrarian communities to the natural world.

Conclusion: What Were the Consequences of Permanent Settlements?

The consequences of sedentism have been far-reaching. Hunter–gatherers may have had a deep-seated sense of place, perhaps connected to a foraging range of some considerable size; but fully sedentary communities would have been very focused on a specific village site. And although foraging communities almost certainly felt proprietorial over their ranges, the notion of private property became dramatically more articulated with the onset of sedentism. Along with property, social structure underwent dramatic changes, too, most notably a marked shift toward greater inequality and gender differentiation, as well as

> ☀ The natural world looks very different from a sedentary perspective; along with all the other consequences, major changes took place in our belief systems, such as the birth of established religions, that have determined so much of the rest of history.

much larger group size. Although taking several millennia to play out, this development, in the long view of human history, unfolded relatively quickly. The natural world looks very different from a sedentary perspective; along with all the other consequences, major changes took place in our belief systems, such as the birth of established religions, that have determined so much of the rest of history.

Sedentism is intimately tied to subsistence (which in turn affects all aspects of our lives). Barker points out that today we rely on a fraction of the animals and plants that were important in the Old Way: "A dozen crops make up over 80 percent of the world's annual tonnage of all crops: banana, barley, maize, manioc, potato, rice, sorghum, soybean, sugar beet, sugar cane, sweet potato and wheat. Only five domestic animals over 100 pounds are globally important: cows, sheep, goats, pigs and horses."[44] Why is this significant? Spreading nutritional requirements over multiple species ensures adequate nutrition and hedges against starvation. The Irish potato famine of the nineteenth century (the major reason that so many Irish emigrated to the United States) was caused by the failure of the potato crop. The nation relied so heavily on one crop—which usually produced spectacularly—that when it failed, as crops sometimes do, disaster followed.

While sedentism affected our diet and the social, political, economic, and spiritual aspects of life, it also affected our environment. Tree cutting, à la *Gilgamesh*, began in the Neolithic as farmers cleared land to till. Today, the Amazon is being cleared to plant crops (often expressly to feed to domesticated animals, which we will eat). As we embark on the twenty-first century, rich countries with expanding populations are buying land on other continents to ensure plentiful crops for their populations.

Farming, in freeing us from the endless work of subsistence, by producing surpluses, has allowed us to achieve the kinds of cultural, artistic, and scientific accomplishments that enable us to form our identities as humans. But many historians of our own era are much less enthusiastic. Up until the Industrial Revolution of the nineteenth century the overwhelming majority of people on earth were mired in agricultural labor that usually involved some level of servitude, even slavery (it was, after all, as agricultural laborers that the majority of slaves were transported to the Americas throughout the eighteenth century). Stoll, for example, refers to agriculture as "the most destructive and socially transforming

---

[44] Barker, *The Agricultural Revolution in Prehistory*, 1.

technology we have ever had."[45] He points to endless population growth, environmental degradation, and conflict, spawned of the ceaseless need for new land: "The fearsome growth of agrarians—fueled by wheat, rice, and maize and driven by the need for fresh land—pushes them even farther east of Eden and into bloody territorial wars."[46] Erosion, in particular, has been progressing since the first Neolithic plow broke the first sod in the Middle East thousands of years ago; whenever you open the land like this, rain and wind will carry away the fertile topsoil, which will eventually find its way to the sea. The writer John Robbins has calculated that every year the equivalent of 165,000 Mississippi River barges full of soil is eroded from Iowa's fields alone. The geographer and historian Jared Diamond has called agriculture the "Worst Mistake in the History of the Human Race,"[47] pointing to similar reasons, including the erasing of hunter–gatherers and mobile populations around the world as well as decreased health and nutrition. Historian John Coatsworth, writing about human welfare over the ages, describes how bioarcheologists, in particular, have cataloged the ill effects of agriculture and concludes that, "civilization, we now know, stunted growth, spread disease, shortened life spans, and set people to killing and maiming each other on an unprecedented scale."[48] Suddenly corn flakes seem less wholesome.

How can we reconcile these views with the earlier (and perhaps still prevalent) view that sedentism represented a beneficial development in the human career? Whereas settling in one place may have led to agriculture and population growth and all subsequent ills, the societies that it spawned, beginning with the Neolithic and going on to the more complex ones described in the following chapters, created literature, science, architecture, medicine, and the culture of which we are all a part and from which we all benefit (although some more than others). Clearly, the human experience is not equal the world over, and there are major inequalities even within countries. But the sedentary societies we have developed have generated human rights, democracy, and respect for all peoples, regardless of race, sexual preference, or class. Few would argue that these are values that define us as fully human. The question that sits at the back of our minds, however, is, *Would all of these rights and protections, seen as "progress," have been necessary were it not for the advent of sedentary, agricultural society in the first place?*

---

[45] Stoll, "Agrarian Anxieties," 6.
[46] Ibid.
[47] Jared Diamond, "The Worst Mistake in the History of the Human Race." *Discover Magazine* (May 1987).
[48] John H. Coatsworth, "Welfare," *American Historical Review* 101, no. 1 (February 1996). 1–17

Words to Think About

Agriculture   Domestication   Foraging
Holocene   Hunter–gatherer   Sedentism
Subsistence

Questions to Think About

- Did farming lead to sedentism, or did sedentism lead to farming?
- What were the consequences of sedentism for gender relations?
- Was there a relationship between violence and sedentism?
- In what ways was sedentism the "beginning of history"?

Primary Sources

Epic of Gilgamesh. Translated by Stephen Mitchell. New York: Free Press, 2004.
Genesis, chapters 2–4.

Secondary Sources

Akkermans, Peter M. M. G., and Glenn M. Schwartz. *The Archaeology of Syria: From Complex Hunter–Gatherers to Early Urban Societies (ca. 16,000–300 BC)*. Cambridge: Cambridge University Press, 2003.

Barker, Graeme. *The Agricultural Revolution in Prehistory: Why Did Foragers Become Farmers?* Oxford: Oxford University Press, 2006.

Bar-Yosef, Ofer. "The Natufian Culture in the Levant: Threshold to the Origins of Agriculture." *Evolutionary Anthropology* 6, no. 5 (1998): 159–177.

Bar-Yosef, Ofer. "Warfare in Levantine Early Neolithic: A Hypothesis To Be Considered." *Neo-Lithics* 1 (2010): 6–10.

Bellwood, Peter. *The First Farmers: The Origins of Agricultural Societies*. Malden, MA: Blackwell, 2005.

Brumbach, Hetty Jo, and Robert Jarvenpa. "Woman the Hunter: Ethnoarchaeological Lessons from Chipewyan Life-Cycle Dynamics." In *Women in Prehistory: North America and Mesoamerica*, edited by Cheryl Claassen and Rosemary A. Joyce, 17–32. Philadelphia: University of Philadelphia Press, 1997.

Coatsworth, John H. "Welfare." *American Historical Review* 101, no. 1 (February 1996): 1–17.

Diamond, Jared. *The World Until Yesterday: What Can We Learn from Traditional Societies?* New York: Viking Adult, 2012.

Diamond, Jared. "The Worst Mistake in the History of the Human Race." *Discover Magazine* (May 1987): 64–66.

Ehrenberg, Barbara. *Women in Prehistory*. Norman: University of Oklahoma Press, 1989.

Hobbes, Thomas. *Leviathan: Or the Matter, Forme and Power of a Commonwealth, Ecclesiastical and Civil*. Cambridge: Cambridge University Press, 1904.

Livi-Bacci, Massimo. *A Concise History of World Population*. Oxford: Blackwell, 1992.

Marshall Thomas, Elizabeth. *The Old Way: A Story of the First People*. New York: Farrar, Strauss and Giroux, 2006.

McElrath, Dale L., Andrew C. Fortier, and Thomas Emerson. "An Introduction to the Archaic Societies of the Midcontinent." In *Archaic Societies: Diversity and Complexity Across the Midcontinent*, edited by Thomas E. Emerson, Dale L. McElrath, and Andrew C. Fortier, 3–22. Albany, NY: SUNY Press, 2009.

Mithen, Steven. *After the Ice Age: A Global Human History, 20,000 BC–5000 BC*. Cambridge, MA: Harvard University Press, 2004.

Molleson, Theya. "The Eloquent Bones of Abu Hureya." *Scientific American* (August 1994).

Renfrew, Colin. "Commodification and Institution in Group-Oriented and Individualizing Societies." In *The Origin of Human Social Institutions*, edited by W. G. Runciman. Proceedings of the British Academy 110. Oxford: Oxford University Press, 2001.

Sahlins, Marshall. *Stone Age Economics*. New York: Aldine de Gruyter, 1972.

Simmons, Alan H. *The Neolithic Revolution in the Near East: Transforming the Human Landscape*. Tucson: University of Arizona Press, 2007.

Smith, Bruce D. *The Emergence of Agriculture*. New York: Scientific American Library, 1998.

Stokes Brown, Cynthia. *Big History: From the Big Bang to the Present*. New York: New Press, 2007.

Stoll, Steven. "Agrarian Anxieties." *Harper's Magazine* (July 2010).

Wright, Rita P. "Women's Labor and Pottery Production in Prehistory." In *Engendering Archaeology: Women and Prehistory*, edited by Joan M. Gero and Margaret W. Conkey, 194–223. Oxford: Basil Blackwell, 1991.

Wright, Robert. *NonZero: The Logic of Human Destiny*. New York: Random House, 2000.

For additional resources, including maps, primary sources, and visuals, web links, and quizzes, please go to **www.oup.com/us/cole**

Maybach motor cars sell for hundreds of thousands, sometimes millions, of dollars. Is it an ancient notion of prestige and status that allows them to fetch such prices?

Chapter 3

How Did the Development of Cities Affect the Human Experience?

Are You First-Class Material?

Imagine you are flying from New York to Los Angeles. Let's say, just for fun, that you have a first-class ticket. At the airport the economy passengers are standing in a line several feet long. You waltz up, present your boarding pass, and drop your bags. Then, sure, there is a little snafu at security, but even important people have to take their shoes off! In the first-class lounge you send a few upbeat tweets and post a picture on Facebook from the comfort of an easy chair. When it's time to board, you do so first, before even the struggling parents with small kids. After the hapless economy passengers have filed wearily past you, the flight attendant gives you a glass of champagne, then you sink back (with only a passing feeling of guilt) into the commodious leather, watch a few movies, take a nap, and you are there.

Let's pretend, further, that you are on an assignment for a new job, with a generous expense account. At the car rental office, you see a large sign saying "Prestige Customers" in front of a convertible red Audi. Your eye scans the lot, taking in a few other prestige options—a white Cadillac Escalade, a silver Porsche, and a Shelby Mustang. You are important! So you should look important. Mustang it is.

What's the significance of this little fantasy? For any thinking person with a sense of history, undergoing this experience might well make him or her question the notions of *privilege* and *social status,* upon which our society is built. Nowhere

THINKING ABOUT URBANISM

What Is Civilized About Civilization?
- As far as the human experience is concerned, the advantages of all this "prog-
ress" may have been theoretical. To put it another way, you could say *"The
Man"* had arrived.

What Is the Relationship Between Cities, States, and Civilization?
- Locating temples, ritual sites, and the priestly class in cities lent considerable
mystique to the city and underscored the ruler's proximity to the divine.

How Did River Valley Civilizations Develop?
- Regular flooding deposited fertile soil on the riverbanks and floodplains, providing optimal soil for growing; and irrigation expanded the area of possible
cultivation.

Conclusion
- Neolithic tribes and Paleolithic bands would have been hard-pressed to com-
prehend the experience of a soldier in the Shang army, a conscripted laborer at
Giza, or a Mesopotamian slave.

is this better reflected than in our economy: we speak of *first class, upper class, gold
cards, platinum cards, executive clubs*. Your worth, monetary and often otherwise,
is defined by the size of your house, the style of your clothes, or the price tag on
your car. We are, perhaps now more than ever, status-obsessed. Is this a "natural"
part of human existence, or does it have a backstory that can be illuminated by a
little historical context?

——————— + ———————

Introduction

By 4000 BCE, humanity was embarking on yet another profound transformation, what archeologist V. Gordon Childe called the "urban revolution." Obviously, there was no revolution in the sense that we understand the term today
(just as there was no revolution during the agricultural "revolution"), but the
development of cities was relatively swift—in hindsight—and its consequences

revolutionary in terms of the human experience. As the name suggests, this revolution involved the growth of cities. *(re-h]≋[historych)*

But here, at the threshold between prehistory and history, people lived in a variety of ways across the globe. We discussed life in the Paleolithic, or Old Stone Age, and the transition to the Neolithic in the last chapter. In this chapter we will focus on those societies that were new, both in scale and in structure. The cities and states that arose in a number of different regions in the several millennia BCE transformed life for their inhabitants—and their descendants—profoundly and established many social structures that are still with us today. We will discuss what, exactly, terms such as *city*, *state*, and *civilization* mean and then go on to examine how these new social structures affected the lives of their inhabitants and altered the course of history.

These civilizations appeared in four places on earth: Egypt, the Indus Valley in India/Pakistan, China, with the earliest cities showing up in Mesopotamia ("the land between the rivers"), in today's southern Iraq. All of them developed along major river systems (hence their name, the *river valley civilizations*), not coincidentally, as the irrigation water provided by rivers and the fertile soil deposited by seasonal floods made for optimal agricultural conditions. Neolithic towns such as Jericho and Çatal Hüyük (see Chapter 2) typically had hundreds to several thousand inhabitants, the latter clocking in at around 8,000 at its height. But these new cities had tens of thousands. The early Mesopotamian cities were self-contained polities, controlling a very limited territory—the urban area itself and a small agricultural hinterland around it. In concept, this is what we will see a few thousand years later, with the Greek city states, such as Athens and Sparta, and even much later, with the Italian city states such as Venice. But over time, and through military conquest, the power of certain Mesopotamian rulers extended to encompass increasingly large areas with multiple urban centers, expanding city states into territorial states. Rural, village life has been a global constant since the Neolithic, the difference being that with the growth of cities and states it became increasingly difficult to avoid the reach of the state, even if you were not living in a city.

Most historians agree that life in cities and states was accompanied by a sharp increase in inequality. This is, perhaps, the standout characteristic of the early states. These new social structures created never-before-seen hierarchies and greater imbalances in power. Latent imbalances, for instance, between men and women, were exaggerated; and divisions of labor became more permanent. By now, the "great male takeover bid" that Barbara Ehrenberg talked about (see Chapter 2) was firmly entrenched in patriarchal orders.[1] Within these orders,

---

[1]   Barbara Ehrenberg, *Women in Prehistory* (Norman: University of Oklahoma Press, 1989), 99.

wealth discrepancies widened significantly. Population growth and irrigation produced agricultural surpluses, but they created the need for management and supervision; and in these two concepts lay the seeds for far-reaching inequality.

In the various religions that became dominant among the early civilizations we can see the seeds of later world religions. In every case religion legitimized power, allowing rulers to control millions without relying on physical force. From this point on, religion and power were hand-in-glove conspirators in the human career. These inequalities apply to all these civilizations, with the possible exception of those in the Indus Valley—and there more data are needed for before we can draw solid conclusions. All these civilizations share certain basic similarities, what we shall refer to as "foundational" aspects. Yet historians have long argued over the reasons for the differences, continuing the centuries-long debate between nature and culture—*If all humans are biologically similar, why do they create such different cultures?*

In focusing on these civilizations, you should not come away with the impression that the rest of the world was dark in this period: emphasizing these societies ignores many other important ones, as the archeologist Peter Boguki says: "There is no society from the Pleistocene bands onward which is not complex in some way."[2] To some extent there is a bias at work here: perhaps we study these societies because they are most like our own. Historians have tended to see "history" as beginning with societies that are recognizable to them. The vast majority of people on earth today live in a state. In these earliest of hierarchical, bureaucratic, highly differentiated societies we see reflections of ourselves. But beyond this bias, there is some validity to their place in history because they represent a new development on earth at this point and for this reason merit further consideration. We will also discuss the value judgments implicit in the term *civilization*, especially in light of the apparent inequalities—and violence—that accompany it.

What Is Civilized About Civilization?

With these new civilizations we see the origins of much of our modern world; writing, architecture, literature, science all find some of their earliest expressions here. Surely, these are steps away from the "primitive" Neolithic toward a world we can better recognize, a step toward "progress."

---

2   Peter Boguki, *The Origins of Human Society* (Malden, MA: Blackwell, 1999), 44.

Nefertiti and Isis   In the earliest civilizations discrepancies in power became enormous. Regardless of the dominance of patriarchal structures in ancient civilizations, women did sometimes rule. And just as their male counterparts, they represented themselves as close to, or synonymous with, gods.

And indeed these societies might have provided partial solutions to problems of food insecurity, as well as physical security; and these should not be understated. But if we are to look at what it was like to live in one of these early states, the answer to the progress question will be a definitive yes and no. These urban societies were not just notable for their size and density, reaching tens of thousands of people. For the first time in human history we see clear, indisputable status divisions between rich and poor, slave and master, ruler and ruled. In the Neolithic some differences in status developed, but most of these were based on kinship and did not appear to have a huge impact on daily life. Speaking of the rise of civilizations, the anthropologist Marvin Harris expressed its disadvantages most starkly:

> For the first time there appeared on earth kings, dictators, high priests, emperors, prime ministers, presidents, governors, mayors, generals, admirals, police chiefs, judges, lawyers, and jailers, along with dungeons, jails, penitentiaries, and concentration camps. Under the tutelage of the state, human beings learned for the first time how to bow, grovel, kneel, and kowtow. In many ways the rise of the state was the descent of the world from freedom to slavery.[3]

---

[3]   Marvin Harris, "The Origin of Pristine States," in *Cannibals and Kings* (New York: Vintage, 1978), 102

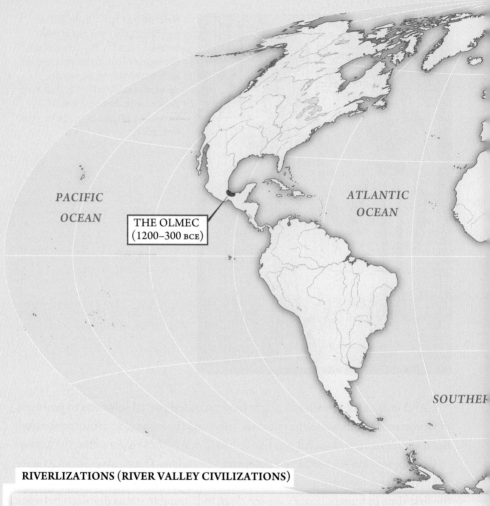

PACIFIC
OCEAN

THE OLMEC
(1200–300 BCE)

ATLANTIC
OCEAN

SOUTHER

RIVERLIZATIONS (RIVER VALLEY CIVILIZATIONS)

All early civilizations developed along river systems, whose flood plains provided fertile agricultural land. Here comp

MAP 3.1   RIVERLIZATIONS (RIVER VALLEY CIVILIZATIONS)

TIMELINE

ca. 3500 BCE
Mesopotamian city states

ca. 2700 BCE
First Egyptian stone pyramid (Saqqar

ca. 3100 BCE
Narmer unifies Upper and Lower Egypt

ca. 3200–2600 BCE
Early Indus Period

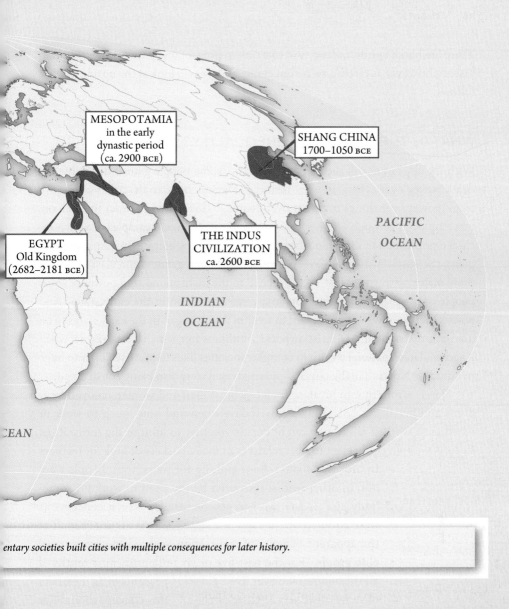

MESOPOTAMIA
in the early
dynastic period
(ca. 2900 BCE)

SHANG CHINA
1700–1050 BCE

EGYPT
Old Kingdom
(2682–2181 BCE)

THE INDUS
CIVILIZATION
ca. 2600 BCE

PACIFIC
OCEAN

INDIAN
OCEAN

CEAN

entary societies built cities with multiple consequences for later history.

ca. 1500–1200 BCE
Shang Dynasty, China

ca. 2600–1500 BCE
Mature Harappan
Period

ca. 1200–400 BCE
Olmecs in Americas

These are harsh words, indeed, and certainly represent one point of view. Human history, however, is rarely a zero-sum game; and we will look at the upside in what follows.

WHAT IS THE SOURCE OF INEQUALITY?

With the appearance of the city and the state, some people gained direct life-or-death power over others, in what historian David Christian describes as a move from "power over things to power over people."[4] This power, in order to catch on, was employed through another innovation, *the institution*, examples of which included priesthood or kingship. The wars between tribes, empires, nations, and religions; the entire history of slavery; struggles between genders and classes—all of these major concerns of history are related to the institutionalized power of some people over others, which finds its first clear expression in the early states. And power, then as now, was connected to wealth, which began in the early states to be unevenly distributed. As Christian puts it, "unlike water, which likes to lie flat when it accumulates, material wealth in complex societies likes to pile itself up into huge pyramids."[5] Not unlike the physical pyramids that were also being constructed.

Harris wrote that in prestate societies most men and women enjoyed freedoms and privileges only a few enjoy today: when and how much to work or whether to work at all. A man might decide whether to hunt or dig for roots or sleep. A woman could elect to visit relatives or make baskets or look for feathers (or, for that matter, hunt and dig for roots, too). People were not, in other words, restricted by the need to work for somebody else or pay taxes, rents, or tributes—such concepts as were codified by the laws of a state.[6] Harris argues that all of the apparent benefits of civilization accrued to a very small elite group: "For the past five or six millennia, nine-tenths of all the people who ever lived did so as peasants or as members of some other servile caste or class."[7] This concept should not be understated: most people in history have left little trace in human records, the lion's share of history being made by a tiny percentage of individuals; and this is largely because power and wealth have generally accrued to small minorities.

> :☀: Most people in history have left little trace in human records, the lion's share of history being made by a tiny percentage of individuals; and this is largely because power and wealth have generally accrued to small minorities.

---

4   David Christian, *Maps of Time: An Introduction to Big History* (Berkeley: University of California Press, 2005), 248.
5   Ibid., 248.
6   Harris, "The Origin of Pristine States," 102
7   Ibid.

Mesopotamian Ziggurat, Iraq, ca. 2100 BCE   Such structures symbolized power, and such power usually accrued to small numbers of individuals. Built as dwelling places for gods, ziggurats were managed by priests who wielded considerable power in their communities through their access to specialized knowledge.

WHY DID BECOMING MORE COMPLEX ENTAIL MORE INEQUALITY?

The urban societies that appeared in four areas of the world after 4000 BCE all exhibited what historians often call "complex" and hierarchical characteristics. No longer did people do everything for themselves—grow food, build houses, and make tools and weapons. Through their development of agricultural surplus, a whole new cast of characters appeared—*specialists*, dedicated to specific tasks and paid in money or kind for their labor. These specialists included metalworkers, boatbuilders, warriors, traders, and priests, all supported by an agricultural surplus created by farmers, still the largest section of the population but no longer making up its entirety.

But the transition from egalitarian societies to hierarchical ones did not happen overnight. Throughout the Neolithic era, villages and towns were ruled by chiefs or families that were able to accumulate more wealth than others. These Neolithic communities were, however, mostly kinship-based, with authority only relevant within a limited physical range and within extended families or clans. Political scientist Francis Fukuyama makes the point that there is a difference between calling someone "king of the Franks" (a tribe) and "king of France" (a territory). "Since membership in a state does not depend on kinship, it can grow much larger than a tribe."[8] With the growth of cities, in other words, the power of some people over others expanded from family relations to encompass strangers, and lots of them.

Societies now required a new way to cement people together and new mechanisms for rulers to extend their reach beyond their tribe. Economics could have provided this new way, but it would have been easy for tribes to break free from the purely fiscal control of foreigners. Instead, religion stepped in to provide "social cement." In all of the early civilizations, the elites wielded their power largely through control of access to the supernatural.

WHAT DID THESE NEW HIERARCHIES LOOK LIKE?

With the possible exception of India, which we will discuss further below (see "India: The Exception?"), in the other three areas of interest to us here we can see the first clear evidence of coercive, or "top-down," power in the remains of lavish royal palaces and tombs, pyramids and ziggurats, and storage facilities where large amounts of food were kept, controlled, and distributed by the authorities. Also notable were what we can think of as the apparatus of violence—signs of a military elite, used both to defend the state from outsiders and to force the ruler's will on his subjects. There is also plenty of archeological evidence of violence and warfare, and it is present in the accounts left behind, chiseled in stone or etched into papyrus or bark, of kings, priests, divine rulers, and god-like warriors. In some cases violence was directly sanctioned by the religious ideology of the time. In many burial sites of early Chinese kings from the Xia (2070–1600 BCE) and Shang (approximately 1500–11200 BCE) dynasties and later, thousands of human sacrifices have been found, following the belief that the social hierarchy continues beyond the grave and that a leader must take his household with him.

WHAT'S THE GOOD NEWS?

But what of the trade-offs? For along with the undoubted servitude, were there not enormous material and cultural "advances" in these civilizations? Writing appears earliest in Mesopotamia around 3500 BCE. This one development has been seen by historians the world over as opening the door for cultural and technological developments that have allowed humans to reach their full potential. Ancient Egyptian hieroglyphics were probably influenced by Mesopotamian writing but evolved along different lines, and the civilizations of the Indus Valley and China both developed their own scripts shortly after Egypt and Mesopotamia.

---

[8]　Francis Fukuyama, *The Origins of Political Order: From Pre-Human Times to the French Revolution* (London: Profile Books, 2011), 56.

But literacy was far from universal, being restricted to a tiny percentage of the population and intimately connected to the elites and their purposes of control and leadership. Sumerian priests (the elite of Sumer) needed a way to record goods that were stored by the state. They also recorded tribute paid to the temple, taxes, and other financial transactions. Writing, in other words, got its break in the service of accountants; and from the very beginning it was also co-opted by propaganda. When written down, ideas and concepts take on a different authority, as archeologist Bruce Trigger puts it: "Traditions and customs become laws and regulations, while memory and sentiments are discounted in favor of authoritative written evidence."[9] Writing, then, was in most cases an elite preserve and remained that way for thousands of years, with literacy still a minority privilege in much of the undeveloped world today.

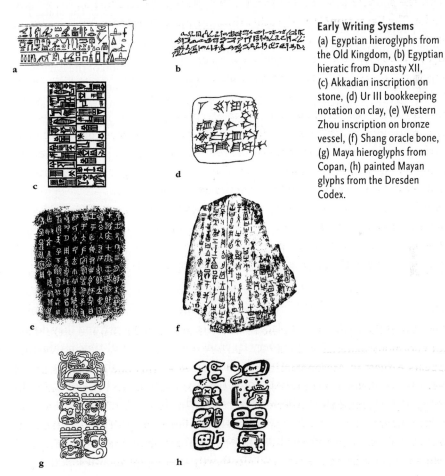

Early Writing Systems
(a) Egyptian hieroglyphs from the Old Kingdom, (b) Egyptian hieratic from Dynasty XII, (c) Akkadian inscription on stone, (d) Ur III bookkeeping notation on clay, (e) Western Zhou inscription on bronze vessel, (f) Shang oracle bone, (g) Maya hieroglyphs from Copan, (h) painted Mayan glyphs from the Dresden Codex.

9   Bruce Trigger, *Understanding Early Civilizations: A Comparative Study* (New York: Cambridge University Press, 2003), 592.

Along with writing, all civilizations discussed here developed sciences, such as mathematics, astronomy, physics, chemistry, and engineering. Their leaders commissioned monuments and buildings, many of which are still standing today. Their traders pioneered routes along which merchants would travel for thousands of years, stitching distant places together in a human network of trade and ideas which steadily expanded, leading to the ever-shrinking, interconnected world that we have inherited today.

By now our heads are spinning with respect for "our" achievement. For the countless individuals who, during the Neolithic, were slaves to their own need for food, some of the pressure was no doubt lifted. Innovations in farming and irrigation increased yields, and this meant that more people could specialize in other productive work. But such achievements came bundled with tribute, an early form of taxation in which a portion of your harvest would have to go to the state. For those people who continued to farm, evolving ideas about private property and ownership meant that land, like everything else, tended to accrue to powerful individuals, who then rented labor to work it for wages or a portion of the harvest.

As far as the human experience is concerned, therefore, the advantages of all of this "progress" may have been theoretical as there was always someone above you who dictated how you should live. To put it another way, you could say "The Man" had arrived.

WHY ARE HIERARCHIES PATRIARCHAL?

"The Man," whether in Sumer or in China, was almost always, well . . . male. The hierarchies we see at this point in history are all *patriarchal*, that is, dominated by men. Judith Brown has made the argument that women's roles were restricted by child raising. She notes how women traditionally worked at tasks that were compatible with watching children. "They do not require rapt concentration and are relatively dull and repetitive; they are easily interruptible, and easily resumed once interrupted; they do not place the child in potential danger, and they do not require the participant to range very far from home."[10] The full-time production of materials for the market outside the home required more than the part-time attention a nursing mother could afford. The "specialist" roles, therefore, went to those members of society who were not needed at home. Men, in other words, were free to go and become warriors, priests, traders, metalworkers, etc. (This might also explain why so many professional chefs, until very recently, have been men, even though traditionally women are the ones who cook most at home.)

---

[10] Judith Brown, quoted in Elizabeth Wayland Barber, *Women's Work: The First 20,000 Years: Women, Cloth and Society in Early Times* (New York: W.W. Norton, 1994), 30.

What Is the Relationship Between "Cities," "States," and "Civilization"?

The word *civilization* comes from the Latin *civis* (or "citizen"). This suggests that to be civilized you need to belong to an entity that has citizens. Since you cannot be a citizen of a tribe, we have to look for civilization (according to this logic) in states. Boguki calls civilization a "cultural term," with a long and distinguished history of use among archeologists. It identifies, he says, "a small group of archaeologically visible and spatially extensive peoples of later prehistory who had produced some degree of monumental construction and sophisticated culture."[11]

But this is a little vague. Trigger gives us a more specific definition, highlighting the role of hierarchies: "Anthropologists apply the term civilization to the earliest and simplest forms of societies in which the basic principle governing social relations was not kinship but a hierarchy of social divisions that cut horizontally across societies and were unequal in power, wealth, and social prestige."[12]

The term *civilization* itself presents other problems, which stem from its evil twin—its opposite. As Boguki puts it, "The classification of a society as civilized suggests that it is in contrast to those that are not."[13] In this sense the term is inherently prejudiced, and it is for this reason that it has largely fallen out of favor since its use suggested a nineteenth-century obsession with "superior" cultures—sedentary, agricultural, complex—which presupposed that all others were "primitive." The more technical, archeological sense of the term is still in circulation, however, and has to some extent lost its associations with superiority, defining instead a set of characteristics which set these societies apart. Historians also use the term from time to time, probably because it is widely accepted, and the alternatives are often cumbersome and equally inexact.

WHAT IS A CITY?

Civilization, whatever it is, certainly requires cities. But weren't the first cities just towns on steroids? Many Neolithic towns were almost as large as smaller, later cities. Can we then define a city by its function? Although farmers often lived in the earliest cities, going out to their fields every day, many city dwellers were non–food producers. "Whatever else their function," says Trigger, "cities were the main locations of high-level political and administrative activities, specialized craft production, marketing, long-distance trade, higher education, artistic and

---

[11] Boguki, *The Origins of Human Society*, 332.
[12] Trigger, *Understanding Early Civilizations*, 44.
[13] Boguki, *The Origins of Human Society*, 332.

cultural achievements, conspicuous display, court life, and religious ritual."[14] Concentrating specialized functions within cities served various purposes and created certain efficiencies. It was easy, for example, for metallurgists to obtain imported metals from traders and then to turn around and sell or consign their products to traders for export.

The example of metallurgy is significant because we are now entering the Bronze Age (often broken down into a chronology of Early, Middle, and Late Bronze Age covering a rough period from 3000 to 1500 BCE). In alloying copper with tin, the resultant metal, bronze, was much stronger than its component parts. Now metal could be used in tools and weapons, whereas copper was too soft for these uses and restricted mostly to decorative functions. By the second millennium BCE, bronze was widely used from the Atlantic coast of Europe all the way to China. Boguki calls the development of bronze technology "the trigger for a number of changes in the organization of human society on a scale comparable to the onset of sedentism and agriculture several millennia earlier."[15]

> Then, as now, cities were glamorous: locating temples, ritual sites, and the priestly class in cities lent considerable mystique and prestige to the city and underscored the ruler's proximity to the divine.

Then, as now, cities were glamorous: locating temples, ritual sites, and the priestly class in cities lent considerable mystique and prestige to the city and underscored the ruler's proximity to the divine. Such concentration also highlighted the relative insignificance of the ordinary citizen or subject—take a trip to Washington, DC, or any national capital, and see how you feel when you are dwarfed by its monumental architecture. Nationalist architecture such as you find in modern capitals often makes the individual—you, for example—feel small, part of something larger than yourself. Religious monuments served the same function in the ancient world.

The archeologist V. Gordon Childe (d. 1957) produced a checklist of 10 points to define a city.[16] Often used to define civilization as well, he wrote that in order to qualify, you need (1) a large population; (2) full-time specialists; (3) surplus concentration, that is, extra food; (4) monumental public buildings; (5) ruling class functionaries; (6) systems of recording, such as writing and numerical notation; (7) exact and predictive sciences, such as math and astronomy; (8) representative art; (9) regular foreign trade; (10) organic social solidarity, in which state organization is dominant.

---

[14]   Trigger, *Understanding Early Civilizations*, 121.

[15]   Boguki, *The Origins of Human Society*, 270.

[16]   V. Gordon Childe, "The Urban Revolution," in *Town Planning Review* 21, no. 1 (1950): 3–17.

There is plenty of disagreement about this list. But at the very least it provides a useful framework for thinking about these early societies. And while there may be other societies that share some of these traits, the river valley civilizations were among the most extensive ever found of their era.

WHAT IS A STATE?

Most of us today know intuitively what a state is, but its definition is surprisingly elusive. States govern, in a variety of styles, over a specific area; and to delineate the area, they employ borders and force to protect and expand them. The state imposes certain rights and obligations upon all of its members but not necessarily in equal measure. Fukuyama sees several important ways in which state societies differ from tribal societies. First of all they are *sovereign*, meaning that a "head of state" exists to whom all levels in the hierarchy defer. This source of authority is backed by a monopoly on "legitimate means of coercion," meaning sanctioned violence. The ability to use force ensures that groups attempting to secede can be bludgeoned back into line, ensuring that the state continues as a whole. The state is territorial, rather than kin-based, and for this reason it is able to expand much farther than any tribe. States are more stratified than tribal societies, recognizing strict rankings in their social orders. Also, religion plays a larger legitimizing role, providing a still wider platform for expansion than kin-based societies.

How Did River Valley Civilizations Develop?

Traditionally called the "river valley civilizations," these early states all grew up along major river systems. Cultivation of the fertile alluvial plains on their banks allowed for population growth. In all cases the rivers are still central to the people living in these areas. Regular flooding deposited fertile alluvium on the riverbanks and floodplains, providing optimal soil for growing; and irrigation expanded the area of possible cultivation. So important was it that irrigation by itself has been proposed as a major reason for the growth of states. Rivers also permitted trade and communication along their length, contributing to the societies' wealth, expansion, and cohesion. Such benefits also came with a cost, which explains why the Chinese refer to the Yellow River as "China's Sorrow" because of its frequent deadly flooding. By paying attention to the needs of the gods, one of the major tasks of the priests of Mesopotamia was to ward off damaging floods (those living along the Mississippi River today can well imagine the concerns of ancient Mesopotamians).

The Green Zone   Herbal Earth from NASA provides images of vegetation worldwide. Here you can see why Egypt was referred to as the "Gift of the Nile," in ancient times. Egyptians have always lived in the "green zones." River valley civilizations developed where they did because of such life-sustaining proximity to freshwater.

WHY MESOPOTAMIA?

Now that we have a broad idea what these civilizations represented, let's look at them in more detail. At 4000 BCE the area between the Tigris and Euphrates Rivers was not, according to historian Andrew Sherratt, "the liveliest place on earth." The people who lived there inhabited grass huts and used clay sickles to harvest grain. Not that this is not thrilling, but the really exciting things were happening to the north, in the Fertile Crescent, where people were painting on pottery and trading in wide varieties of stone and metal, and in the south, along the Persian Gulf, where people were trading with India. But what enabled Mesopotamia to develop beyond its grass huts was the linking of these two areas. Sherratt calls it a "sparking across the gap," and this put Mesopotamia, the middleman, on the map.[17]

By 3500 BCE the area was a dynamic hub of interactivity, with multiple city-states forming a culturally unified "civilization." The cause of this spark was trade, both along the rivers and overland, by caravans of donkeys. But the land between the rivers was largely dry, prompting the need for irrigation; and for this the two rivers (plus other smaller tributaries) came in handy.

Such irrigation required work. Organized labor had been seen before but not on this scale. These projects were of an entirely different magnitude and were continuous, year in and year out; and someone, or some group, was required to manage the work. This is where "The Man" made his appearance.

---

[17]   Andrew Sherratt, "Reviving the Grand Narrative: Archaeology and Long-Term Change," *Journal of European Archaeology* 3, no. 1 (1995): 17.

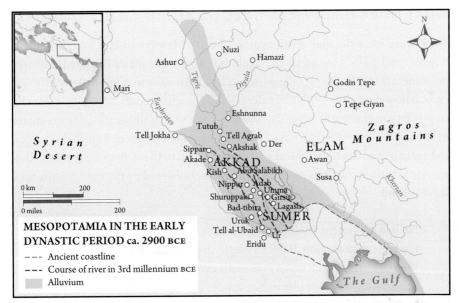

MAP 3.2   MESOPOTAMIA IN THE EARLY DYNASTIC PERIOD   Although the Euphrates and Tigris provided water for irrigation and floods made for fertile land, the rivers shifted courses and rainfall was generally inadequate. Settlements were therefore often abandoned, although many city states lasted for hundreds of years.

Reconstruction Drawing of the Mesopotamian City of Ur, One of the Earliest Cities   Notice the function of the river (transport), the walls (defense), and the central ziggurat complex.

WHAT DOES *GILGAMESH* TELL US ABOUT MESOPOTAMIA?

There were five principal urban centers of early Mesopotamia: Uruk, Eridu, Ur, Nippur, and Kish. One of them, Uruk, just south of today's Baghdad, features prominently in *The Epic of Gilgamesh*, so let's turn back to it briefly here. The excerpt below describes Uruk's wonders—at its height around 2900 BCE it was the largest city in the world so far discovered—as a way of illustrating the greatness of its king, Gilgamesh. There are few better examples of the notion of prestigious individuals, and the hierarchical societies attached to them, than Gilgamesh. This excerpt clearly shows how such individuals are bolstered by the monuments they leave behind.

> He had carved his trials on stone tablets,
> Had restored the holy Eanna Temple and the massive
> Wall of Uruk, which no city on earth can equal.
> See how its ramparts gleam like copper in the sun.
> Climb the stone staircase, more ancient than the mind can imagine,
> Approach the Eanna Temple, sacred to Ishtar,
> A temple that no king has equaled in size or beauty,
> Walk on the wall of Uruk, follow its course
> Around the city, inspect its mighty foundations,
> Examine its brickwork, how masterfully it is built,
> Observe the land it encloses: the palm trees, the gardens,
> The orchards, the glorious palaces and temples, the shops
> And marketplaces, the houses, the public squares.
> Find the cornerstone and under it the copper box
> That is unmarked with his name. Unlock it, open the lid.
> Take out the Tablet of Lapis Lazuli. Read
> How Gilgamesh suffered all and accomplished all.[18]

In a few lines the author of *Gilgamesh* has hit upon the major points of interest to us in Uruk and, by extension, in the entire Sumerian civilization. First, the idea of reading words "carved on a tablet of lapis lazuli" (ironically, we now refer to iPads and their ilk as "tablets," recalling the first reading/writing devices) illustrates that this society was literate, the first in history. Shortly after 3000 BCE, says Boguki, "recorded history emerged from the mists of prehistory with the Sumerian King Lists that document dynastic lineages at several Mesopotamian cities."[19]

---

[18] *Epic of Gilgamesh*, trans. Stephen Mitchell (New York: Free Press, 2004), prologue.
[19] Boguki, *The Origins of Human Society*, 338.

"After the kingship descended from heaven, the kingship was in Eridug. In Eridug, Alulim became king; he ruled for 28,800 years. Alaljar ruled for 36,000 years. 2 kings; they ruled for 64,800 years. Then Eridug fell and the kingship was taken to Bad-tibira. In Bad-tibira, En-men-lu-ana ruled for 43,200 years. En-men-gal-ana ruled for 28,800 years. Dumuzid, the shepherd, ruled for 36,000 years. 3 kings; they ruled for 108,000 years. Then Bad-tibira fell (?) and the kingship was taken to Larag. In Larag, En-sipad-zid-ana ruled for 28,800 years. 1 king; he ruled for 28,800 years. Then Larag fell (?) and the kingship was taken to Zimbir. In Zimbir, En-men-dur-ana became king; he ruled for 21,000 years. 1 king; he ruled for 21,000 years."[20]

It may not read like a Tom Clancy novel, but this passage, along with *Gilgamesh*, is one of the earliest known written documents. What is extraordinary about it—apart from the fact that some of these kings appeared to have lived for thousands of years—is that it is also the beginning of scholarly history. It is, if not wildly informative, a basic record of leaders, giving us evidence of how important the very notion of leadership had become and how important leaders—kings—must have been to have lived so long.

The kind of writing represented by the King's List was derived from earlier notations in pictograms, a kind of precursor to the more legitimate "script" known as "cuneiform." Writing was very much a solution to the pressing needs of Sumerian society to record transactions. Those who could write could also hoard information, and priests were some of the early hoarders of information in Sumer; of particular use was their knowledge of weather, which was vital for agricultural projects.

The author of *Gilgamesh* mentions the temple of Eanna, reflecting the role of religion in Sumer. The temple was the key feature of the Mesopotamian city. Built on a stepped pyramid known as a *ziggurat*, these were located within walled enclosures, priestly precincts. The temples were considered "divine households," and they acted like earthly households. The temple sheltered a statue of the deity, and priests, functionaries, servants, and slaves carried out the day-to-day duties, including labor on the surrounding agricultural lands. The household provided regular and sumptuous sacrifices for the resident gods and goddesses, to ensure their favor. The impetus to please the gods was a key driver of innovation in Sumer as a whole. Uruk's "masterful brickwork," and "glorious temples and palaces," as well as the fashioning—and export—of luxury items, bronze weapons and tools, spun woolen cloth, and the cultivation of diverse fruits and vegetables, as mentioned in *Gilgamesh*, were all part and parcel of this "tribute" paid to the deities.

---

[20] http://www.bibliotecapleyades.net/sitchin/king_list2.htm

Each city had one or more resident gods—Ishtar and An in Uruk, for example—but these deities were not all-powerful, existing alongside seven great gods—Sun, Moon, Earth, Sky, Fresh Water, Salt Water, and Storm—considered to be the most powerful. It is likely that the priests who developed the ideas behind this pantheon modeled it on the way Sumerians themselves organized their lives, with citizens meeting annually to attend to the community's affairs, just as it was believed that the gods met at the beginning of each year to determine the course of events over the next 12 months. In a further example of this model of religious myth making, Mesopotamian myths explained how gods had created men to be their slaves, providing them, in their divine households, with everything they needed, much as earthly slaves provided the elite with the items required to live according to their station.

HOW IS EGYPT "THE GIFT OF THE NILE"?

If we turn to the West, we find a similar, yet different story in Egypt, underscoring the fact that the early civilizations shared certain "foundational" aspects but were distinct in many others. The Greek historian Herodotus called Egypt the "Gift of the Nile," and if you ever need a rock-solid example of geography defining politics, Egypt is where you should turn. Looking at Egypt from above you can see that either side of the thin green strip of the Nile, a few miles at the most, is barren desert, with only a few small oases. Like Sumer, Egyptians needed the water to irrigate their fields.

The Egyptians had irrigated their fields since the dawn of agriculture. But with the growth of the state, far greater resources could be concentrated on this task as the growing population looked to its food needs. Unlike Sumer's unpredictable and damaging floods, the Nile flooded seasonally and relatively gently. Egyptians trapped water behind dikes, allowing surplus water to drain off after depositing silt. Unlike much river silt, the Nile's was not, contrary to popular opinion, particularly fertile. Egyptians therefore enhanced their fields' fertility by allowing them to lie "fallow" with no crops on alternate years or by rotating legumes with cereals. Their irrigation methods prevented salt from building up in the soil—freshwater leaves behind a salt residue as it evaporates, which turns good land into desert over time—as it did in Sumer.

"The River," as ancient Egyptians called the Nile, was also key to its political unity. Travel northward was simply a case of going with the river's current, flowing to the sea.

Going south, you sailed before the trade winds, which blow from the northeast. Such ease of navigation simplified political control as well as trade. But before being unified into a political whole, "Egypt" was made up of multiple small

Felucca (Traditional Nile Trading Boat) on the Nile, Fully Loaded with Goods   Wind transports goods upriver. The current takes them down.

chiefdoms, existing in a state of constant warfare. Eventually, this conflict created two main kingdoms, one based in the southern part of the country, or what is known as Upper Egypt because of its position on the river, and one in Lower, or northern, Egypt. We cannot be completely sure of the exact manner of unification, but "what is clear," says Boguki, "is that by about 3000 BC Egypt was unified into a single state which extended about 1300 kilometers along the Nile."[21] Since that time the country has maintained roughly the same boundaries, even if its leadership and culture have changed periodically.

WHO WERE THE PHARAOHS?

As is the case with Sumer, we can, by about 2500 BCE, hear the voices of the people we are studying. Revealing here are the *Instructions of Ptahhotep*. Believed to be an advisor to the king in the Egyptian Fifth Dynasty (2414–2375 BCE),

---

[21]   Ibid., 358.

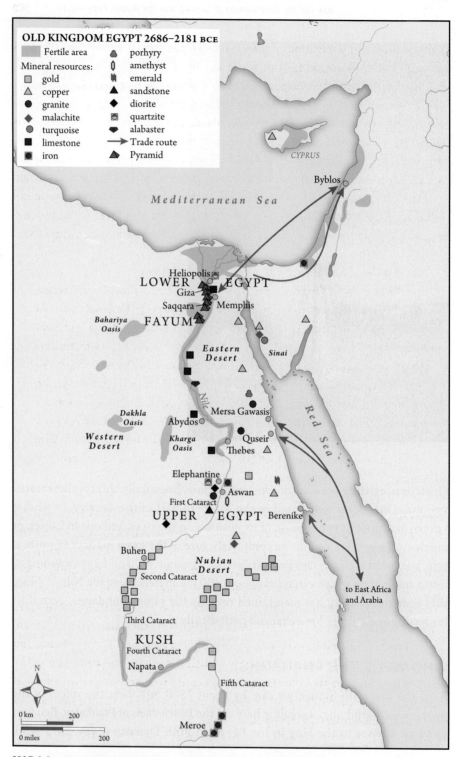

OLD KINGDOM EGYPT 2686–2181 BCE

Fertile area

Mineral resources:
- gold
- copper
- granite
- malachite
- turquoise
- limestone
- iron
- porhyry
- amethyst
- emerald
- sandstone
- diorite
- quartzite
- alabaster
- Trade route
- Pyramid

CYPRUS

Mediterranean Sea

Byblos

LOWER EGYPT
Heliopolis
Giza
Saqqara
Memphis

Bahariya Oasis
FAYUM

Eastern Desert
Sinai

Nile

Dakhla Oasis
Mersa Gawasis
Abydos
Western Desert
Kharga Oasis
Quseir
Thebes

Red Sea

Elephantine
Aswan
First Cataract
UPPER EGYPT
Berenike

Buhen
Nubian Desert
Second Cataract

Third Cataract

to East Africa and Arabia

KUSH
Fourth Cataract
Napata

Fifth Cataract

N

0 km   200

0 miles   200

Meroe

MAP 3.3 OLD KINGDOM EGYPT   While the Nile provided irrigation water and fertile land, the desert supplied stone building materials and security from invasion—usually.

Ptahhotep offered a selection of maxims to his son for his betterment. What is striking here is how modern his advice seems; his "values" are instantly recognizable. But take note of the wider context of his advice: he is instructing his son in ways to succeed in a highly structured and hierarchical society, in which there are leaders and followers, kings and servants, slaves and masters. It sometimes reads like an ancient version of *How to Win Friends and Influence People,* the 1937 self-help bestseller. His admonitions reflect a society in which you need help in order to "get ahead." Indeed, "success" itself is perhaps a new concept historically speaking, arising in civilizations in which the stakes are high and your behavior and skill may determine how well—and perhaps whether—you live. Most ancient societies, however, had caps on success as your station was largely determined at birth.

> "Do that which your master bids you," exhorts Ptahhotep.
>
> "Twice good is the precept of his father, from whom he has issued, from his flesh. What he tells us, let it be fixed in our heart; to satisfy him greatly let us do for him more than he has prescribed. Verily a good son is one of the gifts of Ptah, a son who does even better than he has been told to do. For his master he does what is satisfactory, putting himself with all his heart on the part of right. So I shall bring it about that your body shall be healthful, that the Pharaoh shall be satisfied with you in all circumstances and that you shall obtain years of life without default. It has caused me on earth to obtain one hundred and ten years of life, along with the gift of the favor of the Pharaoh among the first of those whom their works have ennobled, satisfying the Pharaoh in a place of dignity."[22]

A good son, it seems, should serve his father and his "master." The creation of the ancient world's greatest monuments may well have been an expression of this service. The pyramids of Giza, created by several pharaohs over several decades, took the labor of thousands of men. Who were they, and how did they build them?

Like Sumer, the power of the Egyptian rulers only went so far—as far as they could send soldiers. This simple physical limitation on power meant that the elites in Egypt needed another way to ensure obedience from their subjects and, hence, claimed to be living gods, with a combination of earthly and divine powers that greatly enhanced their authority. The easy control over transportation enjoyed by the pharaohs enabled them to transport and concentrate resources anywhere in the state. Conscripted labor provided a workforce capable of creating the kinds of monuments that expressed their power.

---

[22] *Instructions of Ptahhotep,* Papyrus from Egyptian Fifth Dynasty, Prisse Papyrus. (Paris: Bibliotheque Nationale).

We have emphasized how "The Man" was usually male. But in Egypt this rule was occasionally broken. Several pharaohs were, in fact, women, including the famous Cleopatra (r. 51–30 BCE). Ancient Egypt's most illustrious queen, Hatshepsut (r. ca. 1475–1459 BCE), often took the form of a man in pictorial representations, portrayed with a beard. While apparently accepting a woman as a leader, it seems that then, as now, a woman needed to appear "masculine" to achieve her ambitions.

WHAT IS THE SIGNIFICANCE OF THE PYRAMIDS?

The pyramids at Giza represent the most startling testament to the power of Egypt's religious ideology. The largest pyramid is also the oldest. Built for the Pharaoh Khufu, around 2350 BCE (and taking approximately a decade to complete), the pyramid was the largest human structure on the planet until the twentieth century, requiring some 6.5 million tons of stone. All of this was quarried, cut, transported, and raised into place with nothing more than rope, wood, and human muscle.

It has long been assumed that the labor necessary to complete this task must have required thousands of slaves (and there is a healthy Internet-based community convinced that aliens were needed for the project as well). But recent scholarship has questioned the stereotypical version of events as portrayed in movies such as Cecil B. DeMille's *The Ten Commandments* (1956). While it is clear that thousands of people were indeed needed for such an effort, what scholars such as Barry Kemp and Mark Lehner have shown is that they were not necessarily slaves. In uncovering the city built to house the many pyramid workers, Lehner began to form a picture of a conscripted workforce drawn from the Egyptian populace. These workers—stonecutters, masons, haulers, cooks, and support crew—seemed to have come from all parts of the country and were most likely rotated in and out of Giza like conscripts in an army, with a core of several thousand residing there permanently. They were housed and fed in relative comfort; archeological remains near the pyramids reveal barrack-style dormitories, giant bakeries, even tombs apparently belonging to managers of work crews which are richly decorated, suggesting high status. Also present at the site were enormous quantities of bones from young, male cattle—prime beef, in other words, fed to the workers.

Lehner concluded that these were not slaves. Work on the pyramids, the biggest civil engineering project in human history at that point, was mostly conducted by freemen. It is also entirely possible that it was desirable work as it had a sacred purpose, amounting to a form of worship—the pyramids would be

The Pyramids at Giza, Egypt, Seen from Across the Desert   The largest is the oldest (2350 BCE). Until the twentieth century it was the largest human-made structure on earth. What does that say about the society that built it?

an everlasting testament to the greatness of the pharaoh, the "god-king," and as such (if you bought into the ideology) what more important job could there be?

The pyramids had another function, that of cementing the state together: it was not so much, as Lehner put it, that the Egyptians built the pyramids but that the pyramids built Egypt. The work was truly a nationwide effort, which no doubt created a sense of cultural solidarity as well as a national economy. It would also have performed the central role of all monumental architecture, that of inculcating both a sense of pride through association and a sense of personal insignificance in the face of the state. Egyptians owed tribute to the state, a kind of tax payable in different mediums, including obligatory labor.

> It was not so much, as Lehner put it, that the Egyptians built the pyramids but that the pyramids built Egypt.

INDIA: THE EXCEPTION?

The third river valley civilization we have to consider, that of the Indus Valley, has most perplexed historians. It is probably the one we know the least about, having only been unearthed in the 1920s. The Indus is fed by five rivers, which flow across the plains of northwest India and a large part of Pakistan into the Arabian Sea. The life-giving properties of these rivers have made them sacred to Indians throughout the ages. The area that was home to a shared culture, known as the Indus Valley, or Harappan, civilization, after one of its main cities, Harappa, was far larger than either Egypt or Mesopotamia. But while these civilizations were still flourishing, Harappa disappeared. We don't know what caused this collapse, but scholars point to either an environmental event, such as the shifting of river courses, or a series of invasions from outside the region.

Archeology has shown that large Neolithic towns such as Mehrgar, on the Kachi Plain of Pakistan, existed from around 7000 BCE. Historians refer to an "early Indus period" (between 3200 and 2600 BCE) in which agricultural people settled the fertile and well-watered region of the Indus River valley system and developed relatively complex societies. The region consisted of good cropland and a vast expanse for animal herding. Unlike the Euphrates valley, a wealth of minerals, including copper, tin, gold dust, flint, and agate, was also readily available. This period saw the development of towns and multiple agricultural settlements.

Mohenjo-Daro: An Artist's Reconstruction The Harappans seemed to have all the other elements of early civilizations, yet there is doubt as to whether they had powerful military elites. More data are needed.

But in the 100 or so years after 2600 BCE archeologists see a rapid development of the area and the creation of large cities. It is in this period (known as the "Mature Harappan") that a distinctive Indus script shows up, along with widespread evidence of sea trade with Mesopotamia and new styles of pottery and craft. This period concerns us because we see in it many of the items on Childe's list—monumental architecture, dense population, and a marked shift toward craft specialization. But according to archeologist Jane McIntosh, "regional artifact styles had been largely superseded by uniform, high quality products throughout the Indus basin, reflecting cultural and possibly political unity."[23] This evidence would suggest that some sort of central organizing principle was in play, such as a state.

Control of water was pivotal to this civilization. Mohenjo-Daro, a city larger than Harappa and possibly the (or at least *a*) capital, featured a central compound built on a massive raised platform and giant walls for either defense or flood control, a sewage system, and more than 700 deep, skillfully built brick wells. Such features were found in several other cities, revealing that this technology was part of a regional culture. Water was a threat from which they needed protection as well as a commodity that needed to be channeled and preserved for multiple purposes. The city's "bath complex" is widely considered to have religious or ritual significance, especially since bathing has played a part in Indian ritual life for at least 2,500 years.

What is most perplexing, however, and more so because no one has been able to decipher the script, is the seeming lack of a Harappan ruling elite. Even with all this evidence of large-scale architecture and engineering projects, Mark Kenoyer, one of the principal archeologists working in the Indus Valley, points out, "there is a conspicuous absence of central temples, palaces, and elaborate elite burials that are characteristics of other early urban societies in Mesopotamia, Egypt and China."[24]

The earthen mounds upon which the cities were built required in the region of 300,000–400,000 man-days to complete. Such feats of engineering usually presuppose a managerial elite as in Sumer or Egypt. Also suggestive of elite control and supervision is the standardization of weights and measures found throughout the region. Cubical weights were made in graduated sizes, conforming to the standard Harappan binary weight system used throughout the region. Such items were probably used in commercial dealings and possibly in calculating taxes.

---

[23] Jane McIntosh, *The Ancient Indus Valley: New Perspectives* (Santa Barbara, CA: ABC-CLIO, 2008), 84.

[24] Mark Kenoyer, "Cultures and Societies of the Indus Tradition." In *Historical Roots in the Making of "the Aryan,"* edited by R. Thapar (New Delhi, India: National Book Trust), 29.

Although the early British excavators saw signs of a military hierarchy in Harappa, later archeologists have suggested that there is no evidence of violence. But "an entirely peaceful state seems anomalous in the history of world civilization," says McIntosh.[25] If so, how could this condition have arisen? The answer lies partly with our old friend environmental determinism and partly with the specific cultural matrix of this civilization. In other ancient civilizations force was a common means of guaranteeing cooperation. Where it failed, religion was useful, for instance, in compelling men to leave their villages and work on the Giza pyramids. Is it possible that the Harappan religious ideology was sufficiently potent that order was maintained through consent, for fear of offending the religious norms? Environmental causes for conflict may also have been absent, as McIntosh puts it: "The diversity of resources and economic potential of the different regions and the great productivity of its lands and relatively low population meant that there was no spur to conflict."[26] Violence with outsiders was minimized because kin-based associations with nomads and herders to the north of the Indus Valley region resulted, one can imagine, in cooperation rather than conflict. To the south and east protection was provided from invading foreigners by the sea and mountains. Was this combination of factors a "perfect storm" of peace?

Perhaps, but Richard H. Meadow of the Peabody Museum at Harvard University thinks probably not. "There has never been a society without conflict of greater or lesser scale," he says.[27] Because we have not deciphered the Harappan script, we are lacking crucial information that would help us solve this mystery. Archeologists made the same mistake with the Mayan civilization in Mesoamerica, he points out, until they deciphered the Mayan script, which proved that the Maya were as warlike as anybody else.

Less controversial is the apparent lack of a ruling elite. But how did this civilization run itself without a king, emperor, or other supreme leader? Many scholars think Harappa was managed by priest-kings, which would in many ways fit with what we see elsewhere in the ancient world. The difference here, however, is that the religious ideology was so well accepted that top-down coercion was unnecessary. Officials of the "state" were locally appointed in a bottom-up system that focused on responsibility more than on power. If this is true, then the Harappan state truly deserved the term *civilization*, as archeologist Charles Maisels points out: "I see Indus Civilization as an oecumene, or commonwealth, not a state-ordered society. Accordingly it is the only complex society known to history which truly merits the name 'civilization' in the proper, non-technical sense. This

---

[25]   McIntosh, *The Ancient Indus Valley*, 91.
[26]   Ibid., 91.
[27]   Richard H. Meadow, *Harappa.com*, http://a.harappa.com/content/how-peaceful-was-harappan-civilization.

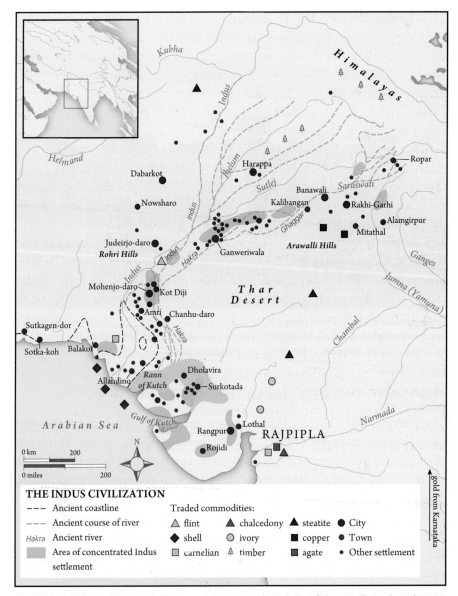

MAP 3.4   THE INDUS CIVILIZATION   Multiple rivers flowed more or less parallel to the Indus several thousand years ago. All entered the Arabian Sea in a large delta, and between the rivers and the delta settlements benefited from ample arable land. The people of the Indus civilization were in constant contact with hunter-gatherers of the surrounding deserts and hills with whom they traded.

is the condition of serving the greatest number through advances in knowledge, civility and economic well-being shared by all."[28]

---

[28]   Charles Keith Maisels, *Early Civilizations of the Old World: The Formative Histories of Egypt, the Levant, Mesopotamia, India and China* (London: Routledge, 1999), 259.

Mohenjo-Daro was built in two sections, the residential area, with a grid pattern, and the citadel. Water management was key to the engineering. In this photo a well shaft is visible. Water and bathing may have had highly ritualistic purposes, as they did in later Indian cultures.

WHAT ARE THE ORIGINS OF THE STATE IN CHINA?

The story of early China is also the story of a river. Starting along the middle reaches of the HuangHe (Yellow) River in northern china, village settlements developed on loess terraces above the river. By about 3000 BCE, burial sites from these villages, known collectively as the Longshan culture (characterized by fine, black-painted pottery), exhibit clear evidence of high-status individuals buried with prestigious grave goods. "Many features of the Longshan period in Northern China," says Boguki, "point to increasing social differentiation, and the concentration of economic and ideological authority in the hands of a limited portion of the population."[29] As is the case with the other river valley civilizations, where agriculture flourished, complex societies were not far behind. Chinese civilization, however, developed more slowly than that in Egypt and Mesopotamia; and it is not until the third millennium BCE that we see comparable urban states. Instead, until the third millennium BCE we see localized tribal chiefdoms in China.

Tribalism has always been important to the Chinese state, from very early times arguably until today. Early Longshan communities were led by chieftains.

---

[29]   Boguki, *The Origins of Human Society*, 323.

YEAR (BCE)	DYNASTY	PERIOD	NO. OF POLITIES
5000		Yangshao	
3000		Longshan	
2000	Xia	Three Dynasties	3,000
1500	Shang		1,800
1200	Western Zhou		170
770	Eastern Zhou	Spring and Autumn (770–476)	23
		Warring States (475–221)	7
221	Qin		1

Ancient China denotes the period from prehistory to the Qin dynasty.

Tribes were organized into lineages, with kings heading groups of lineages. Defined by anthropologists as a corporate group based on proven descent from a common ancestor, *lineages* were strictly patrilineal, descending only through men. Women were not traditionally considered part of the lineage but "assets" to be used in arranging alliances with other lineages, not unlike feudal Europe. Once married into a new lineage, women had no status at all until they bore sons, who provided status for them and security as they aged. The kind of hierarchy we see in early China was therefore distinctly patriarchal. This sidelining of women was only partially offset by the political machinations of "dowagers" attempting to improve their sons' standing in court. If they were successful, they could achieve high status as the mother of an heir; but for the vast majority of ordinary women, power, over self or others, was restricted to the domestic sphere.

From the Longshan period onward, political power was exercised via control over access to ritual sites. It was this function that the Bronze-Age Chinese towns were built to fulfill. Again, we see the hand-in-glove relationship between politics and religion in the early states. Chinese ritual sites were shrines dedicated to specific lineages, which housed the tombs of ancestors. In the temple, worshippers made gifts to their ancestors to ensure successful harvests and encourage favorable outcomes in all walks of life. Wheel pottery and later bronze metallurgy as well as jade carvings were all geared toward these religious rites. This process took on a political significance since those who organized and understood the technologies became the elite.

As population density increased, communities inevitably came into conflict; and such conflict, in turn, likely spurred greater social complexity. Archeological evidence is clear that violence was endemic to the Yellow River valley at this time. Such predominance of conflict continued throughout Chinese history and helps

---

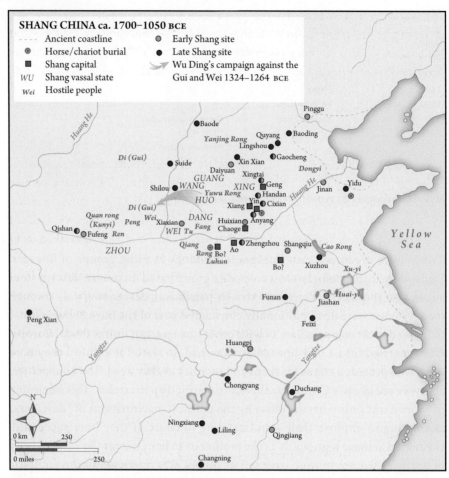

MAP 3.5 **SHANG CHINA**   The Shang Dynasty's last capital was at Anyang, founded about 1350 BCE.

to explain how what was essentially a decentralized feudal territory with multiple centers of power became one large, unified empire. This warfare, although resulting in regular changes in political leadership, did not lead to any significant cultural changes, the like of which might be expected with invasions of "foreigners." Instead, "there seems to have been a rather smooth transition from the innumerable Neolithic villages of the Longshan culture to the Bronze Age capitals of the Three Dynasties, all of which we can view as successive phases of a single cultural development."[30]

---

[30] John K. Fairbanks and Merle Goldman, *China: A New History* (Cambridge, MA: Harvard University Press, 1992), 35.

The three dynasties mentioned here were the Xia, the Shang, and the Zhou, collectively they are referred to as the *San Dai*. The thousands of local polities which struggled for territory gradually shrank to one, by 200 BCE, when the Qin dynasty took control. At this point the foundation of the modern Chinese state had been established.

WHO WERE THE SHANG?

The Xia dynasty has been somewhat mythical until recent decades when archeology began to unearth evidence that confirms later writings about the period. Remains dating to around 2000 BCE have been found at Erlitou and surrounding sites south of the Yellow River, near the city of Yanshi. These sites provide evidence of temples, palaces, and massive defensive walls made of rammed earth, a technique in use in China for thousands of years from this point.

The northernmost city in Henan Province, Anyang, was one of the capitals of the Shang dynasty (1500–1200 BCE). Covering 9.3 square miles, the site encompasses 17 separate cities within its radius. The famous historian of ancient China Sima Qian (ca. 145–86 BCE) said that when the Shang moved their capital to Anyang in 1350 BCE, it began its golden age. Here, archeologists have found palaces and royal tombs, along with what are identified as sacrificial victims,

Shang Bronze Ware   Shang bronze drinking vessel in the form of a bird. The Shang used bronze ware for religious rituals and to provide sustenance for ancestors' spirits.

many with heads separated from torsos. The Shang believed that the social order continued after death; therefore, it was necessary for leaders to go to the grave with their entire retinue, including wives, servants, and even horses. Higher-level burials like the ones at Anyang sometimes contained as many as 500 human sacrifices, and as many as 10,000 sacrificial victims have been found in burial pits in Yinxu. There are few better examples of individuals having to subordinate themselves to the social order.

Increasing levels of hierarchy are seen with the Shang and clear brutality, including severe punishments such as cutting off of feet and castration. There is widespread evidence of slavery and human sacrifice. But although slavery was endemic, it was not the main pillar of the economy as it was, for instance, in the American South centuries later. Like Egypt, labor was conscripted from peasants or lower-ranking members of the society for construction projects such as walls, the one at Zengzhou being 4 miles around and in places 27 feet high. Tribute was made to the rulers in the form of the basic economic commodities of the day: agricultural products and bronze metalwork. Recent scientific analysis of bone remains at the capital suggests that its population was extremely diverse, coming from all parts of China. Anyang, in other words, was a cosmopolitan, even multiethnic center, filled with people from all corners of the empire, and, as such, it was an extraordinarily modern city, created to bring specialists together from all corners of the state.

> Anyang, in other words, was a cosmopolitan, even multiethnic center, filled with people from all corners of the empire, and, as such, it was an extraordinarily modern city, created to bring specialists together from all corners of the state.

Much of what we know of the Shang comes from inscriptions carved on bones. These "oracle bones" have survived because of the materials from which they were made, while others, no doubt made on bamboo, wood, and other materials, did not last. The oracle bones were used to find answers to questions such as whether the harvest would succeed or whether a suitor would make a good husband. The bones were subjected to intense heat, the resultant cracks were interpreted for meaning, and the answers were inscribed on the bones.

WHAT WAS THE FUNCTION OF WRITING IN EARLY CHINA?

The Chinese script in use on these bones originated earlier, within the Xia and even perhaps in embryonic form within the Longshan. But as the society became more complex so did its written medium, largely because administration, as with Mesopotamia, Egypt, and India, required record keeping. The *Book of Songs*, although mostly collected and anthologized during the Zhou period, contains material possibly in circulation as folk poetry and popular songs for generations, well back into the Shang period. The "organization" of all this material is an arresting example of the power of writing to "standardize" ideas and make them canonical. A section of the *Book of Songs* contains songs about the origins of the Shang dynasty, in particular the idea that it was divinely appointed. This concept, which became known later as the *Mandate of Heaven*, was routinely adopted by Chinese dynasties throughout its history. The following "ode" tells of the moment at which the Shang was divinely appointed for kingship:

> Heaven Bade the Dark Bird
> To come down and bear the Shang,
> Who dwelt in the lands of Yin so wide.
> Of old God bade the warlike Tang
> To partition the frontier lands.
> To those lands was he assigned as their lord;
> Into his keeping came all realms.[31]

This notion of divinely appointed leaders is one of the foundational similarities between Egypt, Mesopotamia, and China. Another similarity is that its literature functions to glorify, legitimize, and otherwise praise its leaders; and whereas there may have been songs and poems that were in circulation for generations serving this same purpose, writing them down (initially on wood or bark, or papyrus, as paper was not invented until the Han dynasty of 200 BCE) would have given them canonical power.

But in the voices of the *Book of Songs* we also hear those of the common people, and this represents an exception to the rule of elite use of literature. The delicacy of personal feeling expressed in many of these odes as well as the prominence of features of the natural world show that despite the long reach of the Chinese state in this period the individual was alive and well, and surprisingly lyrical, like the lover's lament in the excerpt below:

> On the willows at the east gate,
> The leaves are very luxuriant. . . .
> The evening was the time agreed on,
> And the morning star is shining bright.
> On the willows at the east gate,
> The leaves are dense.
> The evening was the time agreed on,
> And the morning star is shining bright.[32]

---

[31] *Book of Songs*, Ode 303, trans. Arthur Waley (New York: Grove Press, 1996).
[32] *Book of Songs*, Ode 140.

It may seem paradoxical, but perhaps such lyricism was necessary where the power of the state was strong as it provided an antidote to the dehumanizing effects of the latter. And the Chinese state achieved unprecedented power and scope from early on and never fully relinquished it. Fukuyama points out that state power was consolidated before other social actors could institutionalize themselves, such as "a hereditary, territorially based aristocracy, an organized peasantry, cities based on a merchant class, churches or other autonomous groups." This set of circumstances is why the state in China was "centralized bureaucratic and enormously despotic."[33]

DID NEW WORLD CIVILIZATIONS FOLLOW THE SAME MODEL?

Traditional histories of the earliest civilizations do not tackle the New World in depth. This is generally because Mesoamerican societies, among the earliest in

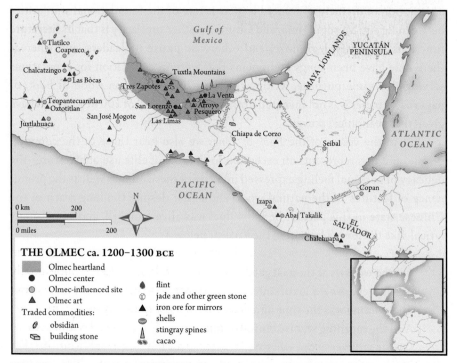

MAP 3.6   THE OLMEC   Archeologists believe that the Olmec dominated this area by 1200 BCE. Their distinctive forms of pottery and other artifacts have been found throughout Mesoamerica, and their influence is visible in later Mesoamerican civilizations.

---

[33] Fukuyama, *The Origins of Political Order*, 93.

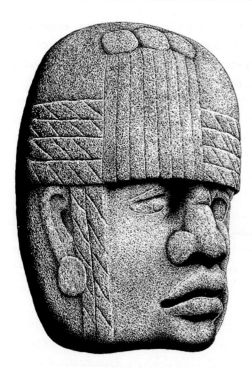

Olmec Achievements   The Olmec created immense stone heads like this one from San Lorenzo, Veracruz, in Mexico. Below is a reconstruction of a ceremonial center at La Venta, Tabasco, Mexico. Less is known of the Olmec than other early civilizations; they had distinct social hierarchies and writing systems, yet there is debate as to how developed their political systems were.

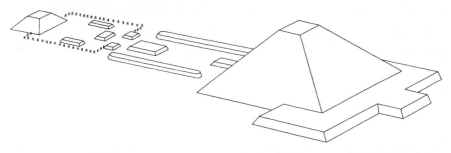

the Americas, did not reach the same level of complexity or scale until somewhat later. And although we have focused on the four societies traditionally seen as "most significant, most early," there are scholars who argue that the Olmecs of Mesoamerica warrant inclusion in this group as they were a "pristine" civilization—in other words, they did not evolve from other civilizations as offshoots but grew independently, in a recognizable sequence from smaller societies to larger, more hierarchical civilizations with elaborate cultures.

The Olmec civilization certainly exhibits many of the traits that Childe listed as necessary for urban civilization; in particular, they are best known for their colossal statues of human heads. These heads were often up to 36,000 pounds in weight and appear to have been transported in some cases over 50 miles. Clearly, these feats required large amounts of that sure sign of civilization, organized labor. In addition to these structures, archeologists have found mirrors of polished iron ore, carvings of humans and animals, and collections of small stone figurines probably representing religious ceremonies.

Flourishing between 1200 and 400 BCE, the most important Olmec centers known to date lie along the Mexican Gulf coast. San Lorenzo Tenochtitlán and La Venta are two of the larger sites, and it is here that archeologists have found clear-cut evidence of social differentiation and hierarchies. The settlements at San Lorenzo, for example, are made up of a three- or four-tiered hierarchy, consisting of subordinate centers, villages, and special-purpose sites. Royal tombs have yielded grave goods consistent with what one would expect from elite burials in Old World tombs, and the colossal heads are believed to represent rulers, suggesting their importance (and probable divinity). There is also evidence here of early writing systems, which may have evolved into the Mayan script, as well as trade networks that extended into the Mexican highlands.

But although several of Childe's criteria appear to have been met by Olmec society, whether or not it represented a "civilization" in the sense of the four other centers we have discussed in this chapter is hotly debated. Specifically, it is not widely accepted that the Olmecs possessed state institutions such as we see in other early civilizations. It may be that they equate better to the Longshan period of state formation in China, predynastic Egypt, and what archeologists call the "Ubaid period" of Mesopotamia, which came before the appearance of state-level society such as the period that produced *Gilgamesh*.

Conclusion: How Did the Development of Cities Affect the Human Experience?

The changes brought to bear on human existence with these early civilizations were far-reaching and created both new opportunities and restrictions. Neolithic tribes and Paleolithic bands would have been hard-pressed to comprehend the experience of a soldier in the Shang army, a conscripted laborer at Giza, or a Mesopotamian slave.

Of particular interest to us in this chapter has been the degree of inequality which was a hallmark of the early civilizations. With agricultural surpluses and specialized labor, some began to use others as what Christian refers to as "human batteries." This idea underscores the role of energy in these societies as well as the dehumanizing consequences of that role; it was energy that created wealth, and energy is always a limited commodity, just as fossil fuels are today. "The importance of human beings as a source of energy," says Christian, "helps explain why forced labor was so ubiquitous in the pre-modern world, just as the existence of fossil fuels helps explain why human slavery has largely vanished today."[34]

Our interest in these early civilizations, if somewhat biased, also suggests that we recognize ourselves in them. Indeed, many of the elements of early civilizations are still with us. Such is the extraordinary staying power of the state as a social structure. For this reason it is easy to look at the early civilizations of Egypt, Mesopotamia, and China as surprisingly modern, even if we do refer to them as "ancient." The educational demands on an apprentice engineer in ancient Egypt would rival those of a university student today. The intrigues and power plays of the Shang court would make modern Washington, DC, look like a picnic. Many such similarities hold for the Harappan civilization of India as well, although it seems to have been the odd one out because we have little evidence of elites or of systematic coercive violence. But notwithstanding these major exceptions, Indus civilization conforms to the pattern of early civilizations on many counts.

These four civilizations were not the only "game in town." To focus on them to this extent might well give the impression that the rest of the world was languishing in illiterate, irreligious, social anarchy. Such was not necessarily the case. "Pristine" states, or states which arose spontaneously, not through conquest or imitation, also appeared in other areas of Afro-Eurasia, the Americas, and the Pacific islands such as Hawaii and Tonga. We have focused here, however, on the four river valley civilizations because they are the earliest and largest examples of so-called civilizations, not to downplay the achievements of other cultures or areas but to be best able to understand what was unique about them, how they arose, and what consequences they had for humanity.

One of the questions a historian asks is, *How did we get here?* To a large extent, when we look hard at our own society, be it globally or locally, we see echoes of these early states. And this comparison is no coincidence; the structures put in place in ancient Mesopotamia, Egypt, India, and China all have modern correlates today, in the spheres of politics, economics, religion, and social relations. To this extent we are all inheritors of the first civilizations.

---

[34] Christian, *Maps of Time*, 263.

Words to Think About

Alluvial	Egalitarian	Hierarchy
Irrigation	Patriarchal	Ziggurat

Questions to Think About

- How did cities change social life for their inhabitants?
- What role did rivers play in the earliest civilizations?
- In what ways might ancient Indian civilization have been different from China, Mesopotamia, and Egypt?
- In what ways did urbanism represent progress? In what ways did it not?

Primary Sources

Book of Songs, Ode 303. Translated by Arthur Waley. New York: Grove Press, 1996.

Epic of Gilgamesh. Translated by Stephen Mitchell. New York: Free Press, 2004.

Instructions of Ptahhotep. Papyrus from Egyptian Fifth Dynasty. Prisse Papyrus. Paris: Bibliotheque Nationale.

Secondary Sources

Barber, Elizabeth Wayland. *Women's Work: The First 20,000 Years: Women, Cloth, and Society in Early Times*. New York: W.W. Norton, 1994.

Boguki, Peter. *The Origins of Human Society*. Malden, MA: Blackwell, 1999.

Childe, V. Gordon. "The Urban Revolution." *Town Planning Review* 21, no. 1 (1950): 3–17.

Christian, David. *Maps of Time: An Introduction to Big History*. Berkeley: University of California Press, 2005.

Ehrenberg, Barbara. *Women in Prehistory*. Norman: University of Oklahoma Press, 1989.

Fairbanks, John King, and Merle Goldman. *China: A New History*. Cambridge, MA: Harvard University Press, 1992.

Fukuyama, Francis. *The Origins of Political Order: From Pre-Human Times to the French Revolution*. London: Profile Books, 2011.

Harris, Marvin. "The Origin of Pristine States." In *Cannibals and Kings*, 101–26. New York: Vintage, 1978.

Kenoyer, Mark. "Cultures and Societies of the Indus Tradition." In *Historical Roots in the Making of "the Aryan,"* edited by R. Thapar, 21–49. New Delhi, India: National Book Trust, 2006.

Maisels, Charles Keith. *Early Civilizations of the Old World: The Formative Histories of Egypt, the Levant, Mesopotamia, India and China*. London: Routledge, 1999.

McIntosh, Jane. *The Ancient Indus Valley: New Perspectives.* Santa Barbara, CA: ABC-CLIO, 2008.

Meadow, Richard H. *Harappa.com*, http://a.harappa.com/content/how-peaceful-was-harappan-civilization.

Sherratt, Andrew. "Reviving the Grand Narrative: Archaeology and Long-Term Change." *Journal of European Archaeology* 3, no. 1 (1995): 1–32.

Trigger, Bruce. *Understanding Early Civilizations: A Comparative Study.* New York: Cambridge University Press, 2003.

For additional resources, including maps, primary sources, and visuals, web links, and quizzes, please go to **www.oup.com/us/cole**

Krishna and Arjuna, Major Antagonists, Leaving for Battle (Eighteenth Century)   A scene repeated throughout history, the world over. Different weapons, different costumes, similar story.

Chapter 4

War (!) What Is It Good For?

War and Poetry

While I watched fearfully under the protection of Vyasa, the derangement of war was all around me; dust that dimmed the sunlight, the noise of crashing chariots, and splintering wood, elephants and horses calling, bones and metal breaking, and the shouts and cries of warriors, telling their names and families, guided by costume and banner and secret words and signs.[1]

MAHABHARATA

The Mahabharata, from which this passage is taken, is one of the two epic poems (the other one being the Ramayana), which together constitute the core of Indian cultural heritage. Composed over several hundred years, between roughly the second century BCE and the second century CE, it tells of events that are believed to have happened some 1,000 years earlier. Specifically, it tells of the dynastic struggle between two branches of a single ruling Indian family, the Kurus and the Pandavas. The ultimate struggle is over the fertile land at the confluence of the Ganges and Yamuna Rivers near Delhi, but the story itself involves multiple long digressions into social, moral, and cosmological areas.

It is no coincidence, however, that the story revolves around military conflict. Many ancient stories, in particular epics, involve war and violence. Why has war been so prominent in human history, and what role has it played?

---

[1]   Mahabharata, retold by William Buck (Berkeley: University of California Press, 1973), 265.

123

THINKING ABOUT WAR

What Is the Origin of War?
- Killing, and possibly war of some form, was familiar to prehistoric humans; as far as the evidence goes back there has been human-on-human violence.

How Did War Change with the Rise of States?
- Instead of struggles over hunting ranges, conflict [among states] ensued over productive agricultural land; slaves were taken as booty because there was work to be done . . . and humans were the only energy source available.

What Role Did War Play in Building Territorial States?
- The notable move from small, less complex societies to larger, more complex ones, which we see the world over, is achieved under both the reality and the threat of war.

Were There Any Peaceful States?
- Buddhism professed a creed of peace, harmony, and equality. . . . But it is likely that Buddhism was a uniquely Indian response to the challenges of ancient life, one of which was constant warfare.

Conclusion
- In the absence of violence and warfare, it remains unclear how human societies would have developed increasingly complex forms, or what the the driving force for such change might have been.

Introduction

War is father of all, king of all. Some it makes gods, some it makes men, some slaves, some free.

HERACLITUS (CA. 535–475 BCE)

It has been estimated that every minute two people are killed in a violent conflict.[2] Like later history, that of the earliest civilizations is drenched in blood. If we

---

[2] "One Day of War," *BBC News*, http://news.bbc.co.uk/2/shared/spl/hi/programmes/this_world/one_day_of_war/clickable_map/html/introduction.stm.

are to look at history unvarnished, it should come with a warning: killing, rape, genocide, and slavery have played a large role in the human experience for much of the past 5,000 years and possibly much, much longer. This may be an unpalatable truth, but truth it is. So why all this war? Is it just that historians have unfairly emphasized the "bad," failing to recognize the many long periods of peace of which we are equally capable? Perhaps. Historians, like journalists, tend to focus on warfare, perhaps out of a prejudice that sees war as an aberration, which in turn suggests that the human "default" is peace. Should we, therefore, be writing about what makes for peace? Well, in many ways we do; when we discuss trade, religion, or science and technology, all of these themes and issues are part of human history and are relevant to periods of peace and of war. But to see peace as a default, or "normal," condition is not far-fetched since wars have generally been short-lived in comparison to periods of peace. Having said that, the consequences of war endure long after the final shots have been fired, suggesting that war and peace are part of an endless dialogue, one unable to exist without the other.

In this chapter we will discuss what motivates humans to participate in violence and war, to better understand war's role in shaping human society. With a focus on the ancient world, we will examine how war and peace formed two inextricably linked parts of the human experience.

War impacted the lives of perhaps millions of people in the ancient world profoundly. Although of little solace for those who lived through it, from the

Soldier with Prisoner, Engraving from Amorite Dynasties, 2000–1595 BCE
Then, as now, certain relationships were conflictual.

wreckage of war there often emerged new relationships, new political entities, and technological, scientific, social, and political innovations. Driven by the needs of defense and aggression, these innovations appeared much in the same way that today's military drives innovations—GPS and the Internet being two prime examples—and in the same way that we now have global political and financial institutions that are the result of two catastrophic twentieth-century world wars.

But these are unintended consequences of, not motivations for, war. Apart from such spin-offs, in this chapter we will explore how in many cases war drives a process of growth from smaller to larger political entities, or *polities*. China's first "unification" came under the Qin dynasty (221–206 BCE) and was wrought out of warfare. Mesopotamia in 3500 BCE was a collection of small city-states, each well defended by walls such as those at Uruk. But 1,000 years later, the "land between the rivers" was largely consolidated under the Akkadian Empire (2334–2154 BCE), ruled over by a very martial royal family from the city of Akkad, who had, by conquest, created one polity. Successions of kings, powerful city states, and empires came and went in the subsequent millennia; and while there were stretches of peace and stability, some of them quite long, this period in history is rich with military chronicles as ruler deposed ruler in gory succession struggles and expansionist campaigns. Ancient Egypt shared with China a large and long-lasting state but one that was born from war as many chiefdoms and kingdoms were brought to heel and incorporated into the larger Egyptian polity. Once unified, Egyptian warfare was focused mostly on its neighbors.

In all of these areas a move from small political units to larger, more coherent ones is evident, even if this process was halting.

Scholars have attempted, largely in vain, to find pacifist societies, hoping to prove that war is not a natural part of human society. Few societies have ever been put forward as "peaceful." Those which have, including the Mbuti pygmies of central Africa, the Shoshone of North America, and some tribes in Malaysia, are mostly hunter–gatherers. Definitions of what constitutes a peaceful society hinge on the longevity of the alleged "peace" and on definitions of war. Some tribes, pushed from their ancestral lands and largely depleted of population, were in no fit state for military operations. Other peoples, like the Swedes, have not taken part in war for several centuries, although they did in the more distant past, when, for example, Scandinavia was known for its fearsome Vikings and not its progressive politics and safe automobiles of today.

Most of the historical evidence from the ancient world comes from archeology, but looking into deep prehistory, with developments in the fields of primatology, evolutionary biology, psychology, and genetics, scholars are now able to put flesh on the bones of archeological evidence and make more confident assertions

KEY DATES	
12,000–10,000 BCE	Bodies with embedded projectiles at Jebel Sahaba, Sudan
8000 BCE	Maces and enlarged projectile points at Qermez Dere, northern Iraq
6000 BCE	Earliest rock art portrayals of group conflict in Australia
5500–5000 BCE	Massacres at Ofnet, Talheim, and Schletz in Germany
5400 BCE	Skeletons show signs of violence in Florida, USA
5000 BCE	Defensive ditches around Yangshao villages in the Yellow River valley, China
4300 BCE	First true fort at Icel on the southern Turkish coast
2600 BCE	Rammed-earth village walls throughout Longshan, China
2500 BCE	Skeletons show signs of violence, Pacific Northwest Coast, USA
2000 BCE	Severed heads, Peruvian coast, South America
1500 BCE	Palisades and settlement destruction at San José Mogote, Oaxaca, Mexico

Key Dates in Humanity's Fighting Career

about our distant past. Recent scholarship suggests that violence might have had an adaptive benefit to the very earliest humans, allowing them to prosper in the brutal struggle for survival. And if violence is the raw material of war, then is it possible that this human characteristic is innate and has played a key role in war in state societies?

Heraclitus's assertion that war was the force which shaped much of human society finds echoes in other ancient writers, for example, China's Sun Tzu, in his *Art of War.* Written in the sixth century BCE, it distills generations of experience in warfare, illustrating how prevalent and important war was to the state. As that text makes clear, warfare became deeply institutionalized from the river valley civilizations onward, and this was true not only in China but everywhere else in the world. "The art of war is of vital importance to the state," says Sun Tzu. "It is a matter of life and death, a road either to safety or ruin. Hence it is a subject of inquiry which can on no account be neglected."[3] These words could have been written yesterday.

What Is the Origin of War?

Did war have a beginning? If it did and we can trace its "invention" back to a historical point, does that mean it is an aberration and can be eradicated, like a disease? But if we can find no start date for war, does that mean that our species was "born" warlike? And if war is innate, does that mean we are destined to always fight?

In order to begin thinking this one through we should define our terms. Like many words, *war* is enormously elastic. Today we tend to think of war as a highly

---

[3]   Sun Tzu, *The Art of War* (Boulder, CO: Westview Press, 1994), 1:1, 2.

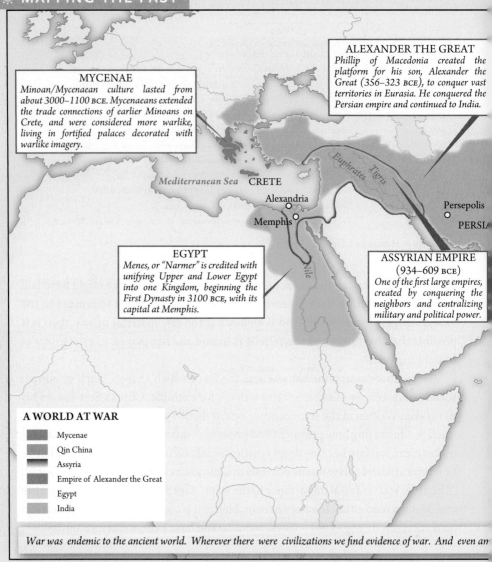

ALEXANDER THE GREAT
Phillip of Macedonia created the platform for his son, Alexander the Great (356–323 BCE), to conquer vast territories in Eurasia. He conquered the Persian empire and continued to India.

MYCENAE
Minoan/Mycenaean culture lasted from about 3000–1100 BCE. Mycenaeans extended the trade connections of earlier Minoans on Crete, and were considered more warlike, living in fortified palaces decorated with warlike imagery.

Mediterranean Sea CRETE

Euphrates

Tigris

Alexandria

Persepolis

Memphis

PERSL

EGYPT
Menes, or "Narmer" is credited with unifying Upper and Lower Egypt into one Kingdom, beginning the First Dynasty in 3100 BCE, with its capital at Memphis.

Nile

ASSYRIAN EMPIRE
(934–609 BCE)
One of the first large empires, created by conquering the neighbors and centralizing military and political power.

A WORLD AT WAR
- Mycenae
- Qin China
- Assyria
- Empire of Alexander the Great
- Egypt
- India

War was endemic to the ancient world. Wherever there were civilizations we find evidence of war. And even an

MAP 4.1 WORLD AT WAR

TIMELINE

☀ **ca. 18,000 years ago**
Wadi Kabbaniya graveyard in Egypt

☀ **ca. 705–681 BCE**
King Sennacherib rules
Neo-Assyrian Empire

☀ **ca. 3000–1100 BCE**
Minoan/Mycenaean civilization

☀ **ca. 2334–2154 BCE**
Akkadian Empire

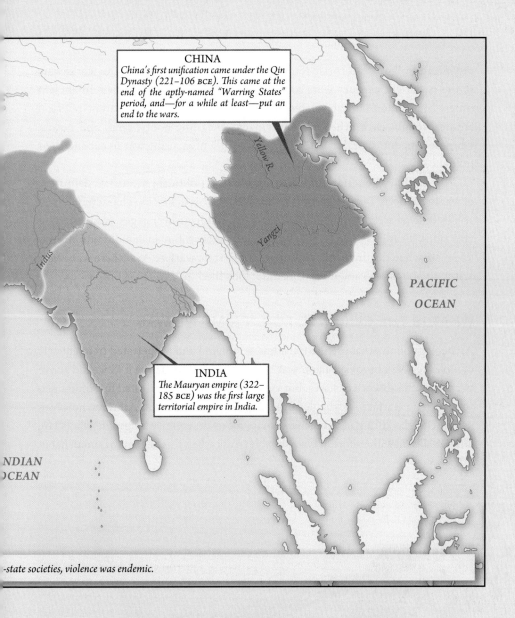

CHINA
China's first unification came under the Qin Dynasty (221–106 BCE). This came at the end of the aptly-named "Warring States" period, and—for a while at least—put an end to the wars.

Yellow R.

Yangzi

Indus

PACIFIC OCEAN

INDIA
The Mauryan empire (322– 185 BCE) was the first large territorial empire in India.

NDIAN
OCEAN

-state societies, violence was endemic.

 461–446 BCE
Peloponnesian Wars

 221–206 BCE
Qin Empire

 480–338 BCE
Classic Greek Civilization

 323 BCE
Death of Alexander the Great

organized military enterprise waged between two nation-states. The world wars of the twentieth century were fought between well-defined parties. In ancient times, Mesopotamian city states, for example, which were coherent political entities, fought each other for "supremacy," meaning booty, land, and power. Chinese kingdoms, or dynasties, fought for millennia, using war to expand their influence.

The military historian John Keegan offers a "political-rationalist" definition of war in his book *The History of Warfare* (1993). This definition characterizes war as a state-level activity in which pitched battles, skirmishes, sieges, easily identifiable sides, clear goals, and even rules are all present. But such a definition is inadequate when dealing with "primitive" or prestate warfare. Was there war *before* states, in prehistory; and if so, what did it look like?

WHAT IS THE EVIDENCE FOR "PRIMITIVE WAR"?

Archeology shows that prehistoric humans suffered and perpetrated frequent acts of violence. We cannot speak of "war" in prehistory if we define it as we did above because of the absence of states. But violence was likely perpetrated for similar reasons to state warfare—struggles over territory and resources. All wars, however, begin with the killing of people who share a certain identity by people who share another identity. Therefore, it is reasonable to ask when this became a human habit.

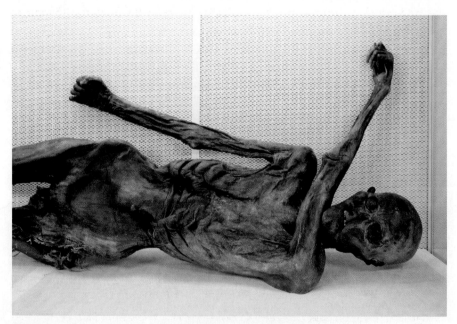

Ötzi, the Ice Man, a probable homicide, was thought to have fallen afoul of enemies 5,000 years ago.

In the caves at Pech Merle and Cougnac in southern France, among more common paintings of animals, Ice-Age humans also depicted what many archeologists consider to be murder. In one painting a man is shown standing with seven spears penetrating him. At Cosquer Cave on the Mediterranean coast, there is an engraving, which has come to be known as the "Killed Man," from 18,500 years ago. It shows a body lying prone with its legs and arms in the air and a deeply engraved line running through its back and up through the skull, possibly a spear or harpoon. Whether this scene portrayed a real event or not, we do not know. But if killing was in the human imagination, was it not happening in reality?

There is considerable evidence—beyond paintings—that it was. In England researchers have found settlements from around 4000 BCE with extensive perimeter walls. Did the walls symbolize the inhabitants' concepts of inclusivity/exclusivity, as some claim? Or were they more simply defensive measures against hostile "others"? Human bones inside the encampment and piles of arrowheads around the gates point to the latter. In one case a man's skeleton was found with an arrowhead lodged in his back. In his arms was an infant who had been crushed to death as he fell.[4]

The famous "Ice Man," a frozen body discovered near the Austrian/Italian border in 1991 (nicknamed Ötzi), also told a dark story. Dated to some 5,000 years ago, multiple theories exist about his death; but the wound from an arrowhead and the evidence of a blow to the head, as well as multiple cuts and abrasions on his body and arms, all point to a violent death.[5] The evidence is by no means limited to Europe. At Wadi Kabbaniya near the Egyptian–Sudanese border, archeologist Fred Wendorf discovered the body of a young man buried around 20,000 years ago, with three wounds: a broken left arm (possibly from warding off a blow), a partly healed wound from a spear tip in the same upper arm, and two spear points in his pelvis. Wendorf thinks that skirmishes over watering holes in that area were frequent and that this individual had experienced several battles. "The last one," he thinks, "got him."[6]

Further archeological evidence points not just to killing on an individual level—more suggestive of murder rather than war—but killing in groups as well. One gruesome example is Cemetery 117, as it's known to archeologists, located in Gebel Sahaba, in Egyptian Nubia. Here, Wendorf discovered 59 bodies of men,

---

4   Lawrence Keeley, *War Before Civilization: The Myth of the Peaceful Savage* (Oxford: Oxford University Press, 1996), 18.

5   Stephanie Pain, "Arrow Points to Foul Play in Ancient Iceman's Death," *New Scientist* (July 2001). For more, see the official website of the South Tyrol Museum of Archaeology in Bolzano, Italy, http://www.iceman.it/en/node/265

6   Quoted in Kirkpatrick Sale, *After Eden: The Evolution of Human Dominance* (Durham, NC: Duke University Press, 2006), 82.

women, and children. Forty percent of the adults had stone projectiles in them. One woman had 29 stone arrow tips in her, and one man exhibited 19 separate wounds, possibly suggesting a ritual killing. Others had multiple arrowheads in the chest and back. The children were mostly executed at short range by arrow shots to the head or neck. This happened 12,000–14,000 years ago, about the same time that the Natufians were building the first villages in the Fertile Crescent (see Chapter 2).

Rock paintings in Arnhem Land, in northern Australia, show groups of men battling with spears, with boomerangs flying overhead. And in the Americas, archeologists found 850-year-old remains of human muscle protein on potsherds and human remains in a piece of fossilized human excrement. As anthropologist Lawrence Keeley puts it, "The Prehistoric New World was also a place where the dogs of war were seldom on a leash."[7] Killing, then, and possibly war of some form, was familiar to prehistoric humans; as far as the evidence goes back there was human-on-human violence.

WHAT DID PREHISTORIC WAR LOOK LIKE?

The standing armies with which we are familiar appeared only with the river valley civilizations. Nomadic tribes and settled hunter–gatherers today, however, still practice several distinct forms of violent conflict, which likely resemble prehistoric warfare. One such type is more "ritualistic" in that it looks like a pitched battle but few people get hurt. The Dani highlanders of New Guinea have been doing this for centuries, if not millennia. Male members of two different communities meet in an open area. Often, much of the battle involves hurling verbal insults at each other, sometimes even ending in hilarity. Exchanges of arrows and spears will likely also take place but at their maximum effective range, and casualties are low, sometimes nil (the stakes have been raised in recent decades, however, with the introduction of guns to the traditional arsenal of spears and arrows).

The other main form of warfare is much more damaging, involving swift and deadly raids on enemy communities. With the element of surprise and overwhelming numbers, there is little risk for the attackers. One technique favored by different groups, including the Bering Straits Eskimos and the Mae Enga of New Guinea, involves surrounding huts at dawn and thrusting spears through the thin walls, pouring arrows into the doorway, and shooting people as they run out. Raids give way to larger enemy actions, what Keeley refers to as "massacres," the aim of which is total annihilation of the enemy—men, women, and children. The

---

[7] Keeley, *War Before Civilization*, 39.

Uncivilized War   If war existed before, or outside of, civilization, it might have looked like this. These are possibly the only photos of an occurrence thought to be global among tribal peoples and hunter–gatherers. Casualties are generally low, but the resemblance to a pitched battle is unmistakable.

subarctic tribe of Kutchin Eskimos habitually attempted to destroy the Mackenzie Eskimos, killing all members of an encampment but one—the "survivor"— who would be left to tell the tale. Something akin to this may have taken place at Cemetery 117 in Gebel Sahaba.

> There are strong taboos against killing in almost all cultures, and this caution is largely understood to be because while violence is a useful tool, it is a tool of last resort.

History attests that killing is, for us, no light matter. Men— and to a lesser extent women—have had to be persuaded, and in many cases forced, to kill in battle. There are strong taboos against killing in almost all cultures, and this caution is largely understood to be because while violence is a useful tool, it is a tool of last resort. Going up against one of your own species supposes an equal match. It does not take much to be injured, possibly fatally, or killed outright. Violence should be undertaken only when absolutely necessary and when the chances of success are high. This is reflected in the advice of Sun Tzu: "If fighting is sure to result in victory then you must fight . . . if fighting will not result in victory, then you must not fight, even if it is a ruler's bidding."[8]

Many historians have noted the reluctance of warriors to kill. Niall Ferguson, for instance, has written that the First World War would have been inconceivable without alcohol because the soldiers could never have committed such atrocities sober.[9] Getting high or drunk is a time-honored wartime practice, from the Vietnam War to ancient India, as the brain needs to be chemically altered to overcome natural inhibitions. There are other ways of overcoming this reluctance, and all have been practiced throughout history. One is propaganda, which broadcasts the "justice" of the cause for which you are fighting and might well portray your enemy as evil, bent on your destruction, or, as was famously the case with the Jews in Nazi Germany, inhuman. *Gooks, Japs, rag heads, camel jockeys*—the list of epithets for perceived enemies is endless and gives away a very human reluctance to kill. Dehumanizing the enemy is therefore often required before killing them.

WHAT IS THE EVOLUTIONARY BACKGROUND OF WAR?

Many evolutionary psychologists now think that humans have always practiced violence against each other. As Steven Pinker of Harvard University puts it, "Any genetic group that has made it into the present probably had pugnacious ancestors in the not-too-distant past."[10] Put simply, human survival over these many

---

8   Sun Tzu, *Art of War*, 10: 23.
9   See David Livingstone Smith, *The Most Dangerous Animal: Human Nature and the Origins of War* (New York: St. Martin's Press, 2007), 154.
10   Steven Pinker, *The Blank Slate: The Modern Denial of Human Nature* (New York: Penguin, 2002), 315.

millennia was always in question; we were up against severe changes in climate, predation from wild beasts, plagues, and famines. Ninety-nine percent of creatures that have ever lived on the planet are now extinct. The evolutionary biologist Richard Dawkins has referred to humans as "survival machines," and key to this was becoming more dangerous than the giant beasts that liked to eat us. This process, however, may have created a new monster, *Humans*, against whom we had to protect ourselves. It is likely that a capacity for violence became a trait that gave tough guys the edge in the game of survival. As philosopher David Livingstone Smith puts it, "These groups flourished while the pacifists withered on the evolutionary vine."[11]

Competition for resources has always been a prompt to violence among individuals and states. Most obviously perhaps, competition arises over food. But beyond this, men, like males of other species, have always competed for women. "This explains," says Pinker, "why men are the violent gender, and also why they always have something to fight over, even when their survival needs have been met."[12] *Sexual selection* is the process by which attractive traits are passed down between generations, becoming increasingly common in a species. Generally, these traits related to reproductive success. In the animal kingdom traits such as birds' plumage or singing ability play a large role in sexual selection. Aggressiveness, as a trait, may have played a part in human sexual selection. Females of our evolutionary ancestors may have favored aggressive mates. Over the generations, increasing numbers of children would have been born to these individuals, who would have inherited the "aggressive gene." As Livingstone Smith conceives it, "Treading the well-worn path of sexual selection, [women] transmitted a proclivity for male coalitionary violence down the generations until it saturated most of humanity."[13]

How Did War Change with the Rise of States?

In the practical art of war, the best thing of all is to take the enemy's country whole and intact; to shatter and destroy it is not so good. So, too, it is better to recapture an army entire than to destroy it, to capture a regiment, a detachment or company entire than to destroy them.

SUN TZU, *THE ART OF WAR*, 3:1

---

[11] Livingstone Smith, *The Most Dangerous Animal*, 81.
[12] Pinker, *The Blank Slate*, 19.
[13] Livingstone Smith, *The Most Dangerous Animal*, 92.

The evidence suggests that prehistoric people practiced warfare and that this behavior had evolutionary roots. But what happened when we became "civilized"? Based on the historical record it seems reasonable to assume that most city states around the ancient world paid little heed to this advice from Sun Tzu (above); conquering enemies was done old-school, besieging them in their citadels, massacring their men, raping their women, and then either enslaving them and their children or butchering them. War, with the advent of civilization, whether Chinese or Olmec, became a major preoccupation, to the extent that states built their economies around the need for defense and the demands of keeping soldiers in the field. It also made war deadlier. "In earliest prehistory," says Livingstone Smith, "the sparseness of human population put a natural brake on the scope of our ancestors' destructiveness. But when agriculture made large concentrations of people possible, and urban centers began to turn nomadic tribesmen into sedentary tillers of the soil, the deadliness of war increased proportionately."[14] The Greek historian Herodotus (ca. 484–425 BCE) recorded that the Greeks killed 200,000 Persians on a single summer day in 479 BCE at the battle of Plataea. Twenty years later, in China, the Qin state slaughtered a quarter of a million combined forces of Han and Wei.[15]

In addition to scale, motivations for war changed somewhat with the rise of cities and states; instead of struggles over hunting ranges, conflict ensued over productive agricultural land; slaves were taken as booty because there was work to be done and, apart from domesticated animals, humans were the only energy source available. Cities also accumulated products and goods, storing either food or valuable items such as precious metals and stones (gold, silver, and jade) and other manufactured goods. Some scholars now think that although warfare increased with civilization, mortality actually declined. This reduction in mortality could be explained by increased warfare being balanced out by long periods of peace. In ancient Egypt, after the country had been unified under one ruler, relative peace was achieved within its boundaries, if not without.

Civilization (that awkward term we discussed in Chapter 3) emerged in the Near East around the fourth millennium BCE. In Mesopotamia, the world's first work crews were assembled to meet the challenges of irrigation and public works, as we discussed in Chapter 3. But organization of men and record keeping are essential ingredients of any effective military. It is therefore no surprise that the shape of the earliest "armies" was related to that of work crews in this region: "In the ancient world, even more so than today, the nature and structure of army,

---

[14] Ibid., 51.
[15] This was "pre-Imperial" Qin, that is to say, the Qin state which existed before it unified China to become the Qin empire (221-106 BCE).

Ashurnasirpal Killing Lions, from the Palace of Ashurnasirpal II, Nimrud, Iraq, ca. 850 BCE
Hunting was often practice for war.

society, economy and state were directly related and interdependent."[16] Armies, therefore, were not conceivable without states, nor states without armies.

And the armies were put to use. Near-Eastern ancient history is a particularly dizzying succession of kings and dynasties. We should look, however, at this warmongering in perspective; although we have many records of wars, for example, from Mesopotamia, these cover several thousand years. "King Hammurabi of Babylon," says historian Benjamin Foster, "was remoter in time from King Assurbanipal of Assyria, than William the Conqueror from Eisenhower."[17] Mesopotamian ancient history was, in other words, long. Conceivably, fairly long periods of peace were scattered among outbursts of war.

DID PEOPLE SETTLE IN CITIES FOR PROTECTION?

With the rise of cities we begin to see the first professional warfare, in which political leaders were often military leaders and could conjure up large numbers of armed men, trained soldiers, and lowly conscripts. City states, whether in Mesopotamia,

---

[16] Nigel Tallis, "Ancient Near Eastern Warfare," in *The Ancient World at War*, ed. Philip De Souza (London: Thames and Hudson, 2008), 47.

[17] Foster, B. "War Under the Straw: Searching for Peace in Mesopotamia," in De Souza, 75.

Greece, or the New World, always appeared in clusters (over 1,000 in ancient Greece, over 30 in Mesopotamia, and several dozen in the Valley of Mexico); and they always appeared in the absence of a larger, territorial state—perhaps because of the absence of such (a larger power being more able to monopolize the use of violence). This clustering suggests a need for defense, probably against each other.

To some extent city state warfare can be seen as an extension of a prehistoric "habit" of warfare, an extension of our natural fear of strangers. As anthropologist Robert Wright puts it, "If two nearby societies are in contact for any length of time, they will either trade or fight."[18] Both of these activities were entered into with gusto. Natural resources provided one motivation for both warfare and trade. Sumerians needed timber and metal ore, neither of which was available locally; and conflict over trade routes was common. Cities also clashed over the waterways and access to productive land, like the protagonists of the Mahabharata. Conflict was also common between sedentary city dwellers and nomadic or semi-nomadic peoples in the region. Sedentary settlements, towns, and cities stockpiled goods of all sorts; and nomadic peoples, who specialized in herding livestock, were adept at lightning raids, used to acquire the products of civilized societies.

As we learned in Chapter 3, unlike today, most inhabitants of early cities were food producers. If this seems counterintuitive, it is—until you begin to perceive the security picture. Archaic references to the Mesopotamian city of Uruk refer to it as "Uruk-the sheep-enclosure," suggesting that the city might have begun as a place of safety where shepherds and goatherds could protect their charges from marauding bands on the lookout for livestock. Protection was written into the DNA of ancient towns and cities. "Centralized ceremonial/cultic/civic centers, marketplaces and artisan workshops," says historian Azar Gat, "would mean little in the development of city-states were it not for the imperatives of defense."[19] The reason that people endured the overcrowding, disease, and inconvenience of a city was the threat posed from other cities, sometimes only a few miles away. Putting it bluntly, Gat makes the point that "City-states were the product of war."[20]

> The reason that people endured the overcrowding, disease, and inconvenience of a city was the threat posed from other cities, sometimes only a few miles away.

But did this kind of clustering together really protect from war? Prehistoric warfare was not as advanced as that which brought down Ur and later Sumerian cities. Tribes have historically "raided" each other in pursuit of booty. Raiding was effective when the target group was small; invaders could swoop in unannounced, grab, and run. If they had a numerical advantage, they enjoyed greater

[18]   Robert Wright, *Nonzero: The Logic of Human Destiny* (New York: Vintage, 2001), 64.
[19]   Azar Gat, *War in Human Civilization* (Oxford: Oxford University Press, 2006), 275.
[20]   Ibid.

security. But when settlements became larger villages, this threw a wrench into the plan. Raiding parties needed to be larger to achieve a numerical advantage, and grab-and-run was no longer an option; instead, fighting would be on a house-to-house basis, each dwelling being a stronghold. A small settlement could be eliminated overnight by a handful of raiders. Not so a town. As populations grew, so did armies; eventually walls went up, and the ante was raised considerably in the scale and scope of warfare.

What Role Did War Play in Building Territorial States?

When there is dust rising in a high column, it is the sign of chariots advancing; when the dust is low, but spread over a wide area, it betokens the approach of infantry. When it branches out in different directions, it shows that parties have been sent to collect firewood. A few clouds of dust moving to and fro signify that the army is encamping.

SUN TZU, *THE ART OF WAR*, 9:23

You know that warfare has become a big deal when you can read an enemy's actions by the behavior of dust clouds on the horizon! While city states increased the deadliness of warfare, the rise of large territorial states, such as the Assyrians and Akkadians in Mesopotamia, ancient Egypt, and, most notably because of its sheer size, China, increased the scale of war further and made it ever more organized, bureaucratic, and central to the state.

The logic of conquest in Mesopotamia led in some periods to greater political unity and larger polities. Lugalzagesi of Uruk established a territorial state in southern Mesopotamia around 2450 BCE. To this point Mesopotamia was inhabited by two major ethnic groups, separated by their language, Sumerians in the south and Akkadians, who were mostly in the north, in today's Syria and southern Turkey. The two groups shared a culture, which archeologists refer to as "Sumerian." But it was not until Sargon the Great (r. ca. 2334–2279 BCE), from the city of Akkad, north of Uruk (he was also known as Sargon of Akkad), conquered the lands of Lugalzagesi and "united" the north and south that this region actually became a single polity under one ruler, around 2330 BCE. Sargon's state is widely considered the world's first "empire."

Sargon's conquests were momentous for the region and beyond as he campaigned far beyond Mesopotamia, including waterborne excursions to what is now Oman and possibly southern Iran, looking to profit economically. If war in Mesopotamia created the need for cities, it subsequently created the idea of

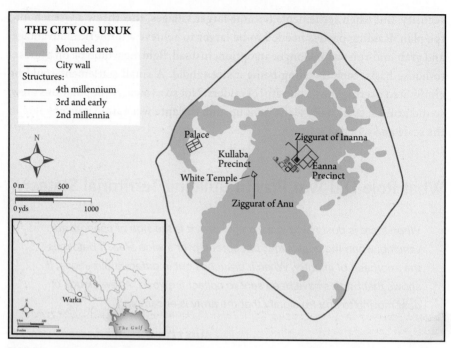

MAP 4.2   THE CITY OF URUK   Cities in Mesopotamia probably originated as defensive sites. The lack of a large territorial state meant they needed protection—from each other.

empire. This model was emulated, reordering the world, as new visions of kingship and the state developed.

As we advance through the centuries in Mesopotamia, the tales of military victories pile up (yet the defeated are silent as ever). Fast-forwarding through the Akkadians and the Babylonians, whose legendary king, Hammurabi, created what some consider the first legal system (Hammurabi's code), we stop next at around 700 BCE. At this point King Sennacherib of the Neo-Assyrian Empire (r. 705–681 BCE) inscribed his valiant deeds on what is known to archeologists as "Sennacherib's Prism," a clay prism inscribed with the text of his annals, mostly concerning graphic accounts of war. Describing his "taming" of the Elamites (a people of southern Mesopotamia), he says, "I cut their throats like sheep . . . my prancing steeds . . . plunged into their welling blood as into a river; the wheels of my battle chariots were bespattered with blood and filth. I filled the plain with the corpses of their warriors."[21]

---

[21]   H.W. F. Saggs, *The Might That Was Assyria* (London: Sidgwick & Jackson, 1984).

Lachish: Sometimes a Hilltop Location Was not Enough for Protection   Lachish was captured by the Assyrian Sennacherib in 701 BCE, who took many of its people into forced exile.

The Assyrians based themselves in the Tigris valley. Wide open plains with no natural defense necessitated a large army. In 700 BCE, when King Hezekiah of Judah, based in Jerusalem, decided he did not need to pay tribute to Sennacherib, the latter mustered his forces. The frieze that he later commissioned to encircle an entire room in his palace in Nineveh in today's Iraq tells the story of the subsequent siege of Lachish, a city south of Jerusalem. The pictures unfold left to right. Images of the Assyrian army marching north read like a graphic novel: the preparations for the siege, the siege itself, and the carrying off of tons of booty. Most poignant, perhaps, are depictions of the more than 200,000 people the Assyrians forcibly relocated to other parts of the empire, evoking scenes familiar to anyone who watches televised news today, wherein can be found images of refugees from war or natural disasters. Deportation was a common Assyrian practice when towns or cities were troublesome and has remained a habit of leaders throughout history.

Assyria came to control most of what is today considered the Middle East, creating one geopolitical region for the first time in history. Whether this was a strategic goal or a side effect of a culture of war is not clear, but the end result, an expanded state, has been repeated in many regions in human history.

KEY DATES	
c. 3500–3100 BCE	Uruk period; expansion; invention of writing
c. 3000–2334 BCE	Early Dynastic; use of early chariots in warfare
c. 2334–2193 BCE	Dynasty of Akkad
c. 2112–2004 BCE	3rd dynasty of Ur
c. 1894–1595 BCE	1st dynasty of Babylon
c. 1700–1450 BCE	Old Hittite Kingdome. Hittites sack Babylon c. 1595 BCE
c. 1550–1250 BCE	Mitannian empire
c. 1450–1200 BCE	Hittite empire
c. 1365–1057 BCE	Middle Assyrian empire
c. 911–605 BCE	Neo-Assyrian empire
883–859 BCE	Assurnasirpal II; successful campaigns to the west
858–824 BCE	Shalmaneser III; mounts major campaigns to extend empire
745–727 BCE	Tiglath-Pileser III; reforms provincial system and standing army
721–705 BCE	Sargon II; Urartu checked
704–681 BCE	Sennacherib; Nineveh developed as imperial capital
680–669 BCE	Esarhaddon; conquest of Egypt
668–c. 627 BCE	Ashurbanipal; Elam ravaged; Babylonian revolt crushed
625–539 BCE	Neo-Babylonian empire
539 BCE	Conquest of Babylon by Cyrus

Timeline of Early Near-Eastern Warfare

HOW DID EGYPT BECOME EGYPT?

The Narmer Palette is carved from a single piece of schist—slate-like rock—dated to around 3200 BCE. Discovered in Upper Egypt in 1897, it was a gift from the Egyptian king to his "father," the god Amun-Ra. The palette tells a tale in pictures and hieroglyphs of military conquest by King Narmer (also associated with Menes, the unifier of Egypt). On one side of the palette the king stands, legs apart, with his right arm raised, grasping a mace, to smash the skull of a kneeling captive, who he holds with his left hand by the hair. The kneeling man's name is inscribed above his head, indicating that he was important, another king, perhaps, or that he symbolized a people. King Narmer is barefoot, signifying that he is on sacred ground, performing a ritual execution. Opposite the king's face we see the falcon Horus of Nehken, representing royalty, standing on six sheaves of papyrus (personified with a human head). The message is clear (at least to Egyptologists): the vignette tells the story of the conquest of Lower Egypt by Upper Egypt. On the reverse side of the palette is another vignette: the king, walking barefoot and holding his mace, approaches 10 decapitated bodies, their heads placed between their legs. Again, we see the king (depicted larger than everyone else) vanquishing his foes.

In the palette, Narmer is shown sporting both the white crown of Upper Egypt and the red crown of Lower Egypt, making it clear that the dominant

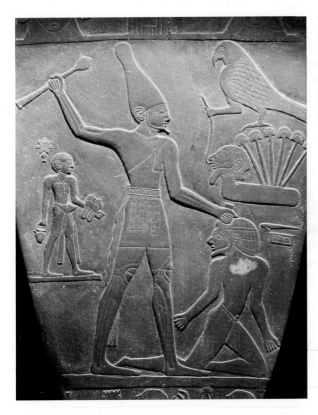

The Narmer Palette
Sometimes you have to break
eggs to make an omelet.
Did Ancient Egypt's unification
came at the cost of warfare?
as this engraving suggests: King
Narmer "unites" Lower and
Upper Egypt.

theme of the work is unification. Is it possible that polities also came together to form larger entities through peaceful means? Clearly, we cannot rule this out, although there is no evidence in the case of Egypt. Trade has often been put forward as an alternative way that mutual interests can converge; economic interaction over time can create commonalities, which may eventually lead to unification under a single leadership.

We can think of different polities coming together out of the pressure of war as a *push* scenario, where unwilling participants are forced to "join or die." Sociologist Robert Carneiro wrote about this push model in the 1970s: "Given the universal disinclination of human groups to relinquish their sovereignty, the surmounting of village autonomy could not have occurred peacefully or voluntarily. It could—and did—occur only by force of arms." Nobody, in other words, would willingly let the neighboring band take over. But the anthropologist Elman Service offered a rebuttal to Carneiro, in which he proposed just that: "It is, in fact, clear from the record in some cases, and probable in many others, that small neighboring societies, or parts of them, often join an adjacent chiefdom quite voluntarily because of the benefits of participation in the total network."[22] Some modern unions have followed this model, the European Union being a case in point; but the Europeans came to this after two world wars, and that was just in the twentieth century.

> The notable move from small, less complex societies to larger, more complex ones, which we see the world over, is therefore achieved under both the reality and the threat of war.

There seems to be less evidence for Elman's theories in the historical record, given the grisly tracks left throughout history by warfare. But if communities did not necessarily join out of force, is it possible that they joined to face a threat of violence from a third entity? This possibility seems more likely, and it is this process that has likely fostered unity, alongside the less subtle method of our hero Narmer and his mace. The notable move from small, less complex societies to larger, more complex ones, which we see the world over, is therefore achieved under both the reality and the threat of war.

While largely mythological, the Narmer Palette celebrates not just royalty, religion, and the forces of order and justice prevailing over chaos but also the unification of the country, whose boundaries would remain essentially unchanged until the present. The Old Kingdom alone lasted a millennium (3100–2100 BCE) and was surprisingly peaceable. Egyptologists believe that the 40 administrative districts of ancient Egypt (or *nomes*) preserved the outlines of the chiefdoms which were conquered to create the state and that the depictions of warfare on the Narmer Palette and another early source, the Towns Palette, show this process of "state consolidation."

What were the consequences of such consolidation? In Egypt, as in other places where similar military campaigns consolidated power, cultural, social, and technological developments followed, which bound the state together, as military historian Azar Gat points out: "Once unified, internal peace was maintained, diverse religious traditions were no doubt standardized and incorporated. A state language was imposed. Royal administration, taxation, economy, justice, and military systems were set up and monumental state construction etc., evolved rapidly."[23] Having been conquered, the vanquished parties became part of the new entity and their former divisions were, if not erased, then at least masked by the state.

WHAT WAS THE RELATIONSHIP BETWEEN WAR AND CULTURE IN ANCIENT CHINA?

China is the longest-lived and largest state entity in history. Competition for supremacy, just as in city state Greece or ancient Mesopotamia, was fierce (even if there were no "flying" martial arts heroes as in the movies). War in China

---

[22] Quoted in Wright, *NonZero*, 59.
[23] Gat, *War in Human Society*, 254.

most probably began under the Shang dynasty (ca.1500–1200 BCE), in that organized royal armies now began to face off against each other. Although you could say that these wars were "expansionist," seeking to conquer neighboring states, control territory, and gain booty of various types, in China there was a complicating feature which continued through the Shang and the Zhou dynasties: the taking of captives for ritual sacrifice. This provided a major motivation for warfare. Sacrifices, of humans and animals, were intended to venerate ancestors; in doing so, the aristocracy maintained the social and cosmic order. War, in this context, was a religious service, or duty, and included rituals of divination, oaths, and prayers before combat, followed by the presentation of booty and captives at ancestral temples.

Sacrificial victims were a part of the religious ideology of the time; therefore, you might argue that war was fought for ideological reasons. However, a well-oiled religious establishment enabled rulers to maintain their legitimacy, and in early China the establishment was oiled with the blood of captives. War enabled the victors to expand their operations and enrich themselves. "Waged against rebellious vassals, other states that were emerging on the Shang's periphery and under its impact, and tribal neighbors, warfare was a constant state occupation."[24]

Heavenly Warriors   As if it was not common enough in life, the emperor's army was ready for war in the afterlife as well. Just in case, 7,000 terra-cotta soldiers were buried with Shi Huangdi.

---

[24] Ibid., 256.

The place of rituals in Chinese warfare illustrates how war is almost always conducted in the face of human reluctance. During the Spring and Autumn Period (771–403 BCE) weapons belonging to the generals were stored in the ancestral temple, taken out only when the head of state had decided on war with other leaders of the lineage and in the presence of the ancestral "tablets" upon which were written the ancestors' names. The leader then purified himself before handing out weapons. The process of the war itself and its end were also marked by specific rituals, making evident that war was a "special" event, fraught with hazards, which necessitated extra observance of religious duties.

Such ritualism continued through the Zhou dynasty, inherited from the Shang, which it supplanted. Continuation of the rituals was one way that the state made clear that the gods approved of the new dynasty. During the Zhou dynasty, and subsequent Chinese dynasties, it was believed that someone who died of unnatural causes could become a dangerous ghost. Killing, therefore, had to be sanctioned by ritual. Dead ancestors enjoyed an afterlife and had the power to affect the living; for this reason, they had to be appeased with constant offerings of food and drink prepared in elaborate ritual vessels made from bronze.

Conquest was also key to the Zhou's motivation for war, and war led to later unification of the country: "War was without question the single most important driver of state formation during China's Eastern Zhou Dynasty," says political scientist Francis Fukuyama.[25] Conquest was responsible for the transition from a decentralized feudal state to a centralized imperial one, and in the process almost every major state institution was intimately connected to this military process. It has been estimated that over 294 years, during the so-called Spring and Autumn Period, there were only 38 years of peace. Some 1,211 separate wars were fought during this period. If the subsequent couple of centuries saw fewer wars, it was only because there were fewer adversaries to fight them; during the aptly named Warring States Period, 16 states fought each other until there were seven. While the frequency of wars declined, their duration and intensity increased. One Chinese historian reported that 245,000 soldiers died in a battle in 293 BCE and 450,000 in 260.

In the early dynasties the focus of fighting was the *chariot*, a wheeled cart pulled by two horses. Charioteers were somewhat equivalent to the European knights of the Middle Ages, in that they were usually aristocratic as the equipment was expensive and the training lengthy. Toward the end of the Zhou, the emphasis on war moved from chariots to infantry as the numbers of aristocrats shrank. Large numbers of peasants, who were cheap to equip and quick to

---

[25] Francis Fukuyama, *The Origins of Political Order: From Prehuman Times to The French Revolution* (New York: Farrar, Strauss and Giroux, 2001), 111.

train, were conscripted by the state. But such militarism was still expensive. War was not possible without money, as every civilization discovered: "If the campaign is protracted," says Sun Tzu, "the resources of the state will not be equal to it."[26] If mass mobilization required money, money meant taxation. To meet this challenge the state of Lu began to tax agricultural land between 594 and 590 BCE. Under similar pressures, in 548 BCE the state of Chu conducted a survey of its lands, villages, households, and agricultural resources, including items such as fishponds and forests, with the goal of reorganizing its tax base and drafting soldiers. Bureaucracy, therefore, was one consequence of such militarization.

The Qin state in particular tightened its hold over its populace via bureaucratic reforms inspired by the legalist school of government, so called because of its reliance on hard and fast rules. These reforms were carried out by Shang Yang, otherwise known as Lord Shang (d. 338 BCE). The state was divided into

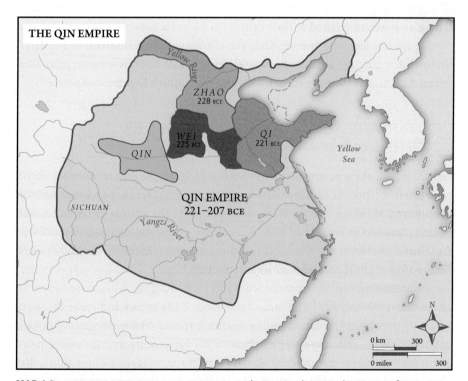

MAP 4.3 THE QIN DYNASTY (221–207 BCE)   Like Rome in the West, the Qin went from a peripheral state to a larger territorial empire by conquering those around in a short period. Organization, force of numbers, and military tactics made it possible.

---

[26] Sun Tzu, *The Art of War*, 2:3.

31 counties, each with an appointed administrator who reported to the capital. A new elite was created within a hierarchy of positions. They replaced the old aristocracy and remained dependent on the ruler. New standardized laws applied to everyone equally, and group responsibility was decreed not just within families but among groups of clans so that entire communities were punished for individual misdeeds. This practice encouraged informing on one's neighbors and undermined individual and family ties, guaranteeing loyalty to the state instead.

China's history of warfare is in many ways no different from that of any other civilization, with age-old reasons driving the conflict: pursuit of an advantage over a rival, struggles over resources and reputation or "honor," as well as more articulated "moral" causes invoked to appease the gods. Ultimately, the Qin, after a 10-year campaign, created the first Chinese empire (221 BCE). Subsequently, this empire dismantled all fortifications and confiscated all weapons, casting them into a series of enormous bronze statues, none of which survive today. The Qin's peace was forged through war and at the time considered to be a renewal of the peace that had reigned at the beginning of cosmic time. China's wars moved outside its borders, and forever after the Chinese saw themselves, as historian Robin Yates puts it, "as a single people living under a single cosmic ruler who linked the three realms, Heaven, Earth, and Man, into a harmonious whole."[27]

DID WARFARE ALSO ACCOMPANY COMPLEX SOCIETIES IN THE NEW WORLD?

Disembodied male heads have been retrieved from the site of Asia on Peru's central coast. These heads signal the beginning of what was to be a long tradition in this area of taking enemy heads as trophies. At the granite temple of Cerro Sechin, dated to around 1500 BCE, you can see gruesome carvings of mutilated and dismembered limbs, the record of ritual sacrifices in which elites displayed their power over others and their link to divinity.

In Mesoamerica, the Olmecs (ca. 1150–400 BCE) used organized force to attain their ends in their heartland and beyond. Early spears and spear throwers quickly give way in Olmec archeology to more specialized weapons of war such as maces, clubs, and stone-tipped spears built for cutting and thrusting more like a sword and for use in close quarters. Historians of the Olmec think that they trained specialized troops in elite warfare and that these individuals are represented in stone carvings; kings are pictured with bound captives, showing

---

[27]   Robin D. S. Yates, "Making War and Making Peace in Early China," in *War and Peace in the Ancient World*, ed. Kurt A. Raaflaub (Malden, MA: Blackwell, 2007), 49.

that projected force was used to build and sustain kingdoms. The Olmec regional centers, however, were not nearly as densely populated as Old World centers of this period, and therefore, we do not see large state armies at this point. Instead, Olmec warriors played a central part in their trading operations, which were conducted elsewhere in Mesoamerica such as Oaxaca, Guatemala, and central Mexico, and as such were instrumental in creating a common cultural area.

After 400 BCE Olmec uniformity was on the decline, and a period of competing cities ensued. Perhaps the largest of these, Monte Alban in southern Mexico, was home to a people now known as the Zapotecs. It began to fortify its perimeter around 200 BCE and was one of the few city sites found with fortifications, allowing it to dominate other cities without being vulnerable itself. Not unlike Mesopotamia, it seems that there was inevitable conflict between cities, and monuments of conquest in Monte Alban portray the vanquished naked and enslaved, bowing to the king. As the polity matures and spreads its influence, however, these monuments begin to portray victims as clothed, sometimes regally, suggesting that there was a new policy of integration of captives into the regional capital. Monte Alban was becoming the region's first—albeit modest—empire.

WHAT WAS THE NATURE OF WAR AMONG THE EARLIEST GREEK CITY STATES?

City states, although originating in Mesopotamia, are often most associated with ancient Greece. Civilization in Greece first appears in Crete around 3000 BCE. Minoan culture, as it is known, was centered around Knossos. Complex palace structures here suggest a hierarchical kingdom, which peaked at about 1600 BCE.

By force or by default, by 1450 BCE Knossos was in the hands of Greeks from Mycenae, a mainland city state. The Mycenaeans expanded the Greek world through trade and conquest. Their military adventures in Asia Minor probably provided the background for Homer's epic poem *The Iliad*, from about the eighth century BCE, which tells the story of the Greek coalition of city states that besieged the city of Troy. In this poem, the Mycenaeans were cast as the leaders of the anti-Troy coalition. The rich archeological record from the Mycenaean period suggests a society of full-time military specialists. Graves reveal armories of weapons and skeletons with multiple wounds, many healed, suggesting men who had long fighting careers. Among their remains were large numbers of double-edged swords; the double edge makes them more likely to be weapons than tools, the extra edge making it hazardous for more innocent uses such as whittling wood or preparing food.

Warrior Elites   Mycenaeans were no strangers to war and violence. Their world required military skill.

For the Mycenaeans war was probably relatively small-scale, involving raids and, if we are to believe Homer, individual combat between elite, aristocratic warriors, producing victories that involved spoils, which in the ancient world included material possessions, such as goods and livestock. Human capital was also transferred upon victory, and this would have included slaves, possibly people enslaved by the war itself, and women, whose fates could be likewise determined by the outcome of conflict. In Book 18 of *The Iliad*, Homer describes the shield of perhaps the Greeks' most prized warrior, Achilles. Designed by the god/metalsmith Hephaestus, it depicted scenes of two cities, one at war and one at peace. The poet says,

> "He made on it two
> cities of mortal men—beautiful in the one there was a wedding
> going on, and a feast. By the light of burning torches the men
> 460   led brides from their chambers through the city—the bridal song
> rose loudly."

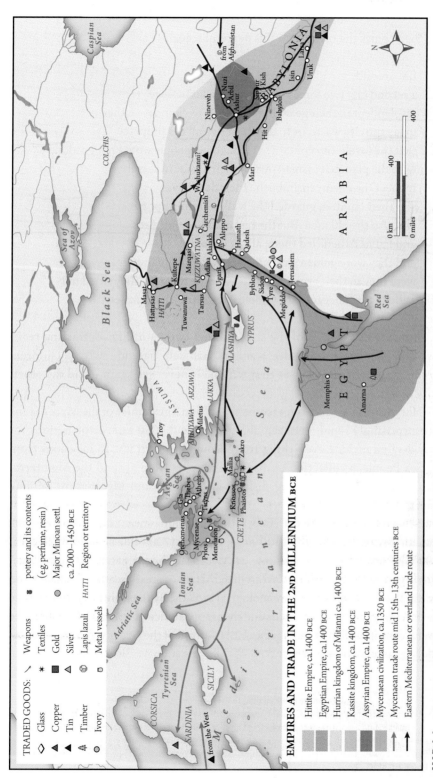

MAP 4.4 EMPIRES AND TRADE IN THE SECOND MILLENIUM BCE Mycenae was a trading empire in the days when trade and raid were close associates.

TRADED GOODS:

◇ Glass
▲ Copper
▲ Tin
▲ Timber
◎ Ivory

✳ Weapons
✳ Textiles
▪ Gold
△ Silver
🜹 Lapis lazuli
○ Metal vessels

▪ pottery and its contents
(e.g. perfume, resin)
◉ Major Minoan settl.
ca. 2000–1450 BCE
HATTI Region or territory

EMPIRES AND TRADE IN THE 2ND MILLENNIUM BCE

Hittite Empire, ca.1400 BCE
Egyptian Empire, ca.1400 BCE
Hurrian kingdom of Mitanni ca.1400 BCE
Kassite kingdom, ca.1400 BCE
Assyrian Empire, ca.1400 BCE
Mycenaean civilization, ca.1350 BCE
Mycenaean trade route mid 15th–13th centuries BCE
Eastern Mediterranean or overland trade route

0 km   400
0 miles   400

Then comes the contrast to this peaceful scene:

> But around
> a second city two forces of armed men sat in siege,
> resplendent in their gear. They were of two minds—either
> to lay the city waste, or to divide in two all the property
> that the lovely city contained.° The townspeople would not go along
> 480   with the plan, but instead put on their armor in secret,
> to meet the enemy in ambush. Their dear wives
> and their children guarded the wall, standing upon it,
> and also the old men. But the rest marched out. Ares
> and Pallas Athena led them, all set in gold,
> 485   and they wore golden clothes—beautiful and majestic
> were they in their armor, as is appropriate to gods! They stood out
> amid the rest because the people were somewhat smaller.²⁸

Homer's description of the shield shows two painfully contrasting realities, one depicting what the warriors had left behind—wives, children, parents, and harmony, such as they will likely never see again—and the other, a city at war.

Notwithstanding their fearsome reputation, the demise of the Mycenaeans was surprisingly rapid, between about 1250 and 1050 BCE. Explanations for their decline include everything from drought to civil war to invasions from the Sea People, a collection of disparate peoples from around the Mediterranean, possibly even including dislocated Minoans and Mycenaeans, among others.

Scholars divide ancient Greek history into three main phases: the Minoan/Mycenaean (3000–1100 BCE), Archaic (700–480 BCE), and Classical (480–338 BCE). After the collapse of Mycenae, Greece entered a "dark age," reverting to some extent to a "precivilized" state of small, scattered villages and little in the way of written or archeological records. By the eighth century BCE we see the emergence of small towns and the reappearance of writing after a hiatus of several centuries. Settlements grew until the form of the Greek city state (or *polis*,

---

°   *...contained*: The besiegers have made an offer to the townspeople: Either be destroyed, or give up half of all their property without a fight, and the attackers will go away. The image of two forces attacking the city may be based on artistic representations from Homer's time that show city walls under attack from both sides: Examples of such a scene survive on a Phoenician metal plate from the eighth century BCE.

²⁸   Barry B. Powell, trans., *The Iliad: Translation, Notes, and Introduction* (New York: Oxford University Press, 2013), 91–92.

Greek for "city") emerged. Multiple city states vied for control throughout the Archaic period, culminating in Sparta's emergence as a regional power by the seventh century BCE. Sparta spent much of its time defending itself from the kingdom of Lydia and its successors, most notably the Persian Empire. Struggles against the Persians continued for many years, until the Greeks, led by the city state of Athens, decisively defeated the Persian armies of Xerxes at the battle of Plataea (479 BCE).

By about 400 BCE, any unity that had been generated by external threats had dissipated, and the cities were at it again. Eventually, there were two primary rivals in Greece, Athens and Sparta. Conflict between them erupted in the Peloponnesian Wars (461–446 BCE and 431–404 BCE). Sparta eventually gained Persian support (it is not uncommon for enemies to become allies, if the interests align). But after defeating Athens, Sparta was beset by new hostile alliances, and wars continued, which by about 350 BCE left Greece largely rudderless. The resulting power vacuum allowed the northern Macedonians to decisively defeat combined Greek forces at the battle of Chaerona in 338 BCE, making Philip of Macedonia the de facto leader of the Greeks.

To what end, all this fighting among Greeks? Greeks themselves talked about "wanting more" (*pleonexia*). Of what? Primarily wealth, but honor to boot. Cities competed for wealth and won honor and respect with acts of military might. Rivalries that in earlier times might have been appeased with raids or a few days of plundering enemy territory developed into a desire for total annihilation of the enemy. Luckily, perhaps, most of the cities of the Classical era lacked the resources for long drawn-out campaigns, and they had to make do with amateur militias and a few seasoned aristocratic warriors who could afford effective weapons.

WHAT WERE THE CONSEQUENCES OF ALEXANDER THE GREAT'S CONQUESTS?

The battle of Chaerona, which established Philip of Macedonia as overlord of Greece, was notable in two ways: first, it demonstrated a new military strategy that would become the norm in the Greek world and beyond: the Macedonians combined the infantry formation known as the *phalanx*, a tightly knit body of infantry, with lighter armed troops and cavalry. The cavalry was commanded by the second notable item: Alexander, son of Philip, to be known later as Alexander the Great. Alexander's greatness, however, was achieved on the shoulders of his father, who was responsible for creating an effective fighting force in Macedonia to unite Greece behind him and to project force outward, toward the ancient Greek enemy, Persia.

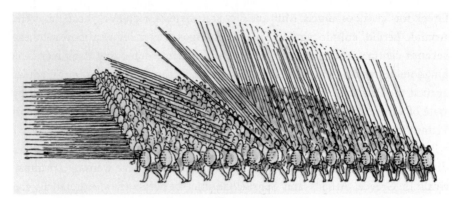

Alexander the Great's Phalanx Formation: 16 files of 16 men   Powerful on flat ground but hard to keep together on the rough.

It would have been helpful to interview Alexander and discover whether he had envisioned an overarching empire or peace through unification. Or did he just feel compelled to wage incessant war and become master of everything—in other words, a god? (Egyptian priests at the oasis of Siwa in the Lybian Desert named him son of Amon-Zeus.) In 334 BCE Alexander crossed into Persian territory, following his father's assasination, and a year later he scored a massive victory over the Persian king Darius III at Issus. Having secured the rest of the Mediterranean coastline from the Persians, he continued inland, confident, no doubt, in his powers. By 329 BCE Alexander had killed or defeated all Persian claimants to the throne and had taken over the empire. Finding it hard to know when enough was enough, he continued headlong into Afghanistan, founding cities as he went, often named by some variation of Alexandria, and entered India in 326. Here his energy—or, at least, that of his soldiers—ran out. He retreated eventually to Persia, where he spent the last year or so of his life grappling with the problem of ruling this empire he had created in such haste.

While his "empire" never really materialized as a coherent, stable unit, Alexander's story is perhaps the clearest example of how war spreads ideas, culture, and ways of life—in this case, *Hellenism*, the exported culture of mainland Greece. Alexander's conquests and founding of multiple cities attracted colonists from mainland Greece, and they contributed to spreading the Greek language as well as religion, philosophy, and the sciences. Alexander was a proponent of incorporating conquered peoples into his empire and even into his army and administration, and in this way he created a hybrid culture which formed the basis of the Hellenistic period throughout North Africa and southwest Asia. Alexandria in

Egypt was perhaps the flagship city in this respect, attracting scholars from around the Hellenistic world. With a first-century population of somewhere between 500,000 and 1 million, the city harbored a large Jewish community; and it was here that the Septuagint, the Greek translation of the Hebrew Bible, was produced. Under the Ptolomies, the descendants of one of Alexander's generals, the library in Alexandria grew to become arguably the most important in the ancient world and the first of its kind to actively collect works on all subjects from other countries.

Quite apart from Alexander's military innovations and successes, he transformed Greece from a place of fragmented warring cities into a regional culture that ultimately affected the world and reached more people than could any number of military campaigns. His physical empire, however, fragmented after his death, and city state Greece continued for several more centuries before succumbing to the military superiority of Rome.

Were There Any Peaceful States?

Therefore the skillful leader subdues the enemy's troops without any fighting; he captures their cities without laying siege to them; he overthrows their kingdoms without lengthy campaigns in the field.

SUN TZU, *THE ART OF WAR*, 3:6

The short answer to this question is no. Not really. But to clarify this point, we need a definition of *peaceful*. This would necessitate agreeing on a length of time in which a society must not fight before being considered peaceful. Matthew Melko and Richard Weigel, for example, define *peace* as the absence of physical conflict in a certain region for at least 100 years. They include in this definition the Ptolemaic Peace of Egypt (332–216 BCE) and the Roman Peace, or *Pax Romana* (27 BCE–180 CE).[29] But just because during these periods there were no wars in Egypt or Italy, respectively, it does not follow that these were "peaceful societies."

Other scholars have searched, largely in vain, for peaceful societies; and many have looked long and hard at hunter–gatherer societies, such as the !Kung or Kalahari Bushmen from southern Africa. But Yale anthropologist

---

[29] Matthew Melko and Richard D. Weigel, *Peace in the Ancient World* (Jefferson, NC: McFarland, 1981).

Carol Ember found that 64% of hunter–gatherers engage in war every 2 years. She rated only 10% as peaceful. While Stephen LeBlanc of Harvard writes that hunter–gatherers, given to regular warfare, rarely take prisoners, preferring annihilation, unless they capture women, who they integrate into their societies.[30]

DID BUDDHISM EXERT A PEACEFUL INFLUENCE IN ANCIENT INDIA?

Ancient India has produced a couple of contenders for the title of "peaceful society" but as we have seen in Chapter 3, one of them, Harappa, is dubious. The other one, also questionable, involves King Asoka (r. ca. 269–232 BCE), of India's Mauryan dynasty. Eight years into his reign, he waged an extensive campaign in the Kalinga territory of the south. By the end of his reign, India was united under one banner, more or less. His annals, inscribed on a rock (known as the Thirteenth Rock Edict) tell of how, in this campaign, 150,000 men were deported from the country (presumably as slaves), 100,000 were slain, and "many times as many those who died."

We might expect this edict to be a Sumerian-style bragging opportunity, in which the great king tells the world that he is not to be trifled with. But Asoka was different. He was repulsed by all this bloodshed and consumed with remorse for the suffering he caused to so many. "For it is considered very painful," he says, "and deplorable by Devanampriya (Asoka) that, while one is conquering an unconquered country, slaughter, death, and deportation of people are taking place there."[31]

Short of having the foresight not to conquer people, he does the next best thing: he regrets it and decrees that people should not engage in this activity again. Is this the beginning of a sensibility of peace, perhaps the first in history? The edict goes on to suggest that future generations should resist the urge to shed blood. In the event that they feel compelled to conquer some territory or other, they consider taking mercy and regard the moral conquest as the only "true" way.

This edict is one of the best-known texts in Indian history. Historian Richard Salomon has read thousands of Indian inscriptions in his multidecade career, carefully looking for signs that someone listened to Asoka and followed his lead. His conclusion? "It is unique . . . I have yet to find a single comparable reference to

---

[30]   Livingstone Smith, *The Most Dangerous Animal*, 40.
[31]   Richard Salomon, "Ancient India: Peace Within and War Without," in *War and Peace in the Ancient World*, edited by Kurt A. Raaflaub (Malden, MA: Blackwell 2007), 55.

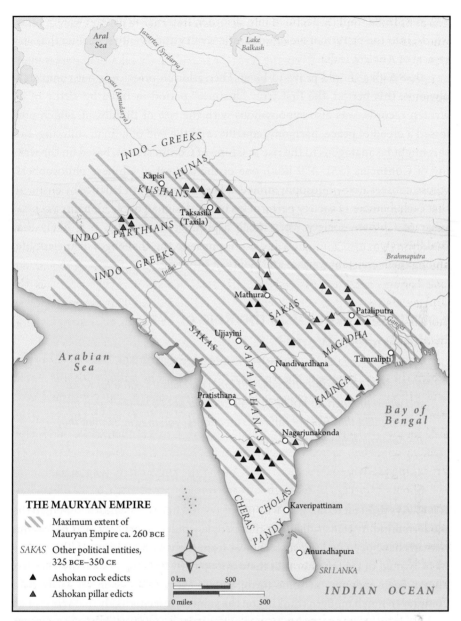

MAP 4.5   THE MAURYAN EMPIRE   The Mauryan Empire's campaigns in the Kalinga territories produced regret on the part of Asoka. The human costs of war appalled him.

the evils of war and the virtues of peace and gentle persuasion."[32] History may well reveal more about this interlude, but as it stands it appears to be an aberration and not an example of a long-standing tradition of peace. After Asoka's death in

---

[32]   Ibid.

232 BCE, India "rapidly declined into disorder, fraternal strife, and war, in other words, into the pattern of violent dynastic rivalry and eventual decline that was typical of Ancient India."[33]

That Asoka should prove to be an aberration in practice is not completely obvious. This period, the first truly "historic" period in India by virtue of its written records, was also synonymous with the rise of Buddhism, which professed a creed of peace, harmony, equality, and the end of human suffering. But this might be analogous to the rise in China of Confucianism, based on the writing of Confucius (551–479 BCE), one of the earliest of Chinese philosophers, whose conservative philosophy, aimed at keeping society in balance by ensuring that each member of society perform his or her designated role, remains a central pillar of Chinese society. Very much a product of its time, it is likely that Buddhism was also a uniquely Indian response to the challenges of ancient life, among them constant warfare and plenty of suffering.

Conclusion: What Was the Role of War in the Ancient World?

When an army feeds its horses with grain and kills its cattle for food, and when the men do not hang their cooking pots over the camp fires, showing that they will not return to their tents, you may know that they are determined to fight to the death.

SUN TZU, *THE ART OF WAR*, 9:34

It is always difficult to imagine why people would fight to the death. Often, to the modern mind it seems ridiculous that people would choose war over peace. But humans have been making such choices from the very beginning of history. We have learned in this chapter that there are no truly "peaceful" societies; war has always been endemic, in some form, among every civilization on earth. And contrary to much modern thinking on the subject, it seems likely that war is not a pathology but instead a common part of the human experience, emanating from conflicts between self-interested, rational beings and societies.

From biologists and geneticists, we have learned that in all likelihood a propensity for violence was a beneficial adaptation. The only reason we have not

---

[33] Ibid.

driven ourselves to extinction—which might seem like a real possibility, especially with nuclear weapons—is that, unlike our violent primate cousins, we have deep-seated inhibitions against violence, which act as a brake to war. The ability to be violent has always been an option for humans, as Steven Pinker notes: "If the brain is equipped with strategies for violence, they are *contingent* strategies, connected to complicated circuitry which computes when and where they should be deployed."[34]

If selective violence was beneficial for individuals and small bands, the same logic applies to larger groups. Therefore, we see warfare blossom and grow with the dawn of civilization. Scholars, such as Pinker, see violence as innate and therefore preceding civilization. Pinker argues, however, that although warfare expanded in scale with the growth of states, mortality dropped because of the increased security that the state offered its citizens. Even if from time to time there would be massive bloodletting, the final tally appears to have been less than the constant attrition experienced by small nonstate societies for whom raids and skirmishes were extremely frequent.[35]

The historical evidence is clear that war played a central role in driving the growth of societies from small bands to larger settlements, cities, and eventually the full-blown civilizations such as we saw in Egypt, Sumer, China, India, and Mesoamerica. Whether war is innate or born with civilization, in the absence of violence and warfare, would human societies have developed increasingly complex forms, and what would have been the driving force for such change? Much of the technological and sociopolitical development we see in the ancient world, from metalworking to shipbuilding, from political standardization to fiscal administration, is directly related to the demands of warfare.

Many people might prefer to see war as an irrational, inexplicable "mistake" that has no basis in human nature. Whether innate or originating in our development of complex society, we should remember Sun Tzu's words and see war as a strategic option, an option of last resort, and hope that all the other human traits, our ability to cooperate, our ability to empathize with others, our respect for human rights, what Pinker, quoting Abraham Lincoln, has called the "better angels of our natures," all conspire to counter the more destructive urges, our collective and personal demons.

---

34   Pinker, *The Blank Slate*, 315.
35   See, for example, Steven Pinker, "Violence Vanquished," *New York Times*, September 9, 2011, or his book *The Better Angels of Our Nature: Why Violence Has Declined* (New York: Viking, 2011).

Words to Think About

Annals	Conscription	Dynasty
Genocide	Hegemonic	Polity
Utopia		

Questions to Think About

- What's the difference between violence and war?
- Is war innate in the human character?
- Did the onset of "civilization" lead to more violence?
- How did war lead to peace?

Primary Sources

Powell, Barry B., trans. *The Iliad: Translation, Notes, and Introduction.* (New York: Oxford University Press, 2013.)

Mahabharata, retold by William Buck. Berkley: University of California Press, 1973.

Sun Tzu, *The Art of War.* Boulder, CO: Westview Press, 1994.

"The Thirteenth Rock Edict of King Asoka." In *Inscriptions of Asoka,* 2nd ed., edited by Eugen Hultzsh. Corpus Inscriptionum Indicarum 1. Calcutta: Superintendent of Government Printing, 1925.

Secondary Sources

Fukuyama, Francis. *The Origins of Political Order: From Prehuman Times to the French Revolution.* New York: Farrar, Strauss and Giroux, 2001.

Gat, Azar. *War in Human Civilization.* Oxford: Oxford University Press, 2006.

Keeley, Lawrence. *War Before Civilization: The Myth of the Peaceful Savage.* Oxford: Oxford University Press, 1996.

Livingstone Smith, David. *The Most Dangerous Animal: Human Nature and the Origins of War.* New York: St. Martin's Press, 2007.

Melko, Matthew, and Richard D. Weigel. *Peace in the Ancient World.* Jefferson, NC: McFarland, 1981.

"One Day of War," *BBC News,* http://news.bbc.co.uk/2/shared/spl/hi/programmes/this_world/one_day_of_war/clickable_map/html/introduction.stm.

Pain, Stephanie. "Arrow Points to Foul Play in Ancient Iceman's Death." *New Scientist* (July 2001).

Pinker, Steven. *The Better Angels of Our Nature: Why Violence Has Declined.* New York: Viking, 2011.

Pinker, Steven. *The Blank Slate: The Modern Denial of Human Nature.* New York: Penguin, 2002.

Pinker, Steven. "Violence Vanquished." *New York Times,* September 9, 2011.

Saggs, H. W. F. *The Might That Was Assyria*. London: Sidgwick & Jackson, 1984.

Sale, Kirkpatrick. *After Eden: The Evolution of Human Dominance*. Durham, NC: Duke University Press, 2006.

Salomon, Richard. "Ancient India: Peace Within and War Without." In *War and Peace in the Ancient World*, edited by Kurt A. Raaflaub, 53–65. Malden, MA: Blackwell, 2007.

Wright, Robert. *Nonzero: The Logic of Human Destiny*. New York: Vintage, 2001.

Yates, Robin D. S. "Making War and Making Peace in Early China." In *War and Peace in the Ancient World*, edited by Kurt A. Raaflaub, 34–52. Malden, MA: Blackwell, 2007.

For additional resources, including maps, primary sources, and visuals, web links, and quizzes, please go to **www.oup.com/us/cole**

American Troops Conducting a Raid in Fallujah, Iraq, 2004

Chapter 5

Was Greece the First Democracy?

The Constant Struggle

In March 2003, a US-led military coalition invaded Iraq and toppled its government. Its stated aim was to end the totalitarian regime of the country's dictator, Saddam Hussein; to negate any threat he posed to the United States; and, most interestingly for our purposes, to allow the Iraqis to develop their own democracy. Within a few short weeks the United States found itself effectively running Iraq, a country of some 31 million people. Then-President George W. Bush put the war in the context of the "2,500-year-old story of democracy." Bush represented the US occupation of Iraq as a continuing effort to bring the benefits of democracy to the rest of the world. In response to his critics he asked, "Are the peoples of the Middle East somehow beyond the reach of liberty? Are millions of men and women and children condemned by history or culture to live in despotism? Are they alone never to know freedom and never even have a choice in the matter?"[1] Skeptics scoffed at the presumption of introducing democracy to the Middle East, arguing that in Western nations it had taken thousands of years for it to evolve, and it was still far from perfect. How, then, could it possibly be imposed from above, by foreign forces? More cynical commentators argued that not only was democracy a foreign invention, it was in fact completely alien to Iraq, and the Middle East in general, both in recent memory and way back into ancient history, which like many peoples' ancient pasts, was filled with despots, absolute monarchs, and emperors.

Subsequent experience has shown that the road to democracy is long and rough, and no one has a clear map. In 2005, Iraq held its first elections for a

---

[1] George W. Bush, "Remarks by President George W. Bush at the 20th Anniversary of the National Endowment for Democracy," November 6, 2003, http://www.ned.org/node/658.

THINKING ABOUT DEMOCRACY

What Is Democracy?
- What kind of regime you have depends upon how the leaders gain leadership positions, how they make decisions, and what role the different members of the community play in those decisions.

What Part Did Participatory Government Play in Early Civilizations?
- [In Mesopotamia] participation by a relatively wide sector of society was most certainly a widespread and a deeply historical characteristic of the region.

Was Greece Exceptional?
- Whereas much of the traditional story of Greek democracy highlights a radical break with the despotic (Eastern) past, much of the thinking, and even some of the institutions that fueled Athens' revolution, were already in place elsewhere.

Conclusion
- Even if forms of democracy differ and even if it's is more or less complete here or there, the underlying quest is the same and is something that mattered in ancient times as much as today.

national assembly, beginning the long process of building democratic institutions. History will ultimately judge Iraq's future democracy, but is participatory government, which is at the heart of democracy, alien to the non-Western world? Or does it have a lineage which has largely been forgotten?

Introduction

Government in the ancient world often appeared to be a minority affair, involving precious few people after you count the elites—royals and their hangers-on. Even then, it almost always excluded women entirely. The history of government, or even of politics, therefore, often looks like a progression from the despotism of ancient men—and, in a few cases, their female heirs—who used force to impose their will upon their subjects to modern democracies, in which people have a say in the running of their own communities (yet for women of many countries the right to vote came only in the twentieth century).

Not only does this optimistic picture of progress ignore modern dictatorships, which, in their deployment of power and authority—if nothing else—often appear to share much with the ancient world but, what is much less often discussed, there were also numerous ancient societies organized around the notion of participatory government. Not all rulers ruled exclusively by the sword, existing only to squeeze taxes and labor out of the inhabitants of the realm, nor was the idea of having a say in running public affairs entirely alien to ancient societies.

In this chapter we examine the early history of politics and question the largely accepted story of the origins of democracy. This story, repeated endlessly, credits the ancient Greeks, in particular the Athenians, with coming up with the idea of democracy, in about 508 BCE, while saying little to nothing of what might have preceded it. The "light" of democracy, as the story has it, moved from Greece to Rome and then, after several centuries of "dark ages," popped up again in Renaissance Europe—and the rest is, well, *history*.

While Athens' contribution to participatory government was enormous, seeing the beginning of democracy's story here is like missing the opening scenes of a movie—without that context, you never quite understand the film. Democracy, like many other human innovations, has a history; and many scholars now believe that Athens was not the beginning of this lineage. As sociologist John Keane puts it, "one of the first matters to be straightened out in any present-minded history of democracy is what might be described as the Greek plagiarism of democracy."[2] British anthropologist Jack Goody, attacking Eurocentric visions of history in general, questions the narrative of democracy, referring to Europe's claims to many of humanity's greatest innovations as the "theft of history."[3] For other scholars, who believe that Athens is the cradle of democracy, these are fighting words, in large part because the Athenian story is one that has developed—largely unchallenged—over several generations of historians and classical scholars. This fact alone, however, does not amount to historical accuracy.

But there were even skeptics on this subject in the ancient world. Flavius Josephus, a Jewish historian of the first century CE, questioned the wisdom of crediting the Greeks with innovations to the detriment of those whom they followed and argued for a continuum of political practices: "[Then we must acknowledge that it was] the Egyptians, the Chaldeans, and the Phoenicians that have preserved the memorials of the most ancient and most lasting traditions of

The Greek did not invent democracy)

---

2   John Keane, *The Life and Death of Democracy* (New York: W.W. Norton, 2009), x.
3   Jack Goody, *The Theft of History* (Cambridge: Cambridge University Press, 2006).

EUROPE

While Athens arguably developed more complex forms of democratic pro- cesses and institutions than any other place for which there are records, it was also a military empire at times, and restricted its citizenship to free men, excluding women and slaves.

Inscriptions from earl[y] Mesopotamian cities suc[h] as Nippur, Ur, and Babylo[n] speak of citizen assemblie[s] and these created checks o[n] royal power. Gods coul[d] also restrain the excesses o[f] kingly power.

Black Sea

GREECE

[Mediterranea]n Sea

PHOENICIA

MESOPOTAMIA

Phoenicians were likely familiar with Mosaic Law, from ancient Israel, which posited a god who monitored the behavior of rulers. Phoenicians governed with assemblies, often filled by merchants and traders.

ARABIA

AFRICA

Zulus of South Africa, Bugandans of Uganda, Akans of Ghana, among others, possessed political cultures with checks on royal power, roles for councils of elders, and processes whereby the people's interests could be furthered.

ATLANTIC OCEAN

ANCIENT POLITIES

Many parts of the ancient world practiced some form of participatory politics. From India to Africa, kings and r[ulers] by their religions.

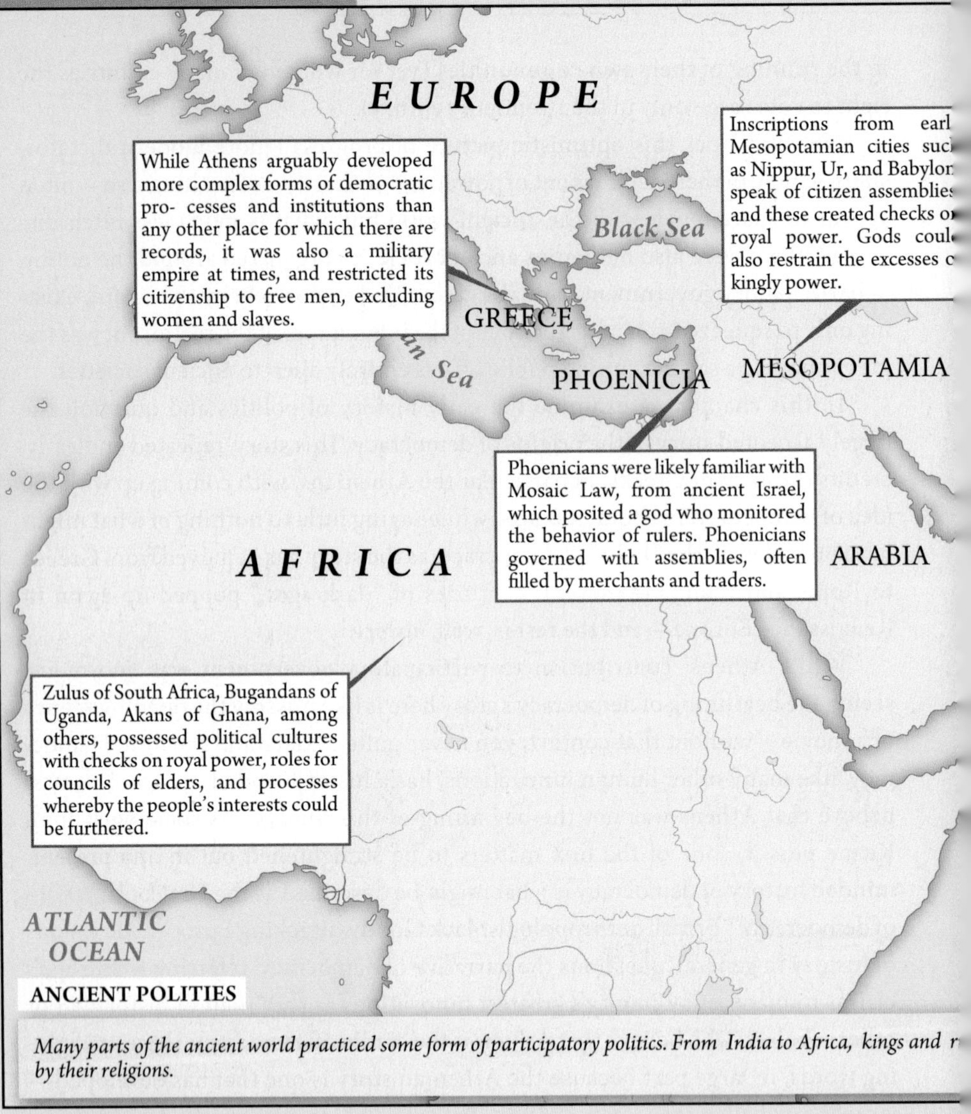

MAP 5.1 ANCIENT POLITIES

TIMELINE

☼ **1785–1760 BCE**
King Zimri Lim of Mari

☼ **508 BCE**
Cleisthenes reforms in Athens

☼ **1550–330 BCE**
Phoenician civilization

☼ **1338 BCE**
Pharaoh Akhenaten dies

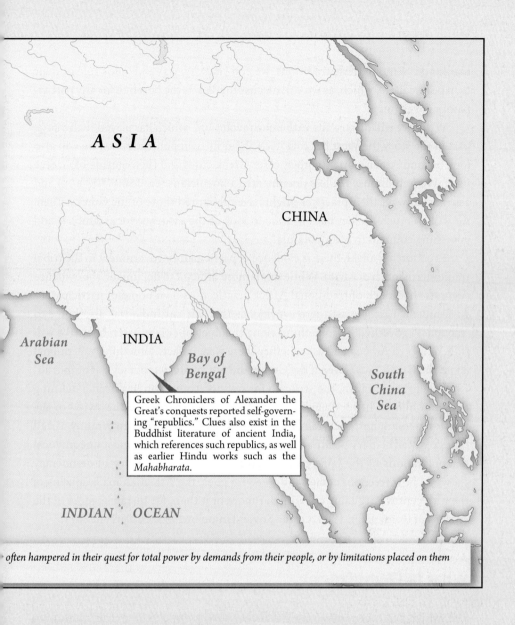

ASIA

CHINA

INDIA

Arabian
Sea

Bay of
Bengal

South
China
Sea

Greek Chroniclers of Alexander the
Great's conquests reported self-governing "republics." Clues also exist in the
Buddhist literature of ancient India,
which references such republics, as well
as earlier Hindu works such as the
Mahabharata.

INDIAN OCEAN

often hampered in their quest for total power by demands from their people, or by limitations placed on them

 327 BCE
Alexander the Great
enters India

 146 BCE
Carthage destroyed
by Rome

338 BCE
Athens occupied
by Macedonia

 ca. 300 BCE
Arthashastra written in India

mankind."[4] Among these traditions, we can surmise, was a people's role in their own political life, which, as we will discuss further, is the baseline for any participatory government.

While we will discuss the "Athenian revolution," which has played such a large part in the story the West has told itself about its own political roots, we will also look beyond Athens, first to other, older Greek cities and then outside of Greece itself. We will discuss the less documented Phoenicians (ca. 1500–300 BCE) and ask in what ways their practices might have prefigured those of the Greeks. Then, we will go much further back in time to look at the evidence for assemblies and governing councils in Mesopotamia.

Even further afield, there is evidence of participatory government in the tribal traditions of much of Africa. While this is more difficult to document, the evidence suggests that much of traditional Africa practiced its own brand of participatory government. Farther east there is evidence that ancient India was also home to "republics" governed by something along the lines of citizen assemblies. We will then return to Athens and ask whether there was, in fact, something exceptional about the Greek "way," even if the Greeks did not create democracy out of thin air.

Whenever it began, the struggle for self-determination has been a defining theme of human history as various peoples have experienced the swing of the political pendulum from tyranny to democracy and back again to tyranny, via all types of intermediary positions. In what is perhaps one of the most unequivocal demonstrations of the fallacy of "progress" in history, the story of democracy shows us how freedom comes and freedom goes, the Athenian male citizens of the fifth century arguably enjoying far more of it than, for instance, most of the citizens of Romania in 1985. Or the Soviet Union in 1935. Or Syria in 2011.

What Is Democracy?

The word *democracy* comes from the ancient Greek *demokratia*—*demos*, meaning "people," and *kratia*, meaning "power."[5] Another reason the West has for so long developed the story of ancient Greek origins of democracy is that the Greeks, such as Aristotle and Plato, wrote about it, in texts that have survived, more than any other people. Therefore, giving their particular form of government a name,

---

[4]   Flavius Josephus, quoted in Benjamin Isakhan and Stephen Stockwell, eds., *The Secret History of Democracy* (Basingstoke, UK, and New York: Palgrave Macmillan, 2011), 21.

[5]   Here, we use Josiah Ober's 2007 definition, using *demos* to mean "people" as opposed to *demes*, the Greek word for "administrative district"—discussed below. Josiah Ober, "The Original Meaning of 'Democracy': Capacity To Do Things, Not Majority Rule" (Princeton/Stanford Working Papers in Classics, Paper no. 090704, September 2007).

discussing it with each other, and writing about it certainly helped to cement the idea that this was their invention. But like many concepts in politics, democracy does not allow itself to be defined in a simple phrase, nor is there a single model for what constitutes democracy. "Democracy does not consist of a single unique set of institutions," say political scientists Phillipe C. Schmitter and Terry Lynn Karl. "There are many types of democracy and their diverse practices produce a similarly varied set of effects."[6] Schmitter and Karl offer a broad definition of *modern democracy*: "a system of governance in which rulers are held accountable for their actions in the public realm by citizens, acting indirectly through the competition and cooperation of their elected representatives."[7] This covers many of the basics, and yet clearly there is room here for considerable differences within political systems—such as how accountable those rulers are, how effective and fair the elections are, and how many people in the community get to vote.

> But like many concepts in politics, democracy does not allow itself to be defined in a simple phrase, nor is there a single model for what constitutes democracy.

What kind of regime you have depends upon how the leaders gain leadership positions, how they make decisions, and what role different members of the community play in those decisions. Democratic states typically allow all their citizens (usually of a certain age) to play a role—*participate*—in government through voting for representatives, who then make decisions on specific public policy issues in their name. The people don't usually "sweat the small stuff" because there is too much small stuff and not enough time. This is known as "representative democracy" and is different from "direct democracy," in which all citizens vote on all key decisions. The US House of Representatives and the British Parliament are good examples of this representative system.

The basic procedures of democracy—voting, elections, etc.—are no doubt familiar to anyone who has taken a basic civics class. Such procedures are the concrete representations of the key principles at stake in a democracy, the biggest one perhaps being the idea of "consent of the people." But this can be expressed in multiple different systems, and it is this diversity of democratic forms that has made *democracy* so slippery to define. Behind the institutions, however, is a basic idea, played out in assemblies of arguing citizens and summed up in the phrase itself—"people power." Economist Amartya Sen says that public debate is at the heart of democracy and is more important than the specifics of the ballot box. "The broader view of democracy," says Sen, "in terms of public reasoning also allows us to understand that the roots of democracy go much beyond the

---

6   Phillipe C. Schmitter and Terry Lynn Karl, "What Democracy Is . . . and Is Not," in *The Global Resurgence of Democracy* (Baltimore: Johns Hopkins University Press, 1994), 50.
7   Ibid.

Democracy Is Seldom Perfect   Often, the institutions of democracy and its processes are hijacked.

narrowly confined chronicles of some designated practices that are now seen as specifically 'democratic institutions.'"[8] Rigged elections and flawed electoral processes occur frequently and in many different places, making it clear that there are "paper democracies" that do not involve real citizen participation.

Sociologist Larry Diamond has boiled democracy down to four essentials: a political system for choosing and replacing the government through free and fair elections; the active participation of the people, as citizens, in politics and civic life; protection of the human rights of all citizens; a rule of law, in which the laws and procedures apply equally to all citizens.[9]

Clearly, there remains plenty to be said about how various democracies actually function. These lists of procedures and principles are subject to disclaimers, caveats, and elaborations. But for our purposes, as we scour the remains of ancient civilizations for signs that there was more to life than unbending tyranny, we should look for the essence of democracy: citizens participating in government in ways that limit the power of the leadership and advance the interests of the governed. So let us dust off the records of the past and see how far back we can trace such principles and practices.

---

[8]   Amartya Sen, "Democracy and Its Global Roots: Why Democracy Is Not the Same as Westernization," *New Republic* (October 6, 2003), 29.

[9]   Larry Diamond, "What Is Democracy," Lecture at Hilla University for Humanistic Studies, January 21, 2004, http://www.stanford.edu/~ldiamond/iraq/WhaIsDemocracy012004.htm.

What Part Did Participatory Government Play in Early Civilizations?

Alexis De Tocqueville (1805–1859) called democracy part of "the most continuous, ancient, and permanent tendency known to history."[10] If this is true, then we should be able to find evidence of it left in the remains of civilizations across the ancient world. Before we look at what exactly happened in Athens in the fifth century BCE, let's tell the story the old-fashioned way—from the beginning. Keane has traced what he believes to be the "seeds" of democracy's basic institution, "self-government through an assembly of equals" through "many different soils and climes, ranging from the Indian sub-continent and the prosperous Phoenician empire to the western shores of provincial Europe."[11] Did these civilizations know any meaningful participation in politics, and therefore, do they present us with a more nuanced vision of ancient government?

HOW WAS TYRANNY KEPT AT BAY IN MESOPOTAMIA?

The "assembly," as we shall learn more below, was the central democratic innovation in Athenian democracy of the fifth century BCE. But, as it turns out, this was not so innovative. Lifting our gaze from the sunny shores of the Aegean, we will shift across the desert to the baking plains of Mesopotamia, which comprised much of what is known as Iraq today. George W. Bush was correct when talking about the present state of Iraqi freedom, which in 2003 was particularly sorry. But was it always so? On first inspection, much of the evidence for early Sumerian life (the earliest civilization that we know of to date) would give it a pretty low ranking on the democracy scale. Historians have given us little reason to believe that there was any meaningful participation in politics on the part of your average Joe (and certainly not by Josephine). In fact, the earliest literature from that part of the world concerns almost exclusively kings and gods, sometimes fighting, sometimes cooperating; but the emphasis is on mighty, powerful figures who few would see as ruling at the pleasure of their people. Scholars have conventionally depicted Sumerian life as overwhelmingly dominated by royalty. "This convention," says Keane, "needs a kick in the pants. Kings, in fact, were neither almighty nor omnipresent—despite whatever those with Western prejudices have said."[12] The "Western

---

[10] Sen, "Democracy and Its Global Roots," 29.
[11] Keane, *The Life and Death of Democracy*, xvi.
[12] Ibid., 109.

prejudices" to which he refers, are those prejudices which suggest that the "West" invented democracy, while the rest of the earth languished in despotism.

But the tribes of Mesopotamia around 3000 BCE, both tent-dwelling, sedentary people and nomadic animal herders, actually possessed an extensive vocabulary relating to notions of shared politics. Much of this would probably have been an ancestral inheritance from hunter–gatherer culture, which is known for being less hierarchical and more egalitarian than settled civilization. But more evidence of assemblies comes from some of the earliest cities in that region (the first on earth), among them Ur, Uruk, Nippur, and Babylon, whose populations left us with not only the remains of their buildings but many of their thoughts and beliefs, written in cuneiform on clay tablets. These cities, built around rich agricultural land, heavily irrigated and inhabited by dense clusters of farmers, artisans, traders, priests, and soldiers, also developed innovative political practices.

Most students of Mesopotamia should be paying attention by now. Were Mesopotamians really freer and more politically engaged than we thought? And in what ways were their mighty kings not so mighty? The kings, Keane argues, were actually "hemmed in" by the omnipresent Sumerian institution of the temple. The temple housed the city god, the entity who held all ultimate power in the city and was believed to maintain the king as one of his or her subjects.

Hammurabi, for example, the legendary lawmaking king of Babylon (d. 1750 BCE) who conquered large parts of southern Mesopotamia, was seen as extending the realm of Marduk, the city god of Babylon. The Mesopotamians, in this context, saw Hammurabi as merely the human steward, or vassal, of the god. In the city of Lagash, to take another example, the temple was dedicated to the god Ningirsu. The temple's "assets," to use a modern term, were considerable and included acres of land and an army of servants to manage them, including goatherds, brewers, and armorers. As Keane puts it, "Such arrangements connected with the sacred served to keep kings in check, making them more humble than they might otherwise have been."[13] This presents a fascinating alternative to the idea that deities in the ancient world served to legitimate the leaders since the leaders often claimed a unique relationship with them, often being semidivine themselves—the "Kings Lists," which represent some of the earliest literature from the area, show that many of them lived for centuries! Clearly, many kings overrode this hierarchy of god over king or found ways around it, but having a belief system in which gods were more powerful than kings could have benefitted the people as much as, or instead of, their king.

The religious beliefs of ancient Mesopotamians played a key role in their politics in other ways. Not only did gods represent a potential check on kingly

---

[13] Ibid., 111.

[margin handwritten notes: "evidence of councils on cuneiform"; "gods above kings"]

power but the social organization of the deities, as laid out in Mesopotamian mythology, provided a blueprint for human society in at least one important way. These myths, originating in the fourteenth century BCE, posited that the world as humans knew it, that often challenging landscape governed by the whim of nature and of the elements, was brought into balance—out of chaos—only through the efforts of the deities, working in *assemblies.* Negotiations between deities in these gatherings, so Mesopotamians believed, decided the unfolding of nothing less than destiny itself and kept the world from disorder. When mere mortals, therefore, gathered together in assemblies to discuss the business of the community—whether or not to wage war, how to distribute goods, to enact laws, etc.— they were engaging in a sacred activity, mimicking the gods themselves and keeping the world from chaos.

> ☀ Negotiations between deities in these gatherings, so Mesopotamians believed, decided the unfolding of nothing less than destiny itself and kept the world from disorder.

But what is the evidence for assemblies? The words *ukkin* in Sumerian and *purhum* in Akkadian refer both to informal gatherings of people and to a governing body. Is it possible that in these humble terms lie the origins of later democracies? Historian Daniel E. Fleming has studied thousands of letters from the palace

Divine Kingship   The sun god, Shamash, is seen here giving Hammurabi of Babylon the laws. The god is dominant, seated, and Hammurabi is supplicant. However, only a king would have the ability to directly address a deity.

of Mari, in what today is Syria. Mari's king, Zimri-Lim (ca. 1785–1760 BCE), was essentially a tribal leader; and we can see the influence of tribal politics on town life through these letters. Key among these influences is the use of assemblies. What is interesting about Mari is that it represents a link between ancestral, tribal/nomadic culture and the "new" Syrian–Mesopotamian sedentary life of cities. "It is in the political life of towns," says Fleming, "that we confront a world before democracy in the Greek sense, certainly not democratic in the Greek sense, but displaying the foundations of collective decision making against which Greek democracy may be profitably examined."[14] Is it possible then that Mesopotamian towns inherited a tendency toward collective decision making from their nomadic ancestors—who, in a world before cities, states, and their attendant inequalities, understood collective action better—and this morphed with city life into more organized assemblies? Such groups kept despots in check, as Fleming puts it: "In much of the Near East, individual rule existed only in dynamic tension with a range of other individual and collective leaderships."[15]

Evidence for assemblies comes from records etched on clay tablets. But if the ancients imagined their deities participating in assemblies, does this not suggest that they were familiar with the idea of assemblies, following Aristotle's observation that humans "imagine not only the forms of their gods but their ways of life to be like their own"?[16] In lamenting the need to destroy humanity in a great flood (the origin of the Bible story of Noah) the goddess Ishtar laments

> How could I in the gods' assembly
> Give such ill counsel,
> To decree the fight
> For the destruction of my mankind?
> I alone give birth to my mankind.
> Now they fill, like the spawn of fishes, the
> sea![17]

From Nippur, 60 miles south of Baghdad, we have evidence of a trial for homicide from the early second century BCE. A tablet reads, "Their case was taken to ... King Ur-Ninurta [who] ordered that their case should be decided by the assembly of Nippur."[18]

---

[14] Daniel E. Fleming, *Democracy's Ancient Ancestors: Mari and Early Collective Governance* (Cambridge and New York: Cambridge University Press, 2004), 171.

[15] Ibid., xi.

[16] Aristotle, *Politics*, 1252b. Cited in Keane, *The Life and Death of Democracy*, 116.

[17] Quoted in Thorkild Jacobsen, "Primitive Democracy in Ancient Mesopotamia," *Journal of Near Eastern Studies* 2, no. 3 (July 1943): 169.

[18] Cited in Keane, *The Life and Death of Democracy*, 118.

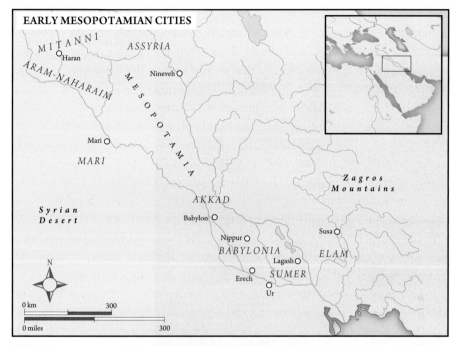

MAP 5.2   **EARLY MESOPOTAMIAN CITIES**

The assembly, which, by the way, was made up of "ordinary people" such as gardeners, bird catchers, and potters, found the defendants guilty: "Nanna-sig, son of Lu-sin, Ku-enlila, son of Ku-Nanna, the barber, Enlil-ennam, slave of Adda-kalla, the gardener, and Nin-dada, daughter of Lu-Ninurta, wife of Lu-Inanna, were given up to be killed. Verdict of the assembly of Nippur."[19]

But these assemblies were more than courts; they did, in fact, have the ability to interfere with kingly authority. A letter from an assembly of Babylon addressed jointly to the king of Babylonia, Shamash-shuma-ukin, and his brother the Assyrian king Assurbanipal reminds the kingly brothers of the earlier Babylonian king's guarantee to protect the inhabitants of Babylon, even those of foreign origins. Another text, *The Advice to a Prince*, from the world's oldest library at Nineveh, around the end of the second millennium BCE, went even further in warning sovereigns that if a prince "takes silver of the citizens of Babylon and adds it to his own coffers [or] if he hears a lawsuit involving men of Babylon and treats it frivolously, Marduk, lord of Heaven and earth, will set his foes upon him [and] will give his property and wealth to his enemy."[20] This text goes on to remind princes that the assemblies of Nippur, Babylon, and Sippar had

---

[19]   Ibid., 119.
[20]   Ibid.

City of Nippur, Being Excavated in the 1920s
One of several ancient cities for which there is evidence of citizen assemblies.

been granted immunity from despots by the gods themselves and that "Anu, Enlil, and Ea the great gods who dwell in heaven and earth, in their assembly, affirmed the freedom of those people from such obligations."[21]

By now we are getting a clearer picture of the culture of assemblies, and the mighty kings appear somewhat diminished. But what was the full range of the assemblies' activities? How much power did they really have? And were they not just stacked with the "king's men"? It is difficult to know this in much detail. Political scientist Benjamin Isakhan sees a little more than "primitive democracy" in the assembly culture of Mesopotamia and the wider Middle East. In law, for example, which was a core element of later Athenian democracy, "it is instructive to turn to the extensive legal codes developed across the region in order to ensure that justice was served in cases as diverse as crime, slavery, agriculture, debts and loans, marriage, property rights, sexual offenses, theft, and, of course, the important matter of goring oxen."[22]

clear pic of assemblies?

---

21   W. G. Lambert, *Babylonian Wisdom Literature* (Oxford: Clarendon Press, 1960), 112–15.
22   Benjamin Isakhan, "What is so 'Primitive' about 'Primitive Democracy'? Comparing the Ancient Middle East and Classical Athens," in Isakhan and Stockwell, *The Secret History of Democracy*, 25.

Even the notion of voting, which is a hallmark of Athenian—and modern—democracies, finds some precedent much earlier: very early city states convened assemblies in order to elect kings in times of military emergencies. Often, these positions were to be terminated upon the cessation of the emergency. Around 2500 BCE the king of Elba was elected by popular vote "for a seven-year-term and shared power with a council of elders."

[margin note: Voting in emergency]

In matters of rights and freedoms, another cornerstone of Athenian democracy, we find similar examples from Mesopotamian cities such as Lagash, around 2500–2300 BCE, where struggles between the king and the temple resulted in the king establishing liberty as one of the main tenets of society (possibly offering the first historical example of the word *freedom*), making the king (Urukagina) the first social reformer in history.

[margin note: Social reform liberty]

Many questions remain, but what we have is a view of ancient Mesopotamia that conflicts with how many scholars have traditionally viewed power in that region. It was not democracy. But participation by a relatively broad sector of society was most certainly a widespread and deeply historical characteristic of this region. "Few ancient voices deny outright the unquestioned authority of the king," says Fleming, "but his actual power seems to be a matter of constant negotiation as he engages a panoply of traditional leaderships, each with its own constituencies and assumed prerogatives."[23] "Constant negotiation" here means both a check on the ruler's power and effective participation—by some part of the population.

WHAT IS THE EVIDENCE FOR PHOENICIAN ASSEMBLIES?

The Phoenicians practiced commerce throughout the Mediterranean and along the coast of West Africa from about 1550 to 330 BCE, some believe even circumnavigating Africa and traveling north to the British Isles, possibly as far as Scandinavia. They established colonies in many of the areas in which they traded. They are also known for having assemblies, which played a considerable role in decision making. Many of these assemblies were comprised of the (male) traders and merchants who were central to the Phoenician culture and economy, and this to a large extent explains their role in government. The evidence suggests that even kings were forced to pay attention to their advice and concerns.

The Phoenicians came from Canaan, in today's Lebanon, and parts of the Israeli coastline; and their roots go back several millennia in that area. This would have put them in touch with the kingdoms of ancient Israel, and central to these

---

23 Fleming, *Democracy's Ancient Ancestors*, xv.

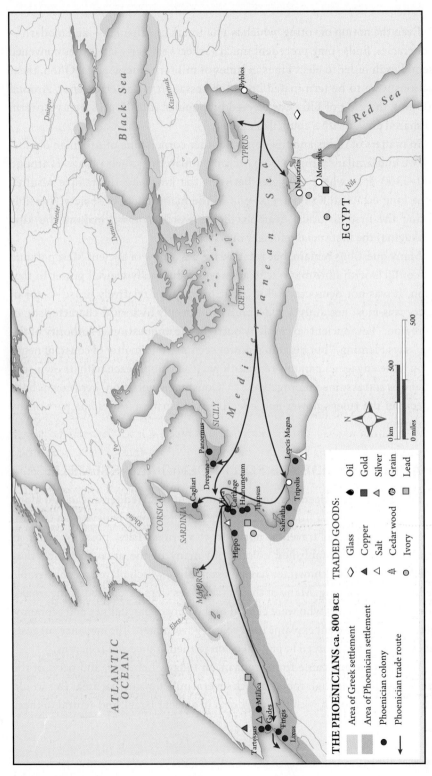

MAP 5.3 THE PHOENICIANS, ca. 800 BCE

Phoenician Bireme: Two Rows of Oars and a Sail, If the Wind Was in the Right Direction   The Phoenicians were some of the earliest Mediterranean traders.

was the creation, in Mosaic law, of the notion of a leader constrained by the laws of god. This echoes the idea that Mesopotamian leaders were restrained in their actions by gods who were looking out for the people.

The evidence for Phoenician assemblies comes largely from what are known as the "Amarna letters." These are diplomatic reports, from the mid-fourteenth century BCE, describing Egyptian dealings with Phoenician cities, over which the Egyptian pharaoh, Akhenaten (d. ca. 1338 BCE), had control. One Egyptian official suggested a high level of cooperation and deliberation among towns in his district when he wrote that "my towns are threatening me (and) have all agreed amongst themselves against me."[24] Other evidence comes from the Report of Wenamun, about 250 years after the Amarna letters, and records the journey of an Egyptian priest to Byblos in search of cedar to use in constructing a sacred river barge. Prince Zakarbaal, with whom he negotiates the purchase of wood, is advised in his dealings by a group of citizens. Wenamun used a hieroglyphic in his report, transcribed as *mw'd*, that has been identified as close to the Hebrew word *mo'ed*, meaning "assembly" or "council."

The Phoenicians, despite their trading strength, were often at the political or military mercy of larger regional states, such as Egypt, Assyria, Babylon, and later Macedonia, Persia, and Rome. It may have been this insecurity which eroded the power of their kings and assisted the growth of councils. The first-century historian

Amarna letters

---

[24]   W. L. Moran, ed. *The Amarna Letters* (Baltimore: Johns Hopkins University Press, 1992), 138.

Detail from the Amarna Letters, Written in Babylonian cuneiform

Flavius Josephus mentions how the city of Tyre was without a monarch for 7 years and describes the "judges" who ruled instead. How did the judges acquire their positions? Some think it most likely that there was an elective mechanism for choosing them. We are not talking about a democracy however. The election would have been in the hands of an assembly; we do not know the makeup of that assembly, but it is most likely that it would have been restricted to prominent, wealthy traders and merchants (all of whom, of course, were men).

Carthage, the Phoenician city that was to cause Rome so much grief in the first century BCE, flourished from before 800 BCE until its destruction by the Romans in 146 BCE. We know more about it than most Phoenician cities thanks to the work of Herodotus, Aristotle, and the later Greek historian Polybius (ca. 150 BCE). The city was ruled by two judges, who were elected annually by city "elders." According to Aristotle, there was also an assembly that stepped in whenever the elders or judges reached a stalemate. Many ancient Greeks, even Athenians, were hostile to democratic ideals. For the wealthy elites, it smacked of mob rule; and it was this that Polybius saw in Carthage. Conducting an autopsy on Carthage after it was defeated—and burned to the ground—by Rome, he says, "the influence of the people in the policy of the state had risen to be supreme, while at Rome the Senate was at the height of its power: and so, as in the one measures were deliberated upon by the many, in the other by the best men."[25] Carthage fell, in other words, because it was *too* democratic.

WHAT DO WE KNOW ABOUT ANCIENT AFRICAN POLITICAL CULTURE?

Some scholars, such as Martin Bernal, have attempted to link Greek democracy to traditions originating in North Africa, including those of the Phoenicians and even some of the tribal/nomadic traditions from farther south. While his thesis in

---

[25]   Polybius, *The Histories of Polybius*, trans. E. Shuckburgh (London: Macmillan 1889), 1:51.

Black Athena (1987) has not been wholly accepted, there is a strong case to be made for the existence of many of the principles and procedures of participatory government among ancient Africans from several regions. Several points should be made at the outset of this discussion however. As with much of early African history, we have little or no documentary evidence for acquiring an understanding of political practices. This leaves us with archeology, which is also limited in some areas and time periods, and ethnology, which allows us to draw conclusions about the past by studying current populations and their habits, customs, and oral traditions. We cannot, therefore, assign specific dates to the developments we cite in this section. However, we can with some confidence point to traditions and customs that most anthropologists (and many historians) see as long-lasting and likely to have origins in the very distant past.

Among these traditions was that of "tribal democracy," which was by no means an African monopoly; it was part of the assembly culture of early Mesopotamia and can be found wherever a tribal culture prevails. South African scholar Joe Teffo has written that many African rulers were, like Mesopotamian kings, restricted in their powers by the need for consensus. Tribal kings ruled at the pleasure of their people, he claims, not *despite* the people. "For every king, the possibility of being deposed by the people on grounds of unpopularity was always a live contingency that it was unwise to discount."[26]

"Tribal Democracy?"   Zulus in South Africa are shown in an assembly in this nineteenth-century drawing.

---

[26]   Joe Teffo, "Democracy, Kingship, and Consensus: A South African Perspective," in *A Companion Guide to African Philosophy*, ed. Kwasi Wiredu (Malden, MA: Blackwell, 2004), 443.

The Ghanaian historian Kwame Gyekye offers a similar insight:

> It appears that the most important injunction was that the chief should never ever act without the advice and full concurrence of his councilors, the representatives of the people. Acting without concurrence and advice of his council was a legitimate cause for his deposition. Thus the chief was bound by law to rule with the consent of his people.[27]

It is not wholly conclusive, of course, that all kings would, indeed, act with such restraint, just as they often would not in China, Europe, or any other place; but the fact is that this idea existed, so the possibility was in place.

As in Mesopotamia and Phoenicia, we hear echoes of a belief system that posits powers greater than those of the king. Potentially, at least, this arrangement considered the welfare of the common people. Discussing the Bugandan traditional political culture of Uganda, historian Edward Wamala makes the point that monarchs represented merely the head of a system of councils: working up from the bottom, heads of families made up tribal councils, the heads of these met in clan councils, and representatives of these advised the monarch. Certainly, there were hierarchies in this system, notably of men over women and of age seniority; but such a system represented a bottom-up approach to government: "Consensus was central to this operation of democracy in Buganda society and, indeed, in many African societies.... If after due deliberations the council reached a consensus, it was taboo for the monarch to oppose or reject it."[28] Anthropologists will debate the role of taboo in political matters, but again, here we can see how political ideas are reflected in political structures and how they provide an ideal, which is realized in differing degrees in different societies.

Such systems were common in Africa, and although there is a lack of precision over dates, these traditional systems generally represented practices that occurred over long stretches of time, very possibly back into the ancient past. Teffo mentions similar practices among the Zulu of South Africa, the Bugandans of Uganda, and the Akans of Ghana. It may be difficult to think of this system as "democratic" because of the presence of an unelected king, but Teffo suggests we can think of the system as a "communocracy" in which consensus is sought out. "Any system that gives such priority to consensus is quite clearly democratic in a far deeper sense than any system in which decision making proceeds on the

---

[27] Kwame Gyekye, *Unexamined Life: Philosophy and the African Experience* (Accra: Ghana Universities Press, 1988), 11.

[28] Edward Wamala, "Government by Consensus: An Analysis of a Traditional Form of Democracy," in *A Companion to African Philosophy*, ed. Kwasi Wiredu (Malden, MA: Blackwell, 2004), 440.

principle that the majority carries the day."[29] There are, in other words, multiple visions of democracy, which go beyond our contemporary notions.

WHAT IS THE EVIDENCE FOR ANCIENT INDIAN REPUBLICS?

Several hundred years after the beginnings of the great Athenian experiment with radical democracy, Alexander of Macedon, the future Alexander the Great, occupied Athens and brought a more or less permanent end to its democracy and its independence. Then he embarked on a whirlwind project to conquer the rest of the world. When he crossed the river Indus and entered India in 327 BCE, according to his chroniclers, he met with some philosophical opposition to the idea of a supremely powerful monarch-like figure—which he represented so audaciously. Having conquered large swathes of the country, Alexander comes across as off-putting to some Indian philosophers, who give him a piece of their mind:

> King Alexander, every man can possess only so much of the earth's surface as this we are standing on. You are but human like the rest of us, save that you are always busy and up to no good, traveling so far from your home, a nuisance to yourself and others! You will soon be dead, and then you will own just as much of the earth as will suffice to bury you.[30]

Alexander was reportedly delighted with this idea (considering himself open-minded) and thought the sages made some excellent points, although this did not appear to change his behavior—it was his troops' exhaustion that forced him to end his frenzy of conquest, not his appreciation of the sages' point of view. But the question for us is: *Was this hostility toward, or distaste for, monarchical power reflected in the political traditions of India at that time? Did the idea of not having a king have legs in India?*

There is reliable evidence that parts of ancient India were, in fact, familiar with the notion of self-governing republics and contained city states which, as historian Steven Muhlburger puts it, have "as good a claim to be called democracies as the communities in the West that gave us the term."[31] This has been largely ignored by Western scholarship, perhaps because most manuscripts from ancient India were written by elite Brahmin sects, who disapproved of people governing themselves. These texts, collectively known as the "Brahmanical literature,"

---

[29] Teffo, "Democracy, Kingship, and Consensus," 445.

[30] From Arrian's *Annabasis of Alexander*, quoted in Sen, *Democracy and Its Global Roots*, 30.

[31] Steven Muhlburger, "Republics and Quasi-Democratic Institutions in Ancient India," in *The Secret History of Democracy*, ed. Benjamin Isakhan and Stephen Stockwell (Basingstoke, UK, and New York: Palgrave Macmillan, 2011), 49.

Alexander the Great in Battle Against the Persian Emperor Darius   When Alexander fought his way eastward to India he encountered self-governing communities.

include works such as the *Manu-Smrti* (ca. 100 BCE) and Kautilya's *Arthashastra* (ca. 300 BCE). Early European readers of these works found it easy to identify with tales of kings and nobles: this matched the European experience. When they looked at modern India, all they saw was kings and nobles, so they imagined an unbroken chain between modern and ancient made of kings and nobles.

Evidence for self-ruling "republics" goes back into the Vedic period (the *Vedas* are hymns and prayers in Sanskrit that form the earliest Hindu literature, dating back as far as 1500 BCE). The bulk of it, however, comes from the later Buddhist period (600–200 BCE). Just as we find words in Mesopotamia and Phoenicia referring to assemblies and councils, there is similar linguistic evidence in India: *gana* and *sangha*, in particular, were different types of self-governing bodies. *Gana* refers to those who claim to be of equal status, and *sangha* means "assembly." These two words signified more than this, however, because they represented communities that were distinct from the kingdoms that were prevalent in many parts of India.

Indian historian Romila Thapar refers to these entities as "proto-states" or possible chiefdoms: "The *gana–sangha* . . . was unlike a kingdom, since power was diffused, the stratification of its society was limited, and the ramifications of

gana- sangha

administration and coercive authority were non-existent."[32] In other words, they lacked the kind of centralized, bureaucratic authority represented by kings and emperors, familiar to us from most ancient civilizations. And these polities were resilient, says Thapar. Despite being repeatedly conquered, they often reappeared, not fully disappearing until the first millennium CE. They were not simply an early form of the state, therefore, but possibly *alternatives* to the state and were found in multiple parts of India. It is possible that more independent-minded peoples, less inclined to submit to the will of a monarchic state, might have occupied these more difficult-to-control areas, comprised of less fertile, hilly terrain. We have to look mostly to the Buddhist, or Pali, canon of literature for mentions of these states in the north; but the Hindu Mahabharata (believed to be dated to the eighth or ninth century BCE) also mentions similar systems, known as *vrishnis* in western India.

Although lacking kings, Thapar thinks that "republic" would be a better description for the *gana–sanghas* than democracy as the participatory piece was likely restricted to certain families and was certainly not universal. "These were systems where the heads of families belonging to a clan, or clan chiefs in a confederacy of clans, governed the territory of the clan, or the confederacy through an assembly, of which they alone were members."[33] The corporate aspect of the *gana–sanghas* was considered their major strength; meetings were held in assemblies presided over by clan heads. Matters of debate were put before them, and members voted on the issues. In addition to these familiar mechanisms of governance, certain democratic principles were in play among *gana–sanghas*. One of these was tolerance for unorthodox views and the ability to express divergent opinions, and it is notable that both Jainism and Buddhism (both offshoots from Brahmanical Hinduism) emerged from these communities.

Apart from the Brahmanical texts and the Buddhist Pali, we also have descriptions of India from Greek sources. One of them, Diodorus of Sicily, from the first century BCE, wrote of how Alexander and his men, having wandered into India regularly, encountered self-governing communities. Having described what seems like a mythical Indian past populated, and ruled, by (what else?) Greek gods, Diodorus, in a somewhat more believable tone, goes on to describe the current state of political affairs in that part of India:

> At last, however, after many years had gone, most of the cities adopted the democratic form of government, though some retained the kingly until the invasion

---

[32] Romila Thapar, *Early India: From the Origins to AD 1300* (Berkeley: University of California Press, 2002), 137.
[33] Ibid., 147.

of the country by Alexander. Of several remarkable customs existing among the Indians, there is one prescribed by their ancient philosophers which one may regard as truly admirable: for the law ordains that no one among them shall, under any circumstances, be a slave, but that, enjoying freedom, they shall respect the principle of equality in all persons.[34]

Even if Indian assemblies were limited in their franchise, restricted as they were by the infamous Indian caste system—which privileged the Kshatriya, or warrior, caste over all others—several scholars have made the point that the caste system was not as rigid as it was later to become. In addition to this, many of the northern city states were, in the Buddhist period, becoming wealthy through trade; and thus evolved a merchant class, which could, by virtue of its economic power, demand an increasing say in government. If all else failed, a group could split off from its polity and form its own *sangha*.

The Buddhist Pali canon provides the clearest descriptions of how the *sanghas* worked, even laying out the process for forming one's own. Here, the participatory model of politics is explicitly recognized. In the *Maha-parinibbana-suttanta*, an early Buddhist text, the king of Maghada sends a minister to the Buddha to ask how he can destroy the Vajjian confederacy. Buddha turns to his disciple Ananda:

> "Have you heard, Ananda, that the Vajjians hold full and frequent public assemblies?"
>
> "Lord, so I have heard," replied he.
>
> "So long, Ananda," rejoined the Blessed One, "as the Vajjians hold the full and frequent public assemblies; so long may they be expected not to decline, but to prosper. . . . So long, Ananda, as the Vajjians meet together in concord, and rise in concord, and carry out their undertakings in concord . . . so long as they enact nothing that has already been enacted, and act in accordance with the ancient institutions of the Vajjians as established in former days . . . so long may they be expected not to decline but to prosper."[35]

Taken as a whole, these different pieces of data provide significant evidence of an ancient and participatory vein in India's early history. Visions of self-rule by members of villages or guilds and other groups with shared interests jostled for position alongside monarchies.

---

[34] Diodorus Siculus, "General Description of India," II:39, quoted in R. C. Majumdar, *The Classical Accounts of India* (Calcutta, 1960), 236.

[35] Quoted in Isakhan and Stockwell, *The Secret History of Democracy*, 54.

Was Greece Exceptional?

Antislavery laws such as were described by Diodorus were not so evident in ancient Greece, for all its laudable institutions and accomplishments. Their massive reliance on slavery and complete exclusion of women, while not uncommon in the ancient world, remain the most evident flaws in their democracy. "An ocean separates the democracy of the ancient polis from the democracies of the western nation-states," says historian Ryan Balot.

> Frankly, modern democracies have progressed beyond the inequalities and abuses of human dignity that were characteristic of the ancient world. We are not slave-holders; modern democrats are repelled by the idea of excluding women from politics; we are attracted by political and cultural pluralism; we have reduced the role of luck in human life in ways that were unimaginable to the ancients; we have developed unthinkably rich private and social lives because of our distinctive individualism; and we have developed much more complete concepts—and practices—of freedom and equality.[36]

These profound differences between ancient and modern must be taken into account while discussing ancient democracy. In Athens, for example, "The good citizen," says Keane, "came equipped with a phallus"; and this fact prompts him to label the Athenian democracy a "phallocracy,"[37] relying as it did exclusively on men. This might appear odd, on the face of it, for *demokratia* is itself a feminine noun. And Athena, the city's patron deity and protector, was a *goddess*, the very goddess, in fact, who presided over and guaranteed the city's democratic institutions—nay, democracy itself! Women played a major role in family life and in the public life of the city that concerned festivals, which were a central feature of Athenian civic life. But when it came to political decision making, they were shut out. Nor were slaves able to participate, lacking any rights whatsoever. Since these two groups comprised a large portion of the population of Athens' hinterland, this falls far short of democracy as we know it.

So far we have discussed societies in which there is evidence—some of which is better than other parts—for democratic or quasi-democratic processes, principles, and institutions. In Athens between 508 and 322 BCE, however, the evidence is far more voluminous and much less equivocal. And while marred by serious shortcomings, it is hard to argue that there is nothing new in

[36] Ryan Balot, *Greek Political Thought* (Malden, MA: Blackwell, 2006), 51-2.
[37] Keane, *The Life and Death of Democracy*, 20.

Athens' Acropolis (in Greek, "Upper City") Housing the Parthenon, a Temple Dedicated to Athena, and Other Civic and Religious Buildings

the historical record, in either quantity or quality. In Athens kings are absent entirely—and thoroughly repudiated; thoughtful mechanisms like elections, people's courts, and assemblies of representative (male) citizens are in evidence. These elements were not all inherited from tradition (although some may have been). But the Athenians of the fifth century BCE generated most of these innovations to solve specific challenges in the wielding of power in their part of Greece. "In a very real sense," notes historian Christopher Blackwell, "the People governed themselves, debating and voting individually on issues great and small, from matters of war and peace to the proper qualifications for ferry-boat captains."[38]

Whereas much of the traditional story of Greek democracy highlights these events as a radical break with the despotic (and Eastern) past, we have argued that

---

[38]   Christopher W. Blackwell, "Athenian Democracy: A Brief Overview," *Dēmos: Classical Athenian Democracy. A Stoa publication.* February 28, 2003, http://www.stoa.org/projects/demos/article_democracy_overview?page=4.

much of the thinking, and even some of the institutions, that fueled Athens' revolution were already in place elsewhere. To that extent Athens represents a continuation of a tradition that began elsewhere—perhaps inherited from the Phoenicians or Mesopotamians. But is it also possible, bearing in mind the history of India and Africa, that democracy is not a Greek invention but part of the human inheritance, pursued by all peoples in their own ways and to no particular schedule? As Jack Goody writes, "'The Greeks, of course, invented the word 'democracy' … but they did not invent the practice of democracy. Representation in one form or other has been a feature of the politics and struggles of many peoples."[39]

> ☀ But is it also possible, bearing in mind the history of India and Africa, that democracy is not a Greek invention but part of the human inheritance, pursued by all peoples in their own ways and to no particular schedule?

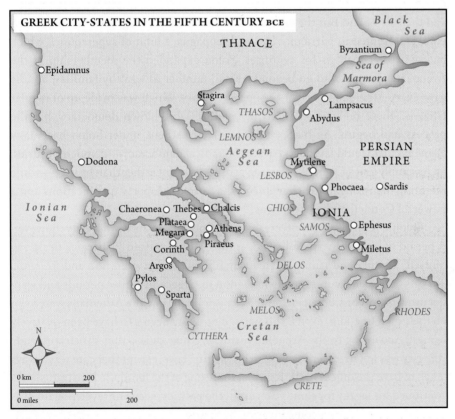

MAP 5.4   ANCIENT GREEK CITY STATES IN THE FIFTH CENTURY BCE

---

[39]   Goody, *The Theft of History*, 50.

HOW DID ATHENIAN DEMOCRACY COME ABOUT?

Most of Greece before about 600 BCE was ruled by kings, the majority of whom acquired their position by birth or good old-fashioned military might. But during the 700s and 600s BCE Athens began to move from the kingship model to a leadership of wealthy aristocrats, and it is with one of these, the lawmaker Solon (d. ca. 558 BCE), that the democratic moment in Athens is thought to have begun. In 594 BCE Solon was called upon by Athenians to resolve a political crisis. Poor Athenian farmers had for years been vulnerable to poverty induced by failed harvests. Hardships were compounded when they were forced to borrow from wealthier citizens and then further impoverished, and often enslaved, by the debt incurred.

Solon was called in to find a solution to this debt crisis, and he initiated reforms that outlawed debt bondage of the poor. Other reforms went further toward the creation of a just and equitable society based on citizen participation and the rule of law. But the aristocratic class was still recognized as a privileged elite, represented in particular by the Areopagus, a kind of supercouncil which had existed in Athens for centuries. Solon expanded the membership of the Areopagus, however, to go beyond a small number of wealthy families; and he gave every Athenian the right to appeal to a jury, which was made up of regular citizens. These reforms fell short of creating a full-blown democracy, but the process had begun. As Blackwell puts it, "So Athens under Solon had many elements that would later be a part of the radical democracy—democratic juries, an Assembly and a Council, selection of officials by lot rather than by vote—while retaining many oligarchic elements in the form of property qualifications and a powerful Council of the Areopagus."[40]

Solon's reforms did not create a lasting peace and prosperity however. A period of political strife followed, ending with a certain Pisistratus declaring himself "tyrant" and ruling in this way off and on between 562 and 527 BCE. Tyrants had been a common phenomenon in Greece in earlier periods and were not universally considered evil. But by this point in time the Athenians were keen on their own freedom, even if this particular tyrant seems to have been relatively benign. According to the Athenian historian Thucydides, after Pisistratus' rule, "the city was left in full enjoyment of its existing laws, except that care was always taken to have the offices in the hands of some one of the family."[41] Pisistratus' sons continued his legacy for some years, until the political scene unraveled again, this time initiating an unwelcome invasion by Sparta.

---

[40]   Blackwell, "Athenian Democracy."
[41]   Thucydides, *History of the Peloponnesian War*, ed. Thomas Hobbes (London: Bohn, 1843), 6.54.6.

The democratic "revolution" did not come until the time of Cleisthenes (b. 570 BCE), largely in response to the Spartan invasion and the various attempts by would-be tyrants and aristocrats to seize the reigns of power in Athens. In 508–507 BCE Cleisthenes initiated further reforms that created the famous Athenian democratic system. The first and perhaps most fundamental step in this process was what you might think of as "redistricting." Cleisthenes took Attica's *demes*—villages—and made them the fundamental political unit of Athens. He even encouraged people to take a last name associated with their village. In all there were 138 demes, spread across the three distinct areas that made up Athens: the rural areas, the port of Pireus, and the city proper. But to get people to think of themselves as Athenians, rather than "urbanites" or "port dwellers" or "country hicks," he created 10 "tribes" whose membership cut across the geographic regions of Athens and divided the demes among the tribes, thus encouraging Athenians to think beyond their local interests.

This move was truly innovative, as political scientist Francis Fukuyama writes: "Most tribal societies are also relatively egalitarian and elect their rulers ... but the Greeks went beyond this by introducing a concept of citizenship that was based on political criteria rather than kinship."[42] Such a move represents a distinct step toward later nation-states, even if kinship continued to play a considerable role in politics.

Each tribe sent 50 men to participate in the Council of 500. Not to be confused with the assembly, which was open to all citizens, the council was a key institution, which set the agenda for the assembly. The 50-man delegations would each hold the presidency of the council for one-tenth of the year, and no individual could serve more than two terms. This meant that a high proportion of the citizen body became acquainted with the affairs of state so that when they participated in other parts of the government, or in the assembly, where debate and voting on issues took place, they did so as informed participants. As historian Josiah Ober puts it, "The army, the assembly, the peoples' courts, and boards of magistrates were all staffed by people with experience of former councilors."[43]

Along with the council and the assembly, the People's Court was the third pillar of the democratic system. All male citizens over 30 were able to sit on the court, as long as they were not in debt to the treasury. "Payment for public duties," wrote Aristotle, "is as follows: first, the people draw a drachma for ordinary meetings of the Assembly, and a drachma and a half for a sovereign meeting; second, the Jury-courts half a drachma; third, the Council five obols; and those acting as

42 Francis Fukuyama, *The Origins of Political Order: From Prehuman Times to the French Revolution* (New York: Farrar Straus and Giroux, 2011), 20.
43 Josiah Ober, "What the Ancient Greeks Can Tell Us About Democracy." Princeton/Stanford Working Papers in Classics, Paper no. 090703, *Annual Review of Political Science* 11(June 2008): 74.

How the Ancient Greeks Dealt with Gridlock   When policymakers became deadlocked, citizens could vote to ostracize—exile—one of them, thus breaking the deadlock. They inscribed the name of the victim on pottery shards such as these. Would such a tactic be useful today?

president have an additional obol for food."[44] Payment for jurors enabled even the poorest Athenian man to partake in legal matters of the city.

The reforms of Cleisthenes therefore had three major consequences: they expanded power from the wealthiest aristocrats down to the poorest citizens, they replaced regional factionalism with what you could call a "pan-Athenian" identity, and they created considerable obstacles to would-be tyrants. But, as may now be apparent, Athenian democracy was always a work in progress; it was constantly being tweaked, refined, threatened, and enforced.

One other major component of the democratic system became paramount in the mid-fifth century BCE, a time of military conflict for Athens. The *strategos*, or "general," was one of the few elected offices, as opposed to being chosen by lot. There were 10 generals who gained positions in this way, at any time. The most influential was Pericles, who was elected on and off multiple times between

---

[44]   *Aristotle in 23 Volumes*, vol. 20, trans. H. Rackham (Cambridge, MA: Harvard University Press; London, William Heinemann, 1952), chap. 62, sec. 2.

The Parthenon Today

454 and 429 BCE. The generals were allowed an unusual privilege; they could introduce their own legislation into the assembly meetings without going through the usual channels. This gave them direct access to the people, who they could then sway with their opinions (if their public speaking skills were up to the job).

Under Pericles' influence as general, Athens embarked on a massive public works building project, which produced much of classical Athens' greatest architecture, such as the Parthenon, and an imperial period that involved projecting their military power across the Aegean, arguably precipitating Athens' eventual downfall.

Some have argued that Pericles overrode the democratic system in which he was an actor. Thucydides himself said,

> Pericles, indeed, by his rank, ability, and known integrity, was enabled to exercise an independent control over the Demos . . . for as he never sought power by improper means . . . but, on the contrary, enjoyed so high an estimation that he could afford to anger them by contradiction. . . . In short, what was nominally a democracy became in his hands government by the first citizen.[45]

The Athenian democratic period ended in fits and starts—much as it had begun, suffering through accelerations and reversals before disappearing

---

[45]   Thucydides, *History of the Peloponnesian War*, 2.65:8–9.

[margin note, handwritten] 50,000 man lost

altogether. In 415 BCE, a botched invasion of Sicily resulted in the destruction of the Athenian fleet and a large army. This disaster impelled the Athenians to reduce the political participation of the community, believing their radical democracy was to blame. Further political crises provoked more tinkering with the makeup of the council, restricting its membership to fewer and wealthier individuals and doing the same for the assembly. Like a concertina, Athens' political enfranchisement expanded and contracted over several decades, its citizens wrestling with each other over the central questions of who and how many should have access to power. Finally, in 338 BCE Athens was occupied by the forces of Alexander of Macedon (the future Alexander the Great). This marked the end of Athens' "golden age."

Was Athens exceptional? In many ways it was. Unlike African tribal democracy, which is a good example of an inherited tradition whose origins are lost in time, the implementation of Athens' democracy had a specific historical origin. It was consciously implemented to resolve conflicts over power in the community. In the process, it was debated and discussed between individuals and examined by writers, whose work has stood the test of time and has been available for historians to chew over ever since. While many of the elements of its democracy may well have originated earlier and farther east, the specific ways in which the Athenians assembled their democracy's component pieces and how far they went with it seem to represent something of an unprecedented nature in the record of history.

Conclusion

The search for self-representation has been a theme of history for generations. It continues unabated today in many parts of the world as British parliamentarian and diplomat Rory Stewart put it, while talking about his experience nation-building in Afghanistan in the first decade of this century: "I have not met, in Afghanistan, in even the most remote community, anybody who does not want a say in who governs them."[46] This is the drive, then, that sets people everywhere searching for a way to control their lives. And even if the forms of "democracy" differ and even if it is more or less complete here or there, the underlying quest is the same and is something that mattered in ancient times as much as today: "Democracy matters because it reflects an idea of equality and an idea of liberty.

---

[46] Rory Stewart, "Why Democracy Matters," London, June 2012, *TED.com*, http://www.ted.com/talks/rory_stewart_how_to_rebuild_democracy.html.

It reflects an idea of dignity, the dignity of the individual, the idea that each individual should have an equal vote, an equal say in the formation of their government."[47] What has changed over the millennia (and only very recently, in fact) are ideas of individualism, human rights, and suffrage, permitting women to gain access to the political process just as men had, and outlawing the practice of slavery. The idea of representation has always been around; the bigger question was who deserved it.

So if the desire for participation is a part of the human heritage, what about the role of Greece? We have seen in this chapter that certain things happened in Greece to advance the cause of democracy, arguably beyond any previous society that we know much about (with the possible exception of tribal societies). But the idea that Athens was the wellspring of this innovative human practice is difficult to swallow, much less that all democracy as we know it today originated there, traveled to Rome, and thence informed modern nation-states. As historian Ian Morris puts it, "It takes a heroically selective reading of history to see a continuous spirit of democratic freedom stretching from classical Greece to the Founding Fathers (who, incidentally, tended to use the word 'democracy' as a term of abuse, just one step above mob rule)."[48] This classic case of Eurocentrism should be seen for what it is, a common tendency of historians to write history without sufficient awareness of the influence of their own era on their perspective.

Ultimately, there are two answers to the question of democracy's origins. One addresses the principles behind the many systems we see as "democratic." The origins of these principles reach as far back as you care to go, intertwined with human DNA. The other looks at the particular practices and institutions that we associate with democracy, and these too have a long lineage. While admirably expressed in classical Athens, that city has a very dubious claim to the patent for democracy. We should recognize its contribution, while also understanding that other places, buried deeper in the dust of history, were major stakeholders in the struggle for a voice in their own governance.

Words to Think About

Brahmin	Ethnology	Oral Tradition
Republic	Taboo	Tyranny

---

[47] Ibid.
[48] Ian Morris, *Why the Rest Rules—For Now: The Patterns of History and What They Reveal About the Future* (New York: Farrar, Straus and Giroux, 2010), 286.

Questions to Think About

- Is democracy a uniquely European practice?
- How can we describe traditional African political practices as "democratic"?
- What was Greece's contribution to participatory politics?

Primary Sources

Aristotle in 23 Volumes. Translated by H. Rackham. Cambridge, MA: Harvard University Press; London, William Heinemann, 1952.

Lambert, W. G. *Babylonian Wisdom Literature*. Oxford: Clarendon Press, 1960.

Moran, W. L., ed. *The Amarna Letters*. Baltimore: Johns Hopkins University Press, 1992.

Polybius. *The Histories of Polybius*. Translated by E. Shuckburgh. London: Macmillan 1889.

Thucydides. *History of the Peloponnesian War*, edited by Thomas Hobbes. London: Bohn, 1843.

Secondary Sources

Balot, Ryan. *Greek Political Thought*. Malden, MA: Blackwell, 2006.

Bernal, Martin. *Black Athena: The Afroasiatic Roots of Classical Civilization*. New Brunswick, NJ: Rutgers University Press, 1987.

Blackwell, Christopher W. "Athenian Democracy: A Brief Overview." *Dēmos: Classical Athenian Democracy. A Stoa Publication*. February 28, 2003, http://www.stoa.org/projects/demos/article_democracy_overview?page=4.

Bush, George W. "Remarks by President George W. Bush at the 20th Anniversary of the National Endowment for Democracy," November 6, 2003, http://www.ned.org/node/658.

Diamond, Larry. "What Is Democracy?" Lecture at Hilla University for Humanistic Studies. January 21, 2004, http://www.stanford.edu/~ldiamond/iraq/WhaIsDemocracy012004.htm.

Fleming, Daniel E. *Democracy's Ancient Ancestors: Mari and Early Collective Governance*. Cambridge and New York: Cambridge University Press, 2004.

Fukuyama, Francis. *The Origins of Political Order: From Prehuman Times to the French Revolution*. New York: Farrar Straus and Giroux, 2011.

Goody, Jack. *The Theft of History*. Cambridge, Cambridge University Press, 2006.

Gyekye, Kwame. *Unexamined Life: Philosophy and the African Experience*. Accra: Ghana Universities Press, 1988.

Isakhan, Benjamin, and Stephen Stockwell, eds. *The Secret History of Democracy*. Basingstoke, UK, and New York: Palgrave Macmillan, 2011.

Jacobsen, Thorkild. "Primitive Democracy in Ancient Mesopotamia." *Journal of Near Eastern Studies* 2, no. 3 (July 1943): 159–172.

Keane, John. *The Life and Death of Democracy*. New York: W.W. Norton, 2009.

Majumdar, R. C. *The Classical Accounts of India*. Calcutta: Firma K.L. Mukhopadyay, 1960.

Morris, Ian. *Why the Rest Rules—For Now: The Patterns of History and What They Reveal About the Future.* New York: Farrar, Straus and Giroux, 2010.

Muhlburger, Steven. "Republics and Quasi-Democratic Institutions in Ancient India." In *The Secret History of Democracy,* edited by Benjamin Isakhan and Stephen Stockwell. Basingstoke, UK, and New York: Palgrave Macmillan, 2011.

Ober, Josiah. "The Original Meaning of 'Democracy': Capacity To Do Things, Not Majority Rule." Princeton/Stanford Working Papers in Classics, Paper no. 090704, September 2007.

Ober, Josiah. "What the Ancient Greeks Can Tell Us About Democracy." Princeton/Stanford Working Papers in Classics, Paper no. 090703. *Annual Review of Political Science* 11 (June 2008): 67–91.

Schmitter, Phillipe C., and Terry Lynn Karl. "What Democracy Is ... and Is Not." In *The Global Resurgence of Democracy.* Baltimore: Johns Hopkins University Press, 1994.

Sen, Amartya. "Democracy and Its Global Roots: Why Democracy Is Not the Same as Westernization." *New Republic* (October 6, 2003): 28–35.

Stewart, Rory. "Why Democracy Matters," London, June 2012. *TED.com,* http://www.ted.com/talks/rory_stewart_how_to_rebuild_democracy.html.

Teffo, Joe. "Democracy, Kingship, and Consensus: A South African Perspective." In *A Companion Guide to African Philosophy,* edited by Kwasi Wiredu. Malden, MA: Blackwell, 2004. 443–450

Thapar, Romila. *Early India: From the Origins to AD 1300.* Berkeley: University of California Press, 2002.

Wamala, Edward. "Government by Consensus: An Analysis of a Traditional Form of Democracy." In *A Companion to African Philosophy,* edited by Kwasi Wiredu. Malden, MA: Blackwell, 2004. 433–435

For additional resources, including maps, primary sources, and visuals, web links, and quizzes, please go to **www.oup.com/us/cole**

Head of the Roman Emperor Augustus   Buried under the threshold of the temple at Meroë and trampled over by worshippers. Not everyone bought that he was a god.

Chapter 6

What Is an Empire?

Candace of Meroë

It was an insult, a humiliation; and that is how it was intended. When the African kingdom of Meroë raided the Egyptian town of Aswan and captured a bronze statue of the Roman emperor Augustus in 25 BCE, the queen, or "candace," of Meroë had the statue's head removed and buried under the threshold of her people's temple. On entering, worshippers stepped on the head of the leader of the most powerful political entity in the world at that time, with the exception, perhaps, of China. The head, unearthed by twentieth-century archeologists, now stands in the British Museum in London. You can still see tiny grains of sand from the Sahara embedded in it.

The head itself was carefully crafted by the top Roman bronze workers of the day. It was designed to show Augustus in the best possible light: strong, young, and powerful. As such, it was a major piece of Rome's propaganda campaign, selling the empire to its conquered provinces. In the years just before the birth of Jesus this empire stretched from the Atlantic coast of Europe in the west, the Rhine and Danube Rivers in the north, Mesopotamia in the east, and in the south, well, it sort of petered out south of Egypt. → Augustus Empire.

Augustus had posted statues like these all over his empire, a means, perhaps, of reminding people far from Rome, the epicenter of the empire, who was in charge. Meroë's leader, referred to by later historians as a "warrior-queen," was clearly not impressed. The Greek geographer Strabo (ca. 63 BCE–ca. 24 CE) described her unflatteringly as "a masculine woman, who had lost one eye," telling the story of how the queen attacked and destroyed several Roman frontier forts when the Roman army was busy fighting border skirmishes elsewhere. She removed Augustus's propagandistic statue and defiled it. A Roman general responded by attacking settlements in Meroë. "He made prisoners of the

199

THINKING ABOUT EMPIRE

Why Was Rome in Meroë and Not Meroë in Rome?
- The comparative population differential made it unlikely that Meroë would project its power far beyond its borders as it would have needed a sizable population itself and dense population in its adjacent areas to bolster its forces.

Are Empires Just Large States?
- Empires are the "Russian doll" of polities, states within states, each state owing allegiance—usually, this means money—to the imperial government.

Who Was the Emperor?
- In contrast to the Chinese and Roman models, the Persian emperor Darius I did not claim to be a god but did allow himself the privilege of being selected by the "Great God" to rule over the earth.

Why Do Empires Exist?
- Empires both are born from expansionist policies and generate them. And strictly hierarchical societies are often more expansionist than others.

Do Empires Survive Through Military Force Alone?
- Apart from the economic benefits of peace . . . the imperial culture would have provided a certain appeal.

Why Do Empires Collapse?
- Many imperial forms—political, social, and economic—continued under different people. The idea of "collapse" . . . gives the impression of instantaneous cessation of existence, as opposed to a process of long, slow decline.

Conclusion
- The inheritors of empire ("barbarians") usually pass along the "goodies" of empire because good ideas are not just good ideas for Romans or Han or Persians. They are good for most people and, as such, eagerly exploited.

inhabitants," says Strabo, "and returned back again with the booty, as he judged any farther advance into the country impracticable on account of the roads."[1]

————— ✦ —————

Introduction

What was Rome doing in Meroë anyway? Why would a western Mediterranean power find it necessary to transport thousands of men across the sea and then march them through Egypt into the eastern reaches of the southern Sahara Desert?

This question is central to any exploration of ancient empires, including those discussed in this chapter: the Persians, or Achaemenids (550–330 BCE); the Romans (ca. 30 BCE–476 CE); the Han Chinese (206 BCE–220 CE); and the Mauryan dynasty of India (522–185 BCE).

All these empires were expansionist, embarking on energetic campaigns of conquest. They wielded great influence in the conquered territories—social, political, economic, and religious—since the "export" of much of the culture of the home country, or *metropole*, became one of the hallmarks of empire. Spanning centuries, if not millennia, such influence resulted in legacies whose traces we can still see in our world today.

This chapter will look at how these empires arose and what motivated their growth. Once established, how did they maintain their possessions? What was life like for the citizens of, and for the conquered people ruled by, such states? How did they balance power between the imperial "center" and the provincial peripheries? What combination of power, both military and other, did they use in this endeavor? Were they generally benign or harmful, destructive or beneficial, and to whom? Finally, we must look at the imperial life cycle and ask questions about their decline, for decline they did, without exception. We will also look at their legacies, for even after collapsing, their memories linger and their political and cultural forms find echoes throughout history—to the extent, in fact, that the idea of complete collapse becomes debatable.

---

[1] *Strabo's Geography*, book XVll, chap. 1.54, http://rbedrosian.com/Classic/strabo17d.htm.

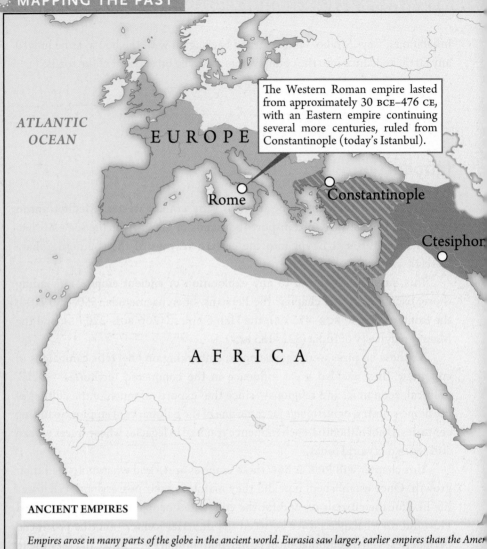

The Western Roman empire lasted from approximately 30 BCE–476 CE, with an Eastern empire continuing several more centuries, ruled from Constantinople (today's Istanbul).

ATLANTIC OCEAN

EUROPE

Rome

Constantinople

Ctesiphor

AFRICA

ANCIENT EMPIRES

Empires arose in many parts of the globe in the ancient world. Eurasia saw larger, earlier empires than the Amer

MAP 6.1   ANCIENT EMPIRES

TIMELINE

550–330 BCE
Achaemenid Empire

333 BCE
Alexander the Great defeats
Darius II of Persia

522–185 BCE
Mauryan Dynasty of India

206 BCE–220 CE
Han Dynasty of China

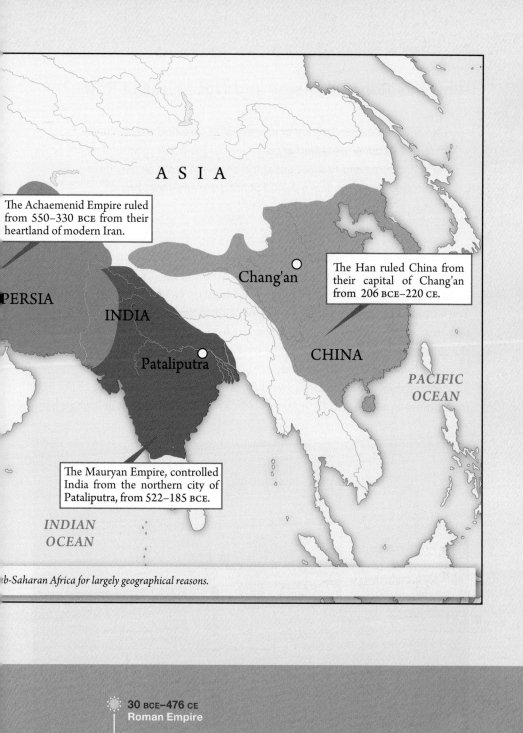

ASIA

The Achaemenid Empire ruled from 550–330 BCE from their heartland of modern Iran.

PERSIA

INDIA

Chang'an ○

The Han ruled China from their capital of Chang'an from 206 BCE–220 CE.

Pataliputra ○

CHINA

PACIFIC OCEAN

The Mauryan Empire, controlled India from the northern city of Pataliputra, from 522–185 BCE.

INDIAN OCEAN

b-Saharan Africa for largely geographical reasons.

30 BCE–476 CE
Roman Empire

232 BCE
Death of Asoka
in India

79 CE
eruption of Italy's Mount
Vesuvius

Why Was Rome in Meroë and Not Meroë in Rome?

Can anyone be so indifferent or idle as not to care to know by what means, and under what kind of polity, almost the whole inhabited world was conquered and brought under the dominion of the single city of Rome, and that too within a period of not quite fifty-three years?[2]

POLYBIUS

Claiming that Rome dominated "almost the whole inhabited world" was a bit of a stretch. Nonetheless, if you were the ruler of Meroë in 25 BCE, you would be wary of this gigantic northern power, apparently intent on swallowing the entire globe. You would likely have felt a deep sense of pride in your position and in the territory over which you held sway. Quite apart from pride in your own identity and the reluctance to have strangers take over your society, this part of Africa was enjoying something of a high point.

Several major contributions swept from eastern to western Africa in the first millennium BCE, specifically ironworking (which some scholars believe to have

Meroë   The ancient city of Meroë stood up to the Romans but fell from a combination of environmental overexploitation, economic decline, and invasion.

---

[2]   Polybius, *The Histories*, vol. 1, trans. Evelyn S. Shuckburgh (London: Macmillan, 1889), 1.

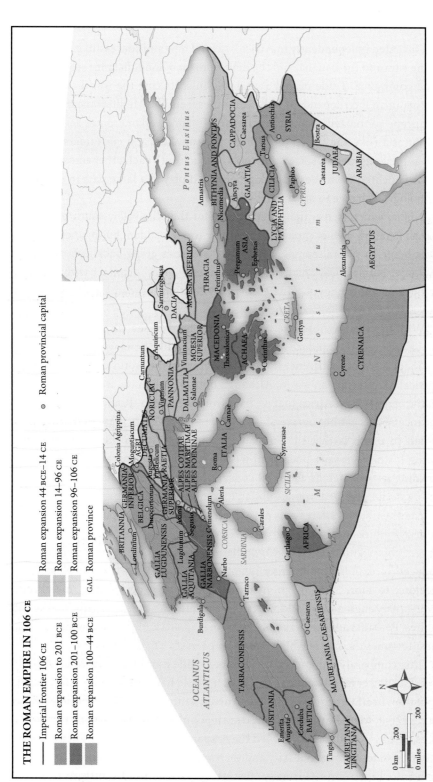

THE ROMAN EMPIRE IN 106 CE

— Imperial frontier 106 CE   ⊙ Roman provincial capital

	Roman expansion 44 BCE–14 CE
	Roman expansion 14–96 CE
	Roman expansion 96–106 CE
GAL	Roman province

Roman expansion to 201 BCE
Roman expansion 201–100 BCE
Roman expansion 100–44 BCE

MAP 6.2 THE ROMAN EMPIRE The Roman Empire united more of the continent of Europe and the Western world than any polity before it. With this unity came a common trade zone, a language, and a notion of citizenship which was unprecedented. This and the prosperity that many found came with a high military cost and constant territorial conflicts.

been invented independently in Africa), several new and successful crops including the yam and the banana, and the development of long-distance sea- and land-
based commerce. Trade played a vital role in shrinking the world and tying it
together in an interdependent web. Sea routes from the Mediterranean to northern Europe connected resources with markets, and overland routes across Africa
and Eurasia (like the fabled Silk Road) put suppliers and consumers of goods
such as precious metals, spices, and tools in touch with each other across Eurasia.
Meroë benefited from these developments and played a large part in spreading
technological change to other parts of Africa.

Nubia, which is also the generic name for the Nile valley south of the first
cataract (shallow area or rapids), is mostly in today's Sudan; but in ancient times
it was home to several complex state-level societies going back as far as about
2400 BCE. Nubia always had close—and often violent—contact with its larger
northern neighbor, Egypt. One Nubian civilization invaded Egypt in 730 BCE
and ruled it for over half a century.

With her wealthy resource base, it is not hard to see why, by the time the
Romans arrived, the candace of Meroë did not feel like bowing to them.

There were big differences, however, between the world of Meroë and the
Classical Mediterranean world. Although both were literate, we do not have the
volume of texts from Africa that we have from the Greco–Roman world. The significance of this cannot be overstated. One of the primary reasons that Rome is
studied so much is that the Romans produced so much literature. We have
diaries, histories, essays, poetry, all written by the historical actors themselves,
providing us with details about all conceivable aspects of their lives. The linear
Merotic script diverged from Egyptian hieroglyphs and remains undeciphered.

Another major difference is population. Some estimates put the Roman and
Chinese Empires together at around half of the world's population at this time.
Why is this significant? Large populations create large economies; food is
produced in exponentially larger quantities, leading to greater surpluses and,
therefore, to more specialization in such pursuits as agriculture, metalwork,
architecture, engineering, and warfare—the building blocks of large states and
empires. Peasants and farmers can be taxed, in goods and cash, allowing states to
amass fortunes the size of which had never been seen in history.

This comparative population difference made it unlikely that Meroë would
project its power far beyond its borders as it would have needed not only a sizable
population itself to begin with but also dense settlement in the conquered areas
adjacent to it. Meroë would have used such population density to bolster its own
forces, just as the Romans did when they expanded, first from a city state among
other city states throughout Italy and then around the Mediterranean world and
north into France and Germany. Just as hurricanes need moisture from the

evaporating water of oceans to maintain their strength, losing force once they hit land, empires tend to lose momentum if they expand into lightly populated areas from which they can glean no new human resources. Meroë was the population center of gravity for its region, but it had sparsely populated desert to the south and west, a powerful neighbor (Egypt) to its north, and the Red Sea to the east.

> Just as hurricanes need moisture from the evaporating water of oceans to maintain their strength, losing force once they hit land, empires tend to lose momentum if they expand into lightly populated areas from which they can glean no new human resources.

WHAT DID EMPIRES LOOK LIKE TO OUTSIDERS?

The theme of resistance is a constant in the history of empires. If Meroë represented the southern extremity of Rome's power, Britain was the northern end. There, resistance is best illustrated by an even more famous female enemy of Rome, the queen of the Iceni tribe, Boudicca. By 40 CE, the Romans had crossed the English Channel and were busy building fortresses in Britain. The island was home to groups of more or less independent tribes and chiefdoms, each with its own territory. Boudicca's husband, Prasutagus, was the leader of one of these and, aware that he could not fight the Romans off forever, had become a client king, an arrangement whereby Rome allowed him to continue business as usual for the payment of tribute. The Roman historian Tacitus heard the story from his father-in-law Agricola, who was a general in Britain at the time:

> Prasutagus, king of the Iceni, famed for his long prosperity, had made the emperor his heir along with his two daughters, under the impression that this token of submission would put his kingdom and his house out of the reach of wrong. But the reverse was the result, so much so that his kingdom was plundered by centurions, his house by slaves, as if they were the spoils of war. First, his wife Boudicea was scourged, and his daughters outraged. All the chief men of the Iceni, as if Rome had received the whole country as a gift, were stripped of their ancestral possessions, and the king's relatives were made slaves.[3]

Inheriting royal property was illegal under Roman law, and Rome was not about to share a kingdom with a woman. The Romans saw in the death of Prasutagus an opportunity to nullify their agreement with him and take over his possessions directly. Boudicca herself was flogged and forced to watch the raping of her teenage daughters. Humiliating and utterly demoralizing one's opponents seems to have been an imperial habit.

---

[3] *Tacitus' Annals*, trans. Ronald Mellor (New York: Oxford University Press, 2010), 14:31.

In a sequence seen repeatedly in the history of empires, the heavy hand of the conqueror created a rebellion. In this case, the outraged Iceni and many surrounding tribes no doubt saw in Boudicca's treatment their own future. They turned on Roman towns in Britain and burned them, including the garrison town of Colchester and Londinium (London), which, as Tacitus says, "though undistinguished by the name of a colony, was much frequented by a number of merchants and trading vessels."[4] Boudicca became the leader of this revolt, which nearly catapulted the Romans out of Britain but instead ended with the tribal alliance broken and Boudicca dead.

If we ask why it was not the candace of Meroë who invaded Rome, we can ask the same of Boudicca or any number of other local kings, queens, or chiefs who interacted with the Roman Empire. We cannot rule out the possibility that they would have invaded, had they been able. And, indeed, more than once "barbarian" tribes did attack Rome, effectively ending Roman control over its western provinces in 410 CE.

But at this point in history, Meroë, no peace-loving utopia itself, lacked the resources to project its power as far as Italy, and evidently did not possess the organizational structure—social, economic, and political—to allow it to generate such resources. Whether they "would have if they could have" is at the heart of whether or not empires are "inevitable" for those who have the means. The same question could be asked about the Britons, who some 1,600 years later would be

Boudicca, Imagined in Today's Britain as a Symbol of Local Resistance to the Imperial Romans

---

4   Ibid., 14:33.

able to expand far beyond their borders (though they did not go to Rome but to Jamestown, Delhi, Cape Town, Cairo, and other distant places). In so doing, the British ironically invoked the "glories" of the Roman Empire, even though that ancient empire had in the all-but-forgotten past defiled their ancestors.

IS EMPIRE A EURASIAN THING?

Although empires show up globally, Eurasia generated larger polities earlier than elsewhere. The kinds of polities we find in Africa at this time, for instance, are all significantly smaller than the "mega"-states of Rome, China, Persia, and India. The same is true of the Americas: the polities of Monte Alban and Teotihuacán, in the Mexican highlands and Mesoamerica, respectively, were far smaller and somewhat later. How can we account for such differences?

Many scholars opt for environmental explanations. It is hard to ignore the influence of environment on humanity, as the historian Erik Gilbert points out: "On some level we are all environmental determinists, after all no one has ever invested a great deal of time in wondering why Eskimos never developed agriculture."[5] Gilbert points to particular challenges to the development of big states in

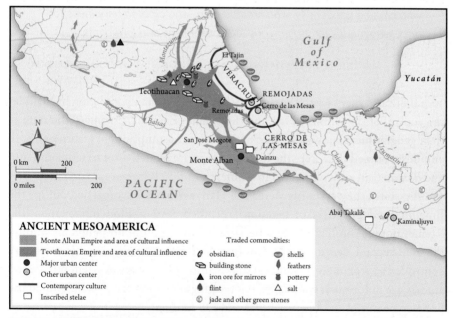

MAP 6.3   ANCIENT MESOAMERICA   Teotihuacán and Monte Alban, New World empires, were later and tended to be smaller, relying less on centralized control and more on tribute payments.

---

[5]   Erik Gilbert, Personal communication with authors, September 2011.

sub-Saharan Africa, in particular the land, which was much wetter. As such, it was not given to the production of storable grains, such as wheat, rice, and maize, which are the engines of all early civilizations. With the (later) appearance of maize in western Africa, there was an explosion of state building; after all, "yams and even bananas are hard to build an empire on."[6] Mega-state building in the Americas had environmental challenges as well, although these were related more to geography than to food staples, the north–south axis of Meso-America and South America being difficult to travel owing to the prevalence of mountain and jungle; this might go a long way to explaining the absence of large empire there until considerably later.

Why Africa did not produce a "Rome" is, ultimately, a misleading question, for by some estimates more than half of the population of Eurasia at this time lived outside of states; you could, therefore, ask why Romania did not produce an empire or northern Thailand or Wales, etc.

Are Empires Just Large States?

> A Great god is Ahuramazda, who created this earth,
> who created yonder sky, who created man, who created happiness for
> man, who made Darius king, one king over many, one lord of many.

INSCRIPTION ON DARIUS I'S ROCK TOMB AT NAQSH-I-RUSTAM

Two thousand years ago approximately half of the human population lived under the control of the Chinese Han and the Roman Empires. Owing to the state of their geographical knowledge (and perhaps their assumptions of greatness), both empires assumed they were the lords of the entire planet, *orbis terrerum* in Latin and *tianxia* ("all under heaven") in Chinese.

Big states they certainly were. The Han census of 2 CE (carried out for the time-honored purposes of taxation) recorded 59.6 million inhabitants. The Roman population had reached between 65 and 75 million people by around the mid-second century CE, according to different estimates. Each empire controlled approximately 4 million square miles of territory. Ancient population studies are notoriously unreliable, but recent guesses put the global figure in the first two centuries CE at between 170 and 330 million.

But apart from size, which is certainly a characteristic of empires, they are different, structurally and functionally. Let's look first at their structure. Empires

---

[6]   Ibid.

are made up of states, they are the "Russian doll" of polities, states-within-states, each state owing allegiance—usually, this means money—to the imperial government. If you imagine your state's governor as a king, then, if the United States were an empire, the president in Washington, DC, would be the emperor. The Persian term that comes closest to "emperor," *shahanshah*, literally means "king of kings," suggesting that the leader of the Achaemenids ruled over subjugated kingdoms, in effect creating a "superstate."

> ☀ Empires are made up of states, they are the "Russian doll" of polities, states-within-states, each state owing allegiance— usually, this means money—to the imperial government.

The early history of the Achaemenid Empire (named after its dynastic founder, Achaemenes) illustrates how this happened. The largest of all the ancient Near-Eastern empires in its heydey, it spanned from Egypt to central Asia and the Indus valley. The Achaemenids began as rulers of a regional state, what we would think of as a kingdom—one "king" ruling an ethnically and linguistically homogenous group of people. How this situation came about involves a history of conquest over several decades: beginning with conquests by King Cyrus the Great (r. ca. 559–530) and his son Cambyses II (r. 530–522 BCE), the Persians defeated the kingdom of the Medes, in modern-day Iran, and then Lydia, in modern-day Turkey, and then Babylon, in Iraq, all between 550 and 539 BCE. A few years later Cambyses II (notice they are keeping it all in the family, another imperial trait) conquered Egypt, helping himself to a rich treasure trove and immense prestige. Imperial expansion slowed under later emperors, notably Xerxes and Darius, who launched multiple campaigns into such areas as Scythia and Greece, with mixed success.[7] This short summary should give you the picture: conquest of neighboring kingdoms and absorption of them under one polity creates the basis of an empire.

The tomb of Darius I (r. ca. 522–486 BCE), carved into a massive rock face at Naqsh-i-Rustam near his capital Persepolis, bears an inscription that neatly illustrates this idea of Persian overlordship. It lists the peoples and kingdoms over which he ruled:

> Media, Elam, Parthia, Aria, Bactria, Sogdiana, Chorasmia, Drangiana, Arachosia, Sattagydia, Gandara, India, Scythians, who drink haoma (an intoxicating ritual drink), Scythians with pointed caps, Babylonia, Assyria, Arabia, Egypt, Armenia, Cappadocia, Sardis, Ionia, Scythians who are across the sea, Thrace, Petasos-wearing Ionians (a type of hat), Libyans, Kushites, men of Maka, Carians.

---

[7]   Darius I, tomb inscription, reproduced in Susan E. Alcock, Terence N. D'Altroy, Kathleen D. Morrison, and Carla M. Sinopoli, eds., *Empires: Perspectives from Archaeology and History* (Cambridge: Cambridge University Press, 2001), 105.

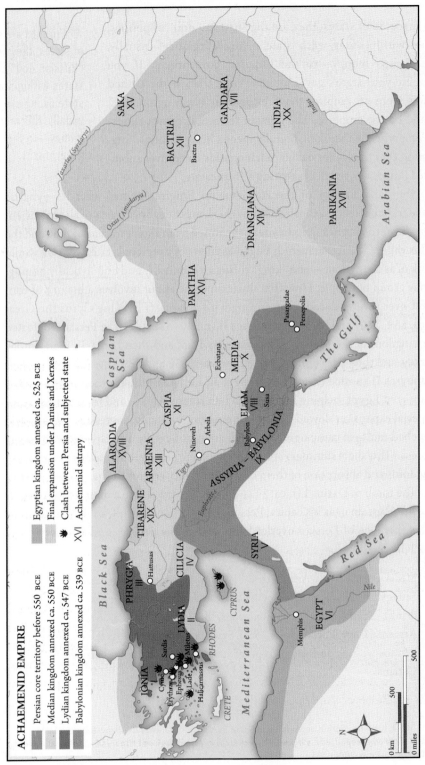

ACHAEMENID EMPIRE

Persian core territory before 550 BCE

Median kingdom annexed ca. 550 BCE

Lydian kingdom annexed ca. 547 BCE

Babylonian kingdom annexed ca. 539 BCE

Egyptian kingdom annexed ca. 525 BCE

Final expansion under Darius and Xerxes

✹ Clash between Persia and subjected state

XVI Achaemenid satrapy

Black Sea

Caspian Sea

Arabian Sea

The Gulf

Red Sea

Mediterranean Sea

Oxus (Amudarya)

Iaxartes (Syrdarya)

Tigris

Euphrates

Nile

Indus

SAKA XV

BACTRIA XII
Bactra ○

GANDARA VII

INDIA XX

DRANGIANA XIV

PARIKANIA XVII

PARTHIA XVI

MEDIA X
Ecbatana ○

ELAM VIII
Susa ○

Pasargadae ○
Persepolis ○

ARMENIA XIII
Arbela ○
Nineveh ○

CASPIA XI

ALARODIA XVIII

TIBARENE XIX

PHRYGIA III
Hattusas ○

CILICIA IV

LYDIA II
Sardis ○

IONIA I
Cyme ○
Erythrae ○
Ephesus ○
Miletus ○
Lade ✹
Halicarnassus ○

RHODES

CYPRUS

CRETE

ASSYRIA – BABYLONIA IX
Babylon ○

SYRIA V

EGYPT VI
Memphis ○

N

0 km   500
0 miles   500

MAP 6.4 ACHAEMENID EMPIRE The Achaemenids were one of the earliest "high-end" empires, directly controlling a large, diverse region. Connected by an extensive system of roads, trade prospered; and the centralized political and administrative system generally accepted local cultures and customs.

Tombs of the Achaemenid Kings, Darius and Xerxes, Province of Fars, Iran   Definition of an emperor? "I am Darius, the Great King, king of kings . . ."

Han China differs from Persia and Rome in that it inherited a largely unified polity from the Qin dynasty, which had created the idea of one entity called "China." To some extent, then, China, having done the work of unification some time before the Han, was on its way to governing more like a state than an empire, albeit a very big one. But the work was not complete, as historian Mark Edward Lewis explains: "One generation of imperial Qin was not sufficient to eradicate local loyalties and secure universal acceptance of an absolute autocrat."[8] After the Qin emperor, Shi Huangdi, died in 210 BCE, the political system he created collapsed. In the ensuing civil war, a general of peasant origin by the name of Liu Bang came to power and, in 202 BCE, proclaimed himself emperor (he was later known as Emperor Han Gaozu). Thus began the Han Empire.

Ancient Indian empires also fit the king-of-kings model. They left much fewer historical data than China and Rome however. The records we have come from Greek writers such as Megasthenes, who was a diplomatic envoy of the Seleucid Empire in Turkey (a dynastic offshoot of Alexander the Great's empire). The *Arthashastra*, an ancient text on Indian statecraft, also tells us something about the empire. But much of our historical data come from rock inscriptions in Greek, Pakrit, and Aramaic, the primary spoken languages in the region, in particular the Rock Edicts of King Asoka, described in Chapter 4.

---

[8]   Mark Edward Lewis, *The Early Chinese Empires: Qin and Han* (Cambridge, MA: Harvard University Press, 2009), 60.

The Mauryan kings of Magadha controlled multiple contemporary city states, which they had conquered in military campaigns. With their intensive agricultural development and participation in trade, principally along the Ganges River, they created a single polity, which controlled a large part of India's Gangetic plain and beyond. Historians generally see Chandragupta (r. ca. 322–293 BCE), the first Mauryan ruler, as having a humble background, although later Buddhist sources claim he was related to the Buddha, which was most likely a political attempt to confer legitimacy on the emperor.

Ruling from their base at Pataliputra, in the far northeast of India, the Maurya conquered a territory that stretched from Bengal in the east to Afghanistan in the west and to most of the southern part of the Deccan peninsula (modern-day India). Their polity was relatively short-lived, however, beginning around 322 BCE and dissolving after the death of Asoka in 232 BCE.

As a result of their conquests, empires ruled over diverse peoples, with multiple linguistic, religious, and ethnic backgrounds. Because of the difficulty of effectively governing such large areas, most empires devolved authority, and running costs, upon local rulers. Ancient empires were, therefore, tolerant of regional diversity and often set modest goals in terms of how much influence they wielded in far-flung provinces, seeing it as sufficient to receive tribute, or taxes, to make the effort of conquest financially worthwhile.

But "tolerant of diversity" did not mean egalitarian. "The concept of empire," say historians Jane Burbank and Frederick Cooper, "presumes that different peoples within the polity will be governed differently."[9] Ethnic differences within the empire ensured differences of treatment, as evidenced by Roman law. In the *provinces*—the conquered territories outside of Italy—Romans had their legal matters decided as in Rome, whereas non-Romans had to rely on local legal practices; and in cases involving Romans and non-Romans, still further sets of legal rules were drawn up.

But, as in nonimperial states, there were other divisions in the social fabric of the empire, most notably that of class. China was populated mainly by rural peasants. Many of these were small landholders, able to farm their land, a few acres under the Han, in return for a large cash or produce tax, which was payable to their local government representative. When payment was impossible, their land was often forfeited; and they would be forced to work harder to rent it back. Apart from peasants, merchants represented another class, often very wealthy.

The Roman republic was built by a system of citizen-soldiery, in which every citizen provided extensive military service. The lower classes, or *plebeians*, therefore actually wielded some power under the republic and had their

---

[9]   Jane Burbank and Frederick Cooper, *Empires in World History* (Princeton, NJ: Princeton University Press, 2010), 8.

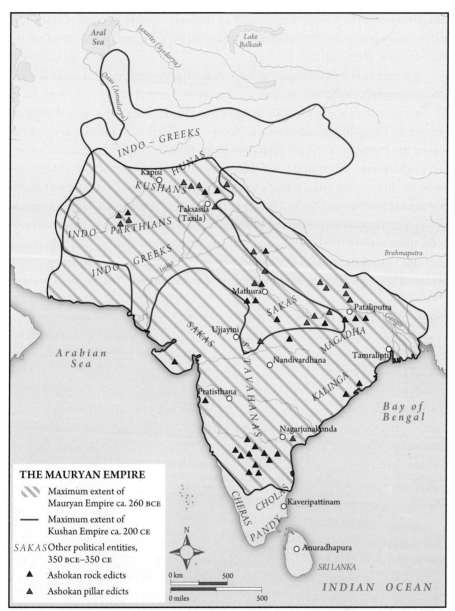

MAP 6.5 THE MAURYAN EMPIRE united large parts of the Indian subcontinent originating in the Magadha region of the Indo-Gangetic plains. Chandragupta's expansion west led him into the former administrative areas left by Alexander the Great.

representative, or *tribune*, in the Senate looking after their interests. With citizen participation at its core, Rome's soldiery felt some sense of ownership of military endeavors. The plebeians were not shy of standing up for their rights; "class struggles," says sociologist Michael Mann, "contributed much to the military effectiveness of the Roman Republic."[10] In the later republic the power of the plebeians waned as aristocratic families, enriched by conquest, gutted the institutional power of the Senate.

During the last two centuries BCE, extraordinary wealth, in the form of coin, precious metals, and other resources, poured into Rome from its conquests. Did a rising tide float all boats? Perhaps. But as archeologists from the Anglo–American project in Pompeii have discovered, Pompeii's society was sharply divided between the haves and the have-nots during the Roman Empire, in contrast to earlier Roman eras.[11] Preserved in volcanic ash from the eruption of Mount Vesuvius in 79 CE, Pompeiian villas tell of a world of elite aristocrats. In some cases multiple houses have been knocked together to make one enormous home, complete with separate quarters for slaves and servants. Earlier archeological remains reveal a far more standardized residential picture, with no such villas. The take-home message is that the wealth of conquest created distinct social inequality, which widened through the late republic into the time of empire. The many eateries or

Pompeii, Destroyed by the Eruption of Mount Vesuvius in 79 CE, a Place of Extreme Income Inequality in the Early Days of the Roman Empire

---

[10]   Michael Mann, *The Sources of Social Power: A History of Power from the Beginning to AD 1760*, vol. 1 (Cambridge: Cambridge University Press, 1986), 252.

[11]   "In Vesuvius' Shadow," InteractiveDig Pompeii, http://www.archaeology.org/interactive/pompeii/.

bars in Pompeii suggest that the majority of the population lived off a kind of ancient fast-food as thousands of peasants, thrown off the land to make room for huge estates worked by foreign slaves, poured into the city to look for work.

In Rome the situation was much worse. With a population of around 1 million in the early empire, it was the largest city on earth and packed with people living on the bread line. Crime was rife, disease endemic. Riches from ceaseless conquest created architectural splendor; the aristocrats to whom the treasure accrued spent most of it on themselves, building lavish houses and country estates and developing ostentatious lifestyles. Social safety nets were not a part of the Roman world, and poverty was such that there may have even been benefits to slavery—slave owners at the very least fed and housed slaves, even if they extended them no civil or human rights whatsoever; slaves could be raped, beaten, even killed with immunity.

Instead of welfare, the emperors instituted what they called "bread and circuses," for the diversion of the population: free bread was often available, and the circuses involved chariot and horse racing, which was wildly popular, as well as gladiatorial battles, which were held in amphitheaters large and small, the largest being the Colosseum in Rome, built around 70 CE under the supervision of the emperor Vespasian. Capable of seating 50,000 people, it hosted mock battles of hundreds of men, mostly captured slaves and some professional gladiators, mercenaries, and ex-soldiers, as well as battles against wild animals, thousands of which were imported from northern Africa, largely depopulating that region of these beasts. Nine thousand wild animals were killed over 100 days in Rome to mark the dedication of the Colosseum. Eleven thousand were killed to celebrate Trajan's conquest of Dacia (106 CE). These isolated "special" orgies of killing do not include the regular massacres. By the early centuries CE, elephant, rhino, and zebra were extinct in northern Africa and hippos, from the Lower Nile.

The circuses were a necessary diversion. Civil disorder was never far away, banditry was common in the countryside, and those lucky enough to have estates kept them well gated and guarded. Roman sources tell us about several slave revolts in the later empire, but whether there were plebeian uprisings is not so clear, as Mann points out: "We cannot really be sure whether it is revolts or records that are absent. The literate class did not seem keen on noticing or chronicling the discontent of their subordinates."[12]

The class and ethnic divisions of empire highlight the deeply stratified and exploitative nature of empires. Elites made history; their footprints remain. Their grand houses, public monuments, and literary records survived, while the remnants of the poor often disappeared with time.

---

[12]   Mann, *The Sources of Social Power*, 263.

The Colosseum   Built 1,900 years ago, it still dominates the modern city of Rome, recalling the grisly scenes that took place there for the amusement of the general public.

Who Was the Emperor?

Even an emperor needs legitimacy. Chinese political theories of legitimacy long preceded the Han. The *Mandate of Heaven* posited that rulers were divinely appointed but at the same time suggested that they could forfeit the position through unjust or foolish policies. The Han built on Qin models and developed more complex forms of legitimacy. Historian of the Han Sima Qian (ca. 145–86 BCE) recorded how, shortly after becoming emperor, Han Gaozu invited his advisers to tell him why he had triumphed in the civil war: "Speak to me frankly, and dare to hide nothing. Why did I gain the empire? Why did Xiang Yu lose it?" According to Sima Qian, it appears that the emperor was more interested in telling his own perspective rather than listening: after naming three of his top aides, whom he considered more skilled than he in their fields, Han Gaozu says, "These three are great men, and I was able to employ them. That is why I gained the empire. Xiang Yu had only Fan Zheng and he could not use him. That is why he was slain by me."[13] So is an emperor just someone who can delegate?

---

[13]   Sima Qian, *Shi Ji*, 8.380–81, quoted in Lewis, *The Early Chinese Empires*, 61.

Uniting the empire won Han Gaozu enormous prestige and helped legitimize his rule; the idea that the emperor should embody excellence and bestow benefits on his people had been part of the Qin's criteria for legitimacy. But there had to be more, and this is where religious ideology and the cosmic order crept in. Sima Qian reports that Gaozu's mother had been impregnated by a dragon, the "Red God," bestowing him with his extraordinary physiognomy. The Han court, at a later date, adopted the Qin's use of the "Five Phase Theory," which suggested that their rise to power represented the arrival of a new cosmic period. A story circulated within the Han that when he rose against the Qin Gaozu had killed a serpent, which was the son of the White God. The succession of the god of one color by another marked the turning over of a new cosmic phase. In this way the emperor was linked to something beyond mere mortal flesh. The implication was clear: his authority was from the heavens and not to be questioned by humans.

In this way the emperor was linked to something beyond mere mortal flesh. The implication was clear: his authority was from the heavens and not to be questioned by humans.

The Han emperor embodied the state. All state employees were his servants. All salaries and positions were gifts from him. In some later Han writing he is even referred to as *Guo Jia* ("the state"). All imperial proclamations had the force of law, and the Han legal code was, in fact, constituted in its entirety by the emperor's decrees, instead of a formal body of accepted legal doctrine, developed by scholars, like the Greco–Roman model.

The Han emperor was enshrouded in a host of rituals and rites whose origins date to much earlier times. Half of the capital, Chang'an, contained residences and palaces of the imperial family. Their tombs created a human-made mountain that loomed over the capital and required several nearby cities to maintain them. The religious leaders organized regular sacrifices and rituals among these tombs. A multitude of rules marked off the imperial being from ordinary humans, and transgressing these rules was often punishable by death.

Lewis makes the point that the formal Chinese bureaucracy had no permanent power base and was usually trumped by the "inner court," which was made up of those close to the emperor, his friends, family, and eunuchs, who frequently enjoyed close ties to the emperor. "As chief administrator, high judge, and chief priest, the emperor knew no limits to his authority, except the not-inconsiderable ones imposed by his biology."[14] Physical limitations sometimes provided a real check to imperial authority—as Lewis points out, some emperors were simply

---

[14]   Ibid., 64.

lazy and left the business of statecraft to the professionals. That may have reduced his authority somewhat, but for those looking for concrete checks on imperial power, it does not stand for much.

The Roman emperor was similarly all-powerful. The English word *empire* is derived from the Latin *imperium*, meaning the power given to the Roman kings to order executions, draft citizens into armies, and collect taxes. Rome, which was a kingdom at 700 BCE, became a republic in the succeeding centuries, in which power was shared between the Senate, a collection of rich old men, and the people (plebeians), collectively known by its acronym *SPQR* (*senatus populusque romanus*, "the Senate and the people of Rome").

Power sharing sounds like a great recipe for democracy; by evolving from a kingdom to a republic, much of the power of *imperium* was transferred to different government agents, such as consuls and praetors, who wielded civic and military authority and staffed major institutions in Rome's administration. But under the later republic, military leaders (such as Julius Caesar and Pompey) wielded disproportionate amounts of power, threatening the very foundation of the state and raising the specter of a return to monarchy. Ultimately, the republic dissolved into one civil war between Caesar, Pompey, and their followers (40s BCE) and another (30s BCE) between the remnants of the senatorial elite and Caesar's nephew and adopted son Octavian (later renamed Augustus), who went on to become Rome's first emperor.

In Augustus' early days, he sported a signet ring with Alexander the Great's head on it, showcasing his role model. When he developed more confidence, he replaced the image on the ring with one of his own profile, feeling no more need for role models. Like the Han emperor, he embodied the state, as his statues reflected (thus explaining why the candace of Meroë garnered so much satisfaction from burying the statue of Augustus underfoot). After his death, the Roman senate declared him a god, and he was worshipped by Romans in cults throughout the empire (this practice was continued with later emperors even if occasionally ridiculed; Emperor Vespasian, feeling he was nearing the end, is said to have quipped, "I think I'm becoming a god!"[15]). His personal finances were almost synonymous with the state treasury; conquests and inheritance had made him so wealthy that he was able to bail out the treasury from his personal property, like the president of the United States paying off the country's national debt from his personal bank account (which, as far as we know, has never happened). A state office called *fiscus* (loosely translated as moneybags) administered both the emperor's personal finances and the state's.

---

[15]   Quoted in Ian Morris, *Why the Rest Rules—For Now: The Patterns of History and What They Reveal About the Future* (New York: Farrar, Straus and Giroux, 2010), 286.

Upon his death, Augustus left instructions that a kind of autobiography, or list of accomplishments (*The Deeds of the Divine Augustus*), be inscribed outside his tomb in Rome and published throughout the empire. "These are the deeds performed by the deified Augustus," it reads, "by which he subjugated the entire world to the power of the Roman people." The use of the term "Roman people" reveals how he saw himself as the embodiment of them and the state itself. "I often waged war," he continues, "civil and foreign, on the earth and sea, in the whole wide world, and as victor I spared all the citizens who sought pardon. As for foreign nations, those which I was able to safely forgive, I preferred to preserve rather than to destroy."[16]

In a contrast to Chinese and Roman models, the Persian emperor Darius I did not claim to be a god but did allow himself the privilege of being selected by the "Great God" to rule over the earth, as recounted in the quote above. "I am Darius, the great king, king of kings," he proclaims, "king of countries containing all kinds of men, king on this great earth far and wide, son of Hystaspes, an Achaemenid, a Persian, son of a Persian, an Aryan, having an Aryan lineage."[17] Here he makes a big deal about his ethnicity, illustrating how the Persian Empire, like many, involved an ethnic hierarchy, privileging the rulers. The great majority of high officials in the Persian Empire were Persians, these positions being reserved, with some exception, for that elite group.

Why Do Empires Exist?

Empires both are born from expansionist policies and generate them. And strictly hierarchical societies are often more expansionist than others. As historian Charles Maier puts it, "Societies in which aristocracies play major roles and have organized their collective consciousness and efforts around military activity generate, and indeed inculcate, military values and often reward aggressive behavior."[18] When the Persian king Cambyses II, consummate warrior from a warlike aristocracy, conquered Egypt in 525 BCE, what greater reward could there have been than its untold riches?

Rome's military aristocracy led it in a similar direction. The origins of the transformation of Rome from republic to empire lie in the concentration of power in individuals, beginning notably with Julius Caesar and his military successes in

---

[16] *The Deeds of the Divine Augustus*, inscription in Rome.

[17] Darius I's rock inscription at Naqsh-i-Rustam.

[18] Charles S. Maier, *Among Empires: American Ascendancy and Its Predecessors* (Cambridge, MA: Harvard University Press, 2006), 45.

Gaul. Conquest made him extremely wealthy. He sent slaves and war treasure back home, bestowing "gifts" on the people, in effect creating an end run around the Senate and making himself popular. Caesar was wanted in Rome to stand trial for illegal activities before he left and for actions carried out in Gaul where he was campaigning (successfully, as it turned out). But Caesar knew that to return to Rome was suicide, and thus, he made the weighty decision to return to Italy at the head of his powerful legion, an action that was punishable by death under Roman law.

When he crossed the small river known as the Rubicon (which separated Italy from Cisalpine Gaul), he became a criminal in the eyes of the Senate. Fortunately for him senators were so terrified by his advance that they fled to country estates, allowing Caesar to enter Rome unchallenged. The ensuing civil wars were played out across the Mediterranean as Caesar pursued Pompey, the leader of the Senate, and his allies for the better part of a decade and ended when Augustus defeated Mark Anthony (Caesar's former ally) and the remnants of the senate leadership at the Battle of Actium in 31 BCE. "I raised an army," says Augustus in his memorial inscription, "with which I set free the state, which was oppressed by the domination of a faction." In terms of its expansionist policies, Rome was already an empire before it had an emperor. With the waning of the republican system it added dictatorship to military expansion, and the package was complete.

WHAT IS THE ECONOMIC MOTIVATION FOR EMPIRE?

Trade and war have always been closely related, for what cannot be bought can sometimes be taken. In commercial relations, parties (be they firms or individuals) require assurances that goods will be available at specific prices, in specific quantities. But in business, as in international relations, how can an entity ensure the benign behavior of partners? The more control one has over them, the better. Power is the only guarantee one's clients, friends, partners will act in accordance with your will. In other words, *if you want something done properly, own the means of doing it.* This is a nutshell explanation of why empires exist: an expansionist, militaristic policy better serves the exploitative and consumptive nature of states.

> This is a nutshell explanation of why empires exist: an expansionist, militaristic policy better serves the exploitative and consumptive nature of states.

The Mauryan Empire was the first polity in India to encompass all the territory from the Arabian Sea in the east to the Bay of Bengal in the west. This feat was accomplished by dogged military action and was probably not undertaken with the explicit intent of "unifying" India. "More probably," says historian John Keay, "its westward extension was intended to engross that lucrative maritime trade pioneered by the Harrapans in timbers, textiles, spices, gems and precious

Lion Pillar of Emperor Asoka (r. ca. 269–232 BCE)   Lions are often used to symbolize the Buddha, but this monument might also represent the power and extent of the Mauryan Empire.

metals between the ports of India's west coast and those of the Persian Gulf."[19] In this case, the Mauryans did not necessarily want to steal all those goods—that would have made too many enemies—but simply to be in a position to trade directly with the suppliers, instead of going through numerous middlemen.

In Han China, as in Rome or India, relying on "friendly princes" to remain friendly did not amount to security. Rome relied increasingly on its provinces for grain, with which it fed its impoverished subjects and its enormous armies. Egypt was famously referred to as the "breadbasket" of Rome; other parts of northern Africa also served this purpose. These areas eventually stumbled in their ability to supply Rome as they lost topsoil to erosion, becoming barren desert instead of

---

[19]   John Keay, *India: A History* (New York: HarperCollins, 2000), 84.

fertile breadbasket. Loss of food supplies has been highlighted as one of many reasons for Roman decline.

Sima Qian reports that toward the end of the first century of Han rule imperial successes had contributed to a very positive effect on economic indicators:

> The granaries in the cities and the countryside were full and the government treasuries were running over with wealth. In the capital the strings of cash had been stacked up by the hundreds of millions until the cords that bound them had rotted away and they could no longer be counted. In the central granary of the government, new grain was heaped on top of the old until the building was full and the grain overflowed and piled up outside, where it spoiled and became unfit to eat.[20]

Indicators of Rome's economic well-being generally rose in periods of expansion, too, and were at their height when the empire's territorial size was greatest. Rome's economy grew between 150 BCE and 150 CE in large part due to the resources that flowed into the empire from its provinces: booty from conquest, taxes from new subject populations, and trade. Slaves added dramatically to the empire's surplus production. In the early years of the empire, they made up an estimated 30%–40% of Rome's imperial population. Estate owners were free to squeeze all the possible labor they could out of slaves should they be so inclined because, as Mann points out, "agricultural slaves were denied membership in the human race."[21]

Do Empires Survive Through Military Force Alone? (Or, What Have the Romans Ever Done for Us?)

The British comedy troupe Monty Python satirized imperial resistance in their film *The Life of Brian*, in which they portray a group of Jewish freedom fighters plotting to kick the Romans out of Judea (modern-day Israel and the Palestinian Territories). Although this is a fictitious story, it refers to the Roman occupation of Judea, which began in 63 BCE. The leader asks his followers, "What have the Romans ever done for us?" The answer to this rhetorical question should, of course, be a resounding "Nothing!" But someone pipes up and mentions "the aqueduct"

---

[20]   Sima Qian, *The Records of the Grand Historian of China*, trans. Burton Watson (New York: Columbia University Press, 1961), 81.

[21]   Mann, *The Sources of Social Power*, 261.

(a structure for transporting water). Then another offers up the roads and another one mentions public safety, law, health, etc. When the list is finally over, the leader admits that, yes, these are all well and good but, apart from all of that, "What have the Romans ever done for us?" A pause. Then someone says, "Brought peace?"

Peace, as it turns out, was no small feat. The Roman and Han Empires had been wrought out of the destruction of massive civil wars. In China, the death of the Qin emperor plunged the country back into the turmoil of the Warring States Period. Liu Bang finally triumphed after several years of struggle, decapitated 80,000 prisoners of war, and pronounced himself emperor. Rome had experienced civil wars for some 50 years before Augustus emerged as the top dog. Both empires then began a prolonged period of internal peace. By any standards, what ensued was a period of remarkable prosperity, in which almost all indicators of productivity and living standards rose. Egyptian records from the Roman era show that their farmers were getting 10 pounds of wheat to every pound sown, a 10:1 ratio that was unprecedented in the ancient world. Technological innovations also greatly increased agricultural output, in particular the harnessing of wind and water. To date, all energy had been produced by human muscle or biomass power. In the first century CE, however, both Rome and China produced the waterwheel, which they employed to power bellows, to heat furnaces, and to grind grain for flour. Increased production at iron foundries and on the farm meant, quite simply, more stuff; and improvements in ship design and building produced better, cheaper, and larger ships that were able to move this "stuff" farther for less, creating economic benefits in the process.[22] All of this amounted to improvement in living conditions—as measured by such indices as overall population growth and average mortality. Notwithstanding the massive wealth inequalities in Rome and China, as archeologist and historian Ian Morris puts it, "Compared to earlier populations, Romans lived in a consumer paradise. Per capita consumption in what became the western provinces of the Roman Empire rose from a level near subsistence around 500 BCE to maybe 50 percent above it six or seven hundred years later." In both Rome and China, while much poorer than today, "compared to all that had gone before, this was a golden age."[23]

To avoid perpetual revolts, an empire must wield what political scientist Joseph Nye has called "soft power."[24] By this Nye is referring to nonphysical

---

[22] The word *stuff* is not particularly academic, we recognize. However, it sums up the meaning we want to convey here. With that proviso, do not use it in papers!

[23] Morris, *Why the West Rules—For Now*, 291.

[24] Joseph S. Nye, Jr., *Soft Power: The Means to Success in World Politics* (New York: Public Affairs, 2004).

Chinese Waterwheel, Invented in the First Century CE
The first conveyor belts, in China and in the Roman world, such innovations allowed for much greater productivity.

inducements for people to see benefit in a political system.[25] In most ancient empires there were, indeed, benefits that would have lessened the burden of being ruled by foreigners (Monty Python's aqueducts, etc.). Apart from the economic benefits of peace experienced by much of the populations within the Roman and Han territories (though not outside), the imperial culture would have provided a certain appeal. Ideas of justice, tolerance, and law, which developed in imperial centers, extended across the provinces. The Indian work *The Arthashastra* combines legalistic proclamations intended to provide a measure of security for the common people and criminalize certain abusive or antisocial behaviors. We find, for example, a section promoting freedom from sexual assault on the part of female slaves: "When a man commits or helps another to commit rape with a girl or a female slave pledged to him, he shall not only forfeit the purchase-value, but also pay a certain amount of money to her and a fine of twice the amount of sulka to the government."[26] And later we read what is probably one of the earliest written prohibitions against nonconsensual sex: "No man shall have sexual intercourse with a woman against her will."

---

[25]   There was considerable interest in soft power in the early years of the twenty-first century when the United States's forays into the Middle East were widely seen as imperial and scholars looked to the past for political models.

[26]   Kautilya, *Arthashastra* (New Delhi, India: Penguin, 2004), book IV, chap. 11.

The Arthashastra contains not only prohibitions but also specific penalties and punishments attached to specific criminal acts, such as this section dealing with marriage:

> If a woman either brings forth no live children, or has no male issue, or is barren, her husband shall wait for eight years before marrying another. If she bears only a dead child, he has to wait for ten years. If she brings forth only females, he has to wait for twelve years. Then, if he is desirous to have sons, he may marry another. . . . If a husband either is of bad character, or is long gone abroad, or has become a traitor to his king, or is likely to endanger the life of his wife, or has fallen from his caste, or has lost virility, he may be abandoned by his wife.[27]

There are ways, to be sure, that a state provides safeguards for its citizens. However, these are often wholly insufficient (as modern Indian women are finding in the case of rape) and often stacked against certain classes (as other laws were against women). But *The Arthashastra* represents the voice of the state as opposed to the voice of what we might call "tradition," such as is represented by the Laws of Manu (ca. 150 CE). These "laws" are a Hindu text, purporting to be a discourse by Manu, the progenitor of humankind, to a group of religious seers. As such, it has a less progressive tone toward women, laying out how women must be placed under male guardianship (father, husband, son) as they are not generally deemed worthy of independence.

All empires involved inequality, and prejudices against gender and ethnicity are near universal. Yet such early expressions of justice and equality, mediated through a body of law, often appealed to the ruling classes and occasionally even benefited the ordinary people, presenting us with a paradoxical view of imperial life. In Rome, law was a part of society from the early republic, and the Romans created the first legal profession, employing lawyers to interpret the law on a case-by-case basis. In the early empire it was not recorded in an orderly way, but from the mid-second century BCE jurists appeared in Rome, advising clients, teaching students, and creating legal documents.

For Romans, respect for law and ideas of civilized behavior were expressed in the word *humanitas*, the root of the English *humanity* or *humanities* in a scholarly context. Generally used to mean civilized behavior, it referred to such areas of life as education, relations with others, and limits on power and abuses thereof. Barbarians, considered the opposite of Romans, were not thought to possess *humanitas*, being instead ignorant, badly behaved, and possessed of poor personal

---

[27] Ibid., book III, chap. 2.

hygiene. While *humanitas* may have been a Roman preoccupation to begin with, the spreading of imperial culture through Rome's absorption of local elites disseminated these cultural ideas and practices beyond the Italian mainland. The concept of *humanitas*, however, also hid the reality of ancient Roman life, its brutality and inequality. The British rebel leader Galgacus, according to Tacitus, described the Roman Empire thus: "To robbery, slaughter, plunder, they give the lying name of empire; they make a solitude and they call it peace."[28]

Just like the ancient Mediterranean world, China had developed multiple philosophical schools, through hundreds of years of civilization. The two predominant schools in the Han era were the Legalists and the Confucians. The Legalist school was most influential during the Warring States Period and gained an important position within the Qin dynasty, under the direction of Shang Yang (Lord Shang, d. 338 BCE), the emperor's adviser. This school influenced the Qin in their rigid centralizing policies and harsh punishments for crime. It also contributed to decisions regarding meritocratic promotion through the ranks of the army and administration and to the sanctioning of private ownership of land for peasants.

The Chinese philosopher Confucius, or Kongzi (551–479 BCE), deplored Legalism and promoted a return to the beliefs and practices of the early Zhou, most centrally, perhaps, the importance of a religious and political elite aristocracy to perform ritual functions which would maintain the "balance" of the cosmos. Under the Han, Confucian ideas were recorded, systematized, and written down as a code of conduct. The ultimately conservative values of stability promoted by Confucianism gave the empire a moral structure (within which there was considerable variation). Burbank and Cooper surmise that "These values, like *humanitas* for Romans, provided a framework for elite education and ideal behavior."[29]

But China's intellectual fervor was not limited to these two ends of the spectrum. Notable for his secular and rationalist thinking, Xunzi (ca. 312–230 BCE), attempted to make Confucianism more relevant to his times and put forward the novel idea that natural disasters were not signs of divine displeasure with the leadership but random acts of nature. What was important about such disasters was how the leadership responded to them, a perspective that would be at home in twenty-first-century politics.

The Chinese were also committed to rule by law but under different assumptions: law was a set of rules emanating from the emperor, sidestepping the need for a separate judiciary as in Rome. But while law emanated from the emperor, it

---

[28] Tacitus, "Agricola 30," http://www.fordham.edu/halsall/ancient/tacitus-galgacus.asp.

[29] Jane Burbank and Frederick Cooper, *Empires in World History* (Princeton, New Jersey: Princeton University Press, UP 2010), 50.

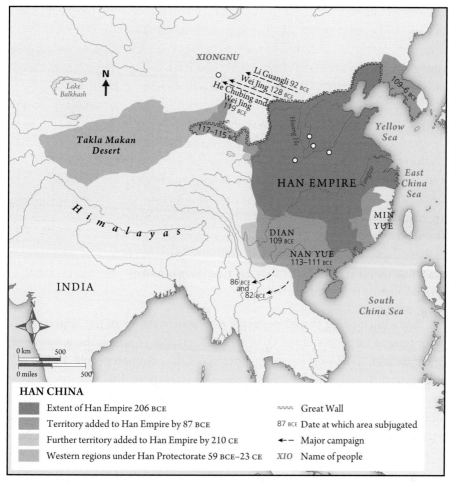

MAP 6.6   **HAN CHINA**   The Han dynasty was aggressively expansionist, colonizing areas as distant as modern Korea and Vietnam, in addition to continuing the Qin's struggle against the Xiongnu nomads in the northwest.

also had to be in accordance with religion. The relationship between Chinese religion and law was close and complex, going back to the time of the Zhou. The government was required to comply with religious beliefs, or the "laws of heaven and nature." Executions, for example, could only be held in autumn and winter, the seasons of death and decay. One story tells of an official at the time of the emperor Wu (156–87 BCE), who was tasked with executing thousands of members of powerful local families, for economic and political misdeeds. When spring came he reportedly stamped his foot and sighed, "If only I could make the winter last one more month it would suffice for me to finish my work!"[30]

---

[30]   Sima Qian, *Records of the Grand Historian*, 441.

Scene from the Life of Confucius (551–479 BCE), From the Qing Dynasty   Confucius was possibly the most influential thinker in China's history.

Notwithstanding the often deeply exploitative stance of the imperial Han state toward its people, Sima Qian tells of instances in which the government could be seen to be working in the interests of the common people. In 120 BCE widespread floods reduced many people to starvation. The emperor ordered provincial granaries to be opened and food to be distributed. More action was needed, however, so he then called upon wealthy families to make loans to the victims. When this was not enough, he resettled some 700,000 people in New Ch'in and south So-fang. "Food and clothing were to be supplied to them for the first few years by the district officials, who were also instructed to lend them what they needed to start a livelihood." The expenses of the move were of "incalculable proportions."[31]

Scant evidence can be found of comparable acts of Roman largess, with the possible exception of the bread and circuses. But the Romans nevertheless practiced a kind of economic development as they advanced through their provinces, usually as a by-product of satisfying their imperial aims. Mann describes this as the "legionnaires economy." The Roman army, divided into legions, was economically productive, building infrastructure as they conquered. Provincial cities were rebuilt with Roman architecture and specific attributes, such as grid systems, sewerage, and civic buildings like amphitheaters and coliseums, giving the conquered people Monty Python's proverbial aqueducts almost as an afterthought or accompaniment of Roman culture.

---

[31]   Ibid., 87.

Roads were essential to all empires; looking across the ancient world we see them spanning enormous distances. Built mostly by the army, Roman roads covered, at the height of the empire, some 52,000 miles. Likewise, a single Chinese road, the north–south highway of the Qin dynasty, finished around 210 BCE, was between 435 and 560 miles long. The Greek historian Herodotus (484–425 BCE) described the Achaemenid road system of the Persians this way: "Now the true account of the road in question is the following: Royal stations exist along its whole length, and excellent caravanserais [rest stops for "caravans"]; and throughout, it traverses an inhabited tract, and is free from danger."[32]

This road linked Susa to Sardis, with way stations providing food and rest at 1-day intervals. Use of these was restricted to imperial officials and controlled by issuing "passports" to users. Different empires had different restrictions on usage, but in many cases these roads lasted, in various states of repair, for centuries. If such roads primarily served the governmental and military needs of the empire, they had a "trickle-down" effect for residents and citizens: travel was facilitated and more goods were available; the economy in general experienced a stimulus from the new ease with which goods could move. If you have ever checked the "no-highways" box on your GPS for directions and driven that route, you will have some appreciation of the extent to which highways improve travel and, therefore, further economic development.

HOW MUCH CONTROL DID EMPIRES REALLY HAVE?

Emperor Han Gaozu began his career by separating the eastern part of the old Qin Empire and giving it to a collection of his relatives and warlords with whom he cut deals. This compromise was no doubt a necessary evil. He ruled the western part directly from his capital. But Gaozu's initial system ultimately proved unsatisfactory because the independent kings acted too independently. Like the Qin, later Han emperors found themselves struggling against powerful lords: "The main problem," say historians Merle Goldman and John Fairbanks, "was how to check the reemergence of aristocratic local families with their own resources of food and fighting men."[33] The later Han centralized increasingly. The emperor Han Wudi, perhaps the most influential of the Han emperors, did the most to increase the government's revenues, in part by establishing centralized

---

[32] Herodotus, *The Histories*, trans. Robin Waterfield (Oxford and New York: Oxford University Press, 2008), book 5.52-4.

[33] John K. Fairbanks and Merle Goldman, *China: A New History* (Cambridge, MA: Harvard University Press, 1992), 59.

government monopolies on salt, iron, copper, bronze, and alcohol. Direct rule of distant lands, however, was expensive; and at the end of his reign Han Wudi left the government struggling to pay its bills.

Some empires left the administrative structures of conquered states in place, using the existing elites to run them; those very elites were usually absorbed over time into the imperial elite and, thus, contributed to spreading the culture and ideals of the "center." This was Rome's *modus operandi*; the local elites were over time Romanized—in other words, taught Latin and educated like Romans of similar social standing. "After about a century of Roman dominance," says Mann, "it generally became impossible to detect local cultural survivals among elites of the western provinces."[34] Lack of obvious regional ties has been a hallmark of many "elites" in large states the world over as they tend to belong to a nonregional, or pan-imperial, culture. This being the case, how would there have been local resistance once the elite leadership had been co-opted? Rome's ability to re-create its class system was at the root of its success.

Even if empires last for centuries, often built-in flaws exist which eventually hit a nerve. The wealth generated by Roman conquests eventually destroyed a central feature of earlier Rome, participatory citizenship, making the naked exploitation and inherent inequality all the more apparent. There was a common saying as early as the third century BCE that provincial governors required three fortunes: one to recoup electoral expenses, another to bribe the jury at his trial for misgovernance, and a third for living expenses. If the fostering of Roman elite culture among the local leadership prevented locals from initiating independence movements, the concentration of power and wealth among so small a class might have played a part in the eventual downfall of the empire.

The Persians used governors, or *satraps*, throughout their empire, who were appointed by the emperor and reported to him. These were almost always drawn from a small ethnic Persian elite and made their capitals often in the former royal capitals that had been conquered; for example, the satrapal center in Egypt was in Memphis, the capital. The satraps collected and stored taxes for the empire, taking what they needed for the running of their province before forwarding the rest to the capital. There is, however, plentiful evidence that local governing structures were often left in place at the level below the satraps and that the Persian provincial authorities used these to carry out the business of government (very limited in terms of what governments today usually do).

> ☀️ This was Rome's *modus operandi*; the local elites were over time Romanized—in other words, taught Latin and educated like Romans of similar social standing.

---

[34] Mann, *The Sources of Social Power*, 269.

WHAT WAS THE ROLE OF THE IMPERIAL COURT?

When Emperor Han Gaozu died in 195 BCE, he left his 15-year-old son on the throne. Because of the boy's youth, the empire was indirectly ruled by his mother, the formidable Empress Lu. When her son died in 188 BCE, she placed an infant on the throne; and when that young emperor died, she replaced him with another baby. With this ruse, she managed to hold on to power until 180 BCE (luckily for her, infant mortality at the time was high). Although a competent leader, she was regarded by later Confucian historians as a ruthless usurper. After her death, her relatives were purged from leadership and power was restored to the Liu family.

As long as an emperor was young, power devolved to whoever could make decisions for him. During the Han's last century no adult ever reached the throne. Even if the emperor was too young to make policy, authority still rested in him; therefore, those closest to him made the decisions. These were often eunuchs, who, in addition to mothers, played a central role in Chinese court politics. Allowed into the emperor's inner circle, originally because they were recruited to look after the imperial harem, many eunuchs became confidantes, friends, and even lovers of emperors. In the later Han there were thousands of eunuchs, becoming so powerful that they were granted the right to adopt heirs of their

Remains of the Han Dynasty Wall, Keeping Out the Nomadic Tribes of the North West; But Sometimes Their Worst Enemies Were Inside, Not Out

own. In 159 CE eunuchs helped an emperor to execute the entire family of the mother of his predecessor, thus eliminating threats to his throne.

Court historian Sima Qian had firsthand knowledge of eunuchs because after enraging the emperor (Han Wudi, r. 141–87 BCE) with his support of a wayward general, the emperor sentenced him to death and then commuted his sentence to castration. He lived out the rest of his life as a eunuch, choosing not to commit suicide (the "honorable" way out) but to finish his historical masterwork, which today serves as the most important primary source for the early Han dynasty.

Why Do Empires Collapse?

"Empires are epics of entropy," says Maier, reminding us that decline is built in to the imperial experience. "Ultimately the lights will go dim on the imperial stage and the curtain will descend."[35]

The idea of "collapse" itself is often taken too literally, then, and gives the impression of instantaneous cessation of existence as opposed to a process of long, slow decline or a change of leadership followed by gradual dissolution.

Most of the ancient world's empires were taken over by outsiders and/or broken up into multiple small nations (as in the case of Rome's western empire, which eventually became the nation-states of western Europe). Such is the strength of ideas, however, that many imperial forms—political, social, and economic—continued under different people. The idea of "collapse" itself is often taken too literally, then, and gives the impression of instantaneous cessation of existence as opposed to a process of long, slow decline or a change of leadership followed by gradual dissolution.

There are lots of ways, however, for empires to collapse. Before Rome becomes a world power, Alexander defeats Darius III in 333 BCE at the battle of Issos. Within 2 years he has taken all of Persia. The Achaemenids are history. How could such an enormous and powerful empire fall apart so quickly? You have to look at the "back story" to answer this question. In 336 BCE, the Persian Empire is in political trouble. Battles over succession have weakened the imperial court; provincial rebellions, notably in Egypt, have weakened the economy and reduced the tax revenue; satraps are increasingly likely to make bids for independence. When Alexander arrives, with radical military strategies and veteran troops, he meets a fatigued imperial power that is in no shape to meet this vigorous challenge.

---

[35] Maier, *Among Empires*, 76.

Rome, by the time it "falls" is in poor shape also. In 410 the Visigothic king Alaric is able to "sack" it, riding roughshod over its cobbled streets. This defeat is, no doubt, crushing for those in Rome; but by this time the empire has already split in two: the eastern part now ruled from Constantinople (today's Istanbul), the west from Rome. Alaric's victory is often seen as a symptom of Rome's internal collapse, and for this there are multiple reasons, such as the profligacy of Rome's government, the incompetence—and assassinations—of its emperors, the overextension of its military, constant and persistent military action on overextended borders, and the influx into the empire of non-Roman people. All of the above cause a historic moan, heard around the imperial domain. As historians Burbank and Cooper say, "The imperial project based on conquest and the projection of a single civilization over the Mediterranean and its hinterland fell on many swords."[36] The rise of Christianity, which appears about the same time as Augustus, reorients Romans as their movement grows away from the focus on the earthly city to the "City of God"; and this arguably plays a part in undermining the empire, reducing Romans' feeling of loyalty and belonging to the state and providing an alternative identity.

In a somewhat similar fashion, after a rebellion in 9 CE under Wang Mang, in which a new dynasty (Xin) holds power briefly, a later, or eastern, Han dynasty (25–220 CE) reemerges with its capital at Luoyang. But after another 200 years, the empire reaches the end of its life cycle. Turmoil at the Han court weakens the government and allows provincial and military leaders to ignore the imperial capital and the dues they owe. As with all empires, cash is king, as our own global economy has learned; without cash, economic activity grinds to a halt and the winds of political change begin to blow. "Barbarians," in the form of nomads in the north and west, in particular the Xiongnu, threaten imperial territory, as they have always. The borders of the empire, extended as they often were, begin to be overwhelmed. The Han has paid the barbarians off for years, to prevent them attacking border towns. It is fruitless to chase them into the steppe territory, from where they emerged: the imperial advantage of huge numbers and concentrated infantry is lost in such a vast featureless landscape, where the enemy melts away. Without payments, the pressure from nomads builds until the dam begins to burst.

The later Han initiate a disastrous policy of ending peasant conscription. Instead, they rely on mercenaries and nomads from outside the empire, who they resettle in walled frontier towns. In the long run, this policy turns against them and creates disloyal units with their own tribal allegiances. In 184 CE a rebellion breaks out among the followers of a Daoist cult known as the Yellow Turbans.

---

[36]   Burbank and Cooper, *Empires*, 41.

This revolt spreads widely, and the country spirals into civil war, with regional leaders declaring their independence. The Han Empire officially comes to an end in 220 CE, splitting into three rival kingdoms.

Over and above these proximate causes of decline, there loomed larger and more menacing issues. In particular, China and Rome were affected by our old friend climate change, which, over the hundreds of years of imperial life cycles, was active once more. Much of the high point of the Roman and Han Empires took place during what scientists call the Roman Warm Period. This made several geographic regions more productive agriculturally, such as England, France, and parts of eastern Europe, as well as Korea, Manchuria, and parts of central Asia. Rome's command of maritime trade in the Mediterranean made it easy for it to exploit the gains to be made by such warming, by shipping goods where they were needed. The same was true, if to a lesser extent, in China, which used its many rivers as trade corridors.

But one consequence of this increase in trade and the mixing of peoples from different regions by trade, war, enslavement, or otherwise was the exchange of microbes. Diseases encountered when the first farmers cohabited with domesticated animals found new populations with little or no immunity to them, just as would happen hundreds of years later when Europeans took their diseases to the Americas. People exposed to such germs for the first time had no defenses. Increased traffic between core settlement areas around the second century CE exposed millions of people to these unfamiliar germs.

In 165 CE Roman soldiers in Syria suffered an unknown pestilence. A few years earlier, Chinese troops fighting nomads succumbed to something similar, losing one-third of their number. In the following decades outbreaks of deadly disease struck repeatedly in China and the Roman provinces, one of which killed one-third of the Egyptian population. Few records tell of similar events in India, and it is therefore possible that the germs passed north of the subcontinent, following the Silk Road routes into Asia. In the middle of the second century CE, for several years, some 5,000 people were reported to have died every day in Rome itself. And in China, especially in the northwest, several decades later, diseases similar to smallpox or measles showed up with deadly consequences.

Subsequently, the weather cooled again. All climatological sources point to a drop of several degrees between 200 and 500 CE. Rainfall diminished, and *monsoons* (annual wind patterns bearing heavy summer rains) lost their strength. With the advent of the Roman Warm Period, the empires in their younger days had responded with innovation; but this time around, hampered by major diseases and structural problems, innovation was not so easy to come by. With ecological factors combining (sometimes causing) political and economic challenges, the cycle of empire took a distinct downward turn.

All Things Come to an End: The Ruins Leptis Magna, a Major Trading City in the Roman Province of Africa in Today's Libya   By the Fourth Century CE much of the city was abandoned; Roman decline, environmental degradation, and a drop-off in trade all contributed.

Rome and China had many things in common over the course of their empires. One major point of divergence, however, is that Rome, once down, did not get up again, at least not in the west; it struck back temporarily in the east under the emperor Justinian. While the Han collapsed under similar pressures and China suffered a terrible setback in terms of its standard of living, successive dynasties ultimately reassembled China, and 2,000 years later its political integrity remains intact.

Conclusion: What Is an Empire?

Empires might decline and fall, but they seldom disappear without a trace. The legacy of Rome has been discussed endlessly in classrooms and lecture halls for generations, and Roman cultural and political forms have been copied repeatedly. One reason for this is the habit of invading barbarians to absorb the culture of the people they invade. Such "barbarians," frequently portrayed as uncultured and bent on destruction, are often quick studies and interested in furthering legacies. Not so "barbarian" after all but just unfairly stigmatized by imperial historians, these inheritors of empire usually pass along the "goodies" of empire because, as it turns out, good ideas are not just good ideas for Romans or Han or Persians. They are good for most people and, as such, eagerly exploited.

Rome's legacy lives on in multitudes of ways that can be seen in language and architecture all over the world. From the Russian *czars*, whose title derives from the Latin word *caesar*, to the emperor Napoleon, the British empress of India (Victoria), and the emperor Bokassa (of the Central African Republic), the ideas and aspirations of ancient empires live on, even if their political viability is limited. Ultimately, the sustainability of great empires is questionable. Such massive aggregations of power and wealth are subject to so much internal and external pressure that survival is a constant battle. Even if they survived for hundreds of years, in one shape or another (which is more, so far, than our present political form, the nation-state), empires and the states which spawned them still only represent a tiny fraction of human history.

Words to Think About

Autocrat	Despotism	Harem
Humanities	Orientalism	Plebeian

Questions to Think About

- Is an empire just a large state?
- Why where all the early large empires located in Eurasia?
- Are empires inherently expansionist?
- Do empires promote equality?

Primary Sources

Darius I's rock inscription at Naqsh-i-Rustam.

Herodotus. *The Histories*. Translated by Robin Waterfield. Oxford and New York: Oxford University Press, 2008.

Kautilya. *Arthashastra*. New Delhi, India: Penguin, 2004.

Polybius. *The Histories*, vol. 1. Translated by Evelyn S. Shuckburgh. London: Macmillan, 1889.

Sima Qian. *The Records of the Grand Historian of China*. Translated by Burton Watson. New York: Columbia University Press, 1961.

Strabo's Geography, book XV11, chap. 1.54. http://rbedrosian.com/Classic/strabo17d.htm.

Tacitus' Annals. Translated by Ronald Mellor. New York: Oxford University Press, 2010.

Tacitus. "Agricola 30." In *Complete Works of Tacitus*. Translated by Alfred John Church and William Jackson Brodribb, edited by Moses Hadas. New York: Modern Library, 1942.

The Deeds of the Divine Augustus. Inscription in Rome.

Secondary Sources

Alcock, Susan E., Terence N. D'Altroy, Kathleen D. Morrison, and Carla M. Sinopoli, eds. *Empires: Perspectives from Archaeology and History.* Cambridge: Cambridge University Press, 2001.

Burbank, Jane, and Frederick Cooper. *Empires in World History: Power and the Politics of Difference.* Princeton, NJ: Princeton University Press, 2010.

Fairbanks, John King, and Merle Goldman. *China: A New History.* Cambridge, MA: Harvard University Press, 1992.

Keay, John. *India: A History.* New York: HarperCollins, 2000.

Lewis, Mark Edward. *The Early Chinese Empires: Qin and Han.* Cambridge, MA: Harvard University Press, 2009.

Maier, Charles S. *Among Empires: American Ascendancy and Its Predecessors.* Cambridge, MA: Harvard University Press, 2006.

Mann, Michael. *The Sources of Social Power: A History of Power from the Beginning to AD 1760,* vol. 1. Cambridge: Cambridge University Press, 1986.

Morris, Ian. *Why the Rest Rules—For Now: The Patterns of History and What They Reveal About the Future.* New York: Farrar, Straus and Giroux, 2010.

Nye, Joseph S., Jr. *Soft Power: The Means to Success in World Politics.* New York: Public Affairs, 2004.

For additional resources, including maps, primary sources, and visuals, web links, and quizzes, please go to **www.oup.com/us/cole**

Maya Fresco from Bonampak The Maya took prisoners to sacrifice to the gods. Often, they were decapitated and the hearts ripped out. Such sacrifices played a central role in the cosmological order and served a sacred purpose.

Chapter 7

How Can We Explain the Similarities and Differences Between Religions?

12,000 BCE to 600 CE

Why the Children Must Die

In about 400 CE, in Meso-America, a Mayan priest cuts into the chest of an orphan, lying on a limestone slab in front of him. Four old men hold down his arms and legs as the priest removes the child's still beating heart, holds it in the air above him for the gods to witness, and utters several prayers. The child's spilling blood is collected and offered to the gods. Then, the priest's assistants take the boy's limp body and hurl it into a narrow hole in the ground, which opens up into a vast underground cavern filled with water. Here, the body will rest along with the bones of other sacrificial victims until discovered hundreds of years later by underwater archeologists.

This is how archeologists think that Mayan sacrifices were performed. Holes in the limestone crust which covers much of Meso-America give way to large caverns, and here large numbers of skeletons have been found. Not all of them were sacrifices; many were actually buried there. But others show distinct signs of sacrifice, such as rib cages broken from the inside as hearts are pulled out. While for us this grisly scene is horrific and unimaginable, to the Maya it represented a central part of a sacred system. Far from a freakish deviation from the cultural "norm," sacrifice was a central part of religious ritual in Meso-America, as it was in many other cultures and eras. Death ensured life's continuity.

THINKING ABOUT RELIGION

What Is Religion?

- World religions all exhibit some elements of these formulations: community is central to religion, the provision of answers also plays a role, relationship to a "higher power" is also key. Gods play a role, though not always.

What Is Tribal or Primal Religion?

- Animists must face spirits, some good and some bad. The major concerns of non-sedentary people—food, fertility, and physical security—can be affected by such spirits, so they must be influenced to act favorably toward their human neighbors.

What Are the Universal Religions?

- The major universal religions all originated between about 1500 BCE and 600 CE, namely, Judaism, Christianity, and Islam in the Middle East; Confucianism and Daoism in China; and Hinduism and Buddhism in India.

How Can We Account for the Rise of the Universal Religions?

- At some point in the first millennium BCE a new way of thinking about the world began to take hold. In certain parts of Eurasia, a new breed of intellectual began asking radical questions and putting forward innovative answers.

Conclusion

- The evolution of religion can be seen as part and parcel of the evolution of human social and political structures.

Introduction

Looking at human history from a big-picture perspective, we can see that what we often think of as "religion" has changed fundamentally over the last 5,000 or so years. The great world religions of today are relatively new, only going back, in most cases, 2,000 or 3,000 years.

The world, or "universal," religions all originated in a relatively short period of time, representing a distinct break from the kind of spiritual belief and practice that preceded them. But while there are clear differences between the universal religions, they also share certain underlying characteristics. What were these, and to what extent were they the product of common historical processes at work in the ancient world?

Some scholars don't even consider the sacred systems that prevailed before the emergence of the world religions as "religion" at all, preferring to call them "magic" or some other, more general term. The belief systems of tribal people[1] lack some of the key attributes that many scholars consider central to religion today, such as a single god; a moral code, usually written down in a sacred text; and a notion of personal salvation toward which the adherent strives. (Historians also refer to such religions as "salvation religions.")

Religion, as most of us know it today, however, is a product of what we have been calling "civilization," that is, agricultural, state societies based largely on urban centers, with distinct social hierarchies, centralized authority, and often imperial—or expansionist—tendencies. But it took several millennia of urban life for the universal religions to emerge; the earliest indications of what became monotheism in the Middle East (Judaism, Christianity, and Islam) can be located somewhere in the first millennium BCE. In China, Confucianism and Daoism also show up with their founders, around the middle of the same millennium. Although Hinduism has its origins long before this date, what most historians see as classical Hinduism emerges at this point in India, while Buddhism, itself a reform movement within Hinduism, get its start at a similar date.

In broad terms, nomadic hunter–gatherers, who accounted for all of the human population until around 10,000 years ago, lived in tribes. Their religious practices were inextricably woven into their daily lives, to the extent that their "religion" was indistinguishable from the rest of their culture. These tribal social systems endured into the era of towns and the earliest cities, and only with several millennia of sedentary life under their belt did major changes occur in religious practices. Among peoples who had never settled down, however, tribal cultural forms remained in place, in some cases until the present.

---

[1]   Terms are important—and complicated. *Tribal* is a case in point. Here, we could alternatively say *hunter–gatherer* or *nomadic*, but there are significant differences between these terms. What we want to highlight here is the difference between sedentary, agricultural societies and those that are not full-time sedentary, not full-time agricultural. Within these parameters there is room for variation.

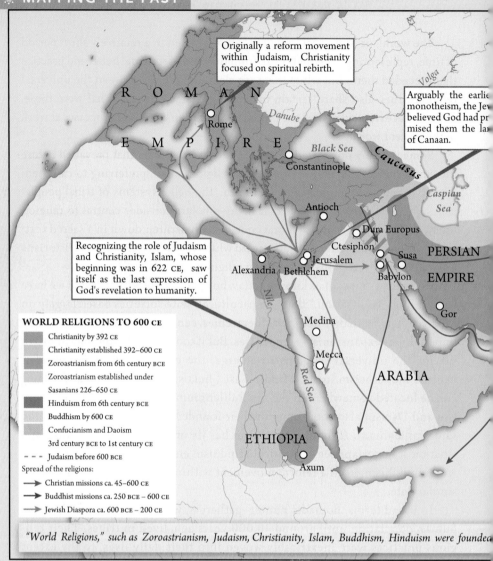

Originally a reform movement within Judaism, Christianity focused on spiritual rebirth.

Arguably the earli⸱ monotheism, the Je⸱ believed God had pr⸱ mised them the la⸱ of Canaan.

Recognizing the role of Judaism and Christianity, Islam, whose beginning was in 622 CE, saw itself as the last expression of God's revelation to humanity.

WORLD RELIGIONS TO 600 CE
- Christianity by 392 CE
- Christianity established 392–600 CE
- Zoroastrianism from 6th century BCE
- Zoroastrianism established under Sasanians 226–650 CE
- Hinduism from 6th century BCE
- Buddhism by 600 CE
- Confucianism and Daoism 3rd century BCE to 1st century CE
- - - - Judaism before 600 BCE

Spread of the religions:
→ Christian missions ca. 45–600 CE
→ Buddhist missions ca. 250 BCE – 600 CE
→ Jewish Diaspora ca. 600 BCE – 200 CE

"World Religions," such as Zoroastrianism, Judaism, Christianity, Islam, Buddhism, Hinduism were founde⸱

MAP 7.1   WORLD RELIGIONS TO 600 CE

◉ **10,000 years ago**
Göbekli Tepe in Turkey

◉ **800–200 BCE**
Axial Age in Eurasia

◉ **ca. 1500–600 BCE**
Zarathrustra

◉ **ca. 1500 BCE**
Vedic Period in India

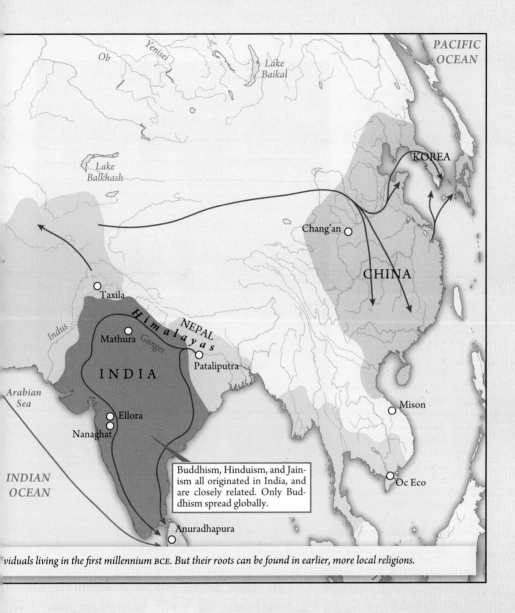

PACIFIC
OCEAN

Ob

Yenisei

Lake
Baikal

Lake
Balkhash

KOREA

Chang'an

CHINA

Taxila

Indus

Himalayas

NEPAL

Mathura   *Ganges*

Pataliputra

INDIA

Arabian
Sea

Ellora

Nanaghat

Mison

INDIAN
OCEAN

Buddhism, Hinduism, and Jainism all originated in India, and
are closely related. Only Buddhism spread globally.

Anuradhapura

Oc Eco

viduals living in the first millennium BCE. But their roots can be found in earlier, more local religions.

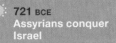

ca. 500 BCE
Siddharta Gutama
(Buddha) born

70 CE
Romans destroy
temple in Jerusalem

721 BCE
Assyrians conquer
Israel

ca. 570 CE
Muhammad born

Doorways to the Afterlife Maya sacrificial victims were sometimes thrown into underwater ponds, or *cenotes*, considered doorways to the afterlife, explored here by a scuba archeologist.

What Is Religion?

This may sound like a sociological question—and it is—but history borrows from sociology, among many other disciplines (and is richer for it); and in order to understand the history, we need to branch out from our narrow discipline on occasion.

Several major thinkers have outlined theories of religion over the last century or two, and these help to clarify the picture. Émile Durkheim (1858–1917), for example, defined *religion* as a "unified system of beliefs and practices relative to sacred things, that is to say, things set apart and forbidden—beliefs and practices which unite into one single moral community called a Church, [and] all those who adhere to them."[2] Notice there is no mention of "God" here since, defined broadly, religions don't always need one—or any. Durkheim focused instead on

---

[2] Émile Durkheim, *The Elementary Forms of Religious Life: A Study in Religious Sociology*, trans. J. W. Swain (London: George Allen and Unwin, 1912), 47.

the notion of "community" as he saw the celebration of community as one of the primary functions of religion, instilling a sense of belonging within members and therefore a sense of meaningfulness, which is central to religious thought.

Somewhat contemporary with Durkheim, Paul Tillich (1886–1965) was a Protestant theologian who penned what many consider the classic definition: "Religion," he wrote, "is the state of being grasped by an ultimate concern which qualifies all other concerns as preliminary and which itself contains the answer to the question of the meaning of our lives."[3] If you ever speak of someone doing something "religiously," this is Tillich's meaning. Again, Tillich does not single out a god and the worship thereof as major elements of his definition, drawing instead on the notion implicit in the Latin origin of the word *religare*, "to be tied or bound" (i.e., to whatever powers you feel might be in charge of your fate—be they God, as in the world's major monotheisms, or the spirits of nature, as in primal, or tribal religions). The "ultimate concerns" become substitutes, in other words, for god so that even the atheist can be religious if she or he is concerned with life's big questions and looks to a philosophy or system to clarify them. (It is as well to bear in mind the definitions of *philosophy* and *theology* here as well: the former means literally "love of wisdom," and the latter means something along the lines of "discussions about God." Philosophy, then, is more concerned with wisdom generally, while theology relates directly to a deity.)

Sigmund Freud (1856–1939), the "father of psychoanalysis," looked for the basis of religion in psychology and in his book *The Future of an Illusion* (1927) wrote that religion was derived from people's profound psychological needs. Gods are an expression of our need for answers to troubling questions central to the human condition. While fathers may have provided these answers for children, adults created a being, or beings, as a substitute for the authority of the father. Interestingly, even if he undermined the notion of a supreme deity, Freud's focus on *patriarchy*—the authority of the father—mirrored monotheism's patriarchal outlook, in which God is variously imagined as male.

All of these definitions get at something, and world religions all exhibit some elements of these formulations: community is central to religion; the provision of answers, or at least frameworks for answers, also plays a role; relationship to a "higher power," purpose, or order is also key. Gods play a role, though not always and not necessarily in a *transcendent* or all-powerful way. Wherever we look, however, and at all times in history, religion or spirituality is an active part of human life.

Wherever we look, however, and at all times in history, religion or spirituality is an active part of human life.

---

3   Paul Tillich, *The Courage to Be* (New Haven: Yale University Press, 1952), 156.

What Is Tribal or Primal Religion?

At the archeological site of Göbekli Tepe in Turkey, researchers found a sprawling complex of exquisitely carved stones protruding from the soil. Each one had scenes of wild animals—wolves, vultures, lions. There were no signs of habitation at this site—no hearths or garbage heaps. Was this, then, a kind of Stone-Age temple? The site dated back 12,000 years, which surprised researchers because this predated sedentism, so it was unlikely to have been a settlement.

☀ Did Göbekli Tepe, in other words, lead to sedentism, instead of sedentism leading to the building of religious monuments as previously thought?

The site clearly had major religious significance; hunter–gatherers were congregating in huge numbers here to perform sacred rituals, which may have led to major innovations in their patterns of subsistence and their use of the environment. (Did they domesticate plants and animals for the consumption of the worshippers? How else would they have fed all those people?) Did Göbekli Tepe, in other words, lead to sedentism, instead of sedentism leading to the building of religious monuments as previously thought?

More research is needed into the Göbekli Tepe site and doubtless others like it that will be discovered. It does, however, provide a tantalizing view into how religion is intimately tied to other elements of human existence. Hunter–gatherers were—and still are—animists. Animists do not worship deities who inhabit a different dimension or realm of reality. The animist world is not split between nature and *supernature*, between the world of humans and that of gods, spirits, demons, and other nonhuman, invisible entities. Nature and supernature are one, all occupying the same universe. This idea is referred to by historians as *immanentism*, the theory that "divine" or sacred presences exist within the material world, as contrasted with *transcendence*, which refers to divine entities existing in a different, transcendent realm.

Along with the challenges of the physical world, animists must also face spirits, some good and some bad. The major concerns of nonsedentary people—food, fertility, and physical security—can be affected by such spirits, so they must be influenced to act favorably toward their human neighbors. Spirits are summoned by group participation in rites and rituals, such as prayers, incantations, songs, and dance. Such practices are found in tribal peoples the world over and throughout history and very possibly were practiced at places such as Göbekli Tepe.

Another important aspect of tribal religion is that it is local by nature. That is to say, tribes inhabit certain territories and, therefore, see spirits as inhabiting certain locales as well. Anthropologists describe how land is of utmost importance to hunter–gatherers and, for that reason, view the forcible removal of tribal

The Göbekli Tepe Site would have taken a large work crew years to construct. But there are no dwellings in evidence. Was it some kind of religious site where hunter–gatherers collected to worship? How did the workers feed themselves?

people from their ancestral lands (a frequent occurrence throughout history) as almost akin to genocide since to divorce people from their land is to separate them from that which structures their sacred universe.

What Are the Universal Religions?

The major universal religions namely, Judaism, Christianity, and Islam (the three great monotheisms), all originated between about 1500 BCE and 600 CE, in the Middle East; Confucianism and Daoism in China; and Hinduism and Buddhism in India. All of these had stark differences, but they also had significant similarities, allowing historians to categorize them together and to recognize that universal religions developed as a response to certain common historical conditions.

WHAT ARE THE ORIGINS OF MONOTHEISM?

There are many indications of "supreme," or "high," gods in the history of early religion; but they often coexist with other gods and are rarely described as the sole deity and creator of the universe. But monotheism itself is a less hard-and-fast term than you might think; Christianity has a central notion of the Trinity, for instance, made up of God, Jesus Christ, and the Holy Spirit. To non-Christians, the Trinity may smack of polytheism. (Is it three-in-one or simply three "gods?") Christians explain this apparent inconsistency in terms of God having three "divine natures." Some commentators have even suggested that the Trinity reflects an earthly family, with God the father, Jesus the son, and the Holy Spirit being identified as feminine, therefore the mother. Even Islam, which arguably places the most emphasis on the singularity of God, has a deep history of almost folkloric spirits and demons, known as *jinn*, which exist in the supernatural realm and can negatively affect human lives. These beings, most likely incorporated from a rich tribal tradition in the pre-Islamic period, are inconsistent with strictly monotheistic ideas.

One of the first people in recorded history to make an explicit case for "one-above-all" was the ancient Egyptian pharaoh Akhenaten, reigning in the fourteenth century BCE. He is sometimes cited as the first monotheist as he destroyed the pervasive images of gods that adorned public places and closed temples in their honor, declaring the sun disk, or *Aten*, to be the source of light and the fundamental reality of the cosmos. Akhenaten's beliefs prefigure later monotheism's concern for a sole deity who is the creator and sustainer of the universe. But Akhenaten's monotheistic revolution did not stick; ultimately, he simply reaffirmed the intimate relationship between god and king (himself), which was traditional among the earliest or "archaic" civilizations and did not present people with a fully transcendent reality that they could access independently of the sovereign.

More or less contemporary with Akhenaten, between 1500 and 600 BCE—we don't know more precisely than that —a prophet appears in Iran by the name of Zarathustra. We use the term *prophet* in its original sense, which is one who transmits the words of god, as opposed to one who tells the future. With Zarathustra begins the Zoroastrian religion, which emphasizes the worship of the god Ahura Mazda, the source of all good in the world, in opposition to Angra Mainyu, the source of all evil.

Ahura Mazda probably originated as a member of the pantheon of Indo-European gods from the Aryan people of the central Asian steppes, several thousand years BCE or earlier. Zarathustra's promotion of Ahura Mazda from one among many to the One may have been a reaction to the popularity of a small

Monotheist
Pharaoh Akhenaten is often considered the first monotheist. But his brand of monotheism didn't stick.

group of gods preferred by a new breed of warlike Aryans, who, having discovered the use of the horse as a means of raiding neighbors' territory and stealing cattle, in the second millennium BCE, initiated a disastrous unraveling of a relatively peaceful way of herding life that had been around for centuries. All reactions have an original "action," and in this case it seems that the herding life of the steppe was affected by the introduction of the new technologies of horse and chariot, ultimately leading the Aryan tribes to commence their march across southwest Asia and eventually into India (either overrunning the Harappan civilization or, as seems more likely, stumbling over its remains—see Chapter 3).

Zarathustra's message was one of the earliest expressions of the dualism between good and evil. Humans, he taught, have the ability to choose between good and evil, and by their actions in life they would be judged by Ahura Mazda and receive their reward or punishment accordingly in heaven or hell. The Achaemenids recognized Ahura Mazda, as we saw in Chapter 6; but whether they actually made Zoroastrianism their official religion or not is still unclear. Unfortunately, there is so much doubt about the historical sources for Zoroastrianism, both its dates and its textual reliability, that scholarship remains largely speculative. What we can say is that the monotheistic idea was in evidence in this region during this time period and that it more than likely influenced later iterations of the one-god concept.

WHO WERE THE ISRAELITES?

Today, Judaism is one of the smallest of the world's great religions, accounting for less than 0.5% of the world's population; but with it monotheism arguably finds its first full expression. The historical records from Judaism's origins are limited, restricted to the Bible and archeology. Historians do not consider the Bible a historical source. There is a very weak consensus on such things as the dating of the biblical texts themselves, and although the Bible presents itself as a historical narrative, as sociologist Robert Bellah contends, "Every page serves a religious purpose and can only be used for the reconstruction of what happened by the most painstaking scholarly analysis, if at all . . . and the 'if at all' is no small problem."[4]

While this history is problematic, the religion is more clear, as the Bible, if nothing else, is a font of stories that reveal the self-image of the religion. We know that the ancient Israelites worshipped Yahweh, a god that may have originated as one of many tribal deities, in the communities of Canaan (today's Israel and Palestinian Territories) or farther to the south, as the Israelites were originally nomadic (tribal) pastoralists.

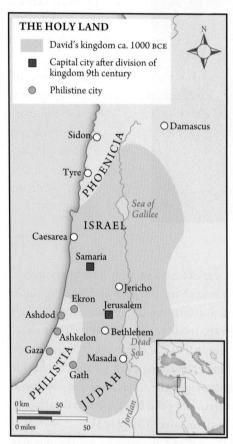

THE HOLY LAND

- David's kingdom ca. 1000 BCE
- ■ Capital city after division of kingdom 9th century
- ● Philistine city

N

Damascus
Sidon
PHOENICIA
Tyre
Sea of Galilee
ISRAEL
Caesarea
Samaria
Jericho
Ekron
Jerusalem
Ashdod
Ashkelon
Bethlehem
Dead Sea
Gaza
Masada
PHILISTIA
Gath
JUDAH
0 km   50
0 miles   50
Jordan

MAP 7.2   THE HOLY LAND   After King Solomon's death in 926 BCE the kingdom of Israel split into those of Judah and Israel. In 70 CE Rome conquered and occupied Judah and destroyed the Jewish Temple.

---

4   Robert Bellah, *Religion in Human Evolution: From the Paleolithic to the Axial Age* (Cambridge, MA: Harvard University Press, 2011), 283.

The people of the hills of Canaan developed a distinctive religion and society, based on the exclusive worship of Yahweh. The Bible says that God told Abraham, the first Jewish patriarch, who likely lived around 1800 BCE, that his descendants would inherit Canaan, the "Promised Land." According to the book of Genesis, the Israelites had been enslaved by the Egyptian pharaohs for several hundred years. God sent Moses as a leader to liberate them. He accomplished this task after parting the Red Sea and walking across to the Sinai Peninsula. Thereafter, according to the Bible, they spent 40 years "wandering" (here we can assume a nomadic, pastoral existence in the Sinai—not unlike some of the remaining Bedouin herders today but without the pickups and televisions) until, under the leadership of Joshua, they entered Canaan. It was during their sojourn in the Sinai that God revealed the *Torah* ("teaching" or "instruction"), which was later organized into the first five books of the Bible.

The Bible tells us how, on Mount Sinai, God makes a covenant (agreement) with the Israelites, via Moses: "'You yourselves have seen what I did to Egypt, and how I carried you on eagles' wings and brought you to myself. Now if you obey me fully and keep my covenant, then out of all nations you will be my treasured possession. Although the whole earth is mine, you will be for me a kingdom of priests and a holy nation'" (Exodus 19:4–6).

The Hebrew word for "holy," *qadosh*, means literally "set apart"; and this is how the Israelites were to be considered.

St. Catherine's Monastery in the Sinai Desert, Egypt, is believed to be the site of the burning bush, where Moses received the Ten Commandments.

Among the revelations to Moses were the famous Ten Commandments, which form the basis of Judaic law. As the Bible tells it, God spoke to Moses:

> I am the LORD your God, who brought you out of Egypt, out of the land of slavery.
>
> You shall have no other gods before me.
>
> You shall not make for yourself an image in the form of anything in heaven above or on the earth beneath or in the waters below. You shall not bow down to them or worship them; for I, the LORD your God, am a jealous God, punishing the children for the sin of the parents to the third and fourth generation of those who hate me, but showing love to a thousand generations of those who love me and keep my commandments. (Exodus 20:2–6)

Idolatry was widespread, and there were plenty of gods to choose from. God's message to the Israelites, though, is that the game is changing. As the sociologist S. N. Eisenstadt puts it, the major characteristic of Israel's cultural change was

> the emergence of the monotheistic conception of God, a transcendental God who created the universe and imposed his will and law on it, who calls many nations to account to His precepts, and who recognizes the people of Israel as having entered into a specific contractual relation with Him, not because he is a tribal deity, but because He is a universal God who has chosen the people of Israel with whom to enter into a covenant.[5]

The human challenge, as conceived in Judaism, is to live in harmony with the will of God; and the greatest obstacle to this is sin. Each individual has free will to follow the ordained path or not, and the surest way to avoid sin and achieve harmony with God is study and practice of the Talmud Torah, God's teaching or revelation. Jews have a particular advantage in that the Torah was revealed only to them, hence the emphasis in Judaism on scholarly study. The Ten Commandments are merely the tip of the iceberg as far as Judaic law is concerned; in total there are some 613 commandments to be followed, together known as the *halakha*.

WHO WAS JESUS?

Judaism created the seedbed for Christianity, and it was as a reform movement that Christianity got its start. Since Jesus was a Jew, it is no surprise that Christianity shares much with Judaism. To Christians, Jesus of Nazareth is

---

[5] S. N. Eisenstadt, "The Axial Age Breakthrough in Ancient Israel," in *The Origins and Diversity of Axial Age Civilizations*, ed. S. N. Eisenstadt (New York: State University of New York Press, 1989), 128.

believed to be the Son of God, or as the Bible puts it, the "Word" of God, made flesh (John 1:14). For Christians, accepting Jesus is the path to salvation: "I am the way and the truth and the life," says Jesus in the gospel of John (14:6). "No one comes to the Father except through me. If you really know me, you will know my Father as well. From now on, you do know him and have seen him."

The main source for Christianity is the New Testament, a collection of four "gospels" as well as letters and other documents describing the life and teaching of Jesus and his disciples. According to Christians, the New Testament bears out the idea that Jesus is the *Christ* or the *Messiah*—literally, "the anointed one"— whose coming was foretold by the Jewish prophets. In addition to the four gospels of Matthew, Mark, Luke, and John, the New Testament includes letters by the apostle Paul (ca. 5–67 CE) and others, in addition to a description of the end of time, in the book of Revelation, and a short history of the early church.

Jesus' message was one of love, compassion, forgiveness, and understanding. Many of these ideals are also expressed in Judaism, but Jesus' teaching pushed these to the fore to become the hallmark of Christianity. The Beatitudes, in the Sermon on the Mount in the gospel of Matthew, express many of the Christian ideals:

> And seeing the multitudes, he went up into the mountain: and when he had sat down, his disciples came unto him: and he opened his mouth and taught them, saying,
>
> "Blessed are the poor in spirit: for theirs is the kingdom of heaven.
>
> Blessed are they that mourn: for they shall be comforted.
>
> Blessed are the meek: for they shall inherit the earth.
>
> Blessed are they that hunger and thirst after righteousness: for they shall be filled.
>
> Blessed are the merciful: for they shall obtain mercy.
>
> Blessed are the pure in heart: for they shall see God.
>
> Blessed are the peacemakers: for they shall be called sons of God.
>
> Blessed are they that have been persecuted for righteousness' sake: for theirs is the kingdom of heaven.
>
> Blessed are ye when [men] shall reproach you, and persecute you, and say all manner of evil against you falsely, for my sake.
>
> Rejoice, and be exceeding glad: for great is your reward in heaven: for so persecuted they the prophets that were before you." (Matthew 5:1–12)

Like Jews, then, Christians believe in one god, who is the creator of the universe and the highest reality and that to act in accordance with His will is the ultimate goal of life. In sending Jesus into the world, God united his divine nature with his human nature, in the process healing the flaws in the latter. But whereas Judaism emphasizes study of the Torah as a major path to righteousness, Christians focus on the concept of spiritual rebirth as the main method for overcoming sin and living close to God's will. Christians are called upon to help bring about the kingdom of God—that is, the new order of love, compassion, and justice, a new existence in which death will be overcome, just like Jesus overcame death on the cross.

WHAT RELATIONSHIP DOES ISLAM HAVE TO JUDAISM AND CHRISTIANITY?

Were you to walk the streets of Cairo, Damascus, Jakarta, or many other cities in the world, you would likely hear this at certain times throughout the day, broadcast through loudspeakers: *Allahu Akbar, Allahu Akbar, la Ila Allah, wa Muhammad Rasoul Allah.* This is the Muslim call to prayer. "God is Great. God is Great." It goes. "There is no god but God, and Muhammad is the Prophet of God." This profession of faith, the *Shahada*, is central to Islam. In saying this, the Muslim witnesses the uniqueness of God, which is the central tenant of the religion.

While the historic heartland of Islam is the Middle East, it is truly a universal religion—in the geographic sense first of all—spreading soon after its arrival with lightning speed across the Middle East, northern Africa, and east into Asia

A Page from a Fifteenth-Century Koran   Muslims believe it to be the literal word of God, as revealed to the prophet Muhammad by the angel Gabriel in a 23-year period starting in 632 CE.

and making up today a body of some 1.2 billion believers. The last great monotheism to appear, the story of its origin is told in the Koran, Islam's holy book. In
about 570 CE, a boy named Muhammad was born in the town of Mecca, halfway
down the western side of the Arabian Peninsula in what is today's Saudi Arabia.
While the place may have seemed somewhat isolated, if you look at a map, it was
in fact a kind of entrepôt, a trading way station between the distant lands of India
and the markets of Mediterranean Africa and the Levant and beyond. It was also
a special site of pilgrimage, housing a large ritual site, known as the Kaaba, to
which people from outlying areas made pilgrimages in order to visit many different gods. Today, the Kaaba is exclusively associated with Islam and is the
religion's holiest place.

The Koran says that when Muhammad was about 40 years old he was medi-
tating in a cave outside the city. Suddenly he was gripped by a powerful force,
which told the terrified Muhammad, "'Recite! Recite in the name of your Lord
who has created, created man out of a germ cell. Recite, for your Lord is the most
generous one, who has taught by the pen, taught man what he did not know.'"[6]
This "force" was the angel Gabriel (*Jibreel*, in Arabic), and thus began years
of revelations from God, which would lay out the foundations of the religion
of Islam.

The revelations that make up the body of the Koran were recorded by
Muhammad's followers and compiled after his death into several versions. The
revelations situate Muhammad in a line of prophets stretching from the earliest
Jewish prophets, like Moses, through to later, Christian ones. The revelation of
the Koran is to be God's last revelation to humanity, Muhammad to be the last
messenger, or "Seal of the Prophets."

The word *Islam* means "surrender" or "submission," and a Muslim, therefore,
is one who surrenders to the will of God and seeks to realize God's will in the
world. Not unlike the message of God to the Jews, the Muslims are told that they
are a special "chosen" people: "You are the best community ever brought forth for
mankind, enjoining what is good and forbidding evil" (Koran 3:110). Despite
significant differences, Islam shares much with Judaism and Christianity, and the
Koran talks about these two religions in a special category as *Ahl al-Kitab*, or
"People of the Book" (i.e., the Bible). All three traditions share a belief in one god,
creator and sustainer of the universe; all believe in moral struggle against sin,
accountability, judgment, and an afterlife comprising either eternal punishment
or reward.

Ultimately, Islam is deeply connected to Judaism and Christianity. Of particular importance is the notion that the Koran's message is not new: it has existed

---

6   *The Koran Interpreted: A Translation*, trans. A. J. Arberry (New York: Touchstone, 2005), 96:1–5.

eternally, outside time, and has been revealed before: "Indeed We sent forth among every nation a messenger saying: Serve your God and shun false gods" (Koran 16:36). The Koran is populated with the same names as the Bible, though in their Arabic form: Ibrahim (Abraham), Musa (Moses), Sulayman (Solomon), etc. Mary, the mother of Jesus, is actually mentioned more often in the Koran than in the Bible. Jesus himself, although held in high esteem by Muslims, is seen as one of the great prophets: "I am God's servant," says an infant Jesus in the Koran, "God has given me the book, and made me a prophet" (Koran 19:30).

It may seem surprising, when you consider the close similarities between the world's largest monotheisms and their shared heritage, that historically so much

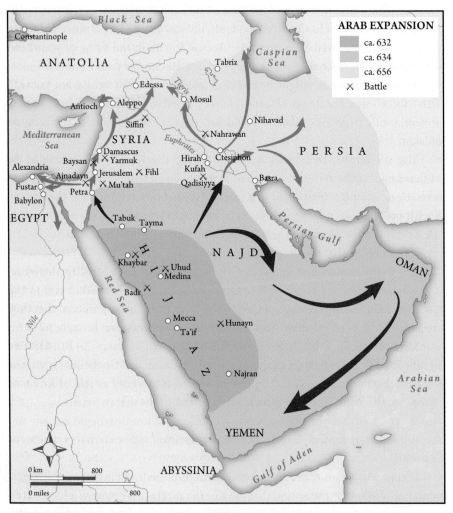

MAP 7.3   ARAB EXPANSION   Once united, the Arab tribes had nowhere to go but out of the Arabian Peninsula, where they encountered the declining and warring Sassanian and Byzantine Empires.

conflict has taken place between their adherents. Such conflict is perhaps a little less hard to understand given the almost
equal conflict within all of these religions as different ideas
and groups competed to establish what was "orthodox" among
an ever-growing body of believers. Religions are intermin-
gled, therefore, with the tensions endemic to political and
economic life and, as such, are vulnerable to conflict.

> It may seem surprising, when you consider the close similarities between the world's largest monotheisms and their shared heritage, that historically so much conflict has taken place between their adherents.

DO YOU NEED A GOD TO QUALIFY AS A "UNIVERSAL RELIGION"?

Three of the world's great religions originated in India: Hinduism, Jainism, and
Buddhism. In much the same way that Middle Eastern religions share commonalities of history as well as theology, the Indian spiritual traditions are intimately
related, sharing concepts, deities, and historical backgrounds.

Hinduism is the oldest of India's religious traditions for which we have any
written records; Buddhism and Jainism developed largely as reform movements
within it. Often considered a collection of religions rather than one, Hinduism
has arguably less unity than any other of the world religions. "Hinduism" was the
name given to practices of the "Hindus," that is, people of the Indus Valley, by the
conquering Muslims in the early middle ages. The British used the same term,
which tended to group all the various gods and practices and beliefs of the Deccan
Peninsula and the Indian subcontinent into one giant religion, even if there was
little evidence for its unity.

The roots of what has also been called "Vedic religion" (following the *Vedas*,
collections of hymns and prayers) go back to before 1500 BCE. Traditionally
thought to have been part of the "Aryan" legacy as the nomadic groups from
the west moved into and across India, historical opinion now tends to look at
the culture of the Aryans as a blending of immigrant and local—Indian—
practices, in particular ritual sacrifices of animals and fire rituals dedicated
to several key gods. These polytheistic beliefs and fire rituals are described
in the earliest texts that remain from this period, four Vedas, collected and read
by the elite between about 1500 and 500 BCE, the oldest of which is the
Rig Veda.

The earliest phase of Vedic hymns was dominated by the notion of *rita,* or the
natural order. Ritual sacrifices maintained this natural order, especially sacrifices
of cattle and other animals, as well as offerings of food. Fire, represented by the
ancient Indo-European god Agni, was, and still is, vital to Hindus; and the rituals
were performed by a special class of priests known as Brahmin, who are still
considered the highest class, or *caste,* in Indian society.

This excerpt from the Rig Veda praises Agni, a central figure in the Vedic pantheon:

> I call upon Agni, the one placed in front, the divine priest of the sacrifice, the invoker, the best bestower of gifts.
>
> Agni is worthy of being called upon by seers past and present: may he bring the gods here!
>
> Through Agni may one obtain wealth and prosperity day by day, splendid and abounding in heroic sons.
>
> O Agni, the sacrifice and work of the sacrifice, which you encompass on all sides—that alone goes to the gods.
>
> May Agni, the invoker who has the powers of a sage, true and most brilliant in glory, come here, a god with the gods![7]

There are clear echoes here of much more ancient religious practices; yet Agni is no abstract force of nature, being compared to a father, something that has clear resonance with later monotheism (and Freud's definition of religion).

Naked, and Liberated   Indian *sadhus* (ascetics) descend steps to bathe in the river Ganges during a religious festival. *Sadhus* dedicate their lives to achieving spiritual liberation (*moksha*) by contemplating Brahman.

---

[7]   Paul Brians, et al., eds. *Reading About the World*, vol. 1, 3rd ed. (San Diego, CA: Harcourt Brace, 1999), http://public.wsu.edu/~brians/world_civ/worldcivreader/world_civ_reader_1/rig_veda.html.

Around 1000 BCE we see a shift of emphasis in Vedic thought. A new collection of hymns, the Upanishads, reflects a tendency toward asceticism; and they
lay out several concepts key to Hinduism. Central among these is the concept of
Brahman. *Brahman* connotes the supreme, or ultimate, reality, a kind of cosmic
consciousness, perhaps synonymous with "God," although Hindus see this as
beyond even gods, who draw their vital energy from Brahman. Amid an ocean of
divinities in the Hindu pantheon, only a few stand out as heavy-hitters; Brahma
(not to be confused with Brahman) is the creator god, who himself proceeds from
Brahman. Vishnu and Shiva also originate in Brahman, Vishnu representing
stability, order, and continuity, while Shiva represents the engine of change in the
world, the beginning and the end. While each of these gods has its own distinct
characteristics, many Hindus see them as different faces of the same god. The
Upanishads puts it like this:

> This is the truth: As from a fire aflame thousands of sparks come forth, even so
> from the Creator an infinity of beings have life and to him return again. . . .
> Radiant in his light, yet indivisible in the secret place of the hearth, the Spirit is
> the supreme abode wherein dwells all that moves and breathes and sees. Know
> him as all that is, and all that is not, the end of love-longing beyond understand-
> ing, the highest in all beings.[8]

Whereas early Vedic texts focus on the maintenance of the natural order, or *rita*,
the Upanishads are more concerned with reincarnation, the law of *karma* and the
idea of *dharma*, or "duty." The basis of this is the quest for liberation (*moksha*) or
release from the world and its hardships (*samsara*). The human quest, then, is to
realize that the individual spirit (*atman*) is part of Brahman and through religious
practice can be reunited with it, through *moksha*, a process sometimes compared
to an air bubble bursting through the surface of the water, its contents mixing
with the air. At the center of the universe is the energy principle of *karma*, which
suggests that all actions create a reaction, in an endless cycle. With proper *karma*,
an individual's incarnations become increasingly better until he or she becomes
one with Brahman, achieving *moksha*.

Anyone going to a yoga studio is partaking in Hinduism's main spiritual
activity; what may sometimes seem like an exotic kind of aerobics actually got its
start several thousand years ago, being the series of disciplined practices which

---

[8] *The Upanishads: Breath of the Eternal*, trans. Frederick Manchester (New York: Mentor Books, 1957),
Mundaka Upanishad a. "Brahman, the Source and End of All," and b. "Brahman, the Infinite, Hidden in
the Heart."

unify and focus spiritual powers. The ultimate aim of this practice is the realization of the "human essence," or *atman*. First described in the Upanishads, these practices were codified later in the *Yoga Sutras*; and they were written with a highly advanced spiritual elite in mind, those aiming to escape the suffering of the world by "burning up" all their past karma.

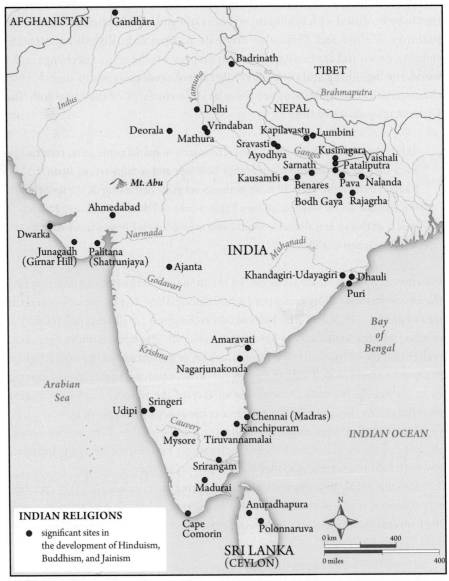

MAP 7.4   INDIAN RELIGIONS   Buddhism, Hinduism, and Jainism are India's contribution to major religions. Buddhism, an outgrowth of Hinduism, was the only one that gained wide popularity outside the Indian subcontinent.

The ultimate goal in yoga—something they don't dwell on much in the studio—is *kaivalya*, an awareness that is perfectly at one with *atman*. The yoga practitioner who reaches this state is said to be able to put an end to *karma* and will experience *moksha*. Thus freed from the darkness of ignorance and desire, the seeker is thought to become capable of supernatural feats, such as clairvoyance, telepathy, and "extraordinary" travel. These skills require more than a few back-bends to achieve.

IS BUDDHISM EVEN A RELIGION?

From Hinduism emerged two other traditions in India, Jainism and Buddhism. Unlike Hinduism, which is unique among all the religions we have discussed so far, for having no central or historic founding figure, Buddhism and Jainism each had founding figures. Mahavira (ca. 599–527 BCE), said to have been a prince from the state of Bihar (near Bengal in northeast India), founded Jainism, preaching a message focusing on the need to free the soul from its continual journey from birth to death, a journey of perpetual suffering. Rejecting the Vedic focus on multiple deities, Mahavira emphasized the veneration of individuals who had lived exemplary lives as well as the need to live a life of absolute respect for other living things. This antipathy to hurting any life form meant that many Jains were restricted from everyday pastimes such as farming or fishing, which tend to involve the taking of lots of innocent (nonhuman) lives. They were strict vegetarians and even sometimes refrained from sitting on chairs so as not to kill microorganisms. But Jainism remained a strictly Indian religion and was mostly confined to that country.

Not so for Buddhism, which, while originating in India, spread globally over several centuries. Buddhism also relies on the teachings of one individual, Siddhartha Gautama, the Buddha or "Enlightened One." The Buddha is usually thought to have been the prince of a small state in northern India, born around 500 BCE, a time in Indian history of multiple small kingdoms and chiefdoms.

Head of the Buddha Carved Into the Roots of a Tree at a Buddhist Temple in Thailand
As the religion spread, likenesses of Siddhartha became objects of meditation and veneration.

According to legendary accounts, Siddhartha's father attempted to shield him from the ugliness and chaos of the world. Some evidence indicates that this was a particularly ugly and chaotic period—unless you were unusually privileged. Such shielding from the world's hardships, however, could only last so long. In his twenties, Siddhartha took a ride outside the palace gates, where he encountered four sights which stayed with him forever and persuaded him of the need to undertake a journey of spiritual discovery: a sick man, an old man, a dead man, and a *sramana* or "seeker," someone who pursued ascetic practices like yoga to discover the essence of life and consciousness.

Having witnessed life with all its flaws—namely, suffering and death—he found it impossible to continue his life as before, living in blissful ignorance, set apart from the world. He made it his priority (we think here of Tillich's definition of *religiare*—that which you are bound to do) to pursue the cause of human suffering and its relief. After several years of traveling as a *sramana*, Siddhartha finally achieved enlightenment, as one of the early sources on the Buddha's life puts it:

> The Boddisatva [literally, "wisdom being"] put himself into a trance ... intent on discerning both the ultimate reality of things and the final goal of existence.
>
> In the first watch of the night he recollected the successive series of his former births. "There was I so and so; that was my name, deceased from there I came here"—in this way he remembered thousands of births, as though living them over again.... Then, as the third watch of the night drew on [he] turned his meditation to the real and essential nature of this world: "Alas, living beings wear themselves out in vain! Over and over again they are born, they age, die, pass on to a new life, and are reborn!"
>
> When the Great Seer had comprehended that where there is no ignorance whatever, there also the karma formations are stopped—then he had achieved a correct knowledge of all there is to be known, and he stood out in the world as a Buddha.[9]

One of the Buddha's earliest teachings, the Four Noble Truths, lays out what has remained central to all later iterations of Buddhism. These "truths" present an analysis of the human condition in addition to a diagnosis, and it was

9   Philip Novak, ed. "The Instructive Legend of the Buddha's Life, 12: The Realization of Nibbana, a) The Progress of Insight," in *The World's Wisdom: Sacred Texts of the World's Great Religions* (San Francisco: HarperCollins, 1995), 50–61.

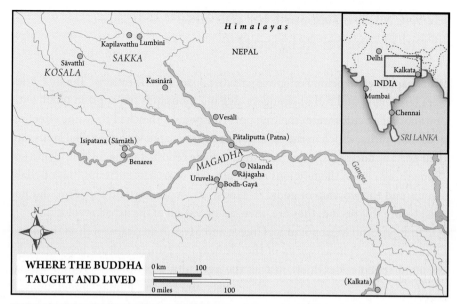

MAP 7.5 **WHERE THE BUDDHA TAUGHT AND LIVED** The Buddha is thought to have started life as a prince in a small north Indian state. Eschewing material life, he promoted a radical idea—human dignity and enlightenment. Did such concern with morality and humanity represent something new globally?

through the realization of these truths that the Buddha reached enlightenment himself. The first truth is that "All life entails suffering." Mortality plays a large part in this as old age, disease, and death are inevitable. The second truth, "The cause of suffering is desire," sees human desires as a thirst for everything, from material possessions to sex, power, and any other kinds of want. The third truth gets at the solution to the problem, "Removing desire removes suffering." And how to do this? Cue the fourth truth: "The way to remove suffering is to follow the eightfold path." Not shy of detailed prescriptions, Buddhism lays out steps toward enlightenment. In most varieties of the religion the steps on the eight-fold path are the following: right views, right thought, right speech, right action, right livelihood, right effort, right mindfulness, right concentration. These are sometimes broken down into three categories: morality, meditation, and insight.

The Buddha was not particularly interested in notions of the afterlife or in the role of gods, seeing neither as helpful to the overwhelming goal of Buddhism: enlightenment. It is for this reason that some people question Buddhism's credentials as a "religion," preferring instead to see it as a philosophical system.

How Can We Account for the Rise of the Universal Religions?

What happened to primal religions with the onset of civilizations? The first cities were large, new, and full of strangers, putting thousands of people in touch with one another. If cities were "melting pots" for people, they had the same effect on gods; old spirits, which in the tribe had been associated with the tribal lands and their specific ancestors, either vanished or were reborn, taking on new identities. "Something new in the religious realm appears in archaic societies," says Bellah, "Gods, and the worship of gods."[10] "Gods," as we understand the term, did not exist before this period; they are, then, an invention of the urban revolution.

In Egypt and Mesopotamia, Greece and Meso-America, as well as India and China, the amorphous spirits of the old ways of human culture began to take on more specific identities: just as the agricultural surpluses created specialists among the human populations—warriors, priests, farmers—so the gods and goddesses took on specific and different characters and skills, representing different areas of life (how could there be a god of the hearth before there were hearths?). The Maya, for example, had multiple deities. The exact number is difficult to determine since each of them had four aspects related to the cardinal points of the compass, as well as old and young and male and female counterparts. Some Maya sources speak of Itzamnaaj ("Lizard House") as a supreme deity, the inventor of writing and the patron of learning and the sciences. His wife was Chak Chell ("Lady Rainbow"), and from this pair all other deities were derived. In Eurasia pantheons included gods of all sorts: gods of war, weather-related gods, fertility gods, domestic gods, servants of gods (who themselves were also gods), divine doorkeepers,

Gods Across the Cultures   Deities take on a bewildering array of forms across cultures.

---

[10]   Bellah, *Religion in Human Evolution*, 212.

Mayan God   Stone sculpture of the Maya god of medicine and science, from Copán, Honduras.

serpent gods, dragon gods, divine giants who held up the earth, and gods for carpenters, smiths, fishermen, even fermentation.

Humans also had to figure out their own identities in this new urban context. If the tribe had lost its meaning upon becoming a part of the urban melting pot, how could people make sense of their lives? How should they live, and what would happen to them after death? City people in archaic civilizations, therefore, faced what historians Esposito, Fasching, and Lewis have called a threefold crisis:

> The loss of the tribal collective life and the emergence of large, impersonal and often brutal urban city-states in Egypt, India, China, and Mesopotamia was in effect a change from paradise to a world of suffering and cruelty. These new city states populated by strangers and ruled by absolute monarchs who were considered to be gods or representatives of gods, were soon enmeshed in a threefold crisis of mortality, morality and meaning.[11]

This "triple M" crisis sums up how people, now seeing themselves as individuals, had to cope with nothing short of the loss of self. Tribal life, with its focus on participatory ritual, answered the *how to live?* question. Tribal myths, told and retold down through hundreds of generations in an oral tradition,

---

[11]   John L. Esposito, Darrell J. Fasching, and Todd Lewis, *World Religions Today* (New York: Oxford University Press, 2006), 15.

explained the big issues such as the creation of the world, the history of the tribe, and the nature of the spirits (as well as giving people something to do at night). These myths answered the *where do we come from?* and *where are we going?* questions.

With the gradual breakdown of tribal myth and ritual in early civilizations, we find instead state laws, setting down a baseline for behavior. Examples of these include the Code of Hammurabi from Babylon and the detailed proscriptions from the (much later) Indian text the *Arthashastra*, discussed in Chapter 6. Since people could not be expected to behave properly out of observance of traditional ritual practice, an alternative means of encouraging decent behavior was required. But a baseline is no more than a bare minimum; it did not provide a code of ethics that could encourage people to aspire to a higher standard of ethics than that required by laws alone. For religions to gain universal appeal more was needed.

At this point in time religions were still localized, gods and goddesses differing according to geography. But there was still only one way of being "religious," which was to make sacrifices to specific gods or goddesses to effect certain desired ends. As Esposito describes it, an inhabitant of ancient Rome would not have understood the question *what religion are you?* People did not think of themselves as belonging to different religious groups; they may have differed in their choices of gods to whom to sacrifice, but these choices did not exclude other deities or other practices. "If you rephrase the original question as 'Are you religious?'" say Fasching, Lewis and Esposito, "you are no longer treating 'religion' as a noun, describing something you join. Instead you are treating it as an adjective, describing an attitude toward the human condition."[12]

True universal religions—which are exclusive—do not develop until what we might think of as a "second wave" of civilizations occurs, and even then this archaic religion persisted alongside them, as in Rome. What we see in the earliest civilizations, then, is an intermediary step, a divergence from tribal religions in which spirits and forces of nature become gods and take on personalities. But this archaic religion offered no sense of transcendence, no overarching morality. Gods and goddesses have certain powers but can still be affected by sacrifices and rituals, and in this sense humans have a certain power over them, which is entirely absent with the universal religions. Nor do the deities of the earliest civilizations have any particular plan for humanity; they do not seem to have anything in mind, in fact, except their own continued power and gratification.

---

[12]   Ibid., 5.

WERE THE FIRST DEITIES INVENTED OR BORROWED?

While many historians see the evolution of religion as a phenomenon welling up from within the various societies in which they appeared, others emphasize the role of influences from outside. Of particular importance in this latter scenario are the Aryans, whose migrations from the central Asian steppes over several millennia before the Common Era introduced many of their notions of "sky gods" to the societies of southern Europe, the Middle East, and Asia. While there is still much debate about the nature of these migrations, it is broadly accepted that the Aryans were relatively warlike, originating as animal herders with great skill on horseback, which they used to become tireless cattle rustlers. But many historians see it as unlikely that the Aryans conquered large cities as they themselves were likely traveling in small, fast-moving bands, unsuitable for the conquering of large populations and incapable of taking over large bureaucracies and administrative duties. Instead, they may well have become dominant over the more rural "horticultural" (or "gardening" rather than farming) societies of villages before the second or third millennium BCE.

Aryan notions of sky gods may have influenced these small societies and found their way into larger ones through them. The traces of these warrior nomads can be seen in the various pantheons of ancient Greece and the Middle East as well as India. Talking about the ancient Greek deities (such as Zeus, Demeter, Hera, Poseidon), historian Bruce Lerro points out that they lived very much like a conquering class would have done: "Just like the warrior overlords, the patriarchal Olympians live off revenues and blast with thunderbolts those who are late with tribute." They are not involved in the day-to-day running of affairs but live off the labor of others, just like a military aristocracy: "They fight, feast, make music, and copulate with whomever they can get their hands on."[13] In the structure of the supernatural world, we can see reflections of the earthly order.

WHAT IS THE AXIAL AGE?

At some point in the first millennium BCE, a certain new way of thinking about the world, the human condition, and society began to take hold, which acted as a kind of midwife for the era of the universal religions. In certain parts of Eurasia a new breed of intellectual began asking radical questions and putting forward

---

[13]   Bruce Lerro, *From Earth Spirits to Sky Gods: The Socioecological Origins of Monotheism, Individualism, and Hyper-Abstract Reasoning, From the Stone Age to the Axial Iron Age* (Lanham, MD: Lexington Books, 2000), 234.

innovative answers. Karl Jaspers, a nineteenth-century German philosopher, coined the term the "Axial Age" to describe this phenomenon and dated it to roughly 800 BCE to 200 BCE. The period was "axial" in two senses: one, that these new intellectual currents occurred along an east–west axis in Eurasia and, two, because they were game-changing.

At this time, said Jaspers, "the spiritual foundations of humanity were laid" in China, India, Persia, ancient Israel, and ancient Greece, "the foundations upon which humanity still subsists today."[14] This new axial thinking was notable for its *transcendental* character, what sociologist Benjamin Schwartz has called a "kind of standing back and looking beyond—a kind of critical, reflective questioning of the actual and a new vision of what lies beyond."[15]

While axial thinking was not synonymous with the universal religions, it was out of this thinking that they all emerged. Axial-Age civilizations posited a higher moral order, a transcendent order beyond the world of humans. Rulers had to be seen to be legitimated by this order, but they did not embody it, as they had in earlier civilizations, until Caesar Augustus and the Roman emperors who considered themselves divine. For the Greeks, although they clung to their old-world gods and goddesses, reason, not a single deity, played the role of the transcendental truth, hence the importance of Greek philosophers such as Socrates, Plato, and Aristotle in the history of Western thought.

The notion that there was something beyond—or greater than—the human world to which leaders must answer, while being a hallmark of the universal religions, also ironically gave birth to the possibility of a secular order—reflected, for example, in ancient Greece—in which the ruler was separate from the gods.

Monotheism was also an outgrowth of the axial transformation as in several contexts many gods turned into one who had power over creation, often acting in historical time and revealing a moral code as well as a history of the creation. In Asia something new appeared that paralleled the Middle Eastern search for salvation: an emphasis on moral behavior and the awareness of a transcendent realm. The Upanishads, which were appended to the earlier Vedic hymns after about 1000 BCE, represented a shift in religious thinking within the Vedic tradition and a certain axial characteristic, that of introspection and questioning, which, while not exactly absent in the Vedas, is more acute now. The word *Upanishad* itself suggested "sitting near devotedly." Gurus and their disciples probed questions which went beyond the largely procedural Vedic sacrifices and

---

[14]   Karl Jaspers, K., *Way to Wisdom: An Introduction to Philosophy,* trans. Ralph Manheim (New Haven, CT: Yale University Press, 1951), 98.

[15]   Benjamin I. Schwartz, "The Age of Transcendence," in "Wisdom, Revelation and Doubt," special issue *Daedelus* 104, no. 2 (Spring 1975): 3–4.

" I'M AFRAID IT'S TIME FOR YOU TO RENDER UNTO
CAESAR THAT WHICH IS CAESAR'S. "

rituals inherited from tradition. The concept of Brahman, originating in the Vedic hymns, was expanded in the Upanishads, which speak of Brahman as both a transcendental and an immanent concept: beyond humanity and within each human: "The being who is in the sky and at the same time in the heart—Him I meditate on as Brahman."[16]

Jesus' famous saying "render unto Caesar what is Caesar's and unto God that which is God's" (Matthew 22:21) represents the culmination of this notion of the difference between God and king, which had begun to be articulated in the early days of Judaism.

At the time this was a highly political message, if you bear in mind the historical context. Judea, where Jesus was preaching, was a Roman province. Suggesting that there was a transcendent realm of greater importance than the political one with which humans could connect was a distinct threat to the Roman authorities as it gave people a potential rallying point for revolt. By Jesus' time the notion of a direct relationship with God had been refined and recast in the idea of personal salvation by accepting Jesus, being spiritually reborn, and gaining access to the kingdom of heaven.

Although it emerges only some 600 years after the beginnings of Christianity, Islam also exhibits this axial character. Before Muhammad, inhabitants of the Arabian Peninsula practiced a tribal polytheism, albeit at times shot through with some Christian or Jewish notions (the heartlands of both religions being only a few

---

[16] "Brihadaranyaka Upanishad," in *The Upanishads: Breath of the Eternal,* trans. Frederick Manchester (New York: Mentor Books, 1957), 80.

days' camel ride from Mecca). The new thinking that came with Islam presented the idea of salvation, which was a personal affair, achievable by submission to God; the path was laid out in detail in the Koran and involved multiple moral injunctions, just as did Christianity and Judaism.

Following from the transcendent nature of the monotheistic gods, such moral injunctions as you find in the teachings of the Talmud, Christianity, and Islam are the other main axial features. Preaxial religious or sacred systems were not big on morality as we understand it. Roman polytheism, for example, was largely a matter of paying attention to the right gods: You want a child? Sacrifice to Alemonia, fertility goddess. Seeking success in battle? Talk to Mars, god of war. Making a sea voyage? Petition Neptune—you get the picture. Nowhere does the "king" of gods, Jupiter, or Mars, or any other deity ever tell a human to spread the word—*don't kill each other! Stop committing adultery! Don't steal each other's stuff!* How could the gods demand moral behavior when they were busy doing the very same thing? Power was their currency, not judgment, and certainly not *goodness.*

While raw power is still very much a hallmark of the God of the Torah, it is tempered by a concern for morality that instantly identifies him as a new type of god. Here, for instance, Yahweh rails against the bad behavior of the Israelites: "Your hands are full of blood! Wash and make yourselves clean. Take your evil deeds out of my sight; stop doing wrong. Learn to do right; seek justice. Defend the oppressed. Take up the cause of the fatherless; plead the case of the widow" (Isaiah 1:15–17). These are the words of a deity appalled by the failings of humanity and intent on his creations turning over a new leaf. The New Testament of Christianity, written down and codified somewhat later than the Axial Age, is clearly heavily influenced by such concern for morality. But if the God of the Israelites shared some traits with the more cantankerous and vengeful sky gods of the early civilizations, the Christian God was further removed from that pedigree. In the Book of Matthew, Jesus tells his followers the Golden Rule: "So in everything, do unto others as you would have them do unto you" (Matthew 7:12). Earlier in the Bible, during the Sermon on the Mount, he demands more of his followers:

> You have heard that it was said, 'Eye for eye, and tooth for tooth.' But I tell you, do not resist an evil person. If anyone slaps you on the right cheek, turn to them the other cheek also. And if anyone wants to sue you and take your shirt, hand over your coat as well. If anyone forces you to go one mile, go with them two miles. Give to the one who asks you, and do not turn away from the one who wants to borrow from you. (Matthew 5:38–42)

Five hundred years before Christ, the Buddha expresses a similar concern for human dignity, which at that time was innovative:

Let no one work another's undoing
Or even slight him at all anywhere;
And never let them wish one another ill
Through provocation or resentful thought.[17]

If axial thinking, characterized by new notions of individualism, morality, and transcendence, emerged at this point, what could have accounted for it? Many historians see the social structures of the early states as producing axial thinking, but it took a millennium or so for this thinking to emerge; so why the delay?

During this time all the societies in question—Greece, Persia, Israel, China, and India—experienced certain things in common: population growth was constant in all of the societies where axial phenomena appear and, with it, war was certainly endemic, as we described in Chapter 4; technological innovation accompanied population growth and war as a habitual sidekick, something we will see throughout the world's history; increasing wealth, unevenly applied, caused great imbalances of power, which have also been discussed in the previous chapters. But the progress of the state was anything but even. There were constant setbacks, as we have seen in the last few chapters. Unlike the preagricultural world, in which dramatic reversals of fortune were much less common, life in large states was prone to calamities, such as famine, war, and economic collapse. In short, over the millennia or two since the appearance of the first "civilizations," humanity had been on a rollercoaster ride; and it was becoming clear that the state, as a social institution, although seemingly here to stay, was highly unstable. As Bellah describes it, in these periods of instability (remember China's Warring States Period?) people began asking uncomfortable questions: "Where is the king? Where is the god? Why are we hungry? Why are we being killed by attackers and no one is defending us?"[18] Such questions addressed not only the political and social disorder but the stability of the very cosmological order itself. While such querulous, perhaps even blasphemous questions had certainly been asked in the

> ☀ In short, over the millennia or two since the appearance of the first "civilizations," humanity had been on a rollercoaster ride; and it was becoming clear that the state, as a social institution, although seemingly here to stay, was highly unstable.

---

[17]   "Metta Sutta," in Novak, *The World's Wisdom*, 74.
[18]   Bellah, *Religion in Human Evolution*, 266.

very earliest societies, they really came to the fore during the Axial Age; and the search for their answers represents the creative energy out of which the world's great religions emerged.

We have discussed China's Warring States Period elsewhere, so let's focus here on the Middle East and India, where political instability in the Axial Age provides a fertile seedbed for religious change. Such instability was a hallmark of the rise of early states. We know that at around 1200 BCE there were small kingdoms in the hills of Canaan. At this point the Israelites are worshipping Yahweh as one among many; his commandment to "have no others beside me" is a statement of *henotheism*—worshipping one god among others—not monotheism, at least not yet. These kingdoms develop into what we know as Israel and Judah, the two kingdoms of the Israelites, by around 1000 BCE; and it is around this point that the reigns of Kings Solomon and David took place. Squabbles among the Israelites led to the rise of the "prophets," such as Amos and Hosea, who channeled God's message to the people and reminded them, among other things, of their tribal roots and values and, most importantly, the covenant made with Yahweh in the Sinai. Punishment would befall them, warned the prophets, if the Israelites failed to follow God's law.

Contrary to some suggestions in the Torah, however, these kingdoms were not major powers. To the east the Neo-Assyrian Empire was growing, and by the eighth century BCE it was a distinct threat to Israel. In 721 BCE the Assyrians conquered Israel and relocated its entire population to a life of slavery in Mesopotamia. Less than two centuries later another calamity struck; in 586 BCE the Babylonians, having conquered the Assyrians, came to Judah and carried off

Mid-13th C. BCE	Moses (traditional dating)
1208	First mention of Israel in Egyptian records
ca. 1200–1000	Premonarchical tribes of Israel and Judah
ca. 1030–1010	Saul as king of Israel
ca. 1010–970	David as king of Judah and Israel
ca. 970–930	Solomon as king of Judah and Israel
ca. 930–722	Divided monarchy of Judah and Israel
722	Assyrian conquest of (northern) kingdom of Israel
640–609	Josiah as king of Judah
587	Babylonian conquest of (southern) kingdom of Judah
587–538	Babylonian exile
539	Conquest of Babylonia by Cyrus the Persian
538	First exiles return to Judah
333	Alexander conquers Persian Empire, including Judah
140–63	Hasmonean monarchy
65	Roman conquest of Palestine

Condensed Chronology of Israelite History

its population as well. It was the Persians who, having conquered Babylon in 538, returned the Jews to Jerusalem. These experiences, of exile and return, helped define Judaism and were fitted into the narrative of the need for fidelity to the covenant with God and the threat of punishment for abandoning it. As Bellah puts it, "Deuteronomy (and perhaps most of the Pentateuch) comes out of a situation of unparalleled violence in which the northern kingdom had already been destroyed and much of its inhabitants deported, and Judah hung by an uneasy thread in a vassal relation to Assyria."[19]

These events represent what Bellah calls an axial breakdown. But what was the breakthrough? The idea of a "portable" religion, made portable in this case by the emphasis on God's Word, the Torah, changed people's beliefs. "The land was never forgotten, but many other Near Eastern peoples would disappear once their land was lost, whereas the Jews could survive and prosper wherever they were as long as they had the Book and a community to interpret it."[20] It was the prevalence of writing, then, that acted as the lifeboat for the Jews, and it remains central to Judaism today.

Calamity struck again, several centuries later, in 70 CE, when the Romans, sick of attacks by the Zealots, a Jewish guerilla movement, marched into Jerusalem and burned the Temple to the ground. Then they drove the Jews out of their city, repeating the much feared cycle of exile. Out of this calamity emerged what became rabbinic, or mainstream, Judaism and the Nazarene movement of early Christianity.

The Holy Land at this time was in flux. The Nazarene movement reflects this instability as it was an apocalyptic movement, expecting the imminent end of the world, as did many other movements. Among these were the Essenes, a Jewish sect in Judea who were probably responsible for collecting and storing the many texts known as the Dead Sea Scrolls. These documents, discovered in a cave in Israel in the 1940s, are made up of versions of the Hebrew Bible, some dating to as early as 300 BCE, and other early religious writings.

The Nazarene movement was concerned with converting as many "gentiles" (non-Jews) as possible before the day of judgment arrived. As increasing numbers of non-Jews flocked to this movement, it became less and less a Jewish movement and developed a more distinct identity, that of the Christian church.

Politically there are similarities to be found in Buddhism's birthplace, northern India of the mid-first century BCE, when the Upanishads began to offer radically new spiritual—and social—insights. Whereas the early Vedas, such as the Rig Veda, reflect a rural, tribal society of mixed Aryan/Indian composition, the

---

[19] Ibid., 338.
[20] Ibid., 315.

Upanishads of the first millennium describe a rapidly urbanizing society, with a growing population. Their metaphors and images come not from agriculture, as is largely true of the Rig Veda, but from weaving, metallurgy, and crafts: "The social background seems to have been courts and crafts, not village and farm."[21] In the context of growing population, urbanization, and incessant conflict among states, the dominant role of Brahmin priests and their sacrifices were becoming less plausible as a method of connecting with the cosmos. Increasingly people were looking for answers outside the Brahminical tradition, including the *sramana*, or ascetic seekers, who questioned everything that the Brahmin stood for, including the rigidity of the caste system of which the Brahmin themselves occupied the highest level.

It was this role of *sramana* that the Buddha embraced in his quest for enlightenment, and early Buddhist texts are full of examples of his questioning of the Brahmin. His rejection of their preeminent position in society is evident in the Buddhist notion that spiritual enlightenment is not reserved for people of high caste but equally available to all people (with the possible exception of women) regardless of status or ethnicity. In this regard Buddhism stands shoulder to shoulder with other Axial-Age religions.

HOW DID UNIVERSAL RELIGIONS SPREAD?

The answer to this question lies largely with the development of new and ever larger political structures, in particular empires. With the exception of Judaism, which needs a slightly different explanation for its endurance, all universal religions piggybacked on enormous and powerful states and empires, which carried them over large geographical distances and embedded them in diverse populations. Under the Han, Confucianism was made the official state religion and, thus, consolidated its hold over China for the rest of its history, playing an intimate part in the empire's cultural and political life.

Christianity, although for the first three centuries of its life as an organized religion under threat of extermination by the Romans, became first legal and then the official Roman religion, ensuring it a cornerstone role in later European and then world culture. The emperor Constantine is largely credited with this as he issued the Edict of Toleration (also known as the edict of Milan) in 313 CE, which permitted Christianity. Constantine was baptized on his deathbed, furthering the Christian cause even more. In 381 Christianity became the official religion of the empire, under Emperor Theodosius, and 10 years later all pagan religion was

---

[21] Ibid., 509.

outlawed. In 325 CE, Constantine convened the Council of Nicaea, a meeting of bishops, the purpose of which was to establish a basis for Christian orthodoxy. Perhaps the most vital issue they settled was the debate over whether Jesus was the figurative or literal son of God (decided in favor of literal). Three centuries had passed since the death of Jesus. In this time considerable diversity had worked its way into Christian belief, and it was the role of the council to establish a certain standardization that would give unity to the newly respectable religion.

Several hundred years later, Islam, carried by the invading Arab armies coming out of the Arabian Peninsula, spread first to northern Africa and the Middle East, then to southern Europe, southwest Asia, and eventually India and China. It was Muhammad who united the tribes of Arabia, and during the following century, under the next four leaders (the "rightly guided" caliphs), the Arab armies overran the Persian and Byzantine Empires (internally weakened by centuries of warfare with each other) then controlling much of the Middle East and Iran. This force was to become the Islamic Caliphate, and it would in various guises rule large areas of the Middle East and southwest Asia for centuries.

In India, as we saw in Chapter 4, the emperor Asoka (r. ca. 269–232 BCE) officially adopted Buddhism as a religion of peace, after his conquest of the Kalinga territory. This imperial support helped to spread Buddhism from Afghanistan to the Bay of Bengal and from northern, Himalayan India to the island of Ceylon in the south. In addition to this early push from the Mauryan Empire, Buddhism expanded across Asia both through further state support and by its extensive system of monasteries, which worked together to expand their reach into many frontier zones. While Hinduism remained a largely Indian religion and recaptured much of the population from early converts to Buddhism, Buddhism itself went on to become a truly global religion.

Conclusion: How Did the Major Religions Develop?

All the universal religions developed over several millennia, originating in prehistory with our hunter–gatherer ancestors who practiced what was a remarkably stable sacred system that answered the needs of their particular lifeway. As societies changed, in particular with the advent of sedentism, urban life, and large states, spirits morphed into gods. Gods were associated with kings, queens, pharaohs, and emperors; and universal religions emerged, during the Axial Age, positing a new concept of personal salvation, liberation, enlightenment, all on the shoulders of the idea of a transcendent realm beyond the purely material. The evolution of religion, then, can be seen as part and parcel of the evolution of human social and political structures, allowing new human perceptions, in particular about identity, the individual self, and the nature of our relationship to the material world.

Ultimately, the settled agricultural societies among which universal religions developed shared similarities as well as differences. Historians have long asked themselves whether there are certain innate human qualities that explain our similarities, while differences are often attributed to material conditions, such as geography and climate. There is no doubt that as a broad approach this has appeal. Religions, as an integral part of human societies, have similarities and differences that can likewise be attributed to both material conditions and profound human constants. The question that persists is, *do these similarities outweigh the differences?*

Words to Think About

Animism	Dualism	Monotheism
Polytheism	Transcendental	

Questions to Think About

- How do universal religions differ from tribal religions?
- Why do some people think Buddhism is not even a religion?
- What do Judaism, Christianity, and Islam have in common?
- How were gods the inventions of cities?

Primary Sources

Novak, Philip, ed. *The World's Wisdom: Sacred Texts of the World Great Religions.* San Francisco: HarperCollins, 1995.

The English Standard Version Bible. New York: Oxford University Press, 2009.

The Koran Interpreted: A Translation. Translated by A. J. Arberry. New York: Touchstone, 2005.

The Upanishads: Breath of the Eternal. Translated by Frederick Manchester. New York: Mentor Books, 1957.

Secondary Sources

Bellah, Robert N. *Religion in Human Evolution: From the Paleolithic to the Axial Age.* Cambridge, MA: Harvard University Press, 2011.

Brians, Paul, Mary Gallwey, Douglas Hughes, Azfar Hussain, Richard Law, Michael Myers Michael Neville, Roger Schlesinger, Alice Spitzer, and Susan Swan, eds. *Reading About the World,* vol. 1, 3rd ed. San Diego, CA: Harcourt Brace, 1999. http://public.wsu .edu/~brians/world_civ/worldcivreader/world_civ_reader_1/rig_veda.html.

Durkheim, Émile. *The Elementary Forms of Religious Life: A Study in Religious Sociology.* Translated by J. W. Swain. London: George Allen and Unwin, 1912.

Eisenstadt, S. N. "The Axial Age Breakthrough in Ancient Israel." In *The Origins and Diversity of Axial Age Civilizations,* edited by S. N. Eisenstadt, 127–34. New York: State University of New York Press, 1989.

Esposito, John L., Darrell J. Fasching, and Todd Lewis. *World Religions Today.* New York: Oxford University Press, 2006.

Freud, Sigmund. *The Future of an Illusion,* trns. James Strachey, New York, W.W. Norton, 1961.

Jaspers, Karl. *Way to Wisdom: An Introduction to Philosophy.* Translated by Ralph Manheim. New Haven, CT: Yale University Press, 1951.

Lerro, Bruce. *From Earth Spirits to Sky Gods: The Socioecological Origins of Monotheism, Individualism, and Hyper-Abstract Reasoning, From the Stone Age to the Axial Iron Age.* Lanham, MD: Lexington Books, 2000.

Schwartz, Benjamin I. "The Age of Transcendence." In "Wisdom, Revelation and Doubt: Perspectives on the First Millennium B.C." Special issue, *Daedelus* 104, no. 2 (Spring 1975): 1–7.

For additional resources, including maps, primary sources, and visuals, web links, and quizzes, please go to **www.oup.com/us/cole**

Gambia on the West African Coast, Part of the Coastline Traveled by Carthaginian Sailors Some 2,500 Years Ago

Chapter 8

What Does Trade Do?

Somewhere Off the Coast of Africa

On a lonely stretch of the western African coast, at some point in the middle of the first millennium BCE, a ragged group of sailors come ashore. They have sailed from Carthage, on Africa's Mediterranean coast, through the Pillars of Hercules (the name the ancient Greeks used to describe the Straits of Gibraltar), and into the Atlantic. With the mass of the African continent on one side and the unending swell of the Atlantic on the other, they had sailed southward, hugging the shore.

According to the ancient Greek historian Herodotus, who wrote this account around 430 BCE, after landing, the sailors proceed to "unload their goods tidily along the beach, and then, returning to their boats, raise a smoke."[1] Some Africans, seeing the smoke, come out of the brush along the beach to inspect the Carthaginian goods. They "place on the ground a certain quantity of gold in exchange for the goods and go off again to a distance." You can see by this point where this is headed. "The Carthaginians," continues Herodotus, "then come ashore and take a look at the gold; and if they think it represents a fair price for their wares, they collect it and go away; if on the other hand, it seems too little, they go back aboard and wait, and the natives come and add to the gold until they are satisfied."

Why wouldn't the natives simply take the goods and run? Well, perhaps at times they did; Herodotus was probably describing an ideal situation, not a real event. Nevertheless, he claims, "There is perfect honesty on both sides; the Carthaginians never touch the gold until it equals in value what they have offered for sale, and the natives never touch the goods until the gold has been taken away."

---

[1] Herodotus, *The Histories* (Baltimore: Penguin, 1968), 307.

THINKING ABOUT TRADE

When Did Trade Begin?

- Some scholars have suggested that the growth of the earliest civilizations was more a function of long-distance trade than it was of irrigation, which produced agricultural surplus.

What Is the Relationship Between Ecological Diversity and Trade?

- If everywhere on earth provided exactly the same raw materials, there would be no need to move anything from one place to another.

What Role Did Trade Play in State Formation?

- While trade may have created states, states created the need for more trade, in a mutually reinforcing relationship.

How Did Trade Spread Religious Ideas?

- Just as the modern American highway and airline systems were pioneered primarily for commerce but are used by everybody, so ancient highways were not restricted to merchants but were used by others, including monks and missionaries.

How Did Trade Spread Disease?

- The Black Death traveled on fleas, hitchhiking on black rats which scrambled down the mooring ropes of Arab dhows and thence across the Indian Ocean.

Conclusion

- Trade has far-reaching cultural, religious, and biological consequences because merchants interact socially, politically, religiously, and sexually.

Introduction

Humans, said the great Scottish economist Adam Smith (1723–1790), are uniquely endowed with the propensity to "truck, barter and exchange, one thing for another."[2] From Stone-Age exchanges of a flint for a piece of meat to information-age "trades" of billions of dollars worth of commodities at the touch of a button,

---

[2]   Adam Smith, *An Inquiry Into the Nature and Causes of the Wealth of Nations* (London: W. Strahan, 1776), book 1, chap. 2.

such habits have been part of the human character for eons. But precisely what part has trade played in the course of human history?

In this chapter we will examine the early history of trade, focusing on the first millennium CE but going back where necessary to set the scene. Trade played a central role in the growth of states, which, as we discussed in Chapter 3, is a perennial subject of scrutiny for historians. The rise and fall of the multiple city states and kingdoms of Mexico and Meso-America, during the first millennium, largely followed the success and failure of trading activity. The western African kingdoms of Ghana and Kanem grew rich on the profit made from the movement of goods on the desert edge. And Silk Road traders enabled parts of Central Asia to flourish, creating kingdoms and empires.

Clearly, trade has always had economic and political consequences. Moving goods from one place to another allows people to do things they were not previously able to do—eat, build, make war, or decorate themselves. The economic consequences of trade also often meant enrichment—of some—and sometimes impoverishment of others.

But trade involved contact with others, and such contact led to noneconomic consequences. These might not always have been friendly or trustworthy. They might even have been considered "unclean" or undesirable in multiple ways. Such suspicion of others explains the Carthaginians' elaborate trading choreography in Herodotus' account, what has been called "dumb barter" or "silent trade." But most exchanges of goods involved more direct contact, and such contact has been the major engine of change throughout history. In addition to spreading things, encounters spread ideas, most notably, perhaps, religions (see Chapter 7). Religions spread along the Silk Road, linking the eastern and western "cores" of civilization, China, and the Mediterranean. Along the way, trade enriched traders and kingdoms, states, and empires arose on the profits. Contact of a more physical nature also spread DNA, mixing the human gene pool, and, more darkly, spread disease, along the Silk Road, in particular, and across the Indian Ocean. As contact grew between these populations, people were exposed to diseases to which they had no immunity and which swept through populations with deadly effect.

Contact also leads to war as sometimes negotiations do not end well. As societies grow, so do their appetites. Feeding large cities is one thing, supplying all the goods their residents need and want is quite another. This is especially true with empires, whose demands for raw materials and consumer goods reached unheard-of levels and whose armies—of soldiers and traders alike—traveled far and wide to fill them. Desire to monopolize both the commodities themselves and the process of their exchange often led to violence—*to trade or to raid?* being the question on many a leader's mind. Sometimes what cannot be bought can be taken. And sometimes stealing is preferable because, simply put, it is cheaper (see Chapters 4 and 6).

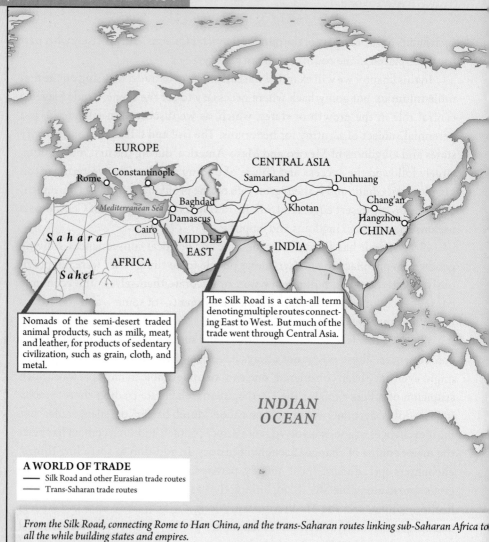

EUROPE

CENTRAL ASIA

Rome

Constantinople

Samarkand

Dunhuang

Mediterranean Sea

Baghdad

Khotan

Chang'an

Damascus

Hangzhou

Cairo

CHINA

S a h a r a

MIDDLE
EAST

INDIA

AFRICA

Sahel

The Silk Road is a catch-all term
denoting multiple routes connecting East to West. But much of the
trade went through Central Asia.

Nomads of the semi-desert traded
animal products, such as milk, meat,
and leather, for products of sedentary
civilization, such as grain, cloth, and
metal.

INDIAN
OCEAN

A WORLD OF TRADE
—— Silk Road and other Eurasian trade routes
—— Trans-Saharan trade routes

*From the Silk Road, connecting Rome to Han China, and the trans-Saharan routes linking sub-Saharan Africa to
all the while building states and empires.*

MAP 8.1   A WORLD OF TRADE

 ca. 3000 BCE
Bronze and iron-age societies trading limited
number of goods

 ca. 1st Century CE
Roman and Han Empires drive
long-distance trade

ca. 200–1100 CE
Classic Maya Period

ca. Second-Fifth Centuries CE
Camel introduced
to Arabia

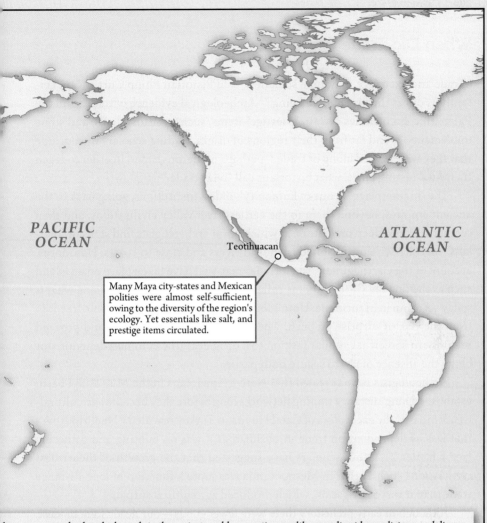

PACIFIC
OCEAN

ATLANTIC
OCEAN

Teotihuacan

Many Maya city-states and Mexican polities were almost self-sufficient, owing to the diversity of the region's ecology. Yet essentials like salt, and prestige items circulated.

...diterranean, trade played a key role in the ancient world, generating wealth, spreading ideas, religions, and disease,

541
Plague of Justinian

750–1258
'Abbasid Dynasty
in Baghdad

220
Collapse of Han Empire

7th C. CE
Muslim conquest
of North Africa

When Did Trade Begin?

"Trade and exchange in human societies," said historian Philip Curtin, "are certainly as old as the first human being."[3] Archeological evidence of trade from the Paleolithic era includes certain "prestige" items, such as beads, shells, and stone implements, found far from their regions of origin, leading scholars to conclude that they were passed along or traded, perhaps numerous times, in order to reach their final resting place, what historians call "relay trade."

The "marketplace" is one of humanity's oldest institutions, going back to the ancient empires, beyond them to the earliest river valley civilizations, and then further still into deep prehistory, at which point archeologists find signs of "markets" on otherwise uninhabited islands in rivers and close to coasts. Herodotus' account of the Carthaginian "silent trade" may well have taken place on an island such as the one the Carthaginians called "Kerne" off the western Sahara, what is today's Arguin in Mauritania. Uninhabited land offered neutrality, some freedom from the risk of surprise ambush, where the exchange of goods could proceed securely, in somewhat similar fashion to a drug deal (the common denominator being the absence of law to secure both parties).

Archeologists have revealed that Native Americans in the Mississippi basin established long-distance trading networks long before they became agriculturalists. Similarly, the excavators of Çatal Hüyük in Turkey revealed a Neolithic town that was as dependent on trade in obsidian as it was on hunting and gathering (see Chapter 2). Other scholars have suggested that the growth of the earliest civilizations such as that in Mesopotamia was more a function of long-distance trade than it was of irrigation, which produced agricultural surplus.

Although in early prehistory there were fewer goods—our needs were modest, perhaps—this changed rapidly in the Neolithic era. Human goods—artifacts,

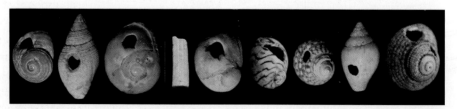

Prehistoric Bling?   These shells were drilled by human hand and probably worn as decoration on a cord as some holes show signs of wear. Shells like these (20,000–35,000 years old, from Greece) were almost universally used for similar purposes in prehistory, often turning up hundreds of miles from their origin (meaning they were probably traded).

---

[3]   Philip D. Curtin, *Cross Cultural Trade in World History* (Cambridge: Cambridge University Press, 1984), 60.

tools, raw materials—increased incrementally until this point, whereupon the streams of goods turned into rivers, with the advent of Bronze- and Iron-Age societies, after about 3000 BCE, and continued to grow in volume and complexity. One single shipwreck from the Bronze-Age Aegean (1350 BCE) has yielded 10 tons of copper and 1 ton of tin (bronze is made from "alloying" tin copper to tin at a ratio of 10:1), in addition to other "high-end" goods such as ivory.[4]

At the height of their powers, the Romans ferried hundreds of items, including Greek wine, Spanish copper, and Egyptian grain, across the Mediterranean; and "caravans" of camels from the first century BCE or earlier conveyed Indian pepper and other spices as well as exotic aromatics such as frankincense and myrrh—of biblical fame—across Arabia and up the Red Sea, to the ports of the Mediterranean, for use in the houses and temples of the Roman Empire. The story is similar in all inhabited parts of the world, the volume of trade being largely determined by population density and demand for items not locally available. As society became increasingly complex, the amount of tradable items only grew.

WHAT WAS THE DIFFERENCE BETWEEN TRADE AND TRIBUTE?

But diverse goods can be moved by different people, for different reasons, some of these amounting to more than "trade," as we understand it today. Historian Karl Polanyi has outlined three types of trade: reciprocity, redistribution, and market exchange. Although this sounds like jargon, these terms are really pretty simple. *Reciprocity* predominates in stateless societies and is characterized by the free exchange of goods—in other words, gift-giving.[5] More than a social nicety, gift-giving serves serious purposes, including alliance building and recognition of allegiances. With the development of the state and institutions of political power, reciprocity gives way to *redistribution*—the movement of goods by political elites, sometimes known as "political economy." Finally, the laws of supply and demand operate in much of the modern world, in which goods move around more or less freely at the hands of multiple (private) players—traders and merchants. But there are lots of exceptions to this model. The

> With the development of the state and institutions of political power, reciprocity gives way to *redistribution*— the movement of goods by political elites, sometimes known as "political economy."

---

[4]   Cemal Pulak, "Discovering a Royal Ship from the Age of King Tut: Uluburun, Turkey," in *Beneath the Seven Seas*, ed. George F. Bass (New York: Thames & Hudson, 2005), 34–47.

[5]   Karl Polyani, Conrad M. Arensberg, and Harry W. Pearson, eds., *Trade and Markets in Early Empires* (New York: Cambridge University Press, 1984).

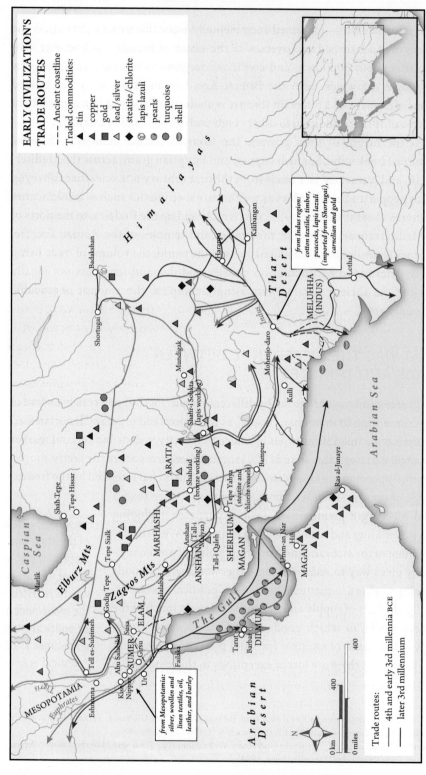

EARLY CIVILIZATION'S TRADE ROUTES

Traded commodities:
- tin
- copper
- gold
- lead/silver
- steatite/chlorite
- lapis lazuli
- pearls
- turquoise
- shell

--- Ancient coastline

from Indus region: cotton textiles, timber, peacocks, lapis lazuli (imported from Shortugai), carnelian and gold

from Mesopotamia: silver, woollen and linen textiles, oil, leather, and barley

Trade routes:
— 4th and early 3rd millennia BCE
— later 3rd millennium

MAP 8.2 EARLY CIVILIZATION'S TRADE ROUTES Trade may be one of the earliest human characteristics, beginning long before "civilization." By the time of the earliest civilizations traders were moving goods in large quantities.

288

Han placated the Xiongnu nomads on the northwest frontier with gifts of silk and princesses—a state society "trading" with a nonstate society. Such activity, they felt, prevented the nomads from raiding along their border and grabbing what they could not get by trade. Mesopotamian merchants seem to have traded more or less independently; while elites also exchanged goods, their model was somewhat hybrid. While Polyani does not necessarily provide explanations for all situations, his model provides a useful theoretical framework for us to tease out the workings of early trade relationships.

These different trade models operated with different types of goods. Prestige goods were often restricted to elites because their ownership suggested status. Other goods were so vital that to control their exchange was to control entire populations—food is a perfect example here, in particular salt, a bulk good that could be traded long-distance because it was nonperishable and that was a necessary dietary supplement.

Other items were moved around as *tribute,* a kind of tax levied by powerful rulers or a gift bestowed upon powerful allies or potential competitors, which often amounted to large sums of money or goods—an early form of the well-known "protection racket." Maya elites in Meso-America, for example, demanded goods—or labor—as tribute; and in this way the ruler and his retinue enriched themselves. Warfare also initiated floods of tribute; conquered Maya kingdoms were required to pay tribute in the form of textiles, foodstuffs, pottery, and other items. "As warfare increased in frequency and intensity during the Classic Period," says historian Arthur Demarest, "the role of such tribute would have gained importance in regional and interregional economies."[6]

Mayan Tribute   This painting adorned a pottery vessel. A ruler, seated, receives basket loads of tribute, all of which is noted in a folded book by a royal courtier seated on the right.

---

6   Arthur Demarest, *Ancient Maya: The Rise and Fall of a Rainforest Civilization* (Cambridge: Cambridge University Press, 2010), 172.

Whether trading, raiding, or paying tribute, people were engaging in the exchange of commodities, with multiple consequences—economic, cultural, political, and historical.

What Is the Relationship Between Ecological Diversity and Trade?

We will revisit tribute below (see "What Role Did Trade Play in the Building of Maya States?"). But first let's look at the most obvious thing that trade does, move goods around—transporting items from where they occur or are made to where they are needed or wanted. From this act there are many *downstream* consequences, or things that trade can be said to achieve. Ecological diversity is a major driver of the movement of goods; different goods are found—grow or are produced—in different areas. China, when unified, encompassed many different ecological regions, all producing different items that could be traded with neighboring regions, some of them worldwide. Here is the Han historian Sima Qian (145–86 BCE), surveying the empire's resources at around 100 BCE:

> The region west of the mountains is rich in timber, paper, mulberry, hemp, oxtails for banner tassels, jade and other precious stones. That east of the mountains abounds in fish, salt, lacquer, silk, singers, and beautiful women. The area south of the Yangtze produces camphor wood, catalpa, ginger, cinnamon, gold, tin, lead, ore, cinnabar, rhinoceros horns, tortoise shell, pearls of various shapes, and elephant tusks and hides, while that north of Lung-men and Chieh-shih is rich in horses, cattle, sheep, felt, furs, tendons, and horns.[7]

(Notice the way he casually lists "women" as a commodity, not uncommon in ancient lists of goods, an indication of the extent to which women were commodities in early civilizations—and beyond.)

To understand the connection between ecological diversity and trade, let us consider an oasis. The word *oasis* is probably used more as a metaphor than a literal term these days, probably because so few people actually live in one. But a literal oasis is a small, well-watered (spring-fed) region surrounded by arid

---

[7]   Sima Qian, *Records of the Grand Historian*, vol. 2, trans. Burton Watson (New York: Columbia University Press, 1961), 477.

desert. For the quintessential oasis you could do worse than look in southern Morocco, in the northern reaches of the world's largest desert, the Sahara ("desert" in Arabic).

The oasis of Tafilalt has a perfect climate—that is, if you happen to be a date palm (*Phoenix dactylifera*). Requiring heat and aridity, with temperatures of around 30 degrees Fahrenheit for several months of the year and water from irrigation, not rain, the date palm is one of the most productive fruit trees in the world. With a high sugar content, it is a perfect supplement to many diets, although it does not qualify as a staple by itself (you cannot survive on dates alone!). The date's prolific growth and durability made it a perfect long-distance trade item. An oasis therefore is a good example of a specialized ecosystem that was made for trade because of its possession of a surplus of one item and a need to import others.

> An oasis therefore is a good example of a specialized ecosystem that was made for trade because of its possession of a surplus of one item and a need to import others.

But there is more to developing a thriving trade than having one item to sell. You need a market in which to sell the item and a means of getting your product to that market. Somewhere around the second to the fifth centuries CE camels were introduced to northern Africa, probably from Arabia. Their ability to travel long distances without water and their large splayed hooves, which did not sink in the soft sand, made them perfectly adapted to be the "ships of the desert." Camels made trans-Saharan trade possible. Innovations in saddle technology allowed traders to load them with up to 500 pounds of merchandise—a lot of dates—which they could carry some 30 miles a day.

We know little for certain about trans-Saharan trade before the Muslim conquest of northern Africa in the seventh century because there are no written records before this point. After this date Arab geographers, such as Al-Bakri (d. 1094), who lived in Muslim Spain, began to leave written accounts of the contacts between northern Africa and western Africa, which had several long-established kingdoms. These kingdoms had been actively trading for generations. But it is not until the advent of Islam and its far-reaching conquests that trade across the Sahara picks up and most importantly is described in writing.

Whereas the trade in slaves, which was prevalent in seventh-century western and northern Africa, suggests hostilities among the various polities in the region—the source of enslaved men and women being raids—trade in agricultural products arose from ecological diversity, which created the incentive to trade. If everywhere on earth provided exactly the same raw materials, there would be no need to move anything from one place to another. As Curtin puts it,

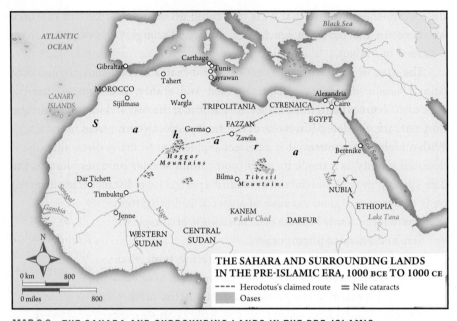

MAP 8.3   THE SAHARA AND SURROUNDING LANDS IN THE PRE-ISLAMIC
ERA   Ecological diversity means that some people have dates, while others have corn or leather.
Trade is simply the circulation of things from where they originate (or grow) to where they are needed.

"The most obvious and ancient explanation of why some people take up commerce and others do not is the differing resource endowments.... Where different environments lie side by side, specialization and trade become likely."[8]

To the south the Sahara turns to savanna grasslands. These in turn give way to tropical forest. To the north the Sahara gives way to the *sahel*, or desert edge, of northern Africa, good pasture for goats and sheep; and this in turn gives onto the coastal plains and Mediterranean Sea, which in Roman times were fertile grain fields. During the first millennium, nomads of the semidesert traded animal products such as milk, meat, and leather for products of sedentary civilization such as grain, cloth, and metal. Like coastal ports, settlements on the desert edge grew and prospered because of their control over the movement of goods between these different ecological zones. Such exchanges were risky however, and history is littered with examples of how trade between farmers and nomads lapsed into violence—where trade became raid. Nomadic men, experts on horses, were able to swoop into villages, seize goods by force, and then disappear into the desert.

Clearly, there were major ecological differences both north and south of the Sahara. In the west, the desert stretched almost to the Atlantic Ocean, leaving

---

[8]   Curtin, *Cross-Cultural Trade in World History*, 16.

little room for agriculture. But in the east the desert ran into the fertile Nile valley, and here was another boundary across which goods could be exchanged.

Salt is an essential mineral in human biology. People living under the intense African sun lose salt through perspiration and need to replenish it. South of the Sahara, in western Sudan, farming populations had no natural source of salt; but it existed in abundance in the desert itself. In the centuries preceding the Arab conquest of northern Africa in the seventh century, the desert nomads, or Berbers, had been mining salt in the Sahara.

Al-Bakri also wrote about the Saharan salt mines in his "Book of Routes and Kingdoms":

> Among the remarkable things found in that desert is the salt mine which is at a distance of two days marching from the Great Waste and twenty days from Sijilmasa. The salt is uncovered by removing a layer of earth as other minerals and precious stones are dug up. The salt is found two fathoms or less below the surface and is cut (in blocks) as stone is cut.... From this mine salt is transported to Sijilmasa, Ghana, and other countries of the land of the Sudan. Work there continues uninterruptedly, and merchants arrive in a constant stream for it has an enormous production.[9]

Salt merchants traded for gold. This came from ancient states such as Ghana, in western Africa. In all likelihood the gold was actually acquired from smaller kingdoms and chiefdoms farther south and traded by the Ghanaians, in whose interest it was to act as middlemen between the producers and the purchasers from the north. Gold was useful to the new Islamic civilization as it played a role in their economy of coinage, like it did for the Romans who preceded them. In addition to gold, dates, textiles, leather, and even books crossed the desert in caravans. Slaves from sub-Saharan Africa for use in the agricultural lands to the north were also a staple of these routes.

HOW DID ECOLOGY AFFECT EARLY TRADE IN THE AMERICAS?

Just as in the Old World, trade played a key role in creating and expanding New World communities. In Meso-America, just as in the areas around the Sahara, ecological diversity acted as the impetus to trade. The Maya kingdoms in Meso-America from the Early Classic period (about 250 CE) to the Terminal

---

[9]   Al-Bakri, "Book of Routes and Kingdoms," in *Corpus of Early Arabic Sources for West African History*, ed. N. Levtzion and F. F. P Hopkins, trans. J. F. P. Hopkins (Cambridge: Cambridge University Press, 1981), 76.

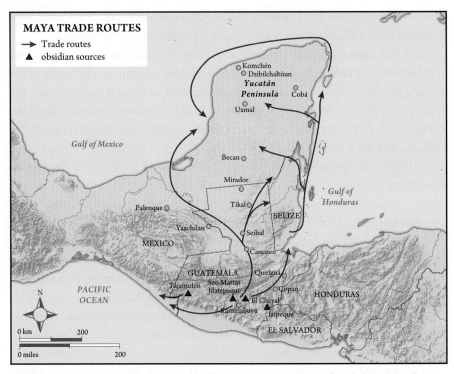

MAP 8.4   MAYA TRADE ROUTES   Much of what the Maya needed was found relatively locally. Long-distance trade was restricted more to luxury goods for the maintenance of the elite.

Classic (1100 CE) circulated both prestige goods, such as shells, beads, metals, and exotic feathers, as well as staples, such as salt. The diversity of the ecological regions of the Maya heartland meant that different commodities originated in different locations, as Robert Sharer puts it: "Differences in elevation, amount of rainfall, availability of water, temperature, distribution of plant and animal life, soil conditions, and location of natural resources combine in the Maya area to produce one of the most diverse environments for its size found anywhere in the world."[10]

But Demarest thinks it likely that most Maya cities of the Classic period derived their subsistence locally, within about 25 miles of population centers, based on the agricultural productivity of the region, and were even able to find most building materials, such as wood, bone, and stone, locally as well. Without pack animals or vehicles (no camels, here), carrying foodstuffs on human backs

---

[10]   Robert J. Sharer and Loa P. Traxler, *The Ancient Maya* (Redwood City, CA: Stanford University Press, 2006), 53.

was expensive as the energy needed to move goods detracted from the energy-producing food that was being transported.

Long-distance trade during the seventh and eighth centuries with the Mexican behemoth of a city Teotihuacán focused on luxury items of great importance to the Maya elites; goods such as feathers, jade, and precious stones were used in religious and public ceremonies that were key to Maya political control and were therefore likely monopolized by the rulers. The exact structure of trade, how it was controlled, and by whom are largely conjecture however. The economic picture of the Maya can be sketched only hypothetically until more evidence is unearthed. Ecological endowments, however, were not always equal. Some cities controlled more valuable resources than others. In particular, access to water influenced political structures because irrigation required higher levels of central coordination, and this led to a larger role for managerial elites. In communities near lakes or rivers this need was absent.

Obsidian, a major trade commodity among the Maya, was heavily traded and played an important part in Maya economics and culture. Obsidian was a favored Neolithic stone and was highly valued in the Americas long after it had been largely replaced by metals in the Old World. The Maya considered it the best cutting tool, whether adhered to wooden swords or knives or fashioned into dart points. Owing to its cryptocrystalline structure, it could be chipped into complex forms known as "eccentrics," used decoratively and in ceremonial functions. Obsidian's cutting properties also made it useful in bloodlettings, which, in contrast to the less frequent human sacrifices, were a large part of Maya everyday life. "The fine, razor–sharp edge of obsidian blades would be effective in the cutting of genitals, ears, cheeks and other tender flesh that was subject to autosacrifice," says Demarest. "If, as many scholars believe, autosacrifice was practiced at all levels of Maya society, this may have been one of its major functions."[11]

Whereas obsidian was essential for many cultural functions, salt was a biological necessity. As in Africa, salt figured prominently in Maya trade and provides an exception to the rule of bulk goods being traded only locally. Salt occurs in *salinas,* or coastal salt flats in the Yucatán. Archeologists have determined that these saline swamps provided somewhere in the region of 20,000 metric tons of salt yearly. The interior of the peninsula, on the other hand, lacked salt altogether; this imbalance between coast and interior prompted an intensive salt trade, and canoe travel up rivers allowed traders to avoid the challenge of transporting goods via human portage through difficult overland terrain. A city such as Tikal, which had an estimated population of some 50,000 during the Classic period, would have needed an average of 130 tons of salt each year.

---

[11]   Demarest, *Ancient Maya*, 158.

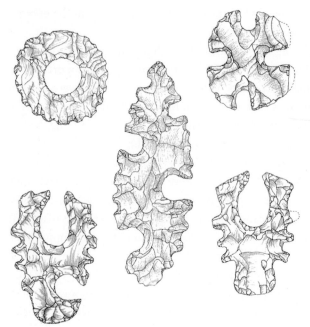

"Eccentrics" were pieces of chipped obsidian used decoratively or in rituals. Obsidian's fine cryptocrystalline structure allows for such fine craftsmanship. Some were also used as weapons or tools for bloodletting. It was a major trade item.

In Mexico, by around by 650, Teotihuacán had about 125,000 inhabitants, making it one of the six largest cities in the world at that time. Occupying a different ecology from the Maya lands to the south, Teotihuacán needed to import many items. Its size, however, allowed it to throw its weight around, and its remains tell the story of a militaristic society that used its power in the time-honored practice of acquiring goods: "The main reason for the use of force," says archeologist Richard Adams, "appears to have been to secure trade routes and access to commodities."[12] In particular, cacao beans (chocolate) from the Pacific coast of Guatemala, tropical bird feathers—largely of the quetzal—from the highlands and lowlands, salt from the lagoons of northern Yucatán, and medicinal herbs from the lowland Maya tropical rain forest.

What is of note about Teotihuacán, apart from its prominence as America's largest city at this time, is that its influence was felt in many parts of the Maya region. Tikal and Copan, in particular, were ruled, from the fourth century, by dynasties with ties to the city. Highland centers, such as Kaminaljuyú, have revealed artifacts, ceramics, and buildings with architectural details clearly influenced by Teotihuacán. Whether these influences suggest trade, war, or marriage alliances is not clear; but in some cases local rulers no doubt enjoyed a certain exotic caché thanks to their foreign associations with such glamorous cities.

[12]   Richard Adams, *Ancient Civilizations of the New World* (San Antonio: University of Texas Press, 1997), 47.

Teotihuacán, Avenue of the Dead, from the Pyramid of the Moon, Looking Toward the Pyramid of the Sun   The city had a population of some 125,000 in 650 CE, making it the sixth largest city in the world at that time. Artifacts from around Meso-America show influence from this city.

What Role Did Trade Play in State Formation?

Ecological diversity partly explains trade. But we also need to consider the social factors, to which we have alluded above. Who controlled trade? How did trade fit into the political systems of civilizations, and what role did it play in their wider culture?

There is a feedback loop at work here, involving trade and the growth of states: trade provided the resources communities needed to grow from settlements to kingdoms, states, and, in some cases, empires. While trade may have created states, states created the need for more trade, in a mutually reinforcing relationship. But the nature of this state-growing trade differed markedly throughout the ancient world.

WHAT ROLE DO PRESTIGE GOODS PLAY IN DEVELOPING STATES?

The difference between want and need in a trade context is the difference between subsistence goods and prestige goods. Humans from way back have dreamed big;

both subsistence and prestige goods played a role in the earliest human societies, suggesting that we are motivated not only by rational needs but also by less than rational wants. Elites have always used prestige goods, which usually came from distant lands, to shore up the mystique of their power. This habit may well have begun with the advent of social stratification with the earliest societies and can be seen in the way that leaders of many societies physically adorn themselves, from the exotic feathers and animal skins of Maya kings to the diamond-encrusted tiaras of European royalty.

Historians Kenneth Pomeranz and Steven Topik pointed out that trade, like speech, can be *expressive*. That is to say, apart from moving things around, trade also signifies things: "Acquiring a particular good or sending it to others was (and still is sometimes) a way of making a statement about who a person or a group was or wanted to be, or about what social relationships people had or desired with others, as much as it was a way of maximizing strictly material comfort."[13] Trade in goods, therefore, is as much a symbolic act as an economic one.

Consider the oyster. Remarkably, the same species of this mollusk, the thorny oyster (*Spondylus*), shows up in large quantities in archeological digs in North and South America, Europe, and the Pacific. This was not just because they were good to eat; shells harvested on the coast of Ecuador over 3,000 years ago were shaped, polished, and made into jewelry to be traded in the Andes. Cowrie shells, another staple of prehistoric trade, can still be found in circulation in western Africa, where millions of them show up in excavations, although they originated in the Indian Ocean. Significantly, such ornamentation was a cultural act, operating by aesthetic and symbolic rules, as well as a medium for communicating meaning between people (signifying understandings of mutual friendship or alliances). These were likely the goods of choice for reciprocal exchanges. Such goods were expressive of relationships between people, as well as of the status of the wearer: in the distant past, just as now, what you owned said something about the person you were. Do you drive a BMW or a beater? Is that real Prada? Were you buried with 10,000 oyster shells and a fancy copper battle-axe, or were you thrown in a hole with a dead puppy?

As a society becomes increasingly complex, the balance between wanted goods and needed goods generally shifts in favor of the wanted. Consider this description by Al-Bakri of the king of Ghana in the eleventh century CE:

> The king adorns himself like a woman [wearing necklaces] round his neck and
> bracelets on his forearms, and he puts on a high cap decorated with gold and

---

[13]   Kenneth Pomeranz and Steven Topik, *The World That Trade Created: Society, Culture and the World Economy, 1400 to the Present*, 2nd ed. (New York: M.E. Sharpe, 2006), 3.

wrapped in a turban of fine cotton. He sits in audience or to hear grievances against officials in a domed pavilion around which stand ten horses covered with gold-embroidered materials. Behind the king stand ten pages holding shields and swords decorated with gold, and on his right are the sons of the vassal kings of his country wearing splendid garments and their hair plaited with gold.[14]

All this finery simply highlights the king's greatness. Some scholars, such as the nineteenth-century historian Thorstein Veblen (1857–1929) and more recently Fernand Braudel (1902–1985), have even suggested that prestige goods played a pivotal role in the evolution of complex societies, the struggle to outspend each other driving economic and political growth.[15]

WHAT ROLE DID TRADE PLAY IN THE BUILDING OF MAYA STATES?

Scholars of the Maya are still challenged by questions such as to what extent the Maya elites were managers of their economy. Were they middlemen in trade networks? Or were they principally warlords who extracted tribute from vassal states? It had been assumed that long-distance trade built and maintained Maya kingdoms, but trade in subsistence goods probably took place more often within what historians call the "social economy," that is, unregulated exchange between producers, such as basket weavers or farmers, and small traders. This might have been as simple as a barter system, wherein you take your excess maize to the market once a week and exchange it for some cloth, chocolate, or a few cutting implements. Long-distance trade between city states or regions, however, was likely in the hands of the political elites and involved exotic goods, such as Caribbean shells, jade, magnetite (a magnetic stone), and feathers.

Long-distance trade may have played a vital role in what Demarest calls "status reinforcement," enhancing the position of rulers (in the same way that gold did with the king of Ghana). Luxury items were key to the maintenance of the Maya elite in the Classic period (200–1100 CE): "All of these materials were part of the costuming regalia of the kings, nobles and priests, without which they could not carry out the public rituals that were their principal duties in the eyes of their followers."[16]

But the extent to which the elites controlled trade probably differed significantly in different Mayan cities. Tikal, for example, had its beginnings in the

[14]   Al-Bakri, "Book of Routes and Kingdoms," 80.
[15]   Fernand Braudel, *Capitalism and Material Life, 1400–1800*, trans. Miriam Kochan (New York: Harper and Row, 1973), 235–36.
[16]   Demarest, *Ancient Maya*, 160.

Rooftops of Tikal's Monumental Architecture Tower Over the Petén Jungle Dominating regional trade in the Fifth Century, it became a tributary power of its rival Calakmul in the Mid-Sixth Century.

Pre-Classic period of Meso-American history (which is divided into several subsections, ending around 250 CE). Much of Tikal's trade focused on Teotihuacán to the north, but its success brought it to the attention of a rival power to its north, Calakmul. Both cities had abundant resources which allowed them to prosper, including deposits of chert, a kind of rock used in making stone tools and useful for starting fires (like flint). Calakmul, situated on the shores of a shallow lake, had not only access to aquatic resources but the ability to transport them by water. Both cities were well positioned to dominate lowland trade by rivers and did so to their advantage. In the mid-sixth century CE, Calakmul dealt Tikal a series of military defeats, which ended its regional influence for more than a century. Tikal became a tributary power of Calakmul, and much of its wealth found its way there.

But the Maya, unlike many Eurasian civilizations, never created a large unified empire. Instead, Maya civilization was comprised of multiple city states, all exhibiting similar cultural traits: religious practices, architectural styles, written script, tools, clothes, and other artifacts. But although city states seemed to rule themselves, they were often dominated by stronger polities. Historians debate the reasons for this lack of political unity among the Maya—thinking, no doubt, of the huge polities that developed in Eurasia at the same time (see Chapter 5). They often point to ecological barriers to explain such a lack of political unity. But it is possible that there were cultural barriers as well. It may well be that Maya beliefs prevented the kind of conquest and destruction that characterizes much of Eurasian history. "As revealed in historical accounts of diplomacy and conquest," say Sharer and Traxler, "Maya kings, in addition to pursuing their practical objectives, also wished to avoid upsetting the established order of their world. One consequence of this concern was that victorious kings allowed defeated polities to maintain their identity, and continue to be ruled by their own kings, as long as proper tribute was paid, and vassalage was acknowledged."[17] This would suggest the importance of tribute in the Maya economy.

WHAT ROLE DID TRADE HAVE IN THE RISE OF THE EARLIEST WESTERN AFRICAN KINGDOMS?

If we look at the early western African kingdoms and empires, we see similar issues at work. Ghana was a little north of the upper Niger and Senegal valleys (not to be confused with modern-day Ghana, which is farther to the south and east).

Al-Bakri described the wealth of Ghana: "The best gold found in this land comes from the town of Ghiyaro, which is eighteen days' travelling form the city of the king."[18] Ghana was probably, therefore, where gold was traded, but it was sourced from producers elsewhere. Jenne, on a southerly tributary of the Niger River, was a city largely built on the trade that it controlled from its favorable position as an entrepôt between producers in the south and Ghana and the northern African merchants who transported it back to the Muslim heartlands in the north and east.

Kanem is the other early kingdom referred to by the Muslim geographers. Lying just to the north of the Lake Chad basin, it was, like Ghana, slightly north of the areas that would have been most favorable to early agricultural and iron development but primed for trade to the north and east. Later caravans would run to the Lake Chad region from the north, and it is likely that these followed more ancient routes that would have included Kanem. It is also likely that Kanem had connections to the civilizations of the east, such as Axum on the river Nile. "It would therefore seem quite probable," say historians J. D. Fage, and William Tordoff, "that commercial motives played at least some part in the emergence of organized government in Kanem. It has been suggested, indeed, that these would relate to the development of a trade to North Africa in black slaves."[19]

Both Ghana and Kanem, therefore, occupied geographical locations that made trade almost unavoidable. Their role as middlemen in a regional network of exchange was consequential for their economic and political development. As Fage puts it, "Very obviously in the case of Ghana, somewhat less clearly perhaps in the case of Kanem, it would seem that an important motive for the development

---

[17] Sharer and Traxler, *The Ancient Maya*, 94.
[18] J. D. Fage and William Tordoff, *A History of Africa*, 4th ed. (London: Routledge, 2002), 57–58.
[19] Ibid.

of considerable kingdoms here was the economic one of engrossing the Sudanic exports which Saharan and North African peoples desired to have, and of controlling the distribution in the Sudan of the goods received in exchange."[20] In addition to the bolstering of elite power, it is likely that both Kanem and Ghana grew rich from the trade in gold and all other items which passed through their hands.

WHAT ROLE DID ARABIA PLAY IN ANCIENT TRADE?

No major powers existed in Arabia until the seventh century, but long before that the peninsula was a major part of the east–west trade routes.

Arabia Felix ("Happy Arabia") is what the Romans called today's Yemen. Although this could conceivably have been coined to celebrate the *joie de vivre* of its inhabitants, it is more likely a reference to the area's dumb luck in being blessed with certain prized items that the Romans bought in camel-loads. The modern city of Aden, on the southern tip of Yemen, receives some 10 inches of rainfall annually, far

View of the Treasury, Petra, in Jordan   Home of the Nabataeans, the spice trade crossed their territory; lots of tired and hungry traders to sell things to meant a good living— until trade shifted farther east.

[20]   Ibid.

more than the rest of the landmass to its back, which is parched desert (known, conversely, as *Arabia Deserta*). Summer monsoon winds account for this rain, which no doubt made the city a relative paradise (*Aden* being the Arabic word for Eden).

Incense is the general term for aromatic plants such as frankincense and myrrh that can be found growing on the mountain slopes of southern Arabia and across the Red Sea in Somalia. What could have accounted for the popularity of these plants? Incense had two main uses. To comprehend the first—covering up unpleasant smells—you need to understand that life in ancient cities stank, quite literally. Lack of public toilets and the inadequacy of ancient personal hygiene created a kind of olfactory nightmare that needed covering up. Myrrh oil does a reasonable job of hiding bodily odors, and in the absence of frequent bathing opportunities, this often had to suffice.

The story of frankincense is somewhat more high-minded. It was traditionally burned at funerary rites in China and India, as well as in the tabernacles of early Judaism. In the Roman republic, sacrifices of animals were usually accompanied by frankincense. Alexander the Great burned lots of it to please the gods. Given the essential uses of both frankincense and myrrh, it is not hard to see why, for thousands of years, they were packed on camels and trekked across the desert to Egypt, Mesopotamia, and the Mediterranean. Frankincense became so central to the Roman economy that it was admitted without tax, a unique privilege. Each camel-load arriving in Rome cost about 1,000 denarii (a denarius was a laborer's day wage). Given the kind of money changing hands around this commodity, it is not hard to see how incense generated wealth all along its supply chain, for camel drivers, middlemen who serviced the camel trains, and tribes who plundered them.

> ☀ Given the kind of money changing hands around this commodity, it is not hard to see how incense generated wealth all along its supply chain, for camel drivers, middlemen who serviced the camel trains, and tribes who plundered them.

Farther north, in the Jordan valley, the ancient city of Petra (which you might recognize from the Indiana Jones movies) was largely dependent upon the trade in incense and spices from Arabia and India. In the first century CE, as the Romans clashed with the Parthian Empire of Iran, Mesopotamia became a battleground for these two adversaries and rendered it unfit for trade. The Nabataeans of the Jordan valley started to profit from the trade in incense and spices that came their way, by providing food and shelter for trading caravans. They built their city in a large ravine between the Dead Sea and the Gulf of Aqaba, which today is one of the most unusual archeological sites in the world. The Nabataeans used existing caves for dwellings and for tombs and adorned their entrances with elaborately carved columns in the Greek style. At its height the city boasted shops and hotels with colonnaded porticos on its main street and rows of houses extending into the hills around. Elevated platforms served as markets for the traders and their goods.

By the second century CE, however, Petra's light was dimming, probably as a result of the growing silk trade between Rome and China, which was being established farther east. This was associated with another great trading center, Palmyra, in the Syrian desert. While already benefiting from trade between India, Arabia, and the Mediterranean, Palmyra also became a conduit for fine textiles from India, China, Persia, and central Asia. But in the city's prosperity lay the seeds of its undoing. The city was essentially a Roman frontier town, and, as such, Rome enjoyed suzerainty over it. But its most famous queen, Zenobia (r. ca. 267–272 CE), ran afoul of this arrangement when, feeling that she did not need Rome anymore, she conquered Egypt, in 269 CE, and declared Palmyra independent from the ancient world's largest superpower.

Like Cleopatra before her, Zenobia was dragged off to Rome and, according to legend, paraded in front of Emperor Aurelian's chariot in gold chains in a triumphal procession in 270.

How Did Trade Spread Religious Ideas?

Trade involved contact between different peoples, and this trade-induced contact led to several consequences, among them the spread of religious ideas. As historian Richard Foltz puts it, "Businessmen do not simply convey, sell, and acquire goods, and move on. They socialize, interact, and observe while on the road, and they take their impressions with them."[21] He points out that just as the modern American highway and airline systems were pioneered primarily for commerce but are also used by everybody else, so the ancient highways were not restricted to merchants but were used by others, prime among them monks, missionaries, and other religious individuals.

Indian Buddhists had developed the Mahayana, or "Great Vehicle," school, through which much larger numbers of adherents could achieve *nirvana*, the ultimate end of suffering; and this version of Buddhism, with its popular appeal, was more easily exported (see Chapter 7). Nestorian Christianity, a sect that had been driven underground by the Byzantine Empire, moved east in the middle centuries of the first millennium and appears, centuries later, as Folz puts it, "like a bad dream to the first Catholic missionaries in China, who find it comfortably entrenched there as the recognized resident Christianity of the East."[22] Islam also spread from west to east during the seventh and eighth centuries, dramatically changing everything in its path. The single commonality among all this religious dissemination was the Silk Road.

---

[21]   Richard Folz, *Religions of the Silk Road: Overland Trade and Cultural Exchange from Antiquity to the Fifteenth Century* (New York: St. Martin's, 1999), 3.

[22]   Ibid., 8.

WHAT WAS THE SILK ROAD?

The *Silk Road* is a catch-all term that encompasses the ancient trade that flowed along an east–west axis from China to the Mediterranean. Although it was the Chinese who were largely responsible for developing the Silk Road into the major commercial highway it was to become under the Han and after, it had likely been a collection of trading routes for centuries, if not millennia. Archeology shows that exchange systems in the steppe lands of inner Eurasia were very old. As historian David Christian says, "The reason is simple. The Inner Eurasian Steppe-lands were occupied, probably since the fourth millennium B.C.E., and certainly by 3000 B.C.E., by communities practicing extensive and mobile forms of horse pastoralism, which ensured that their contacts and influence would extend over large areas."[23] These nomads did everything on horseback, and largely because of their skills, they would play a central role in history, invading empires and states repeatedly.

Such far-roaming horse-riding nomads developed relationships with agrarian civilizations, looking for outlets for their merchandise and for new things to buy from foreigners (exchanging products from different ecologies). The to-and-fro between sedentary and nomadic societies is one of the main themes of history the world over: in China, where the nomads of the northwest often in-migrated, they created ripples of historic change, contributing significantly to China's ethnic and cultural makeup.

In the early years of the first millennium of the Common Era, the Silk Road was bookended to the east by Chang'an, the Han capital, and to the west by Rome. From Chang'an it traveled west to Mongolia and Turkestan (modern Xinjiang). At the Taklimakan Desert it forked north and south and cut through a variety of oasis towns, whence it made its way through Transoxiana, the region between today's Amu Darya and Syr Darya Rivers. The main route traveled west through Persia, eventually to Mesopotamia, the Levant, and the Roman world; but a branch also led from Transoxiana south into India.

Even in times of political stability, such as the high points of the Roman and Han Empires in the first century CE, the Silk Road was not for the idle traveler. Merchants were vulnerable to attack from bandits, hunger, thirst, dehydration, and the depredations of weather. At some time between 399 and 414 CE the Chinese Buddhist monk Faxian (Fa Hien) traveled from China to India in search of Buddhist texts. Heading west from the Great Wall the traveler and his companions encountered deserts "in which there are many evil demons and hot winds

---

[23] David Christian, "Silk Roads or Steppe Roads? The Silk Roads in World History," *Journal of World History* 11, no. 1 (2000): 8.

(travellers) who encounter them perish all to a man."[24] Such dangers often made sea routes more appealing, although they came with the distinct dangers of storms and pirates. These went across the Indian Ocean to Arabia, thence up the Red Sea or overland by camel to the Roman world. Depending on political conditions, the balance of trade shifted back and forth between sea lanes and overland routes.

Silk, originally a Chinese artifact, formed a large part of this trade, although many other commodities accompanied it. Few commodities have had quite such a close relationship with power, prestige, and politics as silk; the Chinese thought so highly of it that at many times its production was monopolized by government workshops and its distribution carefully controlled as it was a signifier of prestige. The nomad leaders prized it above all else because its comfort and luxury differentiated it (and therefore *them*) from all else. "Only rare and luxurious goods from far away could mark the difference between the ruling elite and their subjects."[25]

Precious Commodity   It is difficult to imagine paying top dollar for anything that comes out of these creatures. Emperors and kings did however; and silk was perhaps the most prized commodity traded between east and west for hundreds of years.

---

[24] James Legge, ed., trans., "The Journey of Faxian to India," in *A Record of Buddhistic Kingdoms Being an Account by the Chinese Monk Fa-Hien of His Travels in India and Ceylon (A.D. 399–414) in Search of the Buddhist Books of Discipline*, (Oxford: Clarendon Press, 1886), 9–36, http://depts.washington.edu/silkroad/texts/faxian.html.

[25] Xingru Liu, *The Silk Road in World History* (Oxford: Oxford University Press, 2010), 4.

Probably originating with a trade of silk for horses at the so-called Jade Gate on the Great Wall, silk found its way west; it was traded across central Asia, into Iran and Turkey, and eventually to the Middle East and the Mediterranean, even finding its way south to India. China, which had little high-value coinage of silver or gold, often used silk, along with wheat, as currency. Soldiers posted to the northwest frontier were often paid in silk, which they exchanged for coin; and the silk made its way to Persia and Byzantium with traders.

While silk was gaining popularity in the "western lands" far from the center of imperial China, the Chinese were learning about other commodities they wanted to get their hands on. For the Han, these involved primarily horses. A certain breed of "blood-sweating" horses (so called because of the skin parasites they carried) was of particular interest because of their strength and ability to carry armed men. These horses came from Dawan, a kingdom in central Asia; but when the Han emperor sent out a trade delegation to acquire some, the king of Dawan refused to trade. The emperor changed tactics, from trade to raid; sent an army; and this time took by force what he had been willing to pay for. The upshot of this encounter was that the Chinese realized there were many other items of interest in the western lands, notably Roman woolen textiles, grapes, and wine.

WHAT WERE THE CONSEQUENCES OF BUDDHISM'S SPREAD ALONG THE SILK ROAD?

Buddhism, originating in India, traveled with merchants to the central Asian oases, such as Merv, Bukhara, Samarkand, Kashgar, and Khutan. These oases profited greatly from trade, just as the Nabataeans in Petra did; and they provided services and facilities for merchants, who often formed distinct communities within them. Trade "diasporas"—from the Greek term for "scattering" or "sowing" of grain—were settlements of merchants who learned the ways of their hosts and acted as cultural intermediaries. Diaspora communities were often large, sometimes forming separate cities next to local cities. In the dynamic of the cross-cultural encounter there were strong cultural incentives to maintain distance, stemming from general distrust of foreigners as well as more specific distrust of merchants. Merchants therefore often brought with them all the trappings of home, and among the oases of the Silk Road, these included their monks.

☀ Merchants therefore often brought with them all the trappings of home, and among the oases of the Silk Road, these included their monks.

One of the major ways in which people converted to a new religion was via what historian Jerry Bentley has called "voluntary association," whereby there is some gain to be enjoyed by conversion. As Bentley put it, "The most powerful incentives to conversion through voluntary association were prospects for political, economic or commercial alliance with well-organized foreigners."[26] As communities along the Silk Road became familiar with the Buddhists, both monks and merchants, they began to associate Buddhism with positive and beneficial traditions, to the extent that association with Buddhism appeared attractive. Buddhist principles were often related to familiar cultural ideas in a process referred to by historians as *syncretism*. As Bentley describes it, "Syncretism blended elements from different cultural traditions in such a way that foreign traditions could become intelligible, meaningful and even attractive in a land far from its origin."[27] In addition to lining up new, foreign ideas

175-foot-tall Statue of Buddha in Bamiyan, Afghanistan (One of Two), Built in the Kushan Period (Early Centuries of the Common Era)   Bamiyan was a stopover on the ancient Silk Road, and religions as well as goods passed through it. These statues were destroyed in 2001 by the Taliban, who considered them an affront to Islam.

---

[26] Jerry H. Bentley, *Old World Encounters: Cross-Cultural Contacts and Exchanges in Pre-Modern Times* (New York: Oxford University Press, 1993), 9.

[27] Bentley, 238

with old Chinese ones, other concepts from outside were subtly changed so as to not threaten the status quo. For example, the relatively high status afforded to women in Buddhism was actively changed in the early Chinese translations to reflect the more conservative Chinese approach to gender relations. As the historian Arthur Wright put it, "For example, 'husband supports wife' becomes 'The husband controls his wife,' and 'The wife comforts the husband' became 'The wife reveres her husband.'"[28]

After the collapse of the Han Empire (220 CE), China endured several centuries of turmoil, characterized by frequent warfare and large-scale migrations. Cities were sacked repeatedly as waves of nomads penetrated northern China. With the Roman Empire on the decline as well, trade suffered along the ancient routes. But owing to the enrichment of Buddhist monasteries on many parts of the Silk Road, especially to the north and west of India and among the central Asian oasis towns, trade did not cease. Cave dwellings, used to shelter traders and monks, had been expanded over the centuries; and many had become major shrines devoted to the Buddha. The giant carved Buddhas of Bamiyan in Afghanistan (destroyed by the Taliban in 2001) exemplified this tradition and can be considered the beginning of the central Asian Silk Road.

One consequence of Buddhism's spread along the Silk Road was therefore to keep the east–west trade alive. Another was that it reached China and exerted a strong influence there for several centuries. Chinese historians call the fourth and fifth centuries "sixteen states built by five barbarians," referring to the fact that many nomads in-migrated south of the Great Wall and set up their own states inside China. This had the effect of pushing many Chinese into the marshlands of the south—taking their sericulture with them—overall enlarging the sphere of Chinese culture. Eventually, a clan of the Xianbei nomads united several northern kingdoms and formed the Northern Wei dynasty (386–534 CE).

Confucianism, which emphasized stability of lineage over generations, had little appeal for the rulers of nomadic descent; but Buddhism offered what Bentley has called a kind of "counter cultural appeal for nomads" who traditionally hated the Chinese yet depended on them for trade. From 460 CE onward, in the tradition of other statues such as those at Bamiyan, the Wei emperors had giant statues of the Buddha erected near the capital Pingcheng (modern Yungang). These statues marked the eastern end of the Silk Road and served to legitimize the emperors.

Many Chinese who had suffered generations of migration and instability and had lost track of their lineages found little of relevance in the archaic traditions of an elitist Confucianism. Buddhism, however, seemed a natural fit, especially the Mahayana Buddhism, which was the religion of choice along much of the Silk

---

[28]   Quoted in John King Fairbank and Merle Goldman, *China: A New History* (Cambridge, MA: Harvard University Press, 2006), 75.

Road and which emphasized personal salvation for the common man or woman. Across the board in China, Buddhism had something to offer, as historians Fairbank and Merle put it, "emperors and commoners alike sought religious salvation in an era of disruption."[29] But it took several centuries for Buddhism to find a wide following. Initially, arguments against it were that the support of monasteries was a drag on the economy—all that expensive silk!—and that it was a foreign import associated with shady merchants and scurrilous diplomats.

HOW DID ISLAM SPREAD TO THE EAST?

By the seventh century China had reestablished territorial unity under the Sui and then the Tang dynasties. It controlled the eastern end of the Silk Road, while in the west the Byzantine Empire did the same. Trade once again flourished under conditions of relative security provided by such powerful states. During this century the western end of the Silk Road came under the control of the Muslim Empire as the new religion swept out of Arabia and conquered the Byzantine and Persian Empires. For several centuries subsequently, the Muslim "caliphate" and the Tang Empire jointly controlled all east–west trade. The various Silk Routes had been competing alternatives in the past, according to the geopolitical lay of the land. Under the Muslim Abbasid dynasty (750–1258), everything from the Middle East to the Oxus River in central Asia and the Indian Ocean to the south became essentially a free-trade zone, part of a giant logistics system open to all who recognized the caliph.

"No religious tradition in world history," says Foltz, "favored trade as much as did Islam."[30] Muhammad himself was a merchant by profession, trade being a major part of the Meccan economy of the time—although the details of this trade, how far it went, what was traded, etc., are disputed by scholars. We know that his first wife, Khadijah, employed him to run caravans to Syria, suggesting that she owned the goods and was an independent businesswoman.

The young Muslim community had been driven out of Mecca by opposition from other Meccans, fearing that Muhammad's ideas were bad for business (quite apart from being offensive to their beliefs). It resettled farther north in Yathrib (Medina) in 622. From here they commenced raiding the caravans that passed to and from Mecca. Raiding was a mainstay of the tribal economy of Arabia. There were rules against raiding caravans belonging to your own clan or to tribes with whom you had nonaggression pacts. Increasing numbers of tribes came to the Muslims seeking such pacts, which profession of loyalty became known by later writers as *Islam* or "submission." However, when, by the end of the seventh

---

[29] Ibid.
[30] Foltz, *Religions of the Silk Road*, 89.

century, the Muslims had forged treaties with the majority of the tribes in Arabia, almost everybody appeared on the do-not-raid list.

Given that raiding each other was prohibited, it is no surprise that the new Muslim community looked outside the Arabian Peninsula for economic opportunities. To the north and east, the Byzantine and Sassanian Empires had been locked in a death grip for decades, battling each other for control of what would become the Middle East. Their armies therefore lacked the vigor of the new Arab armies coming out of the desert. As Foltz puts it, "Their success in defeating the armies of both empires probably surprised the armies of the Muslims as much as it did their imperial enemies."[31] Historian Marshall Hodgson described the early campaigns of the Muslims: "From raids for booty, or for, at most, a border lordship over the nearby peasantry, the campaigns were extended into a full-scale conquest of the settled lands."[32] They may have been simply extending their customary raiding practices to the north in search of livelihood and not intending to establish a giant empire, which would, within 100 years or so, span from the Atlantic coast to the Oxus in central Asia and the Indus in India. In other words, the Arabs might have acquired their empire in a fit of absence of mind.[33]

As Muslim armies moved east, much of the conquered population was allowed to maintain their religious affiliations, forced conversions being relatively rare. In 710 the Arabs had crossed the river Oxus and subsequently conquered Samarkand and Bukhara, jewels in the Silk Road's crown. The tenth-century Muslim writer al-Muqadissi recorded the great wealth of resources traded among the oases of central Asia:

> From Tirmidh, soap and asafoetida [a strong-smelling resinous herb]; from Bukhara, soft fabrics, prayer carpets, woven fabrics for covering the floors of inns, copper lamps, Tabari tissues, horse girths (which are woven in places of detention), Ushmuni fabrics [from the Egyptian town of Ushmunayn], grease, sheepskins, oil for anointing the head . . . from Khorezmia, sables, miniver [a white fur], ermines, and the fur of steppe foxes, martens, foxes, beavers, spotted hares, and goats.[34]

All of this, and much more, accrued to the new Muslim overlords as they continued their march east. By the middle of the eighth century the scale of the Muslim

---

[31] Ibid., 92.

[32] Marshall Hodgson, *The Venture of Islam: Conscience and History in a World Civilization*, vol. 1 (Chicago: University of Chicago Press, 1977), 199.

[33] How the British essayist John Robert Seeley described the creation of the British Empire, in *The Expansion of England* (Boston: Roberts Brothers, 1883).

[34] al-Muqadissi, quoted in Christian, "Silk Roads or Steppe Roads?"7.

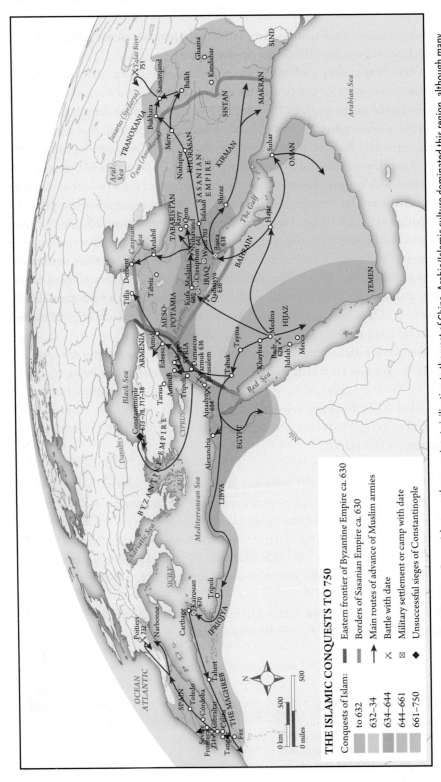

THE ISLAMIC CONQUESTS TO 750

Conquests of Islam:

— Eastern frontier of Byzantine Empire ca. 630

— Borders of Sasanian Empire ca. 630

→ Main routes of advance of Muslim armies

✕ Battle with date

⊠ Military settlement or camp with date

◆ Unsuccessful sieges of Constantinople

to 632

632–34

634–644

644–661

661–750

MAP 8.5 THE ISLAMIC CONQUESTS By 750 Islam was the preeminent civilization to the west of China. Arabic/Islamic culture dominated this region, although many local cultures played a role, as in western and northern Africa, Persia, and central Asia.

conquests and the numbers of people now under their sovereignty made the purity of the Islamic message difficult to maintain, and the historic and sophisticated cultures which they conquered inevitably changed the dynamics of the new empire. By 750 CE, the Abbasids initiated a revolution, set up their own caliphate in the former Sassanian city of Baghdad, and focused their attention to the east.

Forced conversions may have been few in the aftermath of conquest, but along the ancient trade routes people gradually began converting to Islam. With the passage of time, Bentley's "conversion by voluntary association" began to kick in as people saw benefit in being a part of the Islamic community: "A businessman could feel that becoming a Muslim would facilitate contacts and cooperation with other Muslim businessmen both at home and abroad; he would also benefit from favorable conditions extended by Muslim officials and from Islamic laws governing commerce."[35] While this was a largely male conversion, the effects expanded out to the rest of the family. Given that education, conducted at home for small children, was the preserve of women, the new religion was passed on in this way as well. The combination of military conquest and the subsequent Muslim control of trade routes from northern Africa to central Asia resulted in large-scale conversions of populations over the succeeding generations in all these areas.

How Did Trade Spread Disease?

Beyond spreading religion and goods around, trade-driven contact had darker sides; and the darkest, perhaps, was disease. This story starts with a kind of obese squirrel—unlikely culprit, perhaps, for such a narrative. Next time you happen across a groundhog—for they are of the same family—you might think of the relationship between trade and disease. The tarbagan, inhabiting Siberia and parts of Mongolia, is one of the "animal reservoirs" of the plague bacillus, *Yersinia pestis*, otherwise known as the Black Death. Given that the tarbagan did not interact much with humans, the effects of *Yersinia pestis* were generally kept at bay. The disease itself was transferred to other animals by fleas. But one of these provided better access to humans—the rat, known to be a *commensal* species, that is, one sharing its habitation with humans. It was fleas on the backs of black rats which transferred the plague virus to humans.

Although plenty of infectious diseases ravaged various civilizations hundreds of years before what historians can identify as the "plague," they were probably variations of smallpox and measles originating in animal husbandry in the Fertile Crescent. But in 541 CE, during the reign of Byzantine emperor Justinian, a deadly plague occurred which bore the hallmarks of the Black Death. This, in all

---

[35] Foltz, *Religions of the Silk Road*, 96.

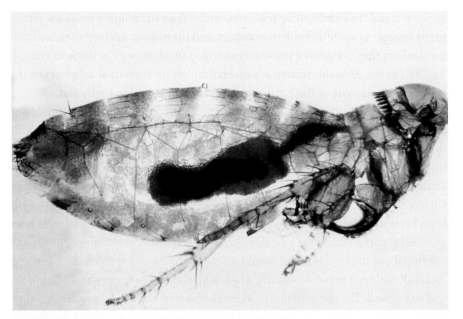

The Downside of Trade: Flea with Plague Pathogens   The rats carried the fleas, and the fleas carried the disease.

probability, had traveled from the animal reservoirs of inner Asia or the Himalayan foothills to the Malabar coast of India on fleas hitchhiking on black rats, which scrambled down mooring ropes of the Arab trading dhows, thence across the Indian Ocean. This route might well have been used more heavily in the sixth century since the Sassanian rulers of Persia had banned the sale of copper and iron to the Roman Byzantine Empire and during the reign of Justinian had also inflated the price of silk. The Byzantines, like the Chinese, exhibited a kind of not-altogether-rational obsession with silk and restricted its use to high officials and clergy. The Indian Ocean route landed goods in Yemen or at the (Christian) kingdom of Axum in today's Eritrea. Thence goods traveled overland by camel to Byzantium.

This is how the contemporary historian Procopius recorded what became known as the "Plague of Justinian":

> At this time it was not easy to see anyone in Byzantium out of doors; all those who were in health sat at home either tending the sick or mourning the dead. If one did manage to see a man actually going out, he would be burying one of the dead. All work slackened; craftsmen abandoned all their crafts, and any task which any man had in hand. In a city which was simply overflowing with good things a harsh famine ran riot. It seemed hard and indeed very remarkable to have enough bread or anything else. As a result even to some of the sick the end of their life came to seem untimely because of the want of provisions. To sum it

up, it was quite impossible to see anyone dressed in Chlamys [cloak used for formal dress] in Byzantium, especially when the emperor fell ill (for he too had a bubonic swelling); in the city which held the sovereignty over the whole Roman Empire everyone was wearing cloaks benefitting private citizens and staying quietly at home. This was the course of the plague in Byzantium and in the rest of the Roman Empire. It also attacked Persian territory and all the other Barbarians.[36]

Contact and exchange, this time largely in the form of merchants, had acted to introduce deadly diseases into hitherto unprotected populations with deadly and historic consequences.

REGION	MOVEMENT OF GOODS	DEVELOPMENT OF STATES	SPREAD OF RELIGION	SPREAD OF DISEASE
Maya	Ecological diversity of Mesoamerica major motivation to trade.	Trade and war enriched communities and supported the elites	Mayan religion was relatively uniform so this does not compare with Eurasia	Disease not a major factor until the arrival of the Europeans
N. Africa	Desert-edge or Sahel, lent itself to trade between differing ecologies	Trade was central to Ghana's growth as a state, and was likely of importance to that of Kanem, both profiting from exchange of gold, slaves and other commodities.	Muslims traders developed diaspora communities in Ghana and beyond, leading to widespread conversions to Islam from the seventh century.	No reports of epidemics to match those in Byzantine world
C. Asia	Oases and steppe lands produced different goods. Trade between sedentary and nomadic peoples.	East-West (Silk Road) goes back to Roman-Han exchange. Oases communities developed into empires and states on trade profits.	Nestorian Christianity, and Buddhism travelled along Silk Roads.	Possible that epidemics in the sixth and seventh centuries greatly facilitated the Arab conquests of C. Asia.
Arabia	Indian Ocean coast received trade goods from the east. Aromatics growing in S. Arabia had a market in the Mediterranean world.	Trade in incense and spices gave rise to states in Yemen as well as Palmyra and Petra in the North	Islam developed in Mecca and Medina. Muslims expanded out of Arabia and conquered to the east and west.	Ocean trade from the east brought rats which conveyed disease to Rome. In Byzantium 10,000 a day die according to Procopius.
China	Varied ecology of China meant that in periods of unity the polity was almost self-sufficient.	China's states developed long before the first millennium CE. War was a major driver of states, but trade played its part.	Silk Road trade brought Buddhism and Nestorian Christianity to China by the third century.	Plague traveled the Silk Roads to China. In 762 half the population of Shantung is said to have succumbed.

What Did Trade Do?

---

[36]   Procopius, *History of the Wars*, trans. Averil Cameron (New York: Washington Square Press, 1967), 121.

Conclusion: What Did Trade Do?

Trade, as we have seen, operates in several different dimensions. The most obvious of these simply moves goods around according to simple laws of supply and demand. Beyond the distinction between political and social economies—which defines who controls trade—there are the consequences of trade, both direct and indirect. If trade moved goods between different ecological zones, such as exist around the Sahara Desert, it also created wealth, for both the owners of the goods and the owners of the caravans that moved them. Wealth also accrued to the places through which trade passed, such as the oases of the Silk Road; and one consequence of this wealth was the establishment of states, which could use resources to grow. We see this pattern in the western African kingdoms, the Maya heartland, and central Asia along the Silk Roads.

Beyond this were the less direct consequences of trade, what we can call the "exchanges." Trade has far-reaching cultural, religious, and biological consequences because merchants and other people traveling the trade routes interacted socially, politically, religiously, and sexually. This led to religious conversion, for many reasons and over many centuries, as well as to population mixing and the spread of deadly diseases. Such exchanges would play a major role in world history from the premodern period and still define our world today, being a pivotal element of what we call "globalization."

Words to Think About

Commodity	Monopoly	Tribute
Sahel	Syncretism	

Questions to Think About

- What noneconomic functions did trade perform in the ancient world?
- Why did ecological diversity act as a spur to trade?
- What is the relationship between trade and war?

Primary Sources

Al-Bakri. "Book of Routes and Kingdoms." In *Corpus of Early Arabic Sources for West African History*. Edited by N. Levtzion and F. F. P. Hopkins. Translated by J. F. P. Hopkins. Cambridge: Cambridge University Press, 1981.

Herodotus. *The Histories*. Baltimore: Penguin, 1968.

Legge, James, ed., trans. "The Journey of Faxian to India." In *A Record of Buddhistic Kingdoms Being an Account by the Chinese Monk Fa-Hien of His Travels in India and Ceylon (A.D. 399–414) in Search of the Buddhist Books of Discipline*, 9–36. Oxford: Clarendon Press, 1886. http://depts.washington.edu/silkroad/texts/faxian.html.

Procopius. *History of the Wars*. Translated by Averil Cameron. New York: Washington Square Press, 1967.

Sima Qian. *Records of the Grand Historian*, vol. 2. Translated by Burton Watson. New York: Columbia University Press, 1961.

Smith, Adam. *An Inquiry Into the Nature and Causes of the Wealth of Nations*. London: W. Strahan, 1776.

Secondary Sources

Adams, Richard. *Ancient Civilizations of the New World*. San Antonio: University of Texas Press, 1997.

Bentley, Jerry H. *Old World Encounters: Cross-Cultural Contacts and Exchanges in Pre-Modern Times*. New York: Oxford University Press, 1993.

Braudel, Fernand. *Capitalism and Material Life, 1400–1800*. Translated by Miriam Kochan. New York: Harper and Row, 1973.

Christian, David. "Silk Roads or Steppe Roads? The Silk Roads in World History." *Journal of World History* 11, no. 1 (2000): 1–26.

Curtin, Philip D. *Cross Cultural Trade in World History*. Cambridge: Cambridge University Press, 1984.

Demarest, Arthur. *Ancient Maya: The Rise and Fall of a Rainforest Civilization*. Cambridge: Cambridge University Press, 2010.

Fage, J. D., and William Tordoff. *A History of Africa*, 4th ed. London: Routledge, 2002.

Fairbank, John King, and Merle Goldman. *China: A New History*. Cambridge, MA: Harvard University Press, 2006.

Folz, Richard. *Religions of the Silk Road: Overland Trade and Cultural Exchange from Antiquity to the Fifteenth Century*. New York: St. Martin's, 1999.

Hodgson, Marshall. *The Venture of Islam: Conscience and History in a World Civilization*, vol. 1. Chicago: University of Chicago Press, 1977.

Liu, Xingru. *The Silk Road in World History*. Oxford: Oxford University Press, 2010.

Polyani, Karl, Conrad M. Arensberg, and Harry W. Pearson, eds. *Trade and Markets in Early Empires*. New York: Cambridge University Press, 1984.

Pomeranz, Kenneth, and Steven Topik. *The World That Trade Created: Society, Culture, and the World Economy, 1400 to the Present*, 2nd ed. New York: M.E. Sharpe, 2006.

Pulak, Cemal. "Discovering a Royal Ship from the Age of King Tut: Uluburun, Turkey." In *Beneath the Seven Seas*, edited by George F. Bass, 34–47. New York: Thames & Hudson, 2005.

Seeley, John Robert. *The Expansion of England*. Boston: Roberts Brothers, 1883.

Sharer, Robert J., and Loa P. Traxler. *The Ancient Maya*. Redwood City, CA: Stanford University Press, 2006.

For additional resources, including maps, primary sources, and visuals, web links, and quizzes, please go to **www.oup.com/us/cole**

The War in Heaven, from John Milton's *Paradise Lost*, Nineteenth-Century Engraving   What the demons needed was better weapons against God. Gunpowder, nuclear fission, "The Force"—technology has always had upsides and downsides. Either way, inventions that change human history have all arisen from the earth and natural processes, from the Acheulian hand axe to iron ore.

Chapter 9

What Role Did Technology Play in Cultural Exchange and Expansion?

Satan, Gunpowder, and Gizmos

In Book 6 of John Milton's epic poem *Paradise Lost*, the fallen angels and "fiends" are at a loss as to how to defeat God. They stand around bemoaning their inadequate weapons, until Satan gives them a morale boost: everything we need, he tells the dejected demons, is right here! "Deep underground, materials dark and crude," can be found with which they can make:

> Such implements of mischief, as shall dash
> To pieces, and o'erwhelm whatever stands
> Adverse, that they shall fear we have disarmed
> The Thunderer of his only dreaded bolt.[1]

Satan recognized what civilizations the world over have figured out: the component parts of everything we need are all here, under our feet. Gunpowder, the quintessentially devilish invention, credited to ninth-century China, was made from saltpeter, sulfur, and charcoal, all naturally occurring substances. Less diabolical things too derive from nature, such as paper, another world-changing early Chinese invention, from hemp, grasses, or wood pulp.

---

[1] John Milton, *Paradise Lost*, Book VI 488–91, https://www.dartmouth.edu/~milton/reading_room/pl/book_6/text.shtml.

THINKING ABOUT TECHNOLOGY

What Were the Contributions of Agricultural Technologies?
- Innovations in techniques and crops have created minirevolutions throughout history, and if we are to feed more than 8 billion on this planet, the innovations must keep coming.

How Did Metal Technology Affect the State?
- [With coal] Song China pioneered the revolution from Stone-Age energy economy in which humans exploited organic resources to a new age of fossil fuels.

What Is Technology Transfer?
- Military technology is the technology of most interest to the state. In the quest for wealth, conquest provided the quickest bang for the buck, so all rulers paid close attention to the arms race.

Is Technology Gender-Blind?
- China's characteristic division of labor was embedded in the notion that "women weave and men farm."

How Did the State Support Science and Technology?
- The Islamic caliphate of Baghdad is more closely associated with support of the "sciences" than perhaps any other classical or medieval state.

How Did Science Support the State?
- Patronage of the sciences created information that when closely guarded could legitimate and empower rulers.

How Did Trade and Communication Needs Spur Technological Innovation?
- Pacific Islanders contributed to a Pacific-wide culture, and this they did at a very early date.

Conclusion
- By about 1000 CE, humanity had reached a technological plateau. Most of the major inventions and discoveries that would carry the human race to the Industrial Revolution were in place, and advances from this position would represent refinements of knowledge already in place.

Notwithstanding the earthly origins of technology, the things we produce have such a dramatic effect on our lives that we often treat them with special reverence. No accident, then, that until very recently in many parts of Africa iron *smelting*—the process of turning oxidized iron ore into usable metal—was accompanied by the sacrifice of an animal, such as a goat's throat being slit and its blood spilled upon the dry earth; the offering of "food" for the furnace; and prayers to spirits and ancestors. The process of turning base lumps of useless ore into things of inestimable value and use, weapons and tools, was itself part magic.

Introduction

It must, I think, be perfectly clear, that to understand lives of the ordinary activities of human beings in ages other than our own, it is indispensible to consider the technologies that served them for they formed in many respects the very framework of those lives themselves.

JACK SIMMON, *HISTORY OF TECHNOLOGY*

Technology is a "big-ticket" item in the history of the world; devices, inventions, processes, and procedures have clearly had a major impact on the course of human events, from the Acheulian hand axe to the atom bomb. In this chapter we will go beyond cataloging the various inventions, to explore how innovation was variously encouraged or stifled, what purposes it was set to, and how it affected men and women, old and young, rich and poor.

Toward the end of the first millennium, certain technologies were in use around the world, with similar consequences. All sedentary societies at this time employed technologies in the fields of agriculture, metallurgy, warfare, construction, and even to some extent religion, for which they all used mathematics and astronomy to establish dates for rituals, festivals, and many other purposes. Much of this technology has been used to better human existence. But as we met basic needs, we turned our attention to less basic needs, always raising the bar on what was considered essential. We turned our attention to efficiency, then comfort, and finally luxury.

Technology does things, but it also conveys and expresses meaning in various ways, for instance, in its role as both creator and reflector of gender roles, as we will learn below in discussions of textiles and ironworking in Africa and Asia.

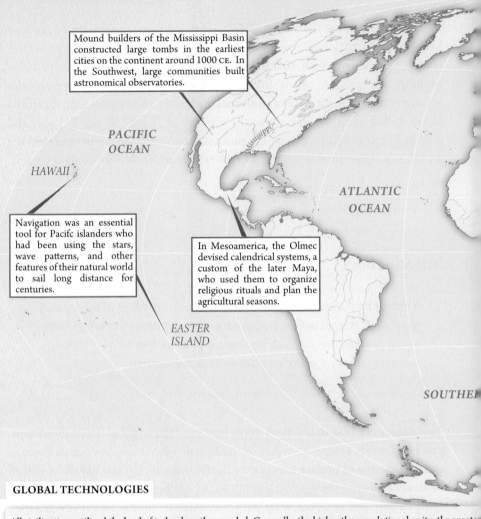

Mound builders of the Mississippi Basin constructed large tombs in the earliest cities on the continent around 1000 CE. In the Southwest, large communities built astronomical observatories.

PACIFIC OCEAN

HAWAII

Navigation was an essential tool for Pacifc islanders who had been using the stars, wave patterns, and other features of their natural world to sail long distance for centuries.

In Mesoamerica, the Olmec devised calendrical systems, a custom of the later Maya, who used them to organize religious rituals and plan the agricultural seasons.

ATLANTIC OCEAN

EASTER ISLAND

SOUTHEI

GLOBAL TECHNOLOGIES

All civilizations utilized the level of technology they needed. Generally, the higher the population density, the greater

MAP 9.1 GLOBAL TECHNOLOGIES

TIMELINE

476 CE
Indian Mathematician Arybhata born

ca. 850 CE
Urban area of Jenne-Jeno reaches maximum geographic area

ca. 700
Stirrups appear in Europe

832
Al Ma'mun founds the House of Wisdom in Baghdad

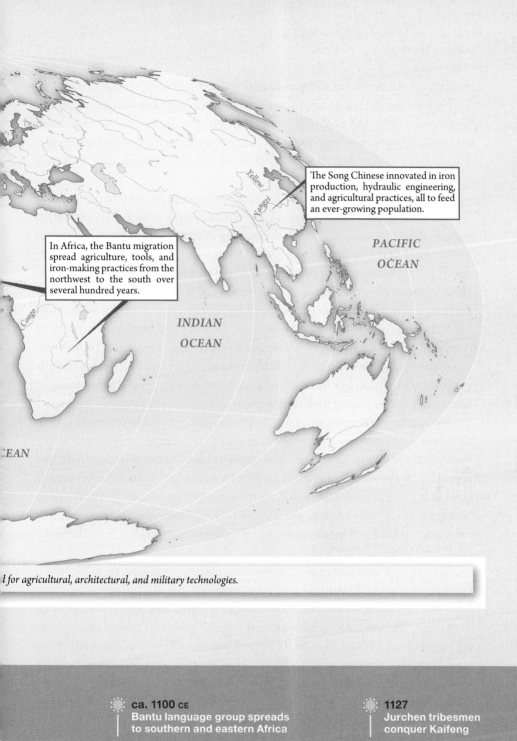

The Song Chinese innovated in iron production, hydraulic engineering, and agricultural practices, all to feed an ever-growing population.

In Africa, the Bantu migration spread agriculture, tools, and iron-making practices from the northwest to the south over several hundred years.

Yellow

Yangzi

PACIFIC OCEAN

Congo

INDIAN

OCEAN

CEAN

d for agricultural, architectural, and military technologies.

ca. 1100 CE
Bantu language group spreads
to southern and eastern Africa

1127
Jurchen tribesmen
conquer Kaifeng

ca. 1000
Horseshoes shoes and
collar harness introduced

960-1279
Song Dynasty

And this is nothing new; anthropologists think that the earliest hand axes may have served communicative purposes, sometimes being more valuable as objects in their own right than as efficient tools. Is this true of devices today? Are various electronic devices more important for the things they can do or for the fact that they signal membership in a group that (1) can afford them, (2) is socially connected, and (3) is cool?

Technology both shapes us as humans and is an expression of the societies that give birth to it. As anthropologist Francesca Bray puts it, "Technology *is* culture, that is its work is as much the making of subjects and the production of meaning as it is the making of objects and the mastery of nature."[2]

What technology does, therefore, will be a major focus of this chapter; and since so much of recorded history has happened within states of one kind or another, we will be considering technology in the context of the state. Most innovation occurred within states because they are the best concentrators of resources. Many states officially supported research in science and technology, usually not out of a disinterested concern for "science" per se, which was not really a subject at this time, but in search of a competitive edge against other states or better ways of controlling their own populations.

But military technology was not the only area of interest to rulers. Research, for instance, in astronomy, gave rulers knowledge of celestial events, legitimizing their claims to power. Even after monotheisms like Christianity and Islam had appeared on the scene, rulers still looked for astrological clues, for propitious signs that a campaign might be successful or a marriage alliance fruitful. Other "sciences," such as alchemy, the forebear of modern chemistry, was often employed in the search for immortality, rulers hoping for a release from the inevitability of death.

Technology undoubtedly improved the human condition in many ways. Food production and medical knowledge increased. Metallurgy and agriculture improved living conditions. But in addition to the good came downsides; resource depletion, pollution, and social inequality were all problems related to burgeoning populations, derived from technological prowess. These problems, which we may think of as a progress trap, illustrate how simplistic narratives highlighting technological advances as a story of human progress are insufficient if we are to understand technology's place in history. All these issues, still pertinent today, were also in operation in the period under consideration here, the late first and early second millennia CE. History is, after all, a continuum; the role of technology, and its consequences 1,000 years ago, has a direct bearing on our own time.

---

2   Francesca Bray, *Technology and Gender: Fabrics of Power in Late Imperial China* (Los Angeles: University of California Press, 1997), 369.

What Were the Contributions of Agricultural Technologies?

When we think of technology today we tend to envision computers, not farmers. But agriculture meets all the criteria of technology: not only do we selectively breed plants and animals to maximize their productivity, disease resistance, and flavor but we develop practices and procedures for germinating, planting, cultivating, and harvesting that maximize results, employing engineering principles and mechanical design in the process. And while the agricultural revolution is ancient history at this date, innovations in techniques and crops have created repeated minirevolutions throughout history; and if we are to feed 8 billion people on this planet, the innovations must keep coming.

HOW DID AFRICA'S TECHNOLOGICAL PROFILE DIFFER FROM EURASIA'S?

One of the key measures of technological development is population and population density. Whereas in Egypt a dense population was made possible by the river Nile, sub-Saharan Africa's population density was far lower. Even today sub-Saharan Africa is half as dense as Europe (and it has quadrupled since about 1960).

Historians often discuss technology in Africa as a story of what was lacking there. The plow, for instance, was notably absent from most of precolonial Africa. This may have been a consequence of Africa's poor soils or of the tsetse fly, a vector of several diseases for humans and other animals. As anthropologist Jack Goody has pointed out, in areas without the plow, states arose later or not at all, whereas in northern Africa including Ethiopia (which had plows and draft animals) large states arose much earlier.[3] Goody also pointed out that where plow agriculture did not obtain, there was no "landlordism" or royal ownership over the land. In *slash-and-burn agriculture*, an area is cleared of forest, then planted in crops. The area is used for a few years until the soil becomes depleted, and the farmers move on to the next piece of land, leaving the used area to regenerate for a decade or so. With this need for constant movement, chiefs established their authority over their people, instead of over their land, as in other parts of Eurasia. This had consequences for later ideas about private property and agricultural development.

But to understand the role of technology in Africa, it is necessary to look beyond the absences and see what technologies were used and how they met the social needs and ecological possibilities of the various regions of the continent.

---

[3]   Jack Goody, *Technology, Tradition and the State in Africa* (London: Oxford University Press, 1971), 30–31.

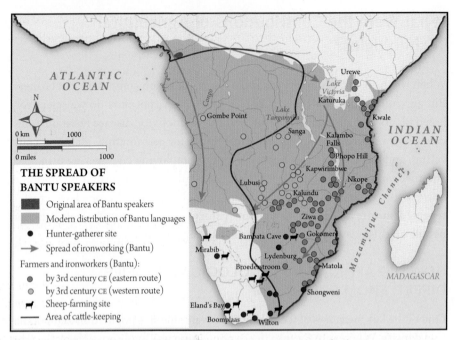

MAP 9.2   THE SPEAD OF BANTU SPEAKERS   Early archeological evidence for the "Bantu migration" made scholars think their progress was driven by warfare. But more recent studies suggest that their spread across the continent was slower and not always violent as nomads gave way to farmers, a process witnessed around the world.

This story is told largely via the movement of the Bantu people, the dominant language group on the continent.

Scholars in the 1960s pinpointed Cameroon and southern Nigeria as the origin of the Bantu family language group, a collection of some 400 closely related languages. People speaking these languages spread across Africa, from west to east and then into southern Africa, up to about 1000 CE. Nineteenth-century scholars of Africa envisioned this movement as conquest, not unlike what the Europeans were in the process of doing to Africa themselves at that time. Later scholars, however, argued that while the Bantu migration theory was essentially correct and the Bantu spread swift, instead of outright conquest, it likely involved assimilation of the hunter–gatherer population by the Bantu as much as, if not more than, extermination.[4] Where neither was the case, the nomadic people were likely pushed onto agriculturally marginal land, such as the Kalahari Desert, today's home of the Khoi-San people, speakers of Khoisan, not Bantu, languages. Other nomads retreated into the forests of the Congo basin or the high and relatively wet and cold Ituri forests of northeastern Zaire.

During the millennia before the Common Era, it was the Bantu's need for new land for farming which pushed them to migrate, and their growing numbers

---

4   See, for example, J. D. Fage and William Todoroff, *A History of Africa*, 4th ed. (London: Routledge, 2002).

would have added urgency to the need for land. Later Bantu worked iron, and this would have greatly facilitated their spread at the expense of hunter–gatherers, being a key component of what historian Jared Diamond termed "farmer power," the farmers' ability to work more land and produce more people who could sustain themselves from that land.[5]

By about 1100 CE Bantu speakers could be found on the eastern African coast and, to a lesser extent, the farther reaches of southern Africa. Africa had few indigenous food crops. The Bantu adopted the banana, originally of southeast Asian origin, which grew well in tropical climates and soils and is a surprisingly varied fruit, with some 200 varieties, able to be consumed as a sweet or savory. In this regard it fulfills the role of a staple food, giving the Bantu a further advantage in their migrations. Other indigenous crops included the yam, mushrooms, and palm oils and kernels. Maize, manioc, and sweet potatoes only arrived after the Europeans had reached the Americas.

The Bantu migration is a good example of the power of agricultural technology, harnessed to iron technology, and its consequences for population growth. Agricultural technology and engineering also enabled western Africans to establish an urban environment several thousand years ago, in what is known as the Upper Inland Niger Delta, between modern Mopti and Segou. People began settling in raised mounds built above the river's floodplain. This region has dozens of such mounds, one of which was the town of Jenne-Jeno, which by 750 CE covered as much as 82 acres of land. Together with all the neighboring mounds, Jenne-Jeno was part of a wider urban area, which at that time would have been home to several hundred thousand people. This area had been a vital crossroads for local trade long before the Arabs arrived in western Africa in the eighth century and connected it to trade networks in northern Africa. Ancient Jenne, 1.9 miles to the south of the modern city, has revealed some 16 centuries of constant occupation beginning around 200 BCE. "The archaeology of Jenne-Jeno," say archeologists Susan Keech McIntosh and Roderick J. McIntosh, "and the surrounding area clearly showed an early, indigenous growth of trade and social complexity."[6] Archeologists also found forges, proving that iron was being produced by 800 CE, with imported ores as there are no local deposits of ore. Wet rice agriculture enabled the region's population to grow, and its position astride the river system allowed traders from the desert to bring in salt, palm dates, and copper ore in exchange for fish and rice.

> ☀ The Bantu migration is a good example of the power of agricultural technology, harnessed to iron technology, and its consequences for population growth.

---

5   See Jared Diamond, *Guns Germs and Steel: The Fates of Human Societies* (New York: W.W. Norton, 1999), chap. 4.

6   Susan Keech McIntosh and Roderick J. McIntosh, "Jenne-Jeno, an Ancient African City," *Anthropology Rice,* http://anthropology.rice.edu/Content.aspx?id=500.

Agricultural technologies, along with metallurgy, gave rise to early—and indigenous—complex societies in this part of Africa. And it was the resultant rise in population that in part spurred the migration of Bantu peoples south and west across the African continent.

HOW DID THE SONG DYNASTY USE TECHNOLOGY IN AGRICULTURE?

Whereas Africa's relatively low population meant that there was little need to develop multiple new technologies to meet the challenge of feeding everybody, China offers a glaring example of how population density and technology create a feedback loop where population growth demands more food and more food means population growth.

Agricultural innovation was the pillar that supported Song China's technological revolution. "From the tenth to the fourteenth century," says historian Mark Elvin, "China advanced to the threshold of a systematic experimentation of nature, and created the world's earliest mechanized industry."[7] These two elements, experimentation of nature and mechanization, correspond directly to the definitions of science and technology. The Song dynasty's unprecedented levels of centralization, population explosion, rapid urbanization, and technological and cultural achievements were unrivaled for the period.

The dynasty's capital at Kaifeng, although only four-fifths the size of the Tang capital at Chang'an, had a population in 1021 of about 500,000 within its walls, with another half a million in the suburbs. By 1100, it had grown to 1.4 million, including military residents. The total population of the country was somewhere in the region of 100 million, growing to 120 million in the twelfth century, compared with the 60 million in Han times and about the same at the height of the Tang.

Where there is a large population there must be a lot of food. Kaifeng, not in the agricultural heartland—that was in the south—was at the junction of the Grand Canal and the Yellow River, allowing grain to travel directly to it from southern China's lower Yangtze grain basket. In 1012 the emperor Zhenzong imported 30,000 bushels of rice seed from Vietnam, specifically Champa rice, which could support two harvests a year and, in tropical climates, three.

Champa, and several other varieties of rice, grow only in water. Fields with heavy, sodden loam had to be plowed with the moldboard plow, a Chinese invention of the third century, which cut the sod, opened up the ground, and turned over the soil in a neat row next to the furrow. Best practices suggested that farmers prepared seedlings in special boxes and then transplanted them by hand

---

[7]   Mark Elvin, *The Pattern of the Chinese Past* (Stanford, CA: Stanford University Press, 1973), 179.

into the rice paddies. Weeding was a particularly important aspect of the process, and for this the Chinese invented a weeding rake or hoe. This invention long preceded the Song but was put into effect energetically, as the fourteenth-century agricultural commentator Wang Zeng noted, somewhat later than the period in question; but it is highly likely that such practices were long established:

> In the villages of the North they frequently form hoeing societies, generally of ten families. First they hoe the fields of one family, which provides all the rest with food and drink, then the other families follow in turn over the ten-day period. . . . This is a quick and pleasant way of performing the task of hoeing, and if one family should fall ill, or meet with an accident, the others will help them out. The fields are free from weeds and the harvests are always bountiful.[8]

Transplanting Rice Seedlings by Hand   Much of Asia still does it the same way.

---

[8]   Robert Temple, *The Genius of China: 3000 Years of Science, Discovery and Invention* (New York: Simon & Schuster, 1986), 15.

The Song provided land grants and loans for peasants to buy seed and equipment. This may sound like a very benevolent state, and perhaps it was in some ways; but the agricultural reforms, especially those of imperial advisor Wang Anshi (1021–1086), were part of an overall redesign of the state's economy with the express purpose of raising cash for the army. Productive peasants would be politically more malleable and fiscally more productive, and the state would benefit from interest on agricultural loans as well as increases in tax revenue. Wang Anshi was proud of his achievements: "Now the poor get loans from the government at a lower rate of interest and the people are thereby saved from poverty."[9] And the government increased its revenue, a medieval win–win situation.

The government oversaw large projects like the draining of marshy areas such as the Yangtze delta, which were then protected by dykes. Smaller projects, such as the reclaiming of hillsides by terraces, leveling of fields, and construction of small-scale dykes and ditches, were carried out by local officials and landowners with corvée labor or associations of farmers. The iconic devices that underpinned the Song agricultural revolution therefore were the dam, the sluice gate, the *noria* (a peripheral pot-wheel), and the treadle pump (for transporting water from low areas to higher fields).

"If carried out with care and diligence," says historian Donald Headrick, "wet rice cultivation provided the highest yields—that is, the most food per acre—of any form of agriculture, one that could support the highest population densities in the world."[10] And this it did. But the labor-intensive nature of such agricultural work made the state almost a prerequisite. Not only did the state provide the impetus for agricultural innovations, but it actively created solutions to the puzzle of feeding so many people. Imperial officials—extension agents—traveled throughout the country spreading agricultural know-how and looking for ways to improve practices.

The invention of woodblock printing in the ninth century also facilitated the spread of knowledge. Printing was a Tang invention and gave rise to new academies, which grew up around collections of books. These soon rivaled the older Buddhist centers of learning and were sponsored either by the state or by wealthy individuals.

While the academies mostly dealt in the currency of traditional "scholarship," reflecting the neo-Confucian concern for literature, poetry, and history, printing also gave rise to books of purely practical application. The government distributed agricultural treatises, written by master farmers, throughout the provinces.

---

[9]   Wang Anshi, "In Defense of Five Major Policies," in *Sources of Chinese Tradition*, 2nd ed., compiled by Wm. Theodore DeBary and Irene Bloom (New York: Columbia University Press, 1999), 619.

[10]   Donald Headrick, *Technology: A World History* (New York: Oxford University Press, 2009), 53.

Set of Chinese Printing Blocks from the Eighteenth Century, a Technology Invented in the Tang Dynasty

In areas where government officials found poor practices, notices would be posted locally, detailing methods of improving yields, like this one from 1180:

> After the autumn harvest has been gathered and before the cold months set in, it is necessary for a household to turn over with the plough all the land that it possesses, so that in the cold season it will be friable [workable]. After the first months of the new year, it should be opened up again several times and ploughed repeatedly. Then sow the seeds.[11]

In 1195, the scholar Zhu Xi outlined his proposals for education, which reflected a neo-Confucian interest in the humanities, that aimed to cultivate character and moral and intellectual qualities but was tempered with a concern for technical specialization. Such balance was not necessarily the rule for Song education, which was often outweighed by neo-Confucian interest in the arts of literature

---

[11] Quoted in Elvin, *The Pattern of the Chinese Past*, 115.

and poetry; in this system high officials had to be well versed but innovation had to come from somewhere, and technical subjects were not totally ignored by officialdom. But as Bray points out,

> it would be a mistake to imagine that the Chinese state was trying to promote agricultural development in the sense we use today.... Such development usually leads to some qualitative change in the mode of production ... but the state perceived the rapid generation of goods and wealth as a threat to social stability and inherently undesirable. It therefore countered this type of growth, directly or indirectly, to the best of its ability.[12]

Its ability, however, was limited, as wealth increased throughout the Song's domains in this period, especially among merchants.

Joseph Needham, the preeminent Western expert on ancient and medieval Chinese technology, saw the importance of the state in agricultural innovation but also pointed to the role of the rural population and the way in which the people were "willing to experiment and improve on their own initiative.... Peasants bred locally new and improved varieties of rice and other crops, some of which travelled hand to hand over vast distances."[13] While the role of the state was no doubt central to the overall program of increased yields, it benefited greatly from the natural inclination of the small farmer to improve his harvests, and innovation came from both directions.

The Szechwan poet Su Tung-Po of the eleventh century penned this ode to the "seedling horse," a kind of boat of indeterminate origin, designed for riding over muddy paddies and planting seedlings, which is still in use today in parts of China:

> My elm wood horse that I can lift with one hand.
> Head and rump are proudly raised, ribs and belly lie deep,
> His back is barreled like a ridge-pole tile.
> My own two feet are his four hoofs
> On which he hops and slides like a drake.
>
> The young lord with his brocade saddle-cloth, riding from the palace gate,
> Mocks me who spend my life plodding behind the plough.
> Little does he know that I too own a high-mettled steed—of wood.[14]

---

[12] Bray, *Technology and Gender*, 26.

[13] Joseph Needham, ed. *Science and Technology in Chinese Civilization*, vol. 6 (Cambridge: Cambridge University Press, 1984), 600.

[14] Ibid., 283.

How Did Metal Technology Affect the State?

Necessity, they say, is the mother of invention. The most conspicuous example from China at this time is the case of iron, which was the other major pillar of the Song economy. Since the Han dynasty the Chinese had known how to raise the temperature of a furnace, using water-powered air pumps to turn iron ore into raw "pig" iron. Tax returns from China suggest that iron production increased sixfold between 800 and 1078, topping out at about 125,000 tons, an amount that would not be reached in Europe until the 1700s at the earliest.

By the early eleventh century, the Song capital at Kaifeng was surrounded by what archeologist and historian Ian Morris, referencing the much later English industrial revolution, describes as "dark satanic mills, belching fire and smoke, sucking in tens of thousands of trees to smelt ores into iron—so many trees in fact that ironmasters bought up and clear cut entire mountains driving the price of charcoal beyond the reach of ordinary homeowners."[15] Wood fires did not produce enough heat, for long enough, to process iron. For this you needed charcoal, which burned hotter and slower, as any barbecue aficionado will tell you.

In 1013 homeowners in need of charcoal for heating fuel hit the streets, leading to hundreds of deaths in riots. The forest cover of most of northern China had been depleted to the extent that a new fuel was needed. The Chinese had known about coal since Han times, but it had never been used to fuel a forge. Budding industrialists, with the capital to recruit hundreds or thousands of workers to mine the rich coal beds in northern China, quickly put coal to use, transporting it to the foundries via the Grand Canal. Soon the state muscled in, and by 1170 there were 48 state foundries, operating with thousands of employees. All the country's natural resources were nominally owned by the state, and iron and coal were to be no exception. China had, for the time being, escaped from the ecological bottleneck created by its material needs; but it had also pioneered the revolution from the Stone-Age energy economy, in which humans exploited organic sources such as plants and animals for energy, to a new age of fossil fuels. The poet Su Shi (1037–1101) wrote,

> Who would have thought
> that in those mountains lay a hidden treasure,

> China had, for the time being, escaped from the ecological bottleneck created by its material needs, but it had also pioneered the revolution from the Stone-Age energy economy in which humans exploited organic sources such as plants and animals for energy to a new age of fossil fuels.

---

[15] Ian Morris, *Why the West Rules—For Now: The Patterns of History and What They Reveal About the Future* (New York: Farrar, Straus and Giroux, 2011), 380.

in heaps, like black jewels, ten thousand cartloads of coal.
Flowing grace and favor, unknown to all.

And what were the consequences of this discovery?

> In the southern mountains, chestnut forests now breathe easy;
> In the Northern Mountains, no need to hammer hard ore.
> They will cast you a sword of a hundred refinings,
> To chop a great whale of a bandit to mincemeat.[16]

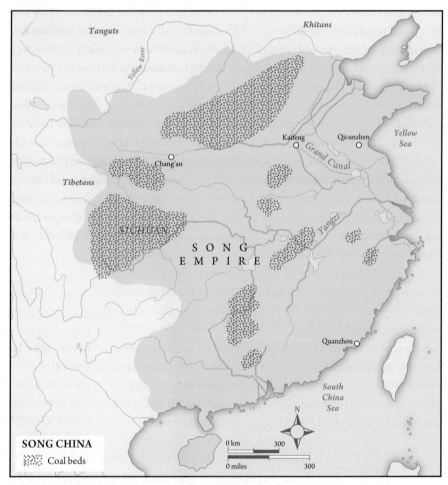

MAP 9.3   SONG CHINA   Song China fell back on technology—coal came to the rescue of the dwindling forests, and iron production subsequently took off in the mid-eleventh century.

---

[16]   Ibid., 382.

What Is Technology Transfer?

But it was ironic to talk so glibly about chopping enemies to pieces. On January 9, 1127, in a blizzard, Kaifeng came under siege from the Jurchen nomads. As the defenders fired iron bolts from their crossbows into a wall of snow, the Jurchens, losing thousands of men to boiling oil, crude incendiary devices, and giant boulders, pushed their massive siege towers against the walls. Gradually, the defenders became unnerved, and soon a widespread panic set in, sending thousands fleeing from the city as the Jurchens made it over the walls, killing and raping as they went. Many fled; some women even drowned themselves to avoid defilement. The emperor was captured and led away.

One reason for this disaster was the Song's own technological success and the logic of technology transfer. New ideas—and weapons in particular—catch on swiftly. The Chinese foundries around Kaifeng equipped the largest army ever seen, some 1.25 million men supplied with 16 million arrowheads and 32,000 suits of armor every year. Ironworkers manufactured steel (harder and lighter than iron) by adjusting the amount of carbon in the iron to precise levels. Military technologists invented the catapult and used gunpowder in grenades and crude bombs. Whereas previously sieges were drawn-out affairs with only a modest chance of success, these new weapons changed the balance and were hard to keep secret. "Unlike agricultural techniques, which are specific to particular environments," says Headrick, "military technology diffuses rapidly from one people to another, as warriors imitate their enemies."[17] The modern world knows this well in the form of the arms race.

HOW DID TECHNOLOGY TRANSFER AFFECT THE BALANCE OF POWER IN EUROPE?

This story of military technology and its transfer applies equally to Europe; military technology is, after all, the technology of most interest to the state. In the quest for wealth, conquest provided the quickest bang for the buck, so all rulers paid close attention to the arms race. Around 1000 CE, mounted knights with lances appeared in Europe. What made them possible was the stirrup, which allowed horsemen to keep their balance while using a weapon. Toe stirrups were known in India by the second century CE and in Afghanistan by the first. The Persians pioneered the first systematic use of the mounted and armored knight, in the first century BCE, with horses large enough to carry the weight.

---

[17] Headrick, *Technology*, 59.

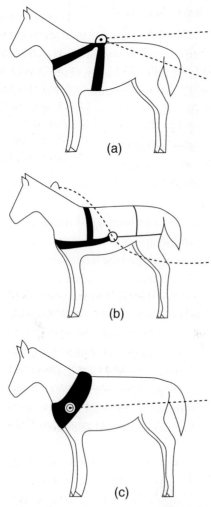

Different Types of Harnesses in China by the Fourth Century BCE   **(a)** This type tended to choke the horse. **(b, c)** These types put pressure on the horse's sternum, allowing it to pull far more weight.

The stirrup showed up in Europe by the eighth century, in the reign of Charles Martel ("Charles the Hammer," ca. 686–741), the leader of the Franks, a confederation of Germanic tribes in western Europe. He saw the advantage of a mounted knight with a heavy lance. Using stirrups, a knight could transfer the weight not only of himself and the lance but also of the horse, therefore making the lance far more powerful than a spear or javelin, so much so that only another mounted knight could stand up to it. French aristocratic knights practiced this form of combat from childhood, needing financial resources to equip a stable and pay a squire to assist. They practiced in tournaments and, when called upon by the king, would offer their services in war, the best among them being rewarded with money and land. When the Norman William the Conqueror crossed the English Channel to fight the English king Harold at the Battle of Hastings (1066), as British and French children learn in school, knights were his secret weapon. The English, on arriving at the battlefield, dismounted, expecting to fight on foot, only to be impaled by the knights' lances.

In short order, however, the Europeans developed the crossbow, which, with its heavier arrows, was able to pierce the armor of a knight, thus canceling out the knightly advantage. These military developments emanated from the constant competition between medieval European states, and the struggle to come up with improved technology on the battlefield still defines warfare today.

After about 1000 CE, Europeans adopted two other horse-related inventions: the horseshoe, which reduced friction, making life easier for the horse, and the collar harness, which came from China. Before this, horses could pull only small loads because their harness would choke them as it pulled on their necks. The Chinese "trace" harness put the strain on the sternum and had a padded collar. Two horses with old-style throat harnesses could pull at most half a ton. With the trace harness, one horse could pull two tons. What difference did this make? Temple thinks that this was the reason that the Romans imported grain from Egypt: there was no way to transport Italian grain to the capital by roads; it was easier to ship it from Egypt. "We often overlook such technological factors," says Temple, "when we seek to interpret events in the ancient world."[18]

☀ These military developments emanated from the constant competition between medieval European states, and the struggle to come up with improved technology on the battlefield still defines warfare today.

Is Technology Gender-Blind?

We mentioned earlier (see "Introduction") how technology affects people. And this is obvious in the case of warfare. But different technologies affected people differently. Throughout Africa, iron technologies were enshrouded in gender-related traditions, taboos, and practices. In sub-Saharan Africa iron smithing was almost exclusively a male preserve. In China ironwork was also largely associated with men, but China's most characteristic division of labor was between textile production and agriculture, embedded in the notion that "women weave and men farm." These roles represented the backbone of China's economy at least until the Song dynasty.

In many parts of sub-Saharan Africa, not only were smiths traditionally male but the process of smelting was surrounded by layers of ritual that related to cosmology and ultimately to notions of power. "Long before the nuclear age," says anthropologist Eugenia Herbert, "they had to confront the terrible ambivalence of a technology that promised so much for good and evil, for increased productivity and increased destruction." What to us today may seem like a routine, industrial process was partly magical in turn of the millennium Africa, as elsewhere. Herbert describes the re-created process of traditional iron smithing that she attended in modern-day Togo:

> The ancestors and the spirits were called upon to bless the enterprise. During the entire process the smelter kept close watch to ensure that no women and no men not observing the prohibition against sexual activity came near the

---

[18] Temple, *The Genius of China*, 21.

furnace. During the smelting itself, food and leaves were offered to the furnace, it was exhorted to be fertile in iron, and a child was beaten and made to cry.[19]

Herbert does not elaborate on why the unfortunate child had to be beaten, but the key notion here is that the production of iron was a transformative and creative process; as such, it was seen to touch upon something supernatural. In this context it was necessary to appease the spirits and one's ancestors, to ensure that one was not undermining the natural order of things. Other transformative activities in parts of Africa, Herbert contends, involved similar ritual practices, notably royal *investiture*—when a prince is turned into a king—or hunting, which involves the taking of an animal's life for human sustenance. Iron-Age people needed to explain how the smithy had the power to effect such transformation, whose feet he might step on in the process, how he should protect himself, and who should benefit from the product—in many cases, a weapon or tool which dramatically affected the balance of power in his community.

In all these activities, the human reproductive cycle was invoked. And it is for this reason that forges in eastern Angola, in southern Tanzania, and among the Shona of Zimbabwe were often decorated with breasts and other female appurtenances. In the Central African Republic, furnaces could be modeled on men or women, "distinguished by appropriate features modeled in clay on the front."[20] In the Western Sudan, the Minyanka people also modeled their furnaces with female or male genitalia. While the processes invoked female (and male) sexuality, female sexuality was not denied but rather appropriated because male power alone was insufficient for the reproductive analogy employed in the process of iron making.

HOW DOES TECHNOLOGY "MAKE" MEN AND WOMEN?

Textile production is another area in which we can see a relationship between technology and gender. "With a few rare exceptions," says Bray, talking about China, "a weaver was by definition a woman, and a woman was by definition a weaver."[21] Until the Song dynasty, textile production was largely women's work. When this began to change, moving in favor of large-scale commercial production which put men in the role of weaver in the later Song and early Ming dynasties, many were concerned that the social order was being turned

[19] Eugenia Herbert, *Iron, Gender and Power: Rituals of Transformation in African Societies* (Bloomington: Indiana University Press, 1993), 4.
[20] Ibid., 32.
[21] Bray, *Technology and Gender*, 183.

Drawing of a Chokwe Furnace from Central Africa   Notice the breasts on the front; in much of Africa the human reproductive cycle was invoked, explaining such decoration.

upside down. Along with coal, the other most radical change in China's techno-logical profile of this period came in textiles, with mechanization. The eleventh century saw the invention of a pedal-powered silk-reeling machine, and in 1313 the scholar Wang Zheng mentioned a water-powered hemp-spinning machine, which was, he noted with glee, "several times cheaper than the women it replaces." In moving textile production from the home to the factory, women were no longer the exclusive weavers; both weaving and gender, therefore, had been redefined.

Until the Song, a woman's role as weaver complemented that of her husband's role as farmer. Together they constituted a taxable unit, producing grain and cloth. "A wife is the fitting partner of her husband," says the *Book of Rites* (ca. first century BCE), "performing all the work with silk and hemp."[22] From the Han to the Ming, tax rates per peasant household varied around two bushels of grain and two bolts of cloth. As such, therefore, a woman was an inte-gral part of the state's economy. Even women in the households of landlords were required to weave or oversee weavers for tax purposes. All but a small percentage of textiles in China until the Song were produced by rural peasant women or by women working in a "manorial" household under the supervision of the mistress of the house.

---

[22]   Ibid., 189.

So technology was often gender-specific. So what? The answer to this question gets to the core of one of the performative characteristics of technology—*what it does*. In addition to the role of technology in subsistence processes, helping humans feed, clothe, or defend themselves, it performs various social, political, and cultural roles. As Bray writes, "The most important work that technologies do is to produce people; the makers are shaped by the making, and the users shaped by the using."[23] How these people are shaped depends upon the technology in question and, of course, the other cultural and social attributes of the society. While women had for millennia been central to China's economy by virtue of their weaving role, China experienced what Europe was to experience hundreds of years later, with traditional crafts, such as weaving, being taken over by mechanization and (in China at least) ultimately relieving women of their economic function.

A Chinese Silk-Reeling Machine, From a Drawing of 1843 but Based on Descriptions Written Around 1090   Operator is unwinding silkworm cocoons in a heated bowl of water while rotating the reel via a treadle crank.

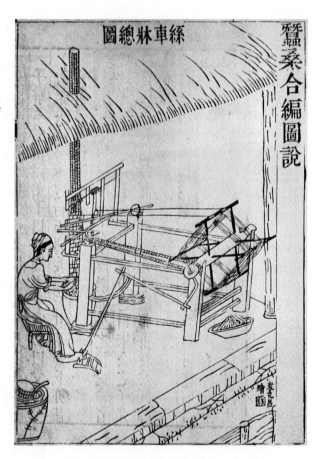

圖總牀車絲

蠶桑合編圖說

---

[23]   Ibid., 19.

How Did the State Support Science and Technology? Islam and India

While technology was a central part of state building, it also had a maintenance function. On the other end of the Silk Road from China, the Arab conquests and the subsequent Islamic caliphate, which ruled from Baghdad between 750 and 1258, initiated their own agricultural revolution, not unlike that under Song China. According to historians James McClellan and Harold Dorn, "The effects of such improved agricultural productivity were typical: unprecedented population increases, urbanization, social stratification, political centralization, and state patronization of higher learning."[24] By the 930s, Baghdad, with a population of 1.1 million, was the largest city on earth, a few steps ahead of Chang'an. Several other Islamic cities had populations of between 100,000 and 500,000, such as Cairo, Damascus, and Cordoba in Islamic Spain.

The Arabs inherited lands that had been irrigated with complex engineering for centuries. Parts of Iran and Iraq in particular had been under Sassanian rule before them and had used the *qanat*, or water storage and moving systems, originally found in Iran in the first millennium BCE. These involved a series of connected wells, which channeled water where it was needed. One of the oldest of these is still in use in the Iranian city of Gonabad; it serves over 40,000 people and was built 2,700 years ago. *Qanats* were adapted for use by the Arabs as far as northern Africa. Islamic engineers also repaired dams, like the one on the Nahrwan Canal, which supplied irrigation water downstream of Baghdad. Waterwheels brought river water up to the levels of fields and were powered by animals or by the energy from the flow of the river itself. Waterwheels were also used to power other devices such as one for processing sugar cane in Iran and Iraq. Cane was crushed, and the juice was boiled to produce a crystalline sugar.

With developments in China and the Islamic world, contacts between them and across Eurasia increased around 1000 CE. Contact, often through trade in luxury goods, was itself a spur to further innovation. As the historian Arnold Pacey describes it, "We can perhaps think in terms of a technological dialogue or an inventive exchange between different regions in Asia, through which techniques were not only transferred from one place to another, but also invention was stimulated in response to the transferred technique."[25]

---

[24] James E. McClellan III and Harold Dorn, *Science and Technology in World History: An Introduction* (Baltimore: Johns Hopkins University Press, 1999), 103.

[25] Arnold Pacey, *Technology in World Civilization: A Thousand-Year History* (Cambridge, MA: MIT Press, 1990), 8.

WHAT IS "ISLAMIC SCIENCE?"

The Islamic caliphate of Baghdad is more closely associated historically with support of the "sciences" than perhaps any other classical or medieval state. Here, it might be worthwhile taking a brief detour to consider the difference between science and technology. The common-sense distinction—which we can stick with here—suggests that technology is applied science. Needham espoused this definition. For him, agriculture was applied botany, alchemy was applied chemistry, engineering was applied physics, etc. Until the twentieth century, however, science and technology, or applied and theoretical fields, remained largely decoupled. There was no pure science, pursued in research institutions, from which innovations in technology flowed.

While the Muslims reinvigorated the agricultural lands they conquered, those same conquests supplied the "brain trust" of Persia and India, which themselves had inherited the Hellenistic traditions of scholarship via Alexander the Great's conquests. In the early centuries of the Islamic caliphate Indian and Persian influences were paramount. Later, the Arabs began to synthesize and translate works from other centers of civilization, such as Alexandria in Egypt and Byzantine centers of learning. The Muslims were able, therefore, to draw upon all of these ancient traditions, inheriting

> While the Muslims reinvigorated the agricultural lands they conquered, those same conquests supplied the "brain trust" of Persia and India, which themselves had inherited the Hellenistic traditions of scholarship via Alexander the Great's conquests.

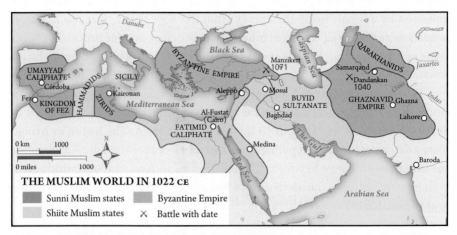

MAP 9.4   THE MUSLIM WORLD IN 1022 CE   By the 930s Baghdad, with a population of over 1 million, was the largest city on earth. But during the tenth century, the political unity of the Muslim world collapsed. Several regional Islamic centers continued to flourish however.

a rich diversity of knowledge. Ibn Sina, known to the West as "Avicenna" (980–1037), described the royal library in Bukhara:

> I found there many rooms filled with books which were arranged in cases, row upon row. One room was allotted to works on Arabic Philology and poetry, another to jurisprudence and so forth, the books on each particular science having a room to themselves. I inspected the catalogue of ancient Greek authors and looked for the books which I required; I saw in this collection of books of which few people have heard even the names, and which I myself have never seen either before or since.[26]

Ibn Sina's experience in central Asia was not unique. Medieval Cairo's research center/library, the Dar Al ʿIlm ("Abode of Learning"), housed 1 million volumes. Cordoba in Islamic Spain had some 70 libraries containing as many as half a million volumes. Europe, meanwhile, lagged far behind; the University of Paris, even by 1400, had only 2,000 titles in its library.

"Medieval Islam became heir to Greek science and was from 800–1300 the world leader in virtually every field of science."[27] The Muslims translated many of the Greek works that they came across. The caliph Al-Ma'mun (r. 813–833) for

Ruins of an Islamic Arch in Cordoba, Spain   Cordoba was a medieval Islamic center of learning, from the eighth to the thirteenth centuries, with a world-class library.

---

[26]   Quoted in McClellan and Dorn, *Science and Technology in World History*, 102.
[27]   Ibid.

example, founded the "House of Wisdom" (*Bayt al-Hikma*) in Baghdad in 832, specifically for translation. His aim was to render the entire corpus of philosophical and scientific Greek work into Arabic—works such as Euclid's *Elements*, Ptolemy's *Almagest* (Arabic for "The Greatest"), as well as the works of Aristotle and Archimedes. Why? Did the caliph have the interests of posterity in mind, seeking to hold aloft the torch of knowledge for future generations? Maybe, but more likely Al-Ma'mun expected to get something practical from all this reading: Aristotle was of interest because of his focus on the art of governing (a complicated subject when one's lands are so extensive). Medicine was also a practical science, and the ninth-century scholar Ishaq Ibn Hunayan alone translated 150 works of the Greek medical writer Galen (ca. 130–200 CE).

Astronomy was also of immediate practical use, in particular for determining calendar dates for religious purposes. The Islamic calendar was lunar, like that of ancient Babylon, comprised of 12 months of 29 or 30 days, revolving in a 30-year cycle. Calculations fixed the dates of Ramadan, the Muslim holy month. Islamic timekeepers (*muwaqquit*) needed precise times for the five daily Muslim prayers. *Muwaqquits* used abstruse instruments such as astrolabes and sundials to determine these times, which were all affected by seasonal and geographical variations. Astronomy was also put in the service of navigation, facilitated by recognition of the stars and their relationship to each other, useful both at sea and in the desert, for traders and pilgrims. And although astrology was frowned upon by religious authorities—superstitious nonsense, which ignored the omniscience of God—it remained popular, so much so that Al-Ma'mun also founded the first Islamic observatory, in Baghdad in 828. Mathematics was used in religiously driven activities as well as others, such as the dividing of personal property upon death, for which a mathematically trained expert, known as *al-faradi*, was necessary.

Academic opinion is divided on the Islamic contribution to science. There are two broad arguments about it. The "marginality" thesis argues that secular, rational sciences inherited from the Greeks never became integrated into Islamic culture but remained on the margins. If true, this may be because in its early years the Islamic empire was a melting pot of ideas and cultures, which informed the governing elite. As time passed and an orthodoxy began to appear in Islamic society, religious authorities selected what was acceptable and what was not. Religious judgments increasingly went against many of the secular sciences: "Consequently the cultural 'space' for creative scientific thinkers narrowed, and so again, the scientific vitality of Islam weakened commensurately."[28]

---

[28] Ibid.

The "assimilationist" argument, however, suggests that the ideas of Hellenism, as well as influences from Persia and India, all found space within Islamic culture, helping to shape the orthodoxy, and remained constituent parts of later philosophy, law, and literature.

WHAT WAS THE SCIENTIFIC AND TECHNOLOGICAL CONTRIBUTION OF EARLY MEDIEVAL INDIA?

Successive Indian dynasties from the middle of the first millennium on were also supportive of scientific activities, the same sciences, in fact, that were of interest to the Islamic state. The Guptas ruled an empire comprising large parts of peninsular India until about 650 CE. And, as in Baghdad, astronomy was front and center. Professional astronomers created calendars to set times for religious observances and cast horoscopes to make predictions. Not remotely theoretical, these activities focused on computational expertise. In many ways, given the goals of this work, the astronomers were more like priests than scientists as their roots were firmly in the Vedic past and its Brahmanical traditions. The Indian astronomers produced a series of textbooks from the fourth to the seventh centuries, known as *siddhantas* ("solutions"), which covered subjects such as the solar year, equinoxes, Metonic cycles (a 19-year cycle devised by the fifth-century Meton of Athens), eclipses, and planetary movements.

Some of the larger kingdoms of post-Gupta India institutionalized medicine. The religious center at Nalanda, for example, in the state of Bihar, sometimes referred to as one of the world's earliest universities, also doubled as a medical school from the fifth to the twelfth centuries. This complex, which boasted some 300 lecture rooms, spread out over a campus of more than one square mile, had anywhere between 4,000 and 10,000 students, all of it supported by the king and free of charge to enrollees. Here, more than perhaps anywhere else at this time, learning began to take on a new meaning as students from as far away as Korea, Turkey, and Indonesia studied astronomy, art, medicine, mathematics, and warfare. King Asoka, hundreds of years before, had established a similar precedent with his medical infirmaries; and the Guptas also had charitable medical dispensaries. Along with medical expertise, the Indians produced some early mathematicians, most notably perhaps Aryabhata (b. ca. 476 CE), who lived in Pataliputra in northern India. He is known for employing decimal notation in his work, in addition to a place-value system which used the nine "Arabic" numerals and zero.

Up until the nineteenth century and British colonial rule, India was also the world's leading producer of textiles. Weavers, like all other professions in India, traditionally belonged to a caste; and theirs was numerically second only to that of farmers. The division of professions into castes became more rigid during the

Gupta period, and the divisions between trades and castes were reflected in the division between crafts and sciences. For this reason, science and technology remained two distinct domains in India, as they did until the modern period in China and most other civilizations.

The unity that classical India had enjoyed under the Guptas and several subsequent kingdoms eventually broke up by 647, after the death of King Harsha. There followed a period of minor Indian states, which continued much of the technological traditions of the classical period, if on a smaller scale. But after 1000 CE the influence of Islam became increasingly felt in India as Muslim conquerors moved into India from the north. This ushered in a new era in Indian history.

In the south, traditional, non-Islamic culture continued, for example, with the Chola kingdom (ca. 800–1300). Here, a large state bureaucracy was responsible for major irrigation works and well-established agriculture, which was able to sustain a large population. In Mysore and Madras, thousands of storage tanks for water were still in existence from this period until the eighteenth and nineteenth centuries. During the Chola period these were part of a complex system of hydraulic engineering that was closely supervised by governing bureaucracy. But perhaps the major legacy of Indian patronage of science and technology remains the spread of Indian influence farther east to what historians refer to as "Greater India."

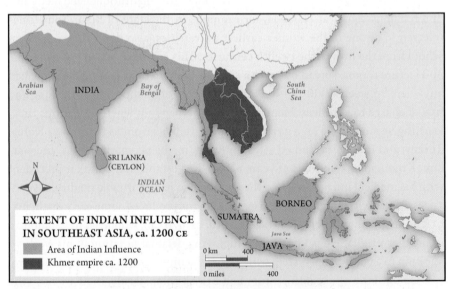

MAP 9.5   EXTENT OF INDIAN INFLUENCE IN SOUTHEAST ASIA, ca. 1200 CE   From early in the first millennium CE Indian traders navigated the Indian Ocean to the east, giving rise to a pan-Indian civilization in Malaysia and southeast Asia. Hinduism and Buddhism spread, and many kingdoms in the region used Sanskrit as their official language.

How Did Science Support the State?

Not only did technological innovations in agriculture and engineering help build prosperous states, which could be taxed in money and goods, but official patronage of the sciences created information that, when closely guarded and studied by the elites and their acolytes, could legitimate and empower rulers. Other technologies, such as engineering—in particular for the construction of monumental architecture—astronomy for calendrical knowledge, and alchemy for immortality were all key to the maintenance of power by elites. Perhaps the best examples of this were the Maya, who we have discussed in several previous chapters. "In a characteristic fashion," say McClellan and Dorn, "and more than in any other American civilization, the Maya came to deploy institutionalized knowledge for the maintenance of their societies."[29]

The *Popul Vuh*, or Mayan "Book of the People," describes the mythic origins of the people of Quiché in the Guatemalan highlands in the Postclassic period (ca. 1000–1600 CE). Much of it talks about the lords of the city, describing their lineages and histories; and they are frequently associated with the monumental architecture, which played such a key role in Mayan society:

> Then splendor and majesty grew among the Quiché. The greatness and weight of the Quiché reached its full splendor and majesty with the surfacing and plastering of the canyon and citadel. The tribes came, whether small or great and whatever titles of their lords, adding to the greatness of the Quiché. As the splendor and majesty grew, so grew the houses of the gods and the houses of the lords.[30]

Similarly, southeast Asian civilizations of the period used technology to enhance the legitimacy and power of elites. The Khmer Empire, part of the greater Indian region, ruled a territory that included parts of modern Cambodia, Thailand, Laos, Burma, Vietnam, and the Malay Peninsula for some six centuries between 802 and 1431. Indian merchants had been sailing across the Indian Ocean since early in the first millennium CE, trading with Java, Sumatra, and Bali in Indonesia. Indian Brahmin were often welcomed as rulers in these areas and brought with them Indian law and administration, as well as Hinduism and Buddhism.

Khmer wealth and longevity were largely due to its irrigation infrastructure, the largest in the history of southeast Asia, which it created along the alluvial plains of the Mekong River. Khmer engineers built an extensive system of lakes,

---

[29] Ibid., 155.
[30] *Popul Vuh*, trans. Dennis Tedlock (New York: Simon and Schuster, 1985), 212.

The Temple of Angkor Watt in Cambodia   The temple required as much stone as the Egyptian pyramid of Cheops. Every square inch is carved in bas-relief. Astronomy, calendrical reckoning, and numerology combine with archeology to serve social and political purposes.

canals, channels, and reservoirs, which they used to meet the challenges of the dry season, to control water supplies, and therefore agriculture, year-round. The resultant bountiful production of rice and many other crops was sufficient to sustain a dense population and large labor force, exactly what every successful royal family needs and yet another example of how agriculture is king.

Along with the Great Wall of China and the pyramids of Giza, the Angkor complex is one of the ancient human-made structures most easily visible from space.

The urban center, the "city" of Angkor Watt, covered over 60 square miles, incorporating a whole series of towns along with 200 temples, the one at Angkor itself being the largest temple in the world. Completed in 1150, the temple took as much stone as the Egyptian pyramid of Cheops, and every square inch is carved in bas-relief. Along with the Great Wall of China and the pyramids of Giza, the Angkor complex is one of the ancient human-made structures most easily visible from space.

The Khmer rulers, like the Maya, used astronomical knowledge politically. At the main temple in Angkor Watt, astronomy, calendrical reckoning, astrology, numerology, and architecture all work together in the design; the complex has built-in astronomical sight lines which functioned to record lunar and solar positions on the horizon, allowing, among other things, the prediction of eclipses.

For the Khmer, like many other civilizations, science worked in the interests of the state more than the state worked in the interests of science. All the technology in play in this empire, from the complex hydraulic engineering to the architectural skill and the astronomical techniques, bolstered the power of the rulers. Successive kings of Angkor outbid each other, as Diamond puts it, "by taking the large building projects of pre-unification kings as models and scaling them up into huge, then gigantic, and finally world-record humungous projects."[31] A thirteenth-century Chinese visitor to the capital was awestruck by the engineering achievements of Angkor and could not help but be impressed by the powers behind it:

> In the center of the capital is a gold tower. . . . To the east of it is a gold bridge flanked by two gold lions . . . about a li (0.3 miles) north of the gold tower there is a bronze tower. It is even taller than the gold tower, and an exquisite sight. . . . Ten li (three miles) to the east of the city lies the East Lake. It is about 100 li (30 miles) in circumference. In the middle of it is a bronze reclining Buddha with water continually flowing from its navel.[32]

The Maya and the Khmer were by no means alone in having elites who used engineering, astronomy, astrology, alchemy, and mathematics to bolster their prestige, underline their power, and manifest their right to rule. But in the event that these were not enough, there was always military technology, which, although vulnerable to being ripped off by one's enemies, could provide the ultimate persuasion.

DID NORTH AMERICAN SOCIETIES USE TECHNOLOGIES DIFFERENTLY?

The Americas followed a different path from Afro-Eurasia in many respects. Yet, underneath the many differences there are several foundational similarities in New and Old World societies. Although the specific technologies may have differed, the uses they were put to and their consequences were often parallel. The use of technology and proto-science to legitimize the state is a universal phenomenon. But while Eurasia had witnessed successive states and empires for centuries

---

[31] Diamond, *Guns, Germs, and Steel*, 533.
[32] Zhou Dagan, *Memoirs on the Customs of Cambodia*, quoted in ibid., 533.

by 1000 CE, like Africa, North America had a low population density, little or no urbanization, and few states.

The warming climate in the years leading up to the eleventh century favored the growth of societies in the region of modern-day St. Louis, Missouri, in the Mississippi valley. Archeologists have unearthed small villages, with huts clustered around a central post, which they think may have acted as ritual markers, perhaps as tokens of ancestors or group identity. Populations here could not become very dense because the economy relied on hunting, especially in winter, and tribes needed large geographical ranges for this. In summer, they supplemented their food with farmed produce, especially corn, which began to make up an increasingly large part of their diet around the turn of the millennium.

By the eleventh century the population of a collection of villages, known as "Old Cahokia," in today's St. Louis, was probably about 1,000. By 1050 some villages were clearly larger than others, and the signs of a complex, urban society were emerging. The area was also full of earthen mounds, used mainly as burial chambers, a cultural artifact common to several areas of North and Central America. Pottery shards and other surviving artifacts suggest that people were migrating to this place, and it is this migration that made it the most populous village in ancient America's "corn belt" by the mid-eleventh century.

Signs of immigration are significant. Unlike today, perhaps, archeologists think that such "immigrants" would have possessed a mystique, a glamorous caché, which would have given them a certain power and might have helped to attract even more immigrants. The residents of Old Cahokia were all crowded into a site of only 100 acres. "This combination of the cultural power of immigrants," says archeologist Timothy R. Pauketat, "and the economic base of Old Cahokia, with its access to large amounts of easy-to-farm river bottom, was a recipe for explosive growth."[33]

On July 4, 1050, a propitious date, it seems, for North America, an event occurred in the sky that was recorded around the world. The people of Old Cahokia noticed it, as did astronomers in China. It was a supernova, a nuclear detonation in the heavens, the last gasp of a dying star, one of only 50 ever recorded. A new luminary appeared in the night sky, still visible today in the Taurus constellation, known as the Crab Nebula. "For ancient people, known to watch the skies carefully," says Pauketat, "a brand new star that shone, initially, day and night, was likely viewed with some combination of wonderment, confusion, and horror. What might the star portend?"[34]

---

[33] Timothy R. Pauketat, *Cahokia: Ancient America's Great City on the Mississippi* (New York: Viking, 2009), 20.
[34] Ibid.

During the weeks and months after July 4, the entire village of Cahokia was razed to the ground and a new, much bigger town built over the top of it, in "what may constitute the first government-sponsored urban renewal project on the continent, north of Mexico."[35] Within a very short span of years the population exploded; this new city may have had as many as 20,000 people, a size to rival many of the city states of the Maya or the larger cities in South America at the time. Cahokia was North America's first city. What is most remarkable about it, however, is how this fact was denied until the second half of the twentieth century. Until that point it was widely believed that the natives of North America were incapable of urban life and had only lived in small, disparate groups, leaving a minimal footprint. This narrative facilitated the early settlement of whites in North America by allowing colonists to believe that they were bringing a superior, urban civilization to a pristine land of savages.

By 1200 the population was between 30,000 and 40,000. The principal features of the city were its mounds, which were not new to North America but had existed along parts of the southern Mississippi in Missouri and Arkansas as

Monks Mound is the centerpiece of Cahokia Mounds, a national park in Illinois. The site went unnoticed until the twentieth century when an archeologist realized that the mounds were human-made. Until then it had been assumed that the Native Americans were incapable of building on this scale and were strangers to the notion of a "city."

---

[35]   Ibid, 21.

far back as 1600 BCE, predating most of the pyramids we know about in Central America. A series of mound-building civilizations also existed around the time of the Common Era in Wisconsin, Ohio, and Illinois.

But most of these mounds existed in areas of relatively light population density, where people were largely nomadic or semisedentary. They served mortuary and ritualistic functions. In areas where population began to increase, along with farming, the mounds became larger. As is the case with all other civilizations, such buildings required organization, engineering skills, and ideological motivations. At Cahokia, earthen mounds were erected in multiple neighborhoods, with one enormous edifice dominating the central plaza, which itself was the size of 35 football fields, the largest public space north of Mexico. The mound presiding over this space rested on a platform that was 25 feet high and carefully engineered for drainage. It was elevated some 150 years after construction, to 100 feet high, making it the world's third largest pyramid.

Around the Midwest, following the construction of New Cahokia, similar cultures appeared, sporting earthen mounds, large open plazas, and objects decorated with images of sky gods and ancestors. Although the Mississippian cultures did not develop the level of bureaucratic, administrative government we see in Eurasia at this time, like their Eurasian cousins, they exhibited keen interest in astronomy and their city planning prioritized astronomical observation and interest in the calendar. This was clearly put in the service of a ruling elite. Mass graves have been found within the mounds at Cahokia, as elsewhere, many of them showing signs of ritual sacrifice and others of burial of high-status individuals, often accompanied by sacrificial victims.

As we have seen, in all civilizations, technologies, from engineering for mound building to the calculations necessary for astronomical predictions, were intimately intertwined with cultural beliefs, religious practices, and, ultimately, political power.

How Did Trade and Communication Needs Spur Technological Innovation?

When Captain James Cook of Britain's Royal Navy arrived in the Pacific in 1769, he could not help but be impressed with the "native" maritime technology. Although Cook's commentary comes from a later period, it also illustrates a European's appreciation for the sophistication of indigenous technology: while, on the one hand, the Europeans generally considered indigenous peoples inferior in many ways, some commentators among them often saw through the ideology of superiority to notice how savvy indigenous peoples really were. Cook's scientific bent of mind and interest in all matters maritime allowed him to see how the Pacific Islanders had a long tradition of building seaworthy craft, "and I believe perform long and distant voyages in them, otherwise they could not have the knowledge of the Islands in these seas they seem to have."[36] The boats were no mere dugout canoes; there were many different designs, from small canoes for coastal fishing to large "war" canoes of much greater size:

> Their Canoes or Proes are built all of them very narrow, and some of the largest are 60 or 70 feet long. These consist of several pieces; the bottom is round and made of large logs hollow'd out to the thickness of about 3 Inches, and may consist of 3 or 4 pieces; the sides are of Plank of nearly the same thickness, and are built nearly perpendicular, rounding in a little towards the Gunwale. The pieces on which they are built are well fitted, and fastend or sewed together with strong platting something in the same manner as old China, Wooden Bowls, etc., are mended.[37]

A Polynesian War Canoe from New Zealand   Some were for coastal voyages, and some were oceangoing. Early European visitors to the Pacific were incredulous at the achievements of native maritime technology.

---

36   From Captain Cooke's Journal, http://ebooks.adelaide.edu.au/c/cook/james/c77j/chapter3.html.
37   Ibid.

European explorers were to find similar skills throughout the Pacific. Some islanders made keels cut from a single tree trunk, for which they needed a specific arc. On some islands the calophyllum tree bends from the darkness of the forest to the light with just the right degree of curve. Islanders removed vegetation around trees to allow them to bend toward the light in the right way as they grew. The Maoris of New Zealand used totara trees to build dugouts up to 70 feet long. They often prepared the trees years in advance of harvesting them, by scraping a line down the trunk of a sapling and allowing the sap to run out. As the tree grew, its trunk rotted on the grooved side, allowing a worker to more easily hollow it out. Europeans were incredulous when they first witnessed this because they could not credit the "primitive" Maoris with such rational foresight.

The Pacific is the world's largest ocean, covering one-third of the earth's surface. It is encircled by a "ring of fire," volcanoes creating frequent eruptions and earthquakes where Pacific tectonic plates collide with the surrounding continental plates. The ecology is as varied as the human population. Some islands are little more than coral atolls; others are mountainous and green, with abundant food resources from land and sea. Many islands are situated within archipelagos of dozens or even hundreds of islands; others are isolated hundreds of miles from the nearest land.

For this obvious reason, Polynesians were obliged to master boatbuilding and navigation. In 1769, when Captain Cook dropped anchor in Tahiti, he brought aboard a man named Tupaia. Cook was amazed at his ability to navigate without the tools that the British found essential: charts, compass, and sextant. Whatever his location at sea, Tupaia was always able to point to Tahiti, with an unerring sense of direction. He used the position of stars to determine his direction at night, having committed whole constellations to memory. Tupaia did not rely on drawn charts but used various memory devices to remember the relationship of islands to each other, the position of reefs, and the direction of currents.

> Tupaia did not rely on drawn charts but used various memory devices to remember the relationship of islands to each other, the position of reefs, and the direction of currents.

And Tupaia was no aberration. These techniques were studied by Pacific navigators all over the region. Such knowledge was essential as many islands were not self-sufficient and relied on resources from elsewhere and, in some cases, even on bringing women from other islands to enable young men to marry outside their families. On the island of Kiribati, for example, locals used the construction of roof beams in their meeting houses to create maps of the stars and to represent the relative positions of different islands. Like Western navigation today, all Pacific navigation was essentially based on "dead reckoning," which calculates present position from last known position, taking into account speed, direction, and time and factoring in drift from possible currents. Islanders threw in some additional skills, such as recognizing the characteristics of ocean swells to determine the direction and distance of islands, something that no Western navigator has ever been able to match.

What were the consequences of these abilities? Why, we might ask, was Tupaia not in London instead of Cook in the Pacific? Some Western commentators, notably Thor Heyerdahl, writing in the 1950s, posited that Pacific Islanders had made it to the South American continent, citing as evidence the existence of the sweet potato, an indigenous South American plant, on some Pacific islands. To prove his thesis, he built a traditional Pacific island boat and sailed it across the Pacific.

Heyerdahl's work is not widely credited today, in part because botanists believe that plant seeds can drift across oceans and still germinate on land. But even if islanders did not unite the Pacific with the continental landmass of the Americas, they did contribute to a Pacific-wide culture; and this they did at a very early date. Austronesians, people from the language-group to which most Pacific Islanders belong, are believed to have originally migrated from the Asian continent several millennia before the Common Era. Gradually, they populated the entire Pacific, and their common traits are visible in their languages and their archeology; their crops and their pottery styles have left clues as to the direction and timing of their migrations. Polynesian seafaring, then, must have started very early on with migratory journeys between islands.

Conclusion: What Is the Relationship Between Technology and the State?

Technology, as we have seen, covers a remarkably wide spectrum of human endeavor. Although many historians have seen technology as a kind of applied science, for most of history until the modern period, technology existed more in the realm of the crafts, rather than the sciences; and this is partly because science as we understand it today did not exist in medieval states. The closest we come, perhaps, in this period were the Islamic and Indian "sciences" of math and astronomy; but they were largely focused on religious functions and lacked the disinterested purpose of exploring the workings of the natural world for "science's sake."

Technology, however, had a massive impact on human lives, with different consequences for different people. While China's agricultural revolution under the Song dynasty created more food and allowed the population to grow, it also underwrote the growth in the iron industry, with all the military consequences that followed, including paradoxically the conquest of China by the Jurchen nomads. As was the case for China over several millennia, the growth of the Chinese state was often mirrored by the simultaneous growth in the nomad empires on its borders.

By about 1000 CE, humanity had reached a technological plateau. Most of the major inventions and discoveries that would carry the human race to the Industrial Revolution were in place, and advances from this position would represent refinements of knowledge already in place. Much has been made of the technical inequality between "the West" and "the East"—we put these terms in quotes because they are not well-defined entities—especially after the Industrial Revolution of the eighteenth and nineteenth centuries. But at 1000 CE China was far ahead of the rest of the world in technological terms. In later centuries this "advantage" would shrink. One possible reason was that much of China's technological innovation was state-driven; the impetus for agricultural developments, water engineering, and administrative organization, as in the Muslim Middle East, often came from above. With the dissolution of the government, therefore, the proverbial rug was pulled out from many technical projects. In Europe, which was politically divided between multiple kings and feudal lords, innovation was often localized. Decentralized innovation was not so vulnerable to interruption.

Another major difference between Europe, China, and the Middle East was their relative use of energy. Europe, with a smaller population than China and the Middle East, was more reliant on animal power. Farmers had larger amounts of land to work, and animals were essential tools for working it. As Headrick puts it, "In the long run, reliance on nonhuman sources of energy was the foundation for improvements in living standards."[38] Whereas animals altered the amount of work that could be accomplished significantly, it was not until the Industrial Revolution of the eighteenth century that human society drastically increased the amount of energy available to it, with dramatic consequences.

Words to Think About

Alchemy	Bas-relief	Numerology
Slash-and-burn agriculture	Technology transfer	

Questions to Think About

- In what ways does technology "make people"?
- What drove the development of technology in the ancient world?

---

[38]   Headrick, *Technology*, 71.

- Which water technologies were significant in the ancient world?
- What is the difference between science and technology?

Primary Sources

Anshi, Wang. "In Defense of Five Major Policies." In *Sources of Chinese Tradition*, 2nd ed. Compiled by Wm. Theodore DeBary and Irene Bloom. New York: Columbia University Press, 1999.

Captain Cooke's Journal.

http://ebooks.adelaide.edu.au/c/cook/james/c77j/chapter3.html.

Popul Vuh. Translated by Dennis Tedlock. New York: Simon & Schuster, 1985.

Secondary Sources

Bray, Francesca. *Technology and Gender: Fabrics of Power in Late Imperial China*. Los Angeles: University of California Press, 1997.

Diamond, Jared. *Guns, Germs, and Steel: The Fates of Human Societies*. New York: W.W. Norton, 1999.

Elvin, Mark. *The Pattern of the Chinese Past*. Stanford, CA: Stanford University Press, 1973.

Fage, J. D., and William Todoroff. *A History of Africa*, 4th ed. London: Routledge, 2002.

Goody, Jack. *Technology, Tradition and the State in Africa*. London: Oxford University Press, 1971.

Headrick, Donald. *Technology: A World History*. New York: Oxford University Press, 2009.

Herbert, Eugenia. *Iron, Gender and Power: Rituals of Transformation in African Societies*. Bloomington: Indiana University Press, 1993.

McClellan, James E., III, and Harold Dorn. *Science and Technology in World History: An Introduction*. Baltimore: Johns Hopkins University Press, 1999.

McIntosh, Susan Keech, and Roderick J. McIntosh. "Jenne-Jeno, an Ancient African City." *Anthropology Rice*. http://anthropology.rice.edu/Content.aspx?id=500.

Milton, John, *Paradise Lost*, Book VI 488-91, https://www.dartmouth.edu/~milton/reading_room/pl/book_6/text.shtml

Morris, Ian *Why the West Rules—For Now: The Patterns of History and What They Reveal About the Future*. New York: Farrar, Straus and Giroux, 2011.

Needham, Joseph, ed. *Science and Technology in Chinese Civilization*, vol. 6 Cambridge: Cambridge University Press, 1984.

Pacey, Arnold. *Technology in World Civilization: A Thousand-Year History*. Cambridge, MA: MIT Press, 1990.

Pauketat, Timothy R. *Cahokia: Ancient America's Great City on the Mississippi*. New York: Viking, 2009.

Temple, Robert. *The Genius of China: 3000 Years of Science, Discovery and Invention*. New York: Simon & Schuster, 1986.

Chinggis Khan, Founder of the Largest Contiguous Empire in History   Mass murderer? Genius military strategist? Brilliant state builder? A little bit of each, and one of history's most controversial characters.

Chapter 10

What Types of Conflicts Existed Between Core Areas and Peripheries?

Chinggis Khan's Soul

In 1937 agents of Stalin's Soviet Union ransacked monasteries in Mongolia, dozens of them, in an organized campaign to destroy Mongol culture. They burned religious texts, destroyed relics, raped nuns, and shot monks. One monastery in particular, the Shankh monastery, along the River of the Moon, had housed a special relic, the soul of Chinggis (or Genghis) Khan; and during these raids it disappeared.

For centuries, Mongol warriors had been in the habit of taking hair from the tails of their horses, their most prized possessions, and attaching them to the shaft of a spear or banner. This artifact, called a *sulde*, or spirit banner, would stand outside a warrior's tent, under the "endless blue sky" that they worshipped as a god (Mongolia, with 250 cloudless days a year, is sunnier than any other region that far north). It proclaimed the warrior's identity and provided him protection. The Mongols believed that as the sun shone on it and the wind passed through it the *sulde* captured their energy and transferred the power of nature to the warrior. The endless twisting of the horsehair in the steppe wind was believed to somehow drive the warrior on toward his destiny, "luring him away from this spot to seek another, to find better pasture, to explore new opportunities and adventures, to create his own fate in his life, in this world."[1] So intimate was the connection

---

[1] Jack Weatherford, *Genghis Khan and the Making of the Modern World* (New York: Random House, 2005), xvi.

THINKING ABOUT CONQUEST

What Is Conquest?

- No single model dominated the desire for expansion and conquest, and conquerors were as different from one another as the people they conquered.

To What Extent Was Conquest Leader-Driven?

- It is tempting to explain the extraordinary Mongol conquests of much of Eurasia as a result of Chinggis Khan losing his wife to a neighboring tribe.

How Did Conquest Relate to Security?

- While confrontations with larger states could be conceived as a form of territorial takeover, in many cases the Mongols only looked to intimidate and exact tribute from their settled neighbors.

What Role Did Religion Play in Conquest?

- Some have suggested that the Reconquest was in reality a mish mash of different ideas and interest groups who signed on to the idea of taking Iberia back. While all paid lip service to recovering lost territories, Christians also competed with one another for resources.

What Were the Consequences and Outcomes of Conquest?

- While conquest had a negative effect not only on those who were conquered but also on future generations, it also brought different groups of people together and established new relationships.

Conclusion

- Like the Mongol pursuit of expansion, conquest during this period was perpetual; territorial gains were constantly challenged by new powers and by the dispossessed, to the extent that conquerors could never rest on their laurels.

between warrior and *sulde* that the Mongols believed his soul came to reside in it after his death. Chinggis Khan, perhaps the greatest conqueror known to history, had two *suldes*: one white, which he used in peacetime, and the other black, reserved for war. The white one disappeared soon after his death, it was his wartime *sulde* that survived, perhaps fittingly.

Introduction

From the distant past to the present, conquest has been a major theme of world history. But certain times are unique in that conquerors went further, established more permanent footprints, and did more to connect disparate people around the world. The time in question (tenth to thirteenth centuries) was characterized by the movement of people and states into new regions. It was an age of empire, similar to Roman and Han times, in which large states dominated significant amounts of territory and conquered large numbers of people. New states initiated connections throughout Eurasia and Africa that stood the test of time and laid the foundations for future states, such as the Ottomans, the Ming, and the Songhay, creating connections from northern Europe to China.

Dwarfing all other expanding polities, however, was the Mongol Empire, the largest contiguous empire in human history. At its height it controlled over 22% of the earth's surface and ruled over 100 million people. Given its territorial reach, it not only was the most important empire of its time but also compared in stature to the British Empire, which ruled half of the world's surface by the beginning of the twentieth century. It is difficult to overstate the significance of the Mongol Empire as it united almost all of Eurasia for the first and only time; all subsequent empires, in Iran, China, or the Middle East and central Asia, bore their stamp in one way or another. As historian Timothy May points out, Columbus was looking for China and the "Great Khan" (the Mongol ruler of China under the Yuan dynasty, 1279–1368), when he bumped into the Americas. "The Mongol moment," says May, "is truly a pivotal and perhaps an axial era in history. In many ways it is the dividing point between the pre-modern and the modern ages."[2] The Romans were a largely Mediterranean phenomenon, the Han Chinese knew little of the world beyond their realms, and the Arab/Islamic conquests of the eighth and ninth centuries linked northern Africa and Persia in a cultural area but rarely in a unified polity. The Mongols, however, achieved unity from the Mediterranean to China and north to Russia, and they did it in record time. "In 25 years," says historian Morris Rossabi, "the Mongol army subjugated more lands and people than the Romans had conquered in 400 years."[3] And, like conquest everywhere, the consequences were widespread. During the *Pax Mongolica*, the peace following the violence, the business of human exchange—of goods, ideas, and genes—received a historic boost.

But while the Mongols dominated Eurasia in this period, they were not the only polity bent on expansion. Their history bears similarities—and key

mobile terror

---

[2]   Timothy May, *The Mongol Conquests in World History* (London: Reaktion Books, 2013), 2.
[3]   Morris Rossabi, *The Mongols: A Very Brief Introduction* (New York: Oxford University Press, 2012), 8.

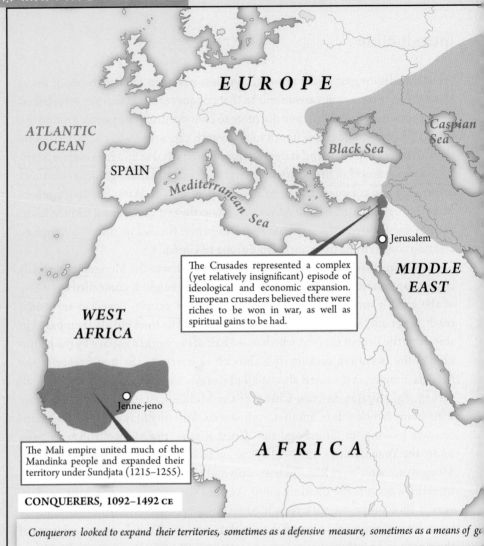

The Crusades represented a complex (yet relatively insignificant) episode of ideological and economic expansion. European crusaders believed there were riches to be won in war, as well as spiritual gains to be had.

The Mali empire united much of the Mandinka people and expanded their territory under Sundjata (1215–1255).

CONQUERERS, 1092–1492 CE

Conquerors looked to expand their territories, sometimes as a defensive measure, sometimes as a means of ga

MAP 10.1   CONQUERERS, 1092–1492 CE

TIMELINE

◇ **1095**
Pope Urban II's speech at Clermont, cAlling for crusade

◇ **1206–1526**
Delhi Sultanate

◇ **1162 (?)–1227**
Genghis Khan

◇ **1279–1368,**
Yuan Dynasty

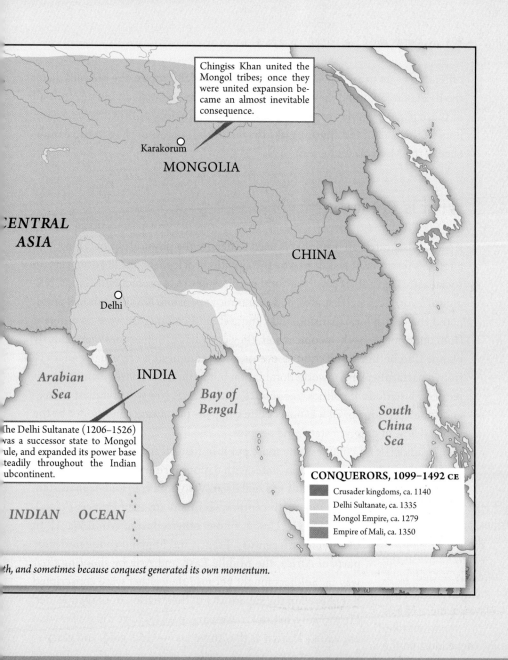

Chingiss Khan united the Mongol tribes; once they were united expansion became an almost inevitable consequence.

Karakorum

MONGOLIA

CENTRAL ASIA

CHINA

Delhi

Arabian Sea

INDIA

Bay of Bengal

South China Sea

The Delhi Sultanate (1206–1526) was a successor state to Mongol rule, and expanded its power base steadily throughout the Indian subcontinent.

INDIAN OCEAN

CONQUERORS, 1099–1492 CE
- Crusader kingdoms, ca. 1140
- Delhi Sultanate, ca. 1335
- Mongol Empire, ca. 1279
- Empire of Mali, ca. 1350

th, and sometimes because conquest generated its own momentum.

1260
Mamluks defeat the Mongols at Ayn Jalut

1215–1255
Sundjata of Mali

1492
Fall of the last Muslim stronghold of Granada

differences—to other powers of the time like the Mali Empire, the Mamluk state, the Iberian *reconquista*, the crusaders, and the Delhi Sultanate in India. While all of these played significant parts in shaping world history at this time and after, none of them achieved anything like the territorial success or the extensive influence of the Mongol conquests.

What Is Conquest?

Conquest is a catch-all term that is used to denote the physical act of taking over another's territory. It was driven by the ambitions of leaders, the needs of certain social actors, an adherence to cultural norms, a desire to protect homelands, religious fervor, factional disputes, and economic expansion. No single model dominated the desire for expansion and conquest, and conquerors were as different from one another as the people whom they conquered. Sometimes meticulously planned, sometimes a reaction to events, most conquests were usually a far cry from a dastardly plan for world domination but, rather, the consequence of complex combinations of politics, economics, and culture. Nor was conquest a once-and-for-all proposition; it was never quite complete but always conditioned by the ebb and flow of different states and peoples.

To understand conquest one must put it in historical context. Modern-day conquest is undertaken by nation-states with national armies. In recent times the United States has sent its army to both Iraq and Afghanistan. In the twentieth century, Germany invaded France, Poland, and the Soviet Union, among others, during World War II. In the nineteenth century, France and England conquered large parts of Africa, the Middle East, and Asia by shooting their way in. Soldiers fought because they either were conscripted or believed in the superiority of their nation or of their leader. Historically, nations, tribes, and peoples have fought for what are widely known as the "three Gs"—God, gold, and glory—each one playing a more or less important role, depending on the context.

> Historically, nations, tribes, and peoples have fought for what are widely known as the "three Gs"—God, gold, and glory—each one playing a more or less important role, depending on the context.

But while the "G factor" was certainly in force in the premodern era, national armies did not exist. "Armies" were made up of mercenaries, tribal members, conquered peoples, unwilling conscripts, and individuals with multiple, diverse motivations—religious, financial, or ideological. Motivations were often different in that their expansion was tied not to national ambition but to the economic, political, cultural, and ideological needs and demands of family, tribe, and religious community.

To What Extent Was Conquest Leader-Driven?

It is tempting to explain the extraordinary Mongol conquests of much of Eurasia as a result of Chinggis Khan losing his wife to a neighboring tribe. While his subsequent spree of world conquering might seem like overkill, there is a certain truth to this, at least in the context of intertribal struggles over the particular resource that women represented. This issue, however, was only a part of the whole experience of being a Mongol at this time in history. Temujin, as Chinggis was known before he achieved prominence, had a particularly harrowing upbringing. We will mention the basics here, but the story is related in some detail in the only primary source we have for Mongol history, the *Secret History of the Mongols*. It sounds like a modern bestseller, but in reality the *History* is the only contemporary book we have that details the life and times of Chinggis. Not to be trusted completely (Rossabi calls it a "semi-mythical and semi-accurate work"[4]), it goes some way to explaining the motivations for Mongol expansion outside their traditional homeland.

Temujin's father was a local chief, or *khan*, presiding over a clan of Mongols, a group of families practicing seasonal herding of sheep and horses. Life on the

Statue of Chinggis Khan East of Ulaanbaatar   Over 130 feet high, it marks the entrance to his ancestral homeland. For today's Mongolians he is a symbol of national pride.

---

[4]   Ibid., 3.

steppe was harsh by most standards. Its continental climate meant hot summers and long, freezing winters, a land that was hostile to agriculture but amenable to animal pasturing. Because of the harsh conditions, population density at the time was tiny compared, for example, with the Mongol neighbor to the south, China. In the twelfth century Mongolia (roughly three times the size of France) had a population of about 1 million, while China had some 75 million.

Geographic conditions doubtless contributed to the social and political life of the Mongols, the major feature of which at this point was disunity. Multiple tribes and clans coexisted uneasily. Theft of animals—and women—was chronic and created a seemingly endless cycle of violence and revenge between constantly shifting groups and alliances. Temujin himself was born of such a theft; his mother, Hogelun, had been kidnapped from her newly married husband on her way back to his tribe. As the *Secret History* tells it, she was riding in a cart with her husband beside her on horseback, when three Mongol horsemen swooped down on them. Understanding how this sort of kidnapping generally unfolded, the young girl, probably not more than 16, knew they would kill her husband if they caught him. She, on the other had, was a valuable asset. She urged her husband to run: "As long as you've got your life you'll be able to find some other girl to marry. When you find her, just name her Hogelun after me."[5] She never saw him again and was instead taken by a man named Yesugi, who was to father Temujin.

History repeats itself, especially in twelfth-century Mongolia. Yesugi died when Temujin was about 9 years old, poisoned by rivals. This left Temujin's family outcasts as their clan decided they could not support a woman with several children. Living off small rodents and the occasional fish, the family scraped a living together by themselves. At about age 16, Temujin set off to claim the bride to whom he had been betrothed before his father had died. The girl, Borte, was still waiting for him; and Temujin and his brother Belgutei took her back to their camp. It is possible that Temujin's life might have been complete at this point, had they been left to live in peace; but such a thing was unlikely on the steppe. The past came back to haunt him. The Merkid tribe, from whom Yesugi had abducted Hogelun, decided to claim vengeance from *him* (in a confusing sort of logic—Temujin, you might think, was an innocent party, the one responsible having died!). They did not want Hogelun back, however, as she was now an old woman, but took Temujin's young bride, Borte. This action, and Temujin's response, was pivotal, as Weatherford points out: "Temujin's response to this crisis, and the challenges of the Merkid would prove the decisive contest that would set him on the path to greatness."[6]

---

[5]   *The Secret History of the Mongols: The Origin of Chingis Khan*, adapted by Paul Khan (San Francisco: North Point Press, 1984), 12.
[6]   Weatherford, *Genghis Khan*, 30.

In the course of rescuing his wife from her abductors, Temujin called upon relationships he had managed to forge with more powerful individuals, most important among them at this point was Ong Khan, a powerful clan leader who had been an *anda*, or blood brother, of Yesugi's. A blood brother of Temujin's from childhood, Jarmukha was another valuable asset to Temujin. These relationships enabled Temujin to strengthen his position and eventually become a clan leader, or *khan*, himself.

But how does this background explain the conquests? Temujin's struggles to, first of all, stay alive and then protect his family led him to develop an increasingly powerful position in Mongol society, based on alliances with others, to the point at which he ultimately became a threat to Ong Khan, who plotted to have him killed. This initiated yet another fateful event in the Great Khan's life, ultimately catapulting him to a position of overall control of the clans and tribes in Mongolia. Chinggis foiled the plot, escaped with a small band of supporters, and regrouped in his ancestral homeland before leading an attack on the Ong Khan, the success of which, in around 1206, led the Mongol "nobility," such as it was, to endorse him as Chinggis, or "Fierce," Khan.

The "great man" school of history, which emphasizes the actions of powerful individuals, has been unfashionable for decades. Yet, when it comes to the Mongols, it might be worth reconsidering. "Whereas the causes and reasons for the pervasiveness of globalization today are multifarious," writes historian George Lane, "the globalization that swept the medieval world can be traced to one man and to one grouping of people. That one man was Genghis Khan ... and the people that he united were the Mongol tribes."[7]

In many ways the phenomenon of the Mongols parallels an earlier expansion, that of the Islamic Empire. Temujin, before expanding out of Mongolia, had to unify his own people. In the same way, Muhammad, in the seventh century, had to unify the Arabs of the Arabian Peninsula, before expanding east and west in an earlier, dynamic period of conquest. Both Mongols and Arabs directed their conquests to richer state societies on their border; if the Mongols lived on the barren steppe, the Arabs inhabited the equally barren—but hotter!—desert of Arabia. And "unifying" the Mongols was a bloody business, relying as it did on warfare and violence. As the *Secret History* tells it, "When on that occasion Çinggis Qa'an plundered the Tayiči'ut he wiped out the men of the Tayiči'ut lineage, such as the Tayiči'ut A'uču Ba'atur, Qoton Örčeng and Qudu'udar—he blew them to the winds like hearth ashes, even to the offspring of the offspring."[8] We have heard language like this before—from Mesopotamian kings, from Chinese warlords,

[7]   George Lane, *Ghengis Khan and Mongol Rule* (Cambridge, MA: Hackett, 2009), xxxiii.
[8]   *The Secret History*, 70.

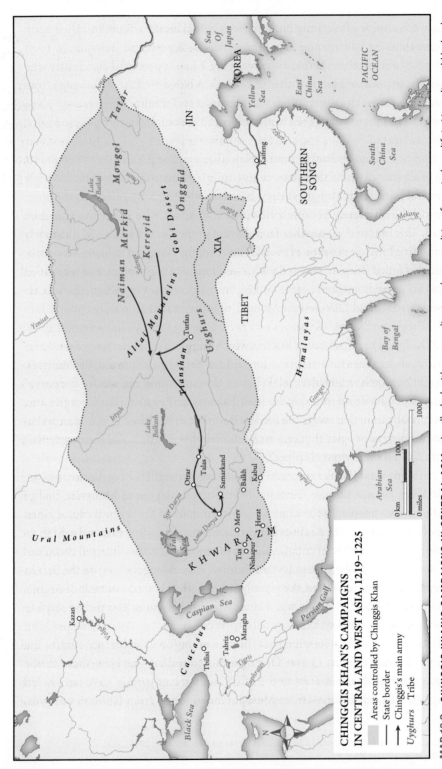

MAP 10.2 CHINGGIS KHAN'S CAMPAIGNS IN CENTRAL AND WEST ASIA Landlocked, with a severe climate and poor conditions for agriculture, life in Mongolia could be harsh. But it was surrounded by wealthier sedentary societies. Is it any surprise, therefore, that once united, they headed abroad?

CHINGGIS KHAN'S CAMPAIGNS IN CENTRAL AND WEST ASIA, 1219–1225

- Areas controlled by Chinggis Khan
- State border
- Chinggis's main army
- *Uyghurs* Tribe

from Roman generals. This kind of desire to obliterate was nothing new in history, and in particular, the desire to wipe out a bloodline can be found in very early Chinese history, where great importance was placed on family lineage. This practice satisfied Chinggis Khan's intolerance of social hierarchy and fulfilled his desire for "total revenge." The authors of the *Secret History* commend him for not only eliminating his rivals but also incorporating their followers into his expanding army (why waste good manpower?). Many who were captured by the Mongols pledged their allegiance willingly, and one tribesman promised, "For the Qa'an I will charge forward, so as to rend the deep water, so as to crumble the shining stone ... so as to crush the black stone at the time when I am told to attack."[9] Many among Chinggis' conquered peoples quickly accepted the idea that he was the "khan of all khans" and "master of all worlds." From the perspective of the *Secret History*, his leadership was the primary reason the Mongols conquered such a vast territory.

> This kind of desire to obliterate was nothing new in history, and in particular, the desire to wipe out a bloodline can be found in very early Chinese history, where great importance was placed on family lineage.

That the drive of one individual should play such a prominent role in the Mongols' story of their own past should be no surprise. They did not have a "state" in any modern sense, and their seminomadic, herding culture allowed individuals to play central leadership roles. But the question remains, *would the Mongols have achieved so much (or so much notoriety!) without Temujin?* Balancing the great man theory somewhat is the idea that, by the late twelfth century, Mongolia was developing and becoming more unified, and their interactions with sedentary civilizations made them increasingly beguiled by the consumer luxuries these societies created. If they could not trade for these items, they were quite willing to raid for them. Additional factors may have been in play, namely, climate change. In the twelfth century the average mean temperature in Mongolia declined. Some scholars suggest that this resulted in poor growth of steppe grass, upon which the Mongol flocks fed. Data on this theory are limited, but the cold spell could well have necessitated the Mongols' finding new pasture outside the steppe. In this period of growth and increasing connection with the world outside Mongolia, would another leader have stepped up in Temujin's absence? Was the time ripe for a Mongol Khan of all Khans?

Leaders had very personal reasons for wanting to conquer other lands, and they were the ones who inspired their peoples to embark on expansionist adventures. But we should not assume that all leaders had similar motivations. The Crusades, for example, were inspired by the political aspirations of a religious

---

9   Ibid., 69.

leader, Pope Urban II (1042–1099). At the end of the eleventh century, this pontiff competed for power and influence with the secular head of the Holy Roman Empire, Henry IV (1050–1106). Urban II believed that religious authority should always trump secular competitors, and in calling for a crusade against Muslims in the Middle East, he hoped to lure soldiers away from Henry IV's army. Putting together a fighting force under the banner of Christendom's struggle against Muslims not only enhanced the position of the church but also consolidated Urban II's own political power. "Let the holy sepulcher of our Lord and Saviour," he announced in a speech at Clermont, France, in 1095, "which is possessed by unclean nations, especially arouse you, and the holy places which are now treated with ignominy and irreverently polluted with the filth of the unclean. Oh, most valiant soldiers and descendants of invincible ancestors, do not degenerate our progenitors, but recall the valor of your progenitors."[10]

During the thirteenth-century reign of Razia Sultan, the only woman to lead India's Delhi Sultanate (1206–1526), personal ambition largely drove the sultanate's expansion. Razia became sovereign simply because her father considered her more competent than her brothers. She established her credentials by leading the charge into battle, riding an elephant while dressed as a man. In a short time she became such a powerful military leader that the people who had initially backed her turned on her and had her killed, reasoning that a woman should not be allowed to have this type of power.

DID SUNDJIATA OF MALI INFLUENCE CONQUEST IN THE SAME WAY?

"Listen there sons of Mali, children of the black people, listen to my word. . . . I am going to tell you of Sundiata, he whose exploits will astonish men for a long time. He was great among kings, he was peerless among men; he was beloved of God because he was the last of the great conquerors."[11] Sundiata, the leader of the Mali Empire (r. ca. 1215–1255), is often referred to as the "Lion King" and has been made famous by the animated Disney film. The story of the king of Mali comes from the Epic of Sundiata, an oral tradition passed down by *griots*, western African storytellers. While the epic's credibility as a historical source is, like that of the *Secret History*, limited, it does tell us something about the Mali conquests and about what motivated people to go to war.

10   Urban II: Speech at Clermont 1095 (Robert the Monk Version), from James Harvey Robinson, ed., *Readings in European History*, vol. 1 (Boston: Ginn, 1904), *Medieval Sourcebook*, http://www.fordham.edu/halsall/source/urban2a.html.

11   D. T. Niane, *Sundiata: An Epic of Old Mali* (London: Longman, 1969), 2.

The story consists of three cycles (slavishly followed by Disney): Sundiata's childhood, his exile, and his triumphant return. He was forced to leave home with his mother because of family rivalries. In exile he became a warrior and established strong ties with important patrons. And on his return he was motivated by the desire to retake lands that his people, the Mandinka tribe, had lost to Sumanguru, the leader of a tribe called the Soso. As the *griots* tell it,

> At the time when Sundiata was preparing to assert his claim over the kingdom of his fathers, Soumaoro [Sumanguru] was the king of kings, the most powerful king in all the lands of the setting sun. The fortified town of Sosso was the bulwark of fetishism against the word of Allah. For a long time Soumaoro defied the whole world. Since his accession to the throne of Sosso he had defeated nine kings whose heads served him as fetishes in his macabre chamber. Their skins served as seats and he cut his footwear from human skin.[12]

We should remember the propagandistic nature of the story, especially bearing in mind how barbaric (and non-Islamic) the people of Soso are made out to be. But Sundiata was interested in defeating the current "strongman" and in gaining redemption after his exile. But was it redemption based on individual desire, or was it redemption tied to tribal interests? One theory is that Sundiata's goal was to win glory by uniting his tribal confederation, the Mandinka. In speaking to tribal leaders opposed to Sumanguru, Sundiata declared, "I have come back and as long as I breathe Mali will never be in thrall—rather death than slavery."[13] The oral narrative supports the idea that a strong leader was needed to unite a divided people.

Yet even during the period of Mandinka subjugation, powerful interests and connections still existed across tribes among groups of hunters who formed associations. The Mandinka revered hunters because they provided the rest of the clan with food and protection, exemplifying the universal connection between hunting and soldiery. Hunters were also able to communicate with spirits of the bush. This power would have afforded them a similar status to that of Sundiata, who was believed to have magical abilities that allowed him to understand the secrets of the cosmos.

In defeating the Soso, Sundiata relied on the hunters' associations, which could overcome clan interests and create a viable fighting force. Shared military and professional interests allowed for the expansion of military organization, and hunters could be promised better access to areas with abundant game and could be given an opportunity to gain more status.

---

[12] Ibid., 41.
[13] Ibid., 56.

Equestrian Figure from Djenne/Mopto Region, Thirteenth to Fourteenth Century   The ornate features on the horse (caparison on nose) and rider (necklace) suggest high status.

By consolidating this alliance, Sundiata might be considered more of a unifier than a conqueror like Chinggis Khan. He rallied together groups of hunters with the common goal of uniting the Mandinka and defeating the Soso. But scholars believe that Sundiata and his forces pushed into areas to the south and west that had formerly been part of the Kingdom of Ghana. This conquest led to the steady flow of Mandinka people into these areas and can be seen as a form of colonization based on territorial control and resource exploitation. This pattern continued under Mansa Uli, the son of Sundiata, who historians believe gained control over the trading cities of Walata, Timbuktu, and Gao, major entrepôts in the African trade network.

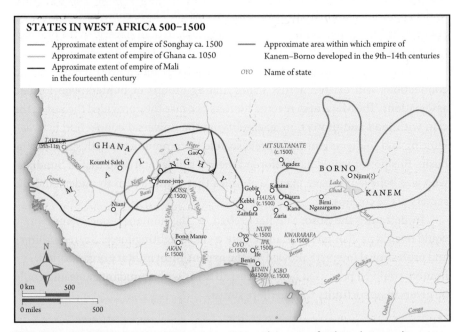

STATES IN WEST AFRICA 500–1500

—— Approximate extent of empire of Songhay ca. 1500
—— Approximate extent of empire of Ghana ca. 1050
—— Approximate extent of empire of Mali in the fourteenth century

—— Approximate area within which empire of Kanem–Borno developed in the 9th–14th centuries

OYO   Name of state

MAP 10.3   STATES IN WEST AFRICA, 500–1500   The empire of Mali was heir to earlier western African states which developed around land and riverine trade routes among differing ecological niches.

How Did Conquest Relate to Security?

That the drive of one individual should play such a prominent role in the Mongols' story of their own past, as related in their *Secret History*, should come as no surprise. They did not have a "state" in any modern sense, and their semi-nomadic, herding culture allowed individuals to play central leadership roles. But while the *Secret History* gives the impression that Chinggis Khan had an abiding desire to control territory far and wide, May suggests that the Mongol appetite for world domination "is debatable." He believes that Chinggis Khan's principal concern was to eliminate threats from his neighbors and that, since the best form of defense, you might argue, is attack, he preempted his neighbors.

One of the problems was that his defeated rivals escaped to other lands and refused to accept the new order, creating ever new enemies and neighbors in a widening sphere of influence. To the north, the Mongols established security by entering into marriage alliances with different groups of the "forest people," who were seminomadic tribes. A *marriage alliance* was an agreement between two peoples, political factions, or families that served as a guarantee of peace. Polities have always spent a good deal of time calculating whether war is viable; while battle often rewarded the victors, losing was disastrous. The decision of the forest people to join rather than oppose the Mongols seemed prudent given the strength of Chinggis Khan's forces. Marriage served not only as a way of building social and political connections but also as a hedge against war.

At other times war was necessary to establish better security and gain more grazing lands. Grazing lands were important because as the Mongols expanded they needed more territory for their horses. While confrontations with larger states could be conceived as a form of territorial takeover, in many cases the Mongols only looked to intimidate and exact tribute from their more settled neighbors, like the Jin dynasty of Manchuria. This had been founded by Jurchen tribesmen in 1115. Migrating south in the middle of the twelfth century, about 3 million Jurchen tribesmen in northern China governed a population of over 25 million, establishing their capital in Zhondu, today's Beijing. In establishing themselves as a resource-dependent state, the Jin came under increasing military pressure from the Mongols in the early half of the thirteenth century. But while Mongols invaded their southern neighbors, they were content to attack and then withdraw. Having devastated the Jin Empire, in 1212 they withdrew to the steppes, retaining only a small part for communications purposes. Defeat in battle, therefore, did not always lead to occupation.

WERE THE MONGOLS DRIVEN BY A PASSION FOR VIOLENCE?

One thing history teaches you is that there are few—very few—exceptional people or societies. Our common human ancestry is largely responsible for this—we are all, in other words, *human*. The likelihood, therefore, of the Mongols possessing some exceptionally violent gene that truly sets them apart from the rest of humanity is, to say the least, small. Instead, we should contextualize their bad behavior in two ways: we should remember that most of what we know about them was written by their enemies or their victims and, as such, is often naturally biased; we should also remember that violence was widespread in the ancient world, as it is in the modern world.

With those caveats, we can look at some of their actions more objectively. In 1220 a dust cloud appeared a few miles from the ancient Silk Road city of Bokhara in central Asia. From the word *Bokhar*, in the Magian language, *Bokhara* means "city of learning"; and Chinggis Khan was about to teach it a lesson. The Mongols had figured out that it was not helpful to approach a city at full gallop—that just gave the game away. Instead, the vast Mongol army ambled toward its victim, in the

Seeker of Riches In a sixteenth-century illustration, Chinggis Khan demands that the rich men of Bokhara lead him to their hidden wealth. Conquest usually resulted in major wealth redistribution.

way a large trading caravan might, like a leopard sauntering toward a gazelle, feigning indifference. It was only when the Mongols were well within reach of the city that its inhabitants realized that the crowd of unruly-looking foreigners was not a group of merchants, bringing desirable luxury goods and intending to exchange wine for silk, but an invading army, peddling death and destruction.

What followed was reported by the Persian historian Juvaini. Included in the Mongol army were many Turks—Mongols, like most conquering armies, employed the services of others, especially those they had conquered. These were men, according to Juvaini, "that knew not clean from unclean, and considered the bowl of war to be a basin of rich soup and held a mouthful of the sword to be a beaker of wine."[14] Not the kind of people you wanted to let into your city.

---

[14]   Ala ad-Din 'Ata Malik Juvaini, *The History of the World Conqueror*, trans. John Andrew Boyle (Cambridge, MA: Harvard University Press, 1958), 58.

After surrounding Bokhara and letting the inhabitants understand that they were not a traveling farmers' market, the Mongols lobbed incendiary bombs over the walls and unleashed arrows, many of them burning, and fire lances. The city ignited, the inhabitants fled, and the Mongols moved in, torching the remaining houses (mostly stick-built). All people taller than the butt of a whip (about 2.5 feet) were killed, amounting to 30,000.

Their enemies were terrified of the Mongol reputation for cruelty, long before they encountered them in the flesh; and this is something the Mongols counted on. The Mongols used prisoners as human shields against the Chinese. "As the captives fell in battle, their bodies helped to fill in the moats and form pathways over defensive holes and structures made by the enemies."[15] The Franciscan monk Giovanni Carpini reported that the Mongols took the fat of the people they killed and threw it on people's houses before setting the houses on fire—to help them burn. The Mongols looked to create the expectation of coming violence; people surrendered to the Mongols sometimes purely on the basis of rumors, being psychologically incapable of fighting back even before the battle began. The Persian chronicler Ibn al Atir claimed (perhaps hyperbolically) that a single Mongol entering a Persian village was sufficient to induce surrender. But the Mongols avoided total extermination if at all possible, restricting their killing principally to those who resisted. Those (men) who survived could be used as recruits in future campaigns.

But were the Mongols any worse than others of the period? Before them, the Romans and other large territorial empires had been similarly violent. When the Byzantines defeated the Bulgarians in 1014, 15,000 captives were blinded; and when the Holy Roman Emperor Barbarossa (ca. 1122–1190) besieged the city of Crema in Italy in 1159, he had his men behead prisoners and play with them on city walls. Mongol violence was not unique, but the speed and success of their conquests were.

Mongol violence coexisted—uneasily, perhaps—with their creativity, evident in other histories. One such includes Marco Polo's account of Chinggis' grandson, Khubilai, the "Great Khan" of China (1215–1294), who sent out agents across the countryside in times of famine, dispensing grain to needy peasants and cancelling their tax bills. The state they created in Eurasia led to more intensive and widespread trade networks than the world had ever seen. The *Pax Mongolica*, which on the face of it sound like an oxymoron, allowed multiple cultures under their supervision to flourish, leaving art, architecture, and literature of unsurpassed quality and endurance. Modern Chinese archeologists working on

---

[15] Weatherford, *Genghis Khan*, 93.

la vicat. x. mille hommes eslont aus.qui sont dut ateconnie. ij. ce. ij. et lequi
lent tasta oz.qui vault a dire hommes qui se prenant garde. Car dare+dare
tenement ca en la. sy que bien tiennent de tune asse.

Khubilai Khan Hunting with a Falcon From Marco Polo's *Book of Marvels*   Some say Polo made it all up. Even if he did, he succeeded in generating enormous interest in Chinese ways among Europeans.

Shangdu, Khubilai's summer palace, have found exquisite Buddhist statues, jewelry, and porcelain, suggesting the elevated tastes of the Mongol rulers—a far cry from the thuggish barbarians often presented in traditional histories.

Clearly, violence would diminish in the postconquest phase, when the Mongols, as with Khubilai Khan in China, were in power. As rulers, the Mongols often adopted the ways of their conquered subjects. Mongol women—or, more specifically, Mongol wives and mothers, who were not always ethnically Mongol—often provided a moderating influence. Perhaps the best example of this is Sorghaghtani Beki (ca. 1204–1252), the wife of Tolui, Chinggis Khan's youngest son. Considered by the Persian historian Rashid-al Din the most intelligent and capable woman in the world, she is credited with persuading the Mongol leadership of northern China to maintain the agricultural economy in that region as it would create the most revenue, instead of ravaging it and turning it into pasture for Mongol ponies. A Nestorian Christian, she also supported the Chinese religions, Buddhism and Daoism, so as to ease the relationship between the Chinese and their new foreign masters. She educated her four sons in the traditional ways of the Mongols—riding, hunting, military skills—as well as in the new Mongol written language and exposed them to the multicultural ways of the empires they were all to rule. Sorghaghtani Beki sought, therefore, to ingratiate herself with her new subjects and understood that it was necessary to reach an accommodation with them and to use their native institutions to rule.

This insight was not shared by all Mongols however. In 1246, Guyug, Chinggis Khan's grandson, was named Great Khan. He moved the capital to Kara Khorum, a city constructed by Chinggis in the steppe but a disconnected and distant place from which to rule. Guyug's reign was characterized by a division among the "old school" Mongols, who wanted to do things the traditional way, and those who, like Sorghaghtani Beki, understood that such a diverse empire needed new thinking to govern.

But a people in the thrall of conquest will act differently once the fighting is over and a status quo is reached. The Mongol reputation for violence is mostly associated with the conquering phase, that of the life of Chinggis and his sons. By the time of his grandson, Khubilai Khan, the Mongol experience was vastly different. They now inhabited a multicultural empire spanning thousands of miles and had access to all of the resources therein. Among these was a wealth of knowledge and tradition developed by their subject peoples. Under Mongol rule many of these people flourished. While the Mongols themselves did not necessarily add to the creative pool of humanity directly, they provided a platform from which others did. As Rossabi puts it, "To be sure, the subjugated populations themselves often developed the economic institutions, the technological innovations, and the literary, religious and artistic texts that characterized their civilizations during the era of Mongol governance. Yet Mongol rule and the stability they brought paved the way for such remarkable developments."[16]

> ☀ By the time of his grandson, Khubilai Khan, the Mongol experience was vastly different. They now inhabited a multicultural empire spanning thousands of miles and had access to all of the resources therein.

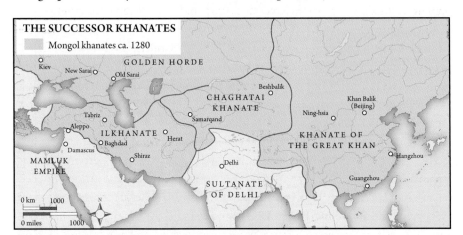

MAP 10.4   **THE SUCCESSOR KHANATES**   In the aftermath of the fourth Great Khan, Mongke, a grandson of Chinggis, the empire split into a number of "khanates." In all of these regions the Mongol conquerors were massively outnumbered by their subjects and absorbed much of the local culture, including converting to local religions and adopting languages.

---

[16]   Rossabi, *The Mongols*, 2.

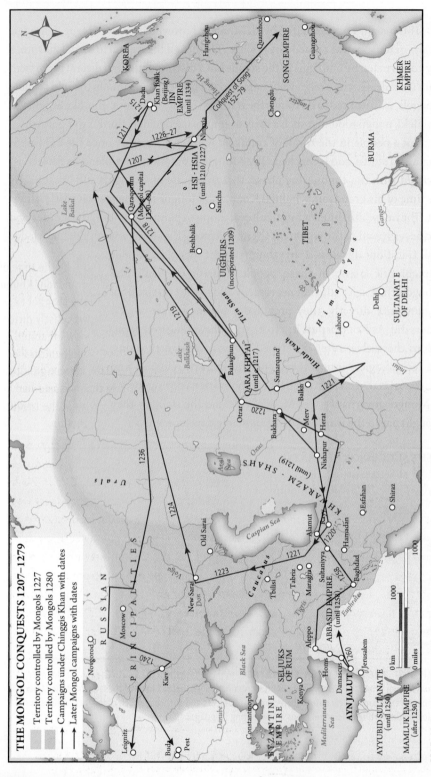

THE MONGOL CONQUESTS 1207–1279

Territory controlled by Mongols 1227

Territory controlled by Mongols 1280

Campaigns under Chinggis Khan with dates

Later Mongol campaigns with dates

MAP 10.5 THE MONGOL CONQUESTS, 1207–1279 Ayn Jalut, 1260: Mamluks stopped the Mongol advance to the west. They decapitated the Mongol leader, no doubt helping to dispel the myth of their invincibility.

HOW DID THE MAMLUKS RESIST THE MONGOLS?

> This country was very far from that land which those infidels had conquered,
> but (then) it became their neighbor. And thus the people (of this country) had
> to fight the infidels and resist them. In order to do so, they had to obtain two
> things, a large army and a brave sultan (to lead them). Without this, it is impos-
> sible to fight these infidels with all their conquests over the many lands, and
> their numerous men and armies.[17]

So writes the Mamluk chronicler Ibn al-Nafis, upon the arrival of the Mongols on
the doorstep of the Mamluk Empire, an Islamic state in Egypt. As we have seen,
the Mongols were able to sweep across central Asia and conquer enormous
amounts of territory, so the possibility of the Mongols entering Mamluk territory
was very real. But the chronicler thought that, with the right army and the right
leadership, the Mongols could be defeated. His idea of war, based on the importance of a defensive response, underscored a fundamental difference in how the
Mongols and the Mamluks viewed their confrontation.

In 1257, Saif ad Din Qutuz defeated his rivals and took control of the Mamluk
state. He justified his taking power on the grounds that Egypt needed a strong leader
to combat the Mongol threat. His claim was justified when in 1260 the Mongol leader
Hulegu, the sacker of Baghdad, sent envoys to Qutuz demanding that he surrender.
Qutuz, following the path of the other Mongol adversaries, chose to ignore the letter
and to kill the hapless envoys, putting their heads on the gates of the city.

Inevitably, this killing led to a direct confrontation between Hulegu and
Qutuz at the battle of Ayn Jalat in present-day Jordan (1260). Qutuz proclaimed
victory over the infidels and declared that he had stood in defense of Islam. Each
side had approached the battle with a different sensibility. Mongol geography was
related to perpetual expansion and to land. In contrast, the type of geography that
defined the Mamluks had more to do with fortified spaces and defense, more specifically citadels. A *citadel* was a fortification that served as the last line of defense
against an attack from the outside. It was the most protected space in the city.
"These citadels," says architectural historian Nasser Rabat, "heralded the new
regime whose roots were foreign and preferences were military. They were built
to be a refuge against attack, a residence for the military elite, a barrier against the
ruled and a symbol of the rulers' valor as defenders of Islam."[18]

Mongols and Mamluks had very different concepts of war and conquest; while
the Mongols did not make distinctions between people of different religions, in theory

---

[17] Reuven Amitai-Preiss, *Mongols and Mamluks: The Mamluk–Ilkhanid War 1260–1281* (Cambridge and
      New York: Cambridge University Press, 1995), 49.
[18] Nasser Rabbat, "The Militarization of Taste in Medieval Bilad al-Sham," in Hugh N. Kennedy (ed),
      Muslim Military Architecture in Greater Syria (Leiden, The Netherlands: E.J. Brill, 2006), 88.

Mamluk Citadel in Aleppo, Syria, Twelfth Century   Mamluks were committed to geographic sites, once they conquered them, as the architecture of this citadel expresses. These people were here to stay.

Muslims believed that two different realms existed, *Dar al Islam* and *Dar al Harb,* the "House of Islam" (where Islam prevailed) and the "House of War" (everywhere else). Mongol incursions into these areas represented both a threat and a challenge to Muslims to protect their lands and motivated the Mamluks to be geared for war.

What Role Did Religion Play in Conquest?

As we have seen in former chapters, empires and universal religions became closely affiliated with one another during periods of territorial expansion. Christianity spread as the Byzantines conquered different parts of the Middle East. Islam became one of the principal religions of Africa and Asia when early Muslims sought to expand their territory beyond the Arabian Peninsula. Even the Mongols believed that their right to rule was conveyed to them by the sky god, the chief deity of nomads. At times, religion and conquest were closely connected to one another.

WHAT WAS THE RECONQUISTA?

The Iberian Peninsula is a case in point. As early as the eighth century, Muslims controlled large parts of contemporary Spain and Portugal. Muslim control was considered unacceptable to many Christians, and by the eleventh century Spanish Christians used the idea of a reconquest, or retaking of former Christian lands, to frame their struggle against Muslims. But the idea that a unified group of Christians pursued a single policy of conquest from the eleventh century until the fall of the last Muslim stronghold in Granada in 1492 has been challenged by many historians. Some have suggested that the reconquest was in reality a mishmash of different ideas and interest groups who signed on to the idea of taking Iberia back. The Iberian Peninsula was a divided place, comprised of different kingdoms, such as Castile-Leon, Navarre, Aragon, and Catalonia, to name a few. While all paid lip service to recovering lost territories, Christians also competed with one another for power and resources.

The Spaniards—at first the Kingdom of Asturias, an area in northwest Spain—came up with a justification for taking back what they thought was rightfully theirs. They saw the Kingdom of Asturias as representing a continuity of the old Visigoth state, a pre-Islamic Christian kingdom. Later Spanish monarchs, such as Isabella and Ferdinand, patrons of Christopher Columbus, also emphasized their Visigoth roots and their ties to a Spain unified by Christianity and free of Muslims.

The idea of a lost past was used to explain the struggle between Muslims and Christians. Sancho Ramirez (ca. 1042–1094), king of Aragon and Navarre, noted that he settled Christians in lands Muslims had conquered "for the recovery and Extension of the Church of Christ, for the destruction of the pagans, the enemies of Christ, and the building up and benefit of the Christians, so that the kingdom invaded and captured by Ishmaelites, might be liberated to the honor and service of Christ."[19] While Christianity served as one of the major rallying points, Muslim and Christian politics were more complicated and based on complex local rivalries. Crossing over to fight for the alleged enemy was not uncommon, and El Cid (ca. 1043–1099), a Spanish nobleman and military legend, ended up fighting for Muslim kings against Christians. Even given these limitations, the Christians were able to reconquer all of the Iberian Peninsula by 1492.

WHAT WAS THE SIGNIFICANCE OF THE CRUSADES?

Some of the Spanish ideology was taken from a crusading spirit that existed in Europe and that looked to take back or "reconquer" Christian lands in the Middle East. In 1095, Pope Urban II, responding to a plea from the Byzantine emperor, offered a call to aid their fellow Christians in the Middle East.

> For, as the most of you have heard, the Turks and Arabs have attacked them and have conquered the territory of Romania [the Greek Empire] as far west as the

---

[19] Joseph O'Callaghan, *Reconquest and Crusade in Medieval Spain* (Philadelphia: University of Pennsylvania Press, 2003), 8.

shore of the Mediterranean and the Hellespont, which is called the Arm of St. George. They have occupied more and more of the lands of those Christians, and have overcome them in seven battles. They have killed and captured many, and have destroyed the churches and devastated the empire. If you permit them to continue thus for a while with impunity, the faithful of God will be much more widely attacked by them. On this account I, or rather the Lord, beseech you as Christ's heralds to publish this everywhere and to persuade all people of whatever rank, foot-soldiers and knights, poor and rich, to carry aid promptly to those Christians and to destroy that vile race from the lands of our friends. I say this to those who are present, it is meant also for those who are absent. Moreover, Christ commands it.[20]

> The long-term influence of the crusaders and the success of their conquest in the region are questionable; they came with big ideas but failed to establish permanent settlements.

The long-term influence of the crusaders and the success of their conquest in the region are questionable; they came with big ideas but failed to establish permanent settlements. They cannot even be compared to a people like the Mongols, who established an empire that covered much of Eurasia, or to the Mamluks, who remained in power until the sixteenth century. Their plans to take back Christian lands fell afoul because, unlike the Spanish, Saladin, a Kurdish Muslim leader, conquered much of the crusader kingdom of Jerusalem in 1187. Other crusader kingdoms also fell shortly after. Oddly, the crusade that resulted in the most significant political development was directed not at Muslims but instead against the Byzantine Empire, the people Urban II had summoned crusaders to help. The Fourth Crusade, initiated by Pope Innocent III and led by the Venetian doge in 1204, was originally designed to regain the Holy Land by first attacking Egypt. Instead, the doge hijacked the crusade and first directed it to the Croatian city of Zadar, to punish the city for its transgressions, before proceeding to Constantinople, where the crusaders sacked the city and placed it under Latin rule. The historical footnote here is that Christians overran Christians and not Muslims.

IN WHAT WAYS CAN THE RELIGIOUS EXPLANATION FOR CONQUEST BE MISLEADING?

If the first thing that you knew about the Delhi Sultanate was that it ruled over a large majority Hindu population in India, it might make sense for you to think that its establishment had to do with a religious clash, like the Crusades. Historians have often emphasized religious motivations in state actions. But while the

---

[20] Urban II: Speech at Clermont 1095, 312–316.

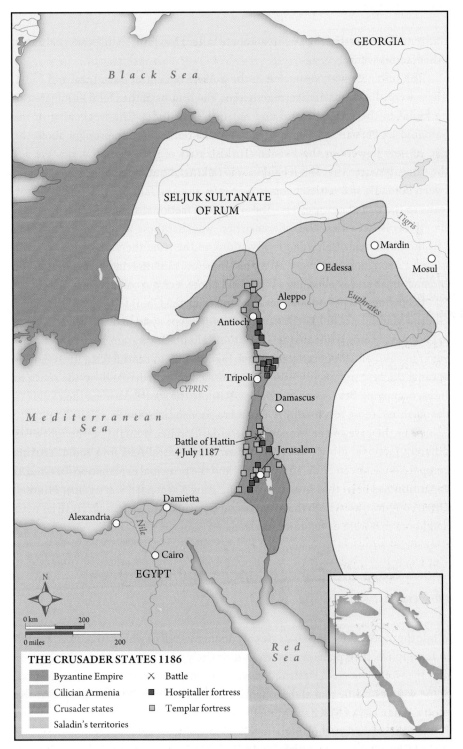

GEORGIA

Black Sea

SELJUK SULTANATE
OF RUM

○ Mardin

Tigris

○ Edessa

○ Mosul

Aleppo ○

Euphrates

Antioch ○

Tripoli ○

CYPRUS

Damascus ○

*M e d i t e r r a n e a n
S e a*

Battle of Hattin
4 July 1187

Jerusalem ○

Damietta ○

Alexandria ○

Nile

○ Cairo

EGYPT

N

0 km   200

0 miles   200

*Red
Sea*

THE CRUSADER STATES 1186

	Byzantine Empire	✕	Battle
	Cilician Armenia	■	Hospitaller fortress
	Crusader states	▫	Templar fortress
	Saladin's territories		

MAP 10.6 THE CRUSADER STATES   States built by crusading Christians in the Near East were
not to last. Crusaders, it turned out, were not colonialists but a strange breed of penitential pilgrims,
not looking to put down roots.

traditional view is that the Delhi Sultanate rallied Muslims to dispossess Hindus, other factors were at play.

The sultanate was connected to the politics of central Asia, Iran, and India. These were all regions of diverse religions. The origins of the Delhi Sultanate can be found in the Islamic world and not in Hindu India. The weakening of the Samanids, a Persian dynasty, at the end of the tenth century, brought about the rise of new powers in the Persian–Turkish part of the Islamic world. We see the same dynamic that Ibn Khaldun was talking about in terms of struggles between nomadic and settled peoples. Societies rise and fall, and this phenomenon leads to the rise of new powers. These types of factional struggles characterized the Mongols' activities. The difference here was that these were Muslims fighting Muslims. Mahmud of Ghazna, a local warlord, and his tribe, the change to Ghaznavid, gained a stronghold in Muslim Afghanistan before raiding Hindu territories in the Indian Punjab and establishing a capital in Lahore, a city in contemporary Pakistan.

Following this period, another Afghan group, the Ghurids, led by Muhammad Ghuri, a Mamluk not unlike the slave soldiers in Egypt, systematically seized change to Ghaznavid lands, while also defeating the shahs of Khwarazam (related to the guy who ran afoul of Chinggis Khan), acquiring territory in central Asia. The Ghurids became the first sultans in Delhi and continued to conquer lands to the south in India, occupying Benares on the Ganges River to the south. Between their lands to the north and those to the south, Delhi was a good location for the Ghurid capital.

As in the case of the Mongols, these developments might be thought of as different factional groups sweeping down from central Asia into India. Yet this comparison has been underemphasized, and the principal explanation for Ghurid expansion has been that Muslims were fighting a sectarian war against Hindus. Often conquest, as in both the Mongol and Ghurid cases, was about rivalries with neighbors that were never quite resolved.

What Were the Consequences and Outcomes of Conquest?

While the motivations and strategies of conquerors tell us what conquerors wanted to accomplish, their plans do not tell us ultimately what conquest brought about or how the world changed. Destruction was certainly one major result of expansion. Some sources claim that the Mongols killed more than 700,000 people in the central Asian city of Merv and more than 1 million in the Persian city of Nishapur. While contemporary scholars claim that these numbers are exaggerated, the scope of the killing and the destruction were considerable. During the Mongol siege, the Abbasid capital of Baghdad was razed to the ground in 1258; and under the

Mongols, the population of China declined by possibly as much as half, from 120 to 60 million. The Mali Empire and the crusaders also engaged in wanton destruction. In celebrating the defeat of the Soso people, the *Epic of Sundiata* notes, "It has disappeared, the proud city of Soumauro. A ghastly wilderness extends over the places where kings came and humbled themselves before the sorcerer king. All traces of the houses have vanished and of Soumaoro's palace there remains nothing more."[21] Also emphasizing the impact of conquest, Ludolph, a Christian chronicler of the siege of Acre, a city in Palestine, during the Crusades commented,

> When the Saracen nobles saw the others lying dead, and themselves unable to escape from the city, they fled for refuge into the mines which they had dug under the great tower, that they might make their way through the wall and so get out. But the Templars (crusaders) and others who were in the castle, seeing that they could not hurt the Saracens with stones and the like, because of the mines wherein they were, undermined the great tower of the castle, and flung it down upon the mines and the Saracens therein, and all perished alike.[22]

Conquest was both violent and destructive and left many cities and communities in ruin. Yet while conquest had a negative effect not only on those who were conquered but also on future generations, it also brought different groups of people together and established new commercial and political relationships. New people were in charge, and they drew up different rules and created new business arrangements.

HOW DID CONQUEST AFFECT TRADE?

The Persian Juvaini, employed by the Mongols, tells how at Chinggis Khan's camp Muslim merchants arrived looking to sell their fabrics. The chief khan of the Mongols was outraged at the merchants' prices and way of doing business and wondered whether these individuals knew that the Mongols were experienced consumers of fabrics. While confiscating the fabrics did not seem the best way to pursue a sound trading policy, Khan was demonstrating that he was willing to conduct a fair business but not to be cheated.

Under Chinggis Khan the basic policy of trade changed because now nomadic people had wealth, much of which they had acquired as booty, that they could exchange with merchants. Even with the changes, this relationship

---

[21]   Niane, *Sundiata*, 61.
[22]   James Brundage, *The Crusades: A Documentary Survey* (Milwaukee, WI: Marquette University Press, 1962), 268–72.

Battle Between Muslims and Christian Crusaders (Fourteenth Century)   Religious zeal was one of many motivations driving crusading knights from Europe to the Holy Land. Promise of financial gain, adventure, and lack of opportunities at home were others.

mirrored in some ways the type of commerce that had always existed between the steppe and settled society. Mutual dependence and reciprocity were quite common during times of peace. Constant hostility was not the order of the day.

Ögödei, Chinggis' son, developed new business practices. He created warehouse spaces, which could be used to store goods. He also expanded a messenger system that had existed under Chinggis Khan that made communication throughout the empire more efficient and created a security force that patrolled caravan routes. These changes provided dividends. Juvaini comments that in regard to Ögödei's business connections, "merchants began to come to his court from every side, and whatever goods they had bought, whether good or bad, he would command that they bought at full price."[23]

After the initial expansion of the Mongols under Chinggis, they begin to show different characteristics once in power, wanting to be connected and in dialogue with the rest of the world. Weatherford says that Chinggis Khan "took the disjointed and languorous trading towns along the Silk Route and organized them into history's largest free trade zone."[24] He was not one who "hoarded wealth and

---

[23]   May, *The Mongol Conquests*, 118–119.
[24]   Weatherford, *Genghis Khan*, xix.

treasure; instead, he widely distributed the goods acquired in combat, so they could make their way back into commercial circulation."[25] For Weatherford, the Mongol desire for unity and standardization literally fueled a commercial revolution.

Weatherford's enthusiasm aside, how realistic is it to talk about a Mongol free trading zone? A time of such great change tears down old structures and creates new opportunities. The Mongol system leveled the playing field somewhat for merchants as they were less interested in ethnic identity or religion than in the booty and trade. The Mongols looked for merchants with goods they desired, and they had loot with which to pay for it. Mongol rule greased the wheels of commerce by providing security along the steppe highways, which were notoriously dangerous for traders.

Skeptics of the idea of a "free trade zone" have argued that the Mongols were a tribute-taking state and made their revenue by extracting fees from people who were subordinate to them. As we know, tribute is a shakedown; it means paying out without getting anything in return. We know, for instance, that in Russia the Golden Horde took 10% of everything from locals. This tribute included both people and goods, and the Mongols relied on local princes to collect the fees. For this responsibility, the princes were able to take a percentage for themselves.

In Africa, evidence suggests that the economics of the gold trade was one of the major factors behind Mandinke expansion. During the Mali Empire, commercial routes were secured and the gold trade with the Mediterranean expanded. Gold was such a prominent part of the Mali economy that when the sultan Mansa Musa traveled to Cairo, he was so liberal with giving his gold as alms that it depressed the price of the commodity in Cairo.

> ☀ Gold was such a prominent part of the Mali economy that when the sultan Mansa Musa traveled to Cairo, he was so liberal with giving his gold as alms that it depressed the price of the commodity in Cairo.

The Dyula traders were important beneficiaries of Mali expansion. The Dyula were native to western Africa and, concurrent with the Mali expansion, led trading expeditions into the forest country to the south, which had remained inaccessible to northern merchants. As Basil Davidson notes, the Dyula were able to establish connections by, "travelling the roads with their own armed escorts, establishing themselves at regular relay stations, patiently linking one production zone with another."[26] Markets were loaded with goods, and exchange was conducted at times with cowrie shells.

Yet other African scholars argue that, like the Mongols, the Mali Empire's desire to expand was connected to an intention to collect tribute. In Mali one subordinated oneself to the person in charge. You handed over a certain percentage of goods, usually food, and in return you could receive protection or support

---

[25] Ibid.
[26] Basil Davidson, *Africa in History* (New York: Collier, 1991), 101.

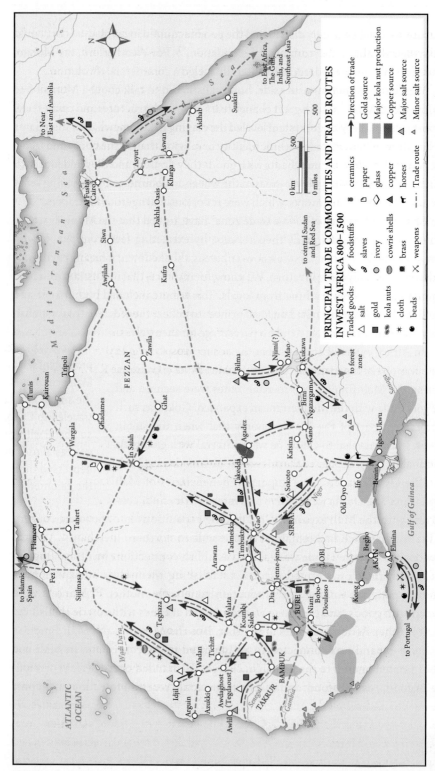

**PRINCIPAL TRADE COMMODITIES AND TRADE ROUTES
IN WEST AFRICA 800–1500**

Traded goods:

△ salt	🐚 foodstuffs	ceramics	
■ gold	✦ slaves	📄 paper	
✴ kola nuts	○ ivory	◇ glass	
● cloth	● cowrie shells	▲ copper	
✱ beads	■ brass	🐴 horses	
	✕ weapons		

→ Direction of trade

Gold source

Major kola nut production

Copper source

▲ Major salt source

▲ Minor salt source

– – – Trade route

MAP 10.7   PRINCIPAL TRADE COMMODITIES AND TRADE ROUTES IN WEST AFRICA   The different ecologies of western Africa led to trade between them, and with the wealth came power and influence—and conquering armies.

from a powerful patron such as the sultan. This practice was not unique to the Mongols or Mali; all states of the period—the Mamluks, the Spanish, and Venice, to name a few—were involved in tribute-taking to greater or lesser extents.

While tribute remained a viable form of revenue generation, the expansion of empires across land and sea routes facilitated the growth of trade in a number of different places. One of the ways that conquerors changed commercial patterns was by directing merchants to places in their domains with an abundance of goods. One of the major centers of the Middle East and the Red Sea was located in Cairo, the Mamluk seat of power. The Mamluk Empire was considered a good place to trade because the state was able to guarantee security. Like the Silk Road, merchants were anxious to find a safe route. Another reason for Cairo's success as a trading center is that it served as an intermediate point between different regions: Circassian slaves arrived from the Black Sea region, gold came from Africa, and spices came from Asia. The Mamluks were also major exporters of sugar, cotton, flax, and manufactured goods (Cairo was one of the leading manufacturing sites in the world, and industries in metallurgy, glass, pottery, leather, food processing, and furniture were all present); and they were anxious to attach themselves to merchants because they wanted to create connections to prospective buyers. One group of merchants whose interests the Mamluk state advanced were the Karimi traders.

HOW DID EUROPE INTERACT WITH MONGOL-ERA EURASIA?

At this time Europe was something of a backwater. The feudal economy that had dominated the previous centuries was gradually ceding position to new mercantile attitudes. *Feudalism* was a relationship in which an individual acquired land in exchange for service. The term refers to a type of subservience that not only subordinated an individual (serf) to another person (lord) but also tethered him or her to a particular place (manor). In the thirteenth century new city states such as Venice and Genoa emerged in Italy. They were different in that many of the leading families were merchants, and these individuals were initially interested more in trade than in agriculture. Champagne fairs in France provided markets where distant merchants from Europe could come to trade and where European goods could be exchanged with those from other parts of the world.

In making commercial connections, the Venetians and the Genoese established their own colonies in the eastern Mediterranean. Each was interested in controlling the Black Sea region, and the struggle between the two was one of the main reasons the Venetians directed the Fourth Crusade to Constantinople. They were not above attacking other merchant ships and were known for their raiding activities. Their operations were a form of "conquest of the sea," parallel to the activities of pirates; and it was not uncommon for so-called upstanding merchants to participate in these types of ventures. Referred to as "privateering," this strategy worked because within a century or two they were the two principal trading groups in the Mediterranean.

The middle of the thirteenth century was a time when Italian merchants first appeared on the Silk Road and when they were first introduced to the large Chinese economy. The principal reason for their presence was the guarantee of Mongol protection. Representing true newbies to the region, anthropologist Janet Abu-Lughod comments that "European ignorance of the east was vast, a simple indicator of how isolated she still was from the system she sought to join."[27] The most famous of the European travelers was Marco Polo, a Venetian merchant who traveled to China to have an audience with Khubilai Khan. While some doubts exist as to whether his story was actually true, it does show how impressed a European was with Chinese life.

WHAT WERE THE LIMITATIONS OF CONQUEST?

To think about change, you must also think beyond economic relations to social and political ones. In considering what might be described here as a "collision" between different peoples (empire did have that quality), recognize that the new social and political relationships that developed did not conform to the wishes of the conquerors.

Different examples provide compelling evidence of resistance. The Mongols were always being forced to defend territories they had conquered. Over a number of years the Mongols made incursions into northern India, which included raiding Lahore and parts of Kashmir. In 1297 Mongol troops met the army of the Delhi Sultanate led by the general Zafar Khan, and they were soundly defeated—2000 Mongols were taken as prisoners and brought back to Delhi. The Mali Empire was in a constant struggle with its periphery, and in the 1340s the Songhay, in present-day Niger and Burkina Faso, who would go on to establish their own empire, were able to gain their independence and liberate their capital of Gao from Mali control. Soon thereafter the Jolof people in Senegal also broke away, and even during the oppressive Mali reign of Mari Djata, who tried to reign in independent-minded tribes, the empire had a difficult time maintaining its control over distant territories like those in the Sahara. Similarly, while the crusaders did manage to take Jerusalem, they also managed to lose it.

You have seen how conquering energy originated on the periphery of states, the Mongols being the best example. They were people who decided to take on states and challenge some of the great centers of power. But was this situation unusual? In addressing this question, anthropologist James Scott, echoing

---

[27] Janet L. Abu-Lughod, *Before European Hegemony: The World System A.D. 1250–1350* (New York: Oxford University Press, 1989), 157.

Ibn Khaldun, believes that stateless people are in an ongoing struggle with states. The history of states cannot be understood without acknowledging the place of stateless people in the historical process. In regard to the hill people of southeast Asia, a region intersecting several states in southeast Asia, referred to as "Zomia," Scott comments that "the ... coevolution of hill and valley, as antagonistic but deeply connected spaces, is, I believe the essential point of departure for making sense of historical change in Southeast Asia."[28] Here, we should point out that the hill people equal the stateless ones and the people of the valley belong to the state. But, Scott points out, it is often the states that are antagonistic to the stateless, attempting to control them, drawing them into the ambit of the state for political and economic reasons. The stateless, on the other hand, withdraw—in this case, to mountainous regions, which, until the arrival of the helicopter, have historically been all but impossible to control. The relationship between the people of the hill and the people of the valley explains a major component of historical change.

While we see societies rise and fall in watching the Mongols romp across Asia and the Ghurids invade India, we must also consider how the ongoing relationship between conquerors and conquered explains not only raiding culture and constant border struggles (the new rich people have the goods, so why not go after them?) but also the autonomy that people were able to gain for themselves before the next conqueror arrived. While conquest produced change, it was never quite complete.

Conclusion: What Motivated Conquerors?

This chapter has explored how conquest shaped the Mongol period. New states and empires, such as the Mongols, Mali, Mamluks, and the Delhi Sultanate, rose to prominence and conquered large swathes of territory. Others, such as crusaders and Iberian Christians, looked to gain lands that they believed were theirs. While the conquerors pursued similar goals of territorial control, they were also very different in the interests they represented and in the way they viewed those with whom they did battle. Part of the reason for these differences was the places that conquerors came from and the worldviews they possessed.

Conquerors brought about change; conquest begat new economic relations, new territorial arrangements, and new politics. But by the time conquerors were able to consolidate their interests and to bring about their desired goals, new challenges appeared. Like the Mongol pursuit of expansion, conquest during this period was perpetual; territorial gains were constantly challenged by new powers and by the dispossessed, to the extent that conquerors could never rest on their laurels. As these

---

[28] James C. Scott, *The Art of Not Being Governed: An Anarchist History of Upland Southeast Asia* (New Haven, CT: Yale University Press, 2009), 16–17.

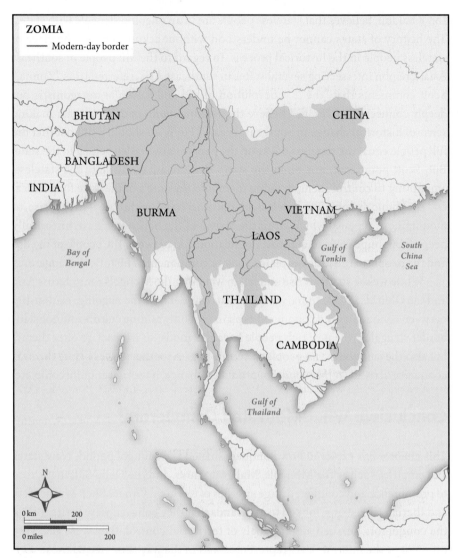

MAP 10.8   ZOMIA   Sometimes the only way to avoid paying taxes and conscription is to take to the hills. Many people did just this in this mountainous region of southeast Asia.

conquerors began to fade in the fourteenth and fifteenth centuries, new groups were on the rise throughout different parts of the world. Incas, Aztecs, Ottomans, Ming, and Songhay came on the scene and began to define new forms of expansion.

Words to Think About

Colonization	Contiguous	Infidel
Steppe		

Questions to Think About

- In what ways were the Mongols destroyers or creators?
- What are the motivations for conquest?
- In what ways were the conquerors in this chapter similar?
- Is conquest a "false" category?

Primary Sources

Juvaini, Ala ad-Din 'Ata Malik. *The History of the World Conqueror*. Translated by John Andrew Boyle. Cambridge, MA: Harvard University Press, 1958.

The Secret History of the Mongols: The Origin of Chingis Khan, adapted by Paul Khan (San Francisco: North Point Press, 1984).

Urban II: Speech at Clermont 1095 (Robert the Monk Version). From James Harvey Robinson, ed., *Readings in European History*, vol. 1. Boston: Ginn, 1904. *Medieval Sourcebook*, http://www.fordham.edu/halsall/source/urban2a.html.

Secondary Sources

Abu-Lughod, Janet L. *Before European Hegemony: The World System A.D. 1250–1350*. New York: Oxford University Press, 1989.

Amitai-Preiss, Reuven. *Mongols and Mamluks: The Mamluk–Ilkhanid War 1260–1281*. Cambridge and New York: Cambridge University Press, 1995.

Brundage, James A. *The Crusades: A Documentary Survey*. Milwaukee, WI: Marquette University Press, 1962.

Davidson, Basil. *Africa in History*. New York: Collier, 1991.

May, Timothy. *The Mongol Conquests in World History*. London: Reaktion Books, 2012.

Morgan, David, *The Mongols*, 2nd ed. Malden, MA: Blackwell, 2007.

Niane, D. T. *Sundiata: An Epic of Old Mali*. London: Longman, 1969.

O'Callaghan, Joseph F. *Reconquest and Crusade in Medieval Spain*. Philadelphia: University of Pennsylvania Press, 2003.

Rabbat, Nasser. "The Militarization of Taste in Medieval Bilad al-Sham." In *Muslim Military Architecture in Greater Syria*, edited by Hugh N. Kennedy, pp. 84–105. Leiden, The Netherlands: E.J. Brill, 2006.

Rossabi, Morris. *The Mongols: A Very Short Introduction*. New York: Oxford University Press, 2012.

Scott, James C. *The Art of Not Being Governed: An Anarchist History of Upland Southeast Asia*. New Haven, CT: Yale University Press, 2009.

Weatherford, Jack. *Genghis Khan and the Making of the Modern World*. New York: Random House, 2004.

For additional resources, including maps, primary sources, and visuals, web links, and quizzes, please go to **www.oup.com/us/cole**

A Nice Vacation Destination? Maybe now. But Lake Issyk Kul in Kyrgyzstan was the probable origin of the plague.

Chapter 11

How Did the Environment Limit Human Endeavors, and How Did It Produce Unpredictable Consequences?

700 CE to 1400 CE

The First Victims?

"In the year of the hare [1339]. This is the grave of Kutluck. He died of the plague with his wife, Magna-Kelka." Thus reads a memorial on a simple headstone, in a desolate place, on the edge of Lake Issyk Kul in today's Kyrgyzstan, which one can only imagine was more desolate 700 years ago. Poignant as it is, this brief inscription barely begins to get at the horror that Kutluk and Magna Kelka must have suffered as some of the very first of the medieval plague victims.

One or two historians have attempted to go beyond the bare facts that the engraving gives us, to flesh out the story.[1] In this case they picture a small cottage or hut; in it live a husband and wife, attached to each other, it is fair to assume. The wife contracts the virulent disease first. Coughing ensues, she brings up blood, pustules appear on her skin. There is no recourse. No medical facilities are available, and even if there were, there is not a soul on the planet at this point in history who has the faintest idea how to treat this condition. It was sent by God, many concluded. Others perhaps saw it as just another incomprehensible event in an incomprehensible universe. Historians of the plague think that Lake Issyk Kul was one of the origins of the disease. From here it spread across Eurasia like a shadow

---

[1] John Kelley, *The Great Mortality: An Intimate History of the Black Death, the Most Devastating Plague of All Time* (New York: Harper Collins, 2005), 92.

THINKING ABOUT THE ENVIRONMENT

What Is Collapse?
- Many historians today urge caution in how we approach the idea of collapse, preferring to see evidence of abandonments of cities as evidence instead of human ability to adapt.

Did the Maya Collapse? And, If So, Was the Environment to Blame?
- There *were* environmental problems, but they were not uniform across the Maya region; and collapse was by no means complete or universal.

Tiwanaku: A Story of Environmental Failure?
- Tiwanaku had reached, and passed, an ecological threshold, beyond which its high levels of population could not be sustained.

Indigenous Cultures of the American Southwest: Collapse or Bad History?
- To suggest that the people of the Southwest were hapless victims of their environment does not take their political lives and land-management skills into account.

Did the Greenland Norse Collapse or Move?
- Not clear is whether they left in an "orderly manner" or whether their last days were marked by starvation, warfare, and chaos.

What Combination of Events in Eurasia Led to the Black Death of 1348–1350?
- Many of those who died would have been developmentally affected by the famine in their youth, which would have damaged their resistance to disease.

Conclusion
- From the very earliest stirrings of our species we have lived hand in glove with our environment. We are a product of it as much as we fashion it, by design as well as by accident.

of death, devastating communities as it went. The plague is illustrative of how human populations are vulnerable to environmental factors, sometimes utterly at their mercy. "Human dominance" (see Chapter 1) may have given us the edge over other species, but the environment is an altogether more challenging adversary.

Introduction

Many histories tell the political stories of rulers, dynasties, and their various friends and enemies. But the story of the human relationship with the environment has been less widely told and is of particular interest today when human environmental impact is so profound. Reading traditional histories, you could easily think that the environment has usually taken a back seat and let humans play out their various dramas on the world stage unimpeded. But, as historian J. Donald Hughes puts it, "The idea of the environment as something separate from the human, and offering merely a setting for human history, is misleading."[2]

Looking at history with an eye on this particular character reveals that the environment has often taken a very active role in human affairs, forcing certain behavior on the animals, human or otherwise, that inhabit the world. We see such environmental "assertiveness" in disasters—earthquakes, hurricanes, droughts, and the like. And such events no doubt demand attention because of their dramatic nature. (Perhaps this is why the National Hurricane Center uses names for hurricanes, giving them a personality.) The affect of the environment can be seen nowhere better than in the evolution of our own species, which was largely prompted by long-term climate change (see Chapter 1). In fact, the relationship of human history to the environment is intimate, as Hughes puts it:

> What has happened to human societies, and what continues to happen to them, is in many important ways an ecological process. The distinction, first made by the ancient Greeks, between "nature" .... and "culture" .... is not an absolute one; in an important sense, culture is part of nature because culture is the product of a species of animal, the human species.[3]

Since the end of the Ice Age, the climatic period known as the Holocene has provided optimal conditions for agriculture in many parts of the world. Humanity assembled its various civilizations on the back of this moderate climatic period, notwithstanding occasional setbacks in the form of cooling or warming. When conditions were stable, therefore, humanity has been able to work with the environment, using the resources it provides—water, plants, soil, animals—to build civilizations.

If environmental history is the story of human interaction with the environment, there are two opposite forces at work in this relationship: one is the basic

---

[2]   J. Donald Hughes, *The Environmental History of the World: Humankind's Changing Role in the Community of Life* (London: Routledge, 2001), 6.

[3]   Ibid.

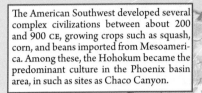

The American Southwest developed several complex civilizations between about 200 and 900 CE, growing crops such as squash, corn, and beans imported from Mesoamerica. Among these, the Hohokum became the predominant culture in the Phoenix basin area, in such as sites as Chaco Canyon.

Vikings crossed the North Atlantic fro Scandinavia, looking for land and weal Between 1000 and 1400 CE they settled many of the places they landed, includi eastern England, Scotland, Iceland, a Greenland. They also made it to mainla North America, but their settlements the were short-lived.

The Maya city-states suffered significant losses of population and in many cases abandonment between the eighth and tenth centuries. While many people have seen this as the period of Maya collapse, others see it simply as change, with some cities declining, others growing, and political systems evolving into different forms.

The pre-Incan civilization of Tiwanaku flourished in western Peru from around 400 to 1400 CE. Its population lived off agricultural systems developed for high altitudes around Lake Titicaca. Scholars cite either climate change or war as the reason for its decline.

ATLANTI
OCEAN

SOUTHE

THE ENVIRONMENT 700 CE – 1400 CE

Although it is just one term, "the environment" has different meanings in different parts of the globe, just as clir

MAP 11.1   **THE ENVIRONMENT, 700 CE–1400 CE**

TIMELINE

 ca. 700 CE
Highpoint of Classic Maya period

 700–1100
Hohokum culture in the American Southwest

793 CE
First recorded Viking raid, on Lindisfarne

 ca. 1000 CE
Highpoint of Tiwanaku

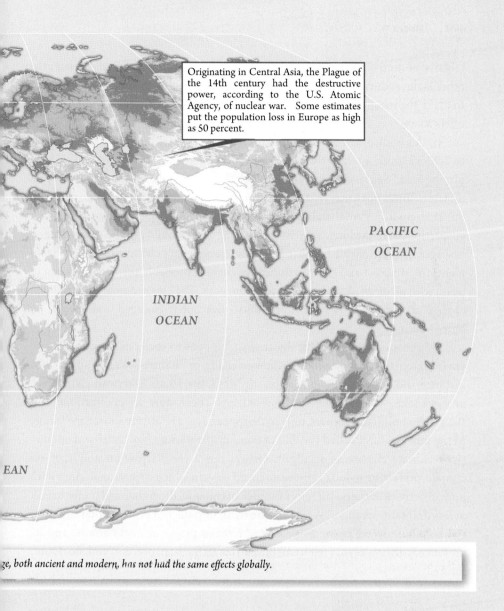

Originating in Central Asia, the Plague of the 14th century had the destructive power, according to the U.S. Atomic Agency, of nuclear war. Some estimates put the population loss in Europe as high as 50 percent.

PACIFIC
OCEAN

INDIAN
OCEAN

EAN

...ge, both ancient and modern, has not had the same effects globally.

ca. 1200
**Height of Norse settlement
in Greenland**

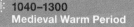

1040–1300
Medieval Warm Period

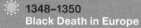

1348–1350
Black Death in Europe

creative or destructive power of the environment to which we are all subject; the other is the enduring human characteristic of adaptability, which has allowed us to make the most of a difficult situation or to seize an opportunity when nature offers it.

In this book much of the story we tell relates to what humans have been able to achieve given a relatively stable environment—what you might call a "level playing field." Sea levels have remained relatively constant, weather relatively predictable. This is not to say that the environment, during this period, was irrelevant but that environmental stability allowed human societies to maintain certain adaptations over the long term. Even this long-term stability of the environment, however, is questionable because human societies enact changes on the environment; the simplest and most historical of these is probably the cutting down of trees, with all of its "downstream" consequences. The environment does not just change according to its own mysterious rules but is changed and shaped by human activity.

This chapter looks specifically at what happens to societies in conditions of environmental change—whether human-made or "natural." What impact, for instance, did climate change have on the Maya, the South American civilization of Tiwanaku, and the Norse of Greenland? These were all civilizations that thrived for hundreds of years, only to disappear over a relatively short time frame. Many scholars have called the end of these civilizations a "collapse" and emphasized climate change as a culprit. Others reject too narrow an emphasis on climate, preferring to look at more nuanced ways in which climate combines with human activity. Others still reject the idea of collapse altogether and prefer to talk of less dramatic "change." Wherever the truth lies, the fact remains that the environment has always been, as it is today, a major player in world affairs; and its presence is always keenly felt by all human societies, past, present, and, no doubt, future.

What Is "Collapse"?

In 1839 John Stephens and Frederick Catherwood came upon the ruins of an ancient Maya city, tangled in the dense jungles of Guatemala. They were stunned as they began to comprehend the true size of the urban site they had stumbled upon and awestruck by the mystery of its abandonment:

> The city was desolate. No remnant of this race hangs round the ruins, with traditions handed down from father to son and from generation to generation.

A Lost Civilization?   For centuries Europeans and Americans believed that some lost, or even alien, civilization built the impressive ruins in the Maya heartlands. No one, apparently not even the modern Maya, considered that it could have been the ancestors of the present inhabitants of the region.

> It lay before us like a shattered bark in the midst of the ocean, her mast gone, her
> name effaced, her crew perished, and none to tell whence she came, to whom
> she belonged, how long her journey, or what caused her destruction[4]

As far as the travelers could see, the people who had created this city had vanished. "Who built it?" they asked their Mayan guides. *¿Quién sabe?* they responded—*Who knows?* The discovery of such ruins always makes us look for the story, and we often expect it to be a tale of dramatic, even catastrophic, failure. But is this fair, and anyway, what do we mean by "collapse"?

"A society has collapsed," says historian Joseph Tainter, "when it displays a rigid, significant loss of an established level of sociopolitical complexity."[5] Such complexity entails having a variety of specialized labor—for example, farmers, potters, weavers, traders, priests, warriors, and rulers. All of the above are found

4   Quoted in Jared Diamond, *Collapse: How Societies Choose to Fail or Succeed* (New York: Viking, 2005), 158.
5   Joseph Tainter, *The Collapse of Complex Societies* (Cambridge: Cambridge University Press, 1988), 3.

in most of the societies we have discussed, including the Maya, Mesopotamians, ancient Egyptians, Chinese, Greeks, and Persians. Clearly, if you take the example of the Maya and imagine a city such as Tikal in, say, 600 CE, when it was at its height, things had changed dramatically by 1000; and today it is in ruins and has been for hundreds of years. At some point in its history it suffered a dramatic turnaround in its fortunes, and the city of Tikal, as the inhabitants knew it, ceased to exist.

Based on historical and archeological records, it is hard to deny that there have been many such incidents of collapse. Abandoned cities speak of mass migrations or of widespread famine, war, and death. Many historians today, however, urge caution in how we approach the idea of collapse, preferring to see evidence of abandonments of cities or "failures" of societies as evidence instead of human ability to adapt, move, or alter their sociopolitical systems, in times of hardship, to survive. Patricia A. McAnany and Norman Yoffee, for example, offer such a corrective: "When closely examined, the overriding human story is one of survival and regeneration. Certainly crises existed, political forms changed, and landscapes were altered, but rarely did societies collapse in an absolute or apocalyptic sense."[6]

> ☀ Many historians today, however, urge caution in how we approach the idea of collapse, preferring to see evidence of abandonments of cities or "failures" of societies as evidence instead of human ability to adapt, move, or alter their sociopolitical systems, in times of hardship, to survive.

When the sixteenth-century Spaniards came to the New World, they considered the mysterious ruins signs of a lost Greco–Roman culture. Later visitors to the Guatemalan Maya ruins also looked upon them as if they were built by a mystery race, rather than looking at the contemporary inhabitants of the region and assuming that their ancestors built the cities that were later abandoned in favor of other sites and other political systems. Perhaps collapse should not be viewed only in quantitative terms, as a decline in population or abandonment of a site, but in terms of the continuation or otherwise of human cultures. As historian J. R. McNeil says, "If a people, a language, and a culture survive, as among the Maya, the Norse, or the Anasazi, is this a collapse?"[7] (We will get to the Norse and Anasazi later.)

But while human cultures often persisted, there is no denying that political forms often changed and populations fluctuated; and without labeling societies as "failures" or "successes," it is certainly possible to see in history the frequent examples of societies which suffered rapid, dramatic, and, as often as not, devastating setbacks to their ways of life.

---

[6]   Patricia A. McAnany and Norman Yoffee, eds., *Questioning Collapse: Human Resilience, Ecological Vulnerability, and the Aftermath of Empire* (New York: Cambridge University Press, 2010), 6.

[7]   J. R. McNeil, quoted in ibid., 359.

The Classic "Imagine" Scenario What would a collapse of modern civilization look like? In the 1968 movie *Planet of the Apes*, the hero sinks to his knees on realizing that the strange planet he has landed on is earth in the future, post-nuclear war. Apes rule; humans are the animals now.

But what is the role of the environment in collapses? "Nature itself changes," says environmental historian Shawn William Miller, "sometimes handing out new, substantial benefits to humans, sometimes painful liabilities, and in a few cases utter destruction."[8] The ultimate extent to which nature has affected history is still heavily debated, and we will look at some of these debates in what follows, acknowledging the good, the bad, and the plain ugly, because the record contains a little of everything. After all, the environment giveth—you might say, echoing the Bible—and the environment taketh away.

Did the Maya Collapse? And, If So, Was the Environment to Blame?

The Maya world that we have discussed as far as trade and war were concerned was in 800 CE a mosaic of competing city states, ruled by charismatic kings, or "holy lords," competing with each other in militaristic struggles. The lowlands of the Yucatán Peninsula supported a dense population through intensive agriculture, which was dependent on irrigation, largely fed from a system of reservoirs.

---

[8]   Shawn William Miller, *An Environmental History of Latin America* (Cambridge: Cambridge University Press, 2007), 45.

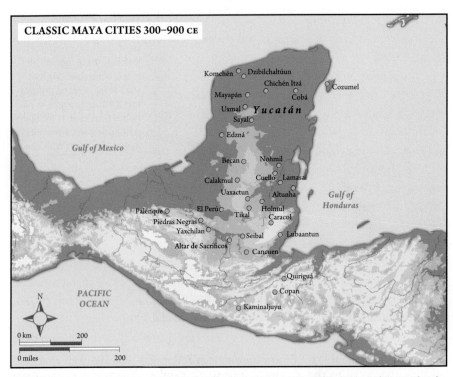

MAP 11.2   THE CLASSICAL MAYAN CITIES, 300–900 CE   Typically, this period is considered the high point for Maya writing, calendrical systems, and powerful city states in the lowland regions. But was their "collapse" just a change by another name?

Cities such as Tikal competed and fought (and sometimes cooperated) in this area for some 1,000 years, but by 900 CE Tikal and others, such as Copan and Palenque, had rapidly declined and ultimately disappeared altogether, serving as jungle-covered mysteries for their descendants and the nosy foreigners who came with notebooks and sketch pads from the north.

The Maya heartlands of the Yucatán Peninsula lacked major rivers. Instead of relying on river floods, therefore, to irrigate their crops, they used a system of what archeologist Vernon Scarborough has called "microwatersheds," in which rainfall filled reservoirs, often created by the quarrying of stone to build their monumental architecture. Relying on these watersheds gave the Maya a certain flexibility and reduced their vulnerability to short-term drought.[9]

At the high point of the Classic period (ca. 700 CE) some 8 to 10 million Maya lived in the lowlands, with a population density of as much as 200 people per square

---

[9]   Vernon L. Scarborough, "Resilience, resource use, and socioeconomic organization: A Mesoamerican pathway," in Garth Bawdon and Richard Martin Reycraft, eds., *Environmental Disaster and the Archeology of Human Response* (Albuquerque: Maxwell Museum of Anthropology, 2000), 195–212.

mile, a high number for the ancient world. Whereas the Maya had been living in this area for hundreds of years and had developed a largely sustainable system of agriculture, they had cultivated all usable farmland and were supporting a large urban population of nonfarmers, in addition to a group of unproductive nobles.

A severe and prolonged drought coincides with the dates for abandonments of several major cities in the southern lowlands, between 750 and 1025. Droughts had caused hardship in the past here, but this prolonged one settled over the Maya heartland at a time when its population was larger than ever before and was demanding unprecedented yields from its land. As historian/archeologist Brian Fagan says, "For nearly three centuries, intense drought lowered the water table, produced inadequate rains, and ravaged an agricultural economy that already had trouble satisfying the accelerating demands of the nobility."[10]

The Maya collapse was a long, drawn-out affair and, according to studies done by archeologist Richardson Benedict Gill, included three main drought-stricken phases, beginning in 810 and affecting the cities of Palenque and Yaxchilan. Another in 860 spelled doom for Caracol and Copan, and the last, between 890 and 910, brought down Tikal and several others.[11]

As Fagan describes it, "In city after city, the great lords were powerless to bring rain; perhaps unrest erupted. Archaeology shows us that these cities' populations either perished or dispersed into small hamlets. The unfortunate Maya had overreached themselves, and their civilization came down around their ears."[12] Other accounts of Maya collapse have also focused on the way in which the "unfortunate" Maya failed to steward their land effectively, to the extent that a "perfect storm" of population growth, overfarming, and climate change finished them off. Peter Bakewell, for instance, offers a familiar version:

> The broad supposition is that overpopulation led to soil depletion and excessive felling of trees (for fuel and building)—with the latter probably bringing erosion of slopes and declining rainfall .... whatever the precise course of events, there is no doubt that, with one exception, the ninth century AD brought to an end almost 1000 years of splendid and distinctive Maya accomplishment.[13]

(The exception was Chichén Itzá, in the north of the Yucatán Peninsula, which continued until the 1200s before being largely abandoned. Thereafter, Mayapan, also in the far north, remained populated until the 1500s.)

---

[10] Brian Fagan, *The Long Summer: How Climate Changed Civilization* (New York: Basic Books, 2004), 237.
[11] See Richardson Benedict Gill, *The Great Maya Droughts: Water, Life, and Death* (Albuquerque: University of New Mexico Press, 2000).
[12] Fagan, *The Long Summer*, 238.
[13] Peter Bakewell, *A History of Latin America to 1825* (New York: Wiley-Blackwell, 2010), 44.

Critiques of this version, however, question the idea that the Maya haplessly overfarmed their land and allowed their population to explode so as to outstrip their ability to feed themselves. Patricia McAnany and Tomás Gallareta Negrón, for example, resist the temptation to see the Maya as helpless victims of their own destructive practices as well as of climate change and point out that the drought scenarios are complex and nuanced and that the evidence for abandonment is protracted. Recent studies of landscape modification, for example, have revealed the extent to which Maya farmers were well aware of the need to conserve soil and its fertility by terracing fields and creating check dams to funnel water across dry slopes. "In other words, Maya farmers of the Late Classic seem to have been doing all that they could to prevent land degradation and promote soil retention and fertility."[14] So much for hapless farmers with insufficient conservation practices.

Archeologist Arthur Demarest also questions the traditional "collapse" story. He points out that many studies of the western Petén area of Maya civilization have found evidence of agricultural systems well adapted to high population levels without any signs of stress. Indeed, there certainly were environmental problems, Demarest says; but they were not uniform across the Maya region, and collapse was by no means complete or universal. "Whatever happened to many of the southern lowland cities," he says, "it was not a uniform, total collapse of these states, and it was in no way an end or even decline of the enduring Maya tradition."[15]

Instead of a collapse, Demarest sees the end of a certain type of polity, the *theater-states*, in which a ruler controls ritual access to the ideological belief system, enacting regular ritual performances atop monumental architecture. Such polities demanded huge amounts of labor to build the temples and palaces of the lords, and they were deeply militaristic. All of this was costly. "In the lowland Maya case," says Demarest, "what actually collapsed, declined, or was transformed at the end of the Classic Period was a particular political system of theater states dominated by the K'uhul Ajaw, or the holy lords."[16] It was these states—remember not only the diversity of the Maya ecology but its political landscape too—that were least able to deal with environmental challenges. *No rain? Let's stage ever more elaborate religious theater to please the gods and to remind people who is in charge, and we'll invade the neighboring city for good measure!*

---

[14] Patricia A. McAnany and Tomás Gallareta Negrón, "Bellicose Rulers and Climatological Peril? Retrofitting Twenty-First-Century Woes on Eighth-Century Maya Society," in McAnany and Yoffee (eds), *Questioning Collapse*, 153.

[15] Arthur Demarest, *The Ancient Maya: The Rise and Fall of a Rainforest Civilization* (Cambridge: Cambridge University Press, 2004), 242.

[16] Ibid.

Temple of the Warriors at Chichén Itzá   Now a tourist attraction for visitors, it was once a site of religious rituals and displays of royal and priestly power.

So did the Maya collapse? Was it because of the environment? As usual, history offers us few clear-cut answers. Certainly, in many parts of the Maya homeland beginning in the ninth century there was a dramatic loss of population, and no one currently lives in Tikal. The cause of this dramatic population loss, we can safely say, was a combination of a drying climate and political conflicts, very likely exacerbated by the climate change. But the process was not uniform, nor was it "game over" for the Maya as a civilization.

Whereas one part of the Maya homeland suffered decline, other parts, most notably the northern and western Yucatán, actually saw population growth in the eighth and ninth centuries (possibly because of refugees from the failing southern states). Chichén Itzá and Mayapan are evidence of this. But new, less hierarchical polities appeared, allowing for greater political participation. Collapse, in this view, begins to look more like "change."

Proponents of the traditional view of Maya collapse might think that calling what happened "change" is tantamount to putting lipstick on a pig: many people died, cities were abandoned, political systems toppled. Sounds like collapse. But to other scholars, the important fact is that the Maya are alive and kicking: visitors to Guatemala will be greeted by Maya. Their culture has endured, as their existence proves; and they would prefer to have that fact recognized, even if, as John Stephens and Frederick Catherwood discovered, many of their cities fell to rack and ruin.

Tiwanaku: A Story of Environmental Failure?

Farther to the south of the Maya heartlands lay the South American civilization of Tiwanaku, with its capital some 9.3 miles from the southern tip of Lake Titicaca, in today's Bolivia. Archeologists here have found a large ceremonial center dominated by an impressive raised platform, called the Akapana, 656 feet long by 49 high. Many more structures around this platform made up a city with houses with water and sewer drains, courtyards, streets, gateways, and residential compounds.

In its heyday, around 1000 CE, the Akapana supported a massive sunken court ringed by stone buildings. Archeologists believe that this precinct was a symbolic island that, like the Maya step pyramids, acted as a venue for religious ceremonies at which the leaders would have appeared, dressed, according to the

Tourists Explore the Akapana, in the Ruins of Tiwanaku, Near La Paz, Bolivia   The civilization thrived on the high-altitude farming techniques developed near Lake Titicaca. Did climate change bring it down? Or was it the neighbors?

evidence of remaining sculptures, like gods or like the native pumas and condors. Ceremonies included human sacrifice to appease the Sun God, whose face appears on the "Gateway of the Sun," which still stands.

Perhaps the most striking innovation of Tiwanaku was in agriculture. At about 900 CE almost 100,000 hectares of land was under cultivation. This was no small feat because the area was at an altitude of 13,123 feet, meaning that it was cold, especially at night, something that cultivators of delicate plants need to bear in mind. Up here, on the Altiplano, Tiwanaku's farmers produced surplus food for centuries, even though experts have long considered this area marginal for agriculture.

But local farmers benefited from the area's high water table. The presence of so much water had a warming effect on the soil, protecting plants from the depredations of night temperatures. Building (literally) on this advantage, farmers created raised fields; they laid down a base of pebbles, then sealed it with clay to prevent the mildly saline water from Lake Titicaca from damaging plant roots. Then they added gravel, sand, and finally topsoil. They augmented this with frequent doses of "green manure," or lake plants, and human excrement for added measure.

This system provided ample food for a reasonable population, as long as the water table remained high and the rains constant. Scientists have taken ice core samples from the Quelccaya ice cap, high in the Andes, some 124 miles north of Lake Titicaca. From these cores they have concluded that there have been many changes in the water table over the long term—at that altitude, some dramatic. There were several wet periods, for instance, from 610 to 650 and from 760 to 1040. There were also several dry periods, the last one coinciding with what climatologists call the Medieval Warm Period from approximately 1040 to 1300; and this was marked by extremely low ice accumulations in the Andes.

What did this mean for those living on the Altiplano? Over about a half-century the raised-field system all but vanished. Tiwanaku, according to several archaeologists had reached and passed an ecological threshold, beyond which its high levels of population could not be sustained. Droughts were not new, but, as Michael Binford and his colleagues put it, "Large urban and rural populations had become dependent upon raised-field systems that relied on abundant water. Increased aridity induced declining agricultural production, progressive raised-field abandonment, population dispersal, and ultimately Tiwanaku cultural collapse."[17]

---

[17]   Michael W. Binford et al., "Climate Variation and the Rise and Fall of an Andean Civilization," *Quaternary Research* 47 (1997): 235–48.

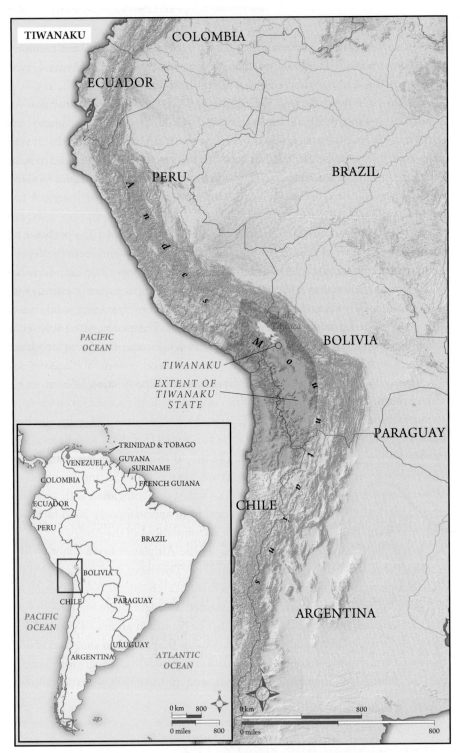

MAP 11.3 TIWANAKU Tiwanaku was the inheritor of earlier civilizations in the region—and ancestor to the Incas. Highland agriculturalists, their fate is still debated by archeologists.

The argument for diminishing rainfall, falling water table, and resultant loss in agricultural productivity is very seductive. Archeologist Bruce Owen, however, is skeptical. His counterargument rests largely on the details of the archeological analysis, in particular the fact that the fields that provided for Tiwanaku were abandoned nearly a century before the climate changed.[18] His culprit in the mystery of collapse and abandonment, therefore, is not drying climate but intergroup rivalry, in particular with a neighboring civilization to the north, the Wari, whose colonies and outposts frequently trespassed on those of Tiwanaku.

Here the debate is to be found in the scientific details of how ice cores are assigned dates; "when you really dig into the evidence for this one," says Owen, "it does not hold up well."[19]

Perhaps the human–environment relationship is more complex and more subtle than we sometimes give it credit for. "By incorporating social elements into the equation," says another archeologist, Patrick Ryan Williams, "we arrive at much more powerful explanatory devices that do not depict human societies as the recipients of environmentally prescribed collapses, but as active agents in the construction of the environment and in their own development."[20] We must look at both social causes and environmental causes of collapse, says Williams, to get the whole picture.

Indigenous Cultures of the American Southwest: Collapse or Bad History?

Archeologists have typically viewed the Southwest as a cultural island, distinct from most of its wider environment but with ties to the more "complex" civilizations of Meso-America and Mexico to their south. Throughout the nineteenth and through much of the twentieth centuries, the area was seen as somewhat ahistorical, existing in a timeless bubble until white people came along (to pop it). It is now recognized that the people of the ancient Southwest, whose descendants still inhabit the area, had a diverse and dynamic history, like any civilization, with seminal political, social, and religious events that changed the course of their history, for better or worse.

---

[18] Bruce Owen, "Distant Colonies and Explosive Collapse: The Two Stages of the Tiwanaku Diaspora in the Osmore Drainage," *Latin American Antiquity* 16, no. 1 (2005): 45–80.

[19] Bruce Owen, Communication with the authors, August 2012.

[20] Patrick Ryan Williams, "Rethinking Disaster-Induced Collapse in the Demise of the Andean Highland States: Wari and Tiwanaku," *World Archaeology* 33, no. 3 (February 2002): 361–74.

Across the Southwest, farmers cultivated maize, beans, and squash. Cultivated food was supplemented with game, such as elk, rabbit, and deer. These subsistence patterns and many other cultural traits were shared across the region.

In the deserts agriculture demanded irrigation and between 400 and 700 a complex system was constructed in the Phoenix basin, around the confluence of the Salt and Gila Rivers, at the site of modern-day Phoenix. Irrigation tethered communities to their land, so these communities were truly sedentary and lasted for generations. As societies became more complex, elite groups developed to manage them. Marked in the archeological record by "big houses," these elites probably dominated civic and economic life in the region.

Away from the irrigated deserts, on the plateau, agriculture was also possible; but it depended not on irrigation but on rainfall. For this reason, it was more risky, and rainfall farmers would have to be prepared to move if the rains failed, as they inevitably did from time to time. Why would people have moved away from the irrigated areas to farm in less secure environments? The most likely answer is that they did not have to endure the demands of "big house" elites. With no complex irrigation system to manage, what was there to be boss of?

WHAT WAS HOHOKAM?

But "big house" society never morphed, as you might have expected it to, into a true Maya-style group of kingdoms, with a highly centralized, parasitic elite. The Hohokam culture that came to dominate a large part of the Southwest from about 700 to 1100 changed the nature of political power in the Phoenix basin. Not a polity or a place, Hohokam was more a group of far-flung communities with shared political and social characteristics, the most important, perhaps, being its lack of centralized authority. As archeologist Stephen Lekson puts it, "It was a supra-governmental or anti-governmental or instead-of-governmental ideology that united large areas and many (perhaps ethnically distinct) people, and got big things done—all without kings."[21]

Hohokam was characterized by a diffused, nonhierarchical leadership, expressed through councils and priesthoods, allowing the elaborate irrigation culture to thrive without centralized political power. Communities carved bivalve shells, often into the likenesses of animals, and wore them on the arm, archeologists think, as a kind of badge of belonging. They also built ball courts—familiar from Mayan and Olmec civilizations—and these might have been used to play out conflicts over land or resources. Although many archeologists prefer to see

---

[21]   Stephen Lekson, "The Southwest in the World," http://stevelekson.com/ancient-southwest/.

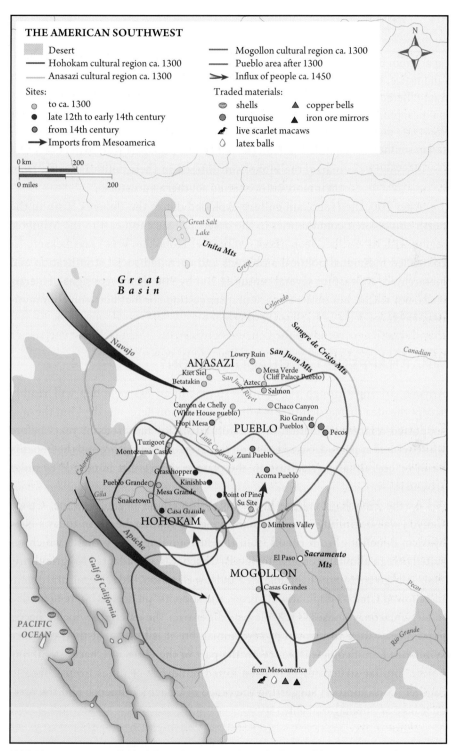

MAP 11.4 THE AMERICAN SOUTHWEST Peoples and cultures of the American Southwest were dependent on either rain or irrigation for their agriculture. Rain may have come with fewer organizational demands and, therefore, might have allowed for less hierarchical political structures.

☀ But apart from ball courts and maize, the Hohokam differed in their political profile from their more authoritarian southern ancestors.

southwestern cultures as distinct from their southern forbears—Maya and Olmec—Felipe Fernández-Armesto makes the point that, "it makes perfect sense to imagine ideas traveling from the south up the Rio Grande."[22] This was, after all, the route traveled by maize cultivation, by far the dominant crop in all the Americas. But apart from ball courts and maize, the Hohokam differed in their political profile from their more authoritarian southern ancestors.

After 700, the Hohokam culture exploded out of the Phoenix basin to the north and colored communities in the desert plateaux and east to the Mimbres region with its distinctive markers. "Whatever Hohokam was," says Lekson, "it controlled individual political ambitions and curtailed social stratification and hierarchy."[23] At least for several centuries. But by 900 there were signs of hierarchies, not within but between societies, suggesting conflict between communities, which needed a centralized response.

WHAT HAPPENED AT CHACO CANYON?

Anyone driving through the southwestern United States today will readily accept the idea that agriculture is a dicey proposition here: it is dry! But the area supported a large population of agriculturalists for hundreds of years before white settlers appeared, based either on the irrigation model around the Phoenix basin or on rainfall agriculture in the plateau deserts for hundreds of miles around it.

As the Hohokam culture in Phoenix's hinterland began to wane, Chaco Canyon was beginning its rise to dominance to the northeast, in today's New Mexico. Benefiting from runoff from the surrounding high ground, which resulted in high alluvial groundwater levels, Chaco was well adapted to agriculture, especially given its large habitable area and low elevation. This agricultural potential allowed Chaco's population to grow, and soon its "pit houses" were upgraded to large masonry houses. Archeologists differ over the extent to which Chaco's great houses were residential or ceremonial, but it is likely that their presence symbolized an ideological stance on the part of the elites of Chaco, signifying power. Similar structures have been found hundreds of miles from Chaco in "outlier" communities, suggesting the range of Chaco's influence and the presence here of a managerial elite.

---

22 Felipe Fernández-Armesto, *Civilizations: Culture, Ambition, and the Transformation of Nature* (New York: Simon & Schuster, 2002), 60.
23 Lekson, "The Southwest in the World."

The Moon Crowds the Sun During a Solar Eclipse, Seen from a Pueblo Bonito Building at Chaco Canyon   Like many other civilizations, including the Meso-American precursors to Chaco, solar and lunar movements played a part in architectural planning.

By the standards of the Southwest, Chaco was big. Nothing of this size had existed before north of the megacities of the Maya in Meso-America (which were much larger). Apart from the overwhelming presence of the great houses, other signs of an elite class have been found, including burials of individuals with unusual amounts of high-value goods. As Lekson puts it, "Who were the inhabitants of Great Houses? Were they chiefs, priests, kings, queens, duly-elected representatives? Who knows? And for now, who cares? They were elite leaders, Major Dudes. That much seems clear."[24] The elite*ness* or otherwise of the inhabitants of the great houses is important because Chaco's social stratification marks a regional cultural and political shift, away from the egalitarianism of the Hohokam culture. And the existence of the outlier communities, some of them more than 100 miles distant, suggests that this shift was occurring not only in the confines of the canyon but in its "cultural shadow" as well, especially between about 1020 and 1125.

Despite its apparently advantageous agricultural position, another archeologist, Michael Wilcox, argues that Chaco was never an agricultural "center," in a surplus-producing sense, and suggests that the canyon's primary function was as

[24]   Ibid.

a multiethnic ritual center, where ideas—as well as some food—were exchanged. This argument suggests that when Chaco's population suffered a dramatic decrease—collapse?—between 1150 and 1200, the cause was more sociopolitical than environmental. The relationship between collapse and agriculture is important because other scholars have suggested that the collapse came about because Chaco Canyon's success in agriculture led to a major increase in population, which, when the climate dried in the late twelfth century, could not be supported by its own agriculture—caught, in other words, in a classic "progress trap."[25]

If Chaco had never, in fact, been a major agricultural producer and had never, therefore, had a large permanent population, it is less likely that drought would have caused such sudden and drastic collapse.

Wilcox's argument directly contradicts that of others, such as Fagan, who points to climate change as the culprit: "But in 1130 fifty years of drought set in. Movement was deeply embedded in their psychology. Within a few generations the pueblos were empty. Well over half Chaco's population had dispersed into villages, hamlets, and pueblos far from the canyon."[26] This is a seductive argument, but for Wilcox, the real story in this mystery is ignored by such a focus on climate. The Chacoans, he says, became embroiled in ideological disputes, in particular over the centralization of power. One of the main differences between contemporary Pueblo communities, notably the Hohokam, and Chaco was the idea that ritual centralization (represented by the great houses) was dangerous. "The relationship between social change and ideology appears to have played a significant role in the history of Chaco," Wilcox says. "Ideology is central to many of the most dramatic changes in western civilization. There is every reason to believe that these types of changes were at least as transformative among Native Americans as they were to Europeans."[27] Wilcox's critique is clear and offers a corrective to some of our historical assumptions: historians for generations have described historical change in Europe and the West by way of political stories, less so via issues such as climate change. Is it right to suppose that Pueblo life was any less driven by ideology rather than climate? Yet here is the problem: *is it simply politically correct to ignore the climate in this case?*

Again, we find ourselves asking, *so did Chaco collapse? And was the environment the cause?* If we take a little from everyone, we have a better chance of coming

---

[25]   Diamond's book *Collapse: How Societies Choose to Fail or Succeed* should be mentioned here, although the term *progress trap* was coined by Canadian writer Ronald Wright.

[26]   Fagan, *The Long Summer*, 226.

[27]   Michael Wilcox, "Marketing Conquest and the Vanishing Indian: An Indigenous Response to Jared Diamond's Archaeology of the American Southwest," in *Questioning Collapse: Human Resilience, Ecological Vulnerability, and the Aftermath of Empire*, edited by Patricia A. McAnany and Norman Yoffee (New York: Cambridge University Press), 134.

up with a convincing answer. Both Lekson and Wilcox highlight the importance of dynamic histories in the Southwest. The people, in other words, had lives; they engaged in politics, experimented with social structures, and struggled over forms of government. To suggest that they were hapless victims of their environment and bad planners to boot does not take their political lives or their land-management skills into account. At the same time, Lekson presses home the point, as do Fagan and Diamond, that collapse happened:

> However we euphemize the dramatic abandonment/depopulation of the Four Corners, the facts seem clear: the region supported tens of thousands of people in the early 13th century and a century later it was essentially empty. Moreover, depopulation was accompanied by political disorder, warfare, and economic disaster punctuated by a final Great Drought. Cities fell, governments crumbled, and whole artistic traditions (and whatever cosmologies they reflected) vanished. All that's missing are rains of fire, plagues of frogs, and seismic convulsions. It's hard to imagine a more complete collapse.[28]

Wilcox makes the point that elements of Chaco culture continued, even if its political, social, and geographic center had changed. The end of Chaco did not mean the end of the Pueblo people, the Chacoans. New Pueblos appeared in different parts of the region, inhabited most likely by descendants of the Chacoans. Are environmental factors and political/cultural factors really braided into one weave that is impossible to disentangle? Or is our tendency toward environmental determinism a case of *post hoc ergo propter hoc* ("after that, therefore because of that")? The debate continues.

Did the Greenland Norse Collapse or Move?

Several hundred years before Christopher Columbus stumbled across the Americas on his way to China, the Norse had picked their way from Scandinavia to the North American coast and made a base camp at L'Anse aux Meadows, on the tip of Newfoundland's northern peninsula.

This story has to do with diminishing land availability on the Scandinavian coast and, as such, is another poignant reminder of how the environment often dictates the terms of human history, for better or worse. Because of its many steep gradients, only about 3% of Norway's land is amenable to agriculture. Its ample

---

[28]   Lekson, "The Southwest in the World."

coastline, indented with long peninsulas known as *fjords*, made seafaring a no-brainer for the local population.

But it was not until the ninth century that a combination of factors came into play that resulted in a Viking explosion away from their homeland. The use of more effective plows enabled farmers to increase their food production. This, as always, meant population growth; the onset of the Medieval Warm Period, while causing droughts and disaster for the Maya and their South American neighbors in the ninth century, provided four centuries of abundant harvests to Europeans. Until the 600s oars had been the only reliable propulsion for seafarers; but thereafter sailing technology developed apace, and the Scandinavians were at the forefront of this.

The Vikings built long, narrow ships with shallow drafts. These allowed them to navigate up rivers and run aground on beaches. While perhaps built with trade in mind, trade, as we learned in previous chapters, often turned into raid. And this was the Vikings, specialty. On June 8, 793, the first recorded Viking raid occurred in Lindisfarne, on the northeast coast of England. Raids continued, doubtless to the exasperation of the locals, the following summers along the English coast.

The Viking raids expanded at such a rate—any young man with a boat could head out and help himself to the goods of nearby England or France—that raiding parties soon began developing bridgeheads on their intended victims' land.

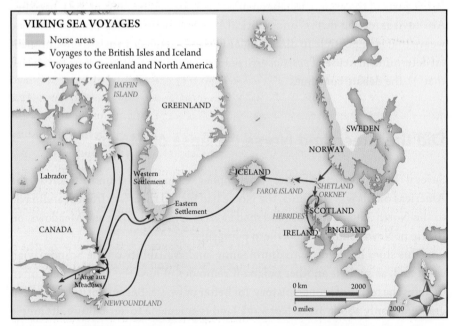

MAP 11.5   VIKING SEA VOYAGES   Although there were long ocean passages in between, the Vikings crossed the Atlantic on stepping-stones instead of in one long passage, as later Europeans would on more southerly routes.

They founded Danelaw, a state on the east coast of England. They settled in Brittany and Normandy and conducted raids into the Mediterranean. In many places they intermarried and became part of the local population. Swedish Vikings went up rivers to Russia, from the Baltic Sea into the Black and Caspian Seas. They traded with Byzantium and founded the principality of Kiev, a precursor to the Russian state.

But this part of the story involved those who went west. The Viking sagas record a progression of discovery. From the English and Irish coasts the Vikings sailed west. On scattered islands such as the Faroes they found Irish monks, who had sequestered themselves on isolated rocks to better contemplate God. On ships designed for longer sea voyages, broader and deeper than their usual raiding vessels, they let the western winds blow them across from the Faroes to Iceland, where, by 930, some 30,000 Scandinavians had settled.

Iceland was a good base for journeys farther west. The saga of Erik the Red, believed to be from the thirteenth century, describes the settlement of Greenland and the exploration of northern North America. From Iceland the Vikings came upon Greenland, which may indeed have been green in summer in the Medieval Warm Period. It may also have been a good name if your intention was to persuade others to move there with you. Green, after all, was the color of grass, upon which the Vikings depended to feed their sheep and cows. From here they eventually made it to the North American continent, a place they called "Vinland" because of the grapevines they found there, much to their delight.

"There is an unbroken chain of inevitable progression," said historian Magnus Magnusson, "between the discovery and subsequent settlement of, first, Iceland, then Greenland, and then Vinland. The discovery and attempted colonization of Vinland were the logical outcome of the great Scandinavian migrations that spilled over northern Europe in the early middle ages, the ultimate reach of the Norse surge to the west."[29] One might quibble with inevitability in history (is anything ultimately inevitable?); but the Vikings expressed a dogged determination to explore, so they kept going until they ran ashore on the New World. But the Norse were conservative sailors: they did not blindly dash into the freezing North Atlantic. "The Norse did not span the Atlantic in one leap, but brachiated across from one island or at least from one indication of land—a gathering of clouds, a flocking of sea fowl—to another."[30] This was only possible in the northern latitudes. The Azores (a good steppingstone between Portugal and New York)

[29] *Vinland Sagas: The Norse Discovery of America*, trans. Magnus Magnusson and Hermann Palsson (London: Penguin, 1965), 11.

[30] Alfred W. Crosby, *Ecological Imperialism: The Biological Expansion of Europe, 900–1900* (Cambridge: Cambridge University Press, 1986), 55.

had not been discovered, and apart from them, there is only open ocean between southern Europe and the New World. But the Norse bounced from the Shetlands to Iceland to Greenland and thence to North America. Good ships, notwith-standing, they were still small, largely open-decked, and devoid of mechanical bilge pumps, all major drawbacks to prolonged ocean sailing.

HOW DID WARFARE, AGRICULTURAL FAILURE, AND CLIMATE CHANGE COMBINE TO END THE NORSE SETTLEMENTS?

Whereas the Vinland colony on the North American mainland was quickly aban-doned, because the indigenous people (referred to as *skraelings*, or "wretches," by the Norse) were too hostile, the settlement of Greenland by Erik the Red, around 982 CE, led to more than four centuries of occupation. At its height in the early 1200s estimates of its population vary between 2,000 and 10,000. Iceland, the other major Norse colony, struggled for several centuries with soil erosion and isolation but emerged as one of the modern world's most successful societies. The Norse lasted in Greenland for almost 500 years. To get some perspective, that is longer than many nations in western Europe have existed and longer than the United States to date. By this measure, then, the Norse settlement of Greenland surely looks like a success. But by the end of the fifteenth century, the Norse com-munity there had vanished. There seems to have been no contact between Greenland and either Norway or Denmark from then until 1721 when a mission-ary appeared, hoping to educate the Norse on the finer points of Christianity, only to find Inuit seal hunters, who became his new target.

Theories about the fate of the Greenland Norse have included reemigration to Iceland or Scandinavia, destruction at the hands of the native Inuit or Thule people, abduction by slave raiders, and starvation brought about by agricultural failure, caused by mismanagement of their farmlands, climate change, or a com-bination of the two.

Diamond has famously depicted the Norse experience in Greenland as a classic case of collapse. His critique points to five main issues that doomed the Norse to failure, a deadly combination which proved impossible to survive in the long term and combined cultural issues (choices) with environmental factors, over which they had little control. These issues included heavy environmental impact based on the Viking imposition on Greenland's fragile ecosystem of a north European agricultural model which worked back home; climate change, which exacerbated the environmental damage and limited their agricultural return; a reduction in friendly trade relations with Norway, which had provided various essential items such as iron; hostility with the Inuit neighbors, who might ultimately have killed them or driven them out; the conservative cultural outlook

Viking Longship: The Vessel That Conquered the Inhospitable North Atlantic   With its ability to enter shallow water, the longship could navigate up rivers. But its sailing ability and beam allowed it to also operate effectively offshore.

of the Norse, which made it difficult for them to jettison cultural practices that were not in the interest of their long-term survival.[31]

Diamond's critique has been controversial, and several archeologists have taken issue with many of the details. Big-picture issues are less contested however; it is clear that the Norse left—or disappeared—over a relatively short period. It is also clear that they employed agricultural techniques from back home, but the extent to which they adapted them is not so clear, nor is their ultimate environmental impact. These included grazing large animals—cows, sheep, goats—on a landscape that was more fragile than that of Scandinavia. Also not clear is whether they left in what you might call an "orderly manner" or whether their last days were marked by starvation, warfare, and chaos. Diamond mentions bones of dogs in the western settlement, with knife marks on them. Societies who use working dogs must be pretty desperate to eat them. Other finds also suggest collapse, such as useful wooden objects, which would, under the "orderly retreat"

---

[31]   Diamond, *Collapse*.

scenario, have been taken with them, and bones of newborn cattle, eaten down to the hoofs. The story, Diamond asserts, is a grim one: "All of these archeological details tell us that the last inhabitants of those Western Settlement farms starved and froze to death in the spring."[32]

But did the Norse really "fail?" Did they misread the environment and flub the adaptation test? Was there warfare with the Inuit, who did know how to work the environment, relying not on agriculture but on the hunting of ring seals, which was the most abundant source of food and raw materials (the Norse never mastered this, and this is another of Diamond's pieces of evidence against them)?

Archeologist Joel Berglund, of the Greenland National Museum, thinks this view fails to recognize the Norse's strengths and successes: "The Greenland Norse were competent farmers," he says, "who knew how to adjust to changing circumstances in their subsistence, to the extent that it was within their power to do so."[33] He points to the fact that the Norse eventually limited the number of cows in favor of smaller ruminants such as sheep and goats, which had less impact on the topsoil and required less hay in winter. It is also likely, although difficult to prove, that they used some sort of rotational grazing system to minimize pasture damage; and there is some evidence (from radioisotope analysis of Norse bones) of a gradual increase in marine animals in the Norse diet, something which would suggest a lessening of emphasis on farmed food and greater exploitation of the abundant ocean resources (Norse becoming a little more Inuit?).

What about their relationship with the Inuit? There is scant record of one of any kind, and when mentioned in Icelandic sagas it is clear that the Norse attitude toward them was negative. Is it possible, then, that the Inuit drove the Norse away from Greenland too? Written evidence is very sparse; a story from an Icelandic annal from 1379, for example, tells of an Inuit raid that killed 18 men and captured two boys. An oral tradition from the nineteenth century tells of the Inuit overrunning a farm at Hvalsey and burning the Norse alive in their houses. Archeological excavations at the site, however, turned up no evidence of fire, leading some historians to conclude, as does Berglund, that "in this case the story or myth was not tied to actual events."[34]

If there was conflict with the Inuit, the Norse did not have much in the way of competitive advantage. They possessed only a small amount of iron; they did not bring horses from Norway, as the Spanish did when they came to Mexico

---

[32] Ibid., 269.

[33] Joel Berglund, "Did the Medieval Norse Society in Greenland Really Fail?" in *Questioning Collapse: Human Resilience, Ecological Vulnerability, and the Aftermath of Empire*, ed. Patricia A. McAnany and Norman Yoffee (New York: Cambridge University Press), 61.

[34] Ibid., 55.

Were the Norse Driven Out by Aggressive Inuit? This woodcut from the eighteenth century suggests so. But archeological evidence is not so clear.

hundreds of years later. What they really needed, as Crosby has pointed out, was biological weapons, in the form of Old World diseases. These opened the way for later European colonization in the New World. But the Norse population was always too small to absorb such epidemics, never allowing them to gain immunity themselves. Instead, the diseases decimated them, as Crosby says: "Fatal infections, off-loaded from European ships time and again, dealt blow after blow to these people for whom survival was difficult under the best of circumstances, knocking back population growth that might have led to healthy societies."[35] Disease counted against them, rather than in their favor; and the Norse were left with little to give them the edge over the Inuit. Even so, it remains inconclusive that Inuit aggression was the primary cause of their disappearance. Rather, we can see it as one piece of the puzzle, perhaps contributing to the ultimate Norse decision to abandon the island.

Other studies have focused on the role of climate change in the Norse disappearance. While most of Europe was experiencing warm weather through the late thirteenth century, Greenland was cooling. Sea ice was collecting around its coast and in the North Atlantic, hampering voyages to and from Scandinavia or even Iceland. This would have prevented new immigrants from arriving, but it also may have cut off a source of income from trade. In particular the Norse had been trading walrus ivory with Scandinavia, and this ceased around this time.

---

[35] Crosby, *Ecological Imperialism*, 52.

But the cooling accelerated, as it did in Europe, in the fourteenth century, limiting grazing potential for animals as the growing season shortened. The population grew in the thirteenth century, placing added stress on the environment as more animals grazed increasingly fragile pasture. Meanwhile, there is archeological evidence that the sea level was rising, which reduced the amount of available pasture even further.

Bearing in mind this potent cocktail of climate change, conflict, and cultural mores, the argument is ultimately one of degree and culpability: did the Norse die in their houses, having haplessly overfarmed the environment, cut down all the trees, and become victim of their aggressive neighbors? Or did the cooling climate, rising seas, and diminution of contact with the "mother country" all contribute to a rational—and perhaps even leisurely—decision to reemigrate to greener pastures? (Pun intended.) By the fifteenth century there were no Norse remaining in not-so-Greenland; whether they died in their beds or packed up slowly and caught the next boat to Iceland is still to be discovered. But one thing remains unquestionable, the Norse in Greenland were never able to take their environment for granted. Their growing season was shorter than it had been back home, the pastures were more fragile, and they were cut off from nearby sources of assistance and trade that may have meant that they lived with a small margin of error and needed to take this into account in all their actions.

 By the fifteenth century there were no Norse remaining in not-so-Greenland; whether they died in their beds or packed up slowly and caught the next boat to Iceland is still to be discovered.

What Combination of Events in Eurasia Led to the Black Death of 1348–1350?

Climate and its effect on agriculture is not the only way in which the environment affects human societies, for better or worse. Another element of the environment that is largely out of the realm of human control—yet influenced by human behaviors—is disease.

When historians speak of the "Black Death," they are generally referring to *Yersinia pestis*, the plague strain that hit Constantinople in the sixth century. Some recent studies, however, suggest that there may have been two distinct diseases in this period, one affecting Europe and one affecting Asia. While the Asian strain is usually considered to have been *Yersinia pestis*, a bacterial disease spread from fleas on rats, some researchers now think the European version may have been an airborne virus, which spread directly between humans. This would account for its rate of travel, estimated by contemporary sources as 2 miles a day, about the distance that leisurely travelers would cross the countryside on foot.[36]

Over the centuries the plague has struck repeatedly and is believed to have been responsible for killing some 200 million people globally. But the medieval plague that struck between 1348 and 1350, killing an estimated 25 million, and then again several times over the succeeding decades, but with diminishing ferocity, was far and away the most extreme of its killing rampages.

Let us try to put this extremity in some perspective. According to the Foster Scale, a scale devised by a Canadian geographer to measure worldwide calamities, the medieval plague is the second worst thing ever to happen to humans. The first was World War II. The third was World War I. The US Atomic Energy Commission considers the plague of the fourteenth century closer than anything to the destructive impact of a nuclear war. Both of these insights look at the plague from the perspective of its death toll and its wider consequences. Although the worst effects in Europe happened over a staggeringly horrific couple of years, around Eurasia the disease stalked the landscape for decades. "In a handful of decades," says historian John Kelley, "*Yersinia pestis* swallowed Eurasia the way a snake swallows a rabbit—whole, virtually in a single sitting."[37]

In the Middle East the Arab historian Ibn Khaldun lamented that it was as if "the voice of existence had called out for oblivion."[38] Many writers give a sense of the world being massively depopulated, so much so that people cast about them for family and friends, most of whom had vanished. "Once we were all together," said the Italian poet Francesco Petrarch, "now we are quite alone. We should make new friends, but where or with whom, when the human race is nearly extinct, and it is predicted that the end of the world is soon at hand?"[39]

HOW DID THE PLAGUE SPREAD SO FAR, SO FAST?

From central Asia and China, across Persia and the Anatolian plain, to Europe and the Middle East, the plague sowed death and devastation wherever it went. As to its origins, most contemporary writers pointed to inner Asia, just as it was in

---

[36] Susan Scott and Christopher J. Duncan, *The Biology of Plagues: Evidence from Historical Populations* (Cambridge: Cambridge University Press, 2004).

[37] Kelley, *The Great Mortality*, 11.

[38] Michael W. Dols, *The Black Death in the Middle East*, Princeton University Press, 1977, 67.

[39] Quoted in John Aberth, *The Black Death: The Great Mortality of 1348–1350: A Brief History with Documents* (New York: Palgrave Macmillan, 2005), 72.

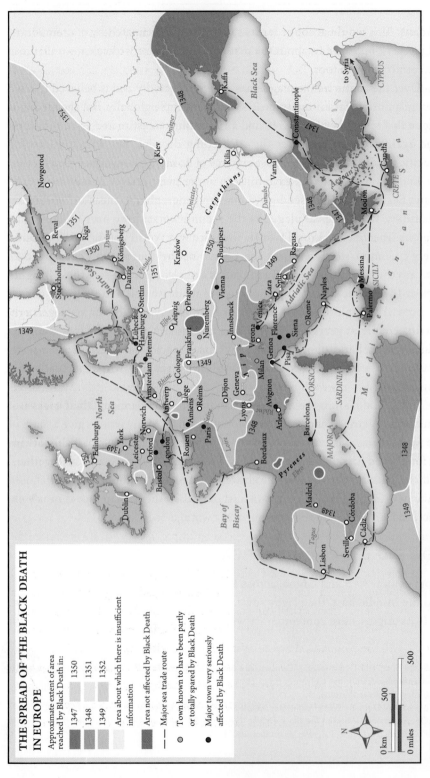

THE SPREAD OF THE BLACK DEATH IN EUROPE

Approximate extent of area reached by Black Death in:

- 1347
- 1348
- 1349
- 1350
- 1351
- 1352

Area about which there is insufficient information

Area not affected by Black Death

- - - Major sea trade route

○ Town known to have been partly or totally spared by Black Death

● Major town very seriously affected by Black Death

0 km   500

0 miles   500

MAP 11.6   THE SPREAD OF THE BLACK DEATH IN EUROPE   Affecting eastern Asia in the 1330s, the plague spread to western Asia a decade later. The town of Kaffa was an important Genoese trading post, and it spread from here to Europe.

the sixth century. Here, we go back to that obese marmot, the tarbagan, whose steppe homeland usually put them out of range of most dense human populations in which disease thrives. But as in the sixth century, when the silk routes were creating much more human traffic and connecting the eastern "core" of China and central Asia and the western core of the Byzantine Empire and the Mediterranean world, the medieval outbreak occurred in an era of growing populations and increasing globalization.

One major "vector" of the disease were the Mongols. For all their destructive powers, the Mongols managed to sew together vast stretches of land (see Chapter 10). This allowed the rats—which carried the fleas, which carried the disease—to overcome barriers of low population. From the Gobi Desert, plague would have infected multiple *caravanserais*—rest stops for medieval travelers—before ascending to Lake Issyk Kul, in today's Kyrgyzstan. From here it would have hitched a ride with merchants heading in all directions, from China to Baghdad.

But the Mongols were only part of the explanation. The western and eastern cores of civilization in the medieval period were considerably larger than they were in the sixth century, so while the Mongols acted as an efficient mode of transport from inner Asia to Europe, the Europeans were experiencing something of a boom and were busily engaged in trade with the east. This made it more likely that, if the Mongols brought pestilence to their doorstep, the Europeans would spread it from there.

Early indications of plague victims appear in the opening stages of the fourteenth century in central Asia. In 1331 it appeared in the middle Yangtze valley in China and is reported to have killed nine out of ten people. In 1334 the Chinese province of Hopei suffered a major outbreak of the disease which killed some 5 million people, about half of the population. In 1345 it ravaged China's east coast, while popping up in multiple locations along the trade routes heading west.

In 1347 the Black Sea port of Caffa (today's Feodosiya) was under the control of the Italian merchant city of Genoa. The Genoese had an agreement with the Mongols to use the town as a trading outpost. This proved of historic importance to Europe; when the Mongol armies besieged Caffa, following a diplomatic hiccup with the Genoese, they brought the plague with them. According to several contemporary sources, the Mongol army catapulted diseased bodies over the city walls, turning Caffa into an oasis of death—perhaps the first recorded incidence of biological warfare. Some historians, however, are skeptical, seeing this as a salacious tidbit, and point out that rats would have entered the city, creating a fast-moving, largely unseen wave of pestilence. Either way, the consequences for Caffa were devastating:

> As the death toll mounted, the streets would have filled with feral animals feeding on human remains, drunken soldiers looting and raping, old women dragging corpses through rubble, and burning buildings spewing jets of flame.... There would have been swarms of rodents with staggering gaits and a strange bloody froth around their snouts.... The scenes in the harbor, the only means of escape in besieged Caffa, would have been especially horrific: surging crowds and sword-wielding guards, children wailing for lost or dead parents, shouting and cursing, everyone pushing toward teeming ships.[40]

Europe's fate was largely sealed by those escaping Genoese galleys; many other ships no doubt passed on the disease, but European records from the time repeatedly single out these:

> It so happened that in the month of October in the year of our lord 1347, around the first of that month, twelve Genoese galleys, fleeing our Lord's wrath which came down upon them for their misdeeds, put in at the port of the city of Messina [in Sicily]. They brought with them a plague that they carried down to the very marrow of their bones, so that if anyone so much as spoke to them, he was infected with a mortal sickness which brought on immediate death that he could in no way avoid.[41]

The galleys did not stay in Sicily; when Sicilians started to die, they were turned away. They then made a catastrophic tour of European ports, and the disease quickly spread. Estimates of the death toll in Europe top out at around 50% or more. The losses were especially great in eastern England and rural France, where mortality was between 40% and 60%. Children and women, especially pregnant women, were disproportionately affected because they spent more time indoors.

So growing populations, European trade, and Mongol conquering successes all had a hand in spreading the plague. But there were several other factors, both human and environmental, which played a key role. Analyzing tree-ring data from the early fourteenth century, scientists discovered that the period witnessed more environmental stress than any time in the preceding 2,000 years.

---

[40] Kelly, *The Great Mortality*, 10.
[41] Michele de Piazza, quoted in Aberth, *The Black Death*, 11.

Global wind patterns changed, resulting in different weather patterns in different regions. In central Asia conditions became drier, causing nomadic herders to migrate into the tarbagan heartland of the northern Eurasian steppe, putting them in contact with the plague source.

Meanwhile the same climatological shifts caused wetter weather in Europe. This followed several hundred years of warm weather across Europe (the Medieval Warm Period) that had provided bumper crops, seen the sea ice melt in the north Atlantic between Iceland and Greenland (good for Norse sailors), and allowed European populations to increase dramatically. Whereas Europe had a population of some 26 million around 700 CE, by 1200 this had tripled to 75 million. The "great clearances" of the twelfth and thirteenth centuries largely denuded the continent of forest, allowing Europeans to create more farmland. Population growth and a rise in living standards had the usual negative consequences: "As greater numbers of Europeans were being clothed," says Hughes, "the land was being unclothed."[42] Forest clearances were followed by armies of sheep, in particular, which take a heavy toll on pasture. The massive changes wrought on Europe's landscape had dire consequences. "The shrinking of forests was a pivotal cause of the environmental crisis of the fourteenth century."[43] Urban life proliferated, with cities such as London, Paris, and Milan having populations of more than 100,000. Trade across the continent, which around 1000 CE had been difficult and hazardous, was now relatively routine.

But by the early 1300s the Medieval Warm Period, which had given most of Europe exceptional harvests for some 400 years, was coming to an end. With a string of excessively wet summers, the European population, bigger than ever before, more connected than ever, and increasingly impoverished, was packed together in unhygienic urban conditions, facing starvation as crops rotted in the fields for several consecutive years.

The "great famine" of 1316 left thousands dead across the continent as farmers failed to recover from these disasters. Farm animals died too, their putrefying remains left to rot in the fields. What relationship did this have to the plague of 1347? Many of those who died would have been developmentally affected by the famine in their youth, which would have damaged their resistance to disease.

But medieval Europe was vulnerable to disease in other ways. The growing urban population was a filthy one. Not only did Christian culture of the time look down on personal hygiene as vanity but its cities were among the most overcrowded and dirty on the planet. Open-air slaughterhouses created stagnant pools of blood and offal,

---

42   Hughes, *The Environmental History of the World*, 91.
43   Ibid., 93.

Not only did Christian culture of the time look down on personal hygiene as vanity, but its cities were among the most overcrowded and dirty on the planet.

with inadequate or nonexistent sewers. Raw human sewage was routinely dumped onto the streets. Rain washed this away—when there was rain. The situation was reflected in Paris' street names, a surprising number of which derive from the word *merde*, literally "shit," as Kelley describes: "Rue Merdeux, rue Merdelet, Rue Merdusson, rue des Merdons, rue Merdiere and rue de pipi. 'Look out below' was the only sanitation ordinance."[44]

The boom of the Medieval Warm Period did not come to an end only with the onset of the Little Ice Age, around 1300, however.[45] Agricultural science and even Malthusian economics played a role: the population expansion in Europe had placed heavy strains on agricultural output, and this was beginning to show. Marginal land that had been plowed under was beginning to give out, and even good land was overfarmed. Food prices collapsed, leaving farmers bankrupt and leading to widespread abandonment of land as people moved into the already crowded cities. Food prices stabilized somewhat by the early 1300s but then skyrocketed shortly thereafter when the endless rains created widespread food shortages throughout northern Europe.

Fourteenth-Century English Engraving Commemorating the Black Death of 1348
Unsanitary urban living, prolonged periods of warfare, and several years of bad harvests led to a weakened population that succumbed in large numbers.

---

44 Kelley, *The Great Mortality*, 17.
45 Dates of the Little Ice Age vary significantly. Some historians point to 1650 as the beginning, while others point to the increase in north Atlantic pack ice in the late 1200s and the European rains that precipitated the great famine of 1316–17 as the onset.

So far we have argued that pre-plague Europe was malnourished, unsanitary, and overcrowded. It was also constantly at war. How did this aid the plague? In the decade leading up to the outbreak, the English army had been roaming the French countryside decimating villages and destroying crops. This was part of its strategy in the dismal episode of European history known as the Hundred Years' War. The *chevauchée* ("raid") was the solution to the problem posed by French nobles locking themselves in their castles and denying the English the pleasure of battling them. Instead of laying siege to a castle for months, the English turned on the noble's peasantry, the very people who provided him with his agricultural wealth. This would draw him out of his castle and onto the battlefield, and it devastated the countryside even further. Not only did endemic warfare compound the food shortages of the civilian population, but it also created a vast reservoir of soldiery weakened and vulnerable to disease.

WHAT WERE THE CONSEQUENCES OF THE BLACK DEATH?

With as much as half the population dead over a 2-year period, the future seemed bleak in Europe, as it did in other parts of Eurasia. Most of Africa, below its northern, Mediterranean fringe, escaped unscathed, as did most of India, possibly because it lay to the south of the major trade routes and was protected by the mountain chains to its north. Japan, which had its island nature to thank for protecting it from the Mongols, was similarly insulated from the plague.

Not surprisingly, people searched for reasons why the plague should have happened. In the medieval world explanations for most occurrences ultimately led to theology, and the plague was often seen as God's wrath. But many Europeans, in keeping with centuries old tradition, blamed the Jews. Interrogations produced fraudulent confessions to ludicrous acts such as the widespread "poisoning" of European populations by secret Jewish groups. In Strasbourg in 1349 some 2,000 Jews were rounded up and forced onto a specially constructed wooden platform, which was then set ablaze. Some of them accepted baptism (maybe as many as half), but the others were burned alive. Some children were reportedly taken from the fire and forcibly baptized. Scenes such as these were repeated in multiple European cities, the Jews being forcibly relieved of all their money and possessions and canceling any debts to non-Jews, before burning.

Such anti-Semitic violence was not unprecedented in Europe, although the circumstances that precipitated it were. Jews were often protected by sovereigns and were sometimes known as the "king's people." Violence against them was therefore sometimes redirected violence against rulers who had failed the people during the plague. Jews were also suspect because of their distinctness.

They usually lived in separate "ghettoes," which provided some insulation from the plague; thus, they died in somewhat smaller numbers. Rabbinical law, which governed much of their daily lives, resulted in higher levels of personal hygiene; and this, again, meant that fewer Jews died of the plague.

The Catholic Church also came in for special criticism, and people became far more cynical about religion in general in the plague's aftermath. Such frustration with the church added to the popularity of fringe religious groups, such as the Flagellants, who paraded through towns flogging themselves to atone for their sins and were often seen as spreading the disease further.

Ultimately, however, the population of Eurasia was able to rebound and grow, strengthened by a new resilience to the specific bacterium that had caused the plague, to the extent that subsequent outbreaks did not come close to the devastation of 1347–48. Growth was slow, however, with population levels in Europe not reaching pre-plague levels until the later fifteenth century. The death of such numbers also created opportunities for many of the survivors, opening up more land and creating labor shortages, which drove wages up and created new opportunities for women in the workplace, although these were not necessarily permanent.

The need for peasant laborers gave incentives for feudal landlords to compete for them, with improvements in pay and conditions. This precipitated perhaps the most long-lasting effects of the plague, a deep evolutionary change that had been under way before the plague struck, a realignment of Europe's feudal system toward greater rights and freedoms for rural laborers.

Conclusion: What Role Does the Environment Play in Human History?

The human relationship with the environment may seem like a recent subject of interest, yet in reality there is a long backstory here. "Current environmental issues," says historian David Christian, "have their roots in, and in some sense express, the very nature of our species and our history."[46] From the very earliest stirrings of our species we have lived hand in glove with our environment. We are a product of it as much as we fashion it, by design as well as by accident.

Clearly, the environment is not the only factor determining historical change, just as human decision making is not either. Ultimately, we need to judge each

---

[46]   David Christian, *Oxford Handbook of World History* (New York: Oxford University Press, 2012), 125.

historical case only after considering all the data. For this reason, the debates about the role of climate in various historical events will be endless. What is clear, however, is that environmental change is rarely a zero-sum game. Certainly, the weather has a profound influence on our lives, and to that extent we must recognize how much the environment determines; there are reasons most of the early civilizations developed in river valleys—there is a link between fertile land and dense human populations. On the other hand, the Aztec and the Inca, who we will discuss in the upcoming chapters, bucked this trend and managed to create densely populated states in steep, mountainous areas that would seem to defy the odds altogether.

This gets at the next proposition: if the environment determines much of what we do, the rest is determined by the human capacity for adaptation. The Norse were able to alter their Scandinavian ways just enough to survive for centuries in Greenland, without actually becoming Inuit (although ultimately the changing climate gave them a stark choice: *become Inuit, if you want to stay, or leave with your Norseness intact*). The natives of the American Southwest adapted to rain-fed agriculture as a means of escaping the burdensome demands of a would-be elite class in the Phoenix basin. And these adaptations bring to mind the subject of Chapter 1, human dominance. Humans are, above all, survivors who do what is necessary to survive; and therein lie the stories of history.

Words to Think About

Collapse	Hohokam	Holocene
Pueblo	Sustainable	Theater-states

Questions to Think About

- In what ways are humans vulnerable to their environment?
- What is the argument against the idea of Maya "collapse"?
- What pressure does technological development put on the environment?

Primary Sources

Aberth, John. *The Black Death: The Great Mortality of 1348–1350: A Brief History with Documents.* New York: Palgrave Macmillan, 2005.

The Vinland Sagas: The Norse Discovery of America. Translated by Magnus Magnusson and Hermann Palsson. London: Penguin, 1965.

Secondary Sources

Bakewell, Peter. *A History of Latin America to 1825*. New York: Wiley-Blackwell, 2010.

Berglund, Joel. "Did the Medieval Norse Society in Greenland Really Fail?" In *Questioning Collapse: Human Resilience, Ecological Vulnerability, and the Aftermath of Empire*, edited by Patricia A. McAnany and Norman Yoffee, pp. 45–70. New York: Cambridge University Press, 2010.

Binford, Michael W., Alan L. Kolata, Mark Brenner, John W. Janusek, Matthew T. Seddon, Mark Abbott, and Jason H. Curtis. "Climate Variation and the Rise and Fall of an Andean Civilization." *Quaternary Research* 47 (1997): 235–48.

Christian, David. *Oxford Handbook of World History*. New York: Oxford University Press, 2012.

Crosby, Alfred W. *Ecological Imperialism: The Biological Expansion of Europe, 900–1900*. Cambridge: Cambridge University Press, 1986.

Demarest, Arthur. *The Ancient Maya: The Rise and Fall of a Rainforest Civilization*. Cambridge: Cambridge University Press, 2004.

Diamond, Jared. *Collapse: How Societies Choose to Fail or Succeed*. New York: Viking, 2005.

Fagan, Brian. *The Long Summer: How Climate Changed Civilization*. New York: Basic Books, 2004.

Fernández-Armesto, Felipe. *Civilizations: Culture, Ambition, and the Transformation of Nature*. New York: Simon & Schuster, 2002.

Gill, Richardson Benedict. *The Great Maya Droughts: Water, Life, and Death*. Albuquerque: University of New Mexico Press, 2000.

Hughes, J. Donald. *The Environmental History of the World: Humankind's Changing Role in the Community of Life*. London: Routledge, 2001.

Kelley, John. *The Great Mortality: An Intimate History of the Black Death, the Most Devastating Plague of All Time*. New York: Harper Collins, 2005.

Lekson, Stephen. "The Southwest in the World." http://stevelekson.com/ancient-southwest/.

McAnany, Patricia A., and Norman Yoffee, eds. *Questioning Collapse: Human Resilience, Ecological Vulnerability, and the Aftermath of Empire*. New York: Cambridge University Press, 2010.

Miller, Shawn William. *An Environmental History of Latin America*. Cambridge: Cambridge University Press, 2007.

Owen, Bruce. "Distant Colonies and Explosive Collapse: The Two Stages of the Tiwanaku Diaspora in the Osmore Drainage." *Latin American Antiquity* 16, no. 1 (2005): 45–80.

Scarborough, Vernon L. "Resilience, Resource Use, and Socioeconomic Organization: A Mesoamerican Pathway." In *Environmental Disaster and the Archeology of Human Response*, edited by Garth Bawdon and Richard Martin Reycraft, pp. 195–212. Albuquerque, NM: Maxwell Museum of Anthropology, 2000.

Scott, Susan, and Christopher J. Duncan. *The Biology of Plagues: Evidence from Historical Populations*. Cambridge: Cambridge University Press, 2004.

Tainter, Joseph. *The Collapse of Complex Societies*. Cambridge: Cambridge University Press, 1988.

Wilcox, Michael. "Marketing Conquest and the Vanishing Indian: An Indigenous Response to Jared Diamond's Archaeology of the American Southwest." In *Questioning Collapse: Human Resilience, Ecological Vulnerability, and the Aftermath of Empire*, edited by Patricia A. McAnany and Norman Yoffee, pp. 113–141. New York: Cambridge University Press, 2010.

Williams, Patrick Ryan. "Rethinking Disaster-Induced Collapse in the Demise of the Andean Highland States: Wari and Tiwanaku." *World Archaeology* 33, no. 3 (2002): 361–74.

For additional resources, including maps, primary sources, and visuals, web links, and quizzes, please go to **www.oup.com/us/cole**

Tomb of Askiya Muhammad, Ruler of Songhay

Chapter 12

Was the European Renaissance Unique?

Taking Power in the Fifteenth Century

Traditional stories related by storytellers, or *griots*, in Mali today tell how the land was ruled by a fish. It swam up the Djoliba River every morning to Kukiya, where it sat on a throne to rule over the people. The *Kitab al fattash* (seventeenth century), an Arabic account of the Songhay Empire, tells how the fish was killed by two brothers from Medina in Arabia.

This may sound outlandishly far-fetched, but the story addresses a very real theme in West African history—the tension between its Islamic culture and its much older traditional culture. For the states in this part of Africa, including Gao, Mali, and Songhay, the Niger River was, like the Nile in Egypt, the source of all life. Little surprise then that myth and history would create such a fabulous character as a fish-king.

If the royal fish in the story represents the Songhay people's deep riverine history, the brothers from Medina represent the coming of Islam to the region. Like all cultures which undergo a change, the ancient traditions of western Africa were not eradicated by the new Islamic culture; the older ways persisted, as reflected in other stories, which tell how the fish did not, in fact, die but continued to rule underwater. This seems a fitting metaphor for how old ways continue, often guiding and informing new traditions from below the surface.

In some stories, the fish is associated with the father of Songhay's best-known leader, the Askiya Muhammad. *Askiyas*, or "leaders," were seen as men with occult powers, relating to ancient African animist religious traditions, as well as devout Muslims, an apparently impossible paradox, according to "orthodox" Islamic notions. But such apparent paradoxes required working out through

THINKING ABOUT RENAISSANCES

What Is a Renaissance?
- In turning to Classical-era texts of Greece and Rome, Petrarch hoped to connect with a lost "spirit" of the antiquity, thereby improving his own times.

How Was the World Shrinking in This Period?
- While there was no doubt panic at the Ottoman conquest, the notion of Europe and the "East" as two distinct entities was, to use a technical term, "fuzzy" at this point in history.

What Is the Role of Cultural Producers?
- While elite intellectuals in several societies turned to ancient texts to explain the present, other societies did not have this option.

What Relevance Does This Period Have for Nonstate Societies?
- Most societies do not preserve their histories in writing; and although they have cultural producers, these tend to be oral in nature and are therefore more difficult to trace historically.

Conclusion
- All societies experience new developments; all of them look over their shoulders for a sense of continuity or to retrieve something they feel they may have lost along the way.

stories, and this is a worldwide phenomenon; new leaders needed to create a basis for their legitimacy, whether in China, the Americas, or Africa. And in Africa this process was mediated by *griots* as much as by official "court" historians.

Introduction

While Islam may have arrived in West Africa with Arab traders of the tenth and eleventh centuries, it took hundreds of years to percolate down and establish its own, unique characteristics there. Likewise, around the world, in the thirteenth and fourteenth centuries, cultures and political entities were encountering each other through trade, war, and migration. In the last quarter of the thirteenth century Marco Polo traveled to China and wrote one of the first Western accounts of life there (*The Travels of Marco Polo*, 1300). In the mid-fourteenth century, Ibn Batutta, a Muslim from Morocco, traveled to India, China, and Mali. He penned an account of his journey (*The Journey of Ibn Batutta*, 1355), in which he covered perhaps as much as three times the distance as Marco Polo. In the early fifteenth century a Chinese eunuch in the court of the Ming dynasty, Admiral Zheng-He (1371–1433) traveled to southern Asia seven times and then sailed as far as the east coast of Africa. And only a few decades later, in 1492, the Genoese sea captain Christoforo Colombo (Christopher Columbus) crossed the Atlantic and bumped into the New World. The anthropologist Eric Wolf argues that "These voyages were not isolated adventures but manifestations of the forces that were drawing the continents into more encompassing relationships and would soon make the world a unified stage for human action."[1] We are not there yet, but the seeds of globalization were stirring.

Bearing in mind the formation of this "unified stage," whatever was happening in Africa was also happening in other places. Not only were people making connections across ever larger distances, but such journeys often resulted from a certain new impetus—part economic, part cultural—that was stitching the world together. Historians have traditionally looked to Europe's "Renaissance" as the epicenter of all global revitalization in this period. And there were many noteworthy developments here at this time. But today's historians are skeptical that the Renaissance represented a genuine historical period—or was really new—or that its attributes were exclusively European. Around the world we see glimmerings of similar characteristics, in particular urbanization, economic expansion, and new stories of legitimation. Just as with the *griots* of Songhay or the *Kitab al-Fattash*, leaders, dynasties, empires, and what we shall call, rather dryly, "cultural producers" began casting around for ways to make sense of their world, legitimize their power, and find a way forward. Often, this entailed looking back and tying oneself into older traditions.

The Songhay revitalization, or Renaissance, was not unlike Europe's or those of the Ottoman Empire in the Middle East and the Ming dynasty in China. In centers of power, politics were changing and new ways of explaining the changes were coming into being that justified the ambitions and traditions of the winners. This was not necessarily a case of "a rising tide floats all boats"; often, one group's success meant another's downfall, or at least stasis.

---

[1]   Eric Wolf, *Europe and the People Without History* (Berkeley: University of California Press, 1982), 24.

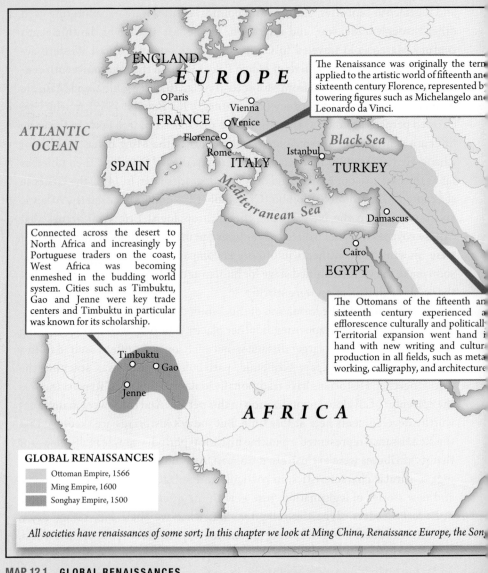

The Renaissance was originally the term applied to the artistic world of fifteenth and sixteenth century Florence, represented by towering figures such as Michelangelo and Leonardo da Vinci.

Connected across the desert to North Africa and increasingly by Portuguese traders on the coast, West Africa was becoming enmeshed in the budding world system. Cities such as Timbuktu, Gao and Jenne were key trade centers and Timbuktu in particular was known for its scholarship.

The Ottomans of the fifteenth and sixteenth century experienced an efflorescence culturally and politically. Territorial expansion went hand in hand with new writing and cultural production in all fields, such as metal working, calligraphy, and architecture.

GLOBAL RENAISSANCES

Ottoman Empire, 1566
Ming Empire, 1600
Songhay Empire, 1500

All societies have renaissances of some sort; In this chapter we look at Ming China, Renaissance Europe, the Song

MAP 12.1   GLOBAL RENAISSANCES

TIMELINE

1368–1644
Ming Dynasty, China

1405–1433
Voyages of Zheng-He,
Chinese admiral

1450
First movable type printing outside China

1452–1519
Leonardo da Vinci

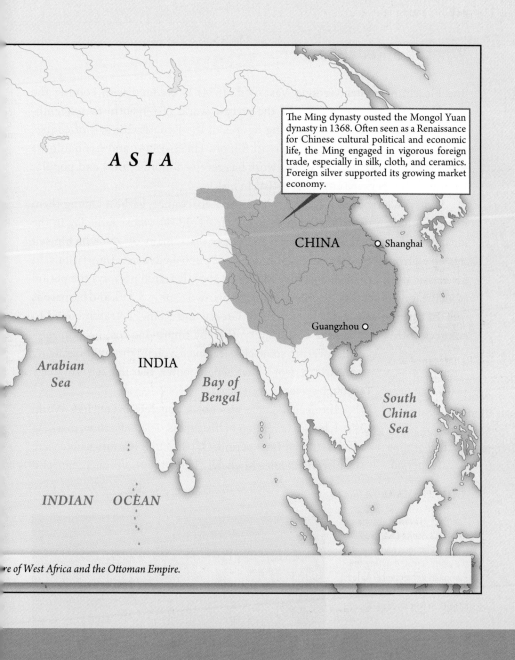

ASIA

The Ming dynasty ousted the Mongol Yuan dynasty in 1368. Often seen as a Renaissance for Chinese cultural political and economic life, the Ming engaged in vigorous foreign trade, especially in silk, cloth, and ceramics. Foreign silver supported its growing market economy.

CHINA

○ Shanghai

Guangzhou ○

Arabian
Sea

INDIA

Bay of
Bengal

South
China
Sea

INDIAN   OCEAN

re of West Africa and the Ottoman Empire.

1520–66
Reign of Ottoman emperor,
Suleyman the Magnificent

1464–1492
Reign of Sonni Ali Ber,
Songhay

What Is a Renaissance?

The Florentine writer Georgio Vasari (d. 1574) is credited with coining the Italian term *Rinascita* to describe the artistic world of fifteenth- to sixteenth-century Florence. The two towering figures of the Renaissance are, of course, Michelangelo di Lodovico Buonarroti Simoni (1475–1564) and Leonardo da Vinci (1452–1519), both of whose work has received more critical and popular attention than perhaps any other artists in history.

Writers also played a central role in the Renaissance, earliest among them being the Italian poet Francesco Petrarch (1304–1374), whose fame lay in the idea of resuscitating ancient Roman and Greek texts, many of which he himself dusted off from shelves in obscure libraries and published in new translations. In his classic work *Letters on Familiar Matters* (1366), Petrarch portrays the period from the fourth-century decline of Rome to his own time as a dark and barbarous one. In turning to Classical-era texts of Greece and Rome, Petrarch hoped to connect with a lost "spirit" of antiquity, thereby improving his own times—rediscovering some classical *mojo*, you might say (borrowing an African word that would enter the English language through slaves in America).

The Renaissance was not a concrete event, like World War I, but an invention of historians, a *periodization*, marking off a particular time period. Of particular relevance here were the historians Jules Michelet (1798–1874), a Frenchman, and

> The Renaissance was not a concrete event, like World War I, but an invention of historians, a *periodization*, marking off a particular time period.

The Eyes Have It   Leonardo da Vinci's *Mona Lisa*, probably the most famous painting in the world, created during the European Renaissance. At least in the art world a new spirit was at work in certain places.

the Swiss Jacob Burkhardt (1818–1897). Michelet was writing with the values and concerns of the French Revolution (1789) very much in mind and looked back at the fifteenth century as the beginning of this awakening—of the revolutionary causes of *liberté, egalité, fraternité* ("liberty, equality, fraternity"). Michelet focused on French cultural achievements of that period, including the works of French writers such as François Rabelais (ca. 1494–ca. 1553) and Michel de Montaigne (1533–1592), and he included William Shakespeare (1564–1616), who, although not French, was nonetheless influential. Michelet saw in the literature, politics, and science of the Renaissance nothing less than the "discovery of the world, and the discovery of man." Burkhardt, on the other hand, focused on northern Italy in the same period; and there he saw in the intellectual and artistic achievements the emergence of nothing short of "individualism" and the "modern man." Both these historians could well be accused of *presentism*, something that afflicts many historians, as historian Jerry Brotton explains: "Rather than describing the world of the fifteenth and sixteenth centuries, these writers were in fact describing their own."[2]

For most historians the key lies in the *Re* of *Renaissance*. The concept of rebirth meant that poets, writers, artists, scientists and cultural producers of all kinds, looked back to an earlier "golden age" as a source of inspiration. Petrarch, who lived through the plague, considered Greco–Roman culture, represented by its literature, models to emulate. European society needed a new direction in the aftermath of the plague: "By the fourteenth century, when climate change, famine, and disease undermined so many old certainties, some intellectuals expanded their interpretation of the ancient classics into a general vision of social rebirth."[3]

In around 1450 three individuals, Johann Gutenburg, Peter Schoffer, and Johan Fust, in Mainz, Germany, engineered the first movable type printing (outside of China, which did it several hundred years earlier), which allowed the mass production of books. A goldsmith, a calligrapher, and a financier, respectively, these three brought about what many considered the most important invention of the era. As literature became increasingly available, at the same time whole new areas of inquiry were introduced from the ancient world, to be studied alongside the strictly theological: medicine, philology, history, politics, and astronomy. There emerged a new breed of scholars, known as "humanists" (responsible for establishing the predominant Western educational model—the humanities),

---

[2]   Jerry Brotton, *The Renaissance Bazaar: From the Silk Road to Michelangelo* (New York: Oxford University Press, 2002), 33.

[3]   Ian Morris, *Why the West Rules—For Now: The Patterns of History and What They Tell Us About the Future* (New York: Farrar, Strauss and Giroux, 2011), 418.

who took all subjects under their wing, able to move seamlessly between poetry and astronomy and back, often with a stopover to practice statecraft.

Politics is a key ingredient here, for many humanist scholars looked for employment in government positions, using literary and rhetorical skills such as translation, critical reading, negotiation, and composition in the service of the state. Examples of such "Renaissance men" include Niccolò Machiavelli (1469–1527), author of the infamous government handbook *The Prince*, written originally in the hope of gaining employment with the Medici family of Florence, and Desiderius Erasmus of Rotterdam (1466–1536), who wrote, among other books, *The Education of a Christian Prince*, originally for the future Hapsburg emperor Charles V (r. 1519–1558). When no official position was forthcoming from him, he sent a copy to England's King Henry VIII (r. 1509–1547). These were two very different Christian princes, but with honed, humanist-inspired rhetorical skills, Erasmus could construct any argument upon demand, like the best PR firm today. Humanist politicians, however, were as diverse as the subjects in which they excelled, which famously crossed the line between the theoretical and the practical: the creative minds of such Renaissance men "moved effortlessly between studios and the corridors of power, taking time off from theorizing to lead armies, hold office, and advise rulers."[4]

Because it is an artificial historical period, historians today argue over the dates of the Renaissance and even over whether there was a Renaissance—the doubters not denying that "new things were happening" in Europe but suggesting that such developments were a continuation of the Middle Ages. This point of view, referred to somewhat dramatically as the "revolt of the medievalists," sees many of the traits associated with the Renaissance by scholars such as Burkhardt as already in place in the twelfth century. For this reason, many historians prefer to use the term "early modern" or "late medieval" to describe this period. These arguments have resulted in divided views over the Renaissance, leading historians, as William Bowsma puts it, to "sorting data into two heaps, one marked 'continuities,' the other marked 'innovations.'"[5] Such is the business of historians. If it was just a continuation of historical trends, then is the focus on this period another example of Eurocentric history, in which European historians have described Europe's "brilliance" so as to legitimate its conquest of large parts of the globe which followed? Jerry Brotton suggests that, "Disputes about dating the Renaissance have become so intense that the validity of the term is now in doubt. Does it have any meaning at all any more? Is it really possible to separate the

---

4   Ibid., 419.
5   William J. Bowsma, "The Renaissance and the Drama of Western History," in *A Usable Past: Essays in European Cultural History* (Berkeley: University of California Press, 1990), 350.

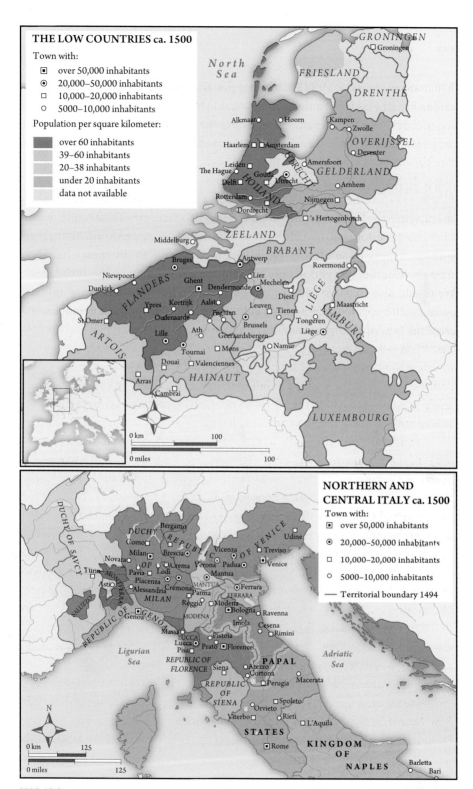

North Sea

GRONINGEN
▢ Groningen
FRIESLAND
DRENTHE

Alkmaar ▢ ○ Hoorn Kampen ○
Haarlem ▢ ⊡ Amsterdam ○ Zwolle
OVERIJSSEL
Leiden ○ ○ Deventer
The Hague ○ Amersfoort ○
Delft ▢ Gouda ○ GELDERLAND
UTRECHT
Rotterdam ▢ ○ Utrecht ○ Arnhem
Dordrecht ▢ Nijmegen ▢
HOLLAND
▢ 's Hertogenbosch
ZEELAND
Middelburg ○
BRABANT
Bruges ⊡ ⊙ Antwerp
Niewpoort ○ Roermond ○
FLANDERS Ghent ⊡ ⊙ Lier
Dunkirk ○ Dendermonde ⊙ Mechelen ⊙
Ypres ⊙ Aalst ⊙ Diest ▢ Maastricht ▢
Kortrijk ⊙ Leuven ⊙ Tienen ○ LIÈGE
St.Omer ▢ Enghien ○ Brussels ⊙ Tongeren ○
Oudenaarde ○ Ath ○ Geeraardsbergen ○ Liège ⊙ LIMBURG
Lille ⊙ Namur ○
Tournai ⊙ ▢ Mons
Douai ▢ ▢ Valenciennes
Arras ▢ HAINAUT
Cambrai ▢

ARTOIS

LUXEMBOURG

0 km   100
0 miles   100

NORTHERN AND
CENTRAL ITALY ca. 1500

DUCHY OF SAVOY
DUCHY
Bergamo ○
Como ▢ REPUBLIC
Milan ⊡ Brescia ⊙
Novara ▢ Crema ○ Vicenza ⊙ OF VENICE
Turin ○ OF Verona ⊙ Treviso ▢ Udine ○
MONFERRATO Pavia ○ Lodi ○ Padua ⊙
Asti ○ Piacenza ○ Mantua ○ Venice ⊡
SALUZZO Alessandria ○ Cremona ⊙ MANTUA Ferrara ⊙
MILAN Reggio ○ Parma ⊙ Modena ▢ FERRARA
REPUBLIC OF GENOA MODENA Bologna ⊡ Ravenna ○
Genoa ⊡ Imola ○ Cesena ○
Massa ○ Rimini ○
LUCCA Pistoia ○
Lucca ▢ Prato ▢ Florence ⊡
Ligurian Pisa ○ PAPAL Adriatic
Sea REPUBLIC OF Siena ⊙ Arezzo ○ Sea
FLORENCE Cortona ○
REPUBLIC Perugia ▢ Macerata ○
OF Spoleto ▢
SIENA Orvieto ○ Rieti ○
Viterbo ○ L'Aquila ▢
STATES
Rome ⊡ KINGDOM
OF
NAPLES Barletta ○
Bari ○

0 km   125
0 miles   125

N

MAP 12.2 THE LOW COUNTRIES AND NORTHERN ITALY, ca. 1500 By 1500 the Low Countries (a) and northern Italy (b) had both developed high-density urban populations. Both areas featured prominently in the European Renaissance. Trade between towns and with the wider world was a major feature of both regions.

Renaissance from the Middle Ages that preceded it, and the modern world that came after it? Has it been invented to establish a convincing myth of European superiority?"[6] And, most importantly, does the idea of a Renaissance pertain to only a few Europeans at the very top of the food chain?

WAS PROSPERITY JUST AN ELITE MALE AFFAIR?

Most figures associated with the period of European growth are elite males: Michelangelo, Botticelli, Columbus, etc. We might be tempted to ask, then, along with the historian Joan Kelley-Gadol, did women have a similar experience, or were the effects of this period only felt among a small number of powerful men?[7] We should also consider whether not only women but nonelite men—ordinary people with less privileged backgrounds—were affected, for these people constituted the overwhelming bulk of the population.

Portrait   The European Renaissance is sometimes credited with the invention of "individuality." Portraits of ordinary people, like this woman by Andrea del Sarto (1486–1530), represented a new ethos. But did women of the Renaissance experience an improved quality of life, or were the gains of the period available only to wealthy men?

---

6   Brotton, *The Renaissance Bazaar*, 20.
7   Joan Kelley-Gadol, "Did Women Have a Renaissance?" in *Becoming Visible: Women in European History*, ed. Renate Bridental, Claudia Koonz, and Susan Stuard, 2nd ed. (Boston: Houghton Mifflin, 1987).

Kelley-Gadol argues that "there was no renaissance for women—at least not during the Renaissance. . . . The startling fact is that women as a group, especially among the classes that dominated Italian urban life, experienced a contradiction of social and personal options that men of their classes either did not, as was the case with the bourgeoisie, or did not experience as markedly, as was the case with the nobility."[8]

Well-born medieval women, Kelley-Gadol argues, enjoyed a certain status that they appeared to have lost in the Renaissance. The "courtly love" culture of the medieval period allowed at least propertied women a certain emotional and even sexual freedom. With the rise of the state, however, and of the business class represented by increasingly wealthy merchants, upper-class women were pushed into less visible roles. Well-born women, therefore, experienced losses, while for the less well-born precious little changed.

Scholars since Kelley-Gadol have mostly agreed with her broad—and pessimistic—conclusions, although they have added some nuance. Evidence from court records, marital documents, and other historical sources shows that women's lives differed greatly from those of men but that they differed from each other as well; and this difference depended upon their class. Much of Renaissance thinking on gender came from scripture and the beloved classical tradition to which Renaissance thinkers looked for inspiration. This was unfortunate for women. Plato, in his work *Timeus*, declared that women began their lives as men and were "regenerated" into women if they lived "cowardly or immoral lives." Aristotle, in his *Politics*, ranks women just above slaves in the natural hierarchy and adds that, because of their natural inferiority, they should always be subject to their husband's authority. Galen, another Greek "expert" on women, saw the vagina, an "internal" sexual organ, as the source of women's obvious inferiority. Little of the much-trumpeted progressive thinking of the Renaissance was used to throw out such ignorant and prejudiced ideas. Instead, these ideas were blended, or "harmonized," with church ideology, which was little better. As William Caferro puts it, the early church fathers, such as St. Jerome and St. Augustine, "expressed an unmistakable misogyny."[9]

Both Christian and Classical traditions, therefore, came to bear on Renaissance women. Writers such as Leon Battista Alberti (*The Book of the Family*, 1432) and Francesco Barbaro (*On Wifely Duties*, 1416) drew upon the unfortunate works of Aristotle, Xenophon, and Augustine to argue for restricting women to the domestic sphere and imposing male authority over them. As if illustrating the dictum that books are made out of other books, humanist authors carried forward the prejudices of the past as they idealized their authors.

---

[8]   Ibid., 19.
[9]   William Caferro, *Contesting the Renaissance* (Malden, MA: Wiley-Blackwell, 2011), 63.

And such ideas often fueled deadly consequences, as Caferro points out: "From 1480 to 1700 more women were executed for witchcraft than for any other crime, and the number of women burned at the stake exceeded those who gained sainthood by 100:1."[10] The church provided one solution to the problem of prostitution and witchcraft, which was to seclude single women in convents, thus taking them, and their nasty habit of inducing social chaos, out of circulation. But although most women managed to avoid burning at the stake, plenty of lesser indignities awaited them. Restricted from property ownership and often from inheritance by variations of Roman law, which posited the idea of *patria potestas*, the ultimate male power in the household, women were also restricted from many types of work. "Alewife" was a common female medieval role, that of beer maker, which, absent modern ideas of artisanal brewing, was a less-than-choice profession. Prostitution was widespread, while "servant" was the most common female occupation in many European countries in this period.

Other historians offer a somewhat more positive view of women's experiences in the Renaissance, promoting the rising-tide-floats-all-boats model. Margaret King, for example, argues that although the majority of women continued to be stifled at home, in the workplace and in the church there were growing numbers who rose above the constraints of their sex. These included the likes of England's Queen Elizabeth I (r. 1558–1603), France's "queen consort" Catherine de Medici (1519–1589), and the Venetian noblewoman Caterina Cornaro (1454–1510), who became queen of Cyprus and, as such, hosted a literary salon that became well known. Such women broke with tradition in multiple ways. King sees a kind of "Renaissance feminism" at work among such women, even if widespread change did not occur on all social levels: "these women wielded the picks of their understanding to build a better city for ladies."[11] But for regular women, residence in such cities was usually precluded.

HOW WAS WEALTH DISTRIBUTED?

History has tended to tell the tale of the wealthy. European revitalization is a perfect example of this, for while wealthy European merchants and princes were paying unprecedented sums for works of art and building palatial homes to commemorate themselves (and indulging in ever more elaborate funerals, of all things), the vast majority of people were continuing to live in the kind of abject poverty that was normal in the premodern world. "European high culture," if not an oxymoron, was at least a distinctly minority affair. One might imagine

---

[10]   Ibid., 76.
[11]   Margaret L. King, *Women of the Renaissance* (Chicago: University of Chicago Press, 1991), 239.

Florence, Italy, as a place with a high standard of living; but this was only true if we define Florence as a society limited to a few elite families and their hangers-on. Material conditions across Europe in this period were highly unstable for most people. Plague popped up frequently, though with nothing like the vicious-ness of its fourteenth-century performance. Hunger was endemic, caused by regular failures of harvests as well as war and the simple limitations of the early modern economy. As the Italian historian Piero Camporesi describes in his book *Bread of Dreams* (1996), the majority of the population lived either near starva-tion or in mortal fear of it. As a result, he argues, most people lived their lives in altered mental states—whether from hunger, the ingestion of rotten foods, or the more purposeful alcoholism, to "take the edge off" their hunger. This gives a new twist to the idea of "high culture." Alternatively, they ate poppy seeds, which were regularly rolled into the bread dough in Italian cities such as Venice, along with half-rotten vegetable matter, fermenting grains, and shop-floor sweepings, in order to get high and forget their misery for a while. Camporesi suggests that this may have been a kind of self-medication and not driven by the leadership, who might well have had incentive to keep the masses drugged: "One could doubtless regard this as having been directed not so much from above (as is sometimes supposed) as desired and sought by the masses themselves, consumed as they were by disease, hunger, nocturnal fears, and daytime obsessions."[12]

Having said that, these conditions may have represented an improvement from what came before. The period from 1450 to 1600 saw population growth in most parts of the globe. That, at the very least, means that more people were surviving into adulthood. The European population had been around 70 million in 1300. Having been devastated by the plague, by 1600 it had rebounded to reach 90 million. While growth was slow in the early decades after the plague, the survivors –especially in the southern states around the Mediterranean, such as the Italian city states—were able to benefit economically from the vibrant commercial activity of that sea, which was connected to the vast empires of Eurasia, including India and China. The popu-lations of Asian states towered over those of Europe. China had as many as 200 million people. France, with 17 million, was dwarfed by the Ottoman Empire's 25 million. India, although not completely unified territorially, had some 110 million people in 1600. These numbers made Europe relatively insignificant.

But this growing population was increasingly urban. Urbanism itself led to intensification of cultural and economic production and ultimately to what many scholars see as the beginnings of capitalism; capitalism's majordomo, Karl Marx, saw the period between 1300 to 1500 as the beginnings of capitalism proper.

---

[12] Piero Camporesi, *Bread of Dreams: Food and Fantasy in Early Modern Europe* (Chicago: Polity Press, 1989), 18.

Cities had been very much on the rise in pre-plague Europe, and these had been new entities, giving birth to distinct modes of behavior. But many of Europe's post-plague cities, in particular Florence, Venice, Genoa, and northern ones such as Antwerp and Amsterdam, were commercial centers where merchants were gaining political and economic power. The self-same merchants, and the princes and sovereigns they served (and to whom they loaned money), in turn represented a clientele for the burgeoning population of artists and scholars who were such a part of the Renaissance.

Was European revitalization, then, just a case of businessmen sponsoring artists? Certainly that was a part of it. The city of Florence commissioned Michelangelo to sculpt the biblical character David, best known to many around the world today as a fridge magnet (he chose to portray him naked, scandalizing many, even though his art referenced the style of the ancient Greeks, which legitimated it in the eyes of many). By the time the sculpture was the talk of the town the world's most famous artist was already in Rome, chasing down more lucrative assignments; he later ended up in the Ottoman sultan's palace in Istanbul, an artist for hire, willing to cross cultural barriers to work where the pay was best.

How Was the World Shrinking in This Period?

The European revitalization was a kind of cultural and economic flowering; it was a looking-back-while-moving-forward, an expression of energetic cultural output in multiple fields, resulting from population growth, cultural exchange, and increasing prosperity. But the word *global* is relevant in two main ways in any discussion about the period. The first is how European economic activity and culture were projected out from Europe via explorers and traders, who, as good Renaissance men, sallied forth to discover, conquer, and harvest the world and its riches.

We will discuss the idea of exploration in Chapter 13, but for now it will suffice to mention Prince Henry "the Navigator" of Portugal (1394–1460), Christopher Columbus (ca. 1451–1506), and Bartolomeu Dias (ca. 1451–1500). Prince Henry poured resources into maritime exploration, no doubt motivated in part by curiosity, greed for African gold and slaves, and, strangely, a desire to discover a mythic Christian king in Africa named Prester John, who, he believed, could aid Europe in its struggle against the infidel Ottoman Empire. Columbus, an Italian in the pay of the Spanish, had read the ancient Greco–Roman geographer Ptolemy (b. ca. 90 CE) and believed that if he sailed west from Portugal he would end up in China. Dias, following Henry's orders, sailed south, until he rounded the southern tip of Africa, the Cape of Good Hope, thus opening up a sea route to the east and its lucrative markets.

All of these events had incalculable consequences for world history, ultimately joining the two hemispheres and making a global history possible, for better or worse. Such events could be considered haphazard and unrelated, but that is not particularly convincing. Technical developments in shipbuilding and navigation allowed for them, and economic and demographic pressures motivated them. Ultimately, they initiated a tsunami of trade, interaction, violence, and disease, which continued for centuries. For Jacob Burkhard—one of the "inventors" of the Renaissance—Columbus was the ultimate Renaissance man, illustrating the spirit of inquiry, his exploration representing the action-oriented spirit of the time yet originating in the thoughtful pursuit of knowledge (and reading of Greek texts). Other scholars have pointed to Columbus' Christian proselytizing, instead, as evidence that he was, in fact, more medieval than modern, pursuing the glory of God, not rational knowledge. As Caferro points out, other explorers exhibited "Renaissance" characteristics as well: "Cortes [who conquered the Aztec Empire in Mexico] grandly described his deeds in his diary, in which he compared himself to Julius Caesar and Alexander the Great. His companion Bernal Diaz gave careful detail of local flora and fauna and wild animals, demonstrating a Renaissance appreciation of nature."[13] Whatever the explorer's motivation, exploration was one major part of the Renaissance's global legacy; and its consequences involved ever more global interaction.

> ☼ Whatever the explorer's motivation, exploration was one major part of the Renaissance's global legacy, and its consequences involved ever more global interaction.

WHAT PART DID NON-EUROPEAN CULTURES PLAY IN REVITALIZATION?

The other sense in which *global* applies to the period is that the European burgeoning of culture was largely spurred by contact with the East. And easterners themselves were also on the move. Looming very large in this picture is the Ottoman Empire. Large parts of northern Africa, Turkey, and the Balkans had been under the control of the Byzantine Empire until the fifteenth century. The Byzantines thought of themselves as the real Romans as they were all that remained of Rome after the empire in the west had been thoroughly routed by waves of barbarians from the fourth century onward. But in the mid-fifteenth century, the group of formerly nomadic Turkish tribes that became the Ottomans captured Constantinople.

---

[13]   Caferro, *Contesting the Renaissance*, 39.

Europe, such as it was back then, was deeply shaken by the Turkish success. Although there had been religious differences between the Byzantines and the Roman Catholics (the Fourth Crusade sacked Constantinople in 1204 and set up a Latin kingdom there until 1266), the Byzantine Empire was the last buffer against "real" infidels—Muslim Turks. For the Europeans, therefore, the Byzantines were decidedly the "devil you know." The humanist scholars—those men whispering in the ears of European princes and writing pamphlets for publication across Europe—saw the fall of Constantinople as another fall of Rome. Pope Pius II called it "a second death for Homer and a second destruction of Plato," referring to the destruction of a shared Western (Greek) heritage by foreigners. Says historian Nancy Bishara, "Hence, in the midst of a golden age of learning and the arts, Renaissance Europeans battled fears that a hostile, Islamic enemy to the east could at any moment destroy their world and hurl them back into the 'dark ages.'"[14] The Genoese merchant Jacopo de Promontorio called the sultan Mehmet II a "horrible, cruel, mad and malignant Turk" and was not alone in leveling such unflattering epithets at him.[15] Such talk was ironic, perhaps, bearing in mind that the Genoese, and de Promontorio in particular, who was a trade envoy in the Ottoman court, had long-standing trading privileges with the Ottomans before the conquest of Constantinople and were quick to reestablish commercial ties after it.

While there was, no doubt, panic at the Ottoman conquest, the notion of Europe and the "East" as two distinct entities was, to use a technical term, "fuzzy" at this point in history. East and West were both interpenetrated with each other's history and religion. Historian Jerry Brotton discusses the painting *St. Mark Preaching in Alexandria* (1504–1507) by Gentile and Giovanni Bellini from Venice. The Bellinis depict St. Mark, by tradition the founder of the Christian church in Alexandria, Egypt, preaching to an ethnically mixed crowd in that city. The buildings look simultaneously Egyptian, Byzantine, and Italian (some of Alexandria's better-known buildings, in fact, served as models for Venetian architects). None of this should come as a surprise. Artists like the Bellinis were aware that Europe's cities wanted many things from the grand, ancient empires of the east, such as Mamluk Egypt, Safavid Persia, and the Ottomans: silks, spices, carpets, porcelain, precious stones, and dyes—in addition, of course, to information. This is why the painting evokes both the Western church and the Eastern bazaar, in addition to the classical and the contemporary; the commonalities between Europe and the "East" were considerable, the boundaries fluid.

---

[14] Nancy Bishara, *Creating East and West: Renaissance Humanists and the Ottoman Turks* (Philadelphia: University of Pennsylvania Press, 2004), 2.

[15] Quoted in Ebru Boyar and Kate Fleet, *A Social History of Ottoman Istanbul* (Cambridge: Cambridge University Press, 2010), 8.

Bellini, Giovanni (ca. 1429–1516) and Gentile (ca. 1429–1507), *St. Mark Preaching in Alexandria*   The Bellinis created a vision of Alexandria in which buildings and people represented a cultural and ethnic mix of East and West, suggesting how each influenced the other at this time.

In the post-Mongol and post-plague years, trade had increased between Europe and points east. Alexandria, being the terminus of the Red Sea trade, bringing goods from India and China, was well known to many in Genoa, Venice, and Florence, which had fought each other over access to its riches. They established trading posts there and in other eastern cities, such as Aleppo and Damascus in modern-day Syria. Painters such as the Bellinis of Venice owed much to certain commodities that came to Europe via the eastern bazaars. Lapis lazuli, vermilion, and cinnabar—pigments that gave the Renaissance painters their brilliant blues and reds—were all imported from the east via Venice. While such commodities revolutionized painting, architecture from cities such as Cairo, Damascus, and Aleppo, among others, directly influenced European tastes. The Rialto market in Venice shows a marked resemblance to certain quarters of Aleppo, Syria's trading entrepôt.

Trade may not be sufficient to break down cultural barriers between people, but notwithstanding European fears, was Mehmet II really as devilish as he was often portrayed? In reality, even as he directed the siege of Constantinople he had scholars read to him daily from the same authorities that appealed so much to the Italian humanists—Herodotus and Livy, among others. Rather than destroy books, Mehmet established a great library, still in existence today, in the Topkapi Palace in Istanbul. Rather than destroy the city, he built edifices reflecting his imperial authority. Ever on the lookout for business opportunities, Venice and Genoa quickly established trading relations with him, and the doge (duke) of Venice wrote letters of friendship to the "Turkish emperor." In 1479 the doge "permitted" Gentile Bellini to work for Mehmet, an example of the considerable cultural as well as economic back-and-forth between Europe and the Ottomans. Historians even question the extent to which historical actors of the time really thought of themselves as absolutely different and separate, as Brotton says: "There were no clear geographical or political barriers east and west in the 15th century. It is a much later, 19th century, belief in the absolute cultural and political separation of the Islamic East and the Christian West that has obscured these two cultures."[16] All this is to say that there was more in common between the Europeans and the Ottomans at this time than has traditionally been supposed.

HOW DID BUSINESS CHANGE?

Historians argue endlessly over whether the plague initiated a prolonged economic slump, which would seem to be at odds with the apparent flowering of everything else in this period. But in many trading cities wealth became more concentrated, adhering especially to merchant families. These people began to spend lavishly and were responsible for much of the conspicuous consumption that was a hallmark of European economic success. Just as in the art world business was open to outside influences. The Pisan merchant known as Fibonacci (1170–1250), used his commercial exposure to Arabic–Islamic culture to write a series of books on math. Working for his father in Algeria, he was instructed in Arabic–Hindu numerals and calculations: "I enjoyed so much the instruction that I later continued to study mathematics while on business trips to Egypt, Syria, Greece, Sicily, and Provence and there enjoyed discussions and disputations with the scholars of those places."[17]

Hindu–Arabic numerals, he realized, were superior for calculating profit and loss. Basic symbols, such as those for addition (+) subtraction (–), and multiplication (×), were unknown in Europe before Fibonacci, yet the Arabs had been using them for centuries. The Arabic term *al jabru* is the origin of the English word *algebra*. A key figure in the history of mathematics was the Persian astronomer Abu Ja'far Muhammad ibn Musa al-Khwarizmi, whose mangled named in Latin languages gave us *algorithm*—without which there would be no Google. Merchants, dealing with bills of exchange—the earliest form of paper money—used the term *check*, which was another bastardization of an Arabic term, *sakk*. Commerce and business, therefore, were the media through which much cross-cultural exchange occurred in the fifteenth and sixteenth centuries, and such exchange influenced the cultural and intellectual lives of all involved.

---

[16] Brotton, *The Renaissance Bazaar*, 53.
[17] Ibid., 43.

WAS THERE AN OTTOMAN REVITALIZATION?

As we have seen, the Ottomans, like the Italians and other Europeans, enjoyed considerable material prosperity in the period following the fall of Constantinople. Along with it came a cultural flowering not unlike that in Europe. This reached its apex under the sultan Suleyman I (r. 1520–1566), known as "the Magnificent" in the West and "the Lawgiver" to the Ottomans. Suleyman more than doubled the area under Ottoman control (suggesting that he should have been known as "the Conqueror," perhaps) but is remembered most for the cultural productivity during his reign. This period had a lasting impact on Turkish art, especially in the material realm: illuminated manuscripts, inlaid woodwork, decorated armaments, tapestries, silk work, and much more.

At the heart of Suleyman's empire, which stretched from Iran to Austria, was Topkapi Palace, which housed his centralized administration. Attached to the palace were numerous workshops for craftspeople and artists, collectively known as the *Ehl-I Hiref,* or "Community of the Talented." This community was made up of dozens of societies of trades and crafts, from leatherworking to gunsmiths, calligraphers to goldsmiths, glassworkers to weavers. The sultan himself was a trained goldsmith, owing to the tradition that the sovereign should have a practical trade. Such centralization of artistic production had a profound effect on the

Suleyman the Lawgiver, known to admiring Europeans as "the Magnificent," presided over the largest expansion of Ottoman territory and a cultural efflorescence, not unlike Europe's Renaissance.

by Titian
1530
Venetian artist

rest of the empire, to which arts and crafts radiated from the center in Istanbul, producing a distinct "Ottoman" style, even if its artists were, variously, from Egypt, northern Africa, Turkey, or Iran.

If the Europeans were having a revitalization, surely the Ottomans were too, especially given that they clearly shared a cultural–economic region with Europe at the time. "During the long sixteenth century," says historian Walter Andrews,

> from approximately 1453 to 1625, Ottoman Turkish culture burgeoned spectacularly, paralleling the broader burgeoning of culture(s) in Europe commonly called "The Renaissance." ... In very general terms, many of the social and material conditions—everything from economics, agriculture, and labor, to modes of rule, demographics, trade, climate, and public health—that made the European Renaissance possible also existed in the Ottoman empire, and had very similar social and cultural consequences.[18]

Yet no one talks about an Ottoman Renaissance. This is partly because European historians wrote much of the history of the Ottoman Empire and reserved the term *Renaissance* for their own culture; they depicted the Ottomans, on the other hand, as a dying Islamic culture, for which a rebirth seemed like an undesirable turn of events.

Just as urbanization in Europe played a large role in the European expansion, so it was central to Ottoman power and influence. A well-established trading power even before they conquered Constantinople, the Ottomans continued this trend afterward. Mehmet II developed more commercial links, making his new city, as historian Lisa Jardine puts it, a "valve through which goods flowed to and from the oriental markets in the east and the Europeans markets in the west."[19] He also forcibly repopulated the new city with ethnically diverse inhabitants: "He gathered them there from all parts of Asia and Europe, and he transferred them with all possible care and speed, people of all nations, but especially Christians. So profound was the passion that came into his soul for the city and its peopling, and for bringing it back to its former prosperity."[20] Such a repopulating would, Mehmet believed, make it a true cosmopolitan city, a capital to impress Ottomans and foreigners alike.

Politics also played a front-and-center role during this period. Historians have traditionally represented the Ottoman sultans as despotic and Ottoman

---

[18] Walter G. Andrews, "Suppressed Renaissance: Q: When Is a Renaissance Not a Renaissance? A: When It Is the Ottoman Renaissance!" In *Other Renaissances: A New Approach to World Literature*, ed. Brenda Deen Schildgen, Gang Zhou, and Sander L. Gilman (New York: Palgrave Macmillan, 2006), 17.

[19] Lisa Jardine, *Worldly Goods: A New History of the Renaissance* (New York: W.W. Norton, 1996), 37.

[20] Asikpasazade, quoted in Boyar and Fleet, *A Social History of Ottoman Istanbul*, 26.

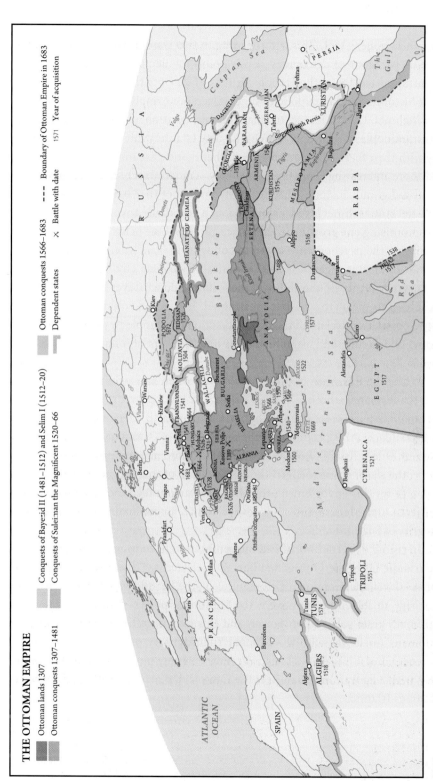

THE OTTOMAN EMPIRE

Ottoman lands 1307	Conquests of Bayezid II (1481–1512) and Selim I (1512–20)
Ottoman conquests 1307–1481	Conquests of Suleiman the Magnificent 1520–66
	Ottoman conquests 1566–1683
	Dependent states

--- Boundary of Ottoman Empire in 1683

× Battle with date   1571 Year of acquisition

MAP 12.3   THE OTTOMAN EMPIRE   The Ottoman Empire saw considerable expansion through the fifteenth and sixteenth centuries, which continued into the seventeenth. In 1683 its troops were defeated outside Vienna, and this is often taken as the turning of the Ottoman tide.

457

politics as nonexistent. This is misleading in two ways. First, European leaders were no paragons of democracy at this point; intellectuals such as Machiavelli often supported the authoritarian regimes of despots themselves. Second, the track history of Ottoman policies suggests a more complicated story. For example, Mehmet II was forced to abandon his taxation plans after conquering Constantinople as the population of the new Istanbul voted against them, literally with their feet—they left the city. Other reports are more "exotic," perhaps, and more interesting than taxation policy. Traders (such as de Promontorio) circulated ghoulish stories that fit the stereotype of the "barbarous Turk." One reported how Mehmet loved melons so much he forbade anyone eating a particularly promising one growing in the palace gardens. One of his boy servants ate it, prompting the psychopathic sultan to cut open 14 boys' stomachs (finding it in the last one). But regardless of the stories of violence (by no means alien to Renaissance princes!), the ability of the sultan to do whatever he liked with or to his subjects appears to have been restrained. "No sultan could rule in disregard of the population of Istanbul, and the reactions of people in the streets had an impact on the ruler and his ministers even to the point of influencing the choice of ruler."[21]

While the Renaissance powers of Europe often had a complex relationship with the Roman Catholic Church, resisting it as their power grew, the Ottomans appointed themselves the guardians of the Islamic faith. One major development in consolidating this position was the recognition of Ottoman supremacy by the *sharif* of Mecca, Islam's holiest city, in 1517. While maintaining some independence, the *sharif* acknowledged the overlordship of the Ottoman sultan; and in exchange for this endorsement, the Ottomans guaranteed the pilgrimage routes to Mecca and Medina and took responsibility for maintaining the territorial integrity of Islamic lands.

In ruling over traditional Islamic centers and becoming the commander of the Islamic faith, the Ottoman sultan was referred as "The Shadow of God on Earth." Given the prominent Ottoman role in the Islamic world, it was necessary for them to look like they were the legitimate power. Cynics will say that legitimacy rests solely upon power, and this may have been the case with the Ottomans (as it was with the Mongol Yuan dynasty or the Medici family of Florence); but it has always been necessary for brute power to dress itself, modestly, with a fig leaf. In this respect the Ottomans strove to have the last word in all things Islamic.

---

[21]   Ibid., 42.

WHAT DID MING CHINA HAVE IN COMMON WITH EUROPE?

But the Ottoman Empire was far from the only power to exert far-reaching influence. Nor was it the only one experiencing something of a golden age. "During the 276 years of the Ming from 1368 to 1644 China's population doubled, from about 80 million to about 160 million. Destructive domestic warfare was largely avoided, and great achievements in education and philosophy, literature and art, reflected the high cultural level of the elite gentry society."[22] So say historians John King Fairbank and Merle Goldman. Was this, then, similar to what

Dragons feature prominently in Chinese art, as in history. In politically uncertain times, sightings of dragons foretold of heaven's disapproval. The Ming, however, witnessed nearly three centuries of relative peace and prosperity.

---

[22]   John King Fairbank and Merle Goldman, *China: A New History* (Cambridge, MA: Harvard University Press, 2006), 128.

happened in Europe? Was it just a golden age like the Ottomans? Historians will no doubt argue it was both and neither—simultaneously. And they would probably be right. There were elements of what you might call the "*very* long sixteenth century" in China that mirrored the European and Ottoman experience. And then there are key areas where China and Europe differed.

Most historians of China see the Song dynasty (960–1279) as more deserving of the word *Renaissance*. In that era China experienced population growth, imperial authority extended farther than ever, technological achievements revolutionized food production and preindustrial processes, and intellectual achievements were as prodigious as Italy's would be later: "Florence in 1500 was crowded with geniuses, moving comfortably between art, literature and politics, but so was Kaifeng in 1100."[23] Like da Vinci in Florence, Shen Kuo (1031–1095) was a Song dynasty statesman whose expertise and learning encompassed mathematics, literature, geology, astronomy, calligraphy, zoology, botany, cartography, agronomy, archeology, ethnography, and finance, among other disciplines. His accomplishments included serving as the minister of astronomy, designing water clocks and pumps for draining thousands of acres of swamps, as well as negotiating treaties with the ever-threatening nomads of the northern frontier. A true "polymath," he was adept in warfare, policymaking, and the fine arts. Like the Europeans, Song emperors looked for ways to continually legitimate their rule and in this endeavor looked back to Confucian texts, like the Europeans who would later look back to Classical ones.

> ☀ Like the Europeans, Song emperors looked for ways to continually legitimate their rule and in this endeavor looked back to Confucian texts, like the Europeans who would later look back to Classical ones.

But contemporary with European revitalization was the Ming dynasty (1368–1644). The origins of the Ming ("Brilliant") dynasty are not so different from those of the Song. Disunity and conflict characterized the period immediately preceding the Ming, following the collapse of the Mongol Yuan dynasty (1271–1368). The need for legitimacy was also front and center, partly because with such a large country there were always challenges to the central government. But there were also specific challenges to China at this time. Historian Timothy Brook paints a picture of China in this period, which, among other challenges, had to endure the Little Ice Age: "Buffeted by weather anomalies, troubled by the insistent presence of foreign traders in their offshore waters, some people clung to past precedents for guidance. Others cast those precedents aside to conceive of new ways to organize the world and find a place for themselves in it."[24] Both of these strategies could have been applied to the humanists of Europe, who were also struggling to explain their rapidly changing world.

---

[23] Morris, *Why the West Rules*, 419.
[24] Timothy Brook, *The Troubled Empire: China in the Yuan and Ming Dynasties* (Cambridge, MA: Harvard University Press, 2010), 1.

In many ways the Ming have even better credentials than the Song for Renaissance status, if only because they were the dynasty that followed nearly a century of hated Mongol rule. The Ming founder, Zhu Yuanzhang (r. 1368–1398), was an orphan at birth and grew up as an impoverished peasant educated by Buddhist monks. After fighting with numerous rebel bands and gangs of outlaws during the series of civil wars accompanying Yuan decline, Zhu began to stitch together an increasingly large territory. Eventually, he felt the time had come to cast modesty aside, name himself *Hongwu* ("Vast Military Power"), and proclaim himself emperor. As Brook describes it, "For most Chinese, 1368 is a key moment in the history of these four centuries, for this is the year in which Zhu's ingenious rebel regime drove out the hated Mongols and re-established China as the realm that the Chinese have come to call 'the Fatherland.'"[25] Historians generally see the Ming as the beginning of China's path to modernity—as the Europeans see their Renaissance. Surely, then, this is a rebirth.

In many ways it was. Confucianism was reestablished as the imperial ideology (a kind of Neo-Neo-Confucianism). This ideology was exemplified by the scholar-bureaucrat Wang Yangming (1472–1529). He was the principal figure behind the Neo-Confucian School of Mind, a school which followed the teachings of Mencius (b. ca. 372 BCE), an earlier Confucian scholar. Like the European scholar-bureaucrats of the time, Wang Yangming was a polymath, quite comfortable in the halls of power, on the battlefield, or in a library. This ideological repositioning occurred during a period of state consolidation as the Ming looked to centralize their control. Commerce, always a major activity in China (regardless of Confucian hostility toward it), benefited from increasing territorial unity and a growing population. The trend toward greater commerce was a continuation of Yuan experience and reflected the age-old Chinese love of material objects; says Brook, "The Yuan and Ming were awash in things. . . . These things were as simple as a chopstick or as common as a teapot, as finely crafted as an eggshell-thin teacup from the Chenghua era (1465–1487) or as elaborate as a sheet of jade carved with miniscule figures playing on a cloud-strewn landscape."[26]

Along with the increase in trade came an increase in urban life. Just as in Europe, population growth and increasing prosperity contributed to an increase in the size of cities. They grew as centers for manufacturing, markets, and residences for the elite. Beijing, with a population of over 500,000, was both a political and a commercial hub. Nanjing boasted up to 700,000 in 1400. Shanghai and Suzhou both had around 1 million people, the former being a major cotton nexus

---

[25] Ibid.
[26] Ibid., 196.

and the latter, the commercial and cultural center of the entire empire. And it was largely commerce that drove this process of growth, more than administration, which was also a contributor.

So far China seems to have had much in common with Renaissance-era Europe and the Ottoman Near East. But Ming trade differed greatly from its European, Indian, Arab, and Turkish counterparts. The Mongols had been keen on trade, although Khubilai Khan (1215–1294) had closed trade with Japan, having failed to conquer the island several times. But he sent naval fleets into southeast Asia, with conquest in mind; and in their wake came Chinese merchants. Merchants on the Yangtze delta built vast ships and traveled to Japan regardless of government prohibitions. But the Yuan were somewhat schizophrenic in their policy on maritime trade, reflecting perhaps their deep ambivalence about the influence of foreigners. In 1289 they imposed a government monopoly on ocean voyages (to earn revenue). They imposed a complete ban on ocean voyaging in 1303 and lifted it in 1307, having nearly destroyed China's coastal economy. For the next decade the ban was lifted and reimposed several times. The Yuan's ability to control this trade may have been limited however, and foreign merchants still profited greatly from coastal trade, while establishing multiple trading posts on Chinese soil.

The Hongwu emperor was more interested in tribute than trade however. He received embassies from foreign rulers and gladly accepted the goods they offered: "I accept them because they come from far away and show the sincerity of distant peoples."[27] But his attitude to merchants was decidedly negative. He did not think it necessary for anyone to travel more than 8 miles from home. Travel 35 and you would receive a whipping. Contrast this with the globe-trotting Italian merchants, and you begin to see a major cultural difference. But the third Ming emperor, Yongle (r. 1402–1424), took a different approach. Instead of waiting for tribute to come to him, he sent out fleets to make diplomatic contact with foreigners and collect their tribute.

On the surface, Yongle's plan might have resembled Prince Henry the Navigator's, if you substitute tribute for trade; but it could not have been more different. The Chinese voyages ultimately ceased after a few decades, and instead of initiating major, irreversible historical change, they were terminated and their legacy was hidden—by Confucian bureaucrats who considered them a waste of money. The "treasure fleets" did not ultimately make it to Europe, much less America, even if it was entirely within their capability to make such enormous voyages.

These were by far the biggest fleets in history to date, representing what Ian Morris calls the "grandest projection of state power the world had ever seen."[28]

---

[27] Emperor Hongwu, quoted in Morris, *Why the West Rules*, 406.
[28] Ibid., 408.

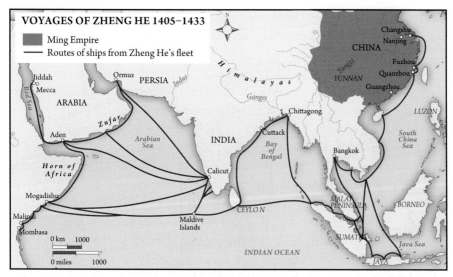

MAP 12.4 **VOYAGES OF ZHENG HE** The Ming voyages of exploration reached as far as the east coast of Africa. But ultimately they were deemed unsupportable. The Chinese already had a large and fertile trade zone in the Indian Ocean, and this provided well for them.

Yongle assembled 25,000 top craftspeople in boatyards in Nanjing. To acquire the lumber, they clear-cut entire forests and floated the trees down the Yangtze. The fleets themselves were made up of more than 300 vessels (compare Columbus' 3), many of them 300 feet long. The fleet was run by a crew of over 27,000 sailors and commanded by Yongle's chief (Muslim) eunuch, Zheng-He. Between 1405 and 1433, Zheng-He conducted seven voyages and is believed to have reached Ceylon, Mecca, and eastern Africa. After Yongle's death, the voyages suffered a similar fate to coastal trade in general, voyages being banned, then permitted again, then banned again, until by 1500 the ships lay rotting in their yards, unable to venture forth even if allowed.

If we were to practice the "what-if" school of history, we might be inclined to ponder what the world would currently look like if Zheng-He had been allowed to continue his voyages and take his ships farther afield. Would he have "discovered" America instead of Columbus? Would New Yorkers be speaking Chinese? (New Beijing?) Would the Incas have fallen to Chinese soldiers, not Spanish conquistadores?

Why did the Chinese cease the explorations? The most likely cause is not the "conservative ideology" of the Ming, as some scholars have argued. It is more likely that the Chinese halted their travels for rational, economic reasons. While for the Europeans all the world's riches lay elsewhere, China saw itself (not unrealistically) as the center of the world. While the Europeans were spurred by commercial interest to go west and east, the Chinese could rely on foreign goods

Ming ships dwarfed later European ships   But ultimately the Chinese did not find it economical to send them around the world. The world came to them instead.

coming to them. Geography put the Chinese much farther from the New World, even had they the desire to explore. They had a large and profitable trading zone already on their doorstep in the Indian Ocean, full of Indian and Arab traders visiting their coast. Emperor Yongle, as one of the first Ming leaders, had a rational incentive to send "diplomatic" fleets into the Indian Ocean to gather tribute and "meet the neighbors." Subsequent leaders did not have such an incentive; the voyages had accomplished their goal, establishing them as the regional heavy hitters. Extending voyages into the Pacific provided no guaranteed returns, yet promised gargantuan costs. Given the Chinese preference for tribute and the fact that foreign merchants already came to China, was it any surprise that while the up-and-coming European states were feverishly looking for more money to buy better weapons to use against each other, the Chinese closed in on themselves? Historians Fairbank and Goldman may be partly right that "anticommercialism and xenophobia won out, and China retired from the world scene,"[29] but such a retirement might also have been the result of rational policies, which saw no tangible benefits in global exploration.

---

[29]   Fairbank and Goldman, *China*, 132.

What Is the Role of "Cultural Producers"?

He who forgets his past cannot understand the present.

SONGHAY PROVERB

So far we have seen that certain characteristics that we might associate with revitalization were present in several places in Eurasia in the period under question: urbanism, economic prosperity, the need to reorient, and a tendency to look to the past in order to do so, in a changing, and even *globalizing*, world.

One major element during this time was the way in which "cultural producers" articulated their sense of the times. But different societies have very different cultural producers—whether they be historians, writers, artists, singers, or storytellers. While elite intellectuals in several societies turned to ancient texts to explain the present and find a "way forward," other societies did not have this option. The western African empire of Songhay (mid-fifteenth to late sixteenth centuries) is a case in point.

Trade and interconnectedness were distinct hallmarks of the western African kingdoms and empires of this period and had been for a long time. As Eric Wolf puts it,

> Africa south of the Sahara was not the isolated, backward area of European imagination, but an integral part of a web of relations that connected forest cultivators and miners with savanna and desert traders and with the merchants and rulers of the north African settled belt.... When the Europeans would enter West Africa from the coast, they would be setting foot in country already dense with towns and settlements, and caught up in networks of exchange that far transcended the narrow enclaves of the European emporia of the coast.[30]

In this sense at least, Songhay shared characteristics with the other Eurasian players of this period as noted cities played a major role here, such as the trading entrepôts of Timbuktu, Gao, and Jenne. Several hundred years of Muslim influence had, together with trade, solidified western Africa's ties with the Islamic world, and European exploration along the western African coast represented another avenue of connectivity. The empire building of the early Songhay leadership had sewn together a diverse group of peoples—traders, farmers, river people, and nomads. But Songhay did not have ancient texts, such as the ones to which the Chinese or Europeans looked for guidance. Although a

---

[30] Wolf, *Europe and the People Without History*, 40.

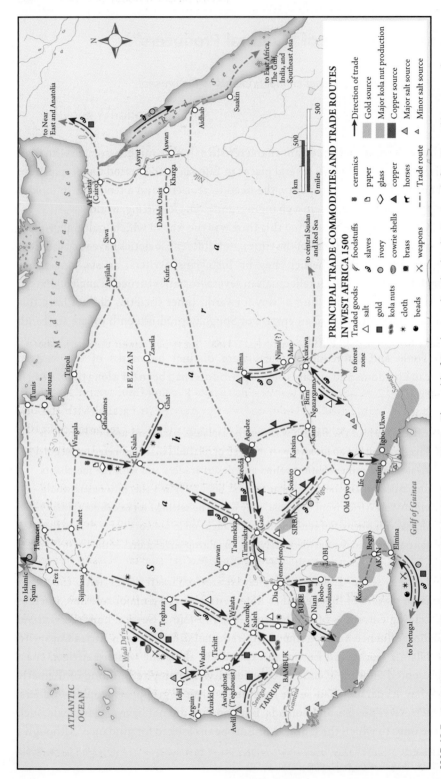

PRINCIPAL TRADE COMMODITIES AND TRADE ROUTES IN WEST AFRICA 1500

Traded goods:

△ salt	🥖 foodstuffs	🏺 ceramics
■ gold	ᨣ slaves	📄 paper
ᨣ kola nuts	○ ivory	◇ glass
✳ cloth	🐚 cowrie shells	▲ copper
● beads	✕ weapons	⋌ brass
		⌇ horses

→ Direction of trade
Gold source
Major kola nut production
Copper source
△ Major salt source
▲ Minor salt source
‒ ‒ Trade route

MAP 12.5 COMMODITIES AND TRADE IN WEST AFRICA, ca. 1500 The wealth of Songhay was directly related to its control of ancient and lucrative trade routes linking different ecological niches such as northern Africa, the coast, sub-Saharan Africa, and the Nile valley.

Today's Timbuktu, Conquered by Sonni Ali Ber in 1468   The tension between Islam and traditional belief systems was central to Mali, as it still is today.

literary tradition developed in cities like Timbuktu and Gao, it came along with the region's conversion to Islam and always existed in parallel with the oral traditions of the Songhay people. Oral traditions were not recorded in books, nor was there a long tradition of written commentary on politics, philosophy, religion, or other cultural matters.

Nonetheless, history, politics, and religion all found a place, as they do to this day, in African oral tradition. And there was nothing anecdotal or haphazard about this; the *marabouts*, or Islamic scholars, of northern and western Africa are part of an organized lineage of specialists who receive the traditions from their seniors and pass them on to their juniors. Malian scholar Hassimi Oumarou Maiga describes the lineage of one such *marabout*, who is the grandson of 34 grandfathers, all of whom have been *marabouts*, many from Goa, the political capital of the Songhay Empire. Such a genealogy qualifies a *marabout* to tell stories, such as that of the origins of the Songhay kingdom (which later became an empire). As Maiga records one tradition, "At that time, (the kingdom of) Koukya, which extended as far as Dahomey (Benin today), and whose capital was Bentia, was administered by Koungorogossi Gariko. He was the son of Gariko Mallenke Songhoy."[31]

---

[31]   Hassimi Oumarou Maiga, *Balancing Written History with Oral Tradition: The Legacy of the Songhoy People* (New York: Routledge, 2010), 34.

In the fifteenth century, however, as the Songhay Empire was reaching the apex of its power, Islamic scholars, many from the city of Timbuktu, began recording the histories of their time in written form. The fact that they were Muslim is of paramount significance here; Islam is a literary religion, one that places great importance on the written word. These histories told the story of the rise of Sonni Ali Ber (r. 1464–1492) and the Askiya dynasty that followed him. Sonni Ali Ber had come from Goa and had conquered the elite (largely Muslim) trading town of Timbuktu in 1468. From here he continued to campaign along the Niger River, using boats to ferry his troops and taking trading towns and cities such as Jenne and Walata. However, there is disagreement among Malians even today as to who was the true "founder" of the Songhay Empire. As we have noted, one of the main themes of the histories is the relationship between Islam and the traditional, pre-Islamic animist religion, which orthodox Muslims regarded as little more than sorcery. Many from Timbuktu believe that Sonni Ali Ber was more aligned with the pre-Islamic traditions and, in fact, persecuted Muslims. Muhammad Askiya, they believe, was the real founder of Songhay. Other people, in particular from cities such as Kukiya, see Sonni Ali Ber as the true founder of the empire and a great sorcerer (who happened to also be a Muslim). The tension between Islamic and animist traditions continues today, as historian Christopher Wise puts it: "In modern-day Timbuktu, the Muslim population continues to venerate the Askiya Muhammad for his piety and for his respect for Islam, whereas the citizens of Gao tend to view him as a great sorcerer."[32]

The writers of the histories (*ta'rikh* in Arabic) tended to be Muslims, many from Timbuktu, while the oral storytellers, *marabouts* and *griots*, tended to be animists. The authors of books such as the *Ta'rikh al fattash* might well be comparable to England's Thomas More or Italy's Machiavelli, who both wrote historical/political works with decidedly political motivations. In the histories we plainly see the contemporary concerns of the historians and a less than objective tone betraying their sycophancy to those in power. Here is the author of the *Ta'rikh al fattash*, the Muslim Hajj Mahmud Kati (b. 1468), praising the Askiya Muhammad, the ruler of the Songhay at the time of the book's writing:

> In the midst of our darkness and obscurity this great prince brought the light of the true faith to shine upon us. He directed us towards the path of

---

[32]   *Ta'rikh al fattash: The Timbuktu Chronicles 1493–1599*, ed. and trans. Christopher Wise (London, Africa World Press, 2011), xiv.

righteousness and extirpated our errors and inequities. Thanks be to God, he subjugated princes and emissaries from far and wide. Some of these submitted to him one-by-one, others in large groups.[33]

As we have seen in the cases of China and the Ottoman Empire, leaders have to constantly legitimize their rule. But as we have also seen repeatedly in this volume, the written word plays a very prominent role in history, particularly in the legitimating process. What anthropologist Jack Goody has called the "tyranny of the text" means that histories that are recorded in books often have the last word. Books, and literature in general, played a very important role in the early modern world, especially in Europe's Renaissance. But oral traditions, such as those of the Songhay, clearly functioned in similar ways to written texts, as a means to legitimate the present. While the Songhay produced textual history, those histories drew upon the ancient oral traditions that preceded them, often reproducing much of the material that was circulated by word of mouth. But because such historical writing was more associated with the elite Muslim communities within the empire, it naturally reflected their point of view.

> But oral traditions, such as those of the Songhay, clearly functioned in similar ways to written texts, as a means to legitimate the present.

What Relevance Does This Period Have for Nonstate Societies?

It would be as well to remember at this point that only what we are calling "state societies" could even be in a position to have a revitalization. The main reason for this is related to literacy and the above-mentioned cultural producers, neither of which pertain to nonstate societies. Most, in other words, do not preserve their histories in writing; and although they have cultural producers, these tend to be oral in nature and are therefore more difficult to trace historically. In the fifteenth century, most people on earth did not live in state societies. Even those who did had only marginal dealings with the authorities since the medieval and early modern states had far less power over their populations than do modern states. Living in the outer reaches of the Ottoman, Ming, or Songhay Empires, one might see evidence of the empire only every few years—usually in the form of some tax collector.

---

[33] Ibid., 24.

But the alternatives to state societies were hunter–gatherer bands and other nomadic, pastoralist groups. These inhabited large territories in agriculturally marginal locations. In the far north, the Inuit hunter–gatherers occupied large parts of what is now Greenland and northern Canada. Farther south, in today's United States, tribal groups made up the bulk of human societies; even though urban centers had flourished previously in Cahokia and Chaco Canyon, these were long gone by 1500. And farther south, in Central and South America, although states had existed since Olmec times, nonstate groups were also very common. In parts of Africa where Bantu farmers had not settled, hunter–gatherers occupied the Kalahari Desert in the south and the jungles and rain forests of central and western Africa. In the Pacific, tribal societies existed in hundreds of islands and archipelagos, most of which did not reach what anthropologists and political scientists would call "states" for several hundred years. The same is true of Australia, Tasmania, and the islands of New Zealand and New Guinea, which were all occupied by hunter–gatherer tribal peoples, practitioners of the "Old Way."

A large section of southeast Asia was similarly devoid of state control until the nineteenth century and after. This area is largely, like many other nonstate regions, inhospitable to the state because its mountainous geography makes the projection of state power challenging. Like deserts, jungles, and frozen tundra, it is impossible to march giant armies into this terrain, let alone resupply troops. Historian Willem van Schendel coined the term *Zomia* to describe this area, deriving from several Tibetan–Burmese languages (*Zo* meaning "remote" and *Mi* meaning "people"); this area comprised parts of today's Burma, Tibet, Vietnam, China, Bangladesh, Thailand, Nepal, Afghanistan, and Pakistan, among others. Many of these areas are still beyond state control, such as Pakistan's infamous Northwest Frontier Province, a haven for the Taliban. In the 1300s, the eastern parts of this area became something of a refuge from the civilizing power of China's early Ming dynasty. People, in other words, retreated from the state into hard-to-reach regions where governments could not penetrate and tribal life could continue.

Prestate societies, therefore, are not just waiting to be "civilized" but have actively sought out places where the state cannot reach them.

Anthropologist James C. Scott, who has written about Zomia (see Chapter 10), argues that these tribal societies are not "our living ancestors," that is to say, simply "prestate," but that they have actively chosen not to develop state institutions as a conscious act of resistance. For all of its much vaunted civilization, he argues, the state is actually a form of repression, involving taxation, forced labor, and serfdom. Prestate societies, therefore, are not just waiting to be "civilized" but have actively sought out places where the state cannot reach them.

In this context, the characteristics of a Renaissance or revitalization—urbanism, prosperity through trade, cultural exchange, and ideological revisionism—are all largely irrelevant to the Zomias of the world. However, the nonstate societies were often influenced by large states; a case in point here are the nomads who frequently threatened China's northern borders. Referred to by anthropologist Thomas Barfield as "shadow empires," such societies on the borders of large states often expanded and contracted as the state did. Expanding states, such as those under the Ming or Song, usually created larger shadow empires in the steppes as the nomads benefited from trade with the expanding state. Such nonstates have often been assumed to have "no history," to have existed unchanged for centuries. In reality, of course, these societies, like all others, have changed, the specific changes being known only in the oral traditions of each society and being largely undocumented.

Conclusion: Was There a Global Renaissance?

We cannot talk about a "global Renaissance" for the simple reason that in the fifteenth century nothing was global. However, the period from the beginning of the fifteenth to the end of the sixteenth centuries does give us the first glimpses of truly global interaction, if for no other reason than the divide between Eurasia and the Americas is permanently bridged (in 1492). Now it is possible to speak about "world history."

In many ways the idea of a renaissance is as old as history. All societies experience new developments; all of them look over their shoulders for a sense of continuity or to retrieve something they feel they may have lost along the way. Clearly, then, the Europeans were not alone in this. The notion of "renaissance" is a universal one, even if the term itself originated in Europe in the nineteenth century to explain revitalization. Whether or not the entire globe experienced a renaissance in this period is doubtful, although many societies experienced some of the attributes that are often associated with it. Looking deeply into the realities of the Renaissance shows us that history is ultimately about rhetoric; historians create stories, some of them more persuasive than others, but many of which take on the luster of reality, according to how many people subscribe to them and for how long.

Words to Think About

Bourgeoisie	Griots	Periodization
Presentism	Renaissance humanism	

Questions to Think About

- In what ways did Renaissance European women benefit or not from the Renaissance?
- Is the Renaissance a meaningful historical period?
- Which Chinese dynasty has a better claim to its own Renaissance, the Ming or the Song?
- In what ways did the Songhay Empire represent a Renaissance?

Primary Sources

Ta'rikh al fattash: *The Timbuktu Chronicles 1493–1599*. Edited and translated by Christopher Wise. London: Africa World Press, 2011.

Secondary Sources

Andrews, Walter G. "Suppressed Renaissance: Q: When Is a Renaissance Not a Renaissance? A: When It Is the Ottoman Renaissance!" In *Other Renaissances: A New Approach to World Literature*, edited by Brenda Deen Schildgen, Gang Zhou, and Sander L. Gilman, pp. 17–34. New York: Palgrave Macmillan, 2006.

Bishara, Nancy. *Creating East and West: Renaissance Humanists and the Ottoman Turks*. Philadelphia: University of Pennsylvania Press, 2004.

Bowsma, William J. "The Renaissance and the Drama of Western History." In *A Usable Past: Essays in European Cultural History*. Berkeley: University of California Press, 1990.

Boyar, Ebru, and Kate Fleet. *A Social History of Ottoman Istanbul*. Cambridge: Cambridge University Press, 2010.

Brook, Timothy. *The Troubled Empire: China in the Yuan and Ming Dynasties*. Cambridge, MA: Harvard University Press, 2010.

Brotton, Jerry. *The Renaissance Bazaar: From the Silk Road to Michelangelo*. New York: Oxford University Press, 2002.

Caferro, William. *Contesting the Renaissance*. Malden, MA: Wiley-Blackwell, 2011.

Camporesi, Piero. *Bread of Dreams: Food and Fantasy in Early Modern Europe*. Chicago: Polity Press, 1989.

Fairbank, John King, and Merle Goldman. *China: A New History*. Cambridge, MA: Harvard University Press, 2006.

Jardine, Lisa. *Worldly Goods: A New History of the Renaissance*. New York: W.W. Norton, 1996.

Kelley-Gadol, Joan. "Did Women Have a Renaissance?" In *Becoming Visible: Women in European History*, edited by Renate Bridental, Claudia Koonz, and Susan Stuard, 2nd ed. Boston: Houghton Mifflin, 1987.

King, Margaret L. *Women of the Renaissance*. Chicago: University of Chicago Press, 1991.

Maiga, Hassimi Oumarou. *Balancing Written History with Oral Tradition: The Legacy of the Songhoy People*. New York: Routledge, 2010.

Morris, Ian. *Why the West Rules—For Now: The Patterns of History and What They Tell Us About the Future*. New York: Farrar, Strauss and Giroux, 2011.

Wolf, Eric. *Europe and the People Without History*. Berkeley: University of California Press, 1982.

For additional resources, including maps, primary sources, and visuals, web links, and quizzes, please go to **www.oup.com/us/cole**

Fateful Encounter One of the most significant encounters in world history, Spaniard Hernán Cortés meets Aztec emperor Moctezuma. Nothing would be the same after this.

Chapter 13

What Changed in Global Interactions Between 1450 and 1750?

Strangers from the East

They came across the ocean, from the east. No one knew what to make of early reports: who were these strange-looking men with pale, hairy faces, riding in vast, dark boats with decorated sails? Were they men or gods or demons? At first they appeared in the islands, and the reports did not bode well; the strangers were very curious. They were unnaturally interested in gold. They had strange, powerful, exploding sticks; huge deer that they rode; dogs of enormous size. Their language was an incoherent babbling.

Then they appeared on the mainland. They fought with the local people, killing many. The emperor sent ambassadors to them with gifts of gold and silver. The strange men wanted more gold because they had a sickness of the heart cured only by it. They spoke of their king across the ocean and of the high god they worshipped who, they claimed, was the god of all peoples. They grew angry at the people's ways of worshipping and abhorred the eating of human flesh more than anything.

Then they left the coast and headed inland, toward the capital, announcing that they wanted to meet the emperor. Confused and anxious, the emperor sent messengers telling them that they needn't bother themselves with the arduous journey. He sent them more gold, hoping they would accept his gifts and go away. Finally, they arrived and met with the emperor, who, still unsure as to who they were, offered them his kingdom. Soon afterward the emperor was dead, the capital was laid waste, and the newcomers had conquered the emperor's lands, scattered his people, or killed them with the deadly diseases that accompanied them.

THINKING ABOUT EXPANSION

How Did Growing States Dodge the Bullet of Development?
- The answer lies partly in the increased ability of states to expand political control and geographic territory and partly in geographical factors that allowed certain states access to new resources.

How Did Expanding States in the New World Affect the European Conquests?
- Where no empires existed Spanish power was much slower to establish, sometimes only succeeding over centuries, such as among the Yucatán Maya.

What Moved Between Empires?
- People moved among and between empires and in the process destroyed old identities and forged new ones. In addition to people, plants, animals, and even microbes slipped easily across borders; and all of these had dramatic impacts on human history.

Conclusion
- Some civilizations came face to face with forces they were utterly unable to control and found themselves engulfed, such as the Aztecs and Incas; others transformed themselves from marginal outsiders (Europe) to globally dominant powers.

Introduction

The story of the first encounter between the Old and New Worlds is about as dramatic, weird, nail-biting, and tragic as any; and we will recount some of it in this chapter. But the kinds of encounters between Europeans and Native Americans—or we should really just call them *Americans*—we will discuss were mirrored by expansions elsewhere. Movement and expansion was not a new phenomenon, but something had changed, as historian Charles H. Parker puts it: "Though peoples from Africa, Asia, and Europe had engaged one another intermittently since ancient times, early modern cross-cultural exchange was distinctive in its worldwide scale and its ongoing regularity."[1] Parker also points out that

---

[1]   Charles H. Parker, *Global Interactions in the Early Modern Age, 1400–1800* (Cambridge: Cambridge University Press, 2010), 3.

while later expansionist eras—notably European colonialism following the Industrial Revolution—involved European powers dominating large parts of the globe through superior firepower and technology, in the early modern period "no region stood at the apex of world dominion."[2]

Historian Victor Lieberman has noted that there was a pattern at play between 1450 and 1830 in which "localized societies in widely separated regions coalesced into larger units—politically, culturally, and commercially."[3] But this sounds unrealistically hygienic: such coalescing created turmoil, forging the world we live in today on an anvil of war, disease, competition, and innovation. Rival powers competed globally, ethnicities blended, religions clashed, merged, splintered, and disappeared. Money and goods were exchanged on an unprecedented scale, and the profits paid armies, explorers, and missionaries, while merchants, princes, and pirates looked for new ways to get rich, generate taxes, and maintain power.

Key to this expansion was the growing population, after it took a dive globally following the plague in the fourteenth century and notwithstanding a slowdown in the middle of the seventeenth. Heading for a resource crisis, as empires and states faced increasingly large numbers of mouths to feed, polities turned to expansion as a solution; and this allowed states to continue growing, even if others were destroyed in the process. A new global community was emerging—at breakneck speed—undermining unique cultural, religious, and economic networks and combining them in new forms. New "half-caste" races emerged and new words to define people's mixed ancestry, such as *mestizo* and *quadroon*. New pidgin languages evolved, amalgams of old ones, while new cultures formed out of the merging of ideas, traditions, and beliefs.

In the east, much of the central Eurasian steppe came under the control of China and Russia by the eighteenth century. This ended a millennia-long conflict between nomadic (or seminomadic) and sedentary, state societies. In India, the Mughals brought virgin land, especially in Bengal, into the empire and Muslim settlers cultivated it. Meanwhile Japan, suffering through decades of civil war in the sixteenth century, became politically unified for the first time and then began to integrate itself with the wider world. Farther west, Ottoman power expanded into Egypt (1517) and thence to the Indian Ocean, the sultans becoming globally recognized as the world's premier Islamic power.

Western and Eastern Hemispheres had been entirely separated by thousands of miles of ocean since the beginning of time. But after Columbus' voyage of

---

[2]   Ibid.

[3]   Victor Liberman, "Transcending East–West Dichotomies: State and Culture Formation in Six Ostensibly Separate Areas," *Modern Asian Studies* 31 (1997): 446.

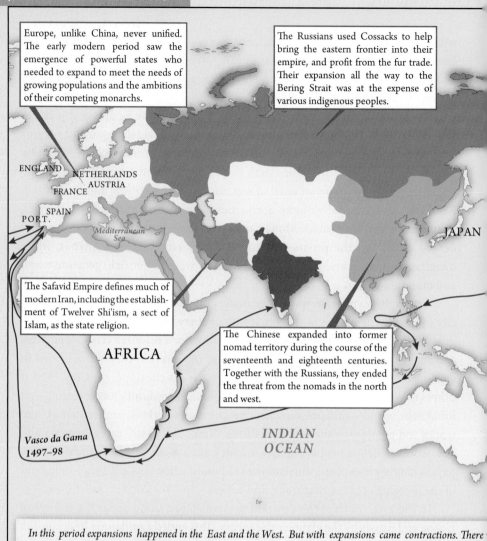

Europe, unlike China, never unified. The early modern period saw the emergence of powerful states who needed to expand to meet the needs of growing populations and the ambitions of their competing monarchs.

The Russians used Cossacks to help bring the eastern frontier into their empire, and profit from the fur trade. Their expansion all the way to the Bering Strait was at the expense of various indigenous peoples.

ENGLAND   NETHERLANDS
              AUSTRIA
    FRANCE

      SPAIN
PORT.
            *Mediterranean
               Sea*

JAPAN

The Safavid Empire defines much of modern Iran, including the establish-ment of Twelver Shi'ism, a sect of Islam, as the state religion.

AFRICA

The Chinese expanded into former nomad territory during the course of the seventeenth and eighteenth centuries. Together with the Russians, they ended the threat from the nomads in the north and west.

Vasco da Gama
1497–98

INDIAN
OCEAN

In this period expansions happened in the East and the West. But with expansions came contractions. There

MAP 13.1   GLOBAL EXPANSIONS

TIMELINE

☀ **1492**
Columbus lands in the New World

☀ **1519**
Cortés enters Tenochtitlán

 1494
Treaty of Tordesillas

 1517
Ottoman conquest
of Egypt

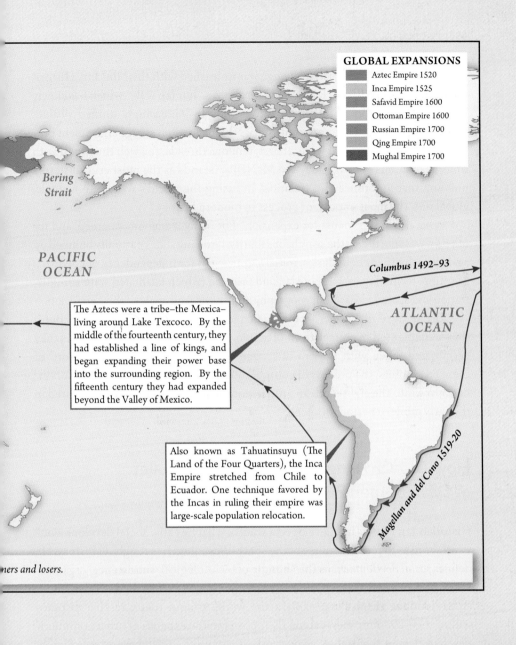

Bering Strait

PACIFIC OCEAN

Columbus 1492–93

ATLANTIC OCEAN

The Aztecs were a tribe–the Mexica– living around Lake Texcoco. By the middle of the fourteenth century, they had established a line of kings, and began expanding their power base into the surrounding region. By the fifteenth century they had expanded beyond the Valley of Mexico.

Also known as Tahuatinsuyu (The Land of the Four Quarters), the Inca Empire stretched from Chile to Ecuador. One technique favored by the Incas in ruling their empire was large-scale population relocation.

Magellan and del Cano 1519-20

ners and losers.

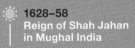

1628–58
Reign of Shah Jahan in Mughal India

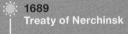

1689
Treaty of Nerchinsk

1616
Foreign merchants banned from Japan

1644
Collapse of Ming dynasty

1750
Height of Atlantic slave trade

1492, cataclysmic and creative change was unleashed with their linking. Historians John R. and William H. McNeill talk about a "human web," which has slowly knitted together the world's populations into an increasingly unified system, turning isolation and ignorance into networks, in an often savage and violent process. Once linked by what were, at first, tenuous threads, the web thickened with time. "Columbus's voyage," say the McNeills, "stands as the most crucial step in undoing that ignorance and isolation, in fusing the world's webs into a single, global one, the most important process in modern history."[4]

What drove this mania for expansion? For many it was simple greed, and for others it was spurred by the search for security. Growing states naturally bumped up against each other's boundaries, initiating struggles for independence or conquest. Maritime technologies, gunpowder, and printing (which facilitated state administration and spread ideas about geography and culture) all enabled this expansion.

The seeds of the modern world were planted in this era of expansion. But if they were planted in a maelstrom of action, that action diminished little as they germinated. Even with the era of second contacts and the "regularization" of these encounters, the process of cultural interaction and political change continued apace into the eighteenth and nineteenth centuries as the dramas initiated in the early modern period unfolded.

How Did Growing States Dodge the Bullet of Development?

Historian Ian Morris has developed a scale of what he calls "social development," which he uses to plot the course of the "East–West divide" throughout history. He defines *social development* as the "bundle of technological, subsistence, organizational and cultural accomplishments through which people feed, clothe, house and reproduce themselves, explain the world around them, resolve disputes within their communities, extend their power at the expense of other communities, and defend themselves against others' attempts to extend power."[5] Simply put, social development is how much a society can get done. This is a neutral value: social development is good (when good things are done) or it may be bad (when not-so-good things are done). In this period, Morris says, both Eastern and Western development "floated upward."

---

4   John R. and William McNeil, *The Human Web: A Bird's Eye View of World History*, (New york, W.W. Norton, 2003), 163.

5   Ian Morris: *Why the West Rules–For Now: The Patterns of History and What They Reveal About the Future* (New York: Farrar, Strauss and Giroux, 2010), 144.

Following the winnowing of population brought about by the plague of the fourteenth century, wages roughly doubled in the West because of labor shortages. But as the population rebounded by the late sixteenth, wages fell to pre-plague levels. If social development had been rising along with population through the sixteenth century in East and West, by the seventeenth large parts of Eurasia were experiencing the consequences. To make matters more complicated, the climate worsened, and colder weather affected everyone from Ireland to Japan between 1645 and 1715. As food became scarce and harvests faltered, people around the world pushed into agriculturally marginal areas, often inhabited by indigenous groups. The Irish (England's oldest colony), the Indians in North America, and the Ainu of Japan suffered similar fates as settlers from large agrarian states occupied their land. The environment, under new pressures to provide for humanity, also suffered; in 1550 only 10% of England and Scotland was still wooded, and this was halved by 1750. In London in the 1650s more than half of the heating needs were met by coal, wood being unavailable. Japan suffered similar widespread deforestation in the 1600s. Such environmental pressure created political pressure. Regular revolts of the poor combined with rebellion by dispossessed gentry, unpaid soldiers, and state officials.

> If social development had been rising along with population through the sixteenth century in East and West, by the seventeenth large parts of Eurasia were experiencing the consequences.

What some historians have seen as a "worldwide crisis of absolutist and agrarian states" in the seventeenth century expressed itself in China with the collapse of the Ming in 1644.[6] The last emperor, Chongzhen, hung himself from a tree behind the imperial palace in the Forbidden City: "Ashamed to face my ancestors, I die," he wrote in a suicide note. "Removing my imperial cap and with my hair disheveled about my face, I leave to the rebels the dismemberment of my body. Let them not harm my people!"[7] They ignored his plea, however, and rebel armies plundered wantonly.

The situation was little better in the West. Absolutist rulers in Europe responded to rebellions by unsubtly reminding the people of the divine legitimacy of their rule, while the Ottoman sultan did the same, stressing the fact that he was God's "shadow" on earth. It didn't work: Sultan Osman II was strangled by his own troops in 1622, rebellions broke out in Anatolia and Egypt between 1629 and 1632, and Istanbul itself was occupied by rebels. Another sultan, Ibrahim, was strangled in 1648. Often treated as signs of much-discussed Ottoman decline, which historians see as starting in the mid- to late sixteenth

---

6   Jack Goldstone, *Revolution and Rebellion in the Early Modern World* (Berkeley: University of California Press, 1991), 3.
7   Quoted in Morris, *Why the West Rules*, 452.

"I Am the State!" Absolutist rulers like Louis XIV of France and Charles I of England believed they were divinely ordained. There were few checks on their power. Their parliaments did not agree.

century, such difficulties as the Ottoman government faced were mirrored almost globally. France was largely crippled through large portions of the seventeenth century by antiabsolutism rebellions. The entire continent of Europe staggered through a series of brutal conflicts known as the Thirty Years' War, between 1618 and 1648; and England's King Charles I was beheaded by representatives of Parliament in 1649, following several years of civil war.

Sociologist Jack Goldstone proposes a partial explanation for such worldwide disruptions. Although his theory focuses mostly on seventeenth-century Europe, he believes it applies to other regions (China, Ottomans) and to later revolutions in Europe and its colonies. He sees such revolutions in the early modern period as stemming from four simultaneous conditions: state financial crises, which crippled governments' ability to meet their expenses; competition between elites for resources and state positions; the mobilization of popular groups by shared grievances; and the emergence of "heterodox cultural and religious beliefs." Groups holding such beliefs acted as leadership for antistate movements.[8]

---

8   Goldstone, *Revolution and Rebellion*, xxiv.

All these criteria applied to varying degrees in the East and the West in the seventeenth century. At a time when both cores seemed to have reached a hard ceiling, which in the past had led to long-term collapses, reducing social development to much lower levels for generations, social development continued to rise. Why? The answer lies partly in the increased ability of states to expand political control and geographic territory and partly in geographical factors that allowed certain states access to new resources.

Historian Felipe Fernández-Armesto argues that Europe's expansion beyond its continent was less a case of a civilization bulging out of the confines of its allotted space—which may fit the bill for Russia and China—than it was a story of smaller states (Portugal, Castile, Holland) grasping for competitive advantage in the face of larger neighbors (the Holy Roman and Ottoman Empires): "Menaced by bigger rivals, they had to increase their resources by means of conquest."[9] Illustrative of the unprecedented Iberian ambition is the Treaty of Tordesillas (1494), signed after Columbus returned from the Indies, by Castile-Aragon and Portugal. It drew a line 370 leagues west of the Cape Verde islands and gave everything to the west to Castile and everything to the east to Portugal. "History may provide other examples of rulers who have staked claims to universal dominion on a similarly tenuous basis, but rarely have these claims anticipated real-world success in such an unexpected and innovative way."[10]

Both the East and the West expanded in ways that ultimately gave them access to almost limitless new resources. China and Russia acquired the central Eurasian steppe, and Europe grabbed the New World. In resource terms this was akin to the modern world getting itself a couple of new planets to mine for space and resources. Europe's exploitation of its new world began in the late fifteenth and early sixteenth centuries and China's and Russia's, in the seventeenth. The results were similar, however, even if the timing was not completely coincidental; the bullet of development was dodged, and social development continued rising, for now.

HOW DID CHINA, RUSSIA, AND INDIA MEET THE NEEDS OF EXPANSION?

The Ming never found a "final solution" to the problem of Mongol raiding, relying on a combination of gift exchanges, controlled trade, and a fully garrisoned Great Wall as a buffer between China and Mongolia. After the Ming collapse in 1644,

---

[9]   Felipe Fernández-Armesto, "Empires in Their Global Context: c. 1500–c. 1800," in *The Atlantic in Global History: 1500–2000*, ed. Jorge Cañizares-Esguerra and Erik R. Seeman (Upper Saddle River, NJ: Pearson, 2006), 96.

[10] Giancarlo Casale, *The Ottoman Age of Exploration* (New York: Oxford University Press, 2010), 5.

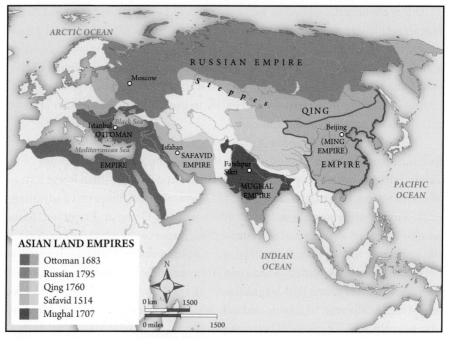

MAP 13.2   ASIAN LAND EMPIRES   Perhaps the overwhelming feature of the early modern period was the growth and reach of states. Better armed, with more control over their territory, and with burgeoning populations, they encroached on hitherto unreachable places, such as the steppe.

the imperial Humpty Dumpty was put back together again by the Manchus from the north, calling themselves the "Qing" dynasty. They built upon much of what the Ming had achieved in the battle with the nomads. But unlike their predecessors, and for the first time in Chinese history, they largely succeeded in bringing the "wild steppe" of Mongolia into the zone of civilization through a combination of military force, diplomacy, and colonial settlement.

Two individuals had a disproportionate influence on events in central Eurasia at this time, the Qing emperor Kangxi (r. 1662–1722) and the Zhunghar Mongol khan Galdan (1644–1697). Emperor and khan were vigorous opponents, representing the two opposing impulses, China's security needs and the Mongols' appetite for territory. The Qing expansion into Mongolia was prompted by the growing threat posed by the Zhunghar Mongols. Kangxi's plan was for Galdan to be China's "tame" Mongol, granted the right to pay tribute to the emperor, even though a top Chinese general reported that he was "violent, evil, and addicted to wine and sex."[11] But in the mid-1680s Galdan's forces abused their trading privileges, as one Qing report put it: "They loot and plunder the horses of

[11]   Quoted in Peter B. Golden, *Central Asia in World History* (New York: Oxford University Press, 2011), 118.

Mongols beyond the pass, and pasture them at will after they enter, trampling fields, and plundering people's goods."[12]

HOW DID THE RUSSIAN EXPANSION AFFECT THE CHINESE IN MONGOLIA?

While Kangxi seemed to possess the political will to take on Galdan, he needed something else to realize his military goals; and history was aligned for this now. It was another competing—and expanding—imperial power which ultimately allowed him to defeat the Mongols. In the 1580s members of the Russian Stroganov family, local salt traders, persuaded the *tsar* (Russian for "Caesar") Ivan the Terrible (1533–1584) to start a fur trade in western Siberia. They recruited Cossacks, a nomadic steppe people equipped with guns, immunity to smallpox, and literacy, to wrest the territory from any nomads they should encounter. By the 1590s, they had crossed the Urals and were headed for Siberia, spearheading the Russian expansion to the east.

Qing Emperor Kangxi (r. 1662–1722) With the treaty of Nerchinsk in 1689 the Chinese and Russians effectively ended the threat from nomadic Mongols. With both states denying them military aid and colonizing much of their territory, the "nomad frontier" was effectively closed.

Siberia: the name brings to mind endless tracts of frozen tundra, emptiness and solitude. It is, in fact, the world's largest continental interior, representing one-quarter of the entire land space of Eurasia. In the mid-sixteenth century it had a population of about 500,000, divided between 100 different language groups. For many Siberians, as historians J. R. and William H. McNeill point out, their introduction to the outside world was often violent, peppered with disease and social disruption; everybody gave up something: "Men paid their tribute. Women took Russian and Cossack men as

> Siberia: the name brings to mind endless tracts of frozen tundra, emptiness and solitude. It is, in fact, the world's largest continental interior, representing one-quarter of the entire land space of Eurasia.

---

[12]   Peter Perdue, *China Marches West: The Qing Conquest of Central Eurasia* (Cambridge, MA: Harvard University Press, 2005), 142.

husbands and masters."[13] In the wake of the Cossacks, trading posts and small settlements sprouted up, driven by trade in luxury items. This expansion spelled destruction for many—humans, for sure, but also the hapless martens, fox, beaver, mink, sables, and countless critters whose numbers were ravaged by the largely European hankering for fur. But for others, in particular settlers from Russia who now had access to virgin land, it spelled opportunity.

Experiences in the Western and Eastern Hemispheres at this time might seem divergent, but they were in many ways similar. It was initially the search for a northwest passage to China that took the French to North America. There, explorers like Samuel de Champlain (ca. 1570–1635) used lucrative beaver pelts to fund exploration. The Native Americans thought the French were fools to give away useful items like knives for smelly old beaver pelts. But beaver fur produced the best felt for the hat industry, and hatters paid through the nose to acquire it back home. "Trade goods valued at one livre when they left France bought beaver skins that were worth 200 livres when they arrived back there."[14]

The belt of tundra that makes up Siberia continues across the Bering Strait into North America, creating one almost continuous ecological zone and allowing Russians and Europeans, looking for pelts, what the Nazis later famously referred to as *lebensraum* ("space for life"). "In both Siberia and America," writes Morris, "tiny bands of desperadoes fanned out, scattering stockades built at their own expense, across mind-boggling expanses of unmapped territory, and constantly writing home for more money and more European women."[15] In both regions, large agrarian empires, outsourcing the work to such "desperadoes," helped themselves to new land and new resources in a process that acted as a pressure-release valve and partly explains how their social development could keep rising.

In 1689 the Russians and the Chinese met on the Armu River at Nerchinsk, and diplomats, using Jesuit translators speaking in Latin, hammered out an agreement to fix the border, putting it roughly where it still lies today. Says Peter Perdue, "The two empires had gradually groped towards each other across vast underpopulated spaces in the seventeenth century."[16] The Russians wanted to trade with the Chinese. The Chinese wanted border security and the ability to settle colonists in the steppe, and all could be accomplished by agreeing not to make deals with the Mongols. Thousands of square miles were now added to the Russian and Chinese states.

Determined to destroy Galdan, Kangxi led one final campaign in 1696. After 90 days, he defeated Galdan's forces. Galdan, unable to persuade the Russians to

---

13   McNeill and McNeill, *The Human Web*, 175.
14   Timothy Brook, *Vermeer's Hat: The Seventeenth Century and the Dawn of the Global World* (New York: Bloomsbury, 2008), 44.
15   Morris, *Why the West Rules*, 460.
16   Perdue, *China Marches West*, 163.

assist him, was isolated. "This time we surrounded them with a pincer movement of troops," said a Chinese imperial report. "Thus we completely eliminated them. This was done by Heaven; no human force could have done it. Now the deserts are permanently cleared, and the border is secure."[17] Regardless of heaven's possible role in the events, three earthly elements converged to enable the Qing to defeat Galdan: horses, gunpowder, and silver. The first were bought in large quantities from other Mongol tribes as the Mongols were the go-to horse traders. Silver currency allowed soldiers to carry pay with them, meaning they could buy provisions along the route if available, instead of carrying a year's worth of grain as salary. The Chinese employed gunpowder in cannons, giving them a decisive advantage. Mongol allies also contributed significantly to the Chinese success. Mongolia was nothing if not a shifting landscape of tribal alliances, and Galdan and his forces had alienated many tribes, creating allies for the Qing. Mongol warriors would prove invaluable, in the same way that Inca and Aztec enemies among the indigenous peoples helped the Spaniards decisively in the sixteenth century.

Galdan escaped the battlefield to die shortly afterward, but the Qing managed to acquire his corpse and had the satisfaction of grinding his bones to dust and scattering them to the wind. "It was a degree of obliteration not found in the penal code; it represented the ultimate in imperial erasure of an enemy from both the human and cosmic realms."[18]

Nomadic pastoralists had represented the largest alternative to settled agrarian societies since the second millennium BCE. Now China's and Russia's steppe frontiers were effectively closed, concluding a major historical theme. Perdue argues that, like the states of Europe, the Russians, Chinese, and Zhungar Mongols were all increasing their "stateness," flexing their muscles and expanding their control of territory and ideological and economic power at this time.[19] But the Zhungars were still nomadic and pastoral and, as such, could not command the resources in men and material that sedentary agricultural states could muster.

Morris echoes this point of view, noting that with the end of the "nomad threat," the Romanovs and the Qing had "effectively killed one of the horsemen of the apocalypse."[20] The pressure of social development did not trigger waves of invading nomads or steppe migration as it had in the second and the twelfth centuries, causing the collapse of the Han and the Song dynasties, respectively. Just like the frontier in North America, expansion provided resources for millions of colonists, and together they (literally) carved up the land, in what Morris calls a "steppe bonanza."

---

[17] *Chronicle of the emperor's personal expeditions to pacify the northwest frontier*, quoted in Ibid., 190.
[18] Ibid., 206.
[19] Ibid.
[20] Morris, *Why the West Rules*, 459.

HOW DID THE MUGHALS EXPAND THEIR CONTROL OF THE SUBCONTINENT?

Firearms and business administration make formidable partners. While the Europeans were busy chartering companies to undertake trading and colonial ventures—the British East India Company (1600), the Dutch East India Company (1602), the Virginia Company (1606)—the Mughals were also using guns and good business practices to expand their resource base. Organized for war, the empire, through the reigns of Akbar (r. 1556–1605) and his successors Jahangir (r. 1605–1627), Shah Jahan (r. 1628–1658), and Aurangzeb (r. 1658–1707), enjoyed military success that expanded its reach across most of the subcontinent. "Tribute, plunder, and new revenues flowed into the imperial coffers in amounts that offset the costs of conquest and expansion," says historian John Richards.[21]

Unlike the empires of the New World, this one was a hands-on operation. Mughal emperors directed legions of officials who were sent across the empire to enact the emperor's wishes. Although many Mughal subjects paid their taxes as a portion of their harvest, the emperors tried to move to a cash basis for taxes, in an attempt to sideline the local aristocracy. The Mughals were still reliant on some local power structures, however; and these local aristocrats were essentially warlords living in compounds with armories and temples. As in many empires, the Mughals tried to restructure villages and warlord territories into provinces defined by the emperor and subject to his tax laws.

"For two centuries," says Richards, "the rulers of Mughal India limited their policy aims to four interconnected goals: military victory, annexation of new territories, imposition of public order, and steadily growing land revenues."[22] During the reign of Shah Jahan, tree cutters and ploughmen accompanied the armies as they expanded into Bihar Province in the eastern Gangetic plain. The government encouraged cultivation and settlement, as a Mughal document explained: "In this manner the people and the ri'aya [peasants] would be attracted by good treatment to come from other regions and subas [provinces] to bring under cultivation wasteland and land under forest."[23]

The most extensive example of this was in the northeast Bengal delta, where the Mughals created the intensively cultivated wet-rice landscape that comprises much of today's Bangladesh. Settlers from the north and west transformed this area of wild wetlands into domesticated agricultural land. The Mughals

---

[21] John F. Richards, *The Unending Frontier: An Environmental History of the Early Modern World* (Berkeley: University of California Press, 2003), 26.

[22] Ibid., 32.

[23] Quoted in Richard Eaton, *The Rise of Islam and the Bengal Frontier, 1204–1760* (Berkeley: University of California Press, 1993), 228.

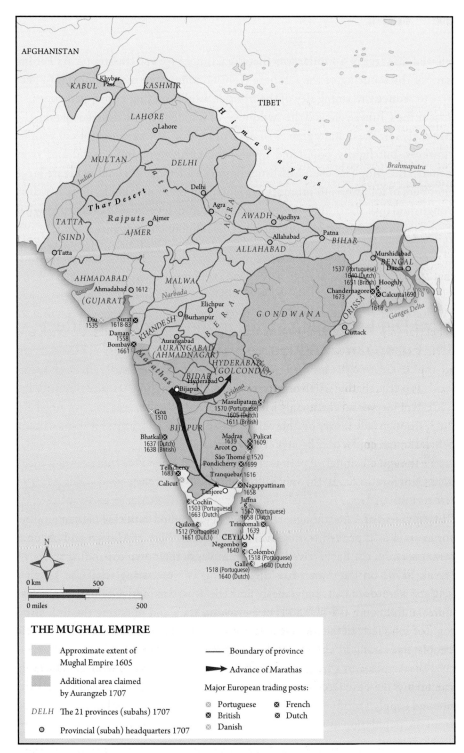

THE MUGHAL EMPIRE

- ▨ Approximate extent of Mughal Empire 1605
- Additional area claimed by Aurangzeb 1707
- *DELH* The 21 provinces (subahs) 1707
- ○ Provincial (subah) headquarters 1707

- —— Boundary of province
- ➤ Advance of Marathas

Major European trading posts:
- ⊠ Portuguese   ⊠ French
- ⊠ British   ⊠ Dutch
- ⊠ Danish

Map labels (from the image):

AFGHANISTAN

KABUL · Khyber Pass · KASHMIR · TIBET

LAHORE · Lahore

MULTAN · DELHI · *Brahmaputra*

Indus · Thar Desert · Jats · Delhi · Agra · AWADH · Ajodhya · Patna · BIHAR · Murshidabad

TATTA (SIND) · Rajputs · Ajmer · AJMER · Allahabad · ALLAHABAD · BENGAL · Dacca

○Tatta

AHMADABAD (GUJARAT) · Ahmadabad ○ 1612 · MALWA · Narbada · Elichpur · 1537 (Portuguese) 1640 (Dutch) 1651 (British) Hooghly · Chandernagore 1673 · Calcutta 1690 · 1616 · Ganges Delta

Diu 1535 · Surat 1618-83 · Daman 1558 · Bombay 1661 · KHANDESH · Burhanpur · BERAR · GONDWANA · ORISSA · Cuttack

Marathas · Aurangabad · AURANGABAD (AHMADNAGAR) · HYDERABAD · GOLCONDA · BIDAR · Hyderabad○ · Krishna

Goa 1510 · Bijapur · BIJAPUR · Masulipatam 1570 (Portuguese) 1605 (Dutch) 1611 (British)

Bhatkal 1637 (Dutch) 1638 (British) · Madras 1639 · Pulicat 1609 · Arcot ○ · São Thomé 1520 · Pondicherry 1699

Telicherry 1683 · Calicut · Tranquebar 1616 · Nagappattinam 1658 · Tanjore ○

Cochin 1503 (Portuguese) 1663 (Dutch) · Jaffna 1560 (Portuguese) 1658 (Dutch) · Trincomali 1639

Quilon 1512 (Portuguese) 1661 (Dutch) · CEYLON · Negombo 1640 · Colombo 1518 (Portuguese) 1640 (Dutch) · Galle 1518 (Portuguese) 1640 (Dutch)

N

0 km 500

0 miles 500

MAP 13.3 THE MUGHAL EMPIRE The Mughal emperor Aurangzeb expanded the empire into much of south and east India in the seventeenth century. By then the Mughals had already annexed much of the Gangetic plain and Bangladesh, where they developed wet-rice cultivation.

viewed this area in a similar way that the Chinese viewed the steppe. As Perdue says of the securing of the Chinese frontier zone, "The most important effect was to reduce the ambiguity of the frontier by eliminating unmapped zones."[24] Just as the Chinese viewed the "wildness" of the steppe with deep suspicion, the Mughals saw the delta region as in need of taming. It was not empty of people, however, but lightly populated by shifting cultivators and coastal and river fishers. The Mughals used Muslim religious leaders, who could generate large numbers of followers, to promote settlement of these new lands, usually riding roughshod over the indigenous people. By the mid-seventeenth century Mughal Bengal was something of a breadbasket, producing large quantities of rice and *ghee* (clarified butter), which was easily moved up and down the coast from Bengal's delta region.

How Did Expanding States in the New World Affect the European Conquests?

> Is it true that on earth one lives?
> Not forever on earth, only a little while.
> Though jade it may be, it breaks;
> Though gold it may be, it is crushed.
> Though it be quetzal plumes, it shall not last.
> Not forever on earth, only a little while.[25]

This fragment of Aztec thought could have been applied to the life of their empire, for as soon as it peaked, ruling over most of the Valley of Mexico and beyond, strangers from the East arrived, representatives of their own expanding states, to wreak havoc on the Americas. These strangers were doing what the Mughal settlers were doing in Bangladesh and the Russians and Chinese in central Eurasia: following the demands of a growing state and pursuing the unfolding logic of conquest. In the process they acquired resources for themselves and their people; like strangers elsewhere, this happened at the expense of others.

The Aztecs' was a tributary empire, in which the lords of Tenochtitlán, their capital in Lake Texcoco, conquered neighbors, who were then obliged to pay tribute and supply sacrificial victims. They had no standing army but raised troops from the population as necessary. They left kings in place after conquering them

---

24   Perdue, *China Marches West*, 161.
25   Aztec poem, quoted in Michael E. Smith, *The Aztecs*, 3rd ed. (Malden, MA: Wiley-Blackwell, 2012), 2.

and had little infrastructure such as roads. However, they did exert political influence, and the peace engendered by Aztec control led to considerable prosperity from trade, evidenced by an increase in population and agricultural output. But in case this sounds too *kumbaya*, there was little love between the Aztecs and their tributary people. Such empires have certain design flaws, as economist David Landes points out: "They rest on no deep loyalty, enjoy no real legitimacy, extort wealth by threat of pain. Replacement of one group of thugs by another is often welcomed by the common folk who hope against hope that change will relieve their oppression."[26]

By the time the Spanish waded ashore on the Mexican coast in the early sixteenth century, the Aztecs had reached the height of their civilization and tensions were showing. Population growth was adding pressure to tense tributary relationships: "Feeding the three million Aztecs was increasingly difficult, and famines occurred with more frequency."[27] Instead of finding a technological or territorial way out from under the hard ceiling of population growth, however, they were invaded by a foreign entity, whose diseases devastated their population and effectively ended their civilization. The Spanish, on the other hand, had discovered a solution to their own hard ceiling.

Tenochtitlán, the Aztec Capital, Site of Modern-Day Mexico City   Its location in a lake connected by causeways made it difficult for the Spaniards to conquer. It took them two attempts and an epidemic of smallpox to take it.

---

[26] David Landes, *The Wealth and Poverty of Nations: Why Some Are So Rich and Some So Poor* (New York: W.W. Norton, 199), 102.
[27] Smith, *The Aztecs*, 280.

HOW WERE THE SPANIARDS ABLE TO CONQUER
THE INCAS AND AZTECS?

This story has often been written as the simple conquest of an underdeveloped civilization by a superior one. In particular, the old story goes, guns, germs, and steel won out over arrows, vulnerability to disease, and wood-obsidian (native swords). Diseases certainly wiped out large parts of the native populations, and European weapon technology was undeniably efficient. But these factors fail to tell the whole story, either in Central and South America or in North America, where the French and British established their New World colonies.

While firearms gave the early French explorers and colonists a distinct advantage against groups like the Mohawks in New England and Canada, other Europeans (the Dutch) traded guns; and the natives quickly learned how to use them. In 1603 Samuel de Champlain formed an alliance with the tribe referred to by the French as the *Montagnais* against the powerful Mohawks in the region. "Champlain understood," writes historian Timothy Brook, "that without the support of the Montagnais, the French could not survive a single winter, let alone insinuate their way into existing trading networks."[28]

The same was true of the Spanish to the south. The story of Spain's conquest of Mexico and Peru is not one of simple military triumph:

> In reality the process was more insidious, more durable, and more believable than any mere feat of arms: the monarchy grew by accommodation with existing elites, by exploiting indigenous rivalries and securing indigenous collaborators. That was how a relatively poor, unpopulated, and peripheral European power came to establish so privileged a position of command in so much of the Americas.[29]

In 1519 the Spanish conquistador Hernán Cortés (1485–1547) entered Tenochtitlán, a city of over 100,000 people, with some 400 Spanish mercenaries. Bernal Díaz (1496–1584), one of the conquistadores who wrote a lengthy account of the conquest, recorded the astonishment of the Spaniards as they took in the sights of the city; and just in case the reader fails to notice their bravery, he writes of his own feat: "What men have there been in the world who have shown such daring?"[30]

But terrifying as entering that strange city was, they were not alone. Historian Ross Hassig has estimated that the Spanish used as many as 200,000 allies

---

[28]   Brook, *Vermeer's Hat*, 32.
[29]   Felipe Fernández-Armesto, *The Americas: A Hemispheric History* (New York: Modern Library, 2003), 58.
[30]   Bernal Díaz, *History of the Conquest of New Spain*, ed. David Carrasco (Albuquerque: University of New Mexico Press, 2008), 158.

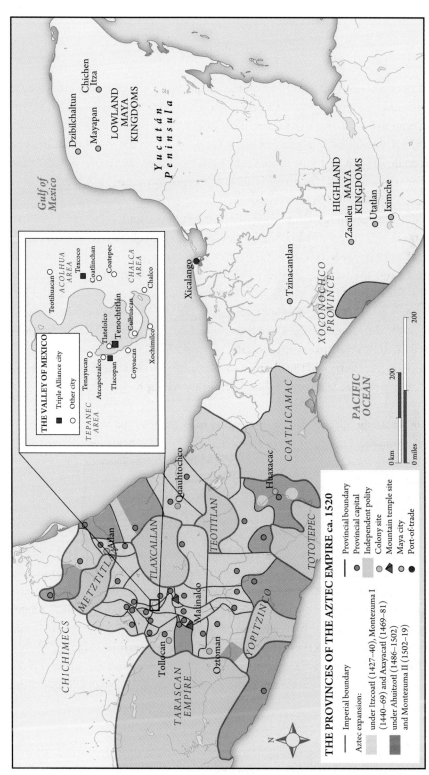

THE PROVINCES OF THE AZTEC EMPIRE ca. 1520

— Imperial boundary

Aztec expansion:

under Itzcoatl (1427–40), Montezuma I (1440–69) and Axayacatl (1469–81)

under Ahuitzotl (1486–1502) and Montezuma II (1502–19)

--- Provincial boundary

● Provincial capital

Independent polity

○ Colony site

▲ Mountain temple site

● Maya city

● Port-of-trade

Gulf of Mexico

Dzibilchaltun

Chichen Itza

Mayapan

LOWLAND MAYA KINGDOMS

Yucatán Peninsula

HIGHLAND MAYA KINGDOMS

Zaculeu

Utatlan

Iximche

Xicalango

THE VALLEY OF MEXICO

■ Triple Alliance city

○ Other city

TEPANEC AREA

ACOLHUA AREA

Teotihuacan

Tenayucan

Texcoco

Coatlinchan

Azcapotzalco

Coatepec

CHALCA AREA

Tlatelolco

Tenochtitlan

Culhuacan

Chalco

Tlacopan

Coyoacan

Xochimilco

Tzinacantlan

XOCONOCHCO PROVINCE

PACIFIC OCEAN

0 km   200

0 miles   200

Quauhtochco

TEOTITLAN

Huaxacac

COATLICAMAC

CHICHIMECS

METZTITLAN

Axtlan

TLAXCALLAN

Malinalco

YOPITZINCO

TOTOTEPEC

Tollocan

Oztoman

TARASCAN EMPIRE

N

MAP 13.4(a) THE AZTEC EMPIRE Both Aztec (**a**) and Inca (**b**) Empires were highly centralized. The Spaniards conquered their capitals and ruled from there. Even so, the Spaniards faced resistance for decades, if not centuries.

493

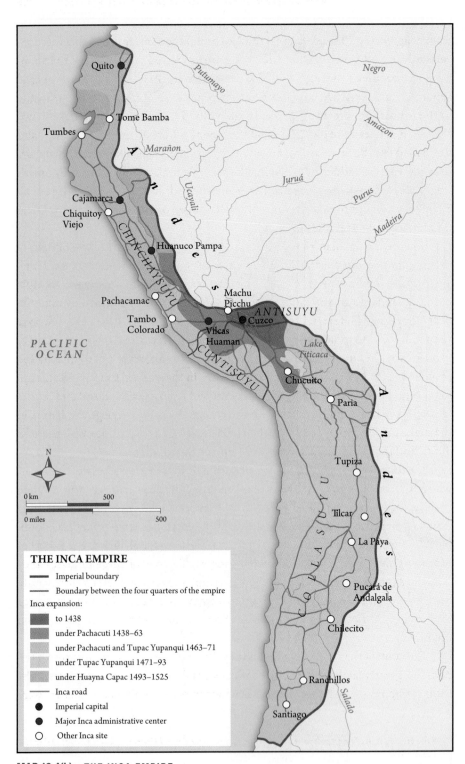

Quito

Tome Bamba

Tumbes

Putumayo

Negro

Marañon

Amazon

Juruá

Cajamarca

Chiquitoy
Viejo

CHINCHAYSUYU

A
n
d
e
s

Ucayali

Purus

Madeira

Huanuco Pampa

Pachacamac

Machu
Picchu

ANTISUYU

Tambo
Colorado

Cuzco

Vilcas
Huaman

CUNTISUYU

*Lake
Titicaca*

PACIFIC
OCEAN

Chucuito

Paria

A
n
d
e
s

N

Tupiza

0 km   500

Tilcar

0 miles   500

La Paya

C
O
L
L
A
S
U
Y
U

Pucará de
Andalgala

THE INCA EMPIRE

Chilecito

Imperial boundary

Boundary between the four quarters of the empire

Inca expansion:

to 1438

under Pachacuti 1438–63

under Pachacuti and Tupac Yupanqui 1463–71

under Tupac Yupanqui 1471–93

under Huayna Capac 1493–1525

Inca road

● Imperial capital

● Major Inca administrative center

○ Other Inca site

Ranchillos

Salado

Santiago

MAP 13.4(b)   THE INCA EMPIRE

from neighboring Tlaxcala against the Aztecs at Tenochtitlán, a fact that was conveniently played down by Díaz, who was more interested in focusing on the Spaniards' "miraculous swordplay."[31] Tlaxcala had resisted the Aztecs' imperial expansion and remained hostile toward them, just as the Montagnais were hostile to the Mohawk in North America. Initially, the Tlaxcalans resisted Cortés, but they soon adopted the old adage that the "enemy of my enemy is my friend" and decided to use the Spaniards against the Aztecs. When the Spaniards showed up, in other words, in addition to playing the star role in their own story, they unwittingly adopted roles in an ongoing Meso-American drama. As Hassig puts it, "The Spaniards were simply another group, albeit an alien one, seeking to gain political dominance in central Mexico."[32]

Initially, the Spaniards were welcomed into the Aztec capital of Tenochtitlán—they had not declared war, and it was not clear what their intentions were. However, while staying as guests of the Aztecs, the Spaniards were notably outnumbered and in the heart of enemy territory. Cortés decided to take the Aztec emperor Moctezuma hostage to ensure their safety. In June 1520, tensions soon erupted into violence; and with the emperor dead, the dwindling group of invaders fought a rear-guard action out of the city (an event referred to by the Spaniards as *la Noche Triste*) and found refuge in their allies' territory. Regrouping there, Cortés had his shipbuilders cut lumber from a nearby forest and build a small fleet of ships, which he used, in the spring of 1521, to besiege the Aztecs in their lake city. Aided by the Tlaxcalans and by a plague of smallpox which gutted Tenochtitlán, the Spaniards were soon able to take the city.

The Spaniards found Peru similarly well put together, courtesy of the Incas, who had been busy expanding and consolidating in the previous century. When the Spaniards captured the capital, Cuzco, they controlled the empire. Stretching from Colombia to Chile—some 2,485.5 miles north to south—the Incas dominated other polities from the coastal plains to the mountains but stopped short of extending their power into the inland jungles. To control these domains they built roads and bridges, which stitched the empire together. Trained from youth, runner relays could cover about 150 miles a day, which meant that Lima to Cuzco took about 3 days, a time that later Spanish horse-drawn carriages could not match.

The control that the fifteenth-century American empires wielded over their domains greatly facilitated Spanish conquest, as Fernández-Armesto notes: "The former empires of the Aztecs and Incas which in the early sixteenth century were

---

[31] Ross Hassig, *Aztec Warfare: Imperial Expansion and Political Control* (Norman, University of Oklahoma Press, 1988).
[32] Ibid., 241.

among the most rapidly growing and ecologically diverse, were virtually swallowed at a gulp."[33] Even their institutions were adopted and utilized, such as the Inca system of *mita*, a tribute payment of labor, which the Spanish put to use in the silver mines of Peru, at the cost of thousands of native lives. Where no empires existed, Spanish power was much slower to establish, sometimes only succeeding over centuries, as among the Yucatán Maya.

And yet we should be cautious in thinking of the Spanish conquest as swift and complete. While the Spanish may have "cut off the head," the body was another issue. "Looking at Spanish America in its entirety," writes Matthew Restall, "the conquest as a series of armed expeditions and military actions against native Americans never ended."[34]

Florida's Seminole Indians were still fighting upon American independence in 1776 and after (Seminole Wars of 1818–1858). The Araucanians of Chile fought the Republic of Chile in the nineteenth century. Other native groups fought governments in Argentina and Central America in the nineteenth century, and a collection of Maya polities existed into the twentieth. The Spanish may have gained control of the reins of government; but ultimate pacification was hard to achieve, and resistance continued indefinitely.

WHAT WAS THE EFFECT OF NEW WORLD SILVER ON THE GLOBAL ECONOMY?

> It was Spanish money, in particular, the silver peso, which made the early modern world go around. It was the first "global" currency, knitting together multiple regions in the East and the West and creating a network between empires.

If it was resources the Europeans were after, they found them, especially in precious metals. It was Spanish money, in particular, the silver peso, which made the early modern world go around. It was the first "global" currency, knitting together multiple regions in the East and the West and creating a network between empires. Spanish exploration in the New World needed to pay; conquistadores were contractually obligated to show a return both to their funders and to the Crown, which licensed their exploration. "Find gold, and—to a slightly lesser extent—silver," might have therefore appeared at the top of Hernán Cortés' to-do list.

At first, it dribbled in. Early expeditions from Hispaniola to the Yucatán in the first decade of the sixteenth century produced tantalizing, yet modest, amounts. Francisco Pizarro kidnapped the Inca emperor Atahualpa and demanded a massive ransom for him. The Incas paid it, filling an entire room with

---

[33] Fernández-Armesto, *The Americas*, 58.
[34] Matthew Restall, *Seven Myths of the Spanish Conquest* (New York: Oxford University Press, 2010), 72.

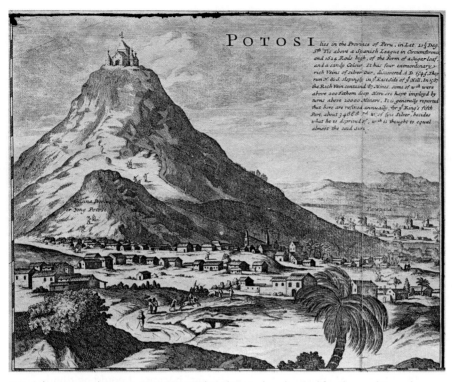

P O T O S I *lies in the Province of Peru, in Lat. 21⅓ Deg. 5th 'Tis above a Spanish League in Circumference, and 1524 Rods high, of the Form of a Sugar-loaf, and a Sandy Colour. It has four extraordinary rich Veins of silver Oar, discovered A.D. 1545. They run N. &. S. sloping in ye East side of ye Hill. In 1587 the Rich Vein contain'd 87 Mines, some of wch were above 200 Fathom deep. Here are kept imploy'd by turns above 20000 Miners. It is generally reported that here are refined annually, for ye King's fifth Part, about 3,466 ℔ wt of fine Silver, besides what he is depriv'd of, wch is thought to equal almost the said Sum.*

Potosí, the mountain known as *Cerro Rico* ("Rich Peak"), was heavily mined for silver; and its produce flooded the world in the sixteenth century, arguably the beginning of the global economy.

precious metals, far in excess of what any European monarch of the time would have been worth. The Spaniards killed him anyway, on charges of "treason."

In the 1540s, pursuing the Incas south, the Spaniards stumbled upon the closest thing to a mother lode: Potosí was a mountain containing a 300-foot outcropping of solid silver ore. The Spaniards soon began tearing into it, christening it *Cerro Rico* ("Rich Peak"). For the next half-century the population of the little town of several thousand at its base mushroomed, and by 1600 it stood at over 150,000, making it the largest city in the Western Hemisphere. Silver poured out of the mountain. It was then packed on mule trains to the Pacific coast, sailed north, then repacked to cross the Isthmus of Panama into the Atlantic, to Havana, Cuba. From here it went on Spanish galleons, "treasure fleets," to Europe and the east. "Many students of international trade," says historian Steven Topik, "date the beginning of the world economy to 1492 with the incorporation of the Americas."[35] But 1540 might be a more precise date as from this

---

[35]   S. Topik, C. Marichal, Z. Frank, *From Silver to Cocaine: Latin American Commodity Chains and the Building of the World Economy (1500–2000)*, (Durham, NC: Duke University Press, 2006).

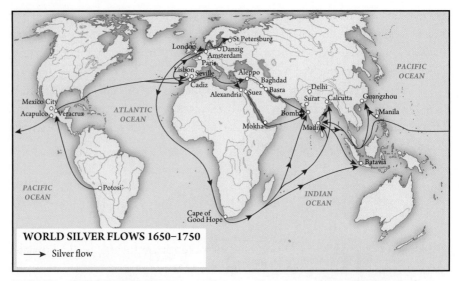

MAP 13.5 WORLD SILVER FLOWS, 1650–1750 The advent of Spanish silver is often considered the origin of the world economy. Its effects were truly international as silver coinage was in high demand from Asia to Europe.

point the silver from Potosí and other (smaller) mines in Central and South America flooded the world.

The silver peso, known as a "piece of eight" because it could be divided into eight parts, played a role in numerous historical processes, like a pecuniary Forrest Gump: it was key to the development of Antwerp's stock market, and it funded the Hapsburg Empire's struggles for European dominance under Holy Roman Emperor Charles V (r. 1519–1558) and Spain's King Phillip II (r. 1556–1598) and King Phillip III (r. 1578–1621). From 1568 to 1648 Spain fought continual wars against rebels in the Spanish-occupied Netherlands; during the eighteenth century, it launched regular offensives against Great Britain (1763–1767, 1779–1783, 1796–1803) and fought France (1793–1795, 1808–1814), not to mention ongoing struggles against the Ottomans. Footing the bill? The silver peso.

Spain, surrounded by enemies, spent it faster than it mined it. "Potosi exists," one commentator claimed, "to serve the imposing aspirations of Spain. It serves to chastise the Turk, humble the Moor, make Flanders tremble, and terrify England."[36] A Chinese tax reform in 1581 demanded that all taxes be paid in silver. With the resultant run on silver (Chinese population then, over 100 million), its value soared; and European and other traders hoarded it especially to trade with China, in the hopes of double profits. American silver also

---

[36] Quoted in Morris, *Why the West Rules*, 461.

played a major part in the Atlantic slave trade, allowing European slavers to buy south Asian goods to sell in western Africa. Receiving silver for slaves, the Africans imported European and Indian cloth, iron, copper, guns, tobacco, cowrie shells (from the Maldives), and alcohol.

"The single product most responsible for the birth of world trade was silver."[37] Yale historian John Demos goes even further, referring to Potosí to suggest that, "if the origins of capitalism . . . can be tied especially to the same period, then the High Place deserves principal credit."[38]

What Moved Between Empires?

Over the course of the sixteenth and seventeenth centuries the old Eurasian empires and the upstart ones of Europe vied for power and resources around the world. But imperial control was never absolute, nor were boundaries impervious. Low-level skirmishes in the form of piracy were endemic in many regions, illustrating how the edges of empires and the spaces in between were often lawless. People moved among and between these empires and in the process destroyed old identities and forged new ones. In addition to people, plants, animals, and even microbes slipped easily across borders; and all of these had dramatic impacts on human history.

> In addition to people, plants, animals, and even microbes slipped easily across borders; and all of these had dramatic impacts on human history.

WHAT WAS EARLY MODERN PIRACY?

So much silver sloshing around the high seas meant easy pickings for anyone with a ship and some cannon. This was the era of Caribbean piracy, described memorably by authors such as Daniel Defoe (1660–1731), who wrote *Robinson Crusoe*, and Robert Louis Stevenson (1850–1894), who wrote *Treasure Island*—surely, the ultimate inspiration for all later pirate movies!

While the Spanish and Portuguese came upon their wealth by plundering and conquering newly "discovered" territories, the Dutch, French, and English resorted to plundering the Spanish and Portuguese possessions: "And when the colonists or natives these adventurers encountered didn't want to trade, the

---

[37] Dennis O. Flynn and Arturo Giraldez, "Born with a Silver Spoon: The Origin of World Trade in 1571," *Journal of World History* 6, no. 2 (1995): 201.

[38] John Demos, "The High Place: Potosi," in "Early Cities of the Americas," special issue *Common-Place* 3, no. 4 (2003), http://www.common-place.org/vol-03/no-04/potosi/.

pirates simply seized goods, raped women, and burned towns."[39] Portuguese and Spanish imperial ambition aimed to bar other Europeans from trade in the East as well. The British and Dutch, although on-and-off enemies through the early modern period, often collaborated against the Iberians, resulting in a running maritime war from southeastern Asia to the Caribbean and necessitating the arming of trading vessels. But piracy was not only an inter-European affair. The residents of Dartmouth in southern England, who were long-distance fishermen and sailors, petitioned their government in the seventeenth century to end the menace of northern African pirates, who routinely captured their ships and sold the crew into slavery.

The earliest piracy that took root in the Caribbean in the sixteenth century was largely government-sponsored. Historian Kenneth Pomeranz claims that of some 13 million pounds invested in joint stock companies in England between 1550 and 1630, more than one-third went toward government-licensed piracy aimed at Spanish possessions. British pirates, he says, made an average of 60% return on their investment in the last quarter of the sixteenth century. Luxury goods led to large profits: spices, gold, silver, quality textiles, slaves, and sugar. One Spanish ship, the *Madre de Deus* ("Mother of God"), was captured by the English in 1592 off the Azores. At 165 feet long, she was three times the size of any ship in England and full of treasure. "Here was the stuff of dreams," says Landes. "Chests bulging with jewels and pearls, gold and silver coins, amber older than England."[40] It contained an amount that was equivalent to approximately half of the entire English treasury. The ship was towed to Dartmouth, where its canny residents looted it before the queen's representatives could arrive to claim its bounty.

But by the mid-seventeenth century bands of "sea rovers" emerged, multiethnic, multinational, democratically run groups—castaways, runaway slaves, political refugees, escaped criminals (a strange hybrid kind of flotsam from the world's empires)—based on a remote part of Hispaniola (the island containing today's Dominican Republic and Haiti). Now we truly enter the world of Defoe and Stevenson, and here is the inspiration for Jack Sparrow. Chased from Hispaniola, they took refuge on the island of Tortuga; and calling themselves the "Brethren of the Coast," they declared war on Spaniards. The piracy that emerged with them was a far cry from the corporate nature of the earlier pirates. These pirates had their own version of justice, shared booty equally among the crew, and generally treated captured crews humanely, leaving them with food and ship or escorting them to a port.

---

[39]   Kenneth Pomeranz and Steven Topik, *The World That Trade Created: Society, Culture and the World Economy, 1400 to the Present* (New York: M.E. Sharpe, 1999), 150.

[40]   Landes, *The Wealth and Poverty of Nations*, 151.

WHAT PART DID SEXUAL POLITICS PLAY
IN THE CONQUEST OF THE NEW WORLD?

New populations appeared on a new scale because of the volume of migrants in this period. In the Atlantic world, the *Carrera de indias* (annual fleets) sailed from Spain (Seville), via the Canary Islands to the Antilles, thence to Havana in Cuba, and to Veracruz on the Mexican coast. They carried materials and people. In the 1500s some 250,000 Spaniards traveled this route; this number almost doubled in the 1600s. By the late 1700s an estimated 800,000 Spaniards had crossed the Atlantic, mostly male and mostly young, able therefore to work and procreate for decades. These people ensured that the Spanish colonial project maintained momentum.

When people move, populations mix. Native women's experience with the Spaniards in America is instructive here, but the experience was repeated globally, wherever conquering or expanding populations met. One of the most popular Disney movies (*Pocahontas*) even deals with this issue in its North American context, fudging the real history. Sexuality was central to the process of the encounter between Europeans and the inhabitants of the New World, and this took many forms, as historian Karen Vieira Powers puts it: "Though rape and betrayal probably represented opposite poles of the spectrum, in its interstices we are likely to find mutual consent, economic opportunism, physical attraction, political alliances, social mobility, genuine love, and other scenarios among the events and motives that catapulted indigenous women into sexual relationships with Spanish men."[41]

The result of these relationships? Children. Spanish imperial policy was built on the idea of a ruling (Spanish) class and an underclass of natives. Mixed children undermined the clarity of this arrangement, leading to an increasingly complex hierarchy of class and race. The Spanish referred to these children as "mixed" (*mestizos*) and the process of such population mixing as *mestizaje*. "In 1521," says Powers, "Cuauhtémoc [Moctezuma's successor] surrendered to Hernan Cortés; it was neither a victory nor a defeat, but the birth of the Mestizo people who are the Mexico of today."[42]

Mixed relationships happened at every level of society. The earliest conquistadores had much to gain by marrying high-born native women. In addition to their hope of acquiring an *encomienda*, or rent-paying estate, Spaniards stood to gain tribal lands through marriage. Perhaps the best-documented relationship was that between the man we might call "Conquistador Number 1," Hernán Cortés, and La Malinche, a woman from the Mexican Gulf coast. Doña Marina, the "Christian" name given her by the Spanish, spoke Nahuatl, the Aztec language, as well as Maya; and she quickly learned Spanish, making herself invaluable to Cortés. She

---

[41] Karen Vieira Powers, "Colonial Sexuality: of Women, Men, and Mestizaje," in *History of the Conquest of New Spain*, ed. Davíd Carrasco (Albuquerque: University of New Mexico Press, 2008), 407.

[42] Ibid., 406.

Cultural Intermediary   La Malinche, or Doña Marina, as the Spaniards called her, was interpreter, diplomat, and sexual partner of the conquistador Hernán Cortés. The early modern period threw multiple identities together in new ways including indigenous female with foreign male.

was "given" to him by the natives of Tabasco, along with some other servants, in 1519; and she was constantly at his side for the next few years. Moctezuma even calls Cortés "Señor Malinche," suggesting he and Doña Marina were one, united in what was to date perhaps the most unusual coupling in history. Malinche bore Cortés a son, Don Martín, proving that sex was part of her job description, although Cortés also made a gift of her to one of his aristocratic captains.

The nature of such relationships is not easy to grasp as they cross so many boundaries—political, religious, economic, linguistic, and sexual. But Cortés did it again, this time with Doña Isabel Moctezuma (the Mexican emperor's daughter), who was forced to have a sexual union with him and bore him a daughter before being married to another Spanish nobleman. In Peru, both Atahualpa's sister and his fiancé became the sexual partners of Pizarro, the man who had executed Atahualpa. Such relationships must have created conflicted loyalties as these women became part of two separate worlds, as Powers says: "They straddled, painfully, the indigenous world of their family, ethnic, and cultural loyalties on the one hand and the Spanish world of their male partners, colonial oppressors, and mestizo children, on the other."[43]

---

[43] Ibid., 411.

In the East, native women who came into contact with the Portuguese, Dutch, and English encountered similar experiences. There were exceptions however. The Dutch formed the East India Company in the early seventeenth century as a vehicle for trading primarily in places such as India, southeast Asia (Malaysia, Indonesia, and the Philippines), Japan, and Taiwan. Given that Dutch women were reluctant to accompany their husbands, Dutch men took native wives. But long before the arrival of Europeans, women had been deeply involved in long-distance trade. As Pomeranz and Topik point out, "Malay proverbs of the 1500s spoke of the importance of teaching daughters how to calculate and make a profit."[44] Commerce was considered a base occupation for men yet too lucrative for elite families to ignore. The Portuguese had profited from intermarriage with such women, gaining access to local networks; and when the Dutch became players in this region, they did as well. What was in it for the women? "Many had also learned from their mothers how useful a European husband could be for protecting their business interests in an increasingly multinational and often violent trading world."[45]

WHAT KINDS OF MIGRANTS MOVED BETWEEN EMPIRES?

While large numbers of Iberians migrated to the New World to find a better life, not all migrants were voluntary. The transporting of African slaves to the New World represented one of the largest human migrations in world history. According to Emory University's Voyages Database, some 12.5 million slaves were transported to the New World between the sixteenth and the nineteenth centuries on about 35,000 voyages.[46] The destinations were mainly Brazil and the Caribbean. Here, the European colonists established large sugar plantations and imported enslaved Africans to work them, Africans being best able to endure the heat and the working hours (7 days week in most places). By 1650 African slaves outnumbered Europeans in Spain's colonies.

The Atlantic slave trade was perhaps *the* most brutal aspect of this era's history. Europeans purchased slaves from Africans, the market for them spawning "raptor" states in Africa, which went to war explicitly to enslave others to sell to Europeans. Often, slaves were captured deep inland, then transported to the coast, where Europeans loaded them on ships to cross the Atlantic. One former slave described the misery of these ships as follows: "two of my wearied countrymen who were chained together . . . preferring death to such a life of misery, somehow made through the netting and jumped into the sea. Immediately another quite dejected fellow, who on account of his illness was suffered to be out of irons,

---

[44]   Pomeranz and Topik, *The World That Trade Created*, 29.
[45]   Ibid.
[46]   Voyages Database 2009, *Voyages: The Trans-Atlantic Slave Trade Database*, http://www.slavevoyages.org/tast/assessment/estimates.faces.

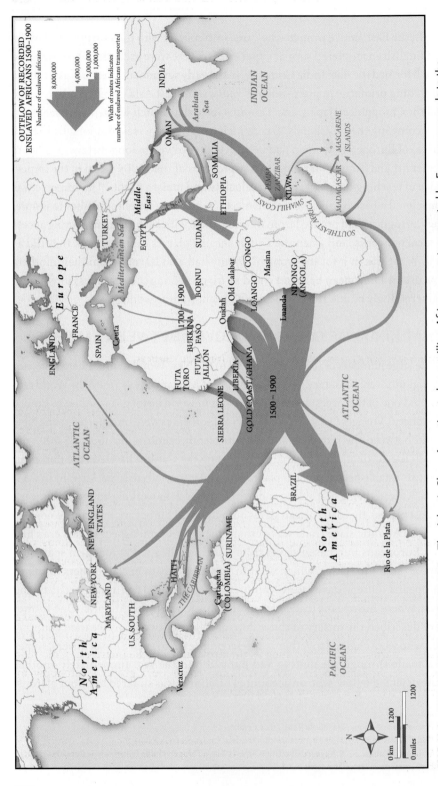

MAP 13.6 **THE ATLANTIC SLAVE TRADE** The Atlantic Slave. An estimated 12.5 million Africans were transported by European vessels to the Americas between the sixteenth and nineteenth centuries.

Within the map:

OUTFLOW OF RECORDED
ENSLAVED AFRICANS 1500–1900

Number of enslaved africans

8,000,000
4,000,000
2,000,000
1,000,000

Width of routes indicates
number of enslaved Africans transported

ENGLAND
FRANCE
SPAIN
Ceuta
Europe
Mediterranean Sea
TURKEY
EGYPT
Middle East
Red Sea
SUDAN
OMAN
Arabian Sea
INDIA
SOMALIA
ETHIOPIA
BORNU
1700–1900
FUTA TORO
FUTA JALLON
BURKINA FASO
Ouidah
Old Calabar
LOANGO
CONGO
Masina
NDONGO (ANGOLA)
Luanda
SIERRA LEONE
LIBERIA
GOLD COAST/GHANA
1500–1900
PEMBA
ZANZIBAR
KILWA
SWAHILI COAST
SOUTHEAST AFRICA
MASCARENE ISLANDS
MADAGASCAR
INDIAN OCEAN
ATLANTIC OCEAN
ATLANTIC OCEAN
North America
U.S. SOUTH
MARYLAND
NEW YORK
NEW ENGLAND STATES
Veracruz
HAITI
THE CARIBBEAN
Cartagena (COLOMBIA)
SURINAME
BRAZIL
South America
Rio de la Plata
PACIFIC OCEAN

N
0 km   1200
0 miles   1200

504

African Slaves Being Loaded into the Hold for the Trip to the Americas

followed their example."[47] In addition to the frequently inhumane treatment of native peoples, from North America to Chile, the experience of African slaves represents the extreme brutality that characterizes the processes of change—and the pursuit of profit—under way in this period.

Such large numbers of Africans transformed an already changing society in the Americas. European culture, adapting to the new environments in which it found itself, was largely eclipsed by African traditions. "From Virginia to Bahía, much of Atlantic-side America became, in early colonial times, a world that was almost uniform in one respect. It was a world 'slaves made,' more African than European."[48]

It took generations for slave culture to abandon its African roots, partly because slave owners did not seek to convert their chattel, uneasy, no doubt, at the proximity of slavery and Christianity. Slaves practiced their own religions, spoke in regional African or pidgin dialects, and ate their own food. Some escaped and formed "maroon" kingdoms, such as the Esmeraldas in the interior of Colombia and others in Jamaica and the Carolinas, which were granted autonomy by Spanish and British authorities, respectively.

---

[47] "The Interesting Narrative of the Life of Olaudah Equiano or Gustavus the African," quoted in Eric Gilbert and Jonathon T. Reynolds, *Africa in World History* (Upper Saddle River, NJ: Pearson, 2008), 159.
[48] Fernández-Armesto, *The Americas*, 64.

Further down the food chain, plants and animals circulated among empires and civilizations. When the Spaniards came to the New World, they missed their staples: wheat bread, pork, olive oil, and wine. A partial solution was to bring some of these things with them. When French fur trappers arrived in the North American interior in the eighteenth century, they found the place largely deserted. They assumed that it had always been thus, but in reality a century before the same place along the Mississippi had been densely populated with Indian towns and villages. The region had been depopulated by smallpox epidemics unleashed by the herds of wild pigs accompanying Spanish explorers of the sixteenth century.

Spaniards always traveled with pigs; they were the fast food of the era. They flourished in most of the Americas, but they were also hyperefficient vectors of disease; and to Indian tribes with no immunity they were deadly. Some explorers left pigs to breed in the wild on Caribbean islands, ensuring a meat supply for future expeditions. While many of the West Indian islands were depopulated by a combination of European slave raids and diseases, the European animals often took over; pigs, sheep, and horses often went feral on deserted islands.

The horse accompanied Columbus on his voyages and was vital to Spanish warfare. But it was altogether fussier than the pig and took longer to find the right environment, suffering in the humid jungles of Central America. But as the Spanish spread across the continent they found new lands that were more pleasing. As historian Alfred Crosby put it, "What happened when the horse reached what is today Argentina and Uruguay is best described as a biological explosion: horses running free on the grassy vastness propagated in a manner similar to the smallpox virus in the salubrious environment of Indian bodies."[49]

But exchange is a reciprocal process. The early Spanish explorers returned home with samples of New World flora and fauna. Maize spread globally; it grows easily and can be stored. The potato is another case in point. It did not succeed immediately in Europe, being long considered a marginal food item; but today it is the second most widespread crop in the world (after wheat). After 1600, Europe's population began to boom, leading to food shortages. The potato liked a good crisis and rose to the occasion. In the mid-seventeenth century the English had been practicing a scorched-earth policy on their Irish colony, burning crops to punish rebels. The potato tolerated wet fields, which were difficult to burn; grew underground; and could be stored indoors for months. "By the end of the century the potato had become the dominant source of Irish food (and drink): an adult male consumed about seven pounds of them a day."[50] This was a miracle

---

[49] Alfred Crosby, *The Columbian Exchange: Biological and Cultural Consequences of 1492* (Westport, CT: Greenwood Press, 1972), 84.

[50] Pomeranz and Topik, *The World That Trade Created*, 145.

solution for the Irish, at least until the famine of the 1840s when crop failure across Ireland caused mass starvation and large-scale emigration to America.

Other New World crops became European staples, and these had as much impact as the potato. "None was very good for you," say Pomeranz and Topik, "but Europeans soon craved them all, and grew none of them at home. Huge plantations were cleared, slaves imported, companies chartered, royal monopolies created. Fortunes made and lost."[51] These included sugar, tobacco, cocoa, and coffee and were all to play a large role in the global economy—and global diet—ever after.

Lower down the food chain still were microbes. There is little debate about the fact that native societies became victims of Old World diseases. The exact numbers are debated, however. Geographer William Denevan concluded in the 1970s that the precontact New World was much more heavily populated than previously assumed, home to anywhere between 43 and 65 million people.[52] There is a growing consensus today that in the early seventeenth century this figure had dropped to 5 or 6 million.

These are shocking numbers to be sure, representing a loss of some 90% of the native population of the entire continent. Disease accounts for the majority of this die-off. "A great many died from this plague," records an Aztec source on the smallpox pandemic that killed thousands in Tenochtitlán, "and many others died from hunger. They could not get up to search for food, and everyone else was too sick to care for them, so they starved to death in their beds."[53] On the island of Hispaniola, the native Taino population was estimated at about half a million in 1492. By 1542 there were some 2,000 left. For many Spaniards these epidemics seemed like a divine message of approval, and they were content to think no further. "This was the Columbian Exchange," says Morris, "Europeans got a new continent and Native Americans got smallpox."[54]

WHAT PART DID RELIGION PLAY IN GLOBAL EXPANSIONS?

When people move, their gods tend to travel with them. From the end of the fifteenth century onward, the scale of global interaction ushered in reforms and revolutions within and among religions. At roughly the same time that Cortés was preparing to sail for Mexico (1517), Martin Luther was about to launch the Protestant Reformation, which would give Europeans something to fight over for centuries. Ottoman conquests in Egypt (1517) and expansion into the Indian

---

[51]   Ibid., 143.

[52]   William H. Denevan, *The Native Population of the Americas in 1492*, 2nd ed. (Madison: University of Wisconsin Press, 1992).

[53]   Miguel Leon Portilla and Lysander Kemp, *The Broken Spears: The Aztec Account of the Conquest of Mexico* (Boston: Beacon Press, 1962), 92–93.

[54]   Morris, *Why the West Rules*, 464.

Ocean made them the predominant multiethnic Islamic power, and the Mughals spread Islam into the jungles and deltas of Bangladesh. Animist religions of nomadic pastoralists gave way to universal religions of sedentary states in many areas. For example, the 1640 Mongol–Oirat *quriltai* ("assembly") produced the Mongol–Oirat code, which, among other things, established Buddhism as the pan-Mongol religion and fined the practice of shamanism. In the West, African religions became established in the Americas with African slave communities.

But, as historian Charles H. Parker points out, the expansion of religions was not a one-directional process, especially in the case of the more hegemonic cases: "Rather indigenous peoples engaged Christianity and Islam with their own cultural frameworks, molding these universal faiths into religious systems they could comprehend and act on."[55] And just as the world's universal religions had developed in an era of growing interaction, a similar process may have been in train now, with new pressures and traditions coming to bear on old religions: "In some ways the religious tumult of the fifteenth to seventeenth centuries was a reprise of the era in which the world's great religions took hold."[56] Increasing urbanism prompted a search for new moral codes and new guidelines for interactions with others. But by 1400, say the McNeills, the old religions invited new intellectual and religious movements because they had to varying degrees become plagued by careerism, corruption, and cronyism.

To many Japanese in the mid-sixteenth century, Christianity had a certain appeal over long-established Buddhist and Shinto traditions. The historian James L. Huffman tells a story about the Japanese introduction to Dutch anatomical studies. In 1771, he relates, the physician Sugita Genpaku watched while the corpse of a criminal known as Old Mother Green Tea was dissected. Genpaku had recently acquired some Dutch books on anatomy and was intrigued that they showed a very different picture of the human body from his Chinese books. To see which were right, Old Mother Green Tea had to be cut open. "Comparing the things we saw with the pictures in the Dutch book," he reported, "we were amazed at their perfect agreement."[57]

The first Westerners to arrive in Japan were, like those in the Yucatán, shipwrecked in 1543. Soon more Europeans came with tradeables, guns, and Christianity. By mid-century the Japanese were welcoming "hundreds of gun-and bible-bearing Westerners who had come to make a profit and save souls."[58] The Portuguese were the most energetic in early interactions as they could reach Japan easily from their trade entrêpot in Macao. The Japanese were initially open to foreign goods and ideas. Possibly as many as 300,000 Japanese embraced

---

[55] Parker, *Global Interactions in the Early Modern Age*, 218.
[56] McNeill and McNeill, *The Human Web*, 181.
[57] James L. Huffman, *Japan in World History* (New York: Oxford University Press, 2010), 55.
[58] Ibid., 57.

Christianity. As with all conversions, there were many reasons; some needed the spiritual nourishment, and some wanted access to the European goods. Some followed their political leaders. Even the *daimyo* ("lord") Oda Nobunaga (1534–1582), credited with setting the stage for Japan's unification, converted.

But foreigners, especially in a relatively small island nation, can be threatening. In 1597 a valuable Spanish galleon ran aground on Japan's coast. Appealing to the shogun, Toyotomi Hideyoshi (1536–1598), to keep his cargo, the captain boasted of his master King Philip II's power. How come so much power from such a small nation? asked Hideyoshi. The answer: the king sends out priests to Christianize the population, softening them up for the military invasion. Hideyoshi promptly kept the cargo and for good measure crucified 26 Christians.

The problem for the Japanese was not just the fear that Europeans wanted

Toyotomi Hideyoshi, the Shogun of Japan (1536–1598), Credited with Being Japan's Second Great Unifier After Oda Nobunaga (1534–1582)   An island nation, Japan was suspicious of the consequences of letting foreigners in, although their goods were appealing.

to Christianize, then conquer; but Christians owed ultimate allegiance to God, thus eliminating the traditional Japanese social hierarchy in which loyalty was to one's earthly lord. In 1612 the Tokugawa Shogunate formally banned Christianity. But European merchants brought their Christianity with them, so by 1616 all except Chinese merchants were restricted from all ports except Nagasaki and Hirado. Eventually only the Dutch were left, and they were restricted to an island in Nagasaki Bay. "They drank, smoked, played cards," says Landes, "and languished in boredom and stupefaction. Not a good assignment. The Japanese wanted it that way."[59] By now Christians, Japanese converts or foreigners, were the victims of full-scale persecution, which lasted for over 100 years.

For Portuguese and Spanish alike, Christianity was woven into the fabric of the violent process of colonization; and they saved many souls, even if ending lives in the process. Wherever they went in Mexico, the Spaniards erected crosses, berated the locals for human sacrifice, and baptized when they could. Cortés was

---

[59]   Landes, *The Wealth and Poverty of Nations*, 356.

✦ The existence of the Christian God did not, therefore, contradict Aztec beliefs, whereas Aztec polytheism was incompatible with biblical monotheism.

quick to raise the subject of religion with Moctezuma, but the emperor's response was underwhelming. As Bernal Díaz recorded it, calling him "Senior Malinche," Moctezuma reminded Cortés that "Throughout all time we have worshipped our own gods, and thought they were good, as no doubt yours are, so do not trouble to speak to us anymore about them at present."[60] The main difference between the Spanish god and those of the Aztecs was that the Aztec gods were not exclusive. The existence of the Christian God did not, therefore, contradict Aztec beliefs, whereas Aztec polytheism was incompatible with biblical monotheism.

The history of Christianity in the New World has often been written in the shadow of one overwhelming aspect of the native religion: cannibalism and human sacrifice. Díaz mentions sacrifice frequently: "That very night five Indians had been sacrificed before them; their chests had been cut open, and their arms and thighs had been cut off and the walls were covered with blood."[61] The Spaniards were particularly horrified when the Aztecs attempted to spice their food with fresh human blood. Such practices may have been exaggerated by the conquistadores, yet it is clear that they were a central part of Aztec religion. Moctezuma explained to Cortés how this practice was demanded of them by their deities. It could not be abandoned for fear of angering the gods.

Human sacrifice was a reflection of Aztec creation myths. In one, the gods burned themselves alive to create the sun. In another they spilled their blood to create humans. "These myths created a reciprocal relationship of obligation between humankind and the gods—and these obligations could be repaid only through offerings of human blood and life."[62] But human sacrifice became another justification for conquest and the spread of Christianity, most immediately during conquest and for decades, even centuries, as the conquest was repeatedly portrayed as a victory of a superior race over an inferior one.

Europeans brought African slaves to the New World, and as with other aspects of their culture, African religions left a lasting impression there, despite the fact that many Africans adopted Christianity. These religions were by and large polytheistic and by that measure essentially different from Christianity. But most Africans and Europeans of the early modern period shared a belief in spirits and believed that ritual practices held the power to control them. The Puritans of the Massachusetts Bay Colony of the seventeenth century, for example, saw Tituba, a slave from the West Indies, as a manipulator of evil spirits

---

[60]   Díaz, *History of the Conquest of New Spain*, 16.
[61]   Ibid., 54.
[62]   Smith, *The Aztecs*, 197.

The Spirit World   African slaves brought their animist and polytheistic religions with them, and even if they became Christian, the syncretic nature of conversion ensured that cultures blended. Early modern Europeans often believed in spirits also, as the Salem witch trials of 1692 proved.

during the Salem witch trials of 1692. African religions had a direct impact on the wider American culture, in particular in the southern United States, as evidenced by the "syncretic" folk magic beliefs such as *juju, hoodoo,* and *mojo.* Other religious ideas blended African elements with foreign ones, such as Santería in Cuba, Macumba and Candomblé in Brazil, and voodoo in Haiti and the southern United States.

Conclusion: What Changed in Global Interactions Between 1450 and 1750?

From China and Japan to Russia and Europe and the Americas, populations grew, came into contact, and entered into multiple relationships—economic, political, military, sexual, and religious. In the East, Russia and China together brought irreversible change to the central Eurasian steppe. In doing so they effectively ended the millennia-long process in which agrarian states had been threatened by pastoral groups and at the same time dodged the bullet of population growth and resource depletion by grabbing for themselves millions of acres of new land for cultivation.

In the West, European demands for new resources were met by the opening up of new sea routes, both to the Americas and to the old empires of Eurasia, where lay rich pickings in spices and other luxury goods. In the process the Portuguese laid the foundations of the Atlantic slave trade and challenged the centuries-old networks of exchange they found in the Indian Ocean. The Spanish effectively overwhelmed the New World civilizations of the Aztec and Inca, whose own expansions had created polities that were vulnerable to conquest.

All of these worlds were stitched together by the resultant economies revolving around commodities from these various regions and to a large extent by the enormous influx of American silver, which facilitated this early modern world economy. Some civilizations came face to face with forces they were utterly unable to control and found themselves engulfed, such as the Aztec and Inca; others transformed themselves from marginal outsiders (Europeans) to globally dominant powers.

Lastly, the movement of people—and animals—brought a host of diseases, which devastated native populations in the New World and to a much lesser extent central Eurasian populations with little resistance. If we have been calling this the "early modern" period, it is because it prefigures many of the modern world's historical characteristics: the capitalist monetary system, the nation-state, industrialization, colonialism and revolution, large-scale environment changes, and globalization—all of which form the basis of modern world history.

Words to Think About

Conquistador	Mestizo	Pidgin
Privateer	Quadroon	Syncretic

Questions to Think About

- Why did states expand in this period?
- What was new about the way states expanded?
- Was early modern expansion an inevitable prelude to European global domination?

Secondary Sources

Brook, Timothy. *Vermeer's Hat: The Seventeenth Century and the Dawn of the Global World.* New York: Bloomsbury, 2008.

Casale, Giancarlo. *The Ottoman Age of Exploration.* New York: Oxford University Press, 2010.

Crosby, Alfred. *The Columbian Exchange: Biological and Cultural Consequences of 1492.* Westport, CT: Greenwood Press, 1972.

Demos, John. "The High Place: Potosi." In "Early Cities of the Americas." Special issue, *Common-Place* 3, no. 4 (2003), http://www.common-place.org/vol-03/no-04/potosi/.

Denevan, William H. *The Native Population of the Americas in 1492*, 2nd ed. Madison: University of Wisconsin Press, 1992.

Diaz, Bernal. *History of the Conquest of New Spain*, edited by Davíd Carrasco. Albuquerque: University of New Mexico Press, 2008.

Eaton, Richard. *The Rise of Islam and the Bengal Frontier, 1204–1760.* Berkeley: University of California Press, 1993.

Fernández-Armesto, Felipe. "Empires in Their Global Context: c. 1500–c. 1800." In *The Atlantic in Global History: 1500–2000*, edited by Jorge Cañizares-Esguerra and Erik R. Seeman. Upper Saddle River, NJ: Pearson, 2006.

Fernández-Armesto, Felipe. *The Americas: A Hemispheric History.* New York: Modern Library Chronicles, 2003.

Flynn, Dennis O., and Arturo Giraldez. "Born with a Silver Spoon: The Origin of World Trade in 1571." *Journal of World History* 6, no. 2 (1995): 201–221.

Gilbert, Eric, and Jonathon T. Reynolds. *Africa in World History.* Upper Saddle River, NJ: Pearson, 2008.

Golden, Peter B. *Central Asia in World History.* New York: Oxford University Press, 2011.

Goldstone, Jack. *Revolution and Rebellion in the Early Modern World.* Berkeley: University of California Press, 1991.

Hassig, Ross. *Aztec Warfare: Imperial Expansion and Political Control.* Norman: University of Oklahoma Press, 1988.

Huffman, James L. *Japan in World History.* New York: Oxford University Press, 2010. Landes, David. *The Wealth and Poverty of Nations: Why Some Are So Rich and Some So Poor.* New York: W.W. Norton, 1999.

Liberman, Victor. "Transcending East–West Dichotomies: State and Culture Formation in Six Ostensibly Separate Areas." *Modern Asian Studies* 31 (1997): 463–546.

McNeill, William H., and J. R. McNeill. *The Human Web: A Bird's Eye View of World History.* New York: W.W. Norton, 2003.

Morris, Ian. *Why the West Rules—For Now: The Patterns of History and What They Reveal About the Future.* New York: Farrar, Strauss and Giroux, 2010.

Parker, Charles H. *Global Interactions in the Early Modern Age, 1400–1800.* Cambridge: Cambridge University Press, 2010.

Perdue, Peter. *China Marches West: The Qing Conquest of Central Eurasia.* Cambridge, MA: Harvard University Press, 2005.

Pomeranz, Kenneth, and Steven Topik. *The World That Trade Created: Society, Culture and the World Economy, 1400 to the Present.* New York: M.E. Sharpe, 1999.

Portilla, Miguel Leon, and Lysander Kemp. *The Broken Spears: The Aztec Account of the Conquest of Mexico.* Boston: Beacon Press, 1962.

Powers, Karen Vieira. "Colonial Sexuality: of Women, Men, and Mestizaje." In *History of the Conquest of New Spain,* edited by Davíd Carrasco. Albuquerque: University of New Mexico Press, 2008.

Restall, Matthew. *Seven Myths of the Spanish Conquest.* New York: Oxford University Press, 2010.

Richards, John F. *The Unending Frontier: An Environmental History of the Early Modern World.* Berkeley: University of California Press, 2003.

Smith, Michael E. *The Aztecs,* 3rd ed. Malden, MA: Wiley-Blackwell, 2012.

Voyages Database 2009, *Voyages: The Trans-Atlantic Slave Trade Database,* http://www.slavevoyages.org/tast/assessment/estimates.faces.

For additional resources, including maps, primary sources, and visuals, web links, and quizzes, please go to **www.oup.com/us/cole**

Epilogue:
History and the Future

The only history of the future that we have, a colleague once pointed out to me, is that from the *Star Trek* TV show of Gene Rodenberry, in which each episode begins with a "star date," tracking our heroes' adventures in time. Unfortunately, we cannot really know what the future holds. The relationship of the past to the future, however, is of some interest, for when we contemplate the future it makes us look differently at the past and understanding the past must surely give us some pointers about the future.

Most generations have felt that their times were more difficult than those preceding them and even that those challenges presaged catastrophe of global proportions. The end of times seems to be something every generation has worried about, perhaps because change itself poses such psychological challenges that we see something terminal when faced with it. But looking at our future, from the point of view of the early twenty-first century, even the most stout-hearted among us can, I believe, be forgiven for swallowing hard and wondering how it is all going to play out.

Robert Jay Lifton, the psychiatrist and author, once wrote that nuclear power's destructive potential was so great that we could not appreciate it enough to effectively control it. Since the bombing of Nagasaki and Hiroshima at the end of World War II, humanity has been forced to contemplate its possible extinction. But today nuclear power, the apocalyptic technology we have invented, is but one of the threats to our existence and arrays itself against us along with human-induced climate change, environmental degradation, pollution, and population growth, making the future distinctly worrisome.

Bearing in mind the challenges that face us in the next decades and centuries, how should we look upon our history? Is history even relevant since you could argue that all eyes are needed as we face forward? The political scientist Francis Fukuyama wrote in the 1990s that we were witnessing the "end of history, as such." By this he meant that Western liberal democracy had become—with the end of the Cold War and the failure of communism—the default, and perhaps the "final," system of human government. But, as it turns out, Fukuyama was too quick to snap the book closed and announce "the end," even if in a sense he was right that there was a tectonic change in the content of human history at that time.

Today, however, we may be facing a kind of "end of history 2.0," in the twin phenomena of global climate change and globalization. Why should these phenomena be the end of history? If history has to date been a seemingly endless tale of one polity going up against another—a succession of wars, struggles, battles, and conflicts—are we approaching an age when that is all . . . history? Are we on the verge of an era of global cooperation of an unprecedented level, spurred by a recognition of mutual interest and common crisis? Such cooperation is needed more than ever before if we are to avert global environmental disaster.

Albert Einstein, among others, wrote about the need for world government in the wake of two destructive world wars. Those disasters were purely political. Now we have challenges that face all of humanity equally. If our soil, water, and air are threatened, our species faces an unprecedented challenge to its existence. Granted, the effects of climate change differ according to geography (often affecting the poorer regions more dramatically), but all human life has the same basic requirements, until recently met by the Holocene, our current geological era. Now some suggest that we have entered the *anthropocene*—a human-generated geological era, marked by unpredictable weather, disrupting the delicate balance required for agriculture and thus threatening our food supplies. Not only that, but our population growth, largely unchecked, has created enormous stresses on the human community and the biosphere. While many argue that larger population provides the opportunity for more geniuses to figure out innovative solutions to our problems, others see this as tortured logic.

Globalization, that process of planetary shrinkage, has combined with environmental crisis to generate a sense of global community that is arguably more vivid, real, and immediate than ever before; not only do we have more critical, shared priorities in the need to protect the planet for our children but we are more aware of each other and our interdependence than ever before. Climate change and globalization, therefore, have arguably created a global community, at the same time as they have posed the greatest challenges to the human race.

But in the same way that globalization has also created conflict in raising the specter of greater inequality, awareness of our common humanity does not mean that human conflict (arguably the very content of history) has disappeared.

The proposition that we are all "in it together" may well fly in the face of the experiences of people such as the Israelis and the Palestinians or the warring parties in the wider Middle East or in dozens of other places worldwide. Nor may the disenfranchised feel particularly close to the superwealthy. However, the fact remains that we are all in it together; the only question that remains is whether the prevailing political mood of the future will reflect this and whether nations will cooperate in mutual benefit or continue in the historical tradition, struggling for their narrow interests and thereby jeopardizing the global future. Will humanity face its greatest crises ever as one or allow its divisions to let it fail?

So as we step forward we must look back and take stock. We have seen in several chapters how war drove a process of growth and merging of states and polities, often leading to larger areas united under common leadership. These large states and empires did not always last, but, like the Roman and Mongol Empires, they had legacies that spread ideas, shared cultural forms, and created a certain unity, which shrank the world in multiple ways. In this sense it is worth asking, therefore, whether we can see in history a movement toward at least the *possibility* of unity. Whether it "takes" or lasts remains to be seen. Will planet earth, in 500 years, reflect Gene Rodenberry's vision of a truly multiracial human community, displacing all conflicts into deep space? Or will it continue, deeply riven and conflictual, to give us more history-as-usual, struggles of one group against another over resources and ideas?

Glossary

Adaptation: A biological trait, or facet, adopted within specific ecosystems that enhances survival chances (e.g., bipedalism, cooking).

Bipedalism: An adaptation, restricted today to *Homo sapiens*, of walking upright on two legs.

Ecosystem: A community of biological creatures interacting with nonbiological elements and features. Example: an ocean, a tide pool, a wood.

Evolution: The process by which biological entities change over time. Working through a process of "natural selection," some traits allow certain individuals to survive to reproductive age—and pass on their genes.

Hominid: Refers to any of the family Hominidae, or upright, bipedal apes.

Chapter 2

Agriculture: The practice of growing food by cultivating plants—preparing soil, sowing, watering, weeding—and rearing animals for food.

Domestication: The process of genetically modifying a species by controlling reproduction. Applicable to plants and animals.

Foraging: The practice of finding food by collecting what nature has already grown; used in opposition to "farming," a method of procuring food by growing it.

Holocene: The climatic period following the Pleistocene. Began approximately 11,700 years ago.

Hunter–Gatherer: Of, relating to, or designating (the culture of) a people who live by hunting, fishing, and foraging rather than by farming (growing crops, rearing livestock, etc.).

Sedentism: The practice of permanently residing in one location. Sedentary living.

Subsistence: The earning of a living, such as by foraging or farming.

Chapter 3

Alluvial: From *alluvium*, a deposit of earth, sand, and other transported matter left by water flowing over land not permanently submerged.

Egalitarian: Relating to the equality of all people.

Hierarchy: A body of persons or things ranked in grades, orders, or classes, one above the other.

Irrigation: The action of supplying or the fact of being supplied with moisture; a moistening or wetting. Often used in an agricultural context.

Patriarchal: of, relating to, or characteristic of a system of a society or government controlled by men.

Ziggurat: A stage tower of pyramid form in which each successive story is smaller than the one below.

Chapter 4

Annal: A narrative of events written year by year.

Conscription: Enrollment or enlistment of soldiers.

Dynasty: A group or sequence of rulers, from the same family.

Genocide: The deliberate and systematic extermination of an ethnic or national group.

Hegemony: An indirect form of government in which the ruler exerts influence over less powerful entities through economic or military pressure or threat.

Polity: State or state-like body, such as a prefecture, district, or kingdom.

Utopia: An imaginary island, depicted by Sir Thomas More as enjoying a perfect social, legal, and political system.

Chapter 5

Brahmin: A high-status, or elite, Indian group.

Ethnology: A branch of anthropology that analyzes human social groups.

Oral Tradition: The passing from generation to generation of a group's history and traditions in narrative form.

Republic: From the Latin *res publica* ("public affairs"), a state of government in which people elect their leaders.

Taboo: A ban or inhibition, originating in social customs.

Tyranny: System of government in which all power is vested in one person.

Chapter 6

Autocrat: A leader with no legal or popular restraints on power.

Despotism: A form of government in which a single entity has power. This can be a person (autocrat) or an entity (oligarchy).

Harem: From the Arabic *haram* ("forbidden"), a restricted sanctuary for women, usually multiple wives of one man.

Humanities: An academic discipline using speculative rather than empirical methods—often history/literature—as opposed to scientific disciplines.

Orientalism: A historical and literary term referring to the representation of the East by scholars and critics from the West.

Plebian: Common people of ancient Rome, in contrast to patricians.

Chapter 7

Animism: The belief that the natural world is populated by multiple spiritual entities. Often the belief system of nomadic or tribal peoples.

Dualism: From the Latin *duo* ("two"). Moral dualism denotes a strict binary opposite of good and evil.

Monotheism: The belief in one god, or the one*ness* of God.

Polytheism: The belief in multiple gods.

Transcendental: Implying a fundamental, supernatural realm, separate from the earthly one.

Chapter 8

Commodity: Any item or object that is subject to trade or exchange or that has a monetary value.

Monopoly: The exclusive control by a group or individual over a commodity's sale or possession.

Sahel: The biogeographic zone in Africa between the Sahara Desert to the north and the sub-Saharan tropics to the south.

Syncretism: The blending of elements from different cultures to enable alien ideas to relate to something culturally familiar (in the context of religious conversion).

Tribute: A gift or payment, used in the ancient world as a sign of respect or subservience. Often made in lieu of taxes.

Chapter 9

Alchemy: A proto-science; the role of alchemy has varied over time, but its historical goals have been to turn base metals into precious ones or to find the elixir of life—that is, immortality.

Bas-relief: Sculptures in bas-relief give the impression that they are raised against a lower background.

Numerology: A practice of associating numbers with divine or supernatural events.

Slash-and-Burn Agriculture: Also known as "swidden" agriculture, this is a system in which small farmers, usually in the tropics, cut and burn forest to clear fields. Fields can only be used in the short term as the lack of trees leads to soil erosion.

Technology Transfer: The process by which innovations, processes, or techniques are copied by different groups.

Chapter 10

Colonization: From the Latin *colere* ("to inhabit, occupy"). Occurs when any specific population inhabits a specific area.

Contiguous: Connected, sharing a common border.

Infidel: A term used particularly in Christianity and Islam, denoting one without faith in a particular religion.

Steppe: An ecoregion or area of semiarid grasslands, too dry to support a forest but not dry enough for desert; typified by continental climate (cold winters, hot summers).

Chapter 11

Collapse: a breakdown; a sudden failure of an institution or undertaking

Hohokam: Used to denote a particular culture in the American Southwest characterized in particular by its lack of central authority.

Holocene: Our current geological epoch. Based on an amelioration of the climate at the end of the Ice Age, about 11,500 years before the present.

Pueblo: From the Castilian word for "town," used to denote the communities of natives of the American Southwest.

Sustainable: Refers to methods of agriculture—and lifestyle in general—which allow a people or society to continue in that vein indefinitely, without overtaxing their environment.

Theater-State: A state with a predatory upper class which uses public (religious) rituals to maintain loyalty and order among their subjects by inculcating an ideology.

Chapter 12

Bourgeoisie: From French, denotes middle-class origins, used from around the late Middle Ages.

Griots: West African storytellers, experts in oral tradition.

Periodization: The historian's process of assigning particular attributes to time periods.

Presentism: The projecting of attitudes or values of the present into the past.

Renaissance Humanism: An intellectual/academic movement to rediscover classical texts and learning. Initially an Italian phenomenon, it then spread across Europe.

Chapter 13

Conquistador: An explorer/soldier/adventurer in South or Central America, usually in the service of the Spanish or Portuguese Crown.

Mestizo: Literally "mixed," referring to a person of mixed Spanish and Native American blood.

Pidgin: A simplified version of two different languages, allowing communication between them (e.g., pidgin English or French).

Privateer: A private individual permitted via "letters of marque" to attack foreign shipping in times of war.

Syncretic: Elements from different cultures blended together.

Quadroon: Refers to a person of mixed African and Caucasian ancestry, specifically one-quarter black, or with biracial parents.

Illustration Credits

Chapter 1

p. 2: © Neustockimages; p. 8: A Venerable Orang Outang, from 'The Hornet' (pencil and charcoal on paper) (b/w photo), English School, (19th century)/Private Collection/The Bridgeman Art Library; p. 11: Ian Tattersall, The Fossil Trail. Used with permission; p. 10: Tim Flannery, The Future Eaters: An Ecological History of the Australasian Lands and People (Chatswood, N.S.W.: Reed, 1995), p. 119; p. 13: Diagram by Jennifer Steffey. Ian Tattersall, Masters of the Planet, published 2012, reproduced with permission of Palgrave Macmillan; p. 16: Photo by Dennis Finnin and Craig Chesek. Transparency #4936(7), American Museum of Natural History, Library; p. 18: Cover/Getty Images; p. 20: CALVK KIKE CALVO/Associated Press; p. 22: © Universal Images Group Limited/Alamy; p. 25: © RMN-Grand Palais/Art Resource, NY; p. 27: AFP/Getty Images; p. 31: Image courtesy of Prof Christopher Henshilwood.

Chapter 2

p. 40: Denmark, Copenhagen, amber necklaces and pendants from Laddenhoj/De Agostini Picture Library/The Bridgeman Art Library; p. 45: Getty Images; p. 49: AFP/Getty Images; p. 52: © Alex Gregory/The New Yorker Collection/The Cartoon Bank; p. 55: UIG via Getty Images; p. 57: © Marion Bull/Alamy; p. 60: Peter M. M. G. Akkermans and Glenn M. Schwarts, The Archaeology of Syria: From Complex Hunter-Gatherers to Early Urban Societies (c. 16,000–300 BC), ©2003, p. 51. Reprinted with the permission of Cambridge University Press; p. 63: De Agostini/Getty Images; p. 67: © nsf/Alamy; p. 70: Erich Lessing/Art Resource, NY; p. 73: Courtesy of the Library of Congress; p. 73: Village on the Euphrates: From Foraging to Farming at Abu Hureyra by Moore, Hillman, and Legge (2000). By permission of Oxford University Press, USA; p. 75: © National Geographic Image Collection/Alamy.

Chapter 3

p. 80: © Jim West/Alamy; p. 85: Isis and Nefertari, from the Tomb of Nefertari, New Kingdom (mural), Egyptian 19th Dynasty (c. 1297–1185 BC)/Valley of the Queens, Thebes, Egypt/Giraudon/The Bridgeman Art Library; p. 89: North-eastern facade of the ziggurat, c. 2100 BC (photo), ./Ur, Iraq/© World Religions Photo Library/The Bridgeman Art Library; p. 96: NASA/NOAA/Rex Features/FEREX/ASSOCIATED PRESS; p. 97: © Balage Balogh/Art Resource, NY Barnow (2001, 51) Drawing by Claus Roloff, from the Cities and Modes of Production Project. Reproduced by permission; p. 99: From Trigger, Understanding Early Civilizations: A Comparative Study (New York: Cambridge University Press, 2003), 592. a) from H. Junker, Giza (Vienna, 1922–1955); b) from A. Gardiner 1950, pl. 2; c) from J. Friedrich, Extinct Languages (New York, 1957), 36; d) from C. E. Keiser, Neo-Sumerian Account Texts from Drehem: Babylonian Inscriptions in the Collection of James B. Nies (New Haven, 1971), document 448; e) after K. Chang, The Archaeology of Ancient

China, 2nd ed. (New Haven, 1968), 188; f) from Lo Chen-yu, Yin-hsu, Shu-ch'I Ching-hua (Peking, 1914); p. 101: © Robert Harding World Imagery/Alamy; p. 105: © BANANA PANCAKE/Alamy; p. 106: Reconstruction of the building of Mohenjo Daro (colour litho), ./Private Collection/Ancient Art and Architecture Collection Ltd./The Bridgeman Art Library; p. 110: View of the well shaft in the Lower City (photo), ./Mohenjo-Daro, Sindh Province, Pakistan/Ancient Art and Architecture Collection Ltd./The Bridgeman Art Library; p. 113: Huang jundong sx – Imaginechina; p. 117: Copyright © 2004 Arthur Demarest. Reprinted with the permission of Cambridge University Press.

Chapter 4

p. 122: bpk, Berlin/Museum fuer Asiatische Kunst, Staatliche Museen zu Berlin, Ber/Iris Papadopoulos/Art Resource, NY; p. 125: Erich Lessing/Art Resource, NY; p. 130: Getty Images; p. 133: Photo by Karl G. Heider © President and Fellows of Harvard College, Peabody Museum of Archaeology and Ethnology, Harvard University, PM# 2006.17.1.89.2; p. 133: Photograph by Michael Clark Rockefeller © President and Fellows of Harvard College, Peabody Museum of Archaeology and Ethnology, Harvard University, PM# 2006.12.1.151.17; p. 137: Erich Lessing/Art Resource, NY; p. 141: © Balage Balogh/Art Resource, NY; p. 143: Gianni Dagli Orti/The Art Archive at Art Resource, NY; p. 145: HIP/Art Resource, NY; p. 150: Courtesy of The Department of Classics, University of Cincinnati; p. 154: Getty Images.

Chapter 5

p. 162: Getty Images; p. 173: Erich Lessing/Art Resource, NY; p. 176: NGS Image Collection/The Art Archive at Art Resource, NY; p. 179: Getty Images; p. 180: © The Trustees of the British Museum; p. 181: Group of Zulus having their Scouff, c. 1895 (b/w photo), South African Photographer, (19th century)/Private Collection/The Bridgeman Art Library; p. 184: The Alexander Mosaic, detail depicting Alexander the Great (356–323 BC) at the Battle of Issus against Darius III (399–330 BC) in 333 BC (mosaic) (detail of 154003), Roman, (1st century BC)/Museo Archeologico Nazionale, Naples, Italy/Giraudon/The Bridgeman Art Library; p. 188: The city of Athens in Ancient Greece, English School, (20th century)/Private Collection/© Look and Learn/The Bridgeman Art Library; p. 192: Greek civilization, Ostraka, sherds of broken pots re-used as voting 'ballots' cast by Athenians/De Agostini Picture Library/G. Nimatallah/The Bridgeman Art Library; p. 193: AFP/Getty Images.

Chapter 6

p. 198: Roman/Getty Images; p. 204: David Du Plessis/Getty Images; p. 208: © Trippin' Out/Alamy; p. 213: DEA/N. CIRANI/Getty Images; p. 216: Virginia Star/Getty Images; p. 218: DEA/PUBBLI AER FOTO/Getty Images; p. 223: Lion Pillar of Emperor Ashoka (c. 264–223 BC) at the Monkey Pond (photo), Indian, (3rd century BC)/Vaisali, Bihar, India/The Bridgeman Art Library; p. 226: Chinese Labourers Working on a River (w/c), Alexander, William (1767–1816)/© The Makins Collection/The Bridgeman Art Library; p. 230: Scene from the life of Confucius (c. 551–479 BC) and his disciples, Qing Dynasty (1644–1912) (ink, w/c & sepia wash on paper), Chinese School, (19th century)/Bibliotheque Nationale, Paris, France/Giraudon/The Bridgeman Art Library; p. 233: Remains of the Han Dynasty Wall, Gansu Province, Near Dunhang (photo), ./The Bridgeman Art Library; p. 237: The Old Forum (photo), ./Leptis Magna, Libya/© Julian Chichester/The Bridgeman Art Library.

Chapter 7

p. 240: SEF/Art Resource, NY; p. 246: Barcroft Media via Getty Images; p. 249: Berthold Steinhilber/laif/Redux; p. 251: Head of Amenophis IV (Akhenaten) (c. 1364–47 BC) (stone), Egyptian 18th Dynasty (c. 1567–1320 BC)/Luxor Museum of Ancient Art, Egypt/The Bridgeman Art Library;

p. 253: Erich Lessing/Art Resource, NY; p. 256: © RMN-Grand Palais/Art Resource, NY; p. 260: Naga sadhus walking down the steps of Har-ki-Pauri ghat to take a dip in the river Ganges on the occasion of 'Somvati Amavasya', a no moon day in the traditional Hindu calendar (photo)./Godong/ UIG/The Bridgeman Art Library; p. 263: Album/Art Resource, NY; p. 266: From Trigger, *Understanding Early Civilizations: A Comparative Study* (New York: Cambridge University Press, 2003), 427. a–d) from Gardiner 1961: 215; e–f) from Eduard Seler, *Gesammelte Abhandlungen zur Amerikanischen Sprach – und Alterthumskunde* (Berlin, 1902–1904); g–j) from G. Zimmermann, *Die Hieroglyphen der Maya-Handschriften* (Hamburg, 1956), pls. 6,7; k) from Woolley, *The Sumerians*, 89; p. 267: UIG via Getty Images; p. 271: www.CartoonStock.com adjacent credit.

Chapter 8

p. 280: © Jack Sullivan/Alamy; p. 286: © Mary C. Stiner, 2010; p. 289: Courtesy of Penn Museum, image #245774; p. 296: Copyright © 2004 Arthur Demarest. Reprinted with the permission of Cambridge University Press; p. 297: Avenue of the Dead from the Pyramid of the Moon showing the Pyramid of the Sun in the background (photo), ./Teotihuacan, Valley of Mexico, Mexico/The Bridgeman Art Library; p. 300: Donne Bryant/Art Resource, NY; p. 302: View of The Treasury (photo), ./Petra, Jordan/Photo © Luca Tettoni/The Bridgeman Art Library; p. 306: NGS Image Collection/The Art Archive at Art Resource, NY; p. 308: The Art Archive at Art Resource, NY; p. 314: © Scott Camazine/Alamy.

Chapter 9

p. 318: The War in Heaven, from Book VI of 'Paradise Lost' by John Milton (1608–74) engraved by A. Ligny, c. 1868 (engraving), Dore, Gustave (1832–83) (after)/Private Collection/The Bridgeman Art Library; p. 329: Fairbanks and Merle, *China: A New History* (Harvard: Harvard University Press, 2006), Plate 19. Illustrations from an 1808 edition of Peiwenzhai gengzhitu showing the principal steps in rice cultivation; p. 331: Set of printing blocks (wood), Chinese School, (18th century)/ Private Collection/Photo © Christie's Images/The Bridgeman Art Library; p. 339: *Iron, Gender, and Power* by Eugenia W. Herbert, ©1993. Reprinted with permission of Indiana University Press; p. 340: From Needham, *Science and Civilization in China*, volume IV, part 2, figure 409 and p. 107, by permission of Cambridge University Press. Illustration from the *Tshan Sang Ho Pien* of Sha Shih-An *et al.* (1843); p. 343: Moorish arch Portico on Plaza de Armas, ruins of Medina Azahara medieval palace-city, Cordoba, Andalusia. Detail. Spain, 10th century./De Agostini Picture Library/ C. Sappa/The Bridgeman Art Library; p. 348: Pre Rup (photo), ./Angkor, Cambodia/Photo © Luca Tettoni/The Bridgeman Art Library; p. 351: NGS Image Collection/The Art Archive at Art Resource, NY; p. 353: A War Canoe of New Zealand, c. April 1770, from 'A Collection of Drawings made in the Countries visited by Captain Cook in his First Voyage, 1768–1771', engraved by R.B. Godfrey (engraving), Parkinson, Sydney (c. 1745–71) (after)/British Library, London, UK/ The Bridgeman Art Library.

Chapter 10

p. 358: Portrait of Genghis Khan (c. 1162–1227), Mongol Khan, founder of the Imperial Dynasty, the Yuan, making China the centre of the great Mongol Empire (1260–1368), (ink and w/c on silk, silk patterned border), Chinese School/National Palace Museum, Taipei, Taiwan/The Bridgeman Art Library; p. 365: © Aurora Photos/Alamy; p. 372: Werner Forman/Art Resource, NY; p. 374: Werner Forman/Art Resource, NY; p. 376: Kublai Khan hunting with a falcon, miniature from Livre des merveilles du monde (Book of the Wonders of the World) by Marco Polo and Rustichello, manuscript 2810 folio 42 verso, France 15th Century./De Agostini Picture Library/The Bridgeman Art Library; p. 380: Syria, Aleppo, Citadel/De Agostini Picture Library/C. Sappa/The Bridgeman Art Library;

p. 386: Fr 22495 f.43 Battle between Crusaders and Moslems, from Le Roman de Godefroi de Bouillon (vellum), French School, (14th century)/Bibliotheque Nationale, Paris, France/The Bridgeman Art Library.

Chapter 11

p. 394: De Agostini/Getty Images; p. 401: Gianni Dagli Orti/The Art Archive at Art Resource, NY; p. 403: PLANET OF THE APES, 1968, Statue of Liberty, TM and Copyright © 20th Century Fox Film Corp. All rights reserved. Courtesy: Everett Collection; p. 407: View of the Temple of the Warriors (or 1000 Columms) post 150 AD (photo), Mexican School/Chichen Itza, Yucatan State, Mexico/Giraudon/The Bridgeman Art Library; p. 408: AFP/Getty Images; p. 415: AFP/Getty Images; p. 421: The Oseberg Ship/Werner Forman Archive/The Bridgeman Art Library; p. 423: Greenland National Museum and Archives; p. 430: The Black Death, 1348 (engraving) (b&w photo), English School, (14th century)/Private Collection/The Bridgeman Art Library.

Chapter 12

p. 436: The tomb of Askia Mohammed, ruler of the Songhai empire from 1493 to 1528, at Gao/ Werner Forman Archive/The Bridgeman Art Library; p. 442: Mona Lisa, c. 1503–6 (oil on panel) (detail of 3179), Vinci, Leonardo da (1452–1519)/Louvre, Paris, France/Giraudon/The Bridgeman Art Library; p. 446: Finsiel/Alinari/Art Resource, NY; p. 453: Scala/Art Resource, NY; p. 455: Erich Lessing/Art Resource, NY; p. 459: Altar Frontal, early 17th century (silk in tapestry weave), Chinese School, Ming Dynasty (1368–1644)/Saint Louis Art Museum, Missouri, USA/Gift of Mrs. Samuel C. Davis/The Bridgeman Art Library; p. 464: Pacey, Arnold., Technology in World Civilization: A Thousand-Year History, Figure 16, p. 65, © 1990 Massachusetts Institute of Technology, by permission of The MIT Press; p. 467: Photographed by Pascal Gyot/Pool AFP/ASSOCIATED PRESS.

Chapter 13

p. 474: Fol.208v Meeting of Hernando Cortes (1485–1547) and Montezuma (1466–1520), miniature from the 'History of the Indians' by Diego Duran, 1579 (vellum) (detail of 227180), Duran, Diego (16th century)/Biblioteca Nacional, Madrid, Spain/Giraudon/The Bridgeman Art Library; p. 482: Bernadette Deschaine. http://nicky-v.deviantart.com/art/Absolutism-Political-Cartoon-182565544. Used with permission; p. 485: K'ang-hsi, Chinese School/Private Collection/Peter Newark Military Pictures/The Bridgeman Art Library; p. 491: Island Capital of the Aztecs, Tenochtitlan (mural), Covarrubias, Luis (1919–1987)/Museo Nacional de Antropologia, Mexico City, Mexico/Sean Sprague/Mexicolore/The Bridgeman Art Library; p. 497: Album/Art Resource, NY; p. 502: The Indian princess Malinche or Dona Marina, mistress of Hernando Cortes (1485–1547) interpreting for him (vellum), Duran, Diego (16th century)/Biblioteca Nacional, Madrid, Spain/Giraudon/The Bridgeman Art Library; p. 505: African slaves being taken on board ship bound for USA (coloured engraving), American School, (19th century)/Private Collection/Peter Newark American Pictures/ The Bridgeman Art Library; p. 509: Toyotomi Hideyoshi (colour litho), Japanese School/Private Collection/Peter Newark Military Pictures/The Bridgeman Art Library; p. 511: The Art Archive at Art Resource, NY.

Index

Acknowledgments

W e thank the staff at Oxford University Press, in particular the deft, even-handed guidance from our editor Charles Cavaliere and his assistant Lynn Luecken. Thanks also to the production staff at OUP, in particular Marianne Paul, production editor, George Chakvetadze, mapmaker, and Francelle Carapetyan, photo researcher.

Many reviewers—mostly anonymous—read various versions of our chapters, and the voluminous comments they offered all contributed to the improvement of the text, sometimes slapping us down when we were heading in the wrong direction, sometimes validating the direction we were pursuing. We are grateful for all the feedback, positive and negative, and recognize the benefits of their engagement with the material. Finally, we would like to express our appreciation to Richard Eaton, Guido Ruggiero, and Francesca Trivellato for taking the time out of their busy schedules to read the final manuscript.

Stephen thanks Nasser Rabbat, Kandice Hauf, Beatrice Manz, Cemal Kafadar for their support and advice, as well as colleagues, Laura Prieto, Stephen Berry, Sarah Leonard, Zhigang Liu, Laurie Crumpacker, and students Emilia Mountain Poppe, Cassandra De Alba, and the entire History 100 class of Fall 2013 at Simmons College: "Without you I could never have imagined this project."

Adrian thanks his children, Uriel, Conrad, Gemma, and Esme, for those times they did not run away when he embarked on a historical "discussion." And thanks them for the times they did. Finally, and most significantly, he thanks his wife, Katy: "Thanks for your ear over the last few years, for your willingness to hear me out when I had to lay down the pen and talk to another human being. Your love gives me hope."